APPLYING CULTURAL ANTHROPOLOGY

APPLYING CULTURAL ANTHROPOLOGY

An Introductory Reader

SEVENTH EDITION

Aaron Podolefsky
Central Missouri State University

Peter J. Brown
Emory University

Boston   Burr Ridge, IL   Dubuque, IA   Madison, WI   New York   San Francisco   St. Louis
Bangkok   Bogotá   Caracas   Kuala Lumpur   Lisbon   London   Madrid   Mexico City
Milan   Montreal   New Delhi   Santiago   Seoul   Singapore   Sydney   Taipei   Toronto

Higher Education

APPLYING CULTURAL ANTHROPOLOGY: AN INTRODUCTORY READER

Published by McGraw-Hill, a business unit of The McGraw-Hill Companies, Inc., 1221 Avenue of the Americas, New York, NY, 10020. Copyright © 2007, 2003, 2001, 1999, 1997, 1994, 1991 by The McGraw-Hill Companies, Inc. All rights reserved. No part of this publication may be reproduced or distributed in any form or by any means, or stored in a database or retrieval system, without the prior written consent of The McGraw-Hill Companies, Inc., including, but not limited to, in any network or other electronic storage or transmission, or broadcast for distance learning.

Some ancillaries, including electronic and print components, may not be available to customers outside the United States.

This book is printed on acid-free paper.

1 2 3 4 5 6 7 8 9 0 QPD/QPD 0 9 8 7 6

ISBN-13: 978-0-07-353092-5
ISBN-10: 0-07-353092-1

Vice President and Editor-in-Chief: *Emily Barrosse*
Publisher: *Phillip A. Butcher*
Freelance Developmental Editor: *Pat Forrest, Carlisle Communications, Ltd.*
Editorial Coordinator: *Teresa C. Treacy*
Senior Marketing Manager: *Daniel M. Loch*
Managing Editor: *Jean Dal Porto*
Senior Project Manager: *Rick Hecker*
Art Director: *Jeanne Schreiber*
Designer: *Srdjan Savanovic*
Production Supervisor: *Jason I. Huls*
Composition: *10/12 Palatino, by Interactive Composition Corporation, India*
Printing: *45# New Scholarly Matte*

Library of Congress Cataloging-in-Publication Data

Applying cultural anthropology : an introductory reader / [edited by] Aaron
    Podolefsky, Peter J. Brown.—7th ed.
    p. cm.
    Includes bibliographical references and index.
    ISBN-13: 978-0-07-353092-5 (softcover : alk. paper)
    ISBN-10: 0-07-353092-1 (softcover : alk. paper)
    1. Applied anthropology.   2. Ethnology.   I. Podolefsky, Aaron.
    II. Brown, Peter J.
  GN397.5. A68 2007
  301—dc22   2006044433

The Internet addresses listed in the text were accurate at the time of publication. The inclusion of a Web site does not indicate an endorsement by the authors or McGraw-Hill, and McGraw-Hill does not guarantee the accuracy of the information presented at these sites.

www.mhhe.com

In memory of Benjamin D. Paul,
who spent his life applying anthropology
for the betterment of humanity.
—Peter J. Brown

To the Student

An introductory course in any discipline is full of new terminology, concepts, and facts. Sometimes students forget that these new ideas and vocabulary are actually intellectual tools that can be put to work for analyzing and solving problems. In preparing this book, we have selected readings that will show you how anthropological concepts, discoveries, and methods can be applied in today's world.

The study of anthropology can help you view the world in a completely different way than you ever have before. You can come to appreciate the great diversity of human cultures and the interrelatedness of economic, sociopolitical, and religious systems. Anthropology can give you a broad perspective on humanity and help you understand other people's beliefs and customs. In doing so, it can help you become a better citizen in an increasingly global society. But your motivation need not be completely altruistic—there are many examples in this book of how cross-cultural awareness can improve performances in business, negotiations, and clinical medicine.

The fascinating side of anthropology seems obvious to most educated people, but there is also a lesser-known practical side of the discipline. The readings we have selected demonstrate that practical, applied side. Many of the articles depict anthropological ideas and research methods in action—as they are used to understand and solve practical problems. We have included articles on anthropologists working outside the academic setting to show how they are applying anthropology. We believe that the fundamental lessons of anthropology can be applied to many careers and all areas of human endeavor.

To benefit from the study of anthropology, you need to study effectively. Over the years, we have found that students often read assignments without planning, and this actually makes studying less efficient. Before you read a selection, spend a few moments skimming it to get an idea of what it is about, where it is going, and what you should look for. This kind of preliminary reading is a poor idea for mystery novels but is essential for academic assignments. Without this preparation, the article may become a hodgepodge of facts and figures; details may be meaningless because you have missed the big picture. By planning your reading, you can see how the details are relevant to the central themes of an article.

To help you plan your reading, at the beginning of each article we have included questions and a list of glossary terms. Looking at these questions in advance, you may gain an idea of what is to come and why the article is important. This will help make the time you spend reading more fruitful. Most of the questions highlight the central themes of the selection or draw your attention to interesting details. Some of the questions, however, do not have straightforward answers—they are food for thought and topics for debate. Some of the selections refer directly to current discussions of HIV, migration, obesity, body image, and drug use. Our idea is to challenge you to think about how anthropology can be applied to your own life and education.

These articles have been selected with you, the student, in mind. We hope they convey our excitement about the anthropological adventure, and we trust that you will find them both enjoyable and thought-provoking.

"Applied anthropology" most often refers to a situation in which a client hires an anthropologist to do research that will help the client resolve a particular problem. Some applied anthropologists run their own research companies that bid and win research contracts from clients and funding agencies; other applied anthropologists work directly for corporations. Applied anthropologists write their reports specifically for their clients. A good place to find out about applied anthropology is at the Society for Applied Anthropology's Web site, www.sfaa.net. There are many master's degree programs in this field. You may also run across the term "public anthropology" in your studies. This refers to anthropological research and writing that engages important public issues (like many of those addressed in this book) and whose audience is the lay educated public. As "public scholars," anthropologists want to communicate their perspective on contemporary issues and influence public opinion and policy. A good place to find out what is happening in public anthropology is through the website of the American Anthropological Association (www.aaanet.org) or the Public Anthropology website (www.publicanthropology.org).

If you are interested in reading more about applied anthropology, there are several excellent books available, such as *Applied Anthropology: A Practical Guide,* by Erve Chambers; *Applied Anthropology: An Introduction,* by John van Willigen; *Anthropological Praxis: Translating Knowledge into Action,* by Robert M. Wulff and Shirley J. Fiske; *Applied Anthropology in America,* by Elizabeth M. Eddy and William L. Partridge; and *Making Our Research Useful,* by John van Willigen, Barbara Rylko-Bauer, and Anne McElroy. If you are interested in medical matters, you may want to consult *Understanding and Applying Medical Anthropology,* by Peter J. Brown or *Anthropology and Public Health,* by Robert Hahn. You may also want to look at the journals *Human Organization* and *Practicing Anthropology,* both of which are published by the Society for Applied Anthropology. The National Association of Practicing Anthropologists (NAPA) also publishes interesting works on specific fields such as medical anthropology.

To the Instructor

Introductory anthropology has become an established part of the college curriculum, and through this course our profession communicates with a large and diverse undergraduate audience. Members of that audience differ in experience, academic concentration, and career aspirations. For those students considering anthropology as a major, we need to provide (among other things) a vision of the future, a view of anthropological work to be done in the public domain as well as within academia. For them, we need to provide some answers to the question, What can I do with a degree in anthropology? For students majoring in other areas, such as business, engineering, or psychology, we need to address the question, How can anthropological insights or research methods help me understand and solve human problems? If we can provide such a service, we increase the likelihood that students will find creative solutions to the professional problems that await them, and we brighten the future for our anthropology majors by underscoring the usefulness of an anthropological perspective in attempts to solve the practical problems of today's world.

Over the years we have found that many introductory texts do little more than include a chapter on applied anthropology at the end of the book. This suggests, at least to students, that most of anthropology has no relevance to their lives. Such treatment also implies that the application of anthropological knowledge is a tangent or afterthought—at best an additional subject area, such as kinship or politics.

We disagree. We believe that the applications of anthropology cut across and infuse all the discipline's subfields. This book is a collection of articles that provide examples of both basic and applied research in all four fields of anthropology.

One of our primary goals is to demonstrate some of the ways our discipline is used outside the academic arena. We want anthropology to be seen as a field that is interesting as well as relevant to the real world. Like the public at large, students seem well aware that the subject matter of anthropology is fascinating, but they seem unaware of both the fundamental questions of humanity addressed by anthropologists and the practical applications of the field. Increased public awareness of the practical contributions of anthropology is a goal that we share with many in the profession. In fact,

this is a major long-term goal of the American Anthropological Association.

Since we first started editing these readers in 1989, the general field of anthropology has changed in precisely this direction of emphasizing public relevance. "Public anthropology" refers to anthropological research and writing that engages important public issues (like many of those addressed in this book) and whose audience is the lay educated public. Our discipline has a long history in this regard, as in the work of Franz Boas on racial discrimination and Margaret Mead's famous articles in *Redbook* magazine. As "public scholars," anthropologists must communicate their perspective on contemporary issues and influence public opinion and policy. In this age of globalization and increased cultural intolerance often linked to religious fundamentalism, the basic messages of public anthropology are more important than ever. Being an effective public anthropologist is just being a great teacher in a larger classroom. A good place to find out what is happening in public anthropology is through the website of the American Anthropological Association (www.aaanet.org) or the Public Anthropology Web site (www.publicanthropology.org).

Although people distinguish between basic and applied research, much of anthropology falls into a gray area, having elements of both. Many selections in this book fall into that gray zone—they are brief ethnographic accounts that contain important implications for understanding and resolving problems. We could have included a large number of articles exemplifying strictly applied cultural research—an evaluation report of agency performance, for example. Although this sort of research is fascinating and challenging to do, it is usually not exciting for students to read. We have selected articles that we believe are fascinating for students and convey the dual nature (basic/applied) of social science research. We think that it is not the scholarly writing style that is most important, but rather the content of the research as a way to get students to think and to challenge their own assumptions about the world.

Anthropological research is oriented by certain basic human values. These include being against ethnocentrism, racism, and ignorance. Anthropology is about understanding and appreciating human similarities and difference. Such an understanding can lead students to new attitudes—like tolerance for cultural difference, commitment to human equality, stewardship of the environment, appreciation of the past, and personal dedication to the continued and honest pursuit of knowledge.

Any student who completes an introductory course in anthropology should learn that anthropological work, in its broadest sense, may include (or at least contribute to) international business, epidemiology, program evaluation, social impact studies, conflict resolution, organizational analysis, market research, and nutrition research, even though their introductory anthropology texts make no mention of those fields. The selections in this book should help students understand why anthropology is important in today's world and also make the course more memorable and meaningful.

FEATURES OF THIS EDITION

- To spark student discussion and thinking about controversial issues and issues of public policy, we have included selections dealing with contemporary topics like globalization, HIV/AIDS, racism, cell phones, Barbie, migration, obesity, intelligent design, and the current war. These selections are clearly anthropological in perspective and approach. When students are able to relate the concepts and examples of anthropology to current debates, they recognize the value of their education.

- We chose readings that complement typical courses in introductory cultural anthropology and that reflect new directions in cultural anthropology. The sequence of articles follows the organization of standard anthropology textbooks, grouped under headings with terms such as kinship, ritual, marriage, and religion, rather than headings based on areas of applied anthropology like medical anthropology or the anthropology of development. At the same time, we include headings such as culture and food and globalization, reflecting growth and development in the anthropological discipline and purview. As in most contemporary textbooks, linguistic anthropology is included under culture and communication. Had we meant this book as a reader on applied anthropology, our organization would have been different. Although this book could be used by students in courses on applied anthropology (as earlier editions have been), those students are not our intended audience. For this reason, we have not provided extensive discussion of the history or definition of applied anthropology.

- For students interested in pursuing applied cultural anthropology on their own, there are a number of fine books. These include *Applied Anthropology: A Practical Guide,* by Erve Chambers; *Applied Anthropology: An Introduction,* by John van Willigen; *Anthropological Praxis: Translating Knowledge into Action,* by Robert M. Wulff and Shirley J. Fiske; *Applied Anthropology in America,* by Elizabeth M. Eddy and William L. Partridge; and *Making Our Research Useful,* by John van Willigen, Barbara Rylko-Bauer, and Anne McElroy. Students interested in medical matters may want to consult *Understanding and Applying Medical Anthropology,* by Peter J. Brown or *Anthropology and Public Health* by Robert Hahn.

- To emphasize how anthropology can be put to work in different settings, we include examples of anthropologists whose careers involve applying anthropology outside the university setting.

- To help students better understand the subject matter, we include a number of pedagogical aids: introductions, a list of glossary terms, and guiding questions for each article; a world map that pinpoints the locations of places and peoples discussed in the articles; and, for easy reference, an extensive glossary and index.

- To help busy instructors, we have provided an electronic instructor's manual that includes a brief summary, glossary terms, and test questions for each article.

NEW TO THIS EDITION

In this edition we have continued to juxtapose "classic" anthropological articles with features that highlight issues of this new millennium. One such juxtaposition is the continued issue of the central biological theory of evolution as opposed to creationism that has recently been reborn as "intelligent design." In the field of human paleontology, we have a new article that explores the continuing "big questions" of human evolution, in part because the corpus of fossil evidence has become so large that it is ever more complex for undergraduate students.

There are twelve new articles that refer to contemporary social issues and events, like Hurricane Katrina in 2005 and the current wars in the Middle East. We also have new selections that deal with hot-button issues like illegal migration, alternative forms of marriage, and the teaching of evolution in high schools. Two new articles discuss transnational migration. Several new articles address health and culture, including the

HIV/AIDS pandemic, emerging infectious diseases, and culturally sensitive health care.

We have continued our previous commitment to the discussion of race as a salient topic for introductory anthropology. We continue to put these articles within the cultural anthropology sections because race is a cultural construction, not a biological fact. In this regard, students need to understand that whiteness is also a cultural construction that brings with it certain privileges. Racism, sexism, severe economic inequality, and intolerance for cultural difference are continuing problems of our society. Throughout this edition we have also newly emphasized globalization and its human dimensions.

ACKNOWLEDGMENTS

We especially wish to thank Sarah Willen, Matt Dudgeon, and Svea Closser—all fantastic doctoral students in anthropology at Emory University—whose excellent suggestions and editorial talents made it possible to complete the task. Thank you so much. Phillip Sarnowski has also done great work, and Helen Simmons has played an important role in keeping this organized. PJB would also like to acknowledge the ideas and contributions of Erin Finley, Kate Winskell, Alexa Dietrich, Eric Lindland, Peggy Barlett, and George Armelagos. Also we thank the capable staff at Carlisle Publishing Services, especially Pat Forrest.

We are grateful to the many instructors who returned questionnaires evaluating the selections: C. Adams, Indiana University; S. Adrian, University of Arizona; N. Allison, Toccoa Falls College; L. Ammons, Assumption College; P. Barlett, Emory University; K. Barlow, University of Minnesota; E. Bigler, Rhode Island College; B. Bigony, University of Wisconsin at Menomonie; G. Bogdan, Orange Coast College; A. Bolyanatz, Wheaton College; C. Bretell, Southern Methodist University; J. Brown, Oakland University; D. Bruner, University of North Carolina at Greensboro; J. Cahoon, College of St. Scholastica; D. Chasin, Newport Beach, CA; J. Coggeshall, Clemson University; K. Costa, Fall River, MA; Philip E. Coyle, Western Carolina University; J. Culbert, San Diego State University; D. Darlington, Western Wyoming Community College; S. Dauria, Bloomsburg University; J. Dempsey, Phoenix, AZ; D. Duchon, Georgia State University; M. Findlay, California State University at Chico; T. Fitzgerald, University of North Carolina at Greensboro; M. Fong, Chaffey College; P. Fontane, St. Louis College of Pharmacy; F. Freedman, Syracuse University; D. Gamble, Southwest Baptist University; D. Gibson, El Camino College; D. Gordon, Fort Lewis College; T. Greaves, Bucknell University; Amy Harper, Central Oregon Community College; C. Hartse, Olympic College; T. Headland, Summer Institute of Linguistics; E. Hegeman, John Jay College, City University of New York; M. Helms, University of North Carolina at Greensboro; J. Herron, Ottawa, KS; B. Howell, University of Tennessee at Knoxville; C. Hull, Grand Valley State University; S. Jen, California State University at Fresno; B. Joans, Merritt College; C. Johnson, Indiana University Northwest; C. Kahrs, Saddleback Community College; P. Kilbride, Bryn Mawr College; S. Kus, Rhodes College; S. Lamb, Brandeis University; G. Landsman, State University of New York at Albany; J. Levi, Carleton College; P. Little, University of Kentucky; W. Lohrer, California State University at Chico; K. Lorenz, Shippensburg University; Cherylynn MacGreagor, University of Houston-Downtown; K. Maines, Pennsylvania State University; B. Mathieu, West Los Angeles College; M. Mazzarelli, Massachusetts Bay Community College; C. McCall, Hiwassee College; J. McCall, Southern Illinois University at Carbondale; C. Moyers, Cabrillo College; B. Nelson, University of Utah; C. Nowak, Chicago, IL; B. Pate, University of Tennessee; K. Piatt, Babson College; K. Porter, Rochester, NY; M. Pulford, University of Wisconsin at Superior; Francis Ellen Purifoy, University of Louisville; S. Rachelle, Mt. San Jacinto College; R. Rajner, University of Toledo; S. Rasmussen, University of Houston; Paul Roach, Century College—St. Paul; S. Rorbakken, University of Iowa; J. Ryan, Texas Christian University; B. Schmitz, Orange Coast College; D. Seelow, State University of New York at Old Westbury; D. Shepherd, Rubbindale, MN; V. Smith, California State University at Chico; J. Stimpfl, University of Nebraska at Lincoln; H. Swanson, Mohave Community College; M. Taylor, University of Memphis; T. M. Taylor, University of South Colorado; J. Thompson, Tennessee Wesleyan College; J. Tizon, University of Southern Maine; K. Wilcoxson, University of Sioux Falls; P. Wohlt, Ball State University; Z. Zelazo, Montclair State University.

Contents

Culture and Fieldwork

Culture and Communication

Culture and Food

Culture and Agriculture

works with Paraguay's indigenous Guaraní communities, helped create a forest reserve that would protect native peoples' rights to their traditional lands. Now these communities are denied access to the reserve.

Race and Ethnicity

Economy and Business

Gender and Sexuality

Kinship, Marriage & Family

Politics, Conflict, and the Law

Culture, Religion, and Ritual

Culture and Health

Globalization and Culture Change

INTRODUCTION

Understanding Humans and Human Problems

To the uninitiated, the term *anthropology* conjures up images of mummies' tombs, Indiana Jones, and treks through steaming jungles or over high alpine peaks. Anthropologists agree that their chosen field is exciting, that they have been places and seen things that few experience firsthand, and that they have been deeply and emotionally involved in understanding the human condition. At the same time, however, the vision of anthropology presented by Hollywood has probably done more to obscure the true nature of the profession than it has to enlighten the public about what we really do.

Providing an accurate image of anthropology and anthropological work is both simple and complex. Essentially, anthropology is the study of people, or more properly, of humankind. But, you may say, many disciplines study people: psychology, sociology, history, biology, medicine, and so on. True, but anthropology is different in that it seeks to integrate these separate and perhaps narrower views of humanity. To understand ourselves, we need to join these disparate views into a single framework, a process that begins with our biological and evolutionary roots, explores the development of culture through the prehistoric and historical periods, probes the uniquely human ability to develop culture through communication, and examines the diversity of recent and present-day cultures that inhabit the globe.

From this conception of the *holistic* and *comparative* study of humankind emerge what are termed the four fields of anthropology: biological (or physical) anthropology, archaeology, anthropological linguistics, and cultural anthropology. Some universities offer an introductory course that covers all four subfields. Other schools cover the subfields in two or three separate introductory courses. Each approach has its advantage. The former may more fully integrate the biocultural and historical dimensions of humanity; the latter allows students to explore each subfield in greater depth. This book introduces you to the four fields of anthropology and how they are used in today's world.

Another way to divide the discipline—in fact almost any discipline—is into *basic* and *applied* research. These categories are important in this reader because we would like students to appreciate both the basic and the applied sides of anthropology. A survey of natural and social scientists and engineers conducted by the U.S. Census Bureau for the National Science Foundation used the following definitions of these fundamental concepts: *Basic research* is study directed toward gaining scientific knowledge primarily for its own sake. *Applied research* is study directed toward gaining scientific knowledge in an effort to meet a recognized need.

Anthropology is a discipline concerned primarily with basic research. It asks "big" questions concerning the origins of humankind, the roots of human nature, the development of civilization, and the functions of our major social institutions (such as marriage and religion). Nevertheless, anthropologists have put the methods and skills developed in basic research to use in solving human problems and fulfilling the needs of society. Anthropologists have, for example, worked with medical examiners in the identification of skeletal remains. They have also helped communities preserve their cultural heritage and businesses and government agencies understand the social impact of programs or development projects.

Although the application of anthropology has a long history, it has until recent years remained in the shadows of pure or basic research. The last twenty-five years have seen a change. Anthropologists have moved beyond their traditional roles in universities and museums and now work in a broad range of settings. They are employed in many government agencies, in the private sector, and in a variety of nonresearch capacities (such as administrator, evaluator, or policy analyst).

In response to the growing opportunities for anthropologists outside academia and to the demands of students, an increasing number of master's degree and doctoral programs provide training specifically in the applications of anthropology. This is not to say that the classified ads list jobs titled "anthropologist." Rather, for those interested in anthropology, there are increasing opportunities to find careers that draw on anthropological training and skills. Profiles of people in nonacademic careers (consumer marketing, high-tech industry, and refugee policy) can be found in this reader. At the same time, studies have shown that there will be increasing job opportunities for anthropologists in universities and colleges during the next decade and beyond.

These new opportunities are particularly evident in this era of multiculturalism and in the increasing public recognition that our society must be a culturally diverse social mosaic. Exploration of this reality has always been the domain of cultural anthropology; a usual pedagogical goal of teachers of cultural anthropology is to increase a student's appreciation and tolerance of cultural differences. Living in a multicultural society presents real challenges of social tensions caused by chronic persistent ethnocentrism and racism. But living in a multicultural society also brings a cultural richness, a luxuriant wealth, to our lives.

School administrators, engineers, doctors, business leaders, lawyers, medical researchers, and government officials have become aware that the substantive knowledge, the unique perspective, and the research skills of anthropologists are applicable to practical problems—in the United States as well as other countries.

As we explore anthropology, keep in mind the interplay between and interdependence of basic cultural research and the applications of anthropological knowledge and research methods to the solution of human problems.

CULTURAL ANTHROPOLOGY

Cultural anthropology is concerned with the description and analysis of people's lives and traditions. In the past, cultural anthropologists almost always did research in far-off "exotic" societies, but today we have expanded our research interests to include our own society. Cultural anthropology can add much to both the basic and the applied scientific understanding of human behaviors and beliefs. The study and interpretation of other societies—of their traditions, history, and view of the world—is inherently interesting and important because it documents the diversity of human lifestyles. The anthropological approach to understanding other societies also has practical value for addressing contemporary human problems and needs.

The concept of *culture* is central to anthropology. It refers to the patterns of economy, social organization, and belief that are learned and shared by members of a social group. Culture is traditional knowledge that is passed down from one generation to the next. Although generally stable over time, culture is flexible and fluid, changing through borrowing or invention. The influential American anthropologist Franz Boas championed the concept of culture for understanding

human diversity; culture, Boas argued, is distinct from biological "race" or language. Anthropologists believe that all cultural lifestyles have intrinsic value and validity. Other societies deserve to be studied and understood without being prejudged using our own narrow (and sometimes intolerant) beliefs and values; this universal tendency to prejudge based on the supposed superiority of one's own group, called *ethnocentrism,* is something everyone should avoid.

Culture is the crowning achievement of human evolution. To understand ourselves is to appreciate cultural diversity. Dependence on culture as our primary mechanism of survival sets humans apart from other members of the animal kingdom. This dependence is responsible for the tremendous evolutionary success of our species, which has grown in population (sometimes to the point of overpopulation) and can inhabit nearly every niche on the planet.

The paradox of culture is that, as we humans learn to accept our own cultural beliefs and values, we unconsciously learn to reject those of other peoples. At birth, we are capable of absorbing any culture and language. We are predisposed to cultural learning, but we are not programmed to adopt a particular culture. As we grow, our parents, our schools, and our society teach us what is right and wrong, good and evil, acceptable and unacceptable. At the subconscious level, we learn the symbolic meanings of behavior and through them interpret the meanings of actions. Beliefs, values, and symbols must be understood within the context of a particular culture. This is the principle of *cultural relativity.* At the same time, culture supplies us with the cognitive models—software programs, if you will—that allow us to perceive or "construct" a particular version of reality. Culture permeates our thinking and our expectations; this is the principle of *culture construction.*

In addition to the concept of culture, the anthropological approach to the study of human behavior and belief has two essential characteristics: a holistic approach and a comparative framework. The *holistic approach* means that anthropologists see a particular part of culture—for example, politics, economy, or religion—in relation to the larger social system. Individuals are viewed, not in isolation, but as part of an intricate web of social relationships. Although an anthropological study may have a particular focus, the holistic approach means that the broader cultural context is always considered important because the different parts of a cultural system are interrelated. When, for example, the economy or the technology changes, other aspects of the culture will change as well.

The *comparative framework* means that explanations or generalizations are achieved through cross-cultural research. Questions about humanity cannot be based on information from a single society or a single type of society such as the industrial societies of the United States and Europe. Such a limited framework is simply too narrow for understanding the big picture that basic anthropological research seeks. By studying others within a comparative framework, we can better understand ourselves. If other cultures are a mirror in which we see ourselves, then anthropology is a mirror for humankind.

The broad generalizations about culture and society that we have been talking about are based on detailed knowledge of the world's cultures. To gain this knowledge, anthropologists go to the people. Often accompanied by spouses and children, we pack our bags and travel to far-off lands—to the highlands of New Guinea, the frozen Arctic, the savannas of Africa, or the jungles of South America. Increasingly, anthropologist are bringing their research methods and comparative, holistic perspective into the cities and suburbs of America, the American schoolroom, and the corporate jungle. This "research adventure" has become the hallmark of cultural anthropology.

The research methods used by the cultural anthropologist are distinctive because they depend to a large extend on the firsthand experiences and interpretations of the field researcher. Cultural anthropologists conduct research in natural settings rather than in laboratories or over the telephone. This method for studying another society is often called *participant observation, ethnography,* or *qualitative methods.* The goal of describing, understanding, and explaining another culture is a large task. It is most often accomplished by living in the society for an extended period, by talking with people, and, as much as possible, by experiencing their lives.

One important tool that cultural anthropologists depend on in field research is *language.* They need to learn the local language not only for their own survival in the field but, more important, because language is a key to understanding someone else's culture. Many anthropologists study descriptive linguistics to make it easier for them to learn an unwritten language in the field. By looking at speech and language in Apache culture (Selection 6) or the complex problems of male-female miscommunication (Selection 7), anthropologists can learn a great deal about the culture they are studying.

The fieldwork experience usually involves a kind of culture shock in which the researcher questions his or her own assumptions about the world. In this way, fieldwork is often a rewarding period of personal growth. In their work, anthropologists expect to find that other people's behavior, even when it seems bizarre when seen from the outside, makes sense when viewed from the people's own point of view. This is why anthropological research often means letting people speak for themselves. While doing research, the anthropologist often thinks of herself or himself as a child—as being ignorant or uninformed and needing to be taught by the people being studied. This approach often involves in-depth interviewing with a few key informants and then interpreting (and writing about) that other culture for the researcher's own society. The ethnographic method, pioneered and developed in anthropology, is now being used in a range of applied areas, including marketing, management research, and school evaluation. Although ethnography is an important research style, the selections in this book demonstrate that many different methods are used in anthropology today.

The applications of cultural anthropology are diverse. Internationally, anthropologists are involved in programs of technical assistance and economic aid to Third World nations. These programs address needs in such areas as agriculture and rural development; health, nutrition, and family planning; education; housing and community organizing; transportation and communication; and energy. Anthropologists do many of the same things domestically as well. They evaluate public education, study agricultural extension programs, administer projects, analyze policy (such as U.S. refugee resettlement programs), and research crime and crime prevention, for example.

In the private sector, cultural anthropologists can add a fresh perspective to market research. They analyze office and industrial organization and culture. They create language and cultural training workshops for businesspeople and others who are going overseas. These workshops reduce the likelihood of cross-cultural misunderstanding and the problems of culture shock for the employee and, often more important, for his or her family. A good example is the work of Richard Reeves-Ellington (Selection 18), who has demonstrated how the training of corporate managers in Japanese culture significantly improves their business productivity.

Applied anthropological work can be divided into four categories. In the first group, applied research and basic research look very much alike, except that the goal of applied research is more directly linked to a particular problem or need. For example, in Selection 28, Aaron Podolefsky studies the causes of the reemergence of tribal warfare in New Guinea. Such studies provide planners and policymakers with important insights for understanding the problem. This knowledge can help in the design and implementation of programs that help bring an end to warfare in the region. Similarly, Philippe Bourgois's sensitive ethnography of the culture of crack users may help in the implementation of drug treatment programs (Selection 4).

In the second category, anthropologists may work as researchers for a government agency, corporation, or interest group on a specific task defined by the client.

In the third category, anthropologists work as consultants to business and industry or to government agencies that need in-depth cultural knowledge to solve or prevent a problem. Anthropologists often act as cultural brokers, mediating and translating between groups who are miscommunicating not because of their words but because of cultural meanings.

Finally, a few anthropologists have developed and administered programs. Gerald F. Murray's work in reforestation in Haiti (Selection 12) exemplifies the development and actual administration of a project in which cultural understanding is a fundamental component. The overwhelming success of this agro-forestry project attests to the practical value of cultural understanding for solving human problems.

A great deal of anthropological work remains to be done, although this seems to be a well-kept secret. People have a far easier time focusing on the individual as the level of analysis. When divorce, drug abuse, or suicide affects small numbers of people, we may look to the individual and to psychology for answers. When divorce rates climb to 50 percent of all marriages and the suicide rate increases tenfold, however, we must look beyond the individual to forces that affect society at large. Because we are so immersed in our own culture, we have difficulty seeing it as a powerful force that guides—even controls—our behavior. We begin these readings, therefore, with several selections that convey the hidden, but powerful, nature of culture.

The readings in this book are subdivided into traditional anthropological categories, such as economy, gender, social organization, politics, and religion. In each category you will find reading selections that demonstrate not only the relevance of anthropology theory and methods in the understanding of human problems but also the application of anthropology to specific problems or issues.

1

Body Ritual Among the Nacirema

Horace Miner

Generations of anthropologists have traveled the globe, reaching to the far corners of the five continents to discover and describe the many ways of humankind. Anthropologists have gathered a diverse collection of exotic customs, from the mundane to the bizarre. Understanding and appreciating other societies requires us to be culturally relative. But people tend to judge others by their own cultural values in a way that is *ethnocentric*. This is because people take their cultural beliefs and behaviors for granted; they seem so natural that they are seldom questioned. Among the most interesting social customs on record are the rituals of the Nacirema. By viewing Nacirema behaviors as *rituals*, we gain insight into their culture and into the meaning of the concept of *culture*. We also gain insight into the problem of ethnocentrism.

Ritual is a cultural phenomenon. Ritual can be found in all societies. It can be defined as a set of acts that follow a sequence established by tradition.

Throughout the world, ritual reflects the fundamental cultural beliefs and values of a society by giving order to important activities and particular life crises like death and birth. Every day, however, mundane rituals are performed unconsciously. In fact, most Nacirema people do these things without being aware of their underlying symbolic meanings. Pay particular attention to the quotation at the end of the selection.

As you read this selection, ask yourself the following questions:

- How do the Nacirema feel about the human body?
- Do you think that the charms and magical potions used by the Nacirema really work?
- Can you list those aspects of social life in which magic plays an important role?
- What is your opinion of the importance of body ritual, and if you went to live among the Nacirema, would you tell them of your opinion?
- Living among the Nacirema, you might find that their behaviors sometimes appear bizarre. Do you think the Nacirema themselves feel this way?

The following terms discussed in this selection are included in the Glossary at the back of the book:

clan	ethnocentrism
culture	ritual

The anthropologist has become so familiar with the diversity of ways in which different peoples behave in similar situations that he is not apt to be surprised by even the most exotic customs. In fact, if all of the logically possible combinations of behavior have not been found somewhere in the world, he is apt to suspect that they must be present in some yet undescribed tribe. This point has, in fact, been expressed with respect to clan organization by Murdock (1949:71). In this light, the magical beliefs and practices of the Nacirema present such unusual aspects that it seems desirable to describe them as an example of the extremes to which human behavior can go.

Professor Linton first brought the ritual of the Nacirema to the attention of anthropologists twenty years ago (1936:326), but the culture of this people is still very poorly understood. They are a North American group living in the territory between the Canadian Cree, the Yaqui and Tarahumare of Mexico, and the Carib and Arawak of the Antilles. Little is known of their origin, although tradition states that they came from the east. According to Nacirema mythology, their nation was originated by a culture hero, Notgnihsaw, who is otherwise known for two great feats of strength—the throwing of a piece of wampum across the river Pa-To-Mac and the chopping down of a cherry tree in which the Spirit of Truth resided.

Reproduced by permission of the American Anthropological Association from *American Anthropologist* 58:3, 1956. Not for further reproduction.

Nacirema culture is characterized by a highly developed market economy which has evolved in a rich natural habitat. While much of the people's time is devoted to economic pursuits, a large part of the fruits of these labors and a considerable portion of the day are spent in ritual activity. The focus of this activity is the human body, the appearance and health of which loom as a dominant concern in the ethos of the people. While such a concern is certainly not unusual, its ceremonial aspects and associated philosophy are unique.

The fundamental belief underlying the whole system appears to be that the human body is ugly and that its natural tendency is to debility and disease. Incarcerated in such a body, man's only hope is to avert these characteristics through the use of the powerful influences of ritual and ceremony. Every household has one or more shrines devoted to this purpose. The more powerful individuals in the society have several shrines in their houses and, in fact, the opulence of a house is often referred to in terms of the number of such ritual centers it possesses. Most houses are of wattle and daub construction, but the shrine rooms of the more wealthy are walled with stone. Poorer families imitate the rich by applying pottery plaques to their shrine walls.

While each family has at least one such shrine, the rituals associated with it are not family ceremonies but are private and secret. The rites are normally only discussed with children, and then only during the period when they are being initiated into these mysteries. I was able, however, to establish sufficient rapport with the natives to examine these shrines and to have the rituals described to me.

The focal point of the shrine is a box or chest which is built into the wall. In this chest are kept the many charms and magical potions without which no native believes he could live. These preparations are secured from a variety of specialized practitioners. The most powerful of these are the medicine men, whose assistance must be rewarded with substantial gifts. However, the medicine men do not provide the curative potions for their clients, but decide what the ingredients should be and then write them down in an ancient and secret language. This writing is understood only by the medicine men and by the herbalists who, for another gift, provide the required charm.

The charm is not disposed of after it has served its purpose, but is placed in the charm-box of the household shrine. As these magical materials are specific for certain ills, and the real or imagined maladies of the people are many, the charm-box is usually full to overflowing. The magical packets are so numerous that people forget what their purposes were and fear to use them again. While the natives are very vague on this point, we can only assume that the idea in retaining all the old magical materials is that their presence in the charm-box, before which the body rituals are conducted, will in some way protect the worshipper.

Beneath the charm-box is a small font. Each day every member of the family, in succession, enters the shrine room, bows his head before the charm-box, mingles different sorts of holy water in the font, and proceeds with a brief rite of ablution. The holy waters are secured from the Water Temple of the community, where the priests conduct elaborate ceremonies to make the liquid ritually pure.

In the hierarchy of magical practitioners, and below the medicine men in prestige, are specialists whose designation is best translated "holy-mouth-men." The Nacirema have an almost pathological horror of and fascination with the mouth, the condition of which is believed to have a supernatural influence on all social relationships. Were it not for the rituals of the mouth, they believe that their teeth would fall out, their gums bleed, their jaws shrink, their friends desert them, and their lovers reject them. They also believe that a strong relationship exists between oral and moral characteristics. For example, there is a ritual ablution of the mouth for children which is supposed to improve their moral fiber.

The daily body ritual performed by everyone includes a mouth-rite. Despite the fact that these people are so punctilious about care of the mouth, this rite involves a practice which strikes the uninitiated stranger as revolting. It was reported to me that the ritual consists of inserting a small bundle of hog hairs into the mouth, along with certain magical powders, and then moving the bundle in a highly formalized series of gestures.

In addition to the private mouth-rite, the people seek out a holy-mouth-man once or twice a year. These practitioners have an impressive set of paraphernalia, consisting of a variety of augers, awls, probes, and prods. The use of these objects in the exorcism of the evils of the mouth involves almost unbelievable ritual torture of the client. The holy-mouth-man opens the client's mouth, and using the above mentioned tools, enlarges any holes which decay may have created in the teeth. Magical materials are put into these holes. If there are no naturally occurring holes in the teeth, large sections of one or more teeth are gouged out so

---

The author of this article used the term *man* to refer to humanity in general. This term is not used by modern anthropologists because, to many people, it reflects an unconscious sexist bias in language and rhetoric. At the time that this article was written, however, the generalized *man* was a common convention in writing. In the interest of historical accuracy we have not changed the wording in this article, but students should be aware that nonsexist terms (*humans, people, Homo sapiens,* and so on) are preferred.—The Editors.

that the supernatural substance can be applied. In the client's view, the purpose of these ministrations is to arrest decay and to draw friends. The extremely sacred and traditional character of the rite is evident in the fact that the natives return to the holy-mouth-men year after year, despite the fact that their teeth continue to decay.

It is to be hoped that, when a thorough study of the Nacirema is made, there will be careful inquiry into the personality structure of these people. One has to but watch the gleam in the eye of a holy-mouth-man as he jabs an awl into an exposed nerve, to suspect that a certain amount of sadism is involved. If this can be established, a very interesting pattern emerges, for most of the population shows definite masochistic tendencies. It was to these that Professor Linton referred in discussing a distinctive part of the daily body ritual which is performed only by men. This part of the rite involves scraping and lacerating the surface of the face with a sharp instrument. Special women's rites are performed only four times during each lunar month, but what they lack in frequency is made up in barbarity. As part of this ceremony, women bake their heads in small ovens for about an hour. The theoretically interesting point is that what seems to be a preponderantly masochistic people have developed sadistic specialists.

The medicine men have an imposing temple, or *latipso*, in every community of any size. The more elaborate ceremonies required to treat very sick patients can only be performed at this temple. These ceremonies involve not only the thaumaturge but a permanent group of vestal maidens who move sedately about the temple chambers in distinctive costume and headdress.

The *latipso* ceremonies are so harsh that it is phenomenal that a fair proportion of the really sick natives who enter the temple ever recover. Small children whose indoctrination is still incomplete have been known to resist attempts to take them to the temple because "that is where you go to die." Despite this fact, sick adults are not only willing but eager to undergo the protracted ritual purification, if they can afford to do so. No matter how ill the supplicant or how grave the emergency, the guardians of many temples will not admit a client if he cannot give a rich gift to the custodian. Even after one has gained admission and survived the ceremonies, the guardians will not permit the neophyte to leave until he makes still another gift.

The supplicant entering the temple is first stripped of all his or her clothes. In everyday life the Nacirema avoids exposure of his body and its natural functions. Bathing and excretory acts are performed only in the secrecy of the household shrine, where they are ritualized as part of the body-rites. Psychological shock results from the fact that body secrecy is suddenly lost upon entry into the *latipso*. A man, whose own wife has never seen him in an excretory act, suddenly finds himself naked and assisted by a vestal maiden while he performs his natural functions into a sacred vessel. This sort of ceremonial treatment is necessitated by the fact that the excreta are used by a diviner to ascertain the course and nature of the client's sickness. Female clients, on the other hand, find their naked bodies are subjected to the scrutiny, manipulation and prodding of the medicine men.

Few supplicants in the temple are well enough to do anything but lie on their hard beds. The daily ceremonies, like the rites of the holy-mouth-men, involve discomfort and torture. With ritual precision, the vestals awaken their miserable charges each dawn and roll them about on their beds of pain while performing ablutions, in the formal movements of which the maidens are highly trained. At other times they insert magic wands in the supplicant's mouth or force him to eat substances which are supposed to be healing. From time to time the medicine men come to their clients and jab magically treated needles into their flesh. The fact that these temple ceremonies may not cure, and may even kill the neophyte, in no way decreases the people's faith in the medicine men.

There remains one other kind of practitioner, known as a "listener." This witch-doctor has the power to exorcise the devils that lodge in the heads of people who have been bewitched. The Nacirema believe that parents bewitch their own children. Mothers are particularly suspected of putting a curse on children while teaching them the secret body rituals. The countermagic of the witch-doctor is unusual in its lack of ritual. The patient simply tells the "listener" all his troubles and fears, beginning with the earliest difficulties he can remember. The memory displayed by the Nacirema in these exorcism sessions is truly remarkable. It is not uncommon for the patient to bemoan the rejection he felt upon being weaned as a babe, and a few individuals even see their troubles going back to the traumatic effects of their own birth.

In conclusion, mention must be made of certain practices which have their base in native esthetics but which depend upon the pervasive aversion to the natural body and its functions. There are ritual fasts to make fat people thin and ceremonial feasts to make thin people fat. Still other rites are used to make women's breasts larger if they are small, and smaller if they are large. General dissatisfaction with breast shape is symbolized in the fact that the ideal form is virtually outside the range of human variation. A few women afflicted with almost inhuman hypermammary development are so idolized that they make a handsome living by simply going from village to village and permitting the natives to stare at them for a fee.

Reference has already been made to the fact that excretory functions are ritualized, routinized, and relegated to secrecy.. Natural reproductive functions are similarly distorted. Intercourse is taboo as a topic and scheduled as an act. Efforts are made to avoid pregnancy by the use of magical materials or by limiting intercourse to certain phases of the moon. Conception is actually very infrequent. When pregnant, women dress so as to hide their condition. Parturition takes place in secret, without friends or relatives to assist, and the majority of women do not nurse their infants.

Our review of the ritual life of the Nacirema has certainly shown them to be a magic-ridden people. It is hard to understand how they have managed to exist so long under the burdens which they have imposed upon themselves. But even such exotic customs as these take on real meaning when they are viewed with the insight provided by Malinowski when he wrote (1948:70):

> Looking from far and above, from our high places of safety in the developed civilization, it is easy to see all the crudity and irrelevance of magic. But without its power and guidance early man could not have mastered his practical difficulties as he has done, nor could man have advanced to the higher stages of civilization.

REFERENCES

Linton, Ralph, 1936, *The Study of Man*. New York, D. Appleton-Century Co.

Malinowski, Bronislaw, 1948, *Magic, Science, and Religion*. Glencoe, The Free Press.

Murdock, George P., 1949, *Social Structure*. New York, The Macmillan Co.

2

Slumber's Unexplored Landscape

Bruce Bower

Why might our sleep be shaped by culture? All people need to sleep, but our expectations of what is normal sleep and how we go about arranging sleep are dictated by our cultural background. Therefore, our need for sleep may be a biological universal, but there are significant variations in the way that our need for sleep is satisfied. Similarly, culture shapes the way that our need for food is satisfied—what and when we eat and which foods we most enjoy. Of course, we can learn to enjoy and desire new foods. In fact, expanding our palates through cultural learning can be a delicious experience. From another perspective, we might consider pain as a way that culture shapes biology. All people experience pain, but there are cultural rules about the way in which we communicate our discomfort. For example, some societies may have gender-specific rules about the expression of pain ("boys don't cry") that become internalized so that adult men seek health care less frequently than women and children and consequently die at earlier ages.

Human biologists do not completely understand what the neurophysiological and psychological functions of dreams might be. In this selection, we see that nearly all scientific sleep research is conducted in artificial laboratory settings and based on the particular patterns of sleep found in Western culture. In this way, medical definitions of insomnia are based upon cultural assumptions of what "normal" sleep patterns are.

In traditional societies, sleep is often communal and in contexts that are noisy. People in these societies see the North American pattern of putting babies in their own cribs in their own rooms as strange and barbaric. Cross-cultural comparison based on direct observations of people in the field is the hallmark of research in cultural anthropology. In this selection we find that people in traditional societies sleep in eye-opening ways.

As you read this selection, ask yourself the following questions:

- Many students find that their sleeping patterns change when they go to college. What are the ways that your social and cultural contexts determine your sleep?
- Does the two-phase sleep pattern described at the end of this selection make sense to you?
- When we sleep, we dream. Does culture affect the content of our dreams? Why are dreams more discussed in some other societies?
- What is the value of cross-cultural anthropological research in sleep research?

The following terms discussed in this selection are included in the Glossary at the back of the book:

communal	*rapid eye movement (REM)*
cross-cultural	*séance*

Ah, the sweet simplicity of sleep. You tramp into your bedroom with sagging eyelids and stifle a yawn. After disrobing, you douse the lights and climb into bed. Maybe a little reading or television massages the nerves, loosening them up for slumber's velvet fingers. In a while, you nod off. Suddenly, an alarm clock's shrill blast breaks up the dozefest as the sun pokes over the horizon. You feel a bit drowsy but shake it off and face

the new day. Images of a dream dissolve like sugar in the morning's first cup of coffee.

There's a surprising twist, however, at the heart of this familiar ritual. It simply doesn't apply to people currently living outside of the modern Western world—or even to inhabitants of Western Europe as recently as 200 years ago.

In such contexts, and probably throughout human evolution, solitary shut-eye organized around a regular bedtime and a single bout of sleep proves about as common as stock car racing or teleconferencing. Surprisingly, anthropologists have rarely scrutinized the sleep patterns and practices of different cultures, much less those of different classes and ethnic groups in the United States.

An initial attempt to draw back the veils of sleep in hunter-gatherer groups and other traditional societies has uncovered a wide variety of sleep customs, reports anthropologist Carol M. Worthman of Emory University in Atlanta. None of these snooze styles, however, looks anything like what modern Western folk take for granted.

This finding raises profound questions for the burgeoning discipline of sleep research, Worthman says. Over the past 50 years, scientists have avidly delved into slumber's biology. Early research identified periods of rapid-eye-movement (REM) sleep, during which intense dreams often occur. Current efforts pursue genes involved in wakefulness and sleeping (SN: 8/14/99, p. 100). Researchers have also taken strides toward treating insomnia and other sleep disturbances.

While investigators readily concede that they don't yet know why people sleep and dream, they assume that they at least know how people should sleep: alone or with a partner for a solid chunk of the night. Sleep studies therefore take place in laboratories where individuals catch winks while hooked up to a bevy of brain and body monitors.

However, the distinctive sleep styles of non-Western groups may mold sleep's biology in ways undreamed of in sleep labs, Worthman suggests. They may influence factors ranging from sleep-related genes to the brain's electrical output during various sleep phases.

"It's time for scientists to get out into natural sleep environments," Worthman remarks. "It's embarrassing that anthropologists haven't done this, and the lack of such work is impeding sleep research."

A seemingly innocent question awakened Worthman to her discipline's ignorance of how people sleep. In 1994, she had a conversation with pediatrician Ronald E. Dahl of the University of Pittsburgh School of Medicine, who studies the effects of mood disorders on sleep. He asked the Emory scientist to tell him what anthropologists know about the history and prehistory of sleep. "[My] bald, if somewhat overstated, answer was 'zero,'" she says.

Sleep scarcely figures in the literature on either cross-cultural differences or human evolution, Worthman realized. Investigators generally relegate slumber to the sidelines, treating it as a biological given with little potential for variation from one place to another, she holds.

A few researchers have bucked this trend. For instance, anthropologist James J. McKenna of the University of Notre Dame in Indiana has reported that babies in many countries outside the United States sleep next to or in the same room as their parents. Contact with a parent's body helps regulate an infant's breathing and other physiological functions, he asserts, perhaps lowering the risk for sudden infant death syndrome (SN:12/4/93, p. 380).

McKenna's work should have roused investigators of traditional societies out of their sleep-related torpor, Worthman says. Yet, even seasoned field-workers have tended to ignore sleep—at least in their published works—while describing food production, sexual practices, and other facets of daily life.

So, Worthman contacted seven researchers who she knew had intimate knowledge of one or more traditional societies, including nomadic foragers, herders, and village-based farmers. Among these far-flung populations, none of the investigators, by their own admission, had systematically studied how people sleep. After plumbing what the researchers had absorbed about nighttime activities, Worthman has assembled a preliminary picture of sleep practices in 10 non-Western populations.

Worthman's findings rip the covers off any lingering suspicions that people everywhere sleep pretty much alike. Far from the wallpapered confines of middle-class bedrooms, sleep typically unfolds in shared spaces that feature constant background noise emanating from other sleepers, various domestic animals, fires maintained for warmth and protection from predators, and other people's nearby night-time activities.

Groups in Worthman's analysis include Ache foragers in Paraguay, !Kung hunter-gatherers in Africa, Swat Pathan herders in Pakistan, and Balinese farmers in Indonesia. For all these groups and six others, communal sleep equals safe sleep, because sleepers can count on there being someone else up or easily awakened at all hours of the night to warn others of a threat or emergency.

Adult sleepers in traditional societies recline on skins, mats, wooden platforms, the ground, or just about anything except a thick, springy mattress. Pillows or head supports are rare, and people doze in whatever they happen to be wearing. Virtually no one, including children, keeps a regular bedtime. Individuals tend to slip in and out of slumber several times during the night. In these unplugged worlds, darkness greatly limits activity and determines the time allotted to sleep. Folks there frequently complain of getting too much sleep, not too little.

Many rituals occur at night and exploit the need to sleep. For instance, initiation rites often force participants to cope with sleep deprivation. In other ceremonies, individuals enter somnolent, or near-sleep, states in order to magnify an occasion's psychological impact and to induce spiritual visions.

Consider the communal sleep of the Gebusi, New Guinea, rainforest dwellers, who grow fruit in small gardens and occasionally hunt wild pigs. Women, girls, and babies crowd into a narrow section of a community longhouse to sleep on mats. Men and boys retreat to an adjacent, more spacious longhouse area, where they sleep on wooden platforms.

Gebusi females retire at dark for about 10 hours of rest and sleep. In contrast, the men stay up later and frequently conduct rituals. About once a month, everyone attends an all-night dance and feast, catching up on sleep the next day.

Each week or two, Gebusi men go to séances led by a "spirit medium," at which they try to keep spirits awake throughout the night. Participants attempt to slip in and out of a near-sleep state as the medium, who's usually adept at operating in this half-conscious condition, sings about the spirit world and other matters.

As in most of the other studied societies, the Gebusi express concerns about exposure to ghosts, evil spirits, and witchcraft during sleep. They consider deep sleep risky, since a sleeper's spirit may wander off too far and fail to return. The Gebusi view group slumber as a way to lessen the danger of spirit loss, which they view as especially likely while a person dreams.

Whether or not one believes that sleeping puts a person's spirit at risk, slumber appears to have crucial effects on body and mind. A culture's sleeping style serves as a growing child's training ground for managing biologically based systems of attention and alertness, Worthman contends. Balinese farmers provide a striking example of this sleep-related tutoring.

Balinese infants are carried and held continuously by caregivers so that they learn to fall asleep even in hectic and noisy situations. This grooms them to exhibit what the Balinese call "fear sleep" later in life, Worthman says. Children and adults enter fear sleep by suddenly slumping over in a deep slumber when they or family members confront intense anxiety or an unexpected fright. They are literally scared into sleep.

Infants in middle-class American homes, who usually sleep alone, may not learn to ground their sleeping and waking cycles in a flow of sensations that include bodily contact, smells, and background noises, Worthman proposes. In fact, babies forced to bounce back and forth between the sensory overload of the waking world and the sensory barrenness of dark, quiet bedrooms may often find it difficult to relax, fall asleep, wake up, or concentrate, she theorizes.

Only cross-cultural studies of children's sleep and behavior can clarify such issues, Worthman says.

She described her findings and their implications in June at the annual meeting of the Associated Professional Sleep Societies in Orlando, Fla.

Sleep researchers at the meeting expressed considerable excitement about the potential for cross-cultural studies. "Worthman is doing innovative and important work," comments neuroscientist Robert A. Stickgold of the Massachusetts Mental Health Center in Boston. "It's awakening us to the many different ways in which people organize sleep."

Stickgold has developed snug-fitting, electrode-studded caps that people can wear in their own beds to measure brain activity linked to REM and other sleep stages. Worthman plans to take these "nightcaps," which hook up to mobile recorders, into the field to study sleep biology in traditional societies.

"I've been hoping anthropologists would examine sleep cross-culturally for the past 20 years," remarks psychologist Mary A. Carskadon of the Brown University School of Medicine in Providence, R.I.

Carskadon has directed studies that indicate that the body's so-called biological clock gets pushed back during adolescence. Teenagers may require more sleep than adults and may have a natural tendency to go to sleep later and wake up later than at other ages, she says.

A related study, directed by neuroscientist Louis J. Ptáček of the University of Utah in Salt Lake City, finds that a specific gene yanks the biological clock forward in some adults. People who have this gene tend to fall asleep by 8:30 P.M. and to awaken before 5:30 A.M., the researchers report in the September *Nature Medicine*.

In modern Western cultures, teens' backward shift in sleep timing is considered a nuisance or a sign of rebellion, while extreme early birds get diagnosed as sleep disordered. In traditional settings, however, highly variable sleep schedules among individuals and age groups prove invaluable, since they allow for someone to be awake or easily roused at all times should danger arise, Worthman holds.

If sleeping patterns in traditional societies remain little known, those of prehistoric humans are a total mystery. Still, in settings that roughly mimic ancient night-time conditions, sleep undergoes an intriguing shift, says psychiatrist Thomas A. Wehr of the National Institute of Mental Health (NIMH) in Bethesda, Md.

When prohibited from using artificial light from dusk until dawn, people who formerly slumbered in solid blocks of time begin to sleep in two periods separated by an hour or two of quiet rest and reflection.

Wehr and his coworkers asked 15 healthy adults to rest and sleep in darkness for 14 hours (6 P.M. to 8 A.M.) each night for several weeks. Volunteers slept for 11 hours each of the first few nights, apparently to catch up on their sleep. They then settled into a pattern of lying awake for a couple of hours before falling asleep for 3 to 5 hours in the evening. An hour or so of quiet wakefulness ensued, followed by about 4 more hours of sleep in the early morning.

Many mammals sleep in two major bouts during the night or day, Wehr says. Animals from rodents to giraffes and the experimental human sleepers secrete elevated amounts of the hormone prolactin when they rest quietly, even if they are not asleep. Prolactin may promote a state of calmness that accompanies sleep, the NIMH scientist suggests.

Participants in Wehr's study usually awoke out of REM sleep to end their first slumber session. During REM sleep, the brain becomes about as active as it is when wide awake. One function of this sleep phase may be to set the stage for waking up, Wehr holds.

If prehistoric people slept in two nightly periods, then regularly awakening out of REM sleep may have allowed them to reflect on and remember their dreams in a semiconscious state that's generally unavailable to modern sleepers. Sleep compressed into a single stint may thus encourage modern humans to lose touch with dreams, myths, and fantasies, Wehr argues.

These results, first reported in 1993, also raise the possibility that people who wake up once or twice each night don't necessarily suffer from insomnia. "A natural human sleep pattern may reassert itself in an unwelcome world and get labeled as a disorder," Wehr says.

The two-phase sleep pattern observed by Wehr corresponds remarkably closely to the way in which most Western Europeans slept between 500 to 200 years ago, according to historian A. Roger Ekirch of Virginia Polytechnic Institute and State University in Blacksburg. While doing research for a book on nighttime behaviors during that era, Ekirch came across several hundred references to what he identifies as "segmented sleep."

From country farms and villages to city apartments, early modern Europeans usually sank each evening into what they called a "first sleep," which lasted for several hours. Shortly after midnight, they awoke and spent 1 or 2 hours in a "watching period." A "second," or "morning," sleep followed.

The watching period presented many opportunities, Ekirch notes. People coming out of their first sleep often stayed in bed to pray, converse with a bedfellow, contemplate the day's events or the meaning of a dream, or simply let their minds wander in a semiconscious state of contentment that was prized at the time.

A 16th-century physician wrote that many laborers dozed off exhausted at the start of each night. Sexual intercourse with their wives typically occurred in the watching period, after a recuperative first sleep.

These days, Western societies treat sleep more as an unavoidable stretch of downtime than as a prelude to sex or a time for inner reflection. Only intensive investigations across cultures and classes will illuminate the lushness of sleep's landscape, Worthman predicts.

Adds Wehr, "We're going to have to reconceptualize what it means to sleep normally."

3

Tricking and Tripping: Fieldwork on Prostitution in the Era of AIDS

Claire E. Sterk

Students often think of anthropological fieldwork as requiring travel to exotic tropical locations, but that is not necessarily the case. This reading is based on fieldwork in the United States—on the streets in New York City as well as Atlanta. Claire Sterk is an anthropologist who works in a school of public health and is primarily interested in issues of women's health, particularly as it relates to sexual behavior. In this selection, an introduction to a book by the same title, she describes the basic fieldwork methods she used to study these women and their communities. Like most cultural anthropologists, Sterk's primary goal was to describe "the life" of prostitution from the women's own point of view. To do this, she had to be patient, brave, sympathetic, trustworthy, curious, and nonjudgmental. You will notice these characteristics in this selection; for example, Sterk begins her book with a poem written by one of her informants. Fieldwork is a slow process, because it takes time to win people's confidence and to learn their language and way of seeing the world. In this regard, there are probably few differences between the work of a qualitative sociologist and that of a cultural anthropologist (although anthropologists would not use the term "deviant" to describe another society or a segment of their own society).

Throughout the world, HIV / AIDS is fast becoming a disease found particularly in poor women. Sex workers or prostitutes have often been blamed for AIDS, and they have been further stigmatized because of their profession. In reality, however, entry into prostitution is not a career choice; rather, these women and girls are themselves most often victims of circumstances such as violence and poverty. Public health officials want to know why sex workers do not always protect their health by making men wear condoms. To answer such questions, we must know more about the daily life of these women. The way to do that, the cultural anthropologist would say, is to ask and to listen.

As you read this selection, ask yourself the following questions:

- What happens when Sterk says, "I'm sorry for you" to one of her informants? Why?
- Why do you think fieldwork might be a difficult job?
- Do you think that the fact that Sterk grew up in Amsterdam, where prostitution is legal, affected her research?
- Which of the six themes of this work, described at the end of the article, do you think is most important?

The following terms discussed in this selection are included in the Glossary at the back of the book:

demography   sample
fieldwork   stroll
key respondent

Prostitution is a way of life. IT IS THE LIFE.
We make money for pimps who promise us love and more,
but if we don't produce, they shove us out the door.
We turn tricks who have sex-for-pay.
They don't care how many times we serve every day.

The Life is rough. The Life is tough.
We are put down, beaten up, and left for dead.
It hurts body and soul and messes with a person's head.
Many of us get high. Don't you understand it is a way
*   of getting by?*
The Life is rough. The Life is tough.
We are easy to blame because we are lame.

—Piper, 1987[1]

One night in March of 1987 business was slow. I was hanging out on a stroll with a group of street prostitutes. After a few hours in a nearby diner/coffee shop, we were kicked out. The waitress felt bad, but she needed our table for some new customers. Four of us decided to sit in my car until the rain stopped. While three of us chatted about life, Piper wrote this poem. As soon as she read it to us, the conversation shifted to more serious topics—pimps, customers, cops, the many hassles of being a prostitute, to name a few. We decided that if I ever finished a book about prostitution, the book would start with her poem.

This book is about the women who work in the lower echelons of the prostitution world. They worked in the streets and other public settings as well as crack houses. Some of these women viewed themselves primarily as prostitutes, and a number of them used drugs to cope with the pressures of the life. Others identified themselves more as drug users, and their main reason for having sex for money or other goods was to support their own drug use and often the habit of their male partner. A small group of women interviewed for this book had left prostitution, and most of them were still struggling to integrate their past experiences as prostitutes in their current lives.

The stories told by the women who participated in this project revealed how pimps, customers, and others such as police officers and social and health service providers treated them as "fallen" women. However, their accounts also showed their strengths and the many strategies they developed to challenge these others. Circumstances, including their drug use, often forced them to sell sex, but they all resisted the notion that they might be selling themselves. Because they engaged in an illegal profession, these women had little status: their working conditions were poor, and their work was physically and mentally exhausting. Nevertheless, many women described the ways in which they gained a sense of control over their lives. For instance, they learned how to manipulate pimps, how to control the types of services and length of time bought by their customers, and how to select customers. While none of these schemes explicitly enhanced their working conditions, they did make the women feel stronger and better about themselves.

In this book, I present prostitution from the point of view of the women themselves. To understand their current lives, it was necessary to learn how they got started in the life, the various processes involved in their continued prostitution careers, the link between prostitution and drug use, the women's interactions with their pimps and customers, and the impact of the AIDS epidemic and increasing violence on their experiences. I also examined the implications for women.

Although my goal was to present the women's thoughts, feelings, and actions in their own words, the final text is a sociological monograph compiled by me as the researcher. Some women are quoted more than others because I developed a closer relationship with them, because they were more able to verbalize and capture their circumstances, or simply because they were more outspoken.

THE SAMPLE

The data for this book are qualitative. The research was conducted during the last ten years in the New York City and Atlanta metropolitan areas. One main data source was participant observation on streets, in hotels and other settings known for prostitution activity, and in drug-use settings, especially those that allowed sex-for-drug exchanges. Another data source was in-depth, life-history interviews with 180 women ranging in age from 18 to 59 years, with an average age of 34. One in two women was African-American and one in three white; the remaining women were Latina. Three in four had completed high school, and among them almost two-thirds had one or more years of additional educational training. Thirty women had graduated from college.

Forty women worked as street prostitutes and did not use drugs. On average, they had been prostitutes for 11 years. Forty women began using drugs an average of three years after they began working as prostitutes, and the average time they had worked as prostitutes was nine years. Forty women used drugs an average of five years before they became prostitutes, and on the average they had worked as prostitutes for eight years. Another forty women began smoking crack and exchanging sex for crack almost simultaneously, with an average of four years in the life. Twenty women who were interviewed were ex-prostitutes.

COMMENTS ON METHODOLOGY

When I tell people about my research, the most frequent question I am asked is how I gained access to the women rather than what I learned from the research. For many, prostitution is an unusual topic of conversation, and many people have expressed surprise that I, as a woman, conducted the research. During my research some customers indeed thought I was a working woman, a fact that almost always amuses those who hear about my work. However, few people want to hear stories about the women's struggles and sadness. Sometimes they ask questions about the reasons why women become prostitutes. Most of the time, they are surprised when I tell them that the prostitutes as well as their customers represent all layers of society. Before presenting the findings, it seems important to discuss the research process, including gaining access to the women, developing relationships, interviewing, and then leaving the field.[2]

LOCATING PROSTITUTES AND GAINING ENTREE

One of the first challenges I faced was to identify locations where street prostitution took place. Many of these women worked on strolls, streets where prostitution activity is concentrated, or in hotels known for prostitution activity. Others, such as the crack prostitutes, worked in less public settings such as a crack house that might be someone's apartment.

I often learned of well-known public places from professional experts, such as law enforcement officials and health care providers at emergency rooms and sexually transmitted disease clinics. I gained other insights from lay experts, including taxi drivers, bartenders, and community representatives such as members of neighborhood associations. The contacts universally mentioned some strolls as the places where many women worked, where the local police focused attention, or where residents had organized protests against prostitution in their neighborhoods.

As I began visiting various locales, I continued to learn about new settings. In one sense, I was developing ethnographic maps of street prostitution. After several visits to a specific area, I also was able to expand these maps by adding information about the general atmosphere on the stroll, general characteristics of the various people present, the ways in which the women and customers connected, and the overall flow of action. In addition, my visits allowed the regular actors to notice me.

I soon learned that being an unknown woman in an area known for prostitution may cause many people to notice you, even stare at you, but it fails to yield many verbal interactions. Most of the time when I tried to make eye contact with one of the women, she quickly averted her eyes. Pimps, on the other hand, would stare at me straight on and I ended up being the one to look away. Customers would stop, blow their horn, or wave me over, frequently yelling obscenities when I ignored them. I realized that gaining entree into the prostitution world was not going to be as easy as I imagined it. Although I lacked such training in any of my qualitative methods classes, I decided to move slowly and not force any interaction. The most I said during the initial weeks in a new area was limited to "how are you" or "hi." This strategy paid off during my first visits to one of the strolls in Brooklyn, New York. After several appearances, one of the women walked up to me and sarcastically asked if I was looking for something. She caught me off guard, and all the answers I had practiced did not seem to make sense. I mumbled something about just wanting to walk around. She did not like my answer, but she did like my accent. We ended up talking about the latter and she was especially excited when I told her I came from Amsterdam. One of her friends had gone to Europe with her boyfriend, who was in the military. She understood from her that prostitution and drugs were legal in the Netherlands. While explaining to her that some of her friend's impressions were incorrect, I was able to show off some of my knowledge about prostitution. I mentioned that I was interested in prostitution and wanted to write a book about it.

Despite the fascination with my background and intentions, the prostitute immediately put me through a Streetwalker 101 test, and apparently I passed. She told me to make sure to come back. By the time I left, I not only had my first conversation but also my first connection to the scene. Variations of this entry process occurred on the other strolls. The main lesson I learned in these early efforts was the importance of having some knowledge of the lives of the people I wanted to study, while at the same time refraining from presenting myself as an expert.

Qualitative researchers often refer to their initial connections as gatekeepers and key respondents. Throughout my fieldwork I learned that some key respondents are important in providing initial access, but they become less central as the research evolves. For example, one of the women who introduced me to her lover, who was also her pimp, was arrested and disappeared for months. Another entered drug treatment soon after she facilitated my access. Other key respondents provided access to only a segment of the players on a scene. For example, if a woman worked for a pimp, [she] was unlikely . . . to introduce me to women working for another pimp. On one stroll my initial contact was with a pimp whom nobody liked. By associating with him, I almost lost the opportunity to meet other pimps. Some key respondents were less connected than promised—for example, some of the women who worked the street to support their drug habit. Often their connections were more frequently with drug users and less so with prostitutes.

Key respondents tend to be individuals central to the local scene, such as, in this case, pimps and the more senior prostitutes. Their function as gatekeepers often is to protect the scene and to screen outsiders. Many times I had to prove that I was not an undercover police officer or a woman with ambitions to become a streetwalker. While I thought I had gained entree, I quickly learned that many insiders subsequently wondered about my motives and approached me with suspicion and distrust.

Another lesson involved the need to proceed cautiously with self-nominated key respondents. For example, one of the women presented herself as knowing everyone on the stroll. While she did know everyone, she was not a central figure. On the contrary, the other prostitutes viewed her as a failed streetwalker whose drug use caused her to act unprofessionally. By associating with me, she hoped to regain some of her status. For me, however, it meant limited access to the other women because I affiliated myself with a woman who was marginal to the scene. On another occasion, my main key respondent was a man who claimed to own three crack houses in the neighborhood. However, he had a negative reputation, and people accused him of cheating on others. My initial alliance with him delayed, and almost blocked, my access to others in the neighborhood. He intentionally tried to keep me from others on the scene, not because he would gain something from that transaction but because it made him feel powerful. When I told him I was going to hang out with some of the other people, he threatened me until one of the other dealers stepped in and told him to stay away. The two of them argued back and forth, and finally I was free to go. Fortunately, the dealer who had spoken up for me was much more central and positively associated with the local scene. Finally, I am unsure if I would have had success in gaining entrance to the scene had I not been a woman.

DEVELOPING RELATIONSHIPS AND TRUST

The processes involved in developing relationships in research situations amplify those involved in developing relationships in general. Both parties need to get to know each other, become aware and accepting of each other's roles, and engage in a reciprocal relationship. Being supportive and providing practical assistance were the most visible and direct ways for me as the researcher to develop a relationship. Throughout the years, I have given countless rides, provided child care on numerous occasions, bought groceries, and listened for hours to stories that were unrelated to my initial research questions. Gradually, my role allowed me to become part of these women's lives and to build rapport with many of them.

Over time, many women also realized that I was uninterested in being a prostitute and that I genuinely was interested in learning as much as possible about their lives. Many felt flattered that someone wanted to learn from them and that they had knowledge to offer. Allowing women to tell their stories and engaging in a dialogue with them probably were the single most important techniques that allowed me to develop relationships with them. Had I only wanted to focus on the questions I had in mind, developing such relationships might have been more difficult.

At times, I was able to get to know a woman only after her pimp endorsed our contact. One of my scariest experiences occurred before I knew to work through the pimps, and one such man had some of his friends follow me on my way home one night. I will never know what plans they had in mind for me because I fortunately was able to escape with only a few bruises. Over a year later, the woman acknowledged that her pimp had gotten upset and told her he was going to teach me a lesson.

On other occasions, I first needed to be screened by owners and managers of crack houses before the research could continue. Interestingly, screenings always were done by a man even if the person who vouched for me was a man himself. While the women also were cautious, the ways in which they checked me out tended to be much more subtle. For example, one of them would tell me a story, indicating that it was a secret about another person on the stroll. Although I failed to realize this at the time, my field notes revealed that frequently after such a conversation, others would ask me questions about related topics. One woman later acknowledged that putting out such stories was a test to see if I would keep information confidential.

Learning more about the women and gaining a better understanding of their lives also raised many ethical questions. No textbook told me how to handle situations in which a pimp abused a woman, a customer forced a woman to engage in unwanted sex acts, a customer requested unprotected sex from a woman who knew she was HIV infected, or a boyfriend had unrealistic expectations regarding a woman's earnings to support his drug habit. I failed to know the proper response when asked to engage in illegal activities such as holding drugs or money a woman had stolen from a customer. In general, my response was to explain that I was there as a researcher. During those occasions when pressures became too severe, I decided to leave a scene. For example, I never returned to certain crack houses because pimps there continued to ask me to consider working for them.

Over time, I was fortunate to develop relationships with people who "watched my back." One pimp in particular intervened if he perceived other pimps, customers, or passersby harassing me. He also was the one who gave me my street name: Whitie (indicating my racial background) or Ms. Whitie for those who disrespected me. While this was my first street name, I subsequently had others. Being given a street name was a symbolic gesture of acceptance. Gradually, I developed an identity that allowed me to be both an insider and an outsider. While hanging out on the strolls and other gathering places, including crack houses, I had to deal with some of the same uncomfortable conditions as the prostitutes, such as cold or warm weather, lack of access to a rest room, refusals from owners for me to patronize a restaurant, and of course, harassment by customers and the police.

I participated in many informal conversations. Unless pushed to do so, I seldom divulged my opinions. I was more open with my feelings about situations and showed empathy. I learned quickly that providing an opinion can backfire. I agreed that one of the women was struggling a lot and stated that I felt sorry for her. While I meant to indicate my genuine concern for her, she heard that I felt sorry for her because she was a failure. When she finally, after several weeks, talked with me again, I was able to explain to her that I was not judging her, but rather felt concerned for her. She remained cynical and many times asked me for favors to make up for my mistake. It took me months before I felt comfortable telling her that I felt I had done enough and that it was time to let go. However, if she was not ready, she needed to know that I would no longer go along. This was one of many occasions when I learned that although I wanted to facilitate my work as a researcher, that I wanted people to like and trust me, I also needed to set boundaries.

Rainy and slow nights often provided good opportunities for me to participate in conversations with groups of women. Popular topics included how to work safely, what to do about condom use, how to make more money. I often served as a health educator and a supplier of condoms, gels, vaginal douches, and other feminine products. Many women were very worried about the AIDS epidemic. However, they also were worried about how to use a condom when a customer refused to do so. They worried particularly about condom use when they needed money badly and, consequently, did not want to propose that the customer use one for fear of rejection. While some women became experts at "making" their customers use a condom—for example, by hiding it in their mouth prior to beginning oral sex—others would carry condoms to please me but never pull one out. If a woman was HIV positive and I knew she failed to use a condom, I faced the ethical dilemma of challenging her or staying out of it.

Developing trusting relationships with crack prostitutes was more difficult. Crack houses were not the right environment for informal conversations. Typically, the atmosphere was tense and everyone was suspicious of each other. The best times to talk with these women were when we bought groceries together, when I helped them clean their homes, or when we shared a meal. Often the women were very different when they were not high than they were when they were high or craving crack. In my conversations with them, I learned that while I might have observed their actions the night before, they themselves might not remember them. Once I realized this, I would be very careful to omit any detail unless I knew that the woman herself did remember the event.

IN-DEPTH INTERVIEWS

All interviews were conducted in a private setting, including women's residences, my car or my office, a restaurant of the women's choice, or any other setting the women selected. I did not begin conducting official interviews until I developed relationships with the women. Acquiring written informed consent prior to the interview was problematic. It made me feel awkward. Here I was asking the women to sign a form after they had begun to trust me. However, often I felt more upset about this technicality than the women themselves. As soon as they realized that the form was something the university required, they seemed to understand. Often they laughed about the official statements, and some asked if I was sure the form was to protect them and not the school.[3] None of the women refused to sign the consent form, although some refused to sign it right away and asked to be interviewed later.

In some instances the consent procedures caused the women to expect a formal interview. Some of them were disappointed when they saw I only had a few structured questions about demographic characteristics, followed by a long list of open-ended questions. When this disappointment occurred, I reminded the women that I wanted to learn from them and that the best way to do so was by engaging in a dialogue rather than interrogating them. Only by letting the women identify their salient issues and the topics they wanted to address was I able to gain an insider's perspective. By being a careful listener and probing for additional information and explanation, I as the interviewer, together with the women, was able to uncover the complexities of their lives. In addition, the nature of the interview allowed me to ask questions about contradictions in a woman's story. For example, sometimes a woman would say that she always used a condom. However, later on in the conversation she would indicate that if she needed drugs she would never use one. By asking her to elaborate on this, I was able to begin developing insights into condom use by type of partner, type of sex acts, and social context.

The interviewer becomes much more a part of the interview when the conversations are in-depth than when a structured questionnaire is used. Because I was so integral to the process, the way the women viewed me may have biased their answers. On the one hand, this bias might be reduced because of the extent to which both parties already knew each other; on the other, a woman might fail to give her true opinion and reveal her actions if she knew that these went against the interviewer's opinion. I suspected that some women played down the ways in which their pimps manipulated them once they knew that I was not too fond of these men. However, some might have taken more time to explain the relationship with their pimp in order to "correct" my image.

My background, so different from that of these women, most likely affected the nature of the interviews. I occupied a higher socioeconomic status. I had a place to live and a job. In contrast to the nonwhite women, I came from a different racial background. While I don't know to what extent these differences played a role, I acknowledge that they must have had some effect on this research.

LEAVING THE FIELD

Leaving the field was not something that occurred after completion of the fieldwork, but an event that took place daily. Although I sometimes stayed on the strolls all night or hung out for several days, I always had a home to return to. I had a house with electricity, a warm shower, a comfortable bed, and a kitchen. My house sat on a street where I had no fear of being shot on my way there and where I did not find condoms or syringes on my doorstep.

During several stages of the study, I had access to a car, which I used to give the women rides or to run errands together. However, I will never forget the cold night when everyone on the street was freezing, and I left to go home. I turned up the heat in my car, and tears streamed down my cheeks. I appreciated the heat, but I felt more guilty about that luxury than ever before. I truly felt like an outsider, or maybe even more appropriate, a betrayer.

Throughout the years of fieldwork, there were a number of times when I left the scene temporarily. For example, when so many people were dying from AIDS, I was unable to ignore the devastating impact of this disease. I needed an emotional break.

Physically removing myself from the scene was common when I experienced difficulty remaining objective. Once I became too involved in a woman's life and almost adopted her and her family. Another time I felt a true hatred for a crack house owner and was unable to adhere to the rules of courteous interactions. Still another time, I got angry with a woman whose

steady partner was HIV positive when she failed to ask him to use a condom when they had sex.

I also took temporary breaks from a particular scene by shifting settings and neighborhoods. For example, I would invest most of my time in women from a particular crack house for several weeks. Then I would shift to spending more time on one of the strolls, while making shorter and less frequent visits to the crack house. By shifting scenes, I was able to tell people why I was leaving and to remind all of us of my researcher role.

While I focused on leaving the field, I became interested in women who had left the life. It seemed important to have an understanding of their past and current circumstances. I knew some of them from the days when they were working, but identifying others was a challenge. There was no gathering place for ex-prostitutes. Informal networking, advertisements in local newspapers, and local clinics and community settings allowed me to reach twenty of these women. Conducting interviews with them later in the data collection process prepared me to ask specific questions. I realized that I had learned enough about the life to know what to ask. Interviewing ex-prostitutes also prepared me for moving from the fieldwork to writing.

It is hard to determine exactly when I left the field. It seems like a process that never ends. Although I was more physically removed from the scene, I continued to be involved while analyzing the data and writing this book. I also created opportunities to go back, for example, by asking women to give me feedback on parts of the manuscript or at times when I experienced writer's block and my car seemed to automatically steer itself to one of the strolls. I also have developed other research projects in some of the same communities. For example, both a project on intergenerational drug use and a gender-specific intervention project to help women remain HIV negative have brought me back to the same population. Some of the women have become key respondents in these new projects, while others now are members of a research team. For example, Beth, one of the women who has left prostitution, works as an outreach worker on another project.

SIX THEMES IN THE ETHNOGRAPHY OF PROSTITUTION

The main intention of my work is to provide the reader with a perspective on street prostitution from the point of view of the women themselves. There are six fundamental aspects of the women's lives as prostitutes that must be considered. The first concerns the women's own explanations for their involvement in prostitution and their descriptions of the various circumstances that led them to become prostitutes. Their stories include justifications such as traumatic past experiences, especially sexual abuse, the lack of love they experienced as children, pressures by friends and pimps, the need for drugs, and most prominently, the economic forces that pushed them into the life. A number of women describe these justifications as excuses, as reflective explanations they have developed after becoming a prostitute.

The women describe the nature of their initial experiences, which often involved alienation from those outside the life. They also show the differences in the processes between women who work as prostitutes and use drugs and women who do not use drugs.

Although all these women work either on the street or in drug-use settings, their lives do differ. My second theme is a typology that captures these differences, looking at the women's prostitution versus drug-use identities. The typology distinguishes among (a) streetwalkers, women who work strolls and who do not use drugs; (b) hooked prostitutes, women who identify themselves mainly as prostitutes but who upon their entrance into the life also began using drugs; (c) prostituting addicts, women who view themselves mainly as drug users and who became prostitutes to support their drug habit; and (d) crack prostitutes, women who trade sex for crack.

This typology explains the differences in the women's strategies for soliciting customers, their screening of customers, pricing of sex acts, and bargaining for services. For example, the streetwalkers have the most bargaining power, while such power appears to be lacking among the crack prostitutes.

Few prostitutes work in a vacuum. The third theme is the role of pimps, a label that most women dislike and for which they prefer to substitute "old man" or "boyfriend." Among the pimps, one finds entrepreneur lovers, men who mainly employ streetwalkers and hooked prostitutes and sometimes prostituting addicts. Entrepreneur lovers engage in the life for business reasons. They treat the women as their employees or their property and view them primarily as an economic commodity. The more successful a woman is in earning them money, the more difficult it is for that woman to leave her entrepreneur pimp.

Most prostituting addicts and some hooked prostitutes work for a lover pimp, a man who is their steady partner but who also lives off their earnings. Typically, such pimps employ only one woman. The dynamics in the relationship between a prostitute and her lover pimp become more complex when both partners use drugs. Drugs often become the glue of the relationship.

For many crack prostitutes, their crack addiction serves as a pimp. Few plan to exchange sex for crack when they first begin using; often several weeks or months pass before a woman who barters sex for crack realizes that she is a prostitute.

Historically, society has blamed prostitutes for introducing sexually transmitted diseases into the general population. Similarly, it makes them scapegoats for the spread of HIV/AIDS. Yet their pimps and customers are not held accountable. The fourth theme in the anthropological study of prostitution is the impact of the AIDS epidemic on the women's lives. Although most are knowledgeable about HIV risk behaviors and the ways to reduce their risk, many misconceptions exist. The women describe the complexities of condom use, especially with steady partners but also with paying customers. Many women have mixed feelings about HIV testing, wondering how to cope with a positive test result while no cure is available. A few of the women already knew their HIV-infected status, and the discussion touches on their dilemmas as well.

The fifth theme is the violence and abuse that make common appearances in the women's lives. An ethnography of prostitution must allow the women to describe violence in their neighborhoods as well as violence in prostitution and drug-use settings. The most common violence they encounter is from customers. These men often assume that because they pay for sex they buy a woman. Apparently, casual customers pose more of a danger than those who are regulars. The types of abuse the women encounter are emotional, physical, and sexual. In addition to customers, pimps and boyfriends abuse the women. Finally, the women discuss harassment by law enforcement officers.

When I talked with the women, it often seemed that there were no opportunities to escape from the life. Yet the sixth and final theme must be the escape from prostitution. Women who have left prostitution can describe the process of their exit from prostitution. As ex-prostitutes they struggle with the stigma of their past, the challenges of developing a new identity, and the impact of their past on current intimate relationships. Those who were also drug users often view themselves as ex-prostitutes and recovering addicts, a perspective that seems to create a role conflict. Overall, most ex-prostitutes find that their past follows them like a bad hangover.

NOTES

1. The names of the women who were interviewed for this study, as well as those of their pimps and customers, have been replaced by pseudonyms to protect their privacy. The use of pseudonyms is suggested by guidelines to protect the privacy of study participants (American

Anthropological Association; American Sociological Association).

2. For more information about qualitative research methods, see, for example, Patricia Adler and Peter Adler, *Membership Roles in Field Research* (Newbury Park: Sage, 1987); Michael Agar, *The Professional Stranger* (New York: Academic Press, 1980) and *Speaking of Ethnography* (Beverly Hills: Sage, 1986); Howard Becker and Blanche Geer, "Participant Observation and Interviewing: A Comparison," *Human Organization* 16 (1957): 28–32; Norman Denzin, *Sociological Methods: A Sourcebook* (Chicago: Aldine, 1970); Barney Glaser and Anselm Strauss, *The Discovery of Grounded Theory: Strategies for Qualitative Research* (Chicago: Aldine, 1967); Y. Lincoln and E. Guba, *Naturalistic Inquiry* (Beverly Hills: Sage, 1985); John Lofland, "Analytic Ethnography: Features, Failings, and Futures," *Journal of Contemporary Ethnography* 24 (1996): 30–67; and James Spradley, *The Ethnographic Interview* (New York: Holt, Rinehart and Winston, 1979) and *Participant Observation* (New York: Holt, Rinehart and Winston, 1980).

3. For a more extensive discussion of informed consent procedures and related ethical issues, see Bruce L. Berg, *Qualitative Research Methods for the Social Sciences*, 3rd edition, Chapter 3: "Ethical Issues" (Boston: Allyn and Bacon, 1998).

4

Crack in Spanish Harlem

Philippe Bourgois

Urban America vibrates with the intensity of a taut drum. The cadence of street life is a constant reminder that things are different here. Suburban folks who meander into some of these inner-city neighborhoods immediately notice the contrasts between these streets and their hometowns. Beset by what have been called the "signs of incivility," outsiders are uneasy and often afraid. Outsiders seldom understand the subculture of the inner city, and most don't want to.

Yet it is in the inner city that many of our most serious social problems are found, including unemployment, homelessness, broken families, poor medical care, and crime. Survival in this milieu, particularly in the drug scene, requires a deep understanding of the subculture. In the same way, effective public policy is more likely to result if policymakers understand the cultural meaning of people's behavior. But how can they achieve such an understanding?

This riveting account reveals how anthropological work can lend an important dimension to our comprehension of a way of life almost as foreign to most of us as is the life of an Amazon warrior, a !Kung bushman, or a rain forest pygmy.

As you read this selection, ask yourself the following questions:

- What is meant by the culture of resistance, and what effects does this culture have on a community and society?

- In what ways is the underground economy like a business?

- How is a job in the underground economy different from a legal job in terms of respect and an individual's feeling of self-worth?

- What is meant by the culture of terror, and what is the role of violence in maintaining social status?

- What can be learned through ethnographic fieldwork as opposed to questionnaires and surveys?

The following terms discussed in this selection are included in the Glossary at the back of the book:

cultural reproduction
ethnography
ghetto

A MUGGING IN SPANISH HARLEM

The heavy-set, white undercover policeman pushed me across the ice-cream counter, spreading my legs and poking me around the groin. As he came dangerously close to the bulge in my right pocket I hissed in his ear "It's a tape recorder." He snapped backwards, releasing his left hand's grip on my neck and whispering a barely audible "Sorry." Apparently, he thought he had clumsily intercepted an undercover from another department because before I could get a close look at his face he had left the *bodega* grocery-store cum numbers-joint. Meanwhile, the marijuana sellers stationed in

"Crack in Spanish Harlem: Culture and Economy in the Inner City" by Philippe Bourgois, from *Anthropology Today*, vol. 5, no. 4, 1989. Royal Anthropological Institute of Great Britain and Ireland. Reprinted by permission of Blackwell publishing.

front of the *bodega* that Gato and I had just entered to buy 16-ounce cans of Private Stock (beer), observing that the undercover had been rough with me when he searched through my pants, suddenly felt safe and relieved—finally confident that I was a white drug addict rather than an undercover.

As we hurried to leave this embarrassing scene we were blocked by Bennie, an emaciated teenager high on angel dust who was barging through the door along with two friends to mug us. I ran to the back of the *bodega* but Gato had to stand firmly because this was the corner he worked, and those were his former partners. They dragged him onto the sidewalk surrounding him on all sides, shouting about the money he still owed, and began kicking and hitting him with a baseball bat. I found out later that Gato owed them for his share of the supply of marijuana confiscated in a drug bust last week. . . . After we finished telling the story at the crack/*botanica*[1] house where I had been spending most of my evening hours this summer, Chino, who was on duty selling that night with Julio (pronounced Jew-Lee-oh), jumped up excitedly calling out "what street was that on? Come on, let's go, we can still catch them—How many were they?" I quickly stopped this mobilization for a revenge posse, explaining that it was not worth my time, and that we should just forget about it. Chino looked at me disgustedly sitting back down on the milk crate in front of the *botanica*'s door and turned his face away from me, shrugging his shoulders. Julio, whom I knew better and had become quite close to for a number of weeks last year, jumped up in front of me raising his voice to berate me for being "pussy." He also sat back down shortly afterwards feigning exasperated incredulity with the comment "Man you still think like a *blanquito*." A half dozen spectators—some of them empty-pocketed ("thirsty!") crack addicts, but most of them sharply dressed teenage drug-free girls competing for Chino's and Julio's attentions—giggled and snickered at me.

CULTURE AND MATERIAL REALITY

The above extract from sanitized fieldwork notes is merely a personalized glimpse of the day-to-day struggle for survival *and for meaning* by the people who stand behind the extraordinary statistics on inner city violent crime in the United States.[2] These are the same Puerto Rican residents of Spanish Harlem, New York City, that Oscar Lewis in *La Vida* declared to be victims of a "culture of poverty" enmired in a "self-perpetuating cycle of poverty" (Lewis 1966:5). The culture of poverty concept has been severely criticized for its internal inconsistencies, its inadequate understanding of "culture" and ethnicity, its ethnocentric/middle class bias, its blindness to structural forces, and its blame-the-victim implications (cf. Leacock ed. 1971, Valentine 1968, Waxman 1977, Stack 1974). Despite the negative scholarly consensus on Lewis's theory, the alternative discussions either tend towards economic reductionism (Ryan 1971, Steinberg 1981, Wilson 1978) or else ultimately minimize the reality of profound marginalization and destruction—some of it internalized—that envelop a disproportionate share of the inner city poor (cf. Stack 1974, Valentine 1978; see critiques by Maxwell 1988, Wilson 1987). More importantly, the media, public policy-makers and a large proportion of inner city residents themselves continue to subscribe to a popularized blame-the-victim/culture of poverty concept that has not been adequately rebutted by scholars.

The inner city residents described in the ethnographic vignette above are the pariahs of urban industrial US society. They seek their income and subsequently their identity and the meaning in their life through what they perceive to be high-powered careers "on the street." They partake of ideologies and values and share symbols which form the basis of an "inner city street culture" completely excluded from the mainstream economy and society but ultimately derived from it. Most of them have a few direct contacts with non–inner city residents, and when they do it is usually with people who are in a position of domination: teachers in school, bosses, police officers, and later parole or probation officers.

How can one understand the complicated ideological dynamic accompanying inner city poverty without falling into a hopelessly idealistic culture of poverty and blame-the-victim interpretation? Structural, political economy reinterpretations of the inner city dynamic emphasize historical processes of labour migration in the context of institutionalized ethnic discrimination. They dissect the structural transformations in the international economy which are destroying the manufacturing sector in the United States and are swelling the low wage, low prestige service sector (cf. Davis 1987; Sassen-Koob 1986; Steinberg 1981; Tabb and Sawers, eds., 1984; Wilson 1978, 1987). These analyses address the structural confines of the inner city dynamic but fall prey to a passive interpretation of human action and subscribe to a weakly dialectic interpretation of the relationship between ideological processes and material reality, or between culture and class.

Although ultimately traceable directly to being products of international labour migrations in a transnational world economy, street-level inner city residents are more than merely passive victims of historical economic transformations or of the institutionalized discrimination of a perverse political and economic system. They do not passively accept their fourth-class citizen fate. They are struggling determinedly—just as ruthlessly as the railroad and oil robber-barons of the previous century and the investment-banker "yuppies" of today—to earn money, demand dignity and lead meaningful lives. Tragically, it is that very process of struggle against—yet within—the system which exacerbates the trauma of their community and which destroys hundreds of thousands of lives on the individual level.

In the day-to-day experience of the street-bound inner city resident, unemployment and personal anxiety over the inability to provide one's family with a minimal standard of living translates itself into intra-community crime, intra-community drug abuse, intra-community violence. The objective, structural desperation of a population without a viable economy, and facing systematic barriers of ethnic discrimination and ideological marginalization, becomes charged at the community level into self-destructive channels.

Most importantly, the "personal failure" of those who survive on the street is articulated in the idiom of race. The racism imposed by the larger society becomes internalized on a personal level. Once again, although the individuals in the ethnographic fragment at the beginning of this paper are the victims of long-term historical and structural transformations, they do not analyse their difficult situation from a political economy perspective. In their struggle to survive and even to be successful, they enforce on a day-to-day level the details of the trauma and cruelty of their lives on the excluded margins of US urban society.

CULTURAL REPRODUCTION THEORY

Theorists of education have developed a literature on processes of social and cultural reproduction which focus on the ideological domination of the poor and the working class in the school setting (cf. Giroux 1983). Although some of the social reproduction approaches tend towards an economic reductionism or a simple, mechanical functionalism (cf. Bowles and Gintis 1977), the more recent variants emphasize the complexity and contradictory nature of the dynamic of ideological domination (Willis 1983). There are several ethnographies which document how the very process whereby students resist school channels them into marginal roles in the economy for the rest of their lives (cf. Willis 1977; Macleod 1987). Other ethnographically-based interpretations emphasize how success for inner city African-American students requires a rejection of their ethnic identity and cultural dignity (Fordham 1988).

There is no reason why these theories of cultural resistance and ideological domination have to be limited to the institutional school setting. Cultural reproduction theory has great potential for shedding light on the interaction between structurally induced cultural resistance and self-reinforced marginalization at the street level in the inner city experience. The violence, crime and substance abuse plaguing the inner city can be understood as the manifestations of a "culture of resistance" to mainstream, white racist, and economically exclusive society. This "culture of resistance," however, results in greater oppression and self-destruction. More concretely, refusing to accept the outside society's racist role playing and refusing to accept low wage, entry-level jobs, translates into high crime rates, high addiction rates and high intra-community violence.

Most of the individuals in the above ethnographic description are proud that they are not being exploited by "the White Man," but they feel "like fucking assholes" for being poor. All of them have previously held numerous jobs in the legal economy in their lives. Most of them hit the street in their early teens working odd jobs as delivery boys and baggers in supermarkets and *bodegas*. Most of them have held the jobs that are recognized as among the least desirable in US society. Virtually all of these street participants have had deeply negative personal experiences in the minimum-wage labour market, owing to abusive, exploitative and often racist bosses or supervisors. They see the illegal, underground economy as not only offering superior wages, but also a more dignified workplace. For example, Gato had formerly worked for the ASPCA, cleaning out the gas chambers where stray dogs and cats are killed. Bennie had been fired six months earlier from a night shift job as security guard on the violent ward for the criminally insane on Wards Island; Chino had been fired a year ago from a job installing high altitude storm windows on skyscrapers following an accident which temporarily blinded him in the right eye. Upon being disabled he discovered that his contractor had hired him illegally through an arrangement with a corrupt union official who had paid him half the union wage, pocketing the rest, and who had not taken health insurance for him. Chino also claimed that his foreman from Pennsylvania was a "Ku Klux Klanner" and had been especially abusive to him as he was a black Puerto Rican. In the process of recovering from the accident, Chino had become addicted to crack and ended up in the hospital as a gunshot victim before landing a job at Papito's crack house. Julio's last legal job before selling crack was as an off-the-books messenger for a magazine catering to New York yuppies. He had become addicted to crack, began selling possessions from out of his home and finally was thrown out by his wife who had just given birth to his son, who carried his name as Julio the IIIrd, on public assistance. Julio had quit his messenger job in favour of stealing car radios for a couple of hours at night in the very same neighbourhood where he had been delivering messages for ten hour days at just above minimum wage. Nevertheless, after a close encounter with the police, Julio begged his cousin for a job selling in his crack house. Significantly, the sense of responsibility, success and prestige that selling crack gave him enabled him to kick his crack habit and replace it by a less expensive and destructive powder cocaine and alcohol habit.

The underground economy, consequently, is the ultimate "equal opportunity employer" for inner city youth (cf. Kornblum and Williams 1985). As Davis (1987:75) has noted for Los Angeles, the structural economic incentive to participate in the drug economy is overwhelming:

> With 78,000 unemployed youth in the Watts-Willowbrook area, it is not surprising that there are now 145 branches of the rival Crips and Bloods gangs in South L.A., or that the jobless resort to the opportunities of the burgeoning "Crack" economy.

The individuals "successfully" pursuing careers in the "crack economy" or any other facet of the underground economy are no longer "exploitable" by legal society. They speak with anger at their former low wages and bad treatment. They make fun of friends and acquaintances—many of whom come to buy drugs from them—who are still employed in factories, in service jobs, or in what they (and most other people) would call "shitwork." Of course, many others are less self-conscious about the reasons for their rejection of entry-level, mainstream employment. Instead, they think of themselves as lazy and irresponsible. They claim they quit their jobs in order to have a good time on the street. Many still pay lip service to the value of a steady, legal job. Still others cycle in and out of legal employment supplementing their bouts at entry-level jobs through part-time crack sales in an almost perverse parody of the economic subsidy of the wage labour sector by semi-subsistence peasants who cyclically engage in migratory wage labour in third world economies (cf. Meillassoux 1981; Wallerstein 1977).

THE CULTURE OF TERROR IN THE UNDERGROUND ECONOMY

The culture of resistance that has emerged in the underground street-level economy in opposition to demeaning, underpaid employment in the mainstream economy engenders violence. In the South American context of extreme political repression and racism against Amerindians and Jews, anthropologist Michael Taussig has argued that "cultures of terror" emerge to become ". . . a high-powered tool for domination and a principal medium for political practice" (1984:492). Unlike Taussig's examples of the 1910s Putumayo massacres and the 1970s Argentine torture chambers, domination in the case of the inner city's culture of terror is self-administered even if the root cause is generated or even imposed externally. With the exception of occasional brutality by policemen or the bureaucratized repression of the social welfare and criminal justice institutions (cf. Davis 1988), the physical violence and terror of the inner city are largely carried out by inner city residents themselves.

Regular displays of violence are necessary for success in the underground economy—especially at the street-level drug dealing world. Violence is essential for maintaining credibility and for preventing rip-off by colleagues, customers and hold-up artists. Indeed, upward mobility in the underground economy requires a systematic and effective use of violence against one's colleagues, one's neighbours and, to a certain extent, against oneself. Behaviour that appears irrationally violent and self-destructive to the middle class (or the working class) outside observer, can be reinterpreted according to the logic of the underground economy, as a judicious case of public relations, advertising, rapport building and long-term investment in one's "human capital development."

The importance of one's reputation is well illustrated in the fieldwork fragment at the beginning of this paper. Gato and I were mugged because Gato had a reputation for being "soft" or "pussy" and because I was publicly unmasked as *not being* an undercover cop: hence safe to attack. Gato tried to minimize the damage to his future ability to sell on that corner by not turning and running. He had pranced sideways down the street, though being beaten with a baseball bat and kicked to the ground twice. Significantly, I found out later that it was the second time this had happened to Gato this year. Gato was not going to be upwardly mobile in the underground economy because of his "pussy" reputation and he was further cementing his fate with an increasingly out-of-control addiction to crack.

Employers or new entrepreneurs in the underground economy are looking for people who can demonstrate their capacity for effective violence and terror. For example, in the eyes of Papito, the owner of the string of crack franchises I am currently researching, the ability of his employees to hold up under gunpoint is crucial as stick-ups of dealing dens are not infrequent. In fact, since my fieldwork began in 1986, the *botanica* has been held up twice. Julio happened to be on duty both times. He admitted to me that he had been very nervous when they held the gun to his temple and had asked for money and crack. Nevertheless, not only did he withhold some of the money and crack that was hidden behind the bogus *botanica* merchandise, but he also later exaggerated to Papito the amount that had been stolen in order to pocket the difference.

On several occasions in the midst of long conversations with active criminals (i.e., once with a dealing-den stick-up artist, several times with crack dealers, and once with a former bank robber) I asked them to explain how they were able to trust their partners in crime sufficiently to ensure the longevity and effectiveness of their enterprise. To my surprise I was not given any righteous diatribes about blood-brotherhood trustworthiness or any adulations of boyhood loyalty. Instead, in each case, in slightly different language I was told somewhat aggressively: "What do you mean how do I trust him? You should ask 'How does he trust me?'" Their ruthlessness is their security: "My support network is me, myself and I." They made these assertions with such vehemence as to appear threatened by the concept that their security and success might depend upon the trustworthiness of their partner or their employer. They were claiming—in one case angrily—that they were not dependent upon trust: because they were tough enough to command respect and enforce all contracts they entered into. The "How can they trust me?" was said with smug pride, perhaps not unlike the way a stockbroker might brag about his access to inside information on an upcoming hostile takeover deal.

At the end of the summer Chino demonstrated clearly the how-can-I-be-trusted dynamic. His cocaine snorting habit had been degenerating into a crack addiction by the end of the summer, and finally one night he was forced to flee out of state to a cousin's when he was unable to turn in the night's receipts to his boss Papito following a binge. Chino also owed Papito close to a thousand dollars for bail that Papito had posted when he was arrested for selling crack at the *botanica* a few months ago. Almost a year later when Papito heard that Chino had been arrested for jumping bail he arranged through another associate incarcerated in the same prison (Rikers Island) to have Chino beaten up before his trial date.

My failure to display a propensity for violence in several instances cost me the respect of the members of the crack scene that I frequented. This was very evident when I turned down Julio and Chino's offer to search for Bennie after he mugged Gato and me. Julio had despairingly exclaimed that I "still [thought] like a *blanquito*," genuinely disappointed that I was not someone with common sense and self-respect.

These concrete examples of the cultivation of violent public behaviour are the extreme cases of individuals relying on the underground economy for their income and dependent upon cultivating terror in order to survive. Individuals involved in street activity cultivate the culture of terror in order to intimidate competitors, maintain credibility, develop new contacts, cement partnerships, and ultimately to have a good time. For the most part they are not conscious of this process. The culture of terror becomes a myth and a role model with rules and satisfactions all its own which ultimately has a traumatic impact on the majority of Spanish Harlem residents—who are drug free and who work honestly at poorly remunerated legal jobs, 9 to 5 plus overtime.

PURSUING THE AMERICAN DREAM

It is important to understand that the underground economy and the violence emerging out of it are not propelled by an irrational cultural logic distinct from that of mainstream USA. On the contrary, street participants are frantically pursuing the "American dream." The assertions of the culture of poverty theorists that the poor have been badly socialized and do not share mainstream values is wrong. On the contrary, ambitious, energetic, inner city youths are attracted into the underground economy in order to try frantically to get their piece of the pie as fast as possible. They often even follow the traditional US model for upward mobility to the letter by becoming aggressive private entrepreneurs. They are the ultimate rugged individualists braving an unpredictable frontier where fortune, fame and destruction are all just around the corner. Hence Indio, a particularly enterprising and ambitious young crack dealer who was aggressively carving out a new sales point, shot his brother in the spine and paralysed him for life while he was high on angel dust in a battle over sales rights. His brother now works for him selling on crutches. Meanwhile, the shooting has cemented Indio's reputation and his workers are awesomely disciplined: "If he shot his brother he'll shoot anyone." Indio reaffirms this symbolically by periodically walking his turf with an oversized gold chain and name plate worth several thousand dollars hanging around his neck.

The underground economy and the culture of terror are experienced as the most realistic routes to upward mobility. Entry-level jobs are not seen as viable channels to upward mobility by high school dropouts. Drug selling or other illegal activity appear as the most effective and realistic options for getting rich within one's lifetime. Many of the street dealers claim to be strictly utilitarian in their involvement with crack and they snub their clients despite the fact that they usually have considerable alcohol and powder cocaine habits themselves. Chino used to chant at his regular customers "Come on, keep on killing yourself; bring me that money; smoke yourself to death; make me rich."

Even though street sellers are employed by the owner of a sales point for whom they have to maintain regular hours, meet sales quotas and be subject to being fired, they have a great deal of autonomy and power in their daily (or nightly) routine. The boss only comes once or twice a shift to drop off drugs and pick up money. Frequently, it is a young messenger who is sent instead. Sellers are often surrounded by a bevy of "thirsty" friends and hanger-oners—frequently young teenage women in the case of male sellers—willing to run errands, pay attention to conversations, lend support in arguments and fights and provide sexual favours for them on demand because of the relatively large amounts of money and drugs passing through their hands. In fact, even youths who do not use drugs will hang out and attempt to befriend respectfully the dealer just to be privy to the excitement of people coming and going, copping and hanging; money flowing, arguments, detectives, and stick-up artists—all around danger and excitement. Other nonusers will hang out to be treated to an occasional round of beer, Bacardi or, on an off night, Thunderbird.

The channel into the underground economy is by no means strictly economic. Besides wanting to earn "crazy money," people choose "hoodlum" status in order to assert their dignity at refusing to "sling a mop for the white man" (cf. Anderson 1976:68). Employment or better yet self-employment—in the underground economy—accords a sense of autonomy, self-dignity and an opportunity for extraordinary rapid short-term upward mobility that is only too obviously unavailable in entry-level jobs. Opulent survival without a "visible means of support" is the ultimate expression of success and it is a viable option. There is plenty of visible proof of this to everyone on the street as they watch teenage crack dealers drive by in convertible Suzuki Samurai jeeps with the stereo blaring, "beem" by in impeccable BMWs, or—in the case of the middle-aged dealers—speed around in well waxed Lincoln Continentals. Anyone can aspire to be promoted to the level of a seller perched on a 20-speed mountain bike with a beeper by their side. In fact, many youths not particularly active in the drug trade run around with beepers on their belts just pretending to be big-time. The impact of the sense of dignity and worth that can accompany selling crack is illustrated by Julio's ability to overcome his destructive addiction to crack only after getting a job selling it: "I couldn't be messin' up the money. I couldn't be fucking up no more! Besides, I had to get respect."

In New York City the insult of working for entry-level wages amidst extraordinary opulence is especially painfully perceived by Spanish Harlem youths who have grown up in abject poverty only a few blocks from all-white neighbourhoods commanding some of the highest real estate values in the world. As messengers, security guards or Xerox machine operators in the corporate headquarters of the *Fortune* 500 companies, they are brusquely ordered about by young white executives who sometimes make monthly salaries superior to their yearly wages and who do not even have the time to notice that they are being rude.

It could be argued that Manhattan sports a *de facto* apartheid labour hierarchy whereby differences in job category and prestige correlate with ethnicity and are often justified—consciously or unconsciously—through a racist logic. This humiliating confrontation with New York's ethnic/occupational hierarchy drives the street-bound cohort of inner city youths deeper into the confines of their segregated neighbourhood and the underground economy. They prefer to seek out meaning and upward mobility in a context that does not constantly oblige them to come into contact with people of a different, hostile ethnicity wielding arbitrary power over them. In the underground economy, especially in the world of substance abuse, they never have to experience the silent subtle humiliations that the entry-level labour market—or even merely a daily subway ride downtown—invariably subjects them to.

In this context the crack high and the rituals and struggles around purchasing and using the drug are comparable to the millenarian religions that sweep colonized peoples attempting to resist oppression in the context of accelerated social trauma—whether it be the Ghost dance of the Great Plains Amerindians, the "cargo cults" of Melanesia, the Mamachi movement of the Guaymi Amerindians in Panama, or even religions such as Farrakhan's Nation of Islam and the Jehovah's Witnesses in the heart of the inner city (cf. Bourgois 1986, 1989). Substance abuse in general, and crack in particular, offer the equivalent of a millenarian metamorphosis. Instantaneously users are transformed from being unemployed, depressed high school dropouts, despised by the world—and secretly convinced that their failure is due to their own inherent stupidity, "racial laziness" and disorganization—into being a mass of heart-palpitating pleasure, followed only minutes later by a jaw-gnashing crash and wideawake alertness that provides their life with concrete purpose: get more crack—fast!

One of the most dramatic illustrations within the dynamic of the crack economy of how a cultural dynamic of resistance to exploitation can lead contradictorily to greater oppression and ideological domination is the conspicuous presence of women in the growing cohort of crack addicts. In a series of ten random surveys undertaken at Papito's crack franchises, women and girls represented just under 50% of the customers. This contrasts dramatically to the estimates of female participation in heroin addiction in the late 1970s.

The painful spectacle of young, emaciated women milling in agitated angst around crack copping corners and selling their bodies for five dollars, or even merely for a puff on a crack stem, reflects the growing emancipation of women in all aspects of inner city life, culture and economy. Women—especially the emerging generation which is most at risk for crack addiction—are no longer as obliged to stay at home and maintain the family. They no longer so readily sacrifice public life or forgo independent opportunities to generate personally disposable income. This is documented by the frequent visits to the crack houses by pregnant women and by mothers accompanied by toddlers.

A more neutral illustration of the changed position of women in street culture outside the arena of substance abuse is the growing presence of young women on inner city basketball courts. Similarly, on the national level, there are conclusive statistics documenting increased female participation in the legal labour market—especially in the working class Puerto Rican community. By the same token, more women are also resisting exploitation in the entry-level job market and are pursuing careers in the underground economy and seeking self-definition and meaning through intensive participation in street culture.

Although women are using the drug and participating intensively in street culture, traditional gender relations still largely govern income-generating strategies in the underground economy. Most notably, women are forced disproportionately to rely on prostitution to finance their habits. The relegation of women to the traditional street role of prostitution has led to a flooding of the market for sex, leading to a drop in the price of women's bodies and to an epidemic rise in venereal disease among women and newborn babies.

Contradictorily, therefore, the underlying process of emancipation which has enabled women to demand equal participation in street culture and to carve out an expanded niche for themselves in the underground economy has led to a greater depreciation of women as ridiculed sex objects. Addicted women will tolerate a tremendous amount of verbal and physical abuse in their pursuit of a vial of crack, allowing lecherous men to humiliate and ridicule them in public. Chino, who is married and is the father of nine children, refers to the women who regularly service him with oral sex as "my moufs" [mouths]. He enjoys calling out to these addicted women from across the street, "Yo, there goes my mouf! Come on over here." Such a public degradation of a cohort of women who are conspicuously present on the street cannot be neutral. It ultimately reinforces the ideological domination of women in general.

DE-LEGITIMIZING DOMINATION

How can one discuss and analyse the phenomenon of street-level inner city culture and violence without reproducing and confirming the very ideological relationships that are its basis? In his discussion of the culture of terror, Taussig notes that it is precisely the narratives about the torture and violence of the repressive societies which ". . . are in themselves evidence of the process whereby a culture of terror was created and sustained" (1984:279). The superhuman power that the media has accorded to crack serves a similar mythical function. The *New York Times* has run articles and interviews with scientists that portray crack as if it were a miraculous substance beyond the power of human beings to control (cf. 25 June, 1988: 1). They "prove" this by documenting how quickly rats will ecstatically kill themselves when provided with cocaine upon demand. Catheterized rats push the cocaine lever to the exclusion of the nutrient lever until they collapse exhausted to die of thirst.

The alleged omnipotence of crack coupled with even the driest recounting of the overpowering statistics on violence ultimately allows US society to absolve itself of any real responsibility for the inner city phenomena. The mythical dimensions of the culture of terror push economics and politics out of the picture and enable the US to maintain in some of its larger cities a level of ethnic segregation and economic marginalization that are unacceptable to any of the other wealthy, industrialized nations of the world, with the obvious exception of South Africa. Worse yet, on the level of theory, because of the continued domination—even in their negation—of the North America-centred culture of poverty theories, this discussion of the ideological implications of the underground economy may take readers full circle back to a blame-the-victim interpretation of inner city oppression.

NOTES

1. A *botanica* is a herbal pharmacy and *santeria* utility store.
2. This research was funded by the United States Bureau of the Census, the Wenner-Gren Foundation for Anthropological Research, two Washington University Junior Faculty Summer Research grants, and Lottery Funds and an Affirmative Action Grant from San Francisco State University. An expanded version of this article will be appearing in a special issue of *Contemporary Drug Problems* devoted to crack in the United States.

    Pseudonyms have been used in order to disguise identities of persons referred to.

REFERENCES

Anderson, Elijah. 1976. *A Place on the Corner.* Chicago: U. of Chicago.

Bourgois, Philippe. 1986. The Miskitu of Nicaragua: Politicized Ethnicity. *A.T.* 2(2): 4–9.

——. 1989. *Ethnicity at Work: Divided Labour on a Central American Banana Plantation.* Baltimore: Johns Hopkins U.P.

Bowles, Samuel, and Herbert Gintis. 1977. *Schooling in Capitalist America.* New York: Basic Books.

Davis, Mike. 1987. *Chinatown,* Part Two? The "Internationalization" of Downtown Los Angeles. *New Left Review* 164: 65–86.

Davis, Mike, with Sue Ruddick. 1988. Los Angeles: Civil Liberties Between the Hammer and the Rock. *New Left Review* 1970: 37–60.

Fordham, Signithia. 1988. Racelessness as a Factor in Black Students' School Success: Pragmatic Strategy or Pyrrhic Victory? *Harvard Educational Review* 58(1): 54–84.

Giroux, Henry. 1983. Theories of Reproduction and Resistance in the New Sociology of Education: A Critical Analysis. *Harvard Educational Review* 53(3): 257–293.

Kornblum, William, and Terry Williams. 1985. *Growing Up Poor.* Lexington, MA: Lexington Books.

Leacock, Eleanor Burke, ed. 1971. *The Culture of Poverty: A Critique.* New York: Simon and Schuster.

Lewis, Oscar. 1966. The Culture of Poverty. In *Anthropological Essays*, pp. 67–80. New York: Random House.

Macleod, Jay. 1987. *Ain't No Makin' It.* Boulder, Colorado: Westview P.

Maxwell, Andrew. 1988. The Anthropology of Poverty in Black Communities: A Critique and Systems Alternative. *Urban Anthropology* 17(2&3): 171–191.

Meillassoux, Claude. 1981. *Maidens, Meal and Money.* Cambridge: Cambridge U.P.

Ryan, William. 1986[1971]. Blaming the Victim. In *Taking Sides: Clashing Views on Controversial Social Issues*, pp. 45–52, ed. Kurt Finsterbusch and George McKenna. Guilford, CT: Dushkin Publishing Group.

Sassen-Koob, Saskia. 1986. New York City: Economic Restructuring and Immigration. *Development and Change* 17(1): 87–119.

Stack, Carol. 1974. *All Our Kin: Strategies for Survival in a Black Community.* New York: Harper & Row.

Steinberg, Stephen. 1981. *The Ethnic Myth: Race, Ethnicity and Class in America.* New York: Atheneum.

Tabb, William, and Larry Sawers, eds. 1984. *Marxism and the Metropolis: New Perspectives in Urban Political Economy.* New York: Oxford U.P.

Taussig, Michael. 1984. Culture of Terror—Space of Death, Roger Casement's Putumayo Report and the Explanation of Torture. *Comparative Studies in Society and History* 26(3): 467–497.

Valentine, Charles. 1968. *Culture and Poverty.* Chicago: U. of Chicago P.

Valentine, Bettylou. 1978. *Hustling and Other Hard Work.* NY: Free Press.

Wallerstein, Emanuel. 1977. Rural Economy in Modern World Society. *Studies in Comparative International Development* 12(1): 29–40.

Waxman, Chaim. 1977. *The Stigma of Poverty: A Critique of Poverty Theories and Policies.* NY: Pergamon.

Willis, Paul. 1983. Cultural Production and Theories of Reproduction. In *Race, Class and Education*, pp. 107–138, ed. Len Barton and Stephen Walker. London: Croom-Helm.

——. 1977. *Learning to Labor: How Working Class Kids Get Working Class Jobs.* Aldershot, England: Gower.

Wilson, William Julius. 1978. *The Declining Significance of Race: Blacks and Changing American Institutions.* Chicago: U. of Chicago P.

——. 1987. *The Truly Disadvantaged: The Inner City, the Underclass and Public Policy.* Chicago: U. of Chicago Press.

5

Shakespeare in the Bush

Laura Bohannan

Communication is an essential characteristic of human social life. Through language we socialize our children and pass down cultural values from generation to generation. Communication forms and defines relations among individuals as well as among groups. Because communication is so natural, we seldom ask a critical question: When we speak, does the listener understand?

At a minimum, communication involves a sender, a receiver, and a shared code for exchanging information. When an individual or a group sends a message, the sender anticipates that those who receive the message will interpret and understand the message in the way the sender intended. Miscommunication is, of course, an unfortunately common phenomenon that can lead to fistfights, divorces, and wars.

What most of us do not appreciate is the degree to which culture affects our interpretation of messages. As Laura Bohannan tells the tale of *Hamlet,* we gradually discover how particular behaviors or events can have very different meanings in different places. What is interesting is that the miscommunication of interpretational differences is not a result of poor language or translation abilities. Miscommunication is not a result of speaking too quickly or not loudly enough. It reflects cultural differences.

As you read this selection, ask yourself the following questions:

- What were the author's original beliefs about the universality of the classics—such as *Hamlet?*
- How did the Tiv elders react to the marriage of Hamlet's mother to his uncle? How was this different from Hamlet's own emotional reaction?
- Why do the Tiv believe that a chief should have more than one wife?
- As the author tells the story, consider how the elders interpret various actions to fit Tiv culture and in so doing redefine the central meaning of the play.

The following terms discussed in this selection are included in the Glossary at the back of the book:

age grade	levirate
agnatic	polygyny
chiefdom	socialization
cultural relativism	

J ust before I left Oxford for the Tiv in West Africa, conversation turned to the season at Stratford. "You Americans," said a friend, "often have difficulty with Shakespeare. He was, after all, a very English poet, and one can easily misinterpret the universal by misunderstanding the particular."

I protested that human nature is pretty much the same the whole world over; at least the general plot and motivation of the greater tragedies would always be clear—everywhere—although some details of custom might have to be explained and difficulties of translation might produce other slight changes. To end an argument we could not conclude, my friend gave me a copy of *Hamlet* to study in the African bush: it

would, he hoped, lift my mind above its primitive surroundings, and possibly I might, by prolonged meditation, achieve the grace of correct interpretation.

It was my second field trip to that African tribe, and I thought myself ready to live in one of its remote sections—an area difficult to cross even on foot. I eventually settled on the hillock of a very knowledgeable old man, the head of a homestead of some hundred and forty people, all of whom were either his close relatives or their wives and children. Like the other elders of the vicinity, the old man spent most of his time performing ceremonies seldom seen these days in the more accessible parts of the tribe. I was delighted. Soon there would be three months of enforced isolation and leisure, between the harvest that takes place just before the rising of the swamps and the clearing of new farms when the water goes down. Then, I thought, they

From *Natural History,* 1966. Reprinted by permission of the author.

would have even more time to perform ceremonies and explain them to me.

I was quite mistaken. Most of the ceremonies demanded the presence of elders from several homesteads. As the swamps rose, the old men found it too difficult to walk from one homestead to the next, and the ceremonies gradually ceased. As the swamps rose even higher, all activities but one came to an end. The women brewed beer from maize and millet. Men, women, and children sat on their hillocks and drank it.

People began to drink at dawn. By midmorning the whole homestead was singing, dancing, and drumming. When it rained, people had to sit inside their huts: there they drank and sang or they drank and told stories. In any case, by noon or before, I either had to join the party or retire to my own hut and my books. "One does not discuss serious matters when there is beer. Come, drink with us." Since I lacked their capacity for the thick native beer, I spent more and more time with *Hamlet*. Before the end of the second month, grace descended on me. I was quite sure that *Hamlet* had only one possible interpretation, and that one universally obvious.

Early every morning in the hope of having some serious talk before the beer party, I used to call on the old man at his reception hut—a circle of posts supporting a thatched roof above a low mud wall to keep out wind and rain. One day I crawled through the low doorway and found most of the men of the homestead sitting huddled in their ragged clothes on stools, low plank beds, and reclining chairs, warming themselves against the chill of the rain around a smoky fire. In the center were three pots of beer. The party had started.

The old man greeted me cordially. "Sit down and drink." I accepted a large calabash full of beer, poured some into a small drinking gourd, and tossed it down. Then I poured some more into the same gourd for the man second in seniority to my host before I handed my calabash over to a young man for further distribution. Important people shouldn't ladle beer themselves.

"It is better like this," the old man said, looking at me approvingly and plucking at the thatch that had caught in my hair. "You should sit and drink with us more often. Your servants tell me that when you are not with us, you sit inside your hut looking at a paper."

The old man was acquainted with four kinds of "papers": tax receipts, bride price receipts, court fee receipts, and letters. The messenger who brought him letters from the chief used them mainly as a badge of office, for he always knew what was in them and told the old man. Personal letters for the few who had relatives in the government or mission stations were kept until someone went to a large market where there was a letter writer and reader. Since my arrival, letters were brought to me to be read. A few men also brought me bride price receipts, privately, with requests to change

the figures to a higher sum. I found moral arguments were of no avail, since in-laws are fair game, and the technical hazards of forgery difficult to explain to an illiterate people. I did not wish them to think me silly enough to look at any such papers for days on end, and I hastily explained that my "paper" was one of the "things of long ago" of my country.

"Ah," said the old man. "Tell us."

I protested that I was not a storyteller. Storytelling is a skilled art among them; their standards are high and the audiences critical—and vocal in their criticism. I protested in vain. This morning they wanted to hear a story while they drank. They threatened to tell me no more stories until I told them one of mine. Finally, the old man promised that no one would criticize my style "for we know you are struggling with our language." "But," put in one of the elders, "you must explain what we do not understand, as we do when we tell you our stories." Realizing that here was my chance to prove Hamlet universally intelligible, I agreed.

The old man handed me some more beer to help me on with my storytelling. Men filled their long wooden pipes and knocked coals from the fire to place in the pipe bowls; then, puffing contentedly, they sat back to listen. I began in the proper style, "Not yesterday, not yesterday, but long ago, a thing occurred. One night three men were keeping watch outside the homestead of the great chief, when suddenly they saw the former chief approach them."

"Why was he no longer their chief?"

"He was dead," I explained. "That is why they were troubled and afraid when they saw him."

"Impossible," began one of the elders, handing his pipe on to his neighbor, who interrupted, "Of course it wasn't the dead chief. It was an omen sent by a witch. Go on."

Slightly shaken, I continued. "One of these three was a man who knew things"—the closest translation for scholar, but unfortunately it also meant witch. The second elder looked triumphantly at the first. "So he spoke to the dead chief saying, 'Tell us what we must do so you may rest in your grave,' but the dead chief did not answer. He vanished, and they could see him no more. Then the man who knew things—his name was Horatio—said this event was the affair of the dead chief's son, Hamlet."

There was a general shaking of heads round the circle. "Had the dead chief no living brothers? Or was this son the chief?"

"No," I replied. "That is, he had one living brother who became the chief when the elder brother died."

The old men muttered: such omens were matters for chiefs and elders, not for youngsters; no good could come of going behind a chief's back; clearly Horatio was not a man who knew things.

"Yes, he was," I insisted, shooing a chicken away from my beer. "In our country the son is next to the father. The dead chief's younger brother had become the great chief. He had also married his elder brother's widow only about a month after the funeral."

"He did well," the old man beamed and announced to the others, "I told you that if we knew more about Europeans, we would find they really were very like us. In our country also," he added to me, "the younger brother marries the elder brother's widow and becomes the father of his children. Now, if your uncle, who married your widowed mother, is your father's full brother, then he will be a real father to you. Did Hamlet's father and uncle have one mother?"

His question barely penetrated my mind; I was too upset and thrown off balance by having one of the most important elements of *Hamlet* knocked straight out of the picture. Rather uncertainly I said that I thought they had the same mother, but I wasn't sure—the story didn't say. The old man told me severely that these genealogical details made all the difference and that when I got home I must ask the elders about it. He shouted out the door to one of his younger wives to bring his goatskin bag.

Determined to save what I could of the mother motif, I took a deep breath and began again. "The son Hamlet was very sad because his mother had married again so quickly. There was no need for her to do so, and it is our custom for a widow not to go to her next husband until she has mourned for two years."

"Two years is too long," objected the wife, who had appeared with the old man's battered goatskin bag. "Who will hoe your farms for you while you have no husband?"

"Hamlet," I retorted without thinking, "was old enough to hoe his mother's farms himself. There was no need for her to remarry." No one looked convinced. I gave up. "His mother and the great chief told Hamlet not to be sad, for the great chief himself would be a father to Hamlet. Furthermore, Hamlet would be the next chief: therefore he must stay to learn the things of a chief. Hamlet agreed to remain, and all the rest went off to drink beer."

While I paused, perplexed at how to render Hamlet's disgusted soliloquy to an audience convinced that Claudius and Gertrude had behaved in the best possible manner, one of the younger men asked me who had married the other wives of the dead chief.

"He had no other wives," I told him.

"But a chief must have many wives! How else can he brew beer and prepare food for all his guests?"

I said firmly that in our country even chiefs had only one wife, that they had servants to do their work, and that they paid them from tax money.

It was better, they returned, for a chief to have many wives and sons who would help him hoe his farms and feed his people; then everyone loved the chief who gave much and took nothing—taxes were a bad thing.

I agreed with the last comment, but for the rest fell back on their favorite way of fobbing off my questions: "That is the way it is done, so that is how we do it."

I decided to skip the soliloquy. Even if Claudius was here thought quite right to marry his brother's widow, there remained the poison motif, and I knew they would disapprove of fratricide. More hopefully I resumed, "That night Hamlet kept watch with the three who had seen his dead father. The dead chief again appeared, and although the others were afraid, Hamlet followed his dead father off to one side. When they were alone, Hamlet's dead father spoke."

"Omens can't talk!" The old man was emphatic.

"Hamlet's dead father wasn't an omen. Seeing him might have been an omen, but he was not." My audience looked as confused as I sounded. "It was Hamlet's dead father. It was a thing we call a 'ghost.'" I had to use the English word, for unlike many of the neighboring tribes, these people didn't believe in the survival after death of any individuating part of the personality.

"What is a 'ghost'? An omen?"

"No, a 'ghost' is someone who is dead but who walks around and can talk, and people can hear him and see him but not touch him."

They objected. "One can touch zombis."

"No, no! It was not a dead body the witches had animated to sacrifice and eat. No one else made Hamlet's dead father walk. He did it himself."

"Dead men can't walk," protested my audience as one man.

I was quite willing to compromise. "A 'ghost' is the dead man's shadow."

But again they objected. "Dead men cast no shadows."

"They do in my country," I snapped.

The old man quelled the babble of disbelief that arose immediately and told me with that insincere, but courteous, agreement one extends to the fancies of the young, ignorant, and superstitious, "No doubt in your country the dead can also walk without being zombis." From the depths of his bag he produced a withered fragment of kola nut, bit off one end to show it wasn't poisoned, and handed me the rest as a peace offering.

"Anyhow," I resumed, "Hamlet's dead father said that his own brother, the one who became chief, had poisoned him. He wanted Hamlet to avenge him. Hamlet believed this in his heart, for he did not like his father's brother." I took another swallow of beer. "In the country of the great chief, living in the same homestead, for it was a very large one, was an important elder who was often with the chief to advise and help him. His name was Polonius. Hamlet was courting his daughter, but her father and her brother ... (I cast hastily about for some tribal analogy) warned her not to let Hamlet visit her when she was alone on her farm, for he would be a great chief and so could not marry her."

"Why not?" asked the wife, who had settled down on the edge of the old man's chair. He frowned at her for asking stupid questions and growled, "They lived in the same homestead."

"That was not the reason," I informed them. "Polonius was a stranger who lived in the homestead because he helped the chief, not because he was a relative."

"Then why couldn't Hamlet marry her?"

"He could have," I explained, "but Polonius didn't think he would. After all, Hamlet was a man of great importance who ought to marry a chief's daughter, for in his country a man could have only one wife. Polonius was afraid that if Hamlet made love to his daughter, then no one else would give a high price for her."

"That might be true," remarked one of the shrewder elders, "but a chief's son would give his mistress's father enough presents and patronage to more than make up the difference. Polonius sounds like a fool to me."

"Many people think he was," I agreed. "Meanwhile Polonius sent his son Laertes off to Paris to learn the things of that country, for it was the homestead of a very great chief indeed. Because he was afraid that Laertes might waste a lot of money on beer and women and gambling, or get into trouble by fighting, he sent one of his servants to Paris secretly, to spy out what Laertes was doing. One day Hamlet came upon Polonius's daughter Ophelia. He behaved so oddly he frightened her. Indeed"—I was fumbling for words to express the dubious quality of Hamlet's madness— "the chief and many others had also noticed that when Hamlet talked one could understand the words but not what they meant. Many people thought that he had become mad." My audience suddenly became more attentive. "The great chief wanted to know what was wrong with Hamlet, so he sent for two of Hamlet's age mates (school friends would have taken long explanation) to talk to Hamlet and find out what troubled his heart. Hamlet, seeing that they had been bribed by the chief to betray him, told them nothing. Polonius, however, insisted that Hamlet was mad because he had been forbidden to see Ophelia, whom he loved."

"Why," inquired a bewildered voice, "should anyone bewitch Hamlet on that account?"

"Bewitch him?"

"Yes, only witchcraft can make anyone mad, unless, of course, one sees the beings that lurk in the forest."

I stopped being a storyteller, took out my notebook and demanded to be told more about these two causes of madness. Even while they spoke and I jotted notes, I tried to calculate the effect of this new factor on the plot. Hamlet had not been exposed to the beings that lurk in the forest. Only his relatives in the male line could bewitch him. Barring relatives not mentioned by Shakespeare, it had to be Claudius who was attempting to harm him. And, of course, it was.

For the moment I staved off questions by saying that the great chief also refused to believe that Hamlet was mad for the love of Ophelia and nothing else. "He was sure that something much more important was troubling Hamlet's heart."

"Now Hamlet's age mates," I continued, "had brought with them a famous storyteller. Hamlet decided to have this man tell the chief and all his homestead a story about a man who had poisoned his brother because he desired his brother's wife and wished to be chief himself. Hamlet was sure the great chief could not hear the story without making a sign if he was indeed guilty, and then he would discover whether his dead father had told him the truth."

The old man interrupted, with deep cunning, "Why should a father lie to his son?" he asked.

I hedged: "Hamlet wasn't sure that it really was his dead father." It was impossible to say anything, in that language, about devil-inspired visions.

"You mean," he said, "it actually was an omen, and he knew witches sometimes send false ones. Hamlet was a fool not to go to one skilled in reading omens and divining the truth in the first place. A man-who-sees-the-truth could have told him how his father died, if he really had been poisoned, and if there was witchcraft in it; then Hamlet could have called the elders to settle the matter."

The shrewd elder ventured to disagree. "Because his father's brother was a great chief, one-who-sees-the-truth might therefore have been afraid to tell it. I think it was for that reason that a friend of Hamlet's father—a witch and an elder—sent an omen so his friend's son would know. Was the omen true?"

"Yes," I said, abandoning ghosts and the devil; a witch-sent omen it would have to be. "It was true, for when the storyteller was telling his tale before all the homestead, the great chief rose in fear. Afraid that Hamlet knew his secret, he planned to have him killed."

The stage set of the next bit presented some difficulties of translation. I began cautiously. "The great chief told Hamlet's mother to find out from her son what he knew. But because a woman's children are always first in her heart, he had the important elder Polonius hide behind a cloth that hung against the wall of Hamlet's mother's sleeping hut. Hamlet started to scold his mother for what she had done."

There was a shocked murmur from everyone. A man should never scold his mother.

"She called out in fear, and Polonius moved behind the cloth. Shouting, 'A rat!' Hamlet took his machete and slashed through the cloth." I paused for dramatic effect. "He had killed Polonius!"

The old men looked at each other in supreme disgust. "That Polonius truly was a fool and a man who knew nothing! What child would not know enough to shout, 'It's me!'" With a pang, I remembered that these people are ardent hunters, always armed with bow, arrow, and machete; at the first rustle in the grass an arrow is aimed and ready, and the hunter shouts "Game!" If no human voice answers immediately, the arrow speeds on its way. Like a good hunter Hamlet had shouted, "A rat!"

I rushed in to save Polonius's reputation. "Polonius did speak. Hamlet heard him. But he thought it was the chief and wished to kill him to avenge his father. He had meant to kill him earlier that evening . . ." I broke down, unable to describe to these pagans, who had no belief in individual afterlife, the difference between dying at one's prayers and dying "unhousell'd, disappointed, unaneled."

This time I had shocked my audience seriously. "For a man to raise his hand against his father's brother and the one who has become his father—that is a terrible thing. The elders ought to let such a man be bewitched."

I nibbled at my kola nut in some perplexity, then pointed out that after all the man had killed Hamlet's father.

"No," pronounced the old man, speaking less to me than to the young men sitting behind the elders. "If your father's brother has killed your father, you must appeal to your father's age mates; *they* may avenge him. No man may use violence against his senior relatives." Another thought struck him. "But if his father's brother had indeed been wicked enough to bewitch Hamlet and make him mad that would be a good story indeed, for it would be his fault that Hamlet, being mad, no longer had any sense and thus was ready to kill his father's brother."

There was a murmur of applause. *Hamlet* was again a good story to them, but it no longer seemed quite the same story to me. As I thought over the coming complications of plot and motive, I lost courage and decided to skim over dangerous ground quickly.

"The great chief," I went on, "was not sorry that Hamlet had killed Polonius. It gave him a reason to send Hamlet away, with his two treacherous age mates, with letters to a chief of a far country, saying that Hamlet should be killed. But Hamlet changed the writing on their papers, so that the chief killed his age mates instead." I encountered a reproachful glare from one of the men whom I had told undetectable forgery was not merely immoral but beyond human skill. I looked the other way.

"Before Hamlet could return, Laertes came back for his father's funeral. The great chief told him Hamlet had killed Polonius. Laertes swore to kill Hamlet because of this, and because his sister Ophelia, hearing her father had been killed by the man she loved, went mad and drowned in the river."

"Have you already forgotten what we told you?" The old man was reproachful. "One cannot take vengeance on a madman; Hamlet killed Polonius in his madness. As for the girl, she not only went mad, she was drowned. Only witches can make people drown. Water itself can't hurt anything. It is merely something one drinks and bathes in."

I began to get cross. "If you don't like the story, I'll stop."

The old man made soothing noises and himself poured me some more beer. "You tell the story well, and we are listening. But it is clear the elders of your country have never told you what the story really means. No, don't interrupt! We believe you when you say your marriage customs are different, or your clothes and weapons. But people are the same everywhere; therefore, there are always witches and it is we, the elders, who know how witches work. We told you it was the great chief who wished to kill Hamlet, and now your own words have proved us right. Who were Ophelia's male relatives?"

"There were only her father and her brother." Hamlet was clearly out of my hands.

"There must have been many more; this also you must ask of your elders when you get back to your country. From what you tell us, since Polonius was dead, it must have been Laertes who killed Ophelia, although I do not see the reason for it."

We had emptied one pot of beer, and the old men argued the point with slightly tipsy interest. Finally one of them demanded of me, "What did the servant of Polonius say on his return?"

With difficulty I recollected Reynaldo and his mission. "I don't think he did return before Polonius was killed."

"Listen," said the elder, "and I will tell you how it was and how your story will go, then you may tell me if I am right. Polonius knew his son would get into trouble, and so he did. He had many fines to pay for fighting, and debts from gambling. But he had only two ways of getting money quickly. One was to marry off his sister at once, but it is difficult to find a man who will marry a woman desired by the son of a chief. For if the chief's heir commits adultery with your wife, what can you do? Only a fool calls a case against a man who will someday be his judge. Therefore Laertes had to take the second way: he killed his sister by witchcraft, drowning her so he could secretly sell her body to the witches."

I raised an objection. "They found her body and buried it. Indeed Laertes jumped into the grave to see his sister once more—so, you see, the body was truly there. Hamlet, who had just come back, jumped in after him."

"What did I tell you?" The elder appealed to the others. "Laertes was up to no good with his sister's body. Hamlet prevented him, because the chief's heir, like a chief, does not wish any other man to grow rich and powerful. Laertes would be angry, because he would have killed his sister without benefit to himself. In our country he would try to kill Hamlet for that reason. Is this not what happened?"

"More or less," I admitted. "When the great chief found Hamlet was still alive, he encouraged Laertes to try to kill Hamlet and arranged a fight with machetes between them. In the fight both the young men were wounded to death. Hamlet's mother drank the poisoned beer that the chief meant for Hamlet in case he won the fight. When he saw his mother die of poison,

Hamlet, dying, managed to kill his father's brother with his machete."

"You see, I was right!" exclaimed the elder.

"That was a very good story," added the old man, "and you told it with very few mistakes. There was just one more error, at the very end. The poison Hamlet's mother drank was obviously meant for the survivor of the fight, whichever it was. If Laertes had won, the great chief would have poisoned him, for no one would know that he arranged Hamlet's death. Then, too, he need not fear Laertes' witchcraft; it takes a strong heart to kill one's only sister by witchcraft.

"Sometime," concluded the old man, gathering his ragged toga about him, "you must tell us some more stories of your country. We, who are elders, will instruct you in their true meaning, so that when you return to your own land your elders will see that you have not been sitting in the bush, but among those who know things and who have taught you wisdom."

6

"To Give up on Words"

Silence in Western Apache Culture

Keith H. Basso

Can you imagine working on a four-person cattle crew for several days without being introduced to or speaking with one of the other members, whom you did not know? For the Apache, this is a normal occurrence; they do not feel obligated to introduce strangers to one another. Instead, the Apache believe that when the time is right, the strangers will begin speaking to one another.

Would you find it uncomfortable to go on a date and sit in silence for an hour because you had only recently met your companion? What would you think if after returning home from several months' absence your parents and relatives didn't speak to you for several days? Although these situations seem unusual to us, they are considered appropriate among the Apache. Although it seems natural to us that when people first meet introductions are in order and that when friends and relatives reunite greetings and catching up will immediately follow, this is not the case for all cultures.

Communicating across cultural boundaries can be fraught with uncertainty and misunderstanding. In this selection Keith Basso shows how, among the Apache, certain situations call for silence rather than communication and how silence makes sense within its cultural context.

As you read this selection, ask yourself the following questions:

- What are some of the ways silence is used in European American communication, and how are they different from those in Apache culture?
- How are the meaning and function of silence affected by the social and cultural context?
- What is the critical factor in an Apache's decision to speak or keep silent?
- How do Apaches interact upon meeting a stranger, courting, welcoming children home, "getting cussed out," and being with people who are sad?
- Despite the variety of situations in which Apaches are silent, what is the underlying determinant?

The following terms discussed in this selection are included in the Glossary at the back of the book:

hypothesis	*socialization*
informant	*sociolinguistics*
kinship	*status*

It is not the case that a man who is silent says nothing.

—Anonymous

I[1]

Anyone who has read about American Indians has probably encountered statements which impute to them a strong predilection for keeping silent or, as one

From *Southwestern Journal of Anthropology*, vol. 26, no. 3, Autumn 1970, pp. 213–230. Reprinted with permission.

writer has put it, "a fierce reluctance to speak except when absolutely necessary." In the popular literature, where this characterization is particularly widespread, it is commonly portrayed as the outgrowth of such dubious causes as "instinctive dignity," "an impoverished language," or, perhaps worst of all, the Indians' "lack of personal warmth." Although statements of this sort are plainly erroneous and dangerously misleading, it is noteworthy that professional anthropologists have made few attempts to correct them. Traditionally, ethnographers and linguists have paid little attention to cultural interpretations given to silence or, equally important, to the types of social contexts in which it regularly occurs.

This study investigates certain aspects of silence in the culture of the Western Apache of east-central Arizona. After considering some of the theoretical issues involved, I will briefly describe a number of situations—recurrent in Western Apache society—in which one or more of the participants typically refrain from speech for lengthy periods of time.[2] This is accompanied by a discussion of how such acts of silence are interpreted and why they are encouraged and deemed appropriate. I conclude by advancing an hypothesis that accounts for the reasons that the Western Apache refrain from speaking when they do, and I suggest that, with proper testing, this hypothesis may be shown to have relevance to silence behavior in other cultures.

II

A basic finding of sociolinguistics is that, although both language and language usage are structured, it is the latter which responds most sensitively to extra-linguistic influences (Hymes 1962, 1964; Ervin-Tripp 1964, 1967; Gumperz 1964; Slobin 1967). Accordingly, a number of recent studies have addressed themselves to the problem of how factors in the social environment of speech events delimit the range and condition the selection of message forms (cf. Brown and Gilman 1960; Conklin 1959; Ervin-Tripp 1964, 1967; Frake 1964; Friedrich 1966; Gumperz 1961, 1964; Martin 1964). These studies may be viewed as taking the now familiar position that verbal communication is fundamentally a decision-making process in which, initially, a speaker, having elected to speak, selects from among a repertoire of available codes that which is most appropriately suited to the situation at hand. Once a code has been selected, the speaker picks a suitable channel of transmission and then, finally, makes a choice from a set of referentially equivalent expressions within the code. The intelligibility of the expression he chooses will, of course, be subject to grammatical constraints. But its acceptability will not. Rules for the selection of linguistic alternates operate on features of the social environment and are commensurate with rules governing the conduct of face-to-face interaction. As such, they are properly conceptualized as lying outside the structure of language itself.

It follows from this that for a stranger to communicate appropriately with the members of an unfamiliar society it is not enough that he learn to formulate messages intelligibly. Something else is needed: a knowledge of what kinds of codes, channels, and expressions to use in what kinds of situations and to what kinds of people—as Hymes (1964) has termed it, an "ethnography of communication."

There is considerable evidence to suggest that extra-linguistic factors influence not only the use of speech but its actual occurrence as well. In our own culture, for example, remarks such as "Don't you know when to keep quiet?" "Don't talk until you're introduced," and "Remember now, no talking in church" all point to the fact that an individual's decision to speak may be directly contingent upon the character of his surroundings. Few of us would maintain that "silence is golden" for all people at all times. But we feel that silence is a virtue for some people some of the time, and we encourage children on the road to cultural competence to act accordingly.

Although the form of silence is always the same, the function of a specific act of silence—that is, its interpretation by and effect upon other people—will vary according to the social context in which it occurs. For example, if I choose to keep silent in the chambers of a Justice of the Supreme Court, my action is likely to be interpreted as a sign of politeness or respect. On the other hand, if I refrain from speaking to an established friend or colleague, I am apt to be accused of rudeness or harboring a grudge. In one instance, my behavior is judged by others to be "correct" or "fitting"; in the other, it is criticized as being "out of line."

The point, I think, is fairly obvious. For a stranger entering an alien society, a knowledge of when *not* to speak may be as basic to the production of culturally acceptable behavior as a knowledge of what to say. It stands to reason, then, that an adequate ethnography of communication should not confine itself exclusively to the analysis of choice within verbal repertoires. It should also, as Hymes (1962, 1964) has suggested, specify those conditions under which the members of the society regularly decide to refrain from verbal behavior altogether.

III

The research on which this paper is based was conducted over a period of sixteen months (1964–1969) in the Western Apache settlement of Cibecue, which is located near the center of the Fort Apache Indian Reservation in east-central Arizona. Cibecue's 800 residents participate in an unstable economy that combines subsistence agriculture, cattle-raising, sporadic wage-earning, and Government subsidies in the form of welfare checks and social security benefits. Unemployment is a serious problem, and substandard living conditions are widespread.

Although Reservation life has precipitated far-reaching changes in the composition and geographical distribution of Western Apache social groups, consanguineal kinship—real and imputed—remains the single most powerful force in the establishment and regulation of interpersonal relationships (Kaut 1957; Basso 1970). The focus of domestic activity is the individual "camp," or *gowáá*. This term labels both the occupants and the location of a single dwelling or, as is more apt to be the case, several dwellings built within a few feet of each other. The majority of *gowáá* in Cibecue are occupied by nuclear families. The next largest residential unit is the *gotáá* (camp cluster), which is a group of spatially localized *gowáá*, each having at least one adult member who is related by ties of matrilineal kinship to persons living in all the others. An intricate system of exogamous clans serves to extend kinship relationships beyond the *gowáá* and *gottáá* and facilitates concerted action in projects, most notably the presentation of ceremonials, requiring large amounts of manpower. Despite the presence in Cibecue of a variety of Anglo missionaries and a dwindling number of medicine men, diagnostic and curing rituals, as well as the girls' puberty ceremonial, continue to be performed with regularity (Basso 1966, 1970). Witchcraft persists in undiluted form (Basso 1969).

IV

Of the many broad categories of events, or scenes, that comprise the daily round of Western Apache life, I shall deal here only with those that are coterminous with what Goffman (1961, 1964) has termed "focused gatherings" or "encounters." The concept *situation*, in keeping with established usage, will refer inclusively to the location of such a gathering, its physical setting, its point in time, the standing behavior patterns that accompany it, and the social attributes of the persons involved (Hymes 1962, 1964; Ervin-Tripp 1964, 1967).

In what follows, however, I will be mainly concerned with the roles and statuses of participants. The reason for this is that the critical factor in the Apache's decision to speak or keep silent seems always to be the nature of his relationships to other people. To be sure, other features of the situation are significant, but apparently only to the extent that they influence the perception of status and role.[3] What this implies, of course, is that roles and statuses are not fixed attributes. Although they may be depicted as such in a static model (and often with good reason), they are appraised and acted upon in particular social contexts and, as a result, subject to redefinition and variation.[4] With this in mind, let us now turn our attention to the Western Apache and the types of situations in which, as one of my informants put it, "it is right to give up on words."

V

1. "Meeting strangers" *(nda dòhwáá iłtsééda)*. The term, *nda*, labels categories at two levels of contrast. At the most general level, it designates any person—Apache or non-Apache—who, prior to an initial meeting, has never been seen and therefore cannot be identified. In addition, the term is used to refer to Apaches who, though previously seen and known by some external criteria such as clan affiliation or personal name, have never been engaged in face-to-face interaction. The latter category, which is more restricted than the first, typically includes individuals who live on the adjacent San Carlos Reservation, in Fort Apache settlements geographically removed from Cibecue, and those who fall into the category *kii dòhandáágo* (non-kinsmen). In all cases, "strangers" are separated by social distance. And in all cases it is considered appropriate, when encountering them for the first time, to refrain from speaking.

The type of situation described as "meeting strangers" *(nda dòhwáá iłtsééda)* can take place in any number of different physical settings. However, it occurs most frequently in the context of events such as fairs and rodeos, which, owing to the large number of people in attendance, offer unusual opportunities for chance encounters. In large gatherings, the lack of verbal communication between strangers is apt to go unnoticed, but in smaller groups it becomes quite conspicuous. The following incident, involving two strangers who found themselves part of a four-man round-up crew, serves as a good example. My informant, who was also a member of the crew, recalled the following episode:

> One time, I was with A, B, and X down at Gleason Flat, working cattle. That man, X, was from East Fork [a community nearly 40 miles from Cibecue] where B's wife was from. But he didn't know A, never knew him before, I guess. First day, I worked with X. At night, when we camped, we talked with B, but X and A didn't say anything to each other. Same way, second day. Same way, third. Then, at night on fourth day, we were sitting by the fire. Still, X and A didn't talk. Then A said, "Well, I know there is a stranger to me here, but I've been watching him and I know he is all right." After that, X and A talked a lot. . . . Those two men didn't know each other, so they took it easy at first.

As this incident suggests, the Western Apache do not feel compelled to "introduce" persons who are unknown to each other. Eventually, it is assumed, strangers will begin to speak. However, this is a decision that is properly left to the individuals involved, and no attempt is made to hasten it. Outside help in the form of introductions or other verbal routines is viewed as presumptuous and unnecessary.

Strangers who are quick to launch into conversation are frequently eyed with undisguised suspicion.

A typical reaction to such individuals is that they "want something," that is, their willingness to violate convention is attributed to some urgent need which is likely to result in requests for money, labor, or transportation. Another common reaction to talkative strangers is that they are drunk.

If the stranger is an Anglo, it is usually assumed that he "wants to teach us something" (i.e., give orders or instructions) or that he "wants to make friends in a hurry." The latter response is especially revealing, since Western Apaches are extremely reluctant to be hurried into friendships—with Anglos or each other. Their verbal reticence with strangers is directly related to the conviction that the establishment of social relationships is a serious matter that calls for caution, careful judgment, and plenty of time.

2. "Courting" (líígoláá). During the initial stages of courtship, young men and women go without speaking for conspicuous lengths of time. Courting may occur in a wide variety of settings—practically anywhere, in fact—and at virtually any time of the day or night, but it is most readily observable at large public gatherings such as ceremonials, wakes, and rodeos. At these events, "sweethearts" (zééde) may stand or sit (sometimes holding hands) for as long as an hour without exchanging a word. I am told by adult informants that the young people's reluctance to speak may become even more pronounced in situations where they find themselves alone.

Apaches who have just begun to court attribute their silence to "intense shyness" ('isté) and a feeling of acute "self-consciousness" (dàyéézí) which, they claim, stems from their lack of familiarity with one another. More specifically, they complain of "not knowing what to do" in each other's presence and of the fear that whatever they say, no matter how well thought out in advance, will sound "dumb" or "stupid."[5]

One informant, a youth 17 years old, commented as follows:

> It's hard to talk with your sweetheart at first. She doesn't know you and won't know what to say. It's the same way towards her. You don't know how to talk yet . . . so you get very bashful. That makes it sometimes so you don't say anything. So you just go around together and don't talk. At first, it's better that way. Then, after a while, when you know each other, you aren't shy anymore and can talk good.

The Western Apache draw an equation between the ease and frequency with which a young couple talks and how well they know each other. Thus, it is expected that after several months of steady companionship sweethearts will start to have lengthy conversations. Earlier in their relationship, however, protracted discussions may be openly discouraged. This is especially true for girls, who are informed by their mothers and older sisters that silence in courtship is a sign of modesty and that an eagerness to speak betrays previous experience with men. In extreme cases, they add, it may be interpreted as a willingness to engage in sexual relations. Said one woman, aged 32:

> This way I have talked to my daughter. "Take it easy when boys come around this camp and want you to go somewhere with them. When they talk to you, just listen at first. Maybe you won't know what to say. So don't talk about just anything. If you talk with those boys right away, then they will know you know all about them. They will think you've been with many boys before, and they will start talking about that."

3. "Children, coming home" (čogoše nakáii). The Western Apache lexeme iltá ìnatsáá (reunion) is used to describe encounters between an individual who has returned home after a long absence and his relatives and friends. The most common type of reunion, čogoše nakáii (children, coming home), involves boarding school students and their parents. It occurs in late May or early in June, and its setting is usually a trading post or school, where parents congregate to await the arrival of buses bringing the children home. As the latter disembark and locate their parents in the crowd, one anticipates a flurry of verbal greetings. Typically, however, there are few or none at all. Indeed, it is not unusual for parents and child to go without speaking for as long as 15 minutes.

When the silence is broken, it is almost always the child who breaks it. His parents listen attentively to everything he says but speak hardly at all themselves. This pattern persists even after the family has reached the privacy of its camp, and two or three days may pass before the child's parents seek to engage him in sustained conversation.

According to my informants, the silence of Western Apache parents at (and after) reunions with their children is ultimately predicated on the possibility that the latter have been adversely affected by their experiences away from home. Uppermost is the fear that, as a result of protracted exposure to Anglo attitudes and values, the children have come to view their parents as ignorant, old-fashioned, and no longer deserving of respect. One of my most thoughtful and articulate informants commented on the problem as follows:

> You just can't tell about those children after they've been with White men for a long time. They get their minds turned around sometimes . . . they forget where they come from and get ashamed when they come home because their parents and relatives are poor. They forget how to act with these Apaches and get mad easy.

They walk around all night and get into fights. They don't stay at home.

At school, some of them learn to want to be White men, so they come back and try to act that way. But we are still Apaches! So we don't know them anymore, and it is like we never knew them. It is hard to talk to them when they are like that.

Apache parents openly admit that, initially, children who have been away to school seem distant and unfamiliar. They have grown older, of course, and their physical appearance may have changed. But more fundamental is the concern that they have acquired new ideas and expectations which will alter their behavior in unpredictable ways. No matter how pressing this concern may be, however, it is considered inappropriate to directly interrogate a child after his arrival home. Instead, parents anticipate that within a short time he will begin to divulge information about himself that will enable them to determine in what ways, if any, his views and attitudes have changed. This, the Apache say, is why children do practically all the talking in the hours following a reunion, and their parents remain unusually silent.

Said one man, the father of two children who had recently returned from boarding school in Utah:

Yes, it's right that we didn't talk much to them when they came back, my wife and me. They were away for a long time, and we didn't know how they would like it, being home. So we waited. Right away, they started to tell stories about what they did. Pretty soon we could tell they liked it, being back. That made us feel good. So it was easy to talk to them again. It was like they were before they went away.

4. "Getting cussed out" (*šìłditéé*). This lexeme is used to describe any situation in which one individual, angered and enraged, shouts insults and criticism at another. Although the object of such invective is in most cases the person or persons who provoked it, this is not always the case, because an Apache who is truly beside himself with rage is likely to vent his feelings on anyone whom he sees or who happens to be within range of his voice. Consequently, "getting cussed out" may involve large numbers of people who are totally innocent of the charges being hurled against them. But whether they are innocent or not, their response to the situation is the same. They refrain from speech.

Like the types of situations we have discussed thus far, "getting cussed out" can occur in a wide variety of physical settings: at ceremonial dancegrounds and trading posts, inside and outside wickiups and houses, on food-gathering expeditions and shopping trips—in short, wherever and whenever individuals lose control of their tempers and lash out verbally at persons nearby.

Although "getting cussed out" is basically free of setting self-imposed restrictions, the Western Apache fear it most at gatherings where alcohol is being consumed. My informants observed that especially at "drinking parties" (*dá'idláá*), where there is much rough joking and ostensibly mock criticism, it is easy for well-intentioned remarks to be misconstrued as insults. Provoked in this way, persons who are intoxicated may become hostile and launch into explosive tirades, often with no warning at all.

The silence of Apaches who are "getting cussed out" is consistently explained in reference to the belief that individuals who are "enraged" (*haškéé*) are also irrational or "crazy" (*bìné'idíí*). In this condition, it is said, they "forget who they are" and become oblivious to what they say or do. Concomitantly, they lose all concern for the consequences of their actions on other people. In a word, they are dangerous. Said one informant:

When people get mad they get crazy. Then they start yelling and saying bad things. Some say they are going to kill somebody for what he has done. Some keep it up that way for a long time, maybe walk from camp to camp, real angry, yelling, crazy like that. They keep it up for a long time, some do.

People like that don't know what they are saying, so you can't tell about them. When you see someone like that, just walk away. If he yells at you, let him say whatever he wants to. Let him say anything. Maybe he doesn't mean it. But he doesn't know that. He will be crazy, and he could try to kill you.

Another Apache said:

When someone gets mad at you and starts yelling, then just don't do anything to make him get worse. Don't try to quiet him down because he won't know why you're doing it. If you try to do that, he may just get worse and try to hurt you.

As the last of these statements implies, the Western Apache operate on the assumption that enraged persons—because they are temporarily "crazy"—are difficult to reason with. Indeed, there is a widely held belief that attempts at mollification will serve to intensify anger, thus increasing the chances of physical violence. The appropriate strategy when "getting cussed out" is to do nothing, to avoid any action that will attract attention to oneself. Since speaking accomplishes just the opposite, the use of silence is strongly advised.

5. "Being with people who are sad" (*nde dòbiłgòzóóda bigáá*). Although the Western Apache phrase that labels this situation has no precise equivalent in English, it refers quite specifically to gatherings in which an individual finds himself in the company of someone whose spouse or kinsman has recently died. Distinct from wakes and burials, which follow

considered "crazy." Until he returns to a more rational condition, others in the situation have no way of predicting how he will behave. Situation No. 5 is similar in that the personality of a focal participant is seen to have undergone a marked shift which makes his actions more difficult to anticipate. In both situations, the status of focal participants is uncertain because of real or imagined changes in their psychological makeup.

In Situation No. 6, a focal participant is ritually transformed from an essentially neutral state to one which is contextually defined as "potentially harmful." Ambiguity and apprehension accompany this transition, and, as in Situations No. 4 and 5, established patterns of interaction must be waived until the focal participant reverts to a less threatening condition.

This discussion points up a third feature characteristic of all situations: *the ambiguous status of focal participants is accompanied either by the absence or suspension of established role expectations.* In every instance, nonfocal participants (i.e., those who refrain from speech) are either uncertain of how the focal participant will behave towards them or, conversely, how they should behave towards him. Stated in the simplest way possible, their roles become blurred with the result that established expectations—if they exist—lose their relevance as guidelines for social action and must be temporarily discarded or abruptly modified.

We are now in a position to expand upon our initial hypothesis and make it more explicit.

1. In Western Apache culture, the absence of verbal communication is associated with social situations in which the status of local participants is ambiguous.

2. Under these conditions, fixed role expectations lose their applicability and the illusion of predictability in social interaction is lost.

3. To sum up and reiterate: keeping silent among the Western Apache is a response to uncertainty and unpredictability in social relations.

VII

The question remains to what extent the foregoing hypothesis helps to account for silence behavior in other cultures. Unfortunately, it is impossible at the present time to provide anything approaching a conclusive answer. Standard ethnographies contain very little information about the circumstances under which verbal communication is discouraged, and it is only within the past few years that problems of this sort have engaged the attention of sociolinguists. The result is that adequate cross-cultural data are almost completely lacking.

As a first step towards the elimination of this deficiency, an attempt is now being made to investigate the occurrence and interpretation of silence in other Indian societies of the American Southwest. Our findings at this early stage, though neither fully representative nor sufficiently comprehensive, are extremely suggestive. By way of illustration, I quote below from portions of a preliminary report prepared by Priscilla Mowrer (1970), herself a Navajo, who inquired into the situational features of Navajo silence behavior in the vicinity of Tuba City on the Navajo Reservation in east-central Arizona.

I. *Silence and Courting:* Navajo youngsters of opposite sexes just getting to know one another say nothing, except to sit close together and maybe hold hands. . . . In public, they may try not to let on that they are interested in each other, but in private it is another matter. If the girl is at a gathering where the boy is also present, she may go off by herself. Falling in step, the boy will generally follow. They may just walk around or find some place to sit down. But, at first, they will not say anything to each other.

II. *Silence and Long Absent Relatives:* When a male or female relative returns home after being gone for six months or more, he (or she) is first greeted with a handshake. If the returnee is male, the female greeter may embrace him and cry—the male, meanwhile, will remain dry-eyed and silent.

III. *Silence and Anger:* The Navajo tend to remain silent when being shouted at by a drunk or angered individual because that particular individual is considered temporarily insane. To speak to such an individual, the Navajo believe, just tends to make the situation worse. . . . People remain silent because they believe that the individual is not himself, that he may have been witched, and is not responsible for the change in his behavior.

IV. *Silent Mourning:* Navajos speak very little when mourning the death of a relative. . . . The Navajo mourn and cry together in pairs. Men will embrace one another and cry together. Women, however, will hold one another's hands and cry together.

V. *Silence and the Ceremonial Patient:* The Navajo consider it wrong to talk to a person being sung over. The only people who talk to the patient are the medicine man and a female relative (or male relative if the patient is male) who is in charge of food preparation. The only time the patient speaks openly is when the medicine man asks her (or him) to pray along with him.

These observations suggest that striking similarities may exist between the types of social contexts in which Navajos and Western Apaches refrain from speech. If this impression is confirmed by further research, it will lend obvious cross-cultural support to the hypothesis advanced above. But regardless of the final outcome, the situational determinants of silence seem eminently deserving of further study. For as we become better informed about the types of contextual variables that mitigate against the use of verbal codes, we should also learn more about those variables that encourage and promote them.

NOTES

1. At different times during the period extending from 1964–1969 the research on which this paper is based was supported by U. S. P. H. S. Grant MH-12691-01, a grant from the American Philosophical Society, and funds from the Doris Duke Oral History Project at the Arizona State Museum. I am pleased to acknowledge this support. I would also like to express my gratitude to the following scholars for commenting upon an earlier draft: Y. R. Chao, Harold C. Conklin, Roy G. D'Andrade, Charles O. Frake, Paul Friedrich, John Gumperz, Kenneth Hale, Harry Hoijer, Dell Hymes, Stanley Newman, David M. Schneider, Joel Sherzer, and Paul Turner. Although the final version gained much from their criticisms and suggestions, responsibility for its present form and content rests solely with the author. A preliminary version of this paper was presented to the Annual Meeting of the American Anthropological Association in New Orleans, Louisiana, November 1969. A modified version of this paper is scheduled to appear in *Studies in Apachean Culture and Ethnology* (ed. by Keith H. Basso and Morris Opler), Tucson: University of Arizona Press, 1970.

2. The situations described in this paper are not the only ones in which the Western Apache refrain from speech. There is a second set—not considered here because my data are incomplete—in which silence appears to occur as a gesture of respect, usually to persons in positions of authority. A third set, very poorly understood, involves ritual specialists who claim they must keep silent at certain points during the preparation of ceremonial paraphernalia.

3. Recent work in the sociology of interaction, most notably by Goffman (1963) and Garfinkel (1967), has led to the suggestion that social relationships are everywhere the major determinants of verbal behavior. In this case, as Gumperz (1967) makes clear, it becomes methodologically unsound to treat the various components of communicative events as independent variables. Gumperz (1967) has presented a hierarchical model, sensitive to dependency, in which components are seen as stages in the communication process. Each stage serves as the input for the next. The basic stage, i.e., the initial input, is "social identities or statuses." For further details see Slobin 1967:131–134.

4. I would like to stress that the emphasis placed on social relations is fully in keeping with the Western Apache interpretation of their own behavior. When my informants were asked to explain why they or someone else was silent on a particular occasion, they invariably did so in terms of *who* was present at the time.

5. Among the Western Apache, rules of exogamy discourage courtships between members of the same clan (*kii àɬhánigo*) and so-called "related" clans (*kii*), with the result that sweethearts are almost always "non-matrilineal kinsmen" (*dòhwàkììda*). Compared to "matrilineal kinsmen" (*kii*), such individuals have fewer opportunities during childhood to establish close personal relationships and thus, when courtship begins, have relatively little knowledge of each other. It is not surprising, therefore, that their behavior is similar to that accorded strangers.

6. I have witnessed over 75 curing ceremonials since 1961 and have seen this rule violated only 6 times. On 4 occasions, drunks were at fault. In the other 2 cases, the patient fell asleep and had to be awakened.

REFERENCES

Basso, Keith H. 1966. *The Gift of Changing Woman.* Bureau of American Ethnology, bulletin 196.

———. 1969. *Western Apache Witchcraft.* Anthropological Papers of the University of Arizona, no. 15.

———. 1970. *The Cibecue Apache.* New York: Holt, Rinehart and Winston, Inc.

Brown, R. W., and Albert Gilman. 1960. "The Pronouns of Power and Solidarity," in *Style and Language* (ed. by T. Sebeok), pp. 253–276. Cambridge: The Technology Press of Massachusetts Institute of Technology.

Conklin, Harold C. 1959. Linguistic Play in Its Cultural Context. *Language* 35:631–636.

Ervin-Tripp, Susan. 1964. "An Analysis of the Interaction of Language, Topic and Listener," in *The Ethnography of Communication* (ed. by J. J. Gumperz and D. Hymes), pp. 86–102. *American Anthropologist*, Special Publication, vol. 66, no. 6, part 2.

———. 1967. *Sociolinguistics.* Language-Behavior Research Laboratory, Working Paper no. 3. Berkeley: University of California.

Frake, Charles O. 1964. "How to Ask for a Drink in Subanun," in *The Ethnography of Communication* (ed. by J. J. Gumperz and D. Hymes), pp. 127–132. *American Anthropologist*, Special Publication, vol. 66, no. 6, part 2.

Friedrich, P. 1966. "Structural Implications of Russian Pronominal Usage," in *Sociolinguistics* (ed. by W. Bright), pp. 214–253. The Hague: Mouton.

Garfinkel, H. 1967. *Studies in Ethnomethodology.* Englewood Cliffs, N.J.: Prentice-Hall, Inc.

Goffman, E. 1961. *Encounters: Two Studies in the Sociology of Interaction.* Indianapolis: The Bobbs-Merrill Co., Inc.

———. 1963. *Behavior in Public Places.* Glencoe, Ill.: Free Press.

———. 1964. "The Neglected Situation," in *The Ethnography of Communication* (ed. by J. J. Gumperz and D. Hymes), pp. 133–136. *American Anthropologist*, Special Publication, vol. 66, no. 6, part 2.

Gumperz, John J. 1961. Speech Variation and the Study of Indian Civilization. *American Anthropologist* 63: 976–988.

——. 1964. "Linguistic and Social Interaction in Two Communities," in *The Ethnography of Communication* (ed. by J. J. Gumperz and D. Hymes), pp. 137–153. *American Anthropologist,* Special Publication, vol. 66, no. 6, part 2.

——. 1967. "The Social Setting of Linguistic Behavior," in *A Field Manual for Cross-Cultural Study of the Acquisition of Communicative Competence (Second Draft)* (ed. by D. I. Slobin), pp. 129–134. Berkeley: University of California.

Hymes, Dell. 1962. "The Ethnography of Speaking," in *Anthropology and Human Behavior* (ed. by T. Gladwin and W. C. Sturtevant), pp. 13–53. Washington, D. C.: The Anthropological Society of Washington.

——. 1964. "Introduction: Toward Ethnographies of Communication" in *The Ethnography of Communication* (ed. by J. J. Gumperz and D. Hymes), pp. 1–34. *American Anthropologist,* Special Publication, vol. 66, no. 6, part 2.

Kaut, Charles R. 1957. *The Western Apache Clan System: Its Origins and Development.* University of New Mexico Publications in Anthropology, no. 9.

Martin, Samuel. 1964. "Speech Levels in Japan and Korea," in *Language in Culture and Society* (ed. by D. Hymes), pp. 407–415. New York: Harper & Row.

Mowrer, Priscilla. 1970. Notes on Navajo Silence Behavior. MS, University of Arizona.

Slobin, Dan I. (ed.). 1967. *A Field Manual for Cross-Cultural Study of the Acquisition of Communicative Competence (Second Draft).* Berkeley: University of California.

7

A Cultural Approach
to Male-Female Miscommunication

Daniel N. Maltz and Ruth A. Borker

Of the 60,000 or so words in the English language, the typical educated adult uses about 2,000. Five hundred of these words alone can convey over 14,000 meanings. But even with all these alternatives, this is not the central problem of miscommunication in North America. Rather, interethnic and cross-sex conversations are the central problem, because the participants possess different subcultural rules for speaking.

Conversation is a negotiated activity. Within a given culture, conversations rely on unspoken understandings about tone of voice, visual cues, silence, minimal responses (such as "mm hmm"), and a variety of other subtle conventions. A cultural approach to male-female conversation highlights unconscious meanings that can lead members of one group to misinterpret the intent of others. Evidence suggests, for example, that women use the response "mm hmm" to indicate they are listening, whereas men use the same response to indicate they are agreeing. Thus, a man who does not provide such cues may indicate to a female conversation partner that he is not listening, whereas a woman may appear to keep changing her mind when giving the same cue. This and similar insights are found throughout this selection and indicate the need for paying attention to communication across cultural and subcultural boundaries.

As you read this selection, ask yourself the following questions:

- What are some of the differences in the ways men and women talk to each other that have been noted in earlier research?

- How do differences between men and women in conversational style reflect differences in power in the larger society?

- If men and women exist in different linguistic subcultures, how and when were these subcultures learned? How does the world of girls differ from the world of boys?

- What kinds of miscommunications occur in cross-sex conversation?

- Can you think of situations that have occurred in your own life that can be better understood after reading this cultural analysis of cross-sex conversation?

The following terms discussed in this selection are included in the Glossary at the back of the book:

gender	*social networks*
metalinguistics	*sociolinguistics*
sex roles	*subculture*

INTRODUCTION

This chapter presents what we believe to be a useful new framework for examining differences in the speaking patterns of American men and women. It is based not on new data, but on a reexamination of a wide variety of material already available in the scholarly literature. Our starting problem is the nature of the different

roles of male and female speakers in informal cross-sex conversations in American English. Our attempts to think about this problem have taken us to preliminary examination of a wide variety of fields often on or beyond the margins of our present competencies: children's speech, children's play, styles and patterns of friendship, conversational turn-taking, discourse analysis, and interethnic communication. The research which most influenced the development of our present model includes John Gumperz's work on problems in interethnic communication (1982) and Marjorie Goodwin's study of the linguistic aspects of play among black children in Philadelphia (1978, 1980a, 1980b).

Daniel Maltz and Ruth Borker, "A Cultural Approach to Male-Female Miscommunication," pp. 196–216, from John Gumperz (ed) *Language and Identity*, 1982. © Cambridge University Press. Reprinted with permission of the authors and publisher.

Our major argument is that the general approach recently developed for the study of difficulties in cross-ethnic communication can be applied to cross-sex communication as well. We prefer to think of the difficulties in both cross-sex and cross-ethnic communication as two examples of the same larger phenomenon: cultural difference and miscommunication.

THE PROBLEM OF CROSS-SEX CONVERSATION

Study after study has shown that when men and women attempt to interact as equals in friendly cross-sex conversations they do not play the same role in interaction, even when there is no apparent element of flirting. We hope to explore some of these differences, examine the explanations that have been offered, and provide an alternative explanation for them.

The primary data on cross-sex conversations come from two general sources: social psychology studies from the 1950s such as Soskin and John's (1963) research on two young married couples and Strodbeck and Mann's (1956) research on jury deliberations, and more recent sociolinguistic studies from the University of California at Santa Barbara and the University of Pennsylvania by Candace West (Zimmerman and West 1975; West and Zimmerman 1977; West 1979), Pamela Fishman (1978), and Lynette Hirschman (1973).

WOMEN'S FEATURES

Several striking differences in male and female contributions to cross-sex conversation have been noticed in these studies.

First, women display a greater tendency to ask questions. Fishman (1978:400) comments that "at times I felt that all women did was ask questions," and Hirschman (1973:10) notes that "several of the female-male conversations fell into a question-answer pattern with the females asking the males questions."

Fishman (1978:408) sees this question-asking tendency as an example of a second, more general characteristic of women's speech, doing more of the routine "shitwork" involved in maintaining routine social interaction, doing more to facilitate the flow of conversation (Hirschman 1973:3). Women are more likely than men to make utterances that demand or encourage responses from their fellow speakers and are therefore, in Fishman's words, "more actively engaged in insuring interaction than the men" (1978:404). In the earlier social psychology studies, these features have been coded under the general category of "positive reactions" including solidarity, tension release, and agreeing (Strodbeck and Mann 1956).

Third, women show a greater tendency to make use of positive minimal responses, especially "mm hmm" (Hirschman 1973:8), and are more likely to insert "such comments throughout streams of talk rather than [simply] at the end" (Fishman 1978:402).

Fourth, women are more likely to adopt a strategy of "silent protest" after they have been interrupted or have received a delayed minimal response (Zimmerman and West 1975; West and Zimmerman 1977:524).

Fifth, women show a greater tendency to use the pronouns "you" and "we," which explicitly acknowledge the existence of the other speaker (Hirschman 1973:6).

MEN'S FEATURES

Contrasting contributions to cross-sex conversations have been observed and described for men.

First, men are more likely to interrupt the speech of their conversational partners, that is, to interrupt the speech of women (Zimmerman and West 1975; West and Zimmerman 1977; West 1979).

Second, they are more likely to challenge or dispute their partners' utterances (Hirschman 1973:11).

Third, they are more likely to ignore the comments of the other speaker, that is, to offer no response or acknowledgment at all (Hirschman 1973:11), to respond slowly in what has been described as a "delayed minimal response" (Zimmerman and West 1975:118), or to respond unenthusiastically (Fishman 1978).

Fourth, men use more mechanisms for controlling the topic of conversation, including both topic development and the introduction of new topics, than do women (Zimmerman and West 1975).

Finally, men make more direct declarations of fact or opinion than do women (Fishman 1978:402), including suggestions, opinions, and "statements of orientation" as Strodbeck and Mann (1956) describe them, or "statements of focus and directives" as they are described by Soskin and John (1963).

EXPLANATIONS OFFERED

Most explanations for these features have focused on differences in the social power or in the personalities of men and women. One variant of the social power argument, presented by West (Zimmerman and West 1975; West and Zimmerman 1977), is that men's dominance in conversation parallels their dominance in society. Men enjoy power in society and also in conversation. The two levels are seen as part of a single social-political system. West sees interruptions and topic control as male displays of power—a power based in the larger social order but reinforced and expressed in face-to-face interaction with women. A second variant of this argument, stated by Fishman (1978), is that while the differential power of men and women is crucial, the specific mechanism through which it enters conversation is sex-role definition. Sex roles serve to obscure the issue of power for participants, but the fact is, Fishman argues, that norms of appropriate behavior for women and men serve to give power and interactional control to men while keeping it from women. To be socially acceptable as women, women cannot exert control and must actually support men in their control. In this casting of the social power argument, men are not necessarily seen to be consciously flaunting power, but simply reaping the rewards given them by the social system. In both variants, the link between macro and micro levels of social life is seen as direct and unproblematic, and the focus of explanation is the general social order.

Sex roles have also been central in psychological explanations. The primary advocate of the psychological position has been Robin Lakoff (1975). Basically, Lakoff asserts that, having been taught to speak and act like "ladies," women become as unassertive and insecure as they have been made to sound. The impossible task of trying to be both women and adults, which Lakoff sees as culturally incompatible, saps women of confidence and strength. As a result, they come to produce the speech they do, not just because it is how women are supposed to speak, but because it fits with the personalities they develop as a consequence of sex-role requirements.

The problem with these explanations is that they do not provide a means of explaining why these specific features appear as opposed to any number of others, nor do they allow us to differentiate between various types of male-female interaction. They do not really tell us why and how these specific interactional phenomena are linked to the general fact that men dominate within our social system.

AN ALTERNATIVE EXPLANATION: SOCIOLINGUISTIC SUBCULTURES

Our approach to cross-sex communication patterns is somewhat different from those that have been previously proposed. We place the stress not on psychological differences or power differentials, although these may make some contribution, but rather on a notion of cultural differences between men and women in their conceptions of friendly conversation, their rules for engaging in it, and, probably most important, their rules for interpreting it. We argue that American men and women come from different sociolinguistic subcultures,

having learned to do different things with words in a conversation, so that when they attempt to carry on conversations with one another, even if both parties are attempting to treat one another as equals, cultural miscommunication results.

The idea of distinct male and female subcultures is not a new one for anthropology. It has been persuasively argued again and again for those parts of the world such as the Middle East and southern Europe in which men and women spend most of their lives spatially and interactionally segregated. The strongest case for sociolinguistic subcultures has been made by Susan Harding from her research in rural Spain (1975).

The major premise on which Harding builds her argument is that speech is a means for dealing with social and psychological situations. When men and women have different experiences and operate in different social contexts, they tend to develop different genres of speech and different skills for doing things with words. In the Spanish village in which she worked, the sexual division of labor was strong, with men involved in agricultural tasks and public politics while women were involved in a series of networks of personal relations with their children, their husbands, and their female neighbors. While men developed their verbal skills in economic negotiations and public political argument, women became more verbally adept at a quite different mode of interactional manipulation with words: gossip, social analysis, subtle information gathering through a carefully developed technique of verbal prying, and a kind of second-guessing the thoughts of others (commonly known as "women's intuition") through a skillful monitoring of the speech of others. The different social needs of men and women, she argues, have led them to sexually differentiated communicative cultures, with each sex learning a different set of skills for manipulating words effectively.

The question that Harding does not ask, however, is, if men and women possess different subcultural rules for speaking, what happens if and when they try to interact with each other? It is here that we turn to the research on interethnic miscommunication.

INTERETHNIC COMMUNICATION

Recent research (Gumperz 1977, 1978a, 1978b, 1979; Gumperz and Tannen 1978) has shown that systematic problems develop in communication when speakers of different speech cultures interact and that these problems are the result of differences in systems of conversational inference and the cues for signalling speech acts and speaker's intent. Conversation is a negotiated activity. It progresses in large part because of shared assumptions about what is going on.

Examining interactions between English-English and Indian-English speakers in Britain (Gumperz 1977, 1978a, 1979; Gumperz et al. 1977), Gumperz found that differences in cues resulted in systematic miscommunication over whether a question was being asked, whether an argument was being made, whether a person was being rude or polite, whether a speaker was relinquishing the floor or interrupting, whether and what a speaker was emphasizing, whether interactants were angry, concerned, or indifferent. Rather than being seen as problems in communication, the frustrating encounters that resulted were usually chalked up as personality clashes or interpreted in the light of racial stereotypes which tended to exacerbate already bad relations.

To take a simple case, Gumperz (1977) reports that Indian women working at a cafeteria, when offering food, used a falling intonation, e.g., "gravy," which to them indicated a question, something like "do you want gravy?" Both Indian and English workers saw a question as an appropriate polite form, but to English-English speakers a falling intonation signalled not a question, which for them is signalled by a rising intonation such as "gravy," but a declarative statement, which was both inappropriate and extremely rude.

A major advantage of Gumperz's framework is that it does not assume that problems are the result of bad faith, but rather sees them as the result of individuals wrongly interpreting cues according to their own rules.

THE INTERPRETATION
OF MINIMAL RESPONSES

How might Gumperz's approach to the study of conflicting rules for interpreting conversation be applied to the communication between men and women? A simple example will illustrate our basic approach: the case of positive minimal responses. Minimal responses such as nods and comments like "yes" and "mm hmm" are common features of conversational interaction. Our claim, based on our attempts to understand personal experience, is that these minimal responses have significantly different meanings for men and women, leading to occasionally serious miscommunication.

We hypothesize that for women a minimal response of this type means simply something like "I'm listening to you; please continue," and that for men it has a somewhat stronger meaning such as "I agree with you" or at least "I follow your argument so far." The fact that women use these responses more often than men is in part simply that women are listening more often than men are agreeing.

But our hypothesis explains more than simple differential frequency of usage. Different rules can lead to repeated misunderstandings. Imagine a male speaker who is receiving repeated nods or "mm hmm"s from the woman he is speaking to. She is merely indicating that she is listening, but he thinks she is agreeing with everything he says. Now imagine a female speaker who is receiving only occasional nods and "mm hmm"s from the man she is speaking to. He is indicating that he doesn't always agree; she thinks he isn't always listening.

What is appealing about this short example is that it seems to explain two of the most common complaints in male-female interaction: (1) men who think that women are always agreeing with them and then conclude that it's impossible to tell what a woman really thinks, and (2) women who get upset with men who never seem to be listening. What we think we have here are two separate rules for conversational maintenance which come into conflict and cause massive miscommunication.

SOURCES OF DIFFERENT CULTURES

A probable objection that many people will have to our discussion so far is that American men and women interact with one another far too often to possess different subcultures. What we need to explain is how it is that men and women can come to possess different cultural assumptions about friendly conversation.

Our explanation is really quite simple. It is based on the idea that by the time we have become adults we possess a wide variety of rules for interacting in different situations. Different sets of these rules were learned at different times and in different contexts. We have rules for dealing with people in dominant or subordinate social positions, rules which we first learned as young children interacting with our parents and teachers. We have rules for flirting and other sexual encounters which we probably started learning at or near adolescence. We have rules for dealing with service personnel and bureaucrats, rules we began learning when we first ventured into the public domain. Finally, we have rules for friendly interaction, for carrying on friendly conversation. What is striking about these last rules is that they were learned not from adults but from peers, and that they were learned during precisely that time period, approximately age 5 to 15, when boys and girls interact socially primarily with members of their own sex.

The idea that girls and boys in contemporary America learn different ways of speaking by the age of five or earlier has been postulated by Robin Lakoff (1975), demonstrated by Andrea Meditch (1975), and more fully explored by Adelaide Haas (1979). Haas's research on school-age children shows the early appearance of important male-female differences in patterns of language use, including a male tendency toward direct requests and information giving and a female tendency toward compliance (1979:107).

But the process of acquiring gender-specific speech and behavior patterns by school-age children is more complex than the simple copying of adult "genderlects" by preschoolers. Psychologists Brooks-Gunn and Matthews (1979) have labelled this process the "consolidation of sex roles"; we call it learning of gender-specific "cultures."

Among school-age children, patterns of friendly social interaction are learned not so much from adults as from members of one's peer group, and a major feature of most middle-childhood peer groups is homogeneity; "they are either all-boy or all-girl" (Brooks-Gunn and Matthews 1979). Members of each sex are learning self-consciously to differentiate their behavior from that of the other sex and to exaggerate these differences. The process can be profitably compared to accent divergence in which members of two groups that wish to become clearly distinguished from one another socially acquire increasingly divergent ways of speaking.[1]

Because they learn these gender-specific cultures from their age-mates, children tend to develop stereotypes and extreme versions of adult behavior patterns. For a boy learning to behave in a masculine way, for example, Ruth Hartley (1959, quoted in Brooks-Gunn and Matthews 1979:203) argues that:

> both the information and the practice he gets are distorted. Since his peers have no better sources of information than he has, all they can do is pool the impressions and anxieties they derived from their early training. Thus, the picture they draw is oversimplified and overemphasized. It is a picture drawn in black and white, with little or no modulation and it is incomplete, including a few of the many elements that go to make up the role of the mature male.

What we hope to argue is that boys and girls learn to use language in different ways because of the very different social contexts in which they learn how to carry on friendly conversation. Almost anyone who remembers being a child, has worked with school-age children, or has had an opportunity to observe school-age children can vouch for the fact that groups of girls and groups of boys interact and play in different ways. Systematic observations of children's play have tended to confirm these well-known differences in the ways girls and boys learn to interact with their friends.

In a major study of sex differences in the play of school-age children, for example, sociologist Janet Lever (1976) observed the following six differences between the play of boys and that of girls: (1) girls more often play indoors; (2) boys tend to play in larger groups; (3) boys' play groups tend to include a wider age range of participants; (4) girls play in predominantly male games more often than vice versa; (5) boys more often play competitive games, and (6) girls' games tend to last a shorter period of time than boys' games.

It is by examining these differences in the social organization of play and the accompanying differences in the patterns of social interaction they entail, we argue, that we can learn about the sources of male-female differences in patterns of language use. And it is these same patterns, learned in childhood and carried over into adulthood as the bases for patterns of single-sex friendship relations, we contend, that are potential sources of miscommunication in cross-sex interaction.

THE WORLD OF GIRLS

Our own experience and studies such as Goodwin's (1980b) of black children and Lever's (1976, 1978) of white children suggest a complex of features of girls' play and the speech within it. Girls play in small groups, most often in pairs (Lever 1976; Eder and Hallinan 1978; Brooks-Gunn and Matthews 1979), and their play groups tend to be remarkably homogeneous in terms of age. Their play is often in private or semi-private settings that require participants be invited in. Play is cooperative and activities are usually organized in noncompetitive ways (Lever 1976; Goodwin 1980b). Differentiation between girls is not made in terms of power, but relative closeness. Friendship is seen by girls as involving intimacy, equality, mutual commitment, and loyalty. The idea of "best friend" is central for girls. Relationships between girls are to some extent in opposition to one another, and new relationships are often formed at the expense of old ones. As Brooks-Gunn and Matthews (1979:280) observe, "friendships tend to be exclusive, with a few girls being exceptionally close to one another. Because of this breakups tend to be highly emotional," and Goodwin (1980a:172) notes that "the non-hierarchical framework of the girls provides a fertile ground for rather intricate processes of alliance formation between equals against some other party."

There is a basic contradiction in the structure of girls' social relationships. Friends are supposed to be equal and everyone is supposed to get along, but in fact they don't always. Conflict must be resolved, but a girl cannot assert social power or superiority as an individual to resolve it. Lever (1976), studying fifth-graders, found that girls simply could not deal with quarrels and that when conflict arose they made no attempt to settle it; the group just broke up. What girls learn to do with speech is cope with the contradiction created by an ideology of equality and cooperation and a social reality that includes differences and conflict. As they grow up they learn increasingly subtle ways of balancing the conflicting pressures created by a female social world and a female friendship ideology.

Basically girls learn to do three things with words: (1) to create and maintain relationships of closeness and equality, (2) to criticize others in acceptable ways, and (3) to interpret accurately the speech of other girls.

To a large extent friendships among girls are formed through talk. Girls need to learn to give support, to recognize the speech rights of others, to let others speak, and to acknowledge what they say in order to establish and maintain relationships of equality and closeness. In activities they need to learn to create cooperation through speech. Goodwin (1980a) found that inclusive forms such as "let's," "we gonna," "we could," and "we gotta" predominated in task-oriented activities. Furthermore, she found that most girls in the group she studied made suggestions and that the other girls usually agreed to them. But girls also learn to exchange information and confidences to create and maintain relationships of closeness. The exchange of personal thoughts not only expresses closeness but mutual commitment as well. Brooks-Gunn and Matthews (1979:280) note of adolescent girls:

> much time is spent talking, reflecting, and sharing intimate thought. Loyalty is of central concern to the 12- to 14-year-old girl, presumably because, if innermost secrets are shared, the friend may have "dangerous knowledge" at her disposal.

Friendships are not only formed through particular types of talk, but are ended through talk as well. As Lever (1976:4) says of "best friends," "sharing secrets binds the union together, and 'telling' the secrets to outsiders is symbolic of the 'break-up.'"

Secondly, girls learn to criticize and argue with other girls without seeming overly aggressive, without being perceived as either "bossy" or "mean," terms girls use to evaluate one another's speech and actions. Bossiness, ordering others around, is not legitimate because it denies equality. Goodwin (1980a) points out that girls talked very negatively about the use of commands to equals, seeing it as appropriate only in role play or in unequal relationships such as those with younger siblings. Girls learn to direct things without seeming bossy, or they learn not to direct. While disputes are common, girls learn to phrase their arguments in terms of group needs and situational requirements rather than personal power or desire (Goodwin 1980a). Meanness is used by girls to describe nonlegitimate acts of exclusion, turning on someone, or withholding friendship. Excluding is a frequent occurrence (Eder and Hallinan 1978), but girls learn over time to discourage or even drive away other girls in ways that don't seem to be just personal whim. Cutting someone is justified in terms of the target's failure to meet group norms and a girl often rejects another using speech that

is seemingly supportive on the surface. Conflict and criticism are risky in the world of girls because they can both rebound against the critic and can threaten social relationships. Girls learn to hide the source of criticism; they present it as coming from someone else or make it indirectly through a third party (Goodwin 1980a, 1980b).

Finally, girls must learn to decipher the degree of closeness being offered by other girls, to recognize what is being withheld, and to recognize criticism. Girls who don't actually read these cues run the risk of public censure or ridicule (Goodwin 1980a). Since the currency of closeness is the exchange of secrets which can be used against a girl, she must learn to read the intent and loyalty of others and to do so continuously, given the system of shifting alliances and indirect expressions of conflict. Girls must become increasingly sophisticated in reading the motives of others, in determining when closeness is real, when conventional, and when false, and to respond appropriately. They must learn who to confide in, what to confide, and who not to approach. Given the indirect expression of conflict, girls must learn to read relationships and situations sensitively. Learning to get things right is a fundamental skill for social success, if not just social survival.

THE WORLD OF BOYS

Boys play in larger, more hierarchically organized groups than do girls. Relative status in this everfluctuating hierarchy is the main thing that boys learn to manipulate in their interactions with their peers. Nondominant boys are rarely excluded from play but are made to feel the inferiority of their status positions in no uncertain terms. And since hierarchies fluctuate over time and over situation, every boy gets his chance to be victimized and must learn to take it. The social world of boys is one of posturing and counterposturing. In this world, speech is used in three major ways: (1) to assert one's position of dominance, (2) to attract and maintain an audience, and (3) to assert oneself when other speakers have the floor.

The use of speech for the expression of dominance is the most straightforward and probably the best-documented sociolinguistic pattern in boys' peer groups. Even ethological studies of human dominance patterns have made extensive use of various speech behaviors as indices of dominance. Richard Savin-Williams (1976), for example, in his study of dominance patterns among boys in a summer camp uses the following speech interactions as measures of dominance: (1) giving of verbal commands or orders, such as "Get up," "Give it to me," or "You go over there"; (2) name calling and other forms of verbal ridicule, such as "You're a dolt";

(3) verbal threats or boasts of authority, such as "If you don't shut up, I'm gonna come over and bust your teeth in"; (4) refusals to obey orders; and (5) winning a verbal argument as in the sequence: "I was here first"/"Tough," or in more elaborate forms of verbal duelling such as the "dozens."[2]

The same patterns of verbally asserting one's dominance and challenging the dominance claims of others form the central element in Goodwin's (1980a) observations of boys' play in Philadelphia. What is easy to forget in thinking about this use of words as weapons, however, is that the most successful boy in such interaction is not the one who is most aggressive and uses the most power-wielding forms of speech, but the boy who uses these forms most successfully. The simple use of assertiveness and aggression in boys' play is the sign not of a leader but of a bully. The skillful speaker in a boys' group is considerably more likeable and better liked by his peers than is a simple bully. Social success among boys is based on knowing both how and when to use words to express power as well as knowing when not to use them. A successful leader will use speech to put challengers in their place and to remind followers periodically of their nondominant position, but will not browbeat unnecessarily and will therefore gain the respect rather than the fear of less dominant boys.

A second sociolinguistic aspect of friendly interaction between boys is using words to gain and maintain an audience. Storytelling, joke telling, and other narrative performance events are common features of the social interaction of boys. But actual transcripts of such storytelling events collected by Harvey Sacks (Sacks 1974; Jefferson 1978) and Goodwin (1980a), as opposed to stories told directly to interviewers, reveal a suggestive feature of storytelling activities among boys: audience behavior is not overtly supportive. The storyteller is frequently faced with mockery, challenges and side comments on his story. A major sociolinguistic skill which a boy must apparently learn in interacting with his peers is to ride out this series of challenges, maintain his audience, and successfully get to the end of his story. In Sacks's account (1974) of some teenage boys involved in the telling of a dirty joke, for example, the narrator is challenged for his taste in jokes (an implication that he doesn't know a dirty joke from a non-dirty one) and for the potential ambiguity of his opening line "Three brothers married three sisters," not, as Sacks seems to imply, because audience members are really confused, but just to hassle the speaker. Through catches,[3] put-downs, the building of suspense, or other interest-grabbing devices, the speaker learns to control his audience. He also learns to continue when he gets no encouragement whatever, pausing slightly at various points for possible audience response but going on if there is nothing but silence.

A final sociolinguistic skill which boys must learn from interacting with other boys is how to act as audience members in the types of storytelling situations just discussed. As audience member as well as storyteller, a boy must learn to assert himself and his opinions. Boys seem to respond to the storytelling of other boys not so much with questions on deeper implications or with minimal-response encouragement as with side comments and challenges. These are not meant primarily to interrupt, to change topic, or to change the direction of the narrative itself, but to assert the identity of the individual audience member.

WOMEN'S SPEECH

The structures and strategies in women's conversation show a marked continuity with the talk of girls. The key logic suggested by Kalčik's (1975) study of women's rap groups, Hirschman's (1973) study of students and Abrahams's (1975) work on black women is that women's conversation is interactional. In friendly talk, women are negotiating and expressing a relationship, one that should be in the form of support and closeness, but which may also involve criticism and distance. Women orient themselves to the person they are talking to and expect such orientation in return. As interaction, conversation requires participation from those involved and back-and-forth movement between participants. Getting the floor is not seen as particularly problematic; that should come about automatically. What is problematic is getting people engaged and keeping them engaged—maintaining the conversation and the interaction.

This conception of conversation leads to a number of characteristic speech strategies and gives a particular dynamic to women's talk. First, women tend to use personal and inclusive pronouns, such as "you" and "we" (Hirschman 1973). Second, women give off and look for signs of engagement such as nods and minimal response (Kalčik 1975; Hirschman 1973). Third, women give more extended signs of interest and attention, such as interjecting comments or questions during a speaker's discourse. These sometimes take the form of interruptions. In fact, both Hirschman (1973) and Kalčik (1975) found that interruptions were extremely common, despite women's concern with politeness and decorum (Kalčik 1975). Kalčik (1975) comments that women often asked permission to speak but were concerned that each speaker be allowed to finish and that all present got a chance to speak. These interruptions were clearly not seen as attempts to grab the floor but as calls for elaboration and development, and were taken as signs of support and interest. Fourth, women at the beginning of their utterances explicitly acknowledge and respond to what has been said by others. Fifth, women attempt to link their utterance to the one preceding it by building on the previous utterance or talking about something parallel or related to it. Kalčik (1975) talks about strategies of tying together, filling in, and serializing as signs of women's desire to create continuity in conversation, and Hirschman (1973) describes elaboration as a key dynamic of women's talk.

While the idiom of much of women's friendly talk is that of support, the elements of criticism, competition, and conflict do occur in it. But as with girls, these tend to take forms that fit the friendship idiom. Abrahams (1975) points out that while "talking smart" is clearly one way women talk to women as well as to men, between women it tends to take a more playful form, to be more indirect and metaphoric in its phrasing and less prolonged than similar talk between men. Smartness, as he points out, puts distance in a relationship (Abrahams 1975). The target of criticism, whether present or not, is made out to be the one violating group norms and values (Abrahams 1975). Overt competitiveness is also disguised. As Kalčik (1975) points out, some stories that build on preceding ones are attempts to cap the original speaker, but they tend to have a form similar to supportive ones. It is the intent more than the form that differs. Intent is a central element in the concept of "bitchiness," one of women's terms for evaluating their talk, and it relates to this contradiction between form and intent, whether putting negative messages in overtly positive forms or acting supportive face to face while not being so elsewhere.

These strategies and the interactional orientation of women's talk give their conversation a particular dynamic. While there is often an unfinished quality to particular utterances (Kalčik 1975), there is a progressive development to the overall conversation. The conversation grows out of the interaction of its participants, rather than being directed by a single individual or series of individuals. In her very stimulating discussion, Kalčik (1975) argues that this is true as well for many of the narratives women tell in conversation. She shows how narrative "kernels" serve as conversational resources for individual women and the group as a whole. How and if a "kernel story" is developed by the narrator and/or audience on a particular occasion is a function of the conversational context from which it emerges (Kalčik 1975:8), and it takes very different forms at different tellings. Not only is the dynamic of women's conversation one of elaboration and continuity, but the idiom of support can give it a distinctive tone as well. Hannerz (1969:96), for example, contrasts the "tone of relaxed sweetness, sometimes bordering on the saccharine," that characterizes approving talk between women, to the heated argument found among men. Kalčik (1975:6) even goes so far as to suggest that there is an "underlying esthetic or organizing principle" of "harmony" being expressed in women's friendly talk.

MEN'S SPEECH

The speaking patterns of men, and of women for that matter, vary greatly from one North American subculture to another. As Gerry Philipsen (1975:13) summarizes it, "talk is not everywhere valued equally; nor is it anywhere valued equally in all social contexts." There are striking cultural variations between subcultures in whether men consider certain modes of speech appropriate for dealing with women, children, authority figures, or strangers; there are differences in performance rules for storytelling and joke telling; there are differences in the context of men's speech; and there are differences in the rules for distinguishing aggressive joking from true aggression.

But more surprising than these differences are the apparent similarities across subcultures in the patterns of friendly interaction between men and the resemblances between these patterns and those observed for boys. Research reports on the speaking patterns of men among urban blacks (Abrahams 1976; Hannerz 1969), rural Newfoundlanders (Faris 1966; Bauman 1972), and urban blue-collar whites (Philipsen 1975; LeMasters 1975) point again and again to the same three features: storytelling, arguing and verbal posturing.

Narratives such as jokes and stories are highly valued, especially when they are well performed for an audience. In Newfoundland, for example, Faris (1966:242) comments that "the reason 'news' is rarely passed between two men meeting in the road—it is simply not to one's advantage to relay information to such a small audience." Loud and aggressive argument is a second common feature of male-male speech. Such arguments, which may include shouting, wagering, name-calling, and verbal threats (Faris 1966:245), are often, as Hannerz (1969:86) describes them, "debates over minor questions of little direct import to anyone," enjoyed for their own sake and not taken as signs of real conflict. Practical jokes, challenges, put-downs, insults, and other forms of verbal aggression are a third feature of men's speech, accepted as normal among friends. LeMasters (1975:140), for example, describes life in a working-class tavern in the Midwest as follows:

> It seems clear that status at the Oasis is related to the ability to "dish it out" in the rapid-fire exchange called "joshing": you have to have a quick retort,

and preferably one that puts you "one up" on your opponent. People who can't compete in the game lose status.

Thus challenges rather than statements of support are a typical way for men to respond to the speech of other men.

WHAT IS HAPPENING IN CROSS-SEX CONVERSATION

What we are suggesting is that women and men have different cultural rules for friendly conversation and that these rules come into conflict when women and men attempt to talk to each other as friends and equals in casual conversation. We can think of at least five areas, in addition to that of minimal responses already discussed, in which men and women probably possess different conversational rules, so that miscommunication is likely to occur in cross-sex interaction.

1. There are two interpretations of the meaning of questions. Women seem to see questions as a part of conversational maintenance, while men seem to view them primarily as requests for information.

2. There are two conventions for beginning an utterance and linking it to the preceding utterance. Women's rules seem to call for an explicit acknowledgment of what has been said and making a connection to it. Men seem to have no such rule and in fact some male strategies call for ignoring the preceding comments.

3. There are different interpretations of displays of verbal aggressiveness. Women seem to interpret overt aggressiveness as personally directed, negative, and disruptive. Men seem to view it as one conventional organizing structure for conversational flow.

4. There are two understandings of topic flow and topic shift. The literature on storytelling in particlar seems to indicate that men operate with a system in which topic is fairly narrowly defined and adhered to until finished and in which shifts between topics are abrupt, while women have a system in which topic is developed progressively and shifts gradually. These two systems imply very different rules for and interpretations of side comments, with major potential for miscommunication.

5. There appear to be two different attitudes towards problem sharing and advice giving. Women tend to discuss problems with one another, sharing experiences and offering reassurances. Men, in contrast, tend to hear women, and

other men, who present them with problems as making explicit requests for solutions. They respond by giving advice, by acting as experts, lecturing to their audiences.[4]

CONCLUSIONS

Our purpose in this paper has been to present a framework for thinking about and tying together a number of strands in the analysis of differences between male and female conversational styles. We hope to prove the intellectual value of this framework by demonstrating its ability to do two things: to serve as a model both of and for sociolinguistic research.

As a model *of* past research findings, the power of our approach lies in its ability to suggest new explanations of previous findings on cross-sex communication while linking these findings to a wide range of other fields, including the study of language acquisition, of play, of friendship, of storytelling, of cross-cultural miscommunication, and of discourse analysis. Differences in the social interaction patterns of boys and girls appear to be widely known but rarely utilized in examinations of sociolinguistic acquisition or in explanations of observed gender differences in patterns of adult speech. Our proposed framework should serve to link together these and other known facts in new ways.

As a model *for* future research, we hope our framework will be even more promising. It suggests to us a number of potential research problems which remain to be investigated. Sociolinguistic studies of school-age children, especially studies of the use of speech in informal peer interaction, appear to be much rarer than studies of young children, although such studies may be of greater relevance for the understanding of adult patterns, particularly those related to gender. Our framework also suggests the need for many more studies of single-sex conversations among adults, trying to make more explicit some of the differences in conversational rules suggested by present research. Finally, the argument we have been making suggests a number of specific problems that appear to be highly promising lines for future research:

1. A study of the sociolinguistic socialization of "tomboys" to see how they combine male and female patterns of speech and interaction;

2. An examination of the conversational patterns of lesbians and gay men to see how these relate to the sex-related patterns of the dominant culture;

3. An examination of the conversational patterns of the elderly to see to what extent speech differences persist after power differences have become insignificant;

4. A study of children's cultural concepts for talking about speech and the ways these shape the acquisition of speech styles (for example, how does the concept of "bossiness" define a form of behavior which little girls must learn to recognize, then censure, and finally avoid?);

5. An examination of "assertiveness training" programs for women to see whether they are really teaching women the speaking skills that politically skillful men learn in boyhood or are merely teaching women how to act like bossy little girls or bullying little boys and not feel guilty about it.

We conclude this paper by reemphasizing three of the major ways in which we feel that an anthropological perspective on culture and social organization can prove useful for further research on differences between men's and women's speech.

First, an anthropological approach to culture and cultural rules forces us to reexamine the way we interpret what is going on in conversations. The rules for interpreting conversations are, after all, culturally determined. There may be more than one way of understanding what is happening in a particular conversation and we must be careful about the rules we use for interpreting cross-sex conversations, in which the two participants may not fully share their rules of conversational inference.

Second, a concern with the relation between cultural rules and their social contexts leads us to think seriously about differences in different kinds of talk, ways of categorizing interactional situations, and ways in which conversational patterns may function as strategies for dealing with specific aspects of one's social world. Different types of interaction lead to different ways of speaking. The rules for friendly conversation between equals are different from those for service encounters, for flirting, for teaching, or for polite formal interaction. And even within the apparently uniform domain of friendly interaction, we argue that there are systematic differences between men and women in the way friendship is defined and thus in the conversational strategies that result.

Third and finally, our analysis suggests a different way of thinking about the connection between the gender-related behavior of children and that of adults. Most discussions of sex-role socialization have been based on the premise that gender differences are greatest for adults and that these adult differences are learned gradually throughout childhood. Our analysis, on the other hand, would suggest that at least some aspects of behavior are most strongly gender-differentiated during childhood and that adult patterns of friendly interaction, for example, involve learning to overcome at least partially some of the gender-specific cultural patterns typical of childhood.

NOTES

1. The analogy between the sociolinguistic processes of dialect divergence and genderlect divergence was pointed out to us by Ron Macaulay.

2. In the strict sense of the term, "dozens" refers to a culturally specific form of stylized argument through the exchange of insults that has been extensively documented by a variety of students of American black culture and is most frequently practiced by boys in their teens and preteens. Recently folklorist Simon Bronner (1978) has made a convincing case for the existence of a highly similar but independently derived form of insult exchange known as "ranking," "mocks," or "cutting" among white American adolescents. What we find striking and worthy of note is the tendency for both black and white versions of the dozens to be practiced primarily by boys.

3. "Catches" are a form of verbal play in which the main speaker ends up tricking a member of his or her audience into a vulnerable or ridiculous position. In an article on the folklore of black children in South Philadelphia, Roger Abrahams (1963) distinguishes between catches which are purely verbal and tricks in which the second player is forced into a position of being not only verbally but also physically abused, as in the following example of a catch which is also a trick:

   A. Adam and Eve and Pinch-Me-Tight
   Went up the hill to spend the night.
   Adam and Eve came down the hill.
   Who was left?

   B: Pinch-Me-Tight
   [A pinches B]

   What is significant about both catches and tricks is that they allow for the expression of playful aggression and that they produce a temporary hierarchical relation between a winner and loser, but invite the loser to attempt to get revenge by responding with a counter-trick.

4. We thank Kitty Julien for first pointing out to us the tendency of male friends to give advice to women who are not necessarily seeking it and Niyi Akinnaso for pointing out that the sex difference among Yoruba speakers in Nigeria in the way people respond verbally to the problems of others is similar to that among English speakers in the U.S.

REFERENCES

Abrahams, R. D. 1963. The "Catch" in negro Philadelphia. Keystone Folklore Quarterly 8(3):107–116.

Abrahams, R. D. 1975. Negotiating respect: Patterns of presentation among black women. In *Women in Folklore*. C. R. Farrat, ed. Austin: University of Texas Press.

Abrahams, R. D. 1976. *Talking Black*. Rowley, Mass.: Newbury House.

Bauman, R. 1972. The La Have Island General Store: Sociability and verbal art in a Nova Scotia community. *Journal of American Folklore* 85:330–43.

Bronner, S. J. 1978. A Re-examining of white dozens. *Western Folklore* 37(2):118–28.

Brooks-Gunn, J. and Matthews, W. S. 1979. *He and She: How Children Develop Their Sex-Role Identity.* Englewood Cliffs, NJ: Prentice Hall.

Eder, D. and Hallinan, M. T. 1978. Sex differences in children's friendships. *American Sociological Review* 43:237–50.

Faris, J. C. 1966. The dynamics of verbal exchange: A Newfoundland example. *Anthropologica* (Ottawa) 8(2):235–48.

Fishman, P. M. 1978. Interaction: The work women do. *Social Problems* 25(4):397–406.

Goodwin, M. 1978. Conversational practices in a peer group of urban black children. Doctoral dissertation. University of Pennsylvania, Philadelphia.

Goodwin, M. 1980a. Directive-response speech sequences in girls' and boys' task activities. In *Women and Language in Literature and Society.* S. McConnell-Ginet, R. Borker, and N. Furman, eds. New York: Praeger.

Goodwin, M. 1980b. He-said-she-said: Formal cultural procedures for the construction of a gossip dispute activity. *American Ethnologist* 7(4):674–95.

Gumperz, J. J. 1977. Sociocultural knowledge in conversational inference. In *Linguistics and Anthropology.* M. Saville-Troike, ed. Washington DC: Georgetown University Press (Georgetown University Round Table on Languages and Linguistics), 1977.

Gumperz, J. J. 1978a. The conversational analysis of interethnic communication. In *Interethnic Communication.* E. Lamar Ross, ed. Athens, Ga.: University of Georgia Press.

Gumperz, J. J. 1978b. Dialect and conversational inference in urban communication. *Language in Society* 7(3):393–409.

Gumperz, J. J. 1979. The sociolinguistic basis of speech act theory. In *Speech Act Ten Years After.* J. Boyd and S. Fertara, eds. Milan: Versus.

Gumperz, J. J. 1982. *Discourse Strategies.* Cambridge: Cambridge University Press.

Gumperz, J. J., Agrawal, A., and Aulakh, G. 1977. Prosody, paralinguistics and contextualization in Indian English. Language Behavior Research Laboratory, typescript. University of California, Berkeley.

Gumperz, J. J. and Tannen, D. 1978. Individual and social differences in language use. In *Individual Differences in Language Ability and Language Behavior.* W. Wang and C. Fillmore, eds. New York: Academic Press.

Haas, A. 1979. The acquisition of genederlect. In Language, Sex and Gender: Does La Différence Make a Difference? J. Orasnu, M. Slater, and L. Adler, eds. *Annals of the New York Academy of Sciences* 327:101–13.

Hannerz, U. 1969. *Soulside.* New York: Columbia University Press.

Harding, S. 1975. Women and words in a Spanish village. In *Towards an Anthropology of Women.* R. Reiter, ed. New York: Monthly Review Press.

Hirschman, L. 1973. Female-male differences in conversational interaction. Paper presented at Linguistic Society of America, San Diego.

Jefferson, G. 1978. Sequential aspects of storytelling in conversation. In *Studies in the Organization of Conversation Interaction.* J. Schenker, ed. New York: Academic Press.

Kalčik, S. 1975. ". . . Like Anne's gynecologist or the time I was almost raped": Personal narratives in women's rap groups. In *Women and Folklore.* C. R. Farrar, ed. Austin: University of Texas Press.

Lakoff, R. 1975. *Language and Women's Place.* New York: Harper and Row.

LeMasters, E. E. 1975. *Blue Collar Aristocrats: Life-Styles at a Working-Class Tavern.* Madison: University of Wisconsin Press.

Lever, J. 1976. Sex differences in the games children play. *Social Problems* 23:478–83.

Lever, J. 1978. Sex differences in the complexity of children's play and games. *American Sociological Review* 43:471–83.

Meditch, A. 1975. The development of sex-specific speech patterns in young children. *Anthropological Linguistics* 17:421–33.

Philipsen, G. 1975. Speaking "like a man" in Teamsterville: Cultural patterns of role enactment in an urban neighborhood. *Quarterly Journal of Speech* 61:13–22.

Sacks, H. 1974. An analysis of the course of a joke's telling in conversation. In *Explorations in the Ethnography of Speaking.* R. Bauman and J. Scherzer, eds. Cambridge: Cambridge University Press.

Savin-Williams, R. C. 1976. The ethological study of dominance formation and maintenance in a group of human adolescents. *Child Development* 47:972–79.

Soskin, W. F. and John, V. P. 1963. The study of spontaneous talk. In *The Stream of Behavior.* R. G. Barker, ed. New York: Appleton-Century-Croft.

Strodbeck, F. L. and Mann, R. D. 1956. Sex role differentiation in jury deliberations. *Sociometry* 19:3–11.

West, C. 1979. Against our will: Male interruptions of females in cross-sex conversation. In Language, Sex and Gender: Does La Différence Make a Difference? J. Oranzanu, M. Slater and L. Adler, eds. *Annals of the New York Academy of Sciences* 327:81–100.

West, C. and Zimmerman, D. H. 1977. Women's place in everyday talk: Reflections on parent–child interaction. *Social Problems* 24(5):521–9.

Zimmerman, D. H. and West, C. 1975. Sex roles, interruptions, and silences in conversation. In *Language and Sex: Differences and Dominance.* B. Thorne and N. Henley, eds. Rowley, Mass.: Newbury House.

8

Eating Christmas in the Kalahari

Richard Borshay Lee

An *economy* is a social system for the production, exchange, and consumption of goods and services. Using this definition, anthropologists believe that all human societies have economies and that economic systems can work without money and markets.

People in food-foraging societies, like the !Kung San described in this selection, have received much attention by anthropologists. To a large degree, this is because they represent (at least by analogy) the original lifestyle of our ancestors. A major discovery of research on food foragers is that their life is not "nasty, brutish, and short." In fact, the food forager's diet might be an ideal one for people living in industrialized societies.

In the hunter-gatherer economy, anthropologists have discovered that the exchange of goods is based on rules of gift giving or reciprocity. In this selection, Richard Lee tells of his surprise at the !Kung San's lack of appreciation of a Christmas gift. As we have already seen, a group's customs and rules about appropriate social behavior can reflect important cultural values. When people act in unexpected ways, anthropologists see this as an opportunity to better understand their culture and world view. That is the case in this selection.

All people give gifts to each other, but there are rules and obligations about those gifts. In our own society, there are rules about the polite way to receive a present. We are supposed to act appreciative (even if we hate the gift) because the gift is less important than the social relationship at stake. The !Kung break those rules, but in the process, Richard Lee discovers that there are important cultural messages behind their "impoliteness."

As you read this selection, ask yourself the following questions:

- Why did Richard Lee feel obligated to give a valuable gift to the !Kung at Christmas? Why did they think he was a miser?
- Why did the !Kung people's insults about the impending gift bother the anthropologist so much? Were the people treating him in a special way?
- What does Lee mean by saying, "There are no totally generous acts"? Do you agree?
- What are some cultural rules about gift giving in our own society?

The following terms discussed in this selection are included in the Glossary at the back of the book:

cultural values
economy
egalitarian society
hunter-gatherers
reciprocal gift

The !Kung Bushmen's knowledge of Christmas is thirdhand. The London Missionary Society brought the holiday to the southern Tswana tribes in the early nineteenth century. Later, native catechists spread the idea far and wide among the Bantu-speaking pastoralists, even in the remotest corners of the Kalahari Desert. The Bushmen's idea of the Christmas story, stripped to its essentials, is "praise the birth of white man's god-chief": what keeps their interest in the holiday high is the Tswana-Herero custom of slaughtering an ox for his Bushmen neighbors as an annual goodwill gesture. Since the 1930s, part of the Bushmen's annual round of activities has included a December congregation at the cattle posts for trading, marriage brokering, and several days of trance dance feasting at which the local Tswana headman is host.

As a social anthropologist working with !Kung Bushmen, I found that the Christmas ox custom suited my purposes. I had come to the Kalahari to study the hunting and gathering subsistence economy

From Eating Christmas in the Kalahari, Richard Borshay Lee, NH, pp. 14–22, 60–64. Reprinted from *Natural History* September 2006; copyright © Natural History Magazine, Inc., 2006.

of the !Kung, and to accomplish this it was essential not to provide them with food, share my own food, or interfere in any way with their food-gathering activities. While liberal handouts of tobacco and medical supplies were appreciated, they were scarcely adequate to erase the glaring disparity in wealth between the anthropologist, who maintained a two-month inventory of canned goods, and the Bushmen, who rarely had a day's supply of food on hand. My approach, while paying off in terms of data, left me open to frequent accusations of stinginess and hardheartedness. By their lights, I was a miser.

The Christmas ox was to be my way of saying thank you for the cooperation of the past year; and since it was to be our last Christmas in the field, I determined to slaughter the largest, meatiest ox that money could buy, insuring that the feast and trance dance would be a success.

Through December I kept my eyes open at the wells as the cattle were brought down for watering. Several animals were offered, but none had quite the grossness that I had in mind. Then, ten days before the holiday, a Herero friend led an ox of astonishing size and mass up to our camp. It was solid black, stood five feet high at the shoulder, had a five-foot span of horns, and must have weighed 1,200 pounds on the hoof. Food consumption calculations are my specialty, and I quickly figured that bones and viscera aside, there was enough meat—at least four pounds—for every man, woman, and child of the 150 Bushmen in the vicinity of /ai/ai who were expected at the feast.

Having found the right animal at last, I paid the Herero £20 ($56) and asked him to keep the beast with his herd until Christmas day. The next morning word spread among the people that the big solid black one was the ox chosen by /ontah (my Bushman name; it means, roughly, "whitey") for the Christmas feast. That afternoon I received the first delegation. Ben!a, an outspoken sixty-year-old mother of five, came to the point slowly.

"Where were you planning to eat Christmas?"

"Right here at /ai/ai," I replied.

"Alone or with others?"

"I expect to invite all the people to eat Christmas with me."

"Eat what?"

"I have purchased Yehave's black ox, and I am going to slaughter and cook it."

"That's what we were told at the well but refused to believe it until we heard it from yourself."

"Well, it's the black one," I replied expansively, although wondering what she was driving at.

"Oh, no!" Ben!a groaned, turning to her group. "They were right." Turning back to me she asked, "Do you expect us to eat that bag of bones?"

"Bag of bones! It's the biggest ox at /ai/ai."

"Big, yes, but old. And thin. Everybody knows there's no meat on that old ox. What did you expect to eat off of it, the horns?"

Everybody chuckled at Ben!a's one-liner as they walked away, but all I could manage was a weak grin.

That evening it was the turn of the young men. They came to sit at our evening fire. /gaugo, about my age, spoke to me man-to-man.

"/ontah, you have always been square with us," he lied. "What has happened to change your heart? That sack of guts and bones of Yehave's will hardly feed one camp, let alone all the Bushmen around /ai/ai." And he proceeded to enumerate the seven camps in the /ai/ai vicinity, family by family. "Perhaps you have forgotten that we are not few, but many. Or are you too blind to tell the difference between a proper cow and an old wreck? That ox is thin to the point of death."

"Look, you guys," I retorted, "that is a beautiful animal, and I'm sure you will eat it with pleasure at Christmas."

"Of course we will eat it: it's food. But it won't fill us up to the point where we will have enough strength to dance. We will eat and go home to bed with stomachs rumbling."

That night as we turned in, I asked my wife, Nancy, "What did you think of the black ox?"

"It looked enormous to me. Why?"

"Well, about eight different people have told me I got gypped; that the ox is nothing but bones."

"What's the angle?" Nancy asked. "Did they have a better one to sell?"

"No, they just said that it was going to be a grim Christmas because there won't be enough meat to go around. Maybe I'll get an independent judge to look at the beast in the morning."

Bright and early, Halingisi, a Tswana cattle owner, appeared at our camp. But before I could ask him to give me his opinion on Yehave's black ox, he gave me the eye signal that indicated a confidential chat. We left the camp and sat down.

"/ontah, I'm surprised at you; you've lived here for three years and still haven't learned anything about cattle."

"But what else can a person do but choose the biggest, strongest animal one can find?" I retorted.

"Look, just because an animal is big doesn't mean that it has plenty of meat on it. The black one was a beauty when it was younger, but now it is thin to the point of death."

"Well I've already bought it. What can I do at this stage?"

"Bought it already? I thought you were just considering it. Well, you'll have to kill it and serve it, I suppose. But don't expect much of a dance to follow."

My spirits dropped rapidly. I could believe that Ben!a and /gaugo just might be putting me on about the black ox, but Halingisi seemed to be an impartial critic. I went around that day feeling as though I had bought a lemon of a used car.

In the afternoon it was Tomazo's turn. Tomazo is a fine hunter, a top trance performer . . . and one of my most reliable informants. He approached the subject of the Christmas cow as part of my continuing Bushman education.

"My friend, the way it is with us Bushmen," he began, "is that we love meat. And even more than that, we love fat. When we hunt we always search for the fat ones, the ones dripping with layers of white fat: fat that turns into a clear, thick oil in the cooking pot, fat that slides down your gullet, fills your stomach and gives you a roaring diarrhea," he rhapsodized.

"So, feeling as we do," he continued, "it gives us pain to be served such a scrawny thing as Yehave's black ox. It is big, yes, and no doubt its giant bones are good for soup, but fat is what we really crave and so we will eat Christmas this year with a heavy heart."

The prospect of a gloomy Christmas now had me worried, so I asked Tomazo what I could do about it.

"Look for a fat one, a young one . . . smaller, but fat. Fat enough to make us //gom (evacuate the bowels), then we will be happy."

My suspicions were aroused when Tomazo said that he happened to know a young, fat, barren cow that the owner was willing to part with. Was Tomazo working on commission, I wondered? But I dispelled this unworthy thought when we approached the Herero owner of the cow in question and found that he had decided not to sell.

The scrawny wreck of a Christmas ox now became the talk of the /ai/ai water hole and was the first news told to the outlying groups as they began to come in from the bush for the feast. What finally convinced me that real trouble might be brewing was the visit from u!au, an old conservative with a reputation for fierceness. His nickname meant spear and referred to an incident thirty years ago in which he had speared a man to death. He had an intense manner; fixing me with his eyes, he said in clipped tones:

"I have only just heard about the black ox today, or else I would have come earlier. /ontah, do you honestly think you can serve meat like that to people and avoid a fight?" He paused, letting the implications sink in. "I don't mean fight you, /ontah; you are a white man. I mean a fight between Bushmen. There are many fierce ones here, and with such a small quantity of meat to distribute, how can you give everybody a fair share? Someone is sure to accuse another of taking too much or hogging all the choice pieces. Then you will see what happens when some go hungry while others eat."

The possibility of at least a serious argument struck me as all too real. I had witnessed the tension that surrounds the distribution of meat from a kudu or gemsbok kill, and had documented many arguments that sprang up from a real or imagined slight in meat distribution. The owners of a kill may spend up to two hours arranging and rearranging the piles of meat under the gaze of a circle of recipients before handing them out. And I knew that the Christmas feast at /ai/ai would be bringing together groups that had feuded in the past.

Convinced now of the gravity of the situation, I went in earnest to search for a second cow; but all my inquiries failed to turn one up.

The Christmas feast was evidently going to be a disaster, and the incessant complaints about the meagerness of the ox had already taken the fun out of it for me. Moreover, I was getting bored with the wise-cracks, and after losing my temper a few times, I resolved to serve the beast anyway. If the meat fell short, the hell with it. In the Bushmen idiom, I announced to all who would listen:

"I am a poor man and blind. If I have chosen one that is too old and too thin, we will eat it anyway and see if there is enough meat there to quiet the rumbling of our stomachs."

On hearing this speech, Ben!a offered me a rare word of comfort. "It's thin," she said philosophically, "but the bones will make a good soup."

At dawn Christmas morning, instinct told me to turn over the butchering and cooking to a friend and take off with Nancy to spend Christmas alone in the bush. But curiosity kept me from retreating. I wanted to see what such a scrawny ox looked like on butchering, and if there was going to be a fight, I wanted to catch every word of it. Anthropologists are incurable that way.

The great beast was driven up to our dancing ground, and a shot in the forehead dropped it in its tracks. Then, freshly cut branches were heaped around the fallen carcass to receive the meat. Ten men volunteered to help with the cutting. I asked /gaugo to make the breast bone cut. This cut, which begins the butchering process for most large game, offers easy access for removal of the viscera. But it allows the hunter to spot-check the amount of fat on an animal. A fat game animal carries a white layer up to an inch thick on the chest, while in a thin one, the knife will quickly cut to the bone. All eyes fixed on his hand as /gaugo, dwarfed by the great carcass, knelt to the breast. The first cut opened a pool of solid white in the black skin. The second and third cut widened and deepened the creamy white. Still no bone. It was pure fat; it must have been two inches thick.

"Hey /gau," I burst out, "that ox is loaded with fat. What's this about the ox being too thin to bother eating? Are you out of your mind?"

"Fat?" /gau shot back. "You call that fat? This wreck is thin, sick, dead!" And he broke out laughing. So did everyone else. They rolled on the ground, paralyzed with laughter. Everybody laughed except me; I was thinking.

I ran back to the tent and burst in just as Nancy was getting up. "Hey, the black ox. It's fat as hell! They were kidding about it being too thin to eat. It was a joke or something. A put-on. Everyone is really delighted with it."

"Some joke," my wife replied. "It was so funny that you were ready to pack up and leave /ai/ai."

If it had indeed been a joke, it had been an extraordinarily convincing one, and tinged, I thought, with more than a touch of malice as many jokes are. Nevertheless, that it was a joke lifted my spirits considerably, and I returned to the butchering site where the shape of the ox was rapidly disappearing under the axes and knives of the butchers. The atmosphere had become festive. Grinning broadly, their arms covered with blood well past the elbow, men packed chunks of meat into the big cast-iron cooking pots, fifty pounds to the load, and muttered and chuckled all the while about the thinness and worthlessness of the animal and /ontah's poor judgment.

We danced and ate that ox two days and two nights; we cooked and distributed fourteen potfuls of meat and no one went home hungry and no fights broke out.

But the "joke" stayed in my mind. I had a growing feeling that something important had happened in my relationship with the Bushmen and that the clue lay in the meaning of the joke. Several days later, when most of the people had dispersed back to the bush camps, I raised the question with Hakekgose, a Tswana man who had grown up among the !Kung, married a !Kung girl, and who probably knows the culture better than any other non-Bushman.

"With us whites," I began, "Christmas is supposed to be the day of friendship and brotherly love. What I can't figure out is why the Bushmen went to such lengths to criticize and belittle the ox I had bought for the feast. The animal was perfectly good and their jokes and wisecracks practically ruined the holiday for me."

"So it really did bother you," said Hakekgose. "Well, that's the way they always talk. When I take my rifle and go hunting with them, if I miss, they laugh at me for the rest of the day. But even if I hit and bring one down, it's no better. To them, the kill is always too small or too old or too thin; and as we sit down on the kill site to cook and eat the liver, they keep grumbling, even with their mouths full of meat. They say things like, 'Oh, this is awful! What a worthless animal! Whatever made me think that this Tswana rascal could hunt!'"

"Is this the way outsiders are treated?" I asked.

"No, it is their custom; they talk that way to each other too. Go and ask them."

/gaugo had been one of the most enthusiastic in making me feel bad about the merit of the Christmas ox. I sought him out first.

"Why did you tell me the black ox was worthless, when you could see that it was loaded with fat and meat?"

"It is our way," he said smiling. "We always like to fool people about that. Say there is a Bushman who has been hunting. He must not come home and announce like a braggart, 'I have killed a big one in the bush!' He must first sit down in silence until I or someone else comes up to his fire and asks, 'What did you see today?' He replies quietly, 'Ah, I'm no good for hunting. I saw nothing at all (pause) just a little tiny one.' Then I smile to myself," /gaugo continued, "because I know he has killed something big.

"In the morning we make up a party of four or five people to cut up and carry the meat back to the camp. When we arrive at the kill we examine it and cry out, 'You mean to say you have dragged us all the way out here in order to make us cart home your pile of bones? Oh, if I had known it was this thin I wouldn't have come.' Another one pipes up, 'People, to think I gave up a nice day in the shade for this. At home we may be hungry but at least we have nice cool water to drink.' If the horns are big, someone says, 'Did you think that somehow you were going to boil down the horns for soup?'

"To all this you must respond in kind. 'I agree,' you say, 'this one is not worth the effort; let's just cook the liver for strength and leave the rest for the hyenas. It is not too late to hunt today and even a duiker or steenbok would be better than this mess.'

"Then you set to work nevertheless; butcher the animal, carry the meat back to the camp and everyone eats," /gaugo concluded.

Things were beginning to make sense. Next, I went to Tomazo. He corroborated /gaugo's story of the obligatory insults over a kill and added a few details of his own.

"But," I asked, "why insult a man after he has gone to all that trouble to track and kill an animal and when he is going to share the meat with you so that your children will have something to eat?"

"Arrogance," was his cryptic answer.

"Arrogance?"

"Yes, when a young man kills much meat he comes to think of himself as a chief or a big man, and he thinks of the rest of us as his servants or inferiors. We can't accept this. We refuse one who boasts, for someday his pride will make him kill somebody. So we always speak of his meat as worthless. This way we cool his heart and make him gentle."

"But why didn't you tell me this before?" I asked Tomazo with some heat.

"Because you never asked me," said Tomazo, echoing the refrain that has come to haunt every field ethnographer.

The pieces now fell into place. I had known for a long time that in situations of social conflict with Bushmen I held all the cards. I was the only source of tobacco in a thousand square miles, and I was not incapable of cutting an individual off for noncooperation. Though my boycott never lasted longer than a few days, it was an indication of my strength. People resented my presence at the water hole, yet simultaneously dreaded my leaving. In short I was a perfect target for the charge of arrogance and for the Bushman tactic of enforcing humility.

I had been taught an object lesson by the Bushmen; it had come from an unexpected corner and had hurt me in a vulnerable area. For the big black ox was to be the one totally generous, unstinting act of my year at /ai/ai and I was quite unprepared for the reaction I received.

As I read it, their message was this: There are no totally generous acts. All "acts" have an element of calculation. One black ox slaughtered at Christmas does not wipe out a year of careful manipulation of gifts given to serve your own ends. After all, to kill an animal and share the meat with people is really no more than the Bushmen do for each other every day and with far less fanfare.

In the end, I had to admire how the Bushmen had played out the farce—collectively straight-faced to the end. Curiously, the episode reminded me of the *Good Soldier Schweik* and his marvelous encounters with authority. Like Schweik, the Bushmen had retained a thoroughgoing skepticism of good intentions. Was it this independence of spirit, I wondered, that had kept them culturally viable in the face of generations of contact with more powerful societies, both black and white? The thought that the Bushmen were alive and well in the Kalahari was strangely comforting. Perhaps, armed with that independence and with their superb knowledge of their environment, they might yet survive the future.

9

Chinese Table Manners

You Are How *You Eat*

Eugene Cooper

I had been looking forward to this dinner with an important client for over a week. We were going to close the biggest deal of my career. He arrived on time, and I ordered a bit of wine. It was a fancy restaurant and I was trying to behave appropriately; I tucked my napkin neatly on my lap and lifted my wine glass carefully with my little finger extended in the way I had always seen it done. But what began well began to go awry. I looked on in horror as my client ladled a number of different dishes together into a soup bowl, lifted it to his mouth and began to shovel it in. I was so embarrassed by this display of bad manners that I hoped no one I knew would happen by. My face must have betrayed my thoughts, but my client did not let on. He simply asked if I was not enjoying my food because I had left the dishes flat on the table. This took me by surprise, because I realized for the first time that he was looking at me and finding *my* behavior odd. Our smiles became realizations and turned to laughter. Luckily, we had a good sense of humor about our ethnocentrism. Somebody should have warned us; this could have been a real disaster.

Consider yourself warned. Table manners, like a great many everyday events, are heavily laden with cultural meaning. Understanding culturally prescribed behaviors is of practical importance, not merely interesting. More anthropologists need to be involved in cross-cultural training for situations where there is likely to be interaction between people from different cultures or ethnic groups.

As you read this selection, ask yourself the following questions:

- How does one determine which culture's table manners are better? Why do we judge people by their manners?
- What are the important distinctions in Chinese food?
- Which food is the most basic and a necessary part of every Chinese meal? What about your own culture?
- What does it mean in China if you leave your rice bowl on the table while eating from it?
- What is the overriding rule of Chinese table customs?
- How do the Chinese feel about eating alone? Why?

The following terms discussed in this selection are included in the Glossary at the back of the book:

> *cultural values*
> *ethnology*
> *symbol*

"Etiquette of this kind (not putting half eaten meat back in the bowl, [not] wiping one's nose on one's sleeve) is not superficial, a matter for the surface rather than the depths; refined ways of acting are so internalized as to make alternative behavior truly 'disgusting,' 'revolting,' 'nauseous,' turning them into some of the most highly charged and deeply felt of intra-social differences, so that 'rustic' behavior is not merely quaint but barbarous" (Goody 1982:140).

"Probably no common practice is more diversified than the familiar one of eating in company, for what Europeans consider as correct and decent may by other races be looked upon as wrong or indelicate. Similarly, few social observances provide more opportunities for offending the stranger than the etiquette of the table"(Hammerton 1936:23).

Reproduced by permission of Society for Applied Anthropology from *Human Organization* 45(2):179–184, 1986.

Our shrinking world makes encounters with people of other cultures increasingly common in our life experiences. Whether in the conduct of business, in interactions with our "ethnic" neighbors, or as visitors to other countries, we are frequently called on to communicate with others whose assumptions about what constitutes appropriate behavior are widely different from our own.

In such contexts, it is often difficult to know whether habits and customs one takes for granted in one's own home may be creating unfavorable impressions in one's host's home. No less an authority than Confucius, writing more than two thousand years ago, was aware of the potential difficulties involved in intercultural communication, and provided the following advice: "When entering a country inquire of its customs. When crossing a border, inquire of the prohibitions" (Li Chi 1971:17).

Among such customs and prohibitions, those associated with behavior at the table can make an enormous difference in the way one is perceived by a foreign host.

As regards the Chinese in particular, the way one handles oneself at the table gives off signals of the clearest type as to what kind of a person one is, and it is all too easy to offend, as I hope to show. At the same time, however, it is easy enough to equip oneself with a few simple points to bear in mind that will not only pleasantly surprise one's Chinese host, but also convince him or her that one is a sensitive, cultivated, courteous, respectful, and considerate individual.

Surprisingly, for a civilization which has generated so many handbooks of its various cuisines, China has not produced any popular guidebooks for table manners of the Emily Post variety. The field, of course, has for the most part been preempted by the *Li Chi*—records of etiquette and ceremonial—most of which is said to date from the early Han. Indeed, many of the themes which characterize contemporary Chinese table manners are present in the minute descriptions of behaviors appropriate to people of various stations in all the gradations of Han social structure, such as the prescription to yield or defer. However, one is hard pressed to find a general rough and ready guide to contemporary Chinese table manners of anything more than the most superficial kind, usually present in popular Chinese cookbooks for Western audiences.

The absence of attention to table manners may be the result of the fact that table manners are among those habits most taken for granted—rules no grown-up needs instruction in. A Chinese culinary enthusiast of my acquaintance assures me that table manners are not important in Chinese history, being far outweighed by the scarcity of food generally as the major issue. Nevertheless, an examination of Chinese table manners provides sufficient contrast with Western table habits in terms of structure and performance, as to make significant features of Chinese etiquette emerge in comparison—features taken for granted by the native.

Those few who have written on the subject (Chang 1977; Hsü and Hsü 1977) generally qualify as bi-cultural individuals with sufficient experience of both Chinese and Western rules to tease out the areas of contrastive significance. My five years of field research (and eating) in Hong Kong, and eight years of marriage to a Chinese woman who taught me Chinese table manners as to a child, also qualify me for the assignment, although my former European colleagues at the University of Hong Kong might question my credentials as an expert on Western etiquette, to be sure.

BASIC STRUCTURES AND PARAPHERNALIA

To begin with, it is useful to consider K. C. Chang's (1977) broad outline of the important distinctions in Chinese food between food (*shih*) and drink (*yin*), and then within the category food, between *fan* (grain/rice) and *ts'ai* (dishes). Chang establishes a hierarchy with grain as the base, vegetables and fruit as next least expendable, and meat as most expendable in the preparation of a meal. Fish would probably fall between vegetables and meat at least as far as contemporary Hong Kong is concerned, particularly if one includes the enormous variety of preserved fish available.

In any event, it is fair to say that a Chinese meal is not a meal without *fan*. The morning food event, at which rice is not normally taken, or if so is taken as gruel, is not thought of as a meal. When Chinese speak of a full day's eating fare, it is two square meals per day rather than three. Thus rice (or grain) defines a meal, and its treatment and consumption are circumscribed in a number of ways.

It will be helpful, however, to lay out the general paraphernalia with which the diner is equipped, and the structure in which it is deployed before returning to the rules governing rice. On this subject, Hsü and Hsü (1977:304) have written:

> The typical Chinese dining table is round or square, the *ts'ai* dishes are laid in the center, and each participant in the meal is equipped with a bowl for *fan*, a pair of chopsticks, a saucer, and a spoon. All at the table take from the *ts'ai* dishes as they proceed with the meal.

The *ts'ai* dishes are typically shared by all, and must be treated much as common property, whereas one's bowl is a private place which comes directly in touch with the mouth. The chopsticks are of both the mouth and the table, and mediate between. They are thin, and when employed appropriately only touch the one piece or small quantity a person touches first. Many Westerners find the habit of sharing from a common plate potentially unhygienic, and one might be tempted to dismiss this as a bit of ethnocentricity. However, the point has recently been made by no less an authority than Communist party secretary Hu Yaobang, who called attention to the unsanitary character of traditional Chinese eating habits and urged change.

One employs the chopsticks to take from the common plate and place food in one's bowl, then one raises the bowl to the mouth and pushes food into the mouth with the chopsticks. Hsü and Hsü state, "The diner who lets his *fan* bowl stay on the table and eats by picking up lumps of *fan* from the bowl is expressing disinterest in or dissatisfaction with the food. If he or she is a guest in someone's house, that is seen as an open insult to the host" (1977:304). Since one's bowl is a private place, "good manners do not preclude resting a piece of meat (or other items) in one's bowl between bites" (1977:304). However, one never puts a partially chewed piece of anything back into one of the common plates (I would not have thought this necessary to mention; however, an otherwise culturally sensitive person I know had the audacity to do so recently so it may bear mentioning.) Also, it is extremely poor manners to suck or bite your chopsticks.

In some cases the bowl may be substituted for by a spoon, as, for example, when one goes out to lunch with one's workmates, and each diner is supplied with a flat plate piled high with rice topped with roast pork, chicken, duck and/or *lap cheong* (Chinese sausage), or with a helping of a single *ts'ai* dish (the latter known as *hui fan*).

Eating rice off a flat plate with chopsticks alone is not an easy task. Westerners exasperated with the use of chopsticks often feel their most intense frustration when trying to accomplish this task, and are often reduced to picking up small bits of rice with the ends of their chopsticks and placing them in the mouth. Seeming to pick at one's food in this way is not good manners and marks one as an incompetent foreign devil, confirming in most Chinese minds all of their previous prejudices about *guailos*.

No self-respecting Chinese would attempt to eat rice directly from a flat plate without first piling the rice onto, or scooping the rice into, a spoon. One eats the *ts'ai* or meat with one's chopsticks, but rice is most often carried to the mouth in a spoon. The spoon stands in for the bowl in the mini-context of an individual serving, and one can also think of the bowl itself as serving in the capacity of an enlarged spoon in the context of regular dining as well.

Rice is usually doled out from a common pot by the host or hostess. When someone has filled your rice bowl for you, it is accepted with two hands. To accept rice with one hand suggests disinterest, disrespect, and carelessness. One places the full bowl in front of oneself and waits until everyone has been served. It is very impolite to begin eating before everyone at the table has had his bowl filled with rice. When one has finished the rice in one's bowl, one does not continue to eat of the common *ts'ai* dishes. To eat *ts'ai* without rice in one's bowl is to appear a glutton interested only in *ts'ai*, of which one must consume a great deal to get full without rice. Depending on the degree of intimacy of a relationship, one may, when eating at the home of a friend or acquaintance, rise from the table to refill one's bowl with rice from the rice pot in the kitchen. However, at formal occasions one's host will usually be alert enough to notice when one's rice bowl is empty and move to fill it before one might be forced to request more rice. When one rises to get more rice, the host will usually insist on taking one's bowl and filling it. One may decline such assistance if the host is a close friend by simply saying "I'll serve myself."

At banquets one is expected to fill up on *ts'ai*, and consumption of too much rice may be a sign of disrespect to the quality of the *ts'ai* dishes. No rice should ever be left over in one's bowl at the end of the meal.

> As children we were always taught to leave not a single grain of *fan* in our bowl when we finished. Our elders strongly impressed on us that each single grain of rice or corn was obtained through the drops of sweat of the tillers of the soil (Hsü and Hsü 1977:308).

A corollary of this rule is never to take so much rice, or anything else for that matter, in your bowl as to be unable to finish it. It is also extremely disrespectful of the meal and of one's host to leave bits of rice on the table around one's bowl, and Chinese children are often told that each of these grains will materialize as a pockmark on the face of their future spouse.

As regards the *ts'ai*, it is important to note again that it is arrayed for all to share. Generally speaking, especially on formal occasions, one does not serve oneself without first offering to others, at least those seated immediately to either side. This applies also to the taking of tea, and one generally fills a neighbor's cup before taking tea for oneself. When tea is poured for you, it is customary to tap the table with your fingers to convey your thanks.

The overriding rule of Chinese table customs is deference. Defer to others in everything. Be conscious of the need to share what is placed in common. This means don't eat only from those dishes that you like.

One very common point of instruction from parents to children is that the best mannered person does not allow co-diners to be aware of what his or her favorite dishes are by his or her eating pattern (Hsü and Hsü 1977:304).

When taking from the common dishes one should also only take in such proportions that everyone else will be left with a roughly equivalent amount. It is polite to take the remains of a common *ts'ai* dish after a new dish has been brought out. The desirability of the remains is diminished by the introduction of a new dish, and the remains of the old become fair game. However, it is rather poor manners to incline a common plate toward oneself and scrape the remains into one's bowl. This "looking in the mirror" evokes the idea of narcissistic concern with oneself.

In general, young should defer to old in order of eating, and on formal occasions when guests are present children may even be excluded from the dining table until the adults are finished, or seated at a table separate from the adults. In the household of the boss of the factory where I did my fieldwork, apprentices commonly sat with the boss at the family table, but were relegated to the children's table at the New Year's feast.

A host will usually signal that it is appropriate to begin eating, after each person at the table has taken rice, by picking up his chopsticks and saying "*sik fan*." When a guest has eaten his fill, he indicates that he is finished by putting down his chopsticks and encouraging others still eating to take their time. They in turn will inquire if the guest is full, and if he is he should say so. Upon finishing one may either remain at the table or leave. A guest of honor is expected to remain until all are finished.

In addition, one should be careful not to take large mouthfuls, to refrain from making noise while chewing, and to try to maintain the same pace of eating as others at the table. In contrast to Western etiquette in which "toothpicks are never used outside the privacy of one's room" (McLean 1941:63), toothpicks are provided at most Chinese tables and it is not impolite to give one's teeth a thorough picking at the table, provided one covers one's mouth with the opposite hand.

Spitting is not good manners at a Chinese table, although this is a rule often honored more in the breach. Spittoons are often provided in Chinese restaurants, both as a repository for waste water and tea used to sterilize one's utensils, and for expectorations of various sorts. Often the contents of the spittoons threaten to get up and walk away, so vile are the contents. The floor is fair game in many restaurants for just about anything remaining in one's mouth not swallowable, such as small bits of bone or gristle. Hong Kong has improved considerably in this regard in recent years, but in working-class restaurants and *daipaidongs*, spitting is still quite common.

INFLECTIONS OF GENERAL PRINCIPLES

Having laid out these basic ground rules, it remains to explore how these rules are inflected in the various contexts in which food events occur in contemporary Hong Kong. These contexts are many and varied, ranging from informal and intimate occasions when the family is together at home for a meal, to the more formal occasions involving elaborate feasts usually held in restaurants. Somewhat intermediate between these are the meals eaten out, but in somewhat less formal contexts—from breakfast taken at *dim saam* houses, lunches taken at foodstalls with workmates, to evening meals prepared in restaurants for individual diners (*hak fan*), and midnight snacks. Expectations as to appropriate comportment at the table will also vary with region of origin, age, and class position.

For example, for Cantonese a full meal usually includes soup, and many Cantonese feel uncomfortable leaving the table without having partaken of soup. The minimal structure of the Cantonese meal includes not just *fan* (grain) and *ts'ai* (dishes), but also soup. This minimal structure is served up in what is known as *hak fan*, a specialty of some restaurants (usually Shanghainese) in which one may choose from a daily set menu of *hak* dishes, served with an extra large bowl of rice and the soup of the day. *Hak fan* is designed for people who must eat alone for some reason, not considered the most desirable circumstances. Two Chinese who knew each other would not sit down at the same table and order two individual dishes of *hak fan*. They would surely grasp the opportunity of sharing the greater variety available to each through social eating.

Jack Goody has likened eating alone to defecating in public (1982:306) because of the absence of the social in meeting essentially biological needs. *Hak fan* assures that even taken alone, the minimum structural entity of a Cantonese meal is available to be consumed. This basic structure is also revealed in a variety of thermos containers used for carrying lunch to work which are equipped with compartments for rice, *ts'ai* and soup. Since the contexts in which food events occur in Hong Kong are so varied, soup is not always the focus of attention. Proceeding through the ordinary day's food events from morning to evening will give us occasion to note context-linked inflections of our general principles.

As mentioned previously, the morning food event does not pass muster as a meal, largely due to the absence of rice. Still, there are a variety of contexts in which this event may take place. At home, the morning food event usually involves rice from the evening before boiled down to congee with a variety of pickles and condiments tossed in or served on the side. This is usually grabbed quickly in the kitchen on the way out to work, if it is eaten at all, and seldom involves the entire family seated at a single table.

Eaten out, the morning food event may take several forms. Consistent with the quick and superficial character of the event at home is the food event taken at a food stall or *daipaidong*, of which several different types serve suitable breakfast fare—congee (most commonly with preserved egg and pork), *yautiu* (unsweetened fried dough strips), hot *dao-jeung* (soy bean milk), *jucheung fen* (rolled rice noodles), all served with tea, usually in a glass.

Eating at a *daipaidong*, and even in some restaurants, one assumes the probability that the chopsticks, stuffed together in a can and set at the center of the table for individual diners to take, as well as one's cup, bowl, and spoon, will not have been properly washed. A brief ritualized washing usually precedes the meal in which one pours a glass of boiling hot tea into one's glass, stirring the ends of the chopsticks in the water to sterilize them, pouring the still hot water into one's bowl where one's cup and spoon are immersed and sterilized. The wash water is then thrown out, usually on the street in the case of a *daipaidong*, or in a spittoon at a restaurant, and one is prepared to commence eating. Occasionally, one is even provided with a separate bowl for washing one's eating implements, filled by one's waiter with boiling water from a huge kettle.

At a *daipaidong* for breakfast, one usually shares a table with a stranger, or perhaps a neighbor or workmate, depending on whether one eats near home or near work. In any case, one's portion is usually one's own, and the rules of formal dining apply only in the most general terms. Food is usually taken with dispatch, as one is usually rushing to work or to school, and the idea is just to put something in one's stomach to suppress hunger till the first meal of the day—*ng fan* (lunch).

The slightly more formal morning food event is *dim saam*, referred to most often as *yam ch'a* (drink tea). "Drinking tea" again refers to something less than a "meal," although on weekends, taken with one's family at a large table, *dim saam* often involves the consumption of large quantities of buns, dumplings, rice noodles in various shapes, a variety of innards, and the like. One sits down, is approached by one's waiter, or in fancier restaurants by a host or hostess, who will inquire what kind of tea one will be drinking—*sao mei, bo lei, soy sin*, and that old perceived favorite of *guailos*—*heung pien* (jasmine). When the tea arrives the host will fill everyone's cup and the meal may begin.

One acquires food from carts pushed around by young children and/or aged women, and less frequently by older men. One may find oneself sharing a table with strangers, or with regular customers who eat at the same restaurant at the same time every morning. Going to *yam ch'a* on a regular schedule assures one of continuous contact with the usual crowd, and it is common to find oneself seated at the same table with many of the same people each morning. While polite conversation is the general rule, more juicy gossip is not inappropriate as the relationship between morning diners becomes more familiar.

Generally, each diner is aware of what he has consumed, and the position of the plates may be adjusted where they have been ambiguously placed so the waiter can figure the tab. One eats from one's own plates under such circumstances, and pays for one's own plates; however, it is polite to fill the tea cup of one's neighbor from one's own pot if one is acquainted with him or her. There are still some restaurants in Hong Kong which serve tea in a covered bowl, quite literally stuffed with tea, and poured into a cup to be drunk, extremely dark, but the standard tea pot has replaced the bowl as a tea vessel in most restaurants.

A table shared with strangers or neighbors is usually an informal arrangement in which one eats one's own food. However, taking *dim saam* may also be a more formal occasion, especially on weekends, or when one has been *cheng*-ed (asked out). In such circumstances many of the rules of formal dining apply, i.e., the food on the table is common and should only be taken in such proportions that enough is left for others. One may order dishes one likes from the passing wagons, but one should always offer to others before taking from the dish for oneself. The dishes accumulate somewhat at random due to the vagaries of the itinerary of the carts, so there is no formal order to the dishes' arrival, although sweeter dishes are usually taken last.

Dim saam often trails off into lunch on formal or informal occasions, and by noon after the diners have warmed up with a few *dim saam* dishes, it is polite to inquire of one's fellow diners whether a plate of noodles or rice (a real meal) is in order, and if so, to order such dishes from the kitchen from one's waiter. Varieties of *dim saam* are also available from *daipaidong* as well, sometimes served up in individual portions to go.

The midday food event in Hong Kong includes rice or a reasonable substitute (rice noodles, bean noodles, wheat noodles), and is most often taken during a lunch hour break from factory or office labor. A variety of choices confront the Hong Kong worker eating out for lunch. Food stalls serve a variety of dishes, usually in individual portions on flat plates heaped high with rice, and covered with a single *ts'ai* dish. A glass of tea is usually served, and doubles again as a vessel for sterilizing one's chopsticks and spoon. Blue collar workers I knew in Hong Kong would often consume a full-to-the-brim tea tumbler of high octane spirits with such meals, and trundle back to work with the warm glow and slightly glazed look of a two-martini-lunch executive.

A plate of noodles may also be ordered from stalls specializing in such things. These may be served in individual portions, but given the easy divisibility of noodle dishes it is common for workmates to order a variety of noodle dishes and share them in common. A portion is lifted from the plate to one's bowl; with chopsticks initially, when the noodles are easily grasped in quantity; with help from the spoon as the plate gets progressively emptied. The setting of shared common dishes makes the general rules of the table outlined above once again applicable.

Co-workers will often go out to lunch at large *dim saam* restaurants, catch the tail end of the morning *dim saam* and order a variety of more substantial noodle or rice dishes. Where eating has taken place in common, and occasionally even where individual portions have been served, it is unusual for the check to be divided. Someone usually pays the whole tab. Among workmates, or those who often eat together, there is an implicit assumption that in the long run reciprocity will be achieved. It is not impolite among status equals to grab the check and pay for one's fellow diner, but this is not polite if the status difference is too great. Fights over the check occasionally occur in a way which evokes the potlatches of Northwest Coast Indians in which a status hierarchy is confirmed. Paying the check validates one's status superiority over one's fellow diners. Of course, the wider social setting must also be taken into account. One may be desirous of seeking a favor of an important person, in which case paying the check may serve as a mild form of pressure in which the obligation of reciprocity is finessed, enjoining one's fellow diner to comply with one's request. Food events are first and foremost social events.

The evening meal taken at home usually includes some warmed over *ts'ai* from the previous day's meal plus an increment of newly prepared dishes. It is not good manners to ignore the leftovers, despite the fact that they may not be quite as attractive as when served the day before. The general rules of the table apply, although the intimate setting of the family at home makes their application somewhat less formal. Still and all, parents will most commonly instruct children as to the appropriate forms of behavior at the table in this setting, and the children must show that they understand and are learning. In many working-class homes in Hong Kong it is still common for the men to

eat first, with the women joining later and/or hovering over the meal without ever formally sitting down.

At more formal dinners or at banquets or feasts associated with weddings, New Year's, funerals or festivals, the primacy of the *fan* and the secondary character of the *ts'ai* dishes is reversed, with attention devoted to the quality of the *ts'ai* dishes (Hsü and Hsü 1977:307), and rice not served till last. Thus at a banquet one may eat *ts'ai* without rice in one's bowl, and one is expected to fill up on *ts'ai* such that when the rice is finally served, one can only take a token portion, which is to say, this has been a real feast.

> During festivals and especially when acting as hosts all Chinese seem to ignore their sense of frugality and indulge in extravagance. *Ts'ai* dishes are served in abundance. The host or hostess will heap the guests' saucers with piece after piece of meat, fish, chicken and so on, in spite of repeated excuses or even protests on the guests' part. When *fan* is finally served, most around the table are full and can at best nibble a few grains (Hsü and Hsü 1977:307).

By the time the rice has been served at a banquet the diner has already had a share of cold appetizer, several stir fry dishes, or whole chickens, ducks, fish, soup, and a sweet/salty dessert. The emphasis on whole items (with head and tail attached) symbolizes completeness and fullness, and evokes these meanings at the table. One tries to serve fish, *yü*, a homophone for surplus, *yü*, to sympathetically bring about that condition in one's guests.

It is not polite to turn over a fish at the table. Rather, when the side facing up has been finished, the skeleton is lifted off to leave the meat underneath exposed. Apparently, turning over the fish is taboo among boat people, since the fish symbolizes the boat which will capsize sympathetically if a fish is turned over. Waiters in Hong Kong are never sure which of their customers are boat folk and might take offense, so they generally refrain from turning over any fish and apparently the practice has now become general.

A variety of prestige foods, such as shark's fin soup and the various eight precious dishes, are served at banquets more for the social recognition they confer than for the pleasure derived from their consumption (see de Garine 1976:150).

Conceptually, whiskey belongs with grain from which it is distilled and may be taken with food as a rice substitute. On formal occasions in Hong Kong scotch or VSOP Cognac is the rule, served straight in water tumblers, and often diluted with Seven-Up.

Another food event of note in Hong Kong is *siu yeh*—loosely translated as snacks. Usually taken late in the evening, they may include anything from congee, noodles and won ton, to roast pork, duck or chicken, to *hung dao sa* (sweet red bean soup—hot or iced) and *daofufa* (sweet bean curd usually flavored with almond). *Siu yeh* is usually served in individual portions. If you go out for won ton mein, everyone gets his own bowl. If you order duck's neck soup with rice, you are served an individual helping of soup, and an individual bowl of rice. Depending on the class of restaurant you take your *siu yeh* in, you may or may not find it advisable to wash your utensils with tea.

Itinerant street vendors with wheeled carts dispense a variety of prepared *siu yeh* in some residential neighborhoods, calling housewives and amahs to the street clutching their large porcelain bowls, or doling out cuttlefish parts to schoolchildren on street corners.

In all these contexts the general pattern that emerges is one that centers on deference, in thinking first of the other, in suppressing one's inclination to satiate oneself before the other has had a chance to begin, in humility. One yields to the other before satisfying one's own urges. At the macro level of China's great tradition, one finds such behavior characteristic of the *chün-tzu*, the individual skilled in the *li* (etiquette, rites, and ceremonies). He is one also skilled in the art of *jang*—of yielding, of accomplishing without activity, of boundless generosity, of cleaving to the *li*. There is even something of a Taoist resonance in all this, getting at things indirectly, without obvious instrumental effort.

Generally, it can be stated that the degree to which a Chinese practices the rules of etiquette marks his class position with respect to his fellow Chinese; although the degree to which the behavior of lower-class people at the table is informed by these rules should not be underestimated. Disregard of the rules on the part of a Chinese is regarded with as much distaste by their fellows as the faux pas normally committed by Westerners, except that the latter can be excused by their hopeless, if expected, ignorance.

It does not take much study for a Westerner to perform well enough at the table to impress most Chinese, since their expectations are exceedingly low. Keeping in mind a few simple things without slavishly parading one's knowledge, one can usually avoid provoking disgust and revulsion, and convince one's fellow diners that one is sensitive to others on their own terms, as well as to the world at large. Among the most basic of cultural patterns, learned early in life, the degree to which one observes these patterns has a lot to do with the way one is perceived as a person in Chinese terms.

Simple knowledge of the structural contexts, behavioral expectations, and symbolic associations of food events can provide access across social boundaries that would otherwise be less easily breached, and make it possible to more easily achieve one's goals. Table manners are part of an inventory of symbolic behaviors that may be manipulated, finessed, and encoded to communicate messages about oneself. For the Chinese, as for almost everyone else, you are *how* you eat.

REFERENCES

Chang, K. C. (ed.), 1977, Introduction. In *Food in Chinese Culture*. New Haven: Yale University Press.

de Garine, I., 1976, Food, Tradition and Prestige. In *Food, Man and Society*. D. Walcher, N. Kretchmer, and H. L. Barnett, eds. New York: Plenum Press.

Goody, J., 1982, *Cooking, Cuisine and Class*. Cambridge: Cambridge University Press.

Hammerton, J. A., 1936, *Manners and Customs of Mankind*, Vol. I. New York: W. M. A. Wise.

Hsü, F. L. K., and V. Y. N. Hsü, 1977, Modern China: North. In *Food in Chinese Culture*. K. C. Chang, ed. New Haven: Yale University Press.

Li Chi, 1971, *Chü Li, Part I*. Taipei: World Publishing.

McLean, N. B., 1941, *The Table Graces: Setting, Service and Manners for the American House without Servants*. Peoria, IL: Manual Arts Press.

10

Culture and the Evolution of Obesity

Peter J. Brown

As a people, Americans rank as one of the fattest societies in history. This epidemiological fact remains despite the tremendous amount of money, effort, and worry that Americans put into diet, exercise, and the quest for the perfect body. For some people, particularly young women, the quest to be thin can become such an obsession that they develop life-threatening eating disorders, like anorexia nervosa. But in other cultures, young women may go to great lengths to try to gain weight to look attractive. There are no universal standards of physical beauty; in fact, there is considerable cross-cultural variation. Culture defines normality.

How do conditions like obesity come to be expressed? Biologists usually say that it is a combination of genes and environment. There is good evidence that genes predispose people toward conditions, but there is seldom evidence that the chain of causation is entirely genetic. A complete explanation must be both biological and cultural. In other words, if a condition like obesity is caused by an interaction of genetic and cultural/behavioral predispositions, then both the genes and culture must be the product of evolutionary processes.

In this selection, Peter Brown provides a cross-cultural and evolutionary analysis of how both biological and cultural factors in obesity evolved. This analysis explains the sociological distribution of obesity today. It also emphasizes that peripheral body fat (characteristic of women) is a small health hazard compared to abdominal fat (characteristic of men).

Dietary patterns are obviously shaped by culture. But human tendencies to value meat, fatty foods, and sweets must be understood in the context of our evolutionary past.

As you read this selection, ask yourself the following questions:

- Have you ever noticed that there are gender differences in the locality of fat storage in the body? Why would this be the case?

- Why are fat people ridiculed and discriminated against in the United States? Are these social reactions worse for men or for women?

- What does the author mean when he says that in a rich society, slenderness can be an individual symbol of conspicuous consumption?

- Given the difference in health risk between peripheral body fat and central body fat, why might weight not be the best way to measure one's risk?

- Why do humans like foods that are "bad" for them?

The following terms discussed in this selection are included in the Glossary at the back of the book:

adipose tissue	*gender dimorphism*
cultural ideals	*ideal body images*
culture	*obesity*
epidemiology	*sexual dimorphism*
food scarcity	

T he etiology or cause of obesity can be understood in the context of human cultural and genetic evolution. The cause of human obesity and overweight involves the interaction of genetic traits with culturally patterned behaviors and beliefs. Both these genes and culture traits, remarkably common in human societies, are evolutionary products of similar processes of selection

Reproduced with permission of Peter Brown.

related to past food scarcities. This idea is not new: The notion of "thrifty phenotypes rendered detrimental by progress" was introduced more than a quarter-century ago. In recent years, the evidence for the existence of genes that enable individuals to use food energy efficiently and store energy reserves in the form of fat has been increasingly impressive; those individuals with "fat phenotypes" are likely to develop adult obesity (Stunkard et al. 1986, 1990).

It is important to recognize that these "thrifty" genes are, at least in the human context, necessary but not sufficient factors in the causation of obesity. In actuality, the new discoveries in the genetics of obesity highlight our ignorance about the role of nongenetic or cultural factors, which are usually subsumed in the term *environment* in the medical literature. The purpose of this paper is to examine why and how cultures have evolved behaviors and beliefs that appear to predispose individuals to develop obesity. I believe that an anthropological model of culture has significant advantages over the commonly used undifferentiated concept of "environment" for generating hypotheses about behavioral causes of obesity. This cultural approach is particularly useful for improving our understanding of the social epidemiological distribution of obesity.

It is valuable to raise an obvious question at the outset: Why do people find it very difficult to reduce their intake of dietary fat and sugar even when the medical benefits of this behavioral change are well known to them? The answer is not obvious, since neither the physiological nor the cultural attraction of these foods is well understood. The proximate mechanisms for this attraction are linked to brain physiology and biochemistry (Wurtman and Wurtman 1987). The ultimate answers are linked to our evolutionary heritage. Human predispositions to obesity are found in both genetic and cultural traits that may have been adaptive in the context of past food scarcities but are maladaptive today in the context of affluence and constant food surpluses.

THE PROBLEMS OF OBESITY AND OVERWEIGHT

Throughout most of human history, obesity was neither a common health problem nor even a realistic possibility for most people. Today, particularly in affluent societies like the United States, obesity is very common, affecting about 12 percent of adult men and women; overweight is even more common, affecting an additional 20 to 50 percent of adult Americans depending on the definitions used (Bray 1987). Not only are overweight and obesity relatively common conditions in our society, they are also extremely complex and intractable. Obesity is a serious public health problem because of its causal connection to major causes of morbidity and mortality from chronic diseases, including cardiovascular disease, type 2 diabetes mellitus (NIDDM), and hypertension. On the individual level, obesity and overweight bring with them an enormous amount of personal psychological pain. The fact that the obese are subjected to significant social and economic discrimination is well documented.

Fat is extraordinarily difficult to shed because the body guards its fat stores. The evidence concerning the effectiveness over a 5-year period of diet therapies indicates that nearly all of the weight that is lost through diets is eventually regained. The remarkable failure of diet therapies has made some researchers rethink their commonsensical theory of obesity as being caused by overeating; the clinical evidence of the past 40 years simply does not support this simplistic notion.

Even in the absence of scientific data about the effectiveness of diet therapy, the diet and weight-loss industry in the United States is remarkably successful in its ability to capture the hope and money of people who perceive themselves to be overweight. This industry thrives because of a complex of cultural beliefs about the ideal body and sexual attractiveness rather than medical advice and the prevention of chronic diseases per se. The American cultural concern about weight loss and the positive valuation of slenderness for women of the middle and upper classes are difficult to overemphasize. Chernin (1981) has referred to this cultural theme as an "obsession" and the "tyranny of slenderness." In this light, it is impossible to claim that obesity is purely a medical issue.

OBESITY AND HUNGER

It is important to remember that for most citizens of the world today, as it has been in the past, the possibility of obesity is remote whereas the possibility of hunger is close to home. There is a palpable irony in the fact of an epidemic of obesity in a world characterized by hunger. For example, in the United States an estimated 20 million people are hungry because they are on a "serious diet"; generally these people are of the middle and upper classes, and most are women. At the same time in the same rich nation, another estimated 20 million Americans are hungry and poorly nourished largely because they lack sufficient money; generally these people are elderly, homeless, or rural inhabitants. This sad symmetry in the estimates of voluntary and involuntary hunger in the United States is a valuable starting point for a discussion of the etiology of obesity. From an evolutionary standpoint, past food shortages have acted as powerful agents of natural selection, shaping both human genetics and behavior.

A theory of the etiology of obesity must not only account for the influences of genes and learned behaviors but also explain its social distribution. Before the problem of causation is addressed, it is worthwhile to examine the nature of human obesity.

CHANGING DEFINITIONS OF OBESITY

The most basic scientific issues regarding obesity are, in fact, controversial. The definitions of obesity and overweight have been the subject of substantial medical debate, in part because they must be based on inferred definitions of normality or "ideal" body proportions. Although obesity refers to excessive adiposity (fat deposits), the most common measurement is not of fat tissue at all but an indirect inference based on measures of stature and total body weight (Bray 1987).

The social history of height and weight standards in the United States is interesting. Until recently, the task of defining both obesity and ideal weights has been the domain of the life-insurance industry. The most well-known table of desirable weights was developed by the Metropolitan Life Insurance Company using correlation statistics between height/weight and mortality among insurance applicants. Ideal weights were based on data from 25-year-old insurance applicants, despite the nonrepresentative nature of the "sample" pool and the fact that in most human populations, individuals increase in weight until around age 50. Obesity was defined as 120 percent of the Ideal Body Weight (IBW), and overweight was defined as 110 percent IBW. Individual life-insurance applicants outside the recommended weight range were required to pay a surcharge on insurance premiums. In 1959, the concept of "frame size" was introduced, although the resulting categories were never given operational definitions using anthropometric measures.

Definitions of obesity have changed throughout history. From 1943 to 1980, definitions of "ideal weights" for women of a particular height were consistently lowered, while those for men remained approximately the same. In 1983, a major debate on the definition of obesity began when Metropolitan Life revised its tables upward, based on new actuarial studies of mortality. Many organizations and experts in the diet industry, including experts in medical fields, rejected these new standards.

In the current medical literature, weight and height tables have been replaced by the Body Mass Index (BMI), defined as body weight (in kilograms) divided by the square of body height (in meters). BMI (W/H^2) is strongly correlated with total body fat, and a value greater than 30 is generally considered obese. Current recommendations include slight increases in BMI with age (Bray 1987). Nevertheless, there continues to be little agreement on precise definitions of either overweight or obesity.

An important added dimension to the questions of definition of obesity involves the distribution of fat around the body trunk or on the limbs. Central or trunk body fat distribution is closely correlated with serious chronic diseases, such as cardiovascular disease, whereas peripheral body fat in the hips and limbs does not carry similar medical risks. Because of this clinically important distinction, measures of fat distribution like waist to hips ratio (WHR), wherein lower WHR values indicate lower risk of chronic disease consequences, will be a valuable addition to future definitions of obesity.

FOUR FACTS ABOUT THE SOCIAL DISTRIBUTION OF OBESITY

Humans are among the fattest of all mammals, and the primary function of our fat is to serve as an energy reserve. The nonrandom social distribution of adiposity within and between human populations may provide a key to understanding obesity. Four facts about this social distribution are particularly cogent for an evolutionary reconstruction: (1) the gender difference in the total percent and site distribution of body fat, as well as the prevalence of obesity; (2) the concentration of obesity in certain ethnic groups; (3) the increase in obesity associated with economic modernization; and (4) the powerful and complex relationship between social class and obesity. Any useful theory concerning the etiology of obesity must account for these social epidemiological patterns.

Sexual Dimorphism

Humans show only mild sexual dimorphism in variables like stature. Males are only 5 to 9 percent taller than females. The sample of adults from Tecumseh, Michigan, seen in Figure 1 are typical. Men are larger than women in height and total body mass, but women have more subcutaneous fat as measured by skinfold thicknesses in 16 of 17 sites (the exception is the suprailiac region—so-called "love handles"). The greatest degree of sexual dimorphism is found in the site of distribution of fat tissue; women have much more peripheral fat in the legs and hips (Kissebah et al. 1989). This difference is epidemiologically important because the greater proportion of peripheral fat in females may be associated with reduced morbidity compared to males with identical BMI values.

Sex differences are also seen in the prevalence of obesity. Despite methodological differences in the categorization of obesity, data from the 14 population surveys shown in Figure 2 indicate that in all of the studies, females have a higher prevalence of obesity than males. A greater risk of obesity for females appears to be a basic fact of human biology.

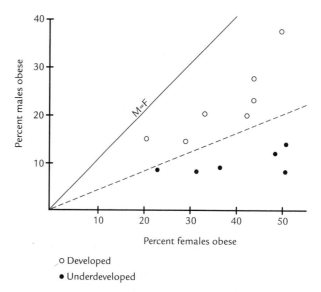

FIGURE 2   Gender differences in prevalences of obesity in 14 populations by general industrial development. Operational definitions of obesity differ between studies. See Brown and Konner (1987) for references. The unbroken line demarcates equal male-female obesity prevalences. The broken line indicates an apparent distinction in gender proportions of obesity in developed and underdeveloped countries. (From Brown, P. J., and M. Konner, An Anthropological Perspective on Obesity. In *Human Obesity*, R. J. Wurtman and J. J. Wurtman, eds. *Annals of New York Academy of Sciences* 499:29–46. Copyright © 1987. Reprinted with permission.)

FIGURE 1   Sexual dimorphism in stature, body mass, and fat measures among white Americans aged 20 to 70 in Techumseh, Michigan. Sexual dimorphism is calculated by comparing male and female means; positive figures refer to greater male measures. Skinfold thicknesses are means of four sites on the trunk or five sites on the arms and legs; the mean dimorphism for all 17 fat measures is –19 percent. (From Brown, P. J., and M. Konner, An Anthropological Perspective on Obesity. In *Human Obesity*, R. J. Wurtman and J. J. Wurtman, eds. *Annals of New York Academy of Sciences* 499:29–46. Copyright © 1987. Reprinted with permission.)

Economic Modernization

The social distribution of obesity varies among societies, depending on their degree of economic modernization. Studies of traditional hunting and gathering populations report *no obesity*. In contrast, numerous studies of traditional societies undergoing the process of economic modernization demonstrate rapid increases in the prevalence of obesity. Trowell and Burkitt's (1981) 15 case studies of epidemiological change in modernizing societies conclude that obesity is the first of the "diseases of civilization" to appear. The rapidity with which obesity becomes a common health problem in the context of modernization underscores the critical role of cultural behaviors in the causation of obesity, since there has been insufficient time for changes in gene frequencies.

Figure 2 also suggests that variations in the male-female ratio of obesity prevalence are related to economic modernization. In less industrially developed societies female obesity is much more common than male obesity, but in more affluent societies the ratio is nearly equivalent. Recent World Health Organization data on global obesity also support this observation (Gurney and Gorstein 1988).

Cultural changes with modernization include the seemingly invariable pattern of diet in industrial countries—decreased fiber intake and increased consumption of fat and sugar. Modernization is also associated with decreased energy expenditures related to work, recreation, or daily activities. From the perspective of the populations undergoing economic modernization, increasing average weight might be seen as a good thing rather than a health problem.

Ethnicity

The idea that particular populations have high rates of a genotype that predisposes individuals to obesity and related diseases is not new but is now supported by a convincing body of adoption and twin data (Stunkard et al. 1986, 1990) and by studies of particular obesity-prone populations like the Pima Indians (Ravussin et al. 1988). In the United States, ethnic groups with elevated rates of obesity include African Americans (particularly in the rural South), Mexican Americans, Puerto Ricans, Gypsies, and Pacific Islanders (Centers for Disease Control 1989).

The fact that certain ethnic groups have high rates of obesity is not easy to interpret because of the entanglement of the effects of genetic heredity, social class, and cultural beliefs. The association of obesity with ethnicity is not evidence for the exclusive role of genetic transmission, since social factors like endogamy (marriage within the group) or group isolation are critical for defining the population structure—that is, the social system through which genes are passed from generation to generation.

Social Class

Social class (socioeconomic status) can be a powerful predictor of the prevalence of obesity in both modernizing and affluent societies, although the direction of the association varies with the type of society. In developing countries, there is a strong and consistent *positive association* between social class and obesity for men, women, and children; correspondingly, there is an inverse correlation between social class and protein-calorie malnutrition. In heterogeneous and affluent societies, like the United States, there is a strong *inverse correlation* of social class and obesity for females. The association between obesity and social class among women in affluent societies is not constant through the life cycle. Economically advantaged girls are initially fatter than their low-income counterparts, but the pattern is reversed beginning at puberty. For females, social class remains the strongest social epidemiological predictor of obesity.

OBESITY AND HUMAN EVOLUTION

Human biology and behavior can be understood in the context of two distinct processes of evolution. Biological evolution involves changes through time in the frequency of particular genes, primarily because of the action of natural selection on individuals. Cultural evolution involves historical changes in the configurations of cultural systems, that is, the learned patterns of behavior and belief characteristics of social groups. Cultural evolution includes the striking and rapid transformation of human lifestyles from small food-foraging societies to large and economically complex states in a span of less than 5,000 years.

The Context of Food Scarcities

Food shortages have been very common in human prehistory and history; in fact, they could be considered a virtually inevitable fact of life for most people. As such, they have been a powerful evolutionary force.

A cross-cultural ethnographic survey of 118 nonindustrial societies (with hunting and gathering, pastoral, horticultural, and agricultural economies) found some form of food shortages for *all* of the societies in the sample (Whiting 1958). Shortages occur annually or even more frequently in roughly half of the societies, and every 2 to 3 years in an additional 24 percent. The shortages are "severe" (i.e., including starvation deaths) in 29 percent of the societies sampled. Seasonal availability of food results in a seasonal cycle of weight loss and weight gain in both hunting and gathering and agricultural societies, although the fluctuation is substantially greater among agriculturalists.

Scarcity and Cultural Evolution

A hunting and gathering economy was characteristic of all human societies for more than 95 percent of our history, yet it is represented by only a handful of societies today. In general, food foragers enjoy high-quality diets, maintain high levels of physical fitness, suffer the risk of periodic food shortages, and are generally healthier than many contemporary populations that rely on agriculture. Without romanticizing these societies, the evidence is persuasive enough to suggest a "paleolithic prescription" of diet and exercise for the prevention of chronic diseases (Eaton et al. 1988). This recommendation refers to the quality of preindustrial diets and not to their dependability or quantity.

Approximately 12,000 years ago, some human groups shifted from a food-foraging economy to one of food production. This economic transformation allowed the evolution of urban civilizations. Many archaeologists believe that people were "forced" to adopt the new agricultural economy because of ecological pressures from population growth and food scarcities or because of military coercion. The archaeological record clearly shows that agriculture was associated with nutritional stress, poor health, and diminished stature (Cohen and Armelagos 1984). The beginning of agriculture is also linked to the emergence of social stratification, a system of inequality that improved the Darwinian fitness of the ruling class relative to that of the lower classes. Social inequality, particularly differential access to strategic resources, plays a critical role in the distribution of obesity in most societies.

Certain ecological zones appear to be prone to severe food shortages. For example, archaeological analysis of tree rings from the southwestern United States shows that the prehistoric past was characterized by frequent and severe droughts. The impressive agricultural societies of the prehistoric Southwest had expanded during an extended period of uncharacteristically good weather and could not be maintained when the lower and more characteristic rainfall patterns resumed. Ecological conditions leading to severe scarcity may have acted as strong forces of selection for "thrifty" genotypes.

Scarcity and Genetic Evolution

Since food shortages were ubiquitous for humans under natural conditions, selection favored individuals who could effectively store calories in times of surplus. For most societies, these fat stores would be called on at least every 2 or 3 years. Malnutrition increases infectious disease mortality, as well as decreasing birth weights and rates of child growth. The evolutionary scenario is this: Females with greater energy reserves in fat would have a selective advantage over their lean counterparts in terms of withstanding the stress of food shortages, not only for themselves but also for their fetuses or nursing children. Humans have evolved the ability to "save up" food energy for inevitable food shortages through the synthesis and storage of fat.

Selection has favored the production of peripheral body fat in females, whose reproductive fitness is influenced by the nutritional demands of pregnancy and lactation. This peripheral fat is usually mobilized after being primed with estrogen during the late stages of pregnancy and during lactation. In addition, a minimal level of fatness increases female reproductive success because of its association with regular cycling and early menarche (Frisch 1987).

In this evolutionary context the usual range of human metabolic variation must have produced many individuals with a predisposition to become obese; yet they would, in all likelihood, never have had the opportunity to do so. Furthermore, in this context there could be little or no natural selection against this tendency. Selection could not provide for the eventuality of continuous surplus simply because it had never existed before.

CULTURE AND ADAPTATIONS TO FOOD SCARCITY

Food scarcities have shaped not only our genes but also, and perhaps more important, human cultures. Because the concept of culture is rarely considered in medical research on obesity, and because I am suggesting that this concept has advantages over the more common and undifferentiated term *environment*, it is

FIGURE 3 A materialist model of culture.

necessary to review some basic aspects of this anthropological term. *Culture* refers to the learned patterns of behavior and belief characteristic of a social group. As such, culture encompasses *Homo sapiens'* primary mechanism of evolutionary adaptation, which has distinct advantages of greater speed and flexibility than genetic evolution.

Cultural behaviors and beliefs are usually learned in childhood and they are often deeply held and seldom questioned by adults, who pass this "obvious" knowledge and habits to their offspring. In this regard, cultural beliefs and values are largely unconscious factors in the motivation of individual behaviors. Cultural beliefs define "what is normal" and therefore constrain the choices of behaviors available to an individual.

One useful way of thinking about culture in relation to obesity is a cultural materialist model as seen in Figure 3. This model divides culture into three layers. The material foundation of a cultural system is the economic mode of production, which includes the technology and the population size that the productive economy allows and requires. Population size is maintained by the social system, sometimes called the mode of reproduction. Contingent on the first layer is the system of social organization, which includes kinship patterns, marriage and family practices, politics, and status differentiation. Contingent on the social structure is the ideology or belief system, including ideas, beliefs, and values, both secular and sacred. Most anthropologists believe that the ideology is an extremely important part of culture, in part because it rationalizes and reinforces the economy and social structure. Ideology enables people to make sense of their world and to share their common world view through symbols. As such, ideology includes sacred concepts from religion as well as secular concepts (with symbolic components) like health or sexual attractiveness.

A culture is an integrated system: A change in one part causes changes in the other layers. The materialist model indicates that the direction of causal change is from the bottom layer upward (the solid arrows in Figure 3). An economic change, like the invention of agriculture or the Industrial Revolution, has drastic implications for population size, social organization, and associated beliefs. On the other hand, most people within a society tend to explain things from the top down. Of course, people can hold contradictory beliefs and values that are not necessarily linked to their actual behavior.

CULTURAL PREDISPOSITIONS TO OBESITY

Obesity is related to culture in all three levels of the materialist model.

Productive Economy and Food Scarcity

Humans have evolved a wide variety of cultural mechanisms to avoid or minimize the effects of food scarcities. The most important adaptation to scarcity is the evolution of systems of food production and storage. As noted previously, the primary weakness of preindustrial systems of food production is a vulnerability to food shortages. The universality of food shortages discussed above is largely because of the technological limitations in food production and storage.

On the other hand, the energy-intensive (and energy-inefficient) system of agriculture in industrialized societies produces large surpluses of food. These agricultural surpluses are seldom used to eliminate hunger; rather they are used to transform and process foods in particular ways—often to add calories, fat, or salt. For example, we feed "extra" grain to beef cattle to increase the proportion of fat in their meat; consumers say that this overfeeding makes the meat "juicy." Similarly, potatoes are transformed into french fries and potato chips. From a nutritional standpoint the original vegetable is actually reduced to a vehicle for fat and salt. Endemic hunger exists even in the most affluent societies, where it is caused not by poor production but by inequitable distribution.

Technological changes associated with cultural evolution almost exclusively reduce the energy requirements of human labor. In general, cultural evolution has meant the harnessing of greater amounts of energy through technology (one aspect of the mode of production). To prevent obesity, people in developed societies must burn energy through daily workouts rather than daily work.

Reproduction and Energy Expenditure

The concept of the *mode of reproduction* is also related to predispositions to obesity. Pregnancy and lactation represent serious and continuing energy demands on women in societies that have not undergone the demographic transition. Industrial and nonindustrial societies differ in terms of the historical changes from high to low fertility and the reduction of mortality attributable to infectious disease. Higher numbers of pregnancies and longer periods of breast-feeding place high energy demands on women, especially if they cannot supplement their diet during these critical periods. As a result, women suffer greater risk of protein-energy malnutrition. Conversely, with fewer pregnancies and the reduction of breast-feeding, women in industrial societies have less opportunity to mobilize peripheral fat stores and suffer greater risk of obesity. In contemporary societies like the United States, mothers in lower social classes tend to have more children and to feed their infants with bottled formula rather than breast milk. Use of infant formulas allows women to retain their fat stores. These different social patterns in reproduction may play a role in the inverse association of obesity and social class for females.

Social Structure and Obesity

Characteristics of social organization may function as predispositions to obesity. In highly stratified and culturally heterogeneous societies, the distribution of obesity is associated with ethnicity and social class. Marriage patterns typically illustrate ethnic or social class endogamy, that is, marriage within the group. In the United States, members of ethnic minorities choose marriage partners from the same group at extremely high rates. This social practice may concentrate the genetic predispositions to conditions like obesity in particular subpopulations. Similarly, data suggest a pattern of "assortative mating" by social class as well as body type (particularly stature), which may be related to the genetic etiology of obesity. Genetic admixture with Native American groups of the Southwest has been suggested as a cause of elevated rates of type 2 diabetes mellitus and obesity among Mexican Americans (Gardner et al. 1984).

The pervasive and complex relationship between obesity and social class, or socioeconomic status (SES), is important. SES is related to particular behavior patterns that cause obesity. This statement underemphasizes the fact that these learned behaviors are *characteristic* of particular social groups or classes. In other words, the cultural patterns of social class groups are primary, not the individual behaviors themselves.

From a cross-cultural perspective, the general association between obesity and social position is positive: The groups with greater access to economic resources have higher rates of obesity. This pattern is logical and expected because socially dominant groups with better access to strategic resources should have better nutrition, better health, and consequently greater reproductive success.

As discussed earlier, the remarkable and important exception is women in industrial societies, who exhibit a strong *inverse* correlation between obesity and social class. The challenge for researchers is to explain why and how upper-class women in industrial societies remain thin. For many women the ideal of thinness requires considerable effort, restrained eating, and often resources invested in exercise. The social origins of the ideal of thinness in American women are associated with historical changes in women's economic roles, marriage patterns, and family size.

Low-income people in industrial societies might be considered well off by worldwide standards, and this access to resources is reflected in obesity prevalences. Yet in the context of perceived relative deprivation and economic stability, many people in societies like the United States live in stressful conditions—just one paycheck away from hunger. In terms of life priorities, economic security may be a higher and more immediate objective than more elusive goals like an "ideal body" or even long-term health. Amid the daily stresses of poverty, food may be the most common avenue of pleasure and psychological relief. Ethnographic studies of low-income urban black communities in the United States show a social emphasis on food sharing as a tool for marking family ties and demonstrating community cohesiveness.

Cultural Beliefs as Predispositions to Obesity

The third and possibly most important level of the model of culture shown in Figure 3 encompasses cultural symbols, beliefs, and values. Aspects of ideology relevant to the etiology of obesity include the symbolic meaning of fatness, ideal body types, and perceived risks of food shortages.

Fatness is symbolically linked to psychological dimensions, such as self-worth and sexuality, in many societies of the world, but the nature of that symbolic association is not constant. In mainstream U.S. culture, obesity is socially stigmatized, but for most cultures of the world, fatness is viewed as a welcome sign of health and prosperity. Given the rarity of obesity in preindustrial societies, it is not surprising that they lack ethnomedical terms for obesity. Much more attention is placed on "thinness" as a symptom of starvation, like among the !Kung San (Lee 1979), or in contemporary Africa as a sign of AIDS (sometimes called "the slim disease"). In the context of the AIDS epidemic, plumpness is indeed a marker of health.

Perhaps it is large body size, rather than obesity per se, that is admired as a symbol of health, prestige, prosperity, or maternity in agricultural societies. The Tiv of Nigeria, for example, distinguish between a very positive category, "too big" *(kehe),* and an unpleasant condition "to grow fat" *(ahon)* (Bohannan and Bohannan 1969). The first is a compliment because it is a sign of prosperity; the second is a rare and undesirable condition.

For women, fatness may also be a symbol of maternity and nurturance. In traditional societies in which women attain status only through motherhood, this symbolic association increases the cultural acceptability of fatness. A fat woman, symbolically, is well taken care of, and in turn she takes good care of her children. Fellahin Arabs in Egypt describe the proper woman as fat because she has more room to bear the child, lactates abundantly, and gives warmth to her children. The cultural ideal of thinness in industrial societies, in contrast, is found where motherhood is not the sole or even primary means of status attainment for woman. The idea that fat babies and children are healthy children is very widespread. Food can be treated as a symbol of love and nurturance; in some cultures it may be impolite for a guest to refuse food that has been offered, but it is taboo to refuse food from one's mother.

In the industrialized United States, ethnic variation in culturally accepted definitions of obesity is significant. Some Mexican Americans have coined a new term, *gordura mala* (bad fatness), because the original term *gordura* continues to have positive cultural connotations (Ritenbaugh 1982). For this group cultural identity has a stronger and independent effect on risk of obesity than socioeconomic status. An ethnographic study of the cultural meanings of weight in a Puerto Rican community in Philadelphia (Massara 1989) documents the positive associations and lack of social stigma of obesity. Additional quantitative evidence suggests significant differences in ideal body preferences between this ethnic community and mainstream American culture. Positive evaluations of fatness may also occur among lower-class African Americans and Mexican Americans. These ethnic groups are heterogeneous, however, and upwardly mobile ethnics tend to resemble mainstream American culture in their attitudes about obesity and ideal body shape.

In a low-income housing project in Atlanta, Georgia, a sociological interviewer was asked by a group of obese black women, "Don't you know how hard it is to keep this weight *on?*" Their views of the advantages of a large body included being given respect and reduced chances of being bothered by young "toughs" in the neighborhood. For these women, fatness was part of their positive self-identity, and if a friend lost weight she was thought to look sickly. Among lower-income groups, the perceived risk of a food shortage—not for the society as a whole but for the immediate family— may be very important, especially if lack of food was personally experienced in the past. The perception of the risk of future "bad times" and insufficient food is the reality upon which people act.

FATNESS AND CROSS-CULTURAL STANDARDS OF BEAUTY IN WOMEN

Culturally defined standards of beauty vary between societies. In a classic example, Malcom (1925) describes the custom of "fattening huts" for elite Efik pubescent girls in traditional Nigeria. A girl spent up to 2 years in seclusion and at the end of this rite of passage possessed symbols of womanhood and marriageability—a three-tiered hairstyle, clitoridectomy, and fatness. Fatness was a primary criterion of beauty as it was defined by the elites, who alone had the economic resources to participate in this custom. Similarly, fatter brides demand significantly higher bridewealth payments among the Kipsigis of Kenya (Borgerhoff Mulder 1988).

Among the Havasupai of the American Southwest, if a girl is thin at puberty, a fat woman "stands" (places her foot) on the girl's back so she will become attractively plump. In this society, fat legs and, to a lesser extent, arms are considered essential to beauty. The Tarahumara of northern Mexico consider fat legs a fundamental aspect of the ideal feminine body; an attractive woman is called a "beautiful thigh." Among the Amhara of Ethiopia in northern East Africa, thin hips are called "dog hips" in a typical insult (Messing 1957).

It is difficult to know how widespread among the world's cultures is the association of plumpness and beauty. A preliminary indication can be found through a cross-cultural survey based on data from the Human Relations Area Files (a cross-indexed compilation of ethnographic information on more than 300 of the most thoroughly studied societies). The results of this survey are summarized in Table 1. Although conclusions made from these data are weak because of the small number and possibly nonrepresentative nature of the cases, as well as the fact that most ethnographies are difficult to code on this variable, some preliminary generalizations are possible. Cultural standards of beauty do not refer to physical extremes. No society on record has an ideal of extreme obesity. On the other hand, the desirability of "plumpness" or being "filled out" is found in 81 percent of the societies for which this variable can be coded. This standard, which probably includes the clinical categories of overweight and mild obesity, apparently refers to the desirability of fat deposits, particularly on the hips and legs.

Although cross-cultural variation is evident in standards of beauty, this variation falls within a certain range. American ideals of thinness occur in a setting in

TABLE 1   Cross-Cultural Standards of Female Beauty

	Number of Societies	Percent of Societies
Overall body		
Extreme obesity	0	0
Plump/moderately fat	31	81
Thin/abhorrence of fat	7	19
Breasts		
Large or long	9	50
Small/abhorrence of large	9	50
Hips and Legs		
Large or fat	9	90
Slender	1	10
Stature		
Tall	3	30
Moderate	6	60
Small	1	10

Source: Brown and Konner 1987.

which it is easy to become fat, and preference for plumpness occurs in settings in which it is easy to remain lean. In context, both standards require the investment of individual effort and economic resources; furthermore, each in its context involves a display of wealth. Cultural beliefs about attractive body shape in mainstream American culture place pressure on females to lose weight and are involved in the etiology of anorexia and bulimia.

IDEAL BODY-TYPE, SIZE, AND SYMBOLIC POWER IN MEN

The ethnographic record concerning body preferences for males is extremely weak, yet preliminary research suggests a universal preference for a muscular physique and for tall or moderately tall stature. In general, members of all human societies appear to admire large body size as an attribute of attractiveness in men, because it symbolizes health, economic success, political power, and social status. "Big men," political leaders in tribal New Guinea, are described by their constituents in terms of their size and physical well-being: He is a man "whose skin swells with 'grease' [fat] underneath" (Strahern 1971). The spiritual power (*mana*) and noble breeding of a Polynesian chief is expected to be seen in his large size. In American society vestiges of a similar idea remain; for example, a "fat cat" is a wealthy and powerful man who can "throw his weight around." The political metaphor of weight and power in American society has been explored by social historians. Most male college students in the U.S., in contrast with women, want to gain weight because it is equivalent to gaining muscle mass and physical power in a process called "bulking up."

CONCLUSIONS

Two sets of conclusions can be drawn from this discussion of culture and its relationship to obesity—one practical and one theoretical. First, recognition of cultural variation in beliefs and behaviors related to obesity needs to be incorporated into health programs aimed at reducing the prevalence of obesity. The second conclusion regards the need for more research on the role of culture, as it interacts with genes, on the etiology of obesity.

The Importance of Culture in Health Interventions

Existing cultural beliefs must be taken into account in the design and implementation of health promotion projects. In an obesity prevention campaign in a Zulu community outside of Durban, one health education poster depicted an obese woman and an overloaded truck with a flat tire, with a caption "Both carry too much weight." Another poster showed a slender woman easily sweeping under a table next to an obese woman who was using the table for support; it had the caption "Who do you prefer to look like?" The intended message of these posters was misinterpreted by the community because of a cultural connection between obesity and social status. The woman in the first poster was perceived to be rich and happy, since she was not only fat but had a truck overflowing with her possessions. The second poster was perceived as a scene of an affluent mistress directing her underfed servant.

Health interventions must be culturally acceptable, and we cannot assume that people place the highest priority on their health. The idea of reducing *risk factors* for chronic diseases that may develop later may not be an effective strategy for populations who do not feel empowered or who live in a fundamentally risky world.

Implications for the Etiology of Obesity

The frequency of past food shortages, the social distribution of obesity, and the cultural meanings of fatness, when taken together, suggest a biocultural hypothesis of the evolution of obesity. Both genetic and cultural predispositions to obesity may be products of the same evolutionary pressures, involving two related processes: first, genetic traits that cause fatness were selected because they improved chances of survival in the face of food scarcities, particularly for pregnant and nursing women; second, in the context of unequal access to food, fatness may have been socially selected because it is a cultural symbol of social prestige and an index of general health. Under Western conditions of abundance, our biological tendency to regulate body weight at levels above our ideal cannot be easily controlled even with a reversal of the widespread cultural ideal of plumpness.

This evolutionary model is obviously congruent with the current etiological theory about obesity, which combines genetic predispositions with "environmental" causes. Recent research both in epidemiology and human laboratory research demonstrates without a doubt the central role of genetic heredity in the etiology of obesity. Similar genetic evidence exists for variables like the distribution of fat on the body and basal metabolic rates. To an anthropologist, these important studies are welcome and expected.

The recent advances in understanding the genetic bases of obesity remind us, however, of our ignorance about the precise role of the "environment." One problem is that "environment" has been poorly defined and treated as if it were idiosyncratic for every individual or family. Another problem is that "environment" is essentially treated as a residual category—one that cannot be explained by genetic heredity. This paper has attempted to show how the anthropological concept of culture may be useful in conceptualization of the different components of the "environment" and the generation of hypotheses for future research in behavioral medicine.

The most convincing demonstrations of a strong genetic component for obesity have been in populations with relatively high levels of cultural homogeneity. In social contexts like Denmark, Iowa, or among Pima Indians, the influence of culture—including learned behaviors and beliefs—is minimized by the sample selected for study in order to emphasize the importance of genotypical variation. Essentially, cultural variation has been treated as if it were "noise." An essential goal in future research must be the identification of specific cultural factors—whether economic, social, or ideological—that predispose people to obesity.

From the standpoint of the prevention of obesity, it is critical to stress that genetic predisposition is not destiny. Genetic predispositions to obesity have apparently been maintained in populations throughout most of our species' history, yet it has rarely been expressed phenotypically. Culture is adaptive because it can be changed. Habitual patterns of behavior—of an individual or an entire society—can be changed to reduce morbidity and mortality linked to obesity and overweight. These changes must include social and political efforts to reduce the risk of hunger and food scarcity, even in affluent societies.

REFERENCES

Bohannan, P., and L. Bohannan. 1969. *A Source Notebook on Tiv Religion*. New Haven, CT: Human Relations Area Files.

Borgerhoff Mulder, M. 1988. Kipsigis Bridewealth Payments. In *Human Reproductive Behavior*, L. Betzig, M. Borgerhoff Mulder, and P. Turke, eds. Pp. 65–82. Cambridge: Cambridge University Press.

Bray, G. A. 1987. Overweight Is Risking Fate: Definition, Classification, Prevalence and Risks. In *Human Obesity*, R. J. Wurtman and J. J. Wurtman, eds. *Annals of the New York Academy of Sciences* 499:14–28.

Brown, P. J., and M. Konner. 1987. An Anthropological Perspective on Obesity. In *Human Obesity*, R. J. Wurtman and J. J. Wurtman, eds. *Annals of the New York Academy of Sciences* 499:29–46.

Centers for Disease Control. 1989. Prevalence of Overweight—Behavioral Risk Factor Surveillance System, 1987. *Morbidity and Mortality Weekly Report* 38:421–423.

Chernin, K. 1981. *The Obsession: Reflections on the Tyranny of Slenderness*. New York: Harper & Row.

Cohen, M. N., and G. J. Armelagos, eds. 1984. *Paleopathology at the Origins of Agriculture*. New York: Academic Press.

Eaton, S. B., M. Shostak, and M. Konner. 1988. *The Paleolithic Prescription*. New York: Harper & Row.

Frisch, R. E. 1987. Body Fat, Menarche, Fitness and Fertility. *Human Reproduction* 2:521–533.

Gardner, L. I., M. P. Stern, S. M. Haffner, S. P. Gaskill, H. Hazuda, and J. H. Relethford. 1984. Prevalence of Diabetes in Mexican Americans. *Diabetes* 33:86–92.

Gurney, M., and J. Gorstein. 1988. The Global Prevalence of Obesity—An Initial Overview of Available Data. *World Health Statistics Quarterly* 41:251–254.

Kissebah, A. H., D. S. Freedman, and A. N. Peiris. 1989. Health Risks of Obesity. *Medical Clinics of North America* 73:11–138.

Lee, R. B. 1979. *The !Kung Sun: Men, Women, and Work in a Foraging Society*. Cambridge, MA: Harvard University Press.

Malcom, L. W. G. 1925. Note on the Seclusion of Girls Among the Efik at Old Calabar. *Man* 25:113–114.

Massara, E. B. 1989. *Que Gordita! A Study of Weight Among Women in a Puerto Rican Community*. New York: AMS Press.

Messing, S. D. 1957. *The Highland Plateau Amhara of Ethiopia*. Ph.D. dissertation, Department of Anthropology, University of Pennsylvania, Philadelphia.

Ravussin, E., S. Lillioja, and W. C. Knowler, et al. 1988. Reduced Rate of Energy Expenditure as a Risk Factor for Body-Weight Gain. *New England Journal of Medicine* 318:467–472.

Ritenbaugh, C. 1982. Obesity as a Culture-Bound Syndrome. *Culture, Medicine and Psychiatry* 6:347–361.

Strahern, A. 1971. *The Rope of Moka*. New York: Cambridge University Press.

Stunkard, A. J., T. I. A. Sorenson, C. Hanis, T. W. Teasdale, R. Chakaborty, W. J. Schull, and F. Schulsinger. 1986. An Adoption Study of Obesity. *New England Journal of Medicine* 314:193–198.

Stunkard, A. J., J. R. Harris, N. L. Pedersen, and G. McClearn. 1990. The Body-Mass Index of Twins Who Have Been Reared Apart. *New England Journal of Medicine* 322:1483–1487.

Trowell, H. C., and D. P. Burkitt. 1981. *Western Diseases: Their Emergence and Prevention*. Cambridge, MA: Harvard University Press.

Whiting, M. G. 1958. *A Cross-Cultural Nutrition Survey*. Doctoral Dissertation, Harvard School of Public Health, Cambridge.

Wurtman, R. J., and J. J. Wurtman, eds. 1987. *Human Obesity*. Annals of the New York Academy of Sciences 499.

11

The Worst Mistake in the History of the Human Race

Jared Diamond

What we eat and how we eat are important both nutritionally and culturally. This selection suggests that how we get what we eat—through gathering and hunting versus agriculture, for example—has dramatic consequences. This seems pretty obvious. We all imagine what a struggle it must have been before the development of agriculture. We think of our ancestors spending their days searching for roots and berries to eat, or out at the crack of dawn, hunting wild animals. In fact, this was not quite the case. Nevertheless, isn't it really better simply to go to the refrigerator, open the door, and reach for a container of milk to pour into a bowl of flaked grain for your regular morning meal? What could be simpler and more nutritious?

There are many things that we seldom question; the truth seems so evident and the answers obvious. One such sacred cow is the tremendous prosperity brought about by the agricultural revolution. This selection is a thought-provoking introduction to the connection between culture and agriculture. The transition from food foraging to farming (what archaeologists call the Neolithic revolution) may have been the worst mistake in human history or its most important event. You be the judge. But for better or worse, this cultural evolution has occurred, and the world will never be the same again.

As you read this selection, ask yourself the following questions:

- What is the fundamental difference between the progressivist view and the revisionist interpretation?
- How did the development of agriculture affect people's health?
- What three reasons explain the changes brought about by the development of agriculture?
- How did the development of agriculture affect social equality, including gender equality?

The following terms discussed in this selection are included in the Glossary at the back of the book:

agricultural development
civilization
domestication of plants and animals
hunter-gatherers
Neolithic
paleontology
paleopathology
social stratification

T o science we owe dramatic changes in our smug self-image. Astronomy taught us that our earth isn't the center of the universe but merely one of billions of heavenly bodies. From biology we learned that we weren't specially created by God but evolved along with millions of other species. Now archaeology is demolishing another sacred belief: that human history over the past million years has been a long tale of progress. In particular, recent discoveries suggest that

the adoption of agriculture, supposedly our most decisive step toward a better life, was in many ways a catastrophe from which we have never recovered. With agriculture came the gross social and sexual inequality, the disease and despotism, that curse our existence.

At first, the evidence against this revisionist interpretation will strike twentieth-century Americans as irrefutable. We're better off in almost every respect than the people of the Middle Ages, who in turn had it easier than cavemen, who in turn were better off than apes. Just count our advantages. We enjoy the most abundant and varied foods, the best tools and material goods, some of the longest and healthiest lives, in history. Most of us are safe from starvation and predators. We get our energy from oil and machines, not from our sweat. What neo-Luddite among us would trade his life for that of a medieval peasant, a caveman, or an ape?

For most of our history we supported ourselves by hunting and gathering: we hunted wild animals and foraged for wild plants. It's a life that philosophers have traditionally regarded as nasty, brutish, and short. Since no food is grown and little is stored, there is (in this view) no respite from the struggle that starts anew each day to find wild foods and avoid starving. Our escape from this misery was facilitated only 10,000 years ago, when in different parts of the world people began to domesticate plants and animals. The agricultural revolution gradually spread until today it's nearly universal, and few tribes of hunter-gatherers survive.

From the progressivist perspective on which I was brought up, to ask "Why did almost all our hunter-gatherer ancestors adopt agriculture?" is silly. Of course they adopted it because agriculture is an efficient way to get more food for less work. Planted crops yield far more tons per acre than roots and berries. Just imagine a band of savages, exhausted from searching for nuts or chasing wild animals, suddenly gazing for the first time at a fruit-laden orchard or a pasture full of sheep. How many milliseconds do you think it would take them to appreciate the advantages of agriculture?

The progressivist party line sometimes even goes so far as to credit agriculture with the remarkable flowering of art that has taken place over the past few thousand years. Since crops can be stored, and since it takes less time to pick food from a garden than to find it in the wild, agriculture gave us free time that hunter-gatherers never had. Thus it was agriculture that enabled us to build the Parthenon and compose the B-minor Mass.

While the case for the progressivist view seems overwhelming, it's hard to prove. How do you show that the lives of people 10,000 years ago got better when they abandoned hunting and gathering for farming? Until recently, archaeologists had to resort to indirect tests, whose results (surprisingly) failed to support the progressivist view. Here's one example of an indirect test: Are twentieth-century hunter-gatherers really worse off than farmers? Scattered throughout the world, several dozen groups of so-called primitive people, like the Kalahari Bushmen, continue to support themselves that way. It turns out that these people have plenty of leisure time, sleep a good deal, and work less hard than their farming neighbors. For instance, the average time devoted each week to obtaining food is only 12 to 19 hours for one group of Bushmen, 14 hours or less for the Hadza nomads of Tanzania. One Bushman, when asked why he hadn't emulated neighboring tribes by adopting agriculture, replied, "Why should we, when there are so many mongongo nuts in the world?"

While farmers concentrate on high-carbohydrate crops like rice and potatoes, the mix of wild plants and animals in the diets of surviving hunter-gatherers provides more protein and a better balance of other nutrients. In one study, the Bushmen's average daily food intake (during a month when food was plentiful) was 2,140 calories and 93 grams of protein, considerably greater than the recommended daily allowance for people of their size. It's almost inconceivable that Bushmen, who eat 75 or so wild plants, could die of starvation the way hundreds of thousands of Irish farmers and their families did during the potato famine of the 1840s.

So the lives of at least the surviving hunter-gatherers aren't nasty and brutish, even though farmers have pushed them into some of the world's worst real estate. But modern hunter-gatherer societies that have rubbed shoulders with farming societies for thousands of years don't tell us about conditions before the agricultural revolution. The progressivist view is really making a claim about the distant past: that the lives of primitive people improved when they switched from gathering to farming. Archaeologists can date that switch by distinguishing remains of wild plants and animals from those of domesticated ones in prehistoric garbage dumps.

How can one deduce the health of the prehistoric garbage makers, and thereby directly test the progressivist view? That question has become answerable only in recent years, in part through the newly emerging techniques of paleopathology, the study of signs of disease in the remains of ancient peoples.

In some lucky situations, the paleopathologist has almost as much material to study as a pathologist today. For example, archaeologists in the Chilean deserts found well preserved mummies whose medical conditions at time of death could be determined by autopsy. And feces of long-dead Indians who lived in dry caves in Nevada remain sufficiently well preserved to be examined for hookworm and other parasites.

Usually the only human remains available for study are skeletons, but they permit a surprising number of deductions. To begin with, a skeleton reveals its owner's sex, weight, and approximate age. In the few cases where there are many skeletons, one can construct mortality tables like the ones life insurance companies use to calculate expected life span and risk of death at any given age. Paleopathologists can also calculate growth rates by measuring bones of people of different ages, examining teeth for enamel defects (signs of childhood malnutrition), and recognizing scars left on bones by anemia, tuberculosis, leprosy, and other diseases.

One straightforward example of what paleopathologists have learned from skeletons concerns historical changes in height. Skeletons from Greece and Turkey show that the average height of hunter-gatherers toward the end of the ice ages was a generous 5'9" for men, 5'5" for women. With the adoption of agriculture, height crashed, and by 3000 B.C. had reached a low of only 5'3" for men, 5' for women. By classical times heights were very slowly on the rise again, but modern Greeks and Turks have still not regained the average height of their distant ancestors.

Another example of paleopathology at work is the study of Indian skeletons from burial mounds in the Illinois and Ohio river valleys. At Dickson Mounds, located near the confluence of the Spoon and Illinois Rivers, archaeologists have excavated some 800 skeletons that paint a picture of the health changes that occurred when a hunter-gatherer culture gave way to intensive maize farming around A.D. 1150. Studies by George Armelagos and his colleagues then at the University of Massachusetts show these early farmers paid a price for their new-found livelihood. Compared to the hunter-gatherers who preceded them, the farmers had a nearly 50 percent increase in enamel defects indicative of malnutrition, a fourfold increase in iron-deficiency anemia (evidenced by a bone condition called porotic hyperostosis), a threefold rise in bone lesions reflecting infectious disease in general, and an increase in degenerative conditions of the spine, probably reflecting a lot of hard physical labor. "Life expectancy at birth in the pre-agricultural community was about twenty-six years," says Armelagos, "but in the post-agricultural community it was nineteen years. So these episodes of nutritional stress and infectious disease were seriously affecting their ability to survive."

The evidence suggests that the Indians at Dickson Mounds, like many other primitive peoples, took up farming not by choice but from necessity in order to feed their constantly growing numbers. "I don't think most hunter-gatherers farmed until they had to, and when they switched to farming they traded quality for quantity," says Mark Cohen of the State University of New York at Plattsburgh, co-editor, with Armelagos, of one of the seminal books in the field, *Paleopathology at the Origins of Agriculture.* "When I first started making that argument ten years ago, not many people agreed with me. Now it's become a respectable, albeit controversial, side of the debate."

There are at least three sets of reasons to explain the findings that agriculture was bad for health. First, hunter-gatherers enjoyed a varied diet, while early farmers obtained most of their food from one or a few starchy crops. The farmers gained cheap calories at the cost of poor nutrition. (Today just three high-carbohydrate plants—wheat, rice, and corn—provide the bulk of the calories consumed by the human species, yet each one is deficient in certain vitamins or amino acids essential to life.) Second, because of dependence on a limited number of crops, farmers ran the risk of starvation if one crop failed. Finally, the mere fact that agriculture encouraged people to clump together in crowded societies, many of which then carried on trade with other crowded societies, led to the spread of parasites and infectious disease. (Some archaeologists think it was crowding, rather than agriculture, that promoted disease, but this is a chicken-and-egg argument, because crowding encourages agriculture and vice versa.) Epidemics couldn't take hold when populations were scattered in small bands that constantly shifted camp. Tuberculosis and diarrheal disease had to await the rise of farming, measles and bubonic plague the appearance of large cities.

Besides malnutrition, starvation, and epidemic diseases, farming helped bring another curse upon humanity: deep class divisions. Hunter-gatherers have little or no stored food, and no concentrated food sources, like an orchard or a herd of cows: they live off the wild plants and animals they obtain each day. Therefore, there can be no kings, no class of social parasites who grow fat on food seized from others. Only in farming populations could a healthy, non-producing elite set itself above the disease-ridden masses. Skeletons from Greek tombs at Mycenae *c.* 1500 B.C. suggest that royals enjoyed a better diet than commoners, since the royal skeletons were two or three inches taller and had better teeth (on the average, one instead of six cavities or missing teeth). Among Chilean mummies from *c.* A.D. 1000, the élite were distinguished not only by ornaments and gold hair clips but also by a fourfold lower rate of bone lesions caused by disease.

Similar contrasts in nutrition and health persist on a global scale today. To people in rich countries like the U.S., it sounds ridiculous to extol the virtues of hunting and gathering. But Americans are an élite, dependent on oil and minerals that must often be imported from countries with poorer health and nutrition. If one could choose between being a peasant farmer in Ethiopia or a Bushman gatherer in the Kalahari, which do you think would be the better choice?

Farming may have encouraged inequality between the sexes, as well. Freed from the need to transport their babies during a nomadic existence, and under pressure to produce more hands to till the fields, farming women tended to have more frequent pregnancies than their hunter-gatherer counterparts—with consequent drains on their health. Among the Chilean mummies, for example, more women than men had bone lesions from infectious disease.

Women in agricultural societies were sometimes made beasts of burden. In New Guinea farming communities today I often see women staggering under loads of vegetables and firewood while the men walk empty-handed. Once while on a field trip there studying birds, I offered to pay some villagers to carry supplies from an airstrip to my mountain camp. The heaviest item was a 110-pound bag of rice, which I lashed to a pole and assigned to a team of four men to shoulder together. When I eventually caught up with the villagers, the men were carrying light loads, while one small woman weighing less than the bag of rice was bent under it, supporting its weight by a cord across her temples.

As for the claim that agriculture encouraged the flowering of art by providing us with leisure time, modern hunter-gatherers have at least as much free time as do farmers. The whole emphasis on leisure time as a critical factor seems to me misguided. Gorillas have had ample free time to build their own Parthenon, had they wanted to. While post-agricultural technological advances did make new art forms possible and preservation of art easier, great paintings and sculptures were already being produced by hunter-gatherers 15,000 years ago, and were still being produced as recently as the last century by such hunter-gatherers as some Eskimos and the Indians of the Pacific Northwest.

Thus with the advent of agriculture an élite became better off, but most people became worse off. Instead of swallowing the progressivist party line that we chose agriculture because it was good for us, we must ask how we got trapped by it despite its pitfalls.

One answer boils down to the adage "Might makes right." Farming could support many more people than hunting, albeit with a poorer quality of life. (Population densities of hunter-gatherers are rarely over one person per ten square miles, while farmers average 100 times that.) Partly, this is because a field planted entirely in edible crops lets one feed far more mouths than a forest with scattered edible plants. Partly, too, it's because nomadic hunter-gatherers have to keep their children spaced at four-year intervals by infanticide and other means, since a mother must carry her toddler until it's old enough to keep up with the adults. Because farm women don't have that burden, they can and often do bear a child every two years.

As population densities of hunter-gatherers slowly rose at the end of the ice ages, bands had to choose between feeding more mouths by taking the first steps toward agriculture, or else finding ways to limit growth. Some bands chose the former solution, unable to anticipate the evils of farming, and seduced by the transient abundance they enjoyed until population growth caught up with increased food production. Such bands outbred and then drove off or killed the bands that chose to remain hunter-gatherers, because a hundred malnourished farmers can still outfight one healthy hunter. It's not that hunter-gatherers abandoned their life style, but that those sensible enough not to abandon it were forced out of all areas except the ones farmers didn't want.

At this point it's instructive to recall the common complaint that archaeology is a luxury, concerned with the remote past, and offering no lessons for the present. Archaeologists studying the rise of farming have reconstructed a crucial stage at which we made the worst mistake in human history. Forced to choose between limiting population or trying to increase food production, we chose the latter and ended up with starvation, warfare, and tyranny.

Hunter-gatherers practiced the most successful and longest-lasting life style in human history. In contrast, we're still struggling with the mess into which agriculture has tumbled us, and it's unclear whether we can solve it. Suppose that an archaeologist who had visited us from outer space were trying to explain human history to his fellow spacelings. He might illustrate the results of his digs by a 24-hour clock on which one hour represents 100,000 years of real past time. If the history of the human race began at midnight, then we would now be almost at the end of our first day. We lived as hunter-gatherers for nearly the whole of that day, from midnight through dawn, noon, and sunset. Finally, at 11:54 p.m., we adopted agriculture. As our second midnight approaches, will the plight of famine-stricken peasants gradually spread to engulf us all? Or will we somehow achieve those seductive blessings that we imagine behind agriculture's glittering façade, and that have so far eluded us?

12

The Domestication of Wood in Haiti

A Case Study in Applied Evolution

Gerald F. Murray

In its annual report on the state of the planet, the Worldwatch Institute describes the growing shortage of wood for fuel and construction throughout the Third World. The problem is most acute in densely populated areas with a long history of agriculture. In these areas, peasant farmers or members of their families can spend several hours each day finding firewood. Because forests take such a long time to grow and such a short time to cut down, reforestation is a worldwide ecological challenge.

As described in this selection, Haiti has a severe deforestation problem that is closely related to wider issues of poverty and overpopulation. In this context, traditional reforestation projects, with ponderous educational components on the value of trees, had failed miserably. Anthropologist Gerald Murray, who had done research on land tenure among rural Haitian peasants, had the rare opportunity to design and implement an alternative project in forestry and agricultural development. His anthropological understanding of the economic system and culture of the Haitian people clearly paid off. The project represents applied cultural anthropology at its best.

As you read this selection, ask yourself the following questions:

- Why does Haiti have a deforestation problem?
- How was Gerald Murray's anthropological alternative project different from traditional reforestation programs?
- Why was using particular kinds of trees important for the project?
- What accounted for the Haitian peasants' enthusiasm for the idea of trees as a cash crop?
- What is meant by the title of this piece?

The following terms discussed in this selection are included in the Glossary at the back of the book:

arable land
cadastral
domestication of plants and animals
horticulture
population pressure
reforestation
swidden cultivation
usufruct rights

PROBLEM AND CLIENT

Expatriate tree lovers, whether tourists or developmental planners, often leave Haiti with an upset stomach. Though during precolonial times the island Arawaks had reached a compromise with the forest, their market-oriented colonial successors saw trees as something to be removed. The Spaniards specialized in exporting wood from the eastern side of the island,

whereas the French on the western third found it more profitable to clear the wood and produce sugar cane, coffee, and indigo for European markets. During the nineteenth century, long after Haiti had become an independent republic, foreign lumber companies cut and exported most of the nation's precious hardwoods, leaving little for today's peasants.

The geometric increase in population since colonial times—from an earlier population of fewer than half a million former slaves to a contemporary population of more than six million—and the resulting shrinkage of average family holding size have led to the evolution of a land use system devoid of systematic fallow periods. A vicious cycle has set in—one that

From *Anthropological Praxis,* by Robert M. Wulff. Copyright © by Westview Press. Reprinted by permission of Westview Press, a member of Perseus Books, L.L.C.

seems to have targeted the tree for ultimate destruction. Not only has land pressure eliminated a regenerative fallow phase in the local agricultural cycle; in addition the catastrophic declines in per hectare food yields have forced peasants into alternative income-generating strategies. Increasing numbers crowd into the capital city, Port-au-Prince, creating a market for construction wood and charcoal. Poorer sectors of the peasantry in the rural areas respond to this market by racing each other with axes and machetes to cut down the few natural tree stands remaining in remoter regions of the republic. The proverbial snowball in Hades is at less risk than a tree in Haiti.

Unable to halt the flows either of wood into the cities or of soil into the oceans, international development organizations finance studies to measure the volume of these flows (50 million trees cut per year is one of the round figures being bandied about) and to predict when the last tree will be cut from Haiti. Reforestation projects have generally been entrusted by their well-meaning but short-sighted funders to Duvalier's Ministry of Agriculture, a kiss-of-death resource channeling strategy by which the Port-au-Prince jobs created frequently outnumber the seedlings produced. And even the few seedlings produced often died in the nurseries because the peasants were understandably reluctant to cover their scarce holdings with state-owned trees. Project managers had been forced to resort to "food for work" strategies to move seedlings out of nurseries onto hillsides. And peasants have endeavored where possible to plant the trees on somebody else's hillsides and to enlist their livestock as allies in the subsequent removal of this dangerous vegetation.

This generalized hostility to tree projects placed the U.S. Agency for International Development (AID)/Haiti mission in a bind. After several years of absence from Haiti in the wake of expulsion by Francois Duvalier, AID had reestablished its presence under the government of his son Jean Claude. But an ambitious Integrated Agricultural Development Project funded through the Ministry of Agriculture had already given clear signs of being a multimillion-dollar farce. And an influential congressman chairing the U.S. House Ways and Means Committee—consequently exercising strong control over AID funds worldwide—had taken a passionate interest in Haiti. In his worldwide travels this individual had become adept at detecting and exposing developmental charades. And he had been blunt in communicating his conviction that much of what he had seen in AID/Haiti's program was precisely that. He had been touched by the plight of Haiti and communicated to the highest AID authorities his conviction about the salvific power of contraceptives and trees and his determination to have AID grace Haiti with an abundant flow of both. And he would

personally visit Haiti (a convenient plane ride from Washington, D.C.) to inspect for himself, threatening a worldwide funding freeze if no results were forthcoming. A chain reaction of nervous "yes sirs" speedily worked its way down from AID headquarters in Washington to a beleaguered Port-au-Prince mission.

The pills and condoms were less of a problem. Even the most cantankerous congressman was unlikely to insist on observing them in use and would probably settle for household distribution figures. Not so with the trees. He could (and did) pooh-pooh nursery production figures and asked to be taken to see the new AID forests, a most embarrassing request in a country where peasants creatively converted daytime reforestation projects into nocturnal goat forage projects. AID's reaction was twofold—first, to commission an immediate study to explain to the congressman and others why peasants refused to plant trees (for this they called down an AID economist); and second, to devise some program strategy that would achieve the apparently unachievable: to instill in cash-needy, defiant, pleasant charcoalmakers a love, honor, and respect for newly planted trees. For this attitudinal transformation, a task usually entrusted to the local armed forces, AID/Haiti invited an anthropologist to propose an alternative approach.

PROCESS AND PLAYERS

During these dynamics, I completed a doctoral dissertation on the manner in which Haitian peasant land tenure had evolved in response to internal population growth. The AID economist referred to above exhaustively reviewed the available literature, also focusing on the issue of Haitian peasant land tenure, and produced for the mission a well-argued monograph (Zuvekas 1978) documenting a lower rate of landlessness in Haiti than in many other Latin American settings but documenting as well the informal, extralegal character of the relationship between many peasant families and their landholdings. This latter observation was interpreted by some in the mission to mean that the principal determinant of the failure of tree planting projects was the absence among peasants of legally secure deeds over their plots. Peasants could not be expected to invest money on land improvements when at mildest the benefits could accrue to another and at worst the very improvements themselves could lead to expropriation from their land. In short, no massive tree planting could be expected, according to this model, until a nationwide cadastral reform granted plot-by-plot deeds to peasant families.

This hypothesis was reputable but programmatically paralyzing because nobody dreamed that the

Duvalier regime was about to undertake a major cadastral reform for the benefit of peasants. Several AID officers in Haiti had read my dissertation on land tenure (Murray 1977), and I received an invitation to advise the mission. Was Haitian peasant land tenure compatible with tree planting? Zuvekas' study had captured the internally complex nature of Haitian peasant land tenure. But the subsequent extrapolations as to paralyzing insecurity simply did not seem to fit with ethnographic evidence. In two reports (Murray 1978a, 1978b) I indicated that peasants in general feel secure about their ownership rights over their land. Failure to secure plot-by-plot surveyed deeds is generally a cost-saving measure. Interclass evictions did occur, but they were statistically rare; instead most land disputes were intrafamilial. A series of extralegal tenure practices had evolved—preinheritance land grants to young adult dependents, informal inheritance subdivisions witnessed by community members, fictitious sales to favored children, complex community-internal share-cropping arrangements. And though these practices produced an internally heterogeneous system with its complexities, there was strong internal order. Any chaos and insecurity tended to be more in the mind of observers external to the system than in the behavior of the peasants themselves. There was a danger that the complexities of Haitian peasant land tenure would generate an unintended smokescreen obscuring the genuine causes of failure in tree planting projects.

What then were these genuine causes? The mission, intent on devising programming strategies in this domain, invited me to explore further, under a contract aimed at identifying the "determinants of success and failure" in reforestation and soil conservation projects. My major conclusion was that the preexisting land tenure, cropping, and livestock systems in peasant Haiti were perfectly adequate for the undertaking of significant tree planting activities. Most projects had failed not because of land tenure or attitudinal barriers among peasants but because of fatal flaws in one or more key project components. Though my contract called principally for analysis of previous or existing projects, I used the recommendation section of the report to speculate on how a Haiti-wise anthropologist would program and manage reforestation activities if he or she had the authority. In verbal debriefings I jokingly challenged certain young program officers in the mission to give me a jeep and carte blanche access to a $50,000 checking account, and I would prove my anthropological assertions about peasant economic behavior and produce more trees in the ground than their current multimillion-dollar Ministry of Agriculture charade. We had a good laugh and shook hands, and I departed confident that the report would be as dutifully perused and as honorably filed and forgotten as similar reports I had done elsewhere.

To my great disbelief, as I was correcting Anthro 101 exams some two years later, one of the program officers still in Haiti called to say that an Agroforestry Outreach Project (AOP) had been approved chapter and verse as I had recommended it; and that if I was interested in placing my life where my mouth had been and would leave the ivory tower to direct the project, my project bank account would have not $50,000, but $4 million. After several weeks of hemming and hawing and vigorous negotiating for leave from my department, I accepted the offer and entered a new (to me) role of project director in a strange upside-down world in which the project anthropologist was not a powerless cranky voice from the bleachers but the chief of party with substantial authority over general project policy and the allocation of project resources. My elation at commanding resources to implement anthropological ideas was dampened by the nervousness of knowing exactly who would be targeted for flak and ridicule if these ideas bombed out, as most tended to do in the Haiti of Duvalier.

The basic structural design of AOP followed a tripartite conceptual framework that I proposed for analyzing projects. Within this framework a project is composed of three essential systemic elements: a technical base, a benefit flow strategy, and an institutional delivery strategy. Planning had to focus equally on all three; I argued that defects in one would sabotage the entire project.

Technical Strategy

The basic technical strategy was to make available to peasants fast-growing wood trees (*Leucaena leucocephala, Cassia siamea, Azadirachta indica, Casuarina equisetifolia, Eucalyptus camaldulensis*) that were not only drought resistant but also rapid growing, producing possible four-year harvest rotations in humid lowland areas (and slower rotations and lower survival rates in arid areas) and that were good for charcoal and basic construction needs. Most of the species mentioned also restore nutrients to the soil, and some of them coppice from a carefully harvested stump, producing several rotations before the need for replanting.

Of equally critical technical importance was the use of a nursery system that produced lightweight microseedlings. A project pickup truck could transport over 15,000 of these microseedlings (as opposed to 250 traditional bag seedlings), and the average peasant could easily carry over 500 transportable seedlings at one time, planting them with a fraction of the ground preparation time and labor required for bulkier bagged seedlings. The anthropological implications of this nursery system were critical. It constituted a technical breakthrough that reduced to a fraction the fossil-fuel and human energy expenditure required to transport and plant trees.

But the technical component of the project incorporated yet another element: the physical juxtaposition of trees and crops. In traditional reforestation models, the trees are planted in large unbroken monocropped stands. Such forests or woodlots presuppose local land tenure and economic arrangements not found in Haiti. For the tree to make its way as a cultivate into the economy of Haitian peasants and most other tropical cultivators, reforestation models would have to be replaced by agroforestry models that entail spatial or temporal juxtaposition of crops and trees. Guided by prior ethnographic knowledge of Haitian cropping patterns, AOP worked out with peasants various border planting and intercropping strategies to make tree planting feasible even for small holding cultivators.

Benefit Flow Strategies

With respect to the second systemic component, the programming of benefit flows to participants, earlier projects had often committed the fatal flaw of defining project trees planted as *pyebwa leta* (the state's trees). Authoritarian assertions by project staff concerning sanctions for cutting newly planted trees created fears among peasants that even trees planted on their own land would be government property. And several peasants were frank in reporting fears that the trees might eventually be used as a pretext by the government or the "Company" (the most common local lexeme used to refer to projects) for eventually expropriating the land on which peasants had planted project trees.

Such ambiguities and fears surrounding benefit flows paralyze even the technically soundest project. A major anthropological feature of AOP was a radical frontal attack on the issue of property and usufruct rights over project trees. Whereas other projects had criticized tree cutting, AOP promulgated the heretical message that trees were meant to be cut, processed, and sold. The only problem with the present system, according to project messages, was that peasants were cutting nature's trees. But once the landowner "mete fos li deyo" (expends his resources) and plants and cares for his or her own wood trees on his or her own land, the landowner has the same right to harvest and sell wood as corn or beans.

I was inevitably impressed at the impact that this blunt message had when I delivered it to groups of prospective peasant tree planters. Haitian peasants are inveterate and aggressive cash-croppers; many of the crops and livestock that they produce are destined for immediate consignment to local markets. For the first time in their lives, they were hearing a concrete proposal to make the wood tree itself one more marketable crop in their inventory.

But the message would ring true only if three barriers were smashed.

1. The first concerned the feared delay in benefits. Most wood trees with which the peasants were familiar took an impractically long time to mature. There fortunately existed in Haiti four-year-old stands of leucaena, cassia, eucalyptus, and other project trees to which we could take peasant groups to demonstrate the growth speed of these trees.

2. But could they be planted on their scanty holdings without interfering with crops? Border and row planting techniques were demonstrated, as well as intercropping. The average peasant holding was about a hectare and a half. If a cultivator planted a field in the usual crops and then planted 500 seedlings in the same field at 2 meters by 2 meters, the seedlings would occupy only a fifth of a hectare. And they would be far enough apart to permit continued cropping for two or three cycles before shade competition became too fierce. That is, trees would be planted on only a fraction of the peasant's holdings and planted in such a way that they would be compatible with continued food growing even on the plots where they stood. We would then calculate with peasants the potential income to be derived from these 500 trees through sale as charcoal, polewood, or boards. In a best-case scenario, the gross take from the charcoal of these trees (the least lucrative use of the wood) might equal the current annual income of an average rural family. The income potential of these wood trees clearly would far offset any potential loss from decreased food production. Though it had taken AID two years to decide on the project, it took about twenty minutes with any group of skeptical but economically rational peasants to generate a list of enthusiastic potential tree planters.

3. But there was yet a third barrier. All this speculation about income generation presupposed that the peasants themselves, and not the government or the project, would be the sole owners of the trees and that the peasants would have unlimited rights to the harvest of the wood whenever they wished. To deal with this issue, I presented the matter as an agreement between cultivator and the project: We would furnish the free seedlings and technical assistance; the cultivators would agree to plant 500 of these seedlings on their own

land and permit project personnel to carry out periodic survival counts. We would, of course, pay no wages or "Food for Work" for this planting. But we would guarantee to the planters complete and exclusive ownership of the trees. They did not need to ask for permission from the project to harvest the trees whenever their needs might dictate, nor would there be any penalties associated with early cutting or low survival. If peasants changed their minds, they could rip out their seedlings six months after planting. They would never get any more free seedlings from us, but they would not be subject to any penalties. There are preexisting local forestry laws, rarely enforced, concerning permissions and minor taxes for tree cutting. Peasants would have to deal with these as they had skillfully done in the past. But from our project's point of view, we relinquish all tree ownership rights to the peasants who accept and plant the trees on their property.

Cash-flow dialogues and ownership assurances such as these were a far cry from the finger-wagging ecological sermons to which many peasant groups had been subjected on the topic of trees. Our project technicians developed their own messages; but central to all was the principle of peasant ownership and usufruct of AOP trees. The goal was to capitalize on the preexisting fuel and lumber markets, to make the wood tree one more crop in the income-generating repertoire of the Haitian peasant.

Institutional Strategy

The major potential fly in the ointment was the third component, the institutional component. To whom would AID entrust its funds to carry out this project? My own research had indicated clearly that Haitian governmental involvement condemned a project to certain paralysis and possible death, and my report phrased that conclusion as diplomatically as possible. The diplomacy was required to head off possible rage, less from Haitian officials than from certain senior officers in the AID mission who were politically and philosophically wedded to an institution-building strategy. Having equated the term "institution" with "government bureaucracy," and having defined their own career success in terms, not of village-level resource flows, but of voluminous and timely bureaucracy-to-bureaucracy cash transfers, such officials were in effect marshaling U.S. resources into the service of extractive ministries with unparalleled track records of squandering and/or pilfering expatriate donor funds.

To the regime's paradoxical credit, however, the blatant openness and arrogance of Duvalierist predation had engendered an angry willingness in much of Haiti's development community to explore other resource flow channels. Though the nongovernmental character of the proposal provoked violent reaction, the reactionaries in the Haiti mission were overridden by their superiors in Washington, and a completely nongovernmental implementing mode was adopted for this project.

The system, based on private voluntary organizations (PVOs), worked as follows.

1. AID made a macrogrant to a Washington-based PVO (the Pan American Development Foundation, PADF) to run a tree-planting project based on the principles that had emerged in my research. At the Haiti mission's urging, PADF invited me to be chief of party for the project and located an experienced accountant in Haiti to be financial administrator. PADF in addition recruited three American agroforesters who, in addition to MA-level professional training, had several years of overseas village field experience under their belts. Early in the project they were supplemented by two other expatriates, a Belgian and a French Canadian. We opened a central office in Port-au-Prince and assigned a major region of Haiti to each of the agroforesters, who lived in their field regions.

2. These agroforesters were responsible for contacting the many village-based PVOs working in their regions to explain the project, to emphasize its microeconomic focus and its difference from traditional reforestation models, to discuss the conditions of entry therein, and to make technical suggestions as to the trees that would be appropriate for the region.

3. If the PVO was interested, we drafted an agreement in which our mutual contributions and spheres of responsibility were specified. The agreements were not drafted in French (Haiti's official language) but in Creole, the only language spoken by most peasants.

4. The local PVO selected *animateurs* (village organizers) who themselves were peasants who lived and worked in the village where trees would be planted. After receiving training from us, they contacted their neighbors and kin, generated lists of peasants interested in planting a specified number of trees, and informed us when the local rains began to fall. At the proper moment we packed the seedlings in boxes customized to the particular region and shipped them on our trucks to the farmers, who would be waiting at specified drop-off points at a specified time. The trees were to be planted within twenty-four hours of delivery.

5. The animateurs were provided with Creole language data forms by which to gather ecological, land use, and land tenure data on each plot where trees would be planted and certain bits of information on each peasant participant. These forms were used to follow up, at periodic intervals, the survival of trees, the incidence of any problems (such as livestock depredation, burning, disease), and—above all—the manner in which the farmer integrated the trees into cropping and livestock patterns, to detect and head off any unintended substitution of food for wood.

RESULTS AND EVALUATION

The project was funded for four years from October 1981 through November 1985. During the writing of the project paper we were asked by an AID economist to estimate how many trees would be planted. Not knowing if the peasants would in fact plant any trees, we nervously proposed to reach two thousand peasant families with a million trees as a project goal. Fiddling with his programmed calculator, the economist informed us that that output would produce a negative internal rate of return. We would need at least two million trees to make the project worth AID's institutional while. We shrugged and told him cavalierly to up the figure and to promise three million trees on the land of six thousand peasants. (At that time I thought someone else would be directing the project.)

Numbers of Trees and Beneficiaries

Though I doubted that we could reach this higher goal, the response of the Haitian peasants to this new approach to tree planting left everyone, including myself, open mouthed. Within the first year of the project, one million trees had been planted by some 2,500 peasant households all over Haiti. My fears of peasant indifference were now transformed into nervousness that we could not supply seedlings fast enough to meet the demand triggered by our wood-as-a-cash-crop strategy. Apologetic village animateurs informed us that some cultivators who had not signed up on the first lists were actually stealing newly planted seedlings from their neighbors' fields at night. They promised to catch the scoundrels. If they did, I told them, give the scoundrels a hug. Their pilfering was dramatic proof of the bull's-eye nature of the anthropological predictions that underlie the project.

By the end of the second year (when I left the project), we had reached the four-year goal of three million seedlings and the project had geared up and decentralized its nursery capacity to produce several million seedlings per season (each year having two planting seasons). Under the new director, a fellow anthropologist, the geometric increase continued. By the end of the fourth year, the project had planted, not its originally agreed-upon three million trees, but twenty million trees. Stated more accurately, some 75,000 Haitian peasants had enthusiastically planted trees on their own land. In terms of its quantitative outreach, AOP had more than quintupled its original goals.

Wood Harvesting and Wood Banking

By the end of its fourth year the project had already received an unusual amount of professional research attention by anthropologists, economists, and foresters. In addition to AID evaluations, six studies had been released on one or another aspect of the project (Ashley 1986; Balzano 1986; Buffum and King 1985; Conway 1986; Grosenick 1985; McGowan 1986). As predicted, many peasants were harvesting trees by the end of the fourth year. The most lucrative sale of the wood was as polewood in local markets, though much charcoal was also being made from project trees.

Interestingly, however, the harvesting was proceeding much more slowly than I had predicted. Peasants were "clinging" to their trees and not engaging in the clear cutting that I hoped would occur, as a prelude to the emergence of a rotational system in which peasants would alternate crops with tree cover that they themselves had planted. This technique would have been a revival, under a "domesticated" mode, of the ancient swidden sequence that had long since disappeared from Haiti. Though such a revival would have warmed anthropological hearts, the peasants had a different agenda. Though they had long ago removed nature's tree cover, they were extremely cautious about removing the tree cover that they had planted. Their economic logic was unassailable. Crop failure is so frequent throughout most of Haiti, and the market for wood and charcoal so secure, that peasants prefer to leave the tree as a "bank" against future emergencies. This arboreal bank makes particular sense in the context of the recent disappearance from Haiti of the peasant's traditional bank, the pig. A governmentally mandated (and U.S. financed) slaughter of all pigs because of fears of African swine fever created a peasant banking gap that AOP trees have now started to fill.

THE ANTHROPOLOGICAL DIFFERENCE

Anthropological findings, methods, and theories clearly have heavily influenced this project at all stages. We are dealing, not with an ongoing project affected by anthropological input, but with a project whose very existence was rooted in anthropological research and whose very character was determined by ongoing anthropological direction and anthropologically informed managerial prodding.

My own involvement with the project spanned several phases and tasks:

1. Proposal of a theoretical and conceptual base of AOP, and concept of "wood as a cash crop."

2. Preliminary contacting of local PVOs to assess preproject interest.

3. Identification of specific program measures during project design.

4. Preparation of social soundness analysis for the AID project paper.

5. Participation as an outside expert at the AID meetings in Washington at which the fate of the project was decided.

6. Participation in the selection and in-country linguistic and cultural training of the agroforesters who worked for the project.

7. Direction and supervision of field operations.

8. Formative evaluation of preliminary results and the identification of needed midcourse corrections.

9. Generation of several hundred thousand dollars of supplemental funding from Canadian and Swiss sources and internationalization of the project team.

10. Preparation of publications about the project (Murray 1984, 1986).

In addition to my own participation in the AOP, four other anthropologists have been involved in long-term commitments to the project. Fred Conway did a preliminary study of firewood use in Haiti (Conway 1979). He subsequently served for two years as overall project coordinator within AID/Haiti. More recently he has carried out revealing case study research on the harvesting of project trees (Conway 1986). Glenn Smucker likewise did an early feasibility study in the northwest (Smucker 1981) and eventually joined the project as my successor in the directorship. Under his leadership, many of the crucial midcourse corrections were introduced. Ira Lowenthall took over the AID coordination of the project at a critical transitional period and has been instrumental in forging plans for its institutional future. And Anthony Balzano has carried out several years of case study fieldwork on the possible impact of the tree-planting activities on the land tenure in participating villages. All these individuals have PhDs, or are PhD candidates, in anthropology. And another anthropologist in the Haiti mission, John Lewis,

succeeded in adapting the privatized umbrella agency outreach model for use in a swine repopulation project. With the possible exception of Vicos, it would be hard to imagine a project that has been as heavily influenced by anthropologists.

But how specifically has anthropology influenced the content of the project? There are at least three major levels at which anthropology has impinged on the content of AOP.

1. *The Application of Substantive Findings.* The very choice of "wood as a marketable crop" as the fundamental theme of the project stemmed from ethnographic knowledge of the cash-oriented foundations of Haitian peasant horticulture and knowledge of current conditions in the internal marketing system. Because of ethnographic knowledge I was able to avoid succumbing to the common-sense inclination to emphasize fruit trees (whose perishability and tendency to glut markets make them commercially vulnerable) and to choose instead a fast-growing wood tree. There is a feverishly escalating market for charcoal and construction wood that cannot be dampened even by the most successful project. And there are no spoilage problems with wood. The peasants can harvest it when they want. Furthermore, ethnographic knowledge of Haitian peasant land tenure—which is highly individualistic—guided me away from the community forest schemes that so many development philosophers seem to delight in but that are completely inappropriate to the social reality of Caribbean peasantries.

2. *Anthropological Methods.* The basic research that led up to the project employed participant observation along with intensive interviewing with small groups of informants to compare current cost/benefit ratios of traditional farming with projected cash yields from plots in which trees are intercropped with food on four-year rotation cycles. A critical part of the project design stage was to establish the likelihood of increased revenues from altered land use behaviors. During project design I also applied ethnographic techniques to the behavior of institutional personnel. The application of anthropological notetaking on 3-by-5 slips, not only with peasants but also with technicians, managers, and officials, exposed the institutional roots of earlier project failures and stimulated the proposal of alternative institutional routes. Furthermore, ethno-scientific elicitation of folk taxonomies led to the realization that whereas fruit trees are classified as a crop by Haitian peasants, wood trees are not so classified. This discovery exposed the need for the creation

of explicit messages saying that wood can be a crop, just as coffee, manioc, and corn can. Finally, prior experience in Creole-language instrument design and computer analysis permitted me to design a baseline data gathering system.

3. *Anthropological Theory.* My own thinking about tree planting was heavily guided by cultural-evolutionary insights into the origins of agriculture. The global tree problem is often erroneously conceptualized in a conservationist or ecological framework. Such a perspective is very short-sighted for anthropologists. We are aware of an ancient food crisis, when humans still hunted and gathered, that was solved, not by the adoption of conservationist practices, but rather by the shift into a domesticated mode of production. From hunting and gathering we turned to cropping and harvesting. I found the analogy with the present tree crisis conceptually overpowering. Trees will reemerge when and only when human beings start planting them aggressively as a harvestable crop, not when human consciousness is raised regarding their ecological importance. This anthropological insight (or bias), nourished by the aggressive creativity of the Haitian peasants among whom I had lived, swayed me toward the adoption of a dynamic "domestication" paradigm in proposing a solution to the tree problem in Haiti. This evolutionary perspective also permitted me to see that the cash-cropping of wood was in reality a small evolutionary step, not a quantum leap. The Haitian peasants already cut and sell natural stands of wood. They already plant and sell traditional food crops. It is but a small evolutionary step to join these two unconnected streams of Haitian peasant behavior, and this linkage is the core purpose of the Agroforestry Outreach Project.

Broader anthropological theory also motivated and justified a nongovernmental implementing mode for AOP. Not only AID but also most international development agencies tend to operate on a service model of the state. This idealized model views the basic character of the state as that of a provider of services to its population. Adherence to this theoretically naive service model has led to the squandering of untold millions of dollars in the support of extractive public bureaucracies. This waste is justified under the rubric of institution building—assisting public entities to provide the services that they are supposed to be providing.

But my anthropological insights into the origins of the state as a mechanism of extraction and control led me to pose the somewhat heretical position that the predatory behavior of Duvalier's regime was in fact not

misbehavior. Duvalier was merely doing openly and blatantly what other state leaders camouflage under rhetoric. AID's search of nongovernmental implementing channels for AOP, then, was not seen as a simple emergency measure to be employed under a misbehaving regime but rather as an avenue of activity that might be valid as an option under many or most regimes. There is little justification in either ethnology or anthropological theory for viewing the state as the proper recipient of developmental funds. This theoretical insight permitted us to argue for a radically nongovernmental mode of tree-planting support in AOP. In short, sensitivity to issues in anthropological theory played a profound role in the shaping of the project.

Would AOP have taken the form it did without these varied types of anthropological input? Almost certainly not. Had there been no anthropological input, a radically different scenario would almost certainly have unfolded with the following elements.

1. AID would probably have undertaken a reforestation project—congressional pressure alone would have ensured that. But the project would have been based, not on the theme of "wood as a peasant cash-crop," but on the more traditional approach to trees as a vehicle of soil conservation. Ponderous educational programs would have been launched to teach the peasants about the value of trees. Emphasis would have been placed on educating the ignorant and on trying to induce peasants to plant commercially marginal (and nutritionally tangential) fruit trees instead of cash-generating wood trees.

2. The project would have been managed by technicians. The emphasis would probably have been on carrying out lengthy technical research concerning optimal planting strategies and the combination of trees with optimally effective bench terraces and other soil conservation devices. The outreach problem would have been given second priority. Throughout Haiti hundreds of thousands of dollars have been spent on numerous demonstration projects to create terraced, forested hillsides, but only a handful of cooperative local peasants have been induced to undertake the same activities on their own land.

3. The project would almost certainly have been run through the Haitian government. When after several hundred thousand dollars of expenditures few trees were visible, frustrated young AID program officers would have gotten finger-wagging lectures about the sovereign right of local officials to use donor money as they see fit. And the few trees planted would have been defined as *pyebwa leta* (the government's trees), and peasants would

have been sternly warned against ever cutting these trees, even the ones planted on their own land. And the peasants would soon turn the problem over to their most effective ally in such matters, the free-ranging omnivorous goat, who would soon remove this alien vegetation from the peasants' land.

Because of anthropology, the Agroforestry Outreach Project has unfolded to a different scenario. It was a moving experience for me to return to the village where I had done my original fieldwork (and which I of course tried to involve in the tree-planting activities) to find several houses built using the wood from leucaena trees planted during the project's earliest phases. Poles were beginning to be sold, although the prices had not yet stabilized for these still unknown wood types. Charcoal made from project trees was being sold in local markets. For the first time in the history of this village, people were "growing" part of their house structures and their cooking fuel. I felt as though I were observing (and had been a participant in) a replay of an ancient anthropological drama, the shift from an extractive to a domesticated mode of resource procurement. Though their sources of food energy had been domesticated millennia ago, my former village neighbors had now begun replicating this transition in the domain of wood and wood-based energy. I felt a satisfaction at having chosen a discipline that could give me the privilege of participating, even marginally, in this very ancient cultural-evolutionary transition.

REFERENCES

Ashley, Marshall D. 1986. *A Study of Traditional Agroforestry Systems in Haiti and Implications for the USAID/Haiti Agroforestry Outreach Project.* Port-au-Prince: University of Maine Agroforestry Outreach Research Project.

Balzano, Anthony. 1986. *Socioeconomic Aspects of Agroforestry in Rural Haiti.* Port-au-Prince: University of Maine Agroforestry Outreach Research Project.

Buffum, William, and Wendy King. 1985. *Small Farmer Decision Making and Tree Planting: Agroforestry Extension Recommendations.* Port-au-Prince: Haiti Agroforestry Outreach Project.

Conway, Frederick. 1979. *A Study of the Fuelwood Situation in Haiti.* Port-au-Prince: USAID.

——. 1986. *The Decision Making Framework for Tree Planting Within the Agroforestry Outreach Project.* Port-au-Prince: University of Maine Agroforestry Outreach Research Project.

Grosenick, Gerald. 1985. *Economic Evaluation of the Agroforestry Outreach Project.* Port-au-Prince: University of Maine Agroforestry Outreach Research Project.

McGowan, Lisa A. 1986. *Potential Marketability of Charcoal, Poles, and Planks Produced by Participants in the Agroforestry Outreach Project.* Port-au-Prince: University of Maine Agroforestry Outreach Research Project.

Murray, Gerald F. 1977. *The Evolution of Haitian Peasant Land Tenure: A Case Study in Agrarian Adaptation to Population Growth.* Ph.D. dissertation, Columbia University, New York.

——. 1978a. *Hillside Units, Wage Labor, and Haitian Peasant Land Tenure: A Strategy for the Organization of Erosion Control.* Port-au-Prince: USAID.

——. 1978b. *Informal Subdivisions and Land Insecurity: An Analysis of Haitian Peasant Land Tenure.* Port-au-Prince: USAID.

——. 1979. *Terraces, Trees, and the Haitian Peasant: An Assessment of 25 Years of Erosion Control in Rural Haiti.* Port-au-Prince: USAID.

——. 1984. "The Wood Tree as a Peasant Cash-Crop: An Anthropological Strategy for the Domestication of Energy." In A. Valdman and R. Foster, eds., *Haiti—Today and Tomorrow: An Interdisciplinary Study.* New York: University Press of America.

——. 1986. "Seeing the Forest While Planting the Trees: An Anthropological Approach to Agroforestry in Rural Haiti." In D. W. Brinkerhoff and J. C. Garcia-Zamor, eds., *Politics, Projects, and Peasants: Institutional Development in Haiti.* New York: Praeger, pp. 193–226.

Smucker, Glenn R. 1981. *Trees and Charcoal in Haitian Peasant Economy: A Feasibility Study.* Port-au-Prince: USAID.

Zuvekas, Clarence. 1978. *Agricultural Development in Haiti: An Assessment of Sector Problems, Policies, and Prospects under Conditions of Severe Soil Erosion.* Washington, D.C.: USAID.

13

Two Rights Make a Wrong

Indigenous Peoples Versus Environmental Protection Agencies

Richard Reed

In today's world, environmentalism has become an almost mainstream cultural ideal, as cereal boxes and pop stars beseech us to "save the rainforest." The question of indigenous rights to traditional lands, however, has not received the same degree of popular attention. Indigenous peoples do not have the same political allies as the forests in which they live. In this selection we see that some environmentalists and anthropologists propose combining these two agendas, arguing that the goals of conservation and defending traditional indigenous land use have much in common. For example, both efforts should be aimed at preventing land from being exploited according to models of nonsustainable agrobusiness.

Neither environmental conservation nor indigenous land rights are simple issues, and the alliance between these two sides is far from harmonious. In this selection, anthropologist Richard Reed describes the history of the creation of a national park (or reserve) in Paraguay where, initially, indigenous people were expected both to have access to land for traditional purposes and to be involved in managing and maintaining the park.

Anthropologists began by calling for the creation of the reserve and the inclusion of indigenous people in its management plan. Anthropologists found a powerful ally to make the reserve a reality: The Nature Conservancy, a U.S.-based nonprofit conservation group. Anthropologists were also called on to facilitate communication among indigenous people, biologists, and personnel in a variety of government and nongovernment organizations. Yet while anthropologists are in a privileged position to understand the viewpoint of these different cultures, they are working in a context of unequal power. By the time the national park was created, only those indigenous people who maintained a traditional economic lifestyle, as defined by The Nature Conservancy, were permitted to have access, while the rest of the "acculturated" indigenous people were excluded.

Indigenous people are not fossils or museum exhibits. They have never been in a "natural" state; they have always had an impact on the local ecology. Indigenous people themselves should ideally decide how to practice their culture and respond to changing political, economic, and ecological traditions. Because native groups remain as disempowered today as they were five hundred years ago when the first Europeans arrived, they profoundly distrust all who want to come and help them, including well-intentioned anthropologists. As Reed says, to the indigenous people of this region, The Nature Conservancy is just another in a long history of outsider plantation owners (*latifundistas*). Until indigenous peoples can become actors with a voice in the environmental movement, this promising alliance will continue to be problematic.

As you read this selection, ask yourself the following questions:

- What are the different goals that the two sides in this alliance have? Are these goals incompatible?
- How did the fact that there were at least two indigenous groups involved in this case make the situation more complicated?
- How did anthropologists play a role as "culture brokers" in this scenario? Did their efforts fail? Why?
- Why was The Nature Conservancy so interested in Mbaracayu Park, whereas the World Bank was not?
- What cultural ideals of the "native" are involved in this case?

The following terms discussed in this selection are included in the Glossary at the back of the book:

foraging	*peasants*
horticulture	*shifting agriculture*
indigenistas	*swidden cultivation*
indigenous	yerba mate
latifundistas	yerbateros

In lowland Latin America, the struggle to save the forests has forged new alliances between indigenous peoples and environmental foundations. Such alliances link the future of the world's indigenous people with the future of the forests, to the benefit of both. The political and economic capital that environmental agencies bring to the conservation struggle can aid indigenous groups. At the same time, environmental groups gain two things: the indigenous knowledge to understand the complex biological communities in these areas as well as a potent symbol of the importance of the mission (Conklin and Graham 1995).

Problems have begun to surface, however, in the relationship between indigenous peoples and the environmental movement. Agencies find that indigenous populations are often internally divided and that their conflicting demands are difficult to reconcile in the larger fight for environmental protection. Indigenous peoples, in turn, are often dissatisfied with the restrictions imposed by environmental protection organizations.

This article examines a case in which The Nature Conservancy (TNC) and several indigenous groups tried to collaborate in the creation and management of a reserve in northeastern Paraguay. In 1989, TNC purchased 53,000 hectares of the last sustainable stands of subtropical deciduous forest that once covered the Paraguay and Brazil's Paraná Plateau—one of the last open forests for the Aché and the Guaraní peoples. In their fight against colonists and cattle ranchers, the Aché, the Guaraní, and TNC were forced to contend with one another. They also had to contend with misunderstandings based on conceptions of nature and indigenous peoples that emerged as environmentalists and anthropologists negotiated access to and management of the region.

MBARACAYU

Until 1970, far eastern Paraguay was undisturbed by intensive development. The region was protected by plantation owners (*latifundistas*) and multinational corporations that were primarily interested in the limited collection of native *yerba mate* (*Ilex paraguayensis*) and harvesting of hardwood trees. Two indigenous groups occupied the forests, the food-foraging Aché and the horticultural Guaraní. These two groups generally lived in a state of mutual fear and permanent conflict; both have had intermittent contact with *yerba mate* collectors and loggers who penetrated the zone. Throughout history, *latifundistas* restricted colonization of the forest by nonindigenous peoples, but the Guaraní

Reprinted by permission of the author.

and Aché were tolerated. As a result, the indigenous groups had free access to sufficient resources to control their own lives.

Over the last twenty years, the forests of eastern Paraguay have been expropriated to satisfy land demands by agro-industrialists and the growing peasant population. Between 1963 and 1976, the Paraguay land reform agency (IBR) distributed about four million hectares to 90,000 families. By 1984, 5.1 million hectares, roughly half of the arable land in eastern Paraguay, had been given to peasant colonists (World Bank 1984:11). Foreign investment accompanied colonization. Brazilian, American, and Japanese companies purchased vast areas of forest for clear-cutting and agriculture (Parquet 1985:37). Soybean production and ranching replaced traditional industries in eastern Paraguay. As a result, the forests were reduced by half by 1989, and the rate of continued deforestation in Paraguay was higher than in any other Latin American country (Hanratty and Meditz 1990).

As rural transformation converts Paraguay's subtropical forests into an international breadbasket, the Aché and Guaraní are losing land. As early as the 1970s, voices were raised in defense of Paraguay's indigenous peoples (AIP/Misión 1977). The Aché became an international concern when they were forced to take refuge with missionaries and exploitative patrons (Arens 1976). Anthropologists and *indigenistas* lobbied the national government for land. Although most Aché and Guaraní received guarantees to some land, these *"colonias nacionales"* were insufficient for hunting and shifting agriculture.

In the early 1980s, anthropologists identified a major tract of remaining forested land called "Mbaracayu," which could allow many of the indigenous people to continue traditional hunting and gathering. Since the World Bank then controlled this land (a lumber company had defaulted on a loan), there was hope that this virgin forest could be secured for the indigenous groups.

Traditionally the Guaraní of the region hunted in the forests and collected a variety of goods, including commodities such as *yerba mate* and skins. In 1971, when the land was sold for lumbering, the families living in Mbaracayu were forced from their homes onto adjacent lands. Today, five hundred Guaraní families are located near the land, supplementing their gardens by hunting and gathering on the few large tracts of forest that remain undeveloped.

Mbaracayu also harbored one of the last groups of hunting and gathering Aché. Since being forced out of the forest in 1976, they had been given fields and houses at a religious mission outside the reserve. Nevertheless, the Aché continued their patterns of intermittent nomadic foraging within the dense forests of Mbaracayu.[1]

TIMELINE OF MBARACAYU RESERVE

- 1531–1960: Indigenous people in Paraguay struggle successfully to maintain traditional lifestyles in the forests of eastern Paraguay.
- 1968: Mbaracayu forest is purchased by timber company.
- 1971: Guaraní communities are forced out of Mbaracayu forest by timber company.
- 1974: Timber company goes bankrupt; World Bank acquires Mbaracayu by default.
- 1976: World Bank and Paraguayan government attempt to force Aché out of Mbaracayu forest.
- 1983: Anthropologists approach World Bank to grant Mbaracayu to indigenous groups.
- 1983: World Bank ignores anthropologists (and their own guidelines on indigenous peoples).

- 1989: TNC purchases 53,000 hectares of the last sustainable stands of subtropical deciduous forest in Paraguay.
- 1989: Anthropologists meet with indigenous groups to discuss the creation of the reserve and its management plan.
- 1989: NGO Fundación Moises Bertoni (FMB) is created to manage the reserve.
- 1991: All Guaraní indigenous people are denied access to the reserve.
- 1991: Aché indigenous people are granted limited access to the reserve, provided they maintain their "traditional," "natural" lifestyles as defined by FMB and TNC.

In 1983, anthropologists approached the World Bank to donate the land for use by Paraguayan indigenous people. When calls to Washington came to naught, the bank was instead asked to provide a small portion of the land to the Aché and Guaraní in compliance with the World Bank's own policy of protecting indigenous peoples in the project areas. Bank personnel ignored the requests, suggesting that the whole idea of indigenous use of the land was preposterous.

Seeking allies, some anthropologists approached TNC. The idea quickly became a plan, was then converted into a project, was embedded in a program, and within days had been granted a budget. There was a reason TNC moved quickly. In the 1980s it was searching for the means to internationalize its work, and Mbaracayu offered a unique opportunity. The region harbored plant and animal life that was disappearing from much of southern Brazil, northern Argentina, and eastern Paraguay. Paraguayan land was cheap and the Paraguayan government was an image-conscious dictatorship. It was a case where a little pull and a little money could accomplish a great deal in a short time.

Whereas anthropologists' inquiries to the World Bank were rebuffed, TNC's interest in acquiring Mbaracayu was warmly received. TNC had important Washington connections, had amassed a considerable war chest for the negotiation of land purchase, and could call on a host of international contacts for such complex transactions as debt-for-nature swaps.

As discussions moved forward quickly, TNC proposed that the land be protected by a joint Paraguayan-international effort. In conformity with World Bank guidelines toward indigenous people, the bank requested that TNC develop a management plan for indigenous peoples' use of the region. To design this component of the management plan, anthropologists (the author included) visited each indigenous community, counted the population, and held a meeting to discuss the plan. In Paraguay, a host country agency called Fundación Moises Bertoni (FMB) was developed to orchestrate the land acquisition and manage the park.

This management plan provided the first arena for the negotiation of the conflicting rights of indigenous people and TNC. The Guaraní and Aché saw the creation of the reserve and TNC's interest in their involvement as a means of acquiring what they considered their primordial right, the forests of Mbaracayu. Although the government's interest in helping indigenous groups was limited, the indigenous groups saw new potential in the international ties and power of TNC. For its part, TNC reinforced the impression that Mbaracayu was a site where indigenous groups could maintain their society and culture. Rhetoric surrounding the project emphasized the agencies' sensitivity to indigenous peoples' needs and rights. Introducing Mbaracayu in its own literature, TNC (1996:17) reported that it purchased the area in 1991 "to help the Aché preserve their traditions and to protect one of the last untouched forest wilderness areas in Paraguay."

In designing the reserve management plan, anthropologists proposed that indigenous people could be important to the future of the region. Guaraní and Aché have the greatest knowledge of the local environment, its resources, and their use. More than a simple biological variable in the forest ecosystem, the plan pointed out that traditional economic activities in the area had directly affected the existing forest. Guaraní and Aché hunting, gathering, fishing, and swidden cultivation had patterned the region's flora and fauna. Anthropologists noted that for five centuries Guaraní had collected *yerba* commercially, while protecting and promoting a series of natural yerba stands (*yerbales*). These activities provided Guaraní with a steady income without destroying the forest. Thus, indigenous commercial extraction had "managed" the so-called "natural" environment (Reed 1997).

Given these models of indigenous resource use, the anthropological team suggested that the indigenous residents be integrated into the maintenance and management of the reserve. Aché would continue to hunt and gather; Guaraní would be allowed to continue traditional, commercial *yerba* gathering. In addition, it was proposed that the Aché be employed as "guarde bosques," manipulating the colonists' fear of "savage Indians" to assure that they remained beyond the park's boundaries. In sum, anthropologists suggested that indigenous groups be given access to the resources that they traditionally used, resources that were vital to their continued social and economic independence (Renshaw and Reed 1989:53).

When the proposed indigenous component of the management plan was presented to the Paraguayan reserve management agency, however, discussions were fraught with conflict and misunderstanding. The team of biologists, TNC, and FMB were skeptical of the plan to give indigenous people rights to use park resources. They were concerned that hunting would undermine endangered animal populations, gardens would damage the forest, and commercial gathering would lead to wholesale destruction of forest resources.

The arguments against the plan rested on two points. First, they suggested that Mbaracayu had been unaffected by past human activity. Second, giving Aché and Guaraní rights to continue hunting, field cutting, or commercial collection would degrade the forest environment.

The management plan that was finally written by the FMB attempted to step gingerly between the conflicting demands. It allowed some Aché limited access to the reserve, provided they had no impact on its floral or faunal populations. The majority of the Aché were to be relocated to land that TNC would purchase elsewhere and title directly to the community. The management plan excluded Guaraní from any access to the land. Instead of being treated as an indigenous people with a right to the reserve, they were integrated into an alternative plan to assist local peasants with agricultural extension work projects.

With the establishment of the reserve, most Aché and Guaraní felt they had lost their primordial right to the forest. They greeted the loss with the same fatalism they had exhibited previously when other large areas were removed from their control. The TNC found that their model was easily imposed on the rural region, creating the reality that fit their ideas. By restricting Guaraní

from this last large parcel of forest, they forced them farther into Paraguayan peasant society. Most Aché, in turn, were forced into a plot where a degree of farming was necessary to augment the meager hunting.

DISCUSSION

It would be easy to blame the unhappy result on the parties involved: the environmentalists' insensitivity, the indigenous communities' naivete; the anthropologists' idealism. The reality is more complex. The negotiations surrounding Mbaracayu suffered from a series of erroneous assumptions and conflicting perceptions. Each party created images of the others based on their differing world views. TNC's ideas of forest peoples, the anthropologists' scientific models, and the indigenous groups' attitudes toward the larger power structure all made it impossible for a meaningful dialogue to take place. Consequently, the plan that was implemented reinforced the inequities of power and resources that characterize other relations between small-scale societies and the larger system.

As instructive as it would be to analyze fully all images used in the discussion, the following discussion focuses on the concept of "natural" that dominates much of our thinking about the environment. Despite the word's ubiquity, the concept of nature remains extremely ambiguous. On one hand, it refers to the inherent qualities of things, as in "the nature of." On the other hand, it refers to the original state, as in "the natural world." In the environmental movement, it has taken on both of these meanings. It signifies the world in its original state, following its own (natural) laws and organized according to the (natural) order of things.

In practice, our ideas of nature are most often defined in relation to their opposites; such as grace, in religion; culture, in anthropology; and history, in philosophy. In the environmental debate, our concept of nature is opposed to civilization. In this romantic vision, for which Rousseau can take much of the credit, human civilization destroys the original ideal order of the world. Where French philosophers found the evils of civilization in the growth of the state, today's evil empire is envisioned in the development of expanding technology, markets, and populations. As humans develop the power and need to dominate nature, they destroy its order, its ecological rationality, and its scientific predictability.

Ecologically Noble Savage

The distinction between nature and civilization helps us understand the position of indigenous peoples in the environmental movement. Rousseau suggested that people's natural humanity was destroyed by civilization. As in the seventeenth century, indigenous peoples today are thought to have the capacity to be *either* natural *or* civilized. Presumably, humans in their original state did not destroy nature but lived in conjunction with it—in ideological and biological harmony with the environment in which they lived. Redford (1990) terms this natural conception of humans the "ecologically noble savage."

Anthropologists' own models of indigenous life also promoted the concept of the ecologically noble savage. Since the nineteenth century, anthropologists have portrayed original human societies as in a state of nature. In the ecological anthropology of the 1960s, this perception developed into models of the idealized ecological relationships of indigenous peoples in biotic communities. Indigenous people are presented as elements in stable ecosystems, their adaptive activity perfectly integrated into the larger environment.

As indigenous people enter into agreements with environmental groups in lowland South America, they are preceived within this dichotomy between "natural" and "civilized." In the planning of Mbaracayu, the Aché—who left the mission, shed superfluous clothing, and lived in the forest—were easily defined as forest savages. In the minds of functionaries in Asunción and Washington, they were perceived to be natural elements of the forest ecosystem. Aché culture was described in biological terms in the forest ecosystem. Aché hunters and gatherers were considered as living in harmony with nature, harvesting enough to survive but not seeking to expand or overexploit the flora or fauna.

This conceptualization found expression in the imagery that TNC used in discussing the Aché and advertising their work to the public. Pictures of Aché in TNC articles emphasized the small, light, forest people as a "Stone Age culture." As one publication put it, "For hundreds of years, the Aché roamed over the dense forest in eastern Paraguay, hunting and gathering with no permanent homes and few possessions" (The Nature Conservancy 1996). A writer for *The Nature Conservancy Magazine* almost fully conflates the categories of Aché and animal:

> "Felipe Jakugi scampers 60 feet up a Lapacho tree that sways like a giant waving hand. Jakugi, an Aché Indian, is at home in the treetops of Mbaracayu forest of northeastern Paraguay. For centuries, the Aché have hunted monkeys and escaped enemies in the forest canopy." (Thigpen 1996)

The anthropologists involved with the project (myself included) made full use of the concept of the noble savage. The indigenous component of the management plan depended more on ethnography and theoretical work in tropical ecology (Posey and Baleé

1989, Treachy 1982) than on the ideas and opinions of the local indigenous communities. It stressed the rationality of traditional indigenous use of natural resources. By arguing that these people would continue to treat the forest as a sacred entity, anthropologists forced the diverse hopes, needs, desires, and plans of all the various individuals of several ethnic groups into one neat political package and then tried to sell it to the environmental agencies.

Ecological Half-Breeds

Few, if any, groups in lowland South America conform to the rigid vision of isolated naturalness. As indigenous people become integrated into the environmental movement, the reality of their attitudes and activities often conflicts with the model of forest people as noble. The vast majority of indigenous peoples enter the market economy for cash crops or wage labor; buy clothes and tools from the world markets; and market natural resources. Once sullied by these activities, they are seen to be forever and utterly changed. Once touched by the market, native peoples are thought to lay down the mantle of noble savage and align with the environmentally destructive society.

Indigenous peoples who fail the litmus test of environmental sensitivity are cast as ignoble savages—ecological half-breeds. Indigenous people in contact with the larger society and international economy are assumed to have acquired only the worst of modern society, having adopted the drives and desires of the poor and destitute. Without considering the long-term implications of these ideas, or their coherence in the face of the actual beliefs of indigenous peoples, researchers assume that these peoples lay down indigenous attitudes en masse as if they were broken tools and pick up new ideas as if they were sharper machetes. These new attitudes are considered destructive and unsustainable in the forest, because forest peoples are believed to be especially vulnerable to irrational desires for commodities. Rousseau, like Marx, pointed to private property as the first step toward both civilization and destruction. Today, we harbor the illusion that exposure to commodities seduces forest peoples into making the most unnecessary demands. With the same smug superiority that is used to describe the sale of Manhattan for a few baubles, we expect indigenous peoples to fall into the commodity trap—machetes and running shorts, followed by unquenchable desires for alcohol, tape players, sunglasses, and a host of other luxuries.

In the case of Mbaracayu, native groups that didn't fit the caricature of the noble savage found no place in TNC's forest. Aché who chose to practice a more complex economy, perhaps integrating swidden cultivation or selling labor for wages, were thought to no longer maintain a "traditional" Aché lifestyle (Thigpen 1996). In fact, as Aché expressed growing discordance over the various options presented by TNC, the population became increasingly divided between those Aché whom TNC considered "real" and those whom they considered somehow less authentic. Those who chose to farm or clear forest were restricted from their native forests and offered a parcel in another region. Only those who subscribed to TNC's model of the Aché were permitted to continue to use Mbaracayu.

TNC considered all Guaraní totally degraded by the larger society. The Guaraní are shifting cultivators; as such, they stepped out of a state of nature and became involved in the market economy, practicing a mix of agriculture, wage labor, and petty commodity production. TNC saw such Guaraní activities as a direct threat to the "virgin" forest that supposedly existed. In many ways, the Guaraní were considered peasants— greedy individuals who acted with unenlightened self-interest, predators who would disrupt the equilibrium of nature and destroy the ecosystem.

THE POLITICAL CONTEXT OF THE DEBATE

The environmental dialogue is locked into a simple dichotomy between the natural and the civilized, despite the many recent advances in theory concerning the complexity of human relations with the environment. Biologists and ecologists are aware that the very concept of "virgin" forest as untouched by human hands ignores millennia of human involvement. Indigenous production has not only been sustained in the forest but is an integral factor in maintaining the "natural" biological diversity (Denevan and Padoch 1987, Hecht and Cockburn 1989). In Mbaracayu, gardening, hunting, and even forestry are important influences on the natural forest ecosystem (Baleé 1992:43). Far from destroying nature, humans have created the natural world.

Anthropologists and ecologists appreciate the resilience of the forest and the tenacity of indigenous cultures, but the new understandings are not readily integrated into the discussion of environmental conservation. Why are misperceptions fostered, and why do simple dichotomies still dominate the dialogue about environmental conservation? An awareness of the political context of dialogue makes it clear that misperceptions are created and reinforced in the contemporary conflict over resources.

Graham and Conklin (1995) point out that the dialogue between indigenous peoples and expanding societies takes place in a frontier area. This "middle ground" is not fully controlled by either the small-scale society or the larger system. Since the time of the Jesuits, the Paraguayan government in Asunción has held tenuous control over its rural area. As recently as the 1880s, Paraguay lost over a third of its territory to Brazil. *Latifundios* were organized to take responsibility for protecting Paraguayan sovereignty. Today, the disassembly of these plantations creates a power vacuum. Brazilian ranchers, Japanese lumber firms, and Paraguayan soybean farmers struggle for remnants of control, and no clear state official has the power to enforce the law.

The dialogue between environmental groups and indigenous peoples is a part of this larger conflict over the resources. As environmental groups move to protect the few remaining stands of forests, they find that they are in conflict not only with developers but also with the claims of primordial rights by indigenous residents. Indigenous groups, on the other hand, find that a new type of plantation owner (*latifundista*) has arrived on the scene. The need to defend their ancestral land demands that they negotiate with this new "developer"—the environmental protection group.

The terms that are chosen in the dialogue over forest rights fall prey to the power relations of the larger system. Worldwide networks of information, international political connections, and a war chest of capital empower environmental groups in the international scramble for land. TNC, World Wildlife Fund, and the Fund for Animals have the economic and political weapons to confront some of the most powerful corporations and many national governments. They hold a vast amount of institutional power in their relations with indigenous groups—relations that reinforce and are reinforced by the terms of the dialogue. By defining indigenous people with respect to a yardstick of savagery, environmental groups can effectively exclude all those who do not conform to their ideal.

Graham and Conklin also point out that it is politically dangerous for environmental groups to ignore indigenous groups. Indians' presence can develop into a political problem if the conflict over resources moves into the national or international consciousness. Environmental groups are better served by defusing confrontation. On the other hand, the involvement of indigenous peoples, even a contentious and divided group such as the Aché, can be a public relations asset. This was clear in the case of Mbaracayu, where TNC was careful to publicize its defense of the Aché along with its program for protecting the environment (The Nature Conservancy 1996).

Indigenous groups have not had the opportunity to establish their own definitions of themselves or their world in the environmental debate. Despite the attempts of anthropologists and Paraguayans to inform

the local residents of TNC and its aims, most indigenous people garnered little understanding of the actors
involved or the complex negotiations that were taking
place over their land. They had little idea of what to
expect, alternating between complete belief that they
would get to use the land exclusively and a lack of confidence that anything would happen.

This is not to say they were confused. In the case
of Mbaracayu, although indigenous groups had only
a hazy idea of TNC, its purpose, or its programs, they
had a very clear idea of the structure of power in the
struggle for the land of Mbaracayu. Their high hopes
and cynicism were born of the long history of relationships with *latifundistas*. From the indigenous
standpoint, the environmental agency was virtually
indistinguishable from previous ranchers and multinational corporations.

As alliances are formed between indigenous
groups and environmental agencies, we are called
upon to facilitate the dialogue concerning reserves
and indigenous peoples. Anthropologists are brought
into the debate because of their distinct knowledge
and perspective. They not only offer accurate information about the people and places involved but are also
in the privileged position of seeing the conflict from
two perspectives. These abilities, however, force
anthropologists into the conflicting roles of scientist
and political actor. Although knowledge gives anthropologists a responsibility to take action, it offers little
power in dictating the terms of the debate or deciding
the outcome.

Thus it was TNC, not the Aché, Guaraní, or
anthropologists, who defined the terms of the debate
over indigenous rights to Mbaracayu in the national
and international sphere. By defining some indigenous
people as threats to the natural environment, TNC
could rally support for the reserve and the relocation
of those indigenous residents. Those who chose to stay
needed to abide by the strictures laid down by the
agency. On the other hand, neither the Aché nor the
Guaraní had the opportunity either to portray themselves in all the complexities of their indigenous identity or to declaim TNC as a *latifundista* that was taking
indigenous land for its own purposes.

In conclusion, environmental groups are integrating indigenous peoples into the day-to-day management of conservation areas. Despite their common
ground, agencies and indigenous groups cannot escape
confrontation. Even when their short-term objectives
are similar, their respective long-term goals are often
very different. Whereas agencies seek to protect the
forests in perpetuity and seek indigenous peoples' assistance in the endeavor, indigenous groups are fundamentally concerned with their own survival and see
the forests as their primary resource in that struggle.

As large areas of the forest are converted to pasture
and field, the two groups remain in contention for the
remaining undisturbed areas.

NOTE

1. This group has been extensively studied by anthropologists and provided data to further a variety of cultural
   ecological models (e.g., Hill and Hurtado 1995).

REFERENCES

AIP/Misión (Asociación Indígena del Paraguay and Misión
de Amistad). 1977. *Población y tierras indígenas en la región
oriental de la República del Paraguay*. Manuscript.

Arens, Richard. 1976. *Genocide in Paraguay*. Philadelphia:
Temple University Press.

Baleé, William. 1992. People of the fallow. In *Conservation of
Neotropical Forests: Working from Traditional Resource Use*,
pp. 35–58, ed. K. Redford and C. Padoch. New York:
Columbia.

Clay, Jason. 1988. *Indigenous Peoples and Tropical Forests:
Models for Land Use and Management from Latin America*.
Cambridge, MA: Cultural Survival.

Denevan, William, and Christine Padoch. 1987. Swidden-
fallow agroforestry in the Peruvian Amazon. *Advances in
Economic Botany* Number 5. New York: New York Botanical
Gardens.

Graham, Laura, and Beth Conklin. 1995. The shifting middle
ground: Amazonian Indians and eco-politics. *American
Anthropologist* 97(4):695–710.

Hanratty, Dennis, and Sandra Meditz, eds. 1990. *Paraguay: A
Country Study*. Washington, DC: U.S. Government Printing Office.

Hecht, Susanna, and Andrew Cockburn. 1989. *The Fate of the
Forest*. New York: Verso.

Hill, Kim, and A. Magdalena Hurtado. 1995. *Aché Life History: The Ecology and Demography of a Foraging People*.
New York: Aldine de Gruyter.

Laino, Domingo. 1997. *Paraguay: Fronteras y penetracion
brasileña*. Asunción: Ediciones Cerro Cora.

The Nature Conservancy. 1996. Profiles: Maracayu. *The
Nature Conservancy*. Nov./Dec.

Padoch, Christine et al. 1985. Amazonian agroforestry: A
market oriented system in Peru. *Agroforestry Systems*
3(1):47–58.

Parquet, Reinerio. 1985. *Las Empresas Transnacionales en la
economia del Paraguay*. Unpublished manuscript prepared for Unidad Conjunta CEPAL/CET: Buenos Aires.

Posey, Darrell, and William Baleé. 1989. Resource management in Amazonia. *Advances in Economic Botany* Number
7. New York: New York Botanical Gardens.

Redford, Kent. 1990. The ecologically noble savage. *Orion Nature Quarterly* 9(3):25–29.

Reed, Richard. 1997. *Forest Dwellers, Forest Protectors: Indigenous Models for International Development.* Boston: Allyn and Bacon.

Renshaw, John, and Richard Reed. 1989. *Analysis socioeconomico y cultural de las poblaciones asentadas in el area de influencia del la reserva Mbaracayu.* Unpublished manuscript prepared for Fundación Moises Bertoni: Asunción.

Thigpen, Jaunita. 1996. Help wanted: Traditional wisdom required. *The Nature Conservancy.* Nov./Dec.

Treachy, Jonathon. 1982. Bora Indian agroforestry: An alternate to deforestation. *Cultural Survival Quarterly* 6(2):16–17.

14

Race Without Color

Jared Diamond

Looking at the title of this selection, you should ask yourself two questions. First, what is a reading about race doing in a cultural anthropology book? After all, it would seem that race is obviously a biological question. Second, what could the author possibly mean by "race without color"? Doesn't that sound like an oxymoron?

An important aspect of anthropological thinking is examining ideas, beliefs, and values within their own cultural context. Our own cultural ideas and concepts, including scientific ones, are grist for the anthropological mill because they are best understood within a larger cultural framework. Sometimes cultural anthropologists focus on a single cultural concept and take it apart, demonstrating its historical roots and its relation to other social beliefs. In postmodern parlance, this kind of intensive analysis can be called "deconstructing" a concept.

In this selection, a well-known natural scientist "deconstructs" the biological concept of race. Although the term *race* seems to have some use in the description of population variation in birds and in creating a taxonomy, the concept doesn't work very well for understanding human variation. In fact, from a biological standpoint, the concept of race based on skin color is scientifically useless. As the reading demonstrates, there are a lot of different ways to categorize human biological diversity, but these variations are independent from one another so that there is more variation within racial categories than between them. By deconstructing race, we see that it is a cultural category, not a biological one.

On the other hand, race is indeed an important historical and political concept—as a cultural construction that functions as a folk-biological rationalization for enforcing social inequalities. We decided to include this reading within this cultural anthropology book to emphasize the fact that race is a cultural invention. Race is not useful for understanding human biological diversity; it is essentially meaningless, like an oxymoron.

As you read this selection, ask yourself the following questions:

- Why does skin color seem to be such an obvious and commonsensical way to make distinctions among people?
- How might it be acceptable to use the concept of race for talking about birds, but not humans?
- What does it mean that taxonomists are "lumpers" and "splitters"?
- How is our understanding of most biological variations—like resistance to malaria or adults' ability to digest milk—not aided by the concept of race?
- If racial classifications are cultural constructions, what does the author think is the purpose of these arbitrary classifications?

The following terms discussed in this selection are included in the Glossary at the back of the book:

lactose intolerance   sickle-cell anemia
race   species

Basing race on body chemistry makes no more sense than basing race on appearance—but at least you get to move the membership around.

Science often violates simple common sense. Our eyes tell us that the Earth is flat, that the sun revolves around the Earth, and that we humans are not animals. But we now ignore that evidence of our senses. We

have learned that our planet is in fact round and revolves around the sun, and that humans are slightly modified chimpanzees. The reality of human races is another commonsense "truth" destined to follow the flat Earth into oblivion. The commonsense view of races goes somewhat as follows. All native Swedes differ from all native Nigerians in appearance: there is no Swede whom you would mistake for a Nigerian, and vice versa. Swedes have lighter skin than Nigerians do. They also generally have blond or light brown hair, while Nigerians have very dark hair. Nigerians usually have more tightly coiled hair than Swedes do, dark eyes as opposed to eyes that are blue or gray, and fuller lips and broader noses.

In addition, other Europeans look much more like Swedes than like Nigerians, while other peoples of sub-Saharan Africa—except perhaps the Khoisan peoples of southern Africa—look much more like Nigerians than like Swedes. Yes, skin color does get darker in Europe toward the Mediterranean, but it is still lighter than the skin of sub-Saharan Africans. In Europe, very dark or curly hair becomes more common outside Scandinavia, but European hair is still not as tightly coiled as in Africa. Since it's easy then to distinguish almost any native European from any native sub-Saharan African, we recognize Europeans and sub-Saharan Africans as distinct races, which we name for their skin colors: whites and blacks, respectively.

What could be more objective?

As it turns out, this seemingly unassailable reasoning is not objective. There are many different, equally valid procedures for defining races, and those different procedures yield very different classifications. One such procedure would group Italians and Greeks with most African blacks. It would classify Xhosas—the South African "black" group to which President Nelson Mandela belongs—with Swedes rather than Nigerians. Another equally valid procedure would place Swedes with Fulani (a Nigerian "black" group) and not with Italians who would again be grouped with most other African blacks. Still another procedure would keep Swedes and Italians separate from all African blacks but would throw the Swedes and Italians into the same race as New Guineans and American Indians. Faced with such differing classifications, many anthropologists today conclude that one cannot recognize any human races at all.

If we were just arguing about races of nonhuman animals, essentially the same uncertainties of classification would arise. But the debates would remain polite and would never attract attention outside the halls of academia. Classification of humans is different "only" in that it shapes our views of other peoples, fosters our subconscious differentiation between "us" and "them," and is invoked to justify political and socioeconomic discrimination. On this basis, many anthropologists therefore argue that even if one *could* classify humans into races, one should not.

To understand how such uncertainties in classification arise let's steer clear of humans for a moment and instead focus on warblers and lions, about which we can easily remain dispassionate. Biologists begin by classifying living creatures into species. A species is a group of populations whose individual members would, if given the opportunity, interbreed with individuals of other populations of that group. But they would not interbreed with individuals of other species that are similarly defined. Thus all human populations, no matter how different they look belong to the same species because they do interbreed and have interbred whenever they have encountered each other. Gorillas and humans, however, belong to two different species because—to the best of our knowledge—they have never interbred despite their coexisting in close proximity for millions of years.

We know that different populations classified together in the human species are visibly different. The same proves true for most other animal and plant species as well, whenever biologists look carefully. For example, consider one of the most familiar species of bird in North America, the yellow-rumped warbler. Breeding males of eastern and western North America can be distinguished at a glance by their throat color, white in the east, yellow in the west. Hence they are classified into two different races, or subspecies (alternative words with identical meanings), termed the myrtle and Audubon races, respectively. The white-throated eastern birds differ from the yellow-throated western birds in other characteristics as well, such as in voice and habitat preference. But where the two races meet, in western Canada, white-throated birds do indeed interbreed with yellow-throated birds. That's why we consider myrtle warblers and Audubon warblers as races of the same species rather than different species.

Racial classification of these birds is easy. Throat color, voice and habitat preference all vary geographically in yellow-rumped warblers, but the variation of those three traits is "concordant"—that is, voice differences or habitat differences lead to the same racial classification as differences in throat color because the same populations that differ in throat color also differ in voice and habitat.

Racial classification of many other species, though, presents problems of concordance. For instance, a Pacific island bird species called the golden whistler varies from one island to the next. Some populations consist of big birds, some of small birds; some have black-winged males, others green-winged males; some have yellow-breasted females, others gray-breasted females; many other characteristics vary as well. But, unfortunately for humans like me who study these birds, those characteristics don't vary concordantly. Islands with green-winged males can have either yellow-breasted or gray-breasted females, and green-winged males are big on some islands but small on other islands. As a result if you classified golden whistlers into races based on single traits, you would set entirely different classifications depending on which trait you chose.

Classification of these birds also presents problems of "hierarchy." Some of the golden whistler races recognized by ornithologists are wildly different from all the other races, but some are very similar to one another.

They can therefore be grouped into a hierarchy of distinctness. You start by establishing the most distinct population as a race separate from all other populations. You then separate the most distinct of the remaining populations. You continue by grouping similar populations, and separating distinct populations or groups of populations as races or groups of races. The problem is that the extent to which you continue the racial classification is arbitrary, and it's a decision about which taxonomists disagree passionately. Some taxonomists, the "splitters," like to recognize many different races, partly for the egotistical motive of getting credit for having named a race. Other taxonomists, the "lumpers," prefer to recognize few races. Which type of taxonomist you are is a matter of personal preference.

How does that variability of traits by which we classify races come about in the first place? Some traits vary because of natural selection: that is, one form of the trait is advantageous for survival in one area, another form in a different area. For example, northern hares and weasels develop white fur in the winter, but southern ones retain brown fur year-round. The white winter fur is selected in the north for camouflage against the snow, while any animal unfortunate enough to turn white in the snowless southern states would stand out from afar against the brown ground and would be picked off by predators.

Other traits vary geographically because of sexual selection, meaning that those traits serve as arbitrary signals by which individuals of one sex attract mates of the opposite sex while intimidating rivals. Adult male lions, for instance, have a mane, but lionesses and young males don't. The adult male's mane signals to lionesses that he is sexually mature, and signals to young male rivals that he is a dangerous and experienced adversary. The length and color of a lion's mane vary among populations, being shorter and blacker in Indian lions than in African lions. Indian lions and lionesses evidently find short black manes sexy or intimidating; African lions don't.

Finally, some geographically variable traits have no known effect on survival and are invisible to rivals and to prospective sex partners. They merely reflect mutations that happened to arise and spread in one area. They could equally well have arisen and spread elsewhere—they just didn't.

RACE BY RESISTANCE

Traditionally we divide ourselves into races by the twin criteria of geographic location and visible physical characteristics. But we could make an equally reasonable and arbitrary division by the presence or absence of a gene, such as the sickle-cell gene, that confers resistance to malaria. By this reckoning, we'd place Yemenites, Greeks, New Guineans, Thai, and Dinkas in one "race," Norwegians and several black African peoples in another.

Nothing that I've said about geographic variation in animals is likely to get me branded a racist. We don't attribute higher IQ or social status to black-winged whistlers than to green-winged whistlers. But now let's consider geographic variation in humans. We'll start with invisible traits, about which it's easy to remain dispassionate.

Many geographically variable human traits evolved by natural selection to adapt humans to particular climates or environments—just as the winter color of a hare or weasel did. Good examples are the mutations that people in tropical parts of the Old World evolved to help them survive malaria, the leading infectious disease of the old-world tropics. One such mutation is the sickle-cell gene, so-called because the red blood cells of people with that mutation tend to assume a sickle shape. People bearing the gene are more resistant to malaria than people without it. Not surprisingly, the gene is absent from northern Europe, where malaria is nonexistent, but it's common in tropical Africa, where malaria is widespread. Up to 40 percent of Africans in such areas carry the sickle-cell gene. It's also common in the malaria-ridden Arabian Peninsula and southern India, and rare or absent in the southernmost parts of South Africa, among the Xhosas who live mostly beyond the tropical geographic range of malaria.

The geographic range of human malaria is much wider than the range of the sickle-cell gene. As it happens, other antimalarial genes take over the protective function of the sickle-cell gene in malarial Southeast Asia and New Guinea and in Italy, Greece, and other warm parts of the Mediterranean basin. Thus human races, if defined by antimalarial genes, would be very different from human races as traditionally defined by traits such as skin color. As classified by antimalarial genes (or their absence), Swedes are grouped with Xhosas but not with Italians or Greeks. Most other peoples usually viewed as African blacks are grouped with Arabia's "whites" and are kept separate from the "black" Xhosas.

RACE BY DIGESTION

We could define a race by any geographically variable trait—for example, the retention in adulthood of the enzyme lactase, which allows us to digest milk. Using this as our divisive criterion, we can place northern and central Europeans with Arabians and such West African peoples as the Fulani; in a "lactase-negative race," we can group most other African blacks with east Asians, American Indians, southern Europeans, and Australian aborigines.

Antimalarial genes exemplify the many features of our body chemistry that vary geographically under the influence of natural selection. Another such feature is the enzyme lactase, which enables us to digest the milk-sugar lactose. Infant humans, like infants of almost all other mammal species, possess lactase and drink milk. Until about 6,000 years ago most humans, like all other mammal species, lost the lactase enzyme on reaching the age of weaning. The obvious reason is that it was unnecessary—no human or other mammal drank milk as an adult. Beginning around 4000 B.C., however, fresh milk obtained from domestic mammals became a major food for adults of a few human populations. Natural selection caused individuals in these populations to retain lactase into adulthood. Among such peoples are northern and central Europeans, Arabians, north Indians, and several milk-drinking black African peoples, such as the Fulani of West Africa. Adult lactase is much less common in southern European populations and in most other African black populations, as well as in all populations of east Asians, aboriginal Australians, and American Indians.

Once again races defined by body chemistry don't match races defined by skin color. Swedes belong with Fulani in the "lactase-positive race," while most African "blacks," Japanese, and American Indians belong in the "lactase-negative race."

Not all the effects of natural selection are as invisible as lactase and sickle cells. Environmental pressures have also produced more noticeable differences among peoples, particularly in body shapes. Among the tallest and most long-limbed peoples in the world are the Nilotic peoples, such as the Dinkas, who live in the hot, dry areas of East Africa. At the opposite extreme in body shape are the Inuit, or Eskimo, who have compact bodies and relatively short arms and legs. The reasons have to do with heat loss. The greater the surface area of a warm body, the more body heat that's lost, since heat loss is directly proportional to surface area. For people of a given weight, a long-limbed, tall shape maximizes surface area, while a compact, short-limbed shape minimizes it. Dinkas and Inuit have opposite problems of heat balance: the former usually need desperately to get rid of body heat, while the latter need desperately to conserve it. Thus natural selection molded their body shapes oppositely, based on their contrasting climates.

(In modern times, such considerations of body shape have become important to athletic performance as well as to heat loss. Tall basketball players, for example, have an obvious advantage over short ones, and slender, long-limbed tall players have an advantage over stout, short-limbed tall players. In the United States, it's a familiar observation that African Americans are disproportionately represented among professional basketball players. Of course, a contributing reason has

to do with their lack of socioeconomic opportunities. But part of the reason probably has to do with the prevalent body shapes of some black African groups as well. However, this example also illustrates the dangers in facile racial stereotyping. One can't make the sweeping generalization that "whites can't jump," or that "blacks' anatomy makes them better basketball players." Only certain African peoples are notably tall and long-limbed; even those exceptional peoples are tall and long-limbed only on the average and vary individually.)

Other visible traits that vary geographically among humans evolved by means of sexual selection. We all know that we find some individuals of the opposite sex more attractive than other individuals. We also know that in sizing up sex appeal, we pay more attention to certain parts of a prospective sex partner's body than to other parts. Men tend to be inordinately interested in women's breasts and much less concerned with women's toenails. Women, in turn, tend to be turned on by the shape of a man's buttocks or the details of a man's beard and body hair, if any, but not by the size of his feet.

But all those determinants of sex appeal vary geographically. Khoisan and Andaman Island women tend to have much larger buttocks than most other women. Nipple color and breast shape and size also vary geographically among women. European men are rather hairy by world standards, while Southeast Asian men tend to have very sparse beards and body hair.

What's the function of these traits that differ so markedly between men and women? They certainly don't aid survival: it's not the case that orange nipples help Khoisan women escape lions, while darker nipples help European women survive cold winters. Instead, these varying traits play a crucial role in sexual selection. Women with very large buttocks are a turn-on, or at least acceptable, to Khoisan and Andaman men but look freakish to many men from other parts of the world. Bearded and hairy men readily find mates in Europe but fare worse in Southeast Asia. The geographic variation of these traits, however, is as arbitrary as the geographic variation in the color of a lion's mane.

RACE BY FINGERPRINTS

Probably the most trivial division of humans we could manage would be based on fingerprint patterns. As it turns out, the prevalance of certain basic features varies predictably among peoples: in the "Loops" race we could group together most Europeans, black Africans, and east Asians. Among the "Whorls" we could place Mongolians and Australian aborigines. Finally, in an "Arches" race, we could group Khoisans and some central Europeans.

Arches   Loops   Whorls

There is a third possible explanation for the function of geographically variable human traits, besides survival or sexual selection—namely, no function at all. A good example is provided by fingerprints, whose complex pattern of arches, loops, and whorls is determined genetically. Fingerprints also vary geographically: for example, Europeans' fingerprints tend to have many loops, while aboriginal Australians' fingerprints tend to have many whorls.

If we classify human populations by their fingerprints, most Europeans and black Africans would sort out together in one race, Jews and some Indonesians in another, and aboriginal Australians in still another. But those geographic variations in fingerprint patterns possess no known function whatsoever. They play no role in survival: whorls aren't especially suitable for grabbing kangaroos, nor do loops help bar mitzvah candidates hold on to the pointer for the Torah. They also play no role in sexual selection: while you've undoubtedly noticed whether your mate is bearded or has brown nipples, you surely haven't the faintest idea whether his or her fingerprints have more loops than whorls. Instead it's purely a matter of chance that whorls became common in aboriginal Australians, and loops among Jews. Our rhesus factor blood groups and numerous other human traits fall into the same category of genetic characteristics whose geographic variation serves no function.

RACE BY GENES

One method that seems to offer a way out of arbitrariness is to classify people's degree of genetic distinctness. By this standard the Khoisans of southern Africa would be in a race by themselves. African blacks would form several other distinct races. All the rest of the world's peoples—Norwegians, Navajo, Greeks, Japanese, Australian aborigines, and so on—would, despite their greatly differing external appearance, belong to a single race.

You've probably been wondering when I was going to get back to skin color, eye color, and hair color and form. After all, those are the traits by which all of us members of the lay public, as well as traditional anthropologists, classify races. Does geographic variation in those traits function in survival, in sexual selection, or in nothing?

The usual view is that skin color varies geographically to enhance survival. Supposedly, people in sunny, tropical climates around the world have generally dark skin, which is supposedly analogous to the temporary skin darkening of European whites in the summer. The supposed function of dark skin in sunny climates is for protection against skin cancer. Variations in eye color and hair form and color are also supposed to enhance survival under particular conditions, though no one has ever proposed a plausible hypothesis for how those variations might actually enhance survival.

Alas, the evidence for natural selection of skin color dissolves under scrutiny. Among tropical peoples, anthropologists love to stress the dark skins of African blacks, people of the southern Indian peninsula, and New Guineans and love to forget the pale skins of Amazonian Indians and Southeast Asians living at the same latitudes. To wriggle out of those paradoxes, anthropologists then plead the excuse that Amazonian Indians and Southeast Asians may not have been living in their present locations long enough to evolve dark skins. However, the ancestors of fair-skinned Swedes arrived even more recently in Scandinavia, and aboriginal Tasmanians were black-skinned despite their ancestors' having lived for at least the last 10,000 years at the latitude of Vladivostok.

Besides, when one takes into account cloud cover, peoples of equatorial West Africa and the New Guinea mountains actually receive no more ultraviolet radiation or hours of sunshine each year than do the Swiss. Compared with infectious diseases and other selective agents, skin cancer has been utterly trivial as a cause of death in human history, even for modern white settlers in the tropics. This objection is so obvious to believers in natural selection of skin color that they have proposed at least seven other supposed survival functions of skin color, without reaching agreement. Those other supposed functions include protection against rickets, frostbite, folic acid deficiency, beryllium poisoning, overheating, and overcooling. The diversity of these contradictory theories makes clear how far we are from understanding the survival value (if any) of skin color.

It wouldn't surprise me if dark skins do eventually prove to offer some advantage in tropical climates, but I expect the advantage to turn out to be a slight one that is easily overridden. But there's an overwhelming importance to skin, eye, and hair color that is obvious to all of us—sexual selection. Before we can reach a condition of intimacy permitting us to assess the beauty of a prospective sex partner's hidden physical attractions, we first have to pass muster for skin, eyes, and hair.

We all know how those highly visible "beauty traits" guide our choice of sex partners. Even the briefest personal ad in a newspaper mentions the advertiser's skin color, and the color of skin that he or she seeks in a partner. Skin color, of course, is also of overwhelming importance in our social prejudices. If you're a black African American trying to raise your children in white U.S. society, rickets and overheating are the least of the problems that might be solved by your skin color. Eye color and hair form and color, while not so overwhelmingly important as skin color, also play an obvious role in our sexual and social preferences. Just ask yourself why hair dyes, hair curlers, and hair straighteners enjoy such wide sales. You can bet that it's not to improve our chances of surviving grizzly bear attacks and other risks endemic to the North American continent.

Nearly 125 years ago Charles Darwin himself, the discoverer of natural selection, dismissed its role as an explanation of geographic variation in human beauty traits. Everything that we have learned since then only reinforces Darwin's view.

We can now return to our original questions: Are human racial classifications that are based on different traits concordant with one another? What is the hierarchical relation among recognized races? What is the function of racially variable traits? What, really, are the traditional human races?

Regarding concordance, we *could* have classified races based on any number of geographically variable traits. The resulting classifications would not be at all concordant. Depending on whether we classified ourselves by antimalarial genes, lactase, fingerprints, or skin color, we could place Swedes in the same race as either Xhosas, Fulani, the Ainu of Japan, or Italians.

Regarding hierarchy, traditional classifications that emphasize skin color face unresolvable ambiguities. Anthropology textbooks often recognize five major races:

"whites," "African blacks," "Mongoloids," "aboriginal Australians," and "Khoisans," each in turn divided into various numbers of sub-races. But there is no agreement on the number and delineation of the sub-races, or even of the major races. Are all five of the major races equally distinctive? Are Nigerians really less different from Xhosas than aboriginal Australians are from both? Should we recognize 3 or 15 sub-races of Mongoloids? These questions have remained unresolved because skin color and other traditional racial criteria are difficult to formulate mathematically.

A method that could in principle overcome these problems is to base racial classification on a combination of as many geographically variable genes as possible. Within the past decade, some biologists have shown renewed interest in developing a hierarchical classification of human populations—hierarchical not in the sense that it identifies superior and inferior races but in the sense of grouping and separating populations based on mathematical measures of genetic distinctness. While the biologists still haven't reached agreement, some of their studies suggest that human genetic diversity may be greatest in Africa. If so, the primary races of humanity may consist of several African races, plus one race to encompass all peoples of all other continents. Swedes, New Guineans, Japanese, and Navajo would then belong to the same primary race; the Khoisans of southern Africa would constitute another primary race by themselves; and African "blacks" and Pygmies would be divided among several other primary races.

As regards the function of all those traits that are useful for classifying human races, some serve to enhance survival, some to enhance sexual selection, while some serve no function at all. The traits we traditionally use are ones subject to sexual selection, which is not really surprising. These traits are not only visible at a distance but also highly variable; that's why they became the ones used throughout recorded history to make quick judgments about people. Racial classification didn't come from science but from the body's signals for differentiating attractive from unattractive sex partners, and for differentiating friend from foe.

Such snap judgments didn't threaten our existence back when people were armed only with spears and surrounded by others who looked mostly like themselves. In the modern world, though, we are armed with guns and plutonium, and we live our lives surrounded by people who are much more varied in appearance. The last thing we need now is to continue codifying all those different appearances into an arbitrary system of racial classification.

15

Official Statement on "Race"

American Anthropological Association

Race is an incredibly important social and political issue in the United States. News items of national interest—from the Los Angeles riots after the Rodney King verdict to the trial of O. J. Simpson—often center on sensitive cultural issues. Questions about the inclusion of mixed race and ethnicity categories for the U.S. Census for the year 2000 have been hotly debated. The publication of Herrnstein and Murray's *The Bell Curve: Intelligence and Class Structure in American Life* raised a remarkable public debate; despite terrible reviews and scientific criticism, the book sold very well. President Clinton identified the need for a national dialogue about race; such a dialogue may well be an uncomfortable conversation.

As we learned in the last selection, race is an out-of-date and useless concept from the viewpoint of understanding and explaining human biological diversity. Although many biological anthropologists have privately come to this conclusion, the public holds on to the belief that race refers to real biological categories. At the same time, discrimination based on skin color—at times overt and at other times subtle and invidious—continues to exist in the United States.

The American Anthropological Association (AAA) is the oldest and largest professional association for all four fields of anthropology as well as applied anthropology. As a professional association, the AAA has drafted a clear statement about the biology and politics of race. The statement is clear and informational.

As you read this selection, ask yourself the following questions:

- Why would members of a professional academic association think that they need to have an official statement about race?
- Why is the history of a concept like race relevant to understanding its current scientific usefulness?
- What is the relationship between racial categorizations and the distribution of privilege, power, and wealth?
- Why does race distort and prejudge our ideas about human differences and group behavior?

The following terms discussed in this selection are included in the Glossary at the back of the book:

> *biophysical diversity*
> *culture*
> *race*

Since the mid-20th century there has been a major transformation in thinking about "race" in the academic world, especially in the fields of anthropology and biology. For several hundred years before this time, both scholars and the public had been conditioned to viewing purported "races" as natural, distinct and exclusive divisions among human populations based on visible physical differences. However, with the vast expansion of scientific knowledge in this century, it is clear that human populations are not unambiguous, clearly demarcated, biologically distinct groups. As a result, we conclude that the concept of "race" has no validity as a biological category in the human species. Because it homogenizes widely varying individuals into limited categories, it impedes research and understanding of the true nature of human biological variations.

The following statement summarizes the findings and conclusions of experts on human biophysical variation. For a more full and extensive exploration of this topic, see the statement published by the American Association of Physical Anthropologists in 1996 (AJPA 101:569–570).

The human species is highly diverse, with individuals and populations varying in observable traits such as body size and shape, skin color, hair texture, facial features and certain characteristics of the skeletal structure. Populations also differ in their percentage frequencies of the blood types (A, B, AB and O) and other

Reprinted by permission of the American Anthropological Association from *Anthropology Newsletter* 38:6, September 1997.

known genetic traits. This variation is a product of evolutionary forces operating on human groups as they have adapted to different environments over thousands of years. Some biogenetic variation results from migration and changes within isolated groups. Yet all human groups are capable of interbreeding with others and producing viable and fertile offspring. Throughout history, whenever different groups have come into contact, they have interbred. As a result, all populations share many features with other, neighboring groups.

Variations in any given trait tend to occur gradually rather than abruptly over geographic areas. And because physical traits vary independently of one another, knowing the frequencies of one trait does not predict the presence or frequencies of others. These facts render any attempt to establish lines of division among biological populations both arbitrary and subjective. Genetically there are greater differences among individuals within large geographic populations than the average differences between them. Because of our complex genetic structure, no human groups can be seen as homogeneous or "pure."

Biophysical diversity has no inherent social meaning except what we humans confer upon it. The concept of "race" is in reality a product of that process. "Race" is a set of culturally created attitudes toward, and beliefs about, human differences developed following widespread exploration and colonization by Western European powers since the 16th century. In the North American colonies, European settlers conquered an indigenous population and brought in as slaves alien peoples from Africa. By the end of the 18th century a rising antislavery movement, produced by liberal and humanistic forces mostly in Europe, compelled slave owners to find new defenses for preserving slavery. "Race" was invented as a social mechanism to justify the retention of slavery. "Race" ideology magnified differences among these populations, established a rigid hierarchy of socially exclusive categories, underscored and bolstered unequal rank and status differences and provided the rationalization that such differences were natural or God-given. The different physical traits became markers or symbols of status differences.

As they were constructing this society, white Americans fabricated the cultural/behavioral characteristics associated with each "race," linking superior traits to Europeans and negative and inferior ones to blacks and Indians. Thus arbitrary beliefs about the different peoples were institutionalized and deeply embedded in American thought. Ultimately "race" as an ideology about human differences was reified and subsequently spread to other areas of the world. It became a mechanism for dividing and ranking people, used by colonial powers everywhere. But it was not limited to the colonial situation; it was employed by Europeans to rank each other and, during World War II, became the motive for the unspeakable brutalities of the Holocaust.

"Race" evolved as a worldview, a body of prejudgments that distorts our ideas about human differences and group behavior. Such beliefs constitute myths about the diversity in the human species and about the abilities and behavior of people homogenized into "racial" categories. The myths fused behavior and physical features together in the public mind, impeding our comprehension of both biology and culture and implying that both are genetically determined. Racial myths bear no relationship to the reality of human capabilities or behavior. Scientists have found that reliance on such folk beliefs about human differences in research has led to countless errors.

At the end of the 20th century, we now understand that human behavior is learned, conditioned into infants beginning at birth and always subject to modification and change. No human is born with built-in culture traits or language. Our temperaments, dispositions and personalities, regardless of genetic propensities, are developed within sets of meanings and values that we call "culture." Studies of infant and early childhood learning and behavior attest to the reality of our cultures in forming who we are.

It is a basic tenet of anthropological knowledge that all normal human beings have the capacity to learn any cultural behavior. In the modern world we humans are constantly experiencing new cultural meanings and are, thus, capable of transforming ourselves. The American experience with immigrants from hundreds of different language and cultural backgrounds who have acquired some variation of American culture traits and behavior is the clearest evidence of this fact. We are all becoming more multicultural as we have access to both material culture and ideas that disseminate around the world.

How people have been accepted and treated within the context of their society and culture has a direct impact on how they perform within that society. The "racial" worldview was invented to assign some groups to perpetual low status while others were permitted access to privilege, power and wealth. The tragedy is that it succeeded all too well in constructing unequal populations. Given what we know about the capacity of normal humans to achieve and function within any culture, we conclude that present-day inequalities between human groups are not consequences of their biological inheritance; rather, these inequalities are products of historical and contemporary social, economic, educational and political circumstances.

16

White Privilege

Unpacking the Invisible Knapsack

Peggy McIntosh

Although many major events of the civil rights movement happened before present-day college students were born, most students have probably seen pictures, films, or videos of police blocking African Americans from entering white schools and signs prohibiting African Americans from sitting at lunch counters or drinking from the same water fountains as whites. Though the signs indicating "for whites only" are fading from the American memory, the legacy of racism certainly remains with us today. In the absence of Cross burnings and other obvious signs of racism, however, there is a tendency for whites to assume that racism is a thing of the past, that inequality no longer plagues our nation.

The frustration in the dialogue about racism in the United States has many of the characteristics of cross-cultural miscommunication. People use the same words but with different meanings. They examine the same social situations and come away with quite different interpretations. The analogy in linguistics is that individuals from one language group may not even hear the phonemes used in a different language. In other words, individuals from one group simply cannot see the world through the eyes of the other. Throughout this book you will be reading about other cultures and trying to understand their lifeways—to see the world as they do. It is often more difficult to set aside our commonsense interpretation of the familiar world that surrounds us each day than to freshly examine a novel situation. We must strive to suspend our judgment and read through this selection with an anthropological imagination.

As you read this selection, ask yourself the following questions:

- What does the author mean by "an invisible package of unearned assets"? How might this relate to the concept of ascribed status?

- Does the author's use of the term *oppressor* imply intentionality, or is this oppression a result of a culture and social organization that is seldom consciously recognized?

- Can you add to the author's list of twenty-six situations that confer privilege?

- Is white privilege a serious threat to equality, or is it merely an inconvenience? What should be done to achieve the U.S. ideal of social equality? Whose responsibility is it to change the culture if it is harmful?

The following terms discussed in this selection are included in the Glossary at the back of the book:

> *hierarchy*
> *meritocracy*
> *privilege*

Through work to bring materials from Women's Studies into the rest of the curriculum, I have often noticed men's unwillingness to grant that they are overprivileged even though they may grant that women are disadvantaged. They may say they will work to improve women's status, in the society, the university, or the curriculum, but they can't or won't support the idea of lessening men's. Denials which amount to taboos surround the subject of advantages which men gain from women's disadvantages. These denials protect male privilege from being fully acknowledged, lessened or ended.

Thinking through unacknowledged male privilege as a phenomenon, I realized that since hierarchies in our society are interlocking, there was most likely a phenomenon of white privilege which was similarly denied and protected. As a white person, I realized I had been taught about racism as something which puts others at a disadvantage, but had been taught not to see one of its corollary aspects, white privilege, which puts me at an advantage.

I think whites are carefully taught not to recognize white privilege, as males are taught not to recognize male privilege. So I have begun in an untutored way to ask what it is like to have white privilege. I have come to see white privilege as an invisible package of unearned assets which I can count on cashing in each day, but about which I was "meant" to remain oblivious. White privilege is like an invisible weightless knapsack of special provisions, maps, passports, codebooks, visas, clothes, tools and blank checks.

Describing white privilege makes one newly accountable. As we in Women's Studies work to reveal male privilege and ask men to give up some of their power, so one who writes about having white privilege must ask, "Having described it, what will I do to lessen or end it?"

After I realized the extent to which men work from a base of unacknowledged privilege, I understood that much of their oppressiveness was unconscious. Then I remembered the frequent charges from women of color that white women whom they encounter are oppressive. I began to understand why we are justly seen as oppressive, even when we don't see ourselves that way. I began to count the ways in which I enjoy unearned skin privilege and have been conditioned into oblivion about its existence.

My schooling gave me no training in seeing myself as an oppressor, as an unfairly advantaged person, or as a participant in a damaged culture. I was taught to see myself as an individual whose moral state depended on her individual moral will. My schooling followed the pattern my colleague Elizabeth Minnich has pointed out: whites are taught to think of their lives as morally neutral, normative, and average, and also ideal, so that when we work to benefit others, this is seen as work which will allow "them" to be more like "us."

I decided to try to work on myself at least by identifying some of the daily effects of white privilege in my life. I have chosen those conditions which I think in my case *attach somewhat more to skin-color privilege* than to class, religion, ethnic status, or geographical location, though of course all these other factors are intricately intertwined. As far as I can see, my African American co-workers, friends and acquaintances with whom I come into daily or frequent contact in this particular time, place, and line of work cannot count on most of these conditions.

1. I can if I wish arrange to be in the company of people of my race most of the time.

2. If I should need to move, I can be pretty sure of renting or purchasing housing in an area which I can afford and in which I would want to live.

3. I can be pretty sure that my neighbors in such a location will be neutral or pleasant to me.

4. I can go shopping alone most of the time, pretty well assured that I will not be followed or harassed.

5. I can turn on the television or open to the front page of the paper and see people of my race widely represented.

6. When I am told about our national heritage or about "civilization," I am shown that people of my color made it what it is.

7. I can be sure that my children will be given curricular materials that testify to the existence of their race.

8. If I want to, I can be pretty sure of finding a publisher for this piece on white privilege.

9. I can go into a music shop and count on finding the music of my race represented, into a supermarket and find the staple foods which fit with my cultural traditions, into a hairdresser's shop and find someone who can cut my hair.

10. Whether I use checks, credit cards, or cash, I can count on my skin color not to work against the appearance of financial reliability.

11. I can arrange to protect my children most of the time from people who might not like them.

12. I can swear, or dress in secondhand clothes. Or not answer letters, without having people attribute these choices to the bad morals, the poverty, or the illiteracy of my race.

13. I can speak in public to a powerful male group without putting my race on trial.

14. I can do well in a challenging situation without being called a credit to my race.

15. I am never asked to speak for all the people of my racial group.

16. I can remain oblivious of the language and customs of persons of color who constitute the world's majority without feeling in my culture any penalty for such oblivion.

17. I can criticize our government and talk about how much I fear its policies and behavior without being seen as a cultural outsider.

18. I can be pretty sure that if I ask to talk to "the person in charge," I will be facing a person of my race.

19. If a traffic cop pulls me over or if the IRS audits my tax return, I can be sure I haven't been singled out because of my race.

20. I can easily buy posters, postcards, picture books, greeting cards, dolls, toys, and children's magazines featuring people of my race.

21. I can go home from most meetings of organizations I belong to feeling somewhat tied in, rather than isolated, out-of-place, outnumbered, unheard, held at a distance, or feared.

22. I can take a job with an affirmative action employer without having co-workers on the job suspect that I got it because of race.

23. I can choose public accommodation without fearing that people of my race cannot get in or will be mistreated in the places I have chosen.

24. I can be sure that if I need legal or medical help, my race will not work against me.

25. If my day, week, or year is going badly, I need not ask of each negative episode or situation whether it has racial overtones.

26. I can choose blemish cover or bandages in "flesh" color and have them more or less match my skin.

I repeatedly forgot each of the realizations on this list until I wrote it down. For me white privilege has turned out to be an elusive and fugitive subject. The pressure to avoid it is great, for in facing it I must give up the myth of meritocracy. If these things are true, this is not such a free country, one's life is not what one makes it; many doors open for certain people through no virtues of their own.

In unpacking this invisible knapsack of white privilege, I have listed conditions of daily experience which I once took for granted. Nor did I think of any of these perquisites as bad for the holder. I now think that we need a more finely differentiated taxonomy of privilege, for some of these varieties are only what one would want for everyone in a just society, and others give license to be ignorant, oblivious, arrogant and destructive.

I see a pattern running through the matrix of white privilege, a pattern of assumptions which were passed on to me as a white person. There was one main piece of cultural turf; it was my own turf, and I was among those who could control the turf. *My skin color was an asset for any move I was educated to want to make.* I could think of myself as belonging in major ways, and of making social systems work for me. I could freely disparage, fear, neglect, or be oblivious to anything outside of the dominant cultural forms. Being of the main culture, I could also criticize it fairly freely.

In proportion as my racial group was being made confident, comfortable, and oblivious, other groups were likely being made inconfident, uncomfortable, and alienated. Whiteness protected me from many kinds of hostility, distress, and violence, which I was being subtly trained to visit in turn upon people of color.

For this reason, the word "privilege" now seems to me misleading. We usually think of privilege as being a favored state, whether earned or conferred by birth or luck. Yet some of the conditions I have described here work to systematically overempower certain groups. Such privilege simply *confers dominance* because of one's race or sex.

I want, then, to distinguish between earned strength and unearned power conferred systematically. Power from unearned privilege can look like strength when it is in fact permission to escape or to dominate. But not all of the privileges on my list are inevitably damaging. Some, like the expectation that neighbors will be decent to you, or that your race will not count against you in court, should be the norm in a just society. Others, like the privilege to ignore less powerful people, distort the humanity of the holders as well as the ignored groups.

We might at least start by distinguishing between positive advantages which we can work to spread, and negative types of advantages which unless rejected will always reinforce our present hierarchies. For example, the feeling that one belongs within the human circle, as Native Americans say, should not be seen as privilege for a few. Ideally it is an *unearned entitlement.* At present, since only a few have it, it is an *unearned advantage* for them. This paper results from a process of coming to see that some of the power which I originally saw as attendant on being a human being in the U.S. consisted [of] *unearned advantage* and *conferred dominance.*

I have met very few men who are truly distressed about systemic, unearned male advantage and conferred dominance. And so one question for me and others like me is whether we will be like them, or whether we will get truly distressed, even outraged, about unearned race advantage and conferred dominance and if so, what we will do to lessen them. In any case, we need to do more work in identifying how they actually affect our daily lives. Many, perhaps most, of our white students in the U.S. think that racism doesn't affect them because they are not people of color; they do not see "whiteness" as a racial identity. In addition, since race and sex are not the only advantaging systems at work, we need similarly to examine the daily experience of having age advantage, or ethnic advantage, or physical ability, or advantage related to nationality, religions or sexual orientation.

Difficulties and dangers surrounding the task of finding parallels are many. Since racism, sexisms and heterosexism are not the same, the advantaging associated with them should not be seen as the same. In addition, it is hard to disentangle aspects of unearned advantage which rest more on social class, economic class, race, religion, sex and ethnic identity than on other factors. Still, all of the oppressions are interlocking, as the Combahee River Collective[1] Statement of 1977 continues to remind us eloquently.

One factor seems clear about all of the interlocking oppressions. They take both active forms which we can see and embedded forms which as a member of the dominant group one is taught not to see. In my class and place, I did not see myself as a racist because I was taught to recognize racism only in individual acts of meanness by members of my group, never in invisible systems conferring unsought racial dominance on my group from birth.

Disapproving of the systems won't be enough to change them. I was taught to think that racism could end if white individuals changed their attitudes. [But] a "white" skin in the United States opens many doors for whites whether or not we approve of the way dominance has been conferred on us. Individual acts can palliate, but cannot end, these problems.

To redesign social systems we need first to acknowledge their colossal unseen dimensions. The silences and denials surrounding privilege are the key political tool here. They keep the thinking about equality or equity incomplete, protecting unearned advantage and conferred dominance by making these taboo subjects. Most talk by whites about equal opportunity seems to me now to be about equal opportunity to try to get into a position of dominance while denying that *systems* of dominance exist.

It seems to me that obliviousness about white advantage, like obliviousness about male advantage, is kept strongly inculturated in the United States so as to maintain the myth of meritocracy, the myth that democratic choice is equally available to all. Keeping most people unaware that freedom of confident action is there for just a small number of people props up those in power and serves to keep power in the hands of the same groups that have most of it already.

Though systemic change takes many decades, there are pressing questions for me and I imagine for some others like me if we raise our daily consciousness on the perquisites of being lightskinned. What will we do with such knowledge? As we know from watching men, it is an open question whether we will choose to use unearned advantage to weaken hidden systems of advantage, and whether we will use any of our arbitrarily awarded power to try to reconstruct power systems on a broader base.

NOTE

1. Combahee River Collective: A group of black feminist women in Boston from 1974 to 1980.

17

Strings Attached

Lee Cronk

Anthropologists have traditionally studied how social ties among people are created through a system of kinship and marriage; this is a universal aspect of human social systems. Marriages link families who were previously strangers into kin (affines). Such new social relations are cemented by the exchange of goods—expected gifts—at the time of the marriage; this appears to be a universal aspect of marriage systems.

People give each other gifts all the time, and in all cultures of the world. According to the French anthropologist Marcel Mauss, who first wrote about this phenomenon in 1924, gift giving is a universal way of creating and maintaining social relations among people. This is because gift giving creates social obligations. Gifts "cement" social relationships, and members of a society understand what the implicit rules of gift giving are.

In the beginning of this selection, Lee Cronk discusses possible cultural misunderstandings that were involved in the creation of the unfortunate (and racist) term *Indian giver*. These misunderstandings were offensive to both Native Americans and whites. Europeans thought that gifts should be freely given and that the gift is less valued when there are strings attached. On a worldwide survey of different cultures, however, it is far more common for the strings themselves to be the main consideration of value. Because of this, when anthropologists study economic exchange, they are more interested in the social relationship between the gift giver and the receiver than in the actual gift.

As we saw in the case of Richard Lee and the gift of the Christmas ox among the !Kung San (Selection 8), the cultural rules behind gift giving often involve the principle of reciprocity. There are also cases when gifts can be used to embarrass rivals or to foster feelings of indebtedness. These cases usually involve social groups or nations rather than individuals. It is valuable to reexamine international political relations and economic aid in light of the cross-cultural context of gift giving.

As you read this selection, ask yourself the following questions:

- Is it really true that "there is no such thing as a free gift"?

- How can gift giving be a question of social power and prestige, as in the case of one chief "burying" another with gifts?

- Why was Russian acceptance of humanitarian aid from the United States after the 1988 Armenian earthquake considered to be a breakthrough?

- How can concessions in arms reduction negotiations be considered as gifts?

- Do Americans devalue a gift that has strings attached? Why?

The following terms discussed in this selection are included in the Glossary at the back of the book:

dependency	*potlatch*
exchange	*reciprocity*
kula	

During a trek through the Rockies in the 1830s, Captain Benjamin Louis E. de Bonneville received a gift of a fine young horse from a Nez Percé chief. According to Washington Irving's account of the incident, the American explorer was aware that "a parting pledge was necessary on his own part, to prove that this friendship was reciprocated." Accordingly, he "placed a handsome rifle in the hands of the venerable chief; whose benevolent heart was evidently touched and gratified by this outward and visible sign of amity."

Even the earliest white settlers in New England understood that presents from natives required reciprocity, and by 1764, "Indian gift" was so common a phrase that the Massachusetts colonial historian Thomas Hutchinson identified it as "a proverbial expression, signifying a present for which an equivalent return is expected." Then, over time, the custom's meaning was

The article is reprinted by permission of *The Sciences* and is from May–June 1989 issue, (3):2–4.

lost. Indeed, the phrase now is used derisively, to refer to one who demands the return of a gift. How this cross-cultural misunderstanding occurred is unclear, but the poet Lewis Hyde, in his book *The Gift,* has imagined a scenario that probably approaches the truth.

Say that an Englishman newly arrived in America is welcomed to an Indian lodge with the present of a pipe. Thinking the pipe a wonderful artifact, he takes it home and sets it on his mantelpiece. When he later learns that the Indians expect to have the pipe back, as a gesture of goodwill, he is shocked by what he views as their short-lived generosity. The newcomer did not realize that, to the natives, the point of the gift was not to provide an interesting trinket but to inaugurate a friendly relationship that would be maintained through a series of mutual exchanges. Thus, his failure to reciprocate appeared not only rude and thoughtless but downright hostile. "White man keeping" was as offensive to native Americans as "Indian giving" was to settlers.

In fact, the Indians' tradition of gift giving is much more common than our own. Like our European ancestors, we think that presents ought to be offered freely, without strings attached. But through most of the world, the strings themselves are the main consideration. In some societies, gift giving is a tie between friends, a way of maintaining good relationships, whereas in others it has developed into an elaborate, expensive, and antagonistic ritual designed to humiliate rivals by showering them with wealth and obligating them to give more in return.

In truth, the dichotomy between the two traditions of gift giving is less behavioral than rhetorical: our generosity is not as unconditional as we would like to believe. Like European colonists, most modern Westerners are blind to the purpose of reciprocal gift giving, not only in non-Western societies but also, to some extent, in our own. Public declarations to the contrary, we, too, use gifts to nurture long-term relationships of mutual obligation, as well as to embarrass our rivals and to foster feelings of indebtedness. And this ethic touches all aspects of contemporary life, from the behavior of scientists in research networks to superpower diplomacy. Failing to acknowledge this fact, especially as we give money, machines, and technical advice to peoples around the world, we run the risk of being misinterpreted and, worse, of causing harm.

Much of what we know about the ethics of gift giving comes from the attempts of anthropologists to give things to the people they are studying. Richard Lee, of the University of Toronto, learned a difficult lesson from the !Kung hunter-gatherers, of the Kalahari desert, when, as a token of goodwill, he gave them an ox to slaughter at Christmas. Expecting gratitude, he was shocked when the !Kung complained about having to make do with such a scrawny "bag of bones." Only later did Lee learn, with relief, that the !Kung belittle all gifts. In their eyes, no act is completely generous, or free of calculation; ridiculing gifts is their way of diminishing the expected return and of enforcing humility on those who would use gifts to raise their own status within the group.

Rada Dyson-Hudson, of Cornell University, had a similar experience among the Turkana, a pastoral people of northwestern Kenya. To compensate her informants for their help, Dyson-Hudson gave away pots, maize meal, tobacco, and other items. The Turkana reaction was less than heartwarming. A typical response to a gift of a pot, for example, might be, "Where is the maize meal to go in this pot?" or, "Don't you have a bigger one to give me?" To the Turkana, these are legitimate and expected questions.

The Mukogodo, another group of Kenyan natives, responded in a similar way to gifts Beth Leech and I presented to them during our fieldwork in 1986. Clothing was never nice enough, containers never big enough, tobacco and candies never plentiful enough. Every gift horse was examined carefully, in the mouth and elsewhere. Like the !Kung, the Mukogodo believe that all gifts have an element of calculation, and they were right to think that ours were no exception. We needed their help, and their efforts to diminish our expectations and lessen their obligations to repay were as fair as our attempts to get on their good side.

The idea that gifts carry obligations is instilled early in life. When we gave Mukogodo children candies after visiting their villages, their mothers reminded them of the tie: "Remember these white people? They are the ones who gave you candy." They also reinforced the notion that gifts are meant to circulate, by asking their children to part with their precious candies, already in their mouths. Most of the youngsters reluctantly surrendered their sweets, only to have them immediately returned. A mother might take, at most, a symbolic nibble from her child's candy, just to drive home the lesson.

The way food, utensils, and other goods are received in many societies is only the first stage of the behavior surrounding gift giving. Although repayment is expected, it is crucial that it be deferred. To reciprocate at once indicates a desire to end the relationship, to cut the strings; delayed repayment makes the strings longer and stronger. This is especially clear on the Truk Islands, of Micronesia, where a special word—*niffag*—is used to designate objects moving through the island's exchange network. From the Trukese viewpoint, to return niffag on the same day it is received alters its nature from that of a gift to that of a sale, in which all that matters is material gain.

After deciding the proper time for response, a recipient must consider how to make repayment, and that is dictated largely by the motive behind the gift. Some exchange customs are designed solely to preserve a relationship. The !Kung have a system, called *hxaro*, in which little attention is paid to whether the items exchanged are equivalent. Richard Lee's informant !Xoma explained to him that "Hxaro is when I take a thing of value and give it to you. Later, much later, when you find some good thing, you give it back to me. When I find something good I will give it to you, and so we will pass the years together." When Lee tried to determine the exact exchange values of various items (Is a spear worth three strings of beads, two strings, or one?), !Xoma explained that any return would be all right: "You see, we don't trade with things, we trade with people!"

One of the most elaborate systems of reciprocal gift giving, known as *kula*, exists in a ring of islands off New Guinea. Kula gifts are limited largely to shell necklaces, called *soulava*, and armbands, called *mwali*. A necklace given at one time is answered months or years later with an armband, the necklaces usually circulating clockwise, and the armbands counterclockwise, through the archipelago. Kula shells vary in quality and value, and men gain fame and prestige by having their names associated with noteworthy necklaces or armbands. The shells also gain value from their association with famous and successful kula partners.

Although the act of giving gifts seems intrinsically benevolent, a gift's power to embarrass the recipient and to force repayment has, in some societies, made it attractive as a weapon. Such antagonistic generosity reached its most elaborate expression, during the late nineteenth century, among the Kwakiutl, of British Columbia.

The Kwakiutl were acutely conscious of status, and every tribal division, clan, and individual had a specific rank. Disputes about status were resolved by means of enormous ceremonies (which outsiders usually refer to by the Chinook Indian term *potlatch*), at which rivals competed for the honor and prestige of giving away the greatest amount of property. Although nearly everything of value was fair game—blankets, canoes, food, pots, and, until the mid-nineteenth century, even slaves—the most highly prized items were decorated sheets of beaten copper, shaped like shields and etched with designs in the distinctive style of the Northwest Coast Indians.

As with the kula necklaces and armbands, the value of a copper sheet was determined by its history—by where it had been and who had owned it—and a single sheet could be worth thousands of blankets, a fact often reflected in its name. One was called "Drawing All Property from the House," and another, "About Whose Possession All Are Quarreling." After the Kwakiutl began to acquire trade goods from the Hudson's Bay Company's Fort Rupert post, in 1849, the potlatches underwent a period of extreme inflation, and by the 1920s,

when items of exchange included sewing machines and pool tables, tens of thousands of Hudson's Bay blankets might be given away during a single ceremony.

In the 1880s, after the Canadian government began to suppress warfare between tribes, potlatching also became a substitute for battle. As a Kwakiutl man once said to the anthropologist Franz Boas, "The time of fighting is past. . . . We do not fight now with weapons: we fight with property." The usual Kwakiutl word for potlatch was *p!Esa*, meaning to flatten (as when one flattens a rival under a pile of blankets), and the prospect of being given a large gift engendered real fear. Still, the Kwakiutl seemed to prefer the new "war of wealth" to the old "war of blood."

Gift giving has served as a substitute for war in other societies, as well. Among the Siuai, of the Solomon Islands, guests at feasts are referred to as attackers, while hosts are defenders, and invitations to feasts are given on short notice in the manner of "surprise attacks." And like the Kwakiutl of British Columbia, the Mount Hagen tribes of New Guinea use a system of gift giving called *moka* as a way of gaining prestige and shaming rivals. The goal is to become a tribal leader, a "big-man." One moka gift in the 1970s consisted of several hundred pigs, thousands of dollars in cash, some cows and wild birds, a truck, and a motorbike. The donor, quite pleased with himself, said to the recipient, "I have won. I have knocked you down by giving so much."

Although we tend not to recognize it as such, the ethic of reciprocal gift giving manifests itself throughout our own society, as well. We, too, often expect something, even if only gratitude and a sense of indebtedness, in exchange for gifts, and we use gifts to establish friendships and to manipulate our positions in society. As in non-Western societies gift giving in America sometimes takes a benevolent and helpful form; at other times, the power of gifts to create obligations is used in a hostile way.

The Duke University anthropologist Carol Stack found a robust tradition of benevolent exchange in an Illinois ghetto known as the Flats, where poor blacks engage in a practice called swapping. Among residents of the Flats, wealth comes in spurts; hard times are frequent and unpredictable. Swapping, of clothes, food, furniture, and the like, is a way of guaranteeing security, of making sure that someone will be there to help out when one is in need and that one will get a share of any windfalls that come along.

Such networks of exchange are not limited to the poor, nor do they always involve objects. Just as the exchange of clothes creates a gift community in the Flats, so the swapping of knowledge may create one among scientists. Warren Hagstrom, a sociologist at the University of Wisconsin, in Madison, has pointed out that papers submitted to scientific journals often are called contributions, and, because no payment is received for them, they truly are gifts. In contrast, articles written for profit—such as this one—often are held in low esteem: scientific status can be achieved only through giving gifts of knowledge.

Recognition also can be traded upon, with scientists building up their gift-giving networks by paying careful attention to citations and acknowledgments. Like participants in kula exchange, they try to associate themselves with renowned and prestigious articles, books, and institutions. A desire for recognition, however, cannot be openly acknowledged as a motivation for research, and it is a rare scientist who is able to discuss such desires candidly. Hagstrom was able to find just one mathematician (whom he described as "something of a social isolate") to confirm that "junior mathematicians want recognition from big shots and, consequently, work in areas prized by them."

Hagstrom also points out that the inability of scientists to acknowledge a desire for recognition does not mean that such recognition is not expected by those who offer gifts of knowledge, any more than a kula trader believes it is all right if his trading partner does not answer his gift of a necklace with an armband. While failure to reciprocate in New Guinean society might once have meant warfare, among scientists it may cause factionalism and the creation of rivalries.

Whether in the Flats of Illinois or in the halls of academia, swapping is, for the most part, benign. But manipulative gift giving exists in modern societies, too—particularly in paternalistic government practices. The technique is to offer a present that cannot be repaid, coupled with a claim of beneficence and omniscience. The Johns Hopkins University anthropologist Grace Goodell documented one example in Iran's Khūzestān Province, which, because it contains most of the country's oil fields and is next door to Iraq, is a strategically sensitive area. Goodell focused on the World Bank–funded Dez irrigation project, a showpiece of the shah's ambitious "white revolution" development plan. The scheme involved the irrigation of tens of thousands of acres and the forced relocation of people from their villages to new, model towns. According to Goodell, the purpose behind dismantling local institutions was to enhance central government control of the region. Before development, each Khūzestāni village had been a miniature city-state, managing its own internal affairs and determining its own relations with outsiders. In the new settlements, decisions were made by government bureaucrats, not townsmen, whose autonomy was crushed under the weight of a large and strategically placed gift.

On a global scale, both the benevolent and aggressive dimensions of gift giving are at work in superpower diplomacy. Just as the Kwakiutl were left only with blankets with which to fight after warfare was banned, the United States and the Soviet Union now find, with war out of the question, that they are left only with gifts—called concessions—with which to do battle. Offers of military cutbacks are easy ways to score points in the public arena of international opinion and to shame rivals, and failure either to accept such offers or to respond with even more extreme proposals may be seen as cowardice or as bellicosity. Mikhail Gorbachev is a virtuoso, a master potlatcher, in this new kind of competition, and, predictably, Americans often see his offers of disarmament and openness as gifts with long strings attached. One reason U.S. officials were buoyed last December, when, for the first time since the Second World War, the Soviet Union accepted American assistance, in the aftermath of the Armenian earthquake, is that it seemed to signal a wish for reciprocity rather than dominance—an unspoken understanding of the power of gifts to bind people together.

Japan, faced with a similar desire to expand its influence, also has begun to exploit gift giving in its international relations. In 1989, it will spend more than ten billion dollars on foreign aid, putting it ahead of the United States for the second consecutive year as the world's greatest donor nation. Although this move was publicly welcomed in the United States as the sharing of a burden, fears, too, were expressed that the resultant blow to American prestige might cause a further slip in our international status. Third World leaders also have complained that too much Japanese aid is targeted at countries in which Japan has an economic stake and that too much is restricted to the purchase of Japanese goods—that Japan's generosity has less to do with addressing the problems of underdeveloped countries than with exploiting those problems to its own advantage.

The danger in all of this is that wealthy nations may be competing for the prestige that comes from giving gifts at the expense of Third World Nations. With assistance sometimes being given with more regard to the donors' status than to the recipients' welfare, it is no surprise that, in recent years, development aid often has been more effective in creating relationships of dependency, as in the case of Iran's Khūzestān irrigation scheme, than in producing real development. Nor that, given the fine line between donation and domination, offers of help are sometimes met with resistance, apprehension and, in extreme cases, such as the Iranian revolution, even violence.

The Indians understood a gift's ambivalent power to unify, antagonize, or subjugate. We, too, would do well to remember that a present can be a surprisingly potent thing, as dangerous in the hands of the ignorant as it is useful in the hands of the wise.

18

Using Cultural Skills
for Cooperative Advantage in Japan

Richard H. Reeves-Ellington

Cultural awareness and sensitivity have significant payoffs, helping people avoid major mistakes resulting from cultural ignorance or cultural misunderstanding. In addition, businesspeople who are more culturally aware are also more successful. In this selection, Reeves-Ellington describes a cross-cultural training program that he designed and implemented for an American company doing business in Japan. About fifty employees participated in the on-site cross-cultural training. The long-term results of their training are impressive. Project managers who took the cultural training program were able to cut project completion time nearly in half and increase the financial returns from the projects threefold (see Table 7). After the training program, managers felt much more comfortable and confident about conducting business in Japan on their own.

What might account for this dramatic success? Do the trained managers make no cultural mistakes, and are there no communication misunderstandings? Obviously, some cultural "horror stories" are instructive, like the case of the nervous American who publicly folded and then tore up a Japanese counterpart's business card during a meeting. But there is also evidence that the American efforts to learn Japanese customs and cultural rules of politeness engendered much goodwill and increased trust between employees involved in multinational business cooperation.

Reeves-Ellington teaches businesspeople to use the basic methods developed by cultural anthropologists to describe and analyze cultural settings. In this selection, he describes the cultural values and behavioral rituals implicit in day-to-day business interactions. In many ways, it is more important to recognize the different ways to observe and interpret cultural patterns than to remember the particular details of the cultural rules of business described here. There are practical advantages to being a participant observer rather than a nonobserving participant.

As you read this selection, ask yourself the following questions:

- What Japanese cultural values are illustrated in the stories about business cards and identity?

- Given the cultural expectations for business entertainment described, do you think there may be special challenges facing American women doing business in Japan?

- What are aspects of American culture that Japanese people might find particularly perplexing?

- In what ways do the rules of a business meeting seem to be ritualized?

- How would you convince an American company of the value of intercultural training?

The following terms discussed in this selection are included in the Glossary at the back of the book:

artifact	*ritual*
intercultural communication	*values*
participant observation	

Reproduced by permission of the Society for Applied Anthropology, from Reeves-Ellington, Richard H., Using Cultural Skills for Comparative Advantage in Japan, SfAA 1993, *Human Organization*, Vol. 52, No. 2, pp. 203–215.

Through trial and error, American managers who do business in Japan have learned to gain insight into the Japanese culture. Nonetheless, most American managers remain uneasy dealing with their Japanese counterparts, and "home office" continues to be suspicious of Japanese business practices. This situation produces ineffective business relationships and poor business results. The paradigm of discomfort and suspicion must be replaced by one of confidence and trust if American business is to succeed in Japan.

Pharmco, a pharmaceutical subsidiary of a major United States multinational, was saddled with this "home office" attitude of suspicion. Having done business in Japan for more than 20 years, it was dissatisfied with the relationships and financial arrangements with its Japanese licensees. The advent of innovative pharmaceutical technologies provided an opportunity to develop a new strategic alliance with a major Japanese company, Diversity KK. Pharmco anticipated that the alliance would facilitate rapid introduction of its technology in Japan, yield tenfold greater financial returns, and furnish the framework for learning to operate more successfully in Japan. Senior managers in the company understood that they and their staff needed to work effectively at many levels with Japanese managers and scientists in both the Japanese and American cultural environments. They had, however, no plan for learning about Japanese culture; the initial meetings between employees of the two companies resulted in more "damage control" than was desirable. The Pharmco senior manager responsible for Japanese operations, a trained anthropologist, proposed a program offering United States-based managers and scientists assistance in learning about Japanese culture. As a result of the program, American-Japanese relations at Pharmco improved considerably and business operations are running smoothly.

This paper . . . demonstrates how individuals used a cultural understanding process, ethnographic data, and participant observation (PO) to get through a business day in Japan, build their own database, and eventually, predict Japanese social behavior in different settings. Empirical evidence is provided to demonstrate the value the program had for one company.

UNDERPINNINGS OF THE PROGRAM

Employee Needs

The purpose of education in the business setting is to resolve problems. . . . Within the Pharmco context, the people who needed cultural information were based in the United States, worked in a variety of functions, and had to operate in several different cultures, not only Japan. Two common learning methods were thereby excluded, i.e., general reading and the use of culture-specific training courses. The manager-anthropologist had to devise another method.

To determine the educational needs, he set up small-group and one-on-one meetings with managers and scientists who would be required to work on the Japanese strategic alliance. He discovered that two questions deterred employees from wanting to work with Japanese in particular and all non-Americans in general: "What

do I do during a business day?" and "How can I learn to respond to the various situations I might find myself in while travelling in foreign cultures?" The initial training objective, therefore, was to offer assistance in getting through a Japanese business day while at the same time providing the tools and processes to enable employees to gain cultural understanding and apply their learning to other cultural contexts.

Involvement of an Insider Anthropologist

The manager-anthropologist responsible for Japan operations provided all training that took place over a five-year period and involved ten sets of employees. Training content included "horror" stories of what goes wrong in U.S.-Japanese relationships, examples of successful activities and processes for increasing the chances of success, and practice in using all the material discussed and presented. Material selection depended on the previous experience of members of the group in multicultural settings. Initial sessions were timed approximately two weeks before contacts with Japanese counterparts. This timing coincided with the peak interest employees had in learning the information. All training was done at the employees' work site, allowing them a greater comfort level. The manager-anthropologist was present at all initial meetings between U.S. employees and their Japanese contacts, and he continued to be present until the Americans expressed confidence that he was not needed at future meetings. . . .

The goal of training was that, through better understanding of Japan, employees would change their normal behavior patterns when working with Japanese counterparts. All improved their ability to work cross-culturally, but not all applied the material learned equally. Managers, in particular, had less patience to learn "how to do things," but rather just wanted to know "what to do." Scientists, on the other hand, tended to apply the models and processes in a much more diligent manner. . . .

Application of the "Understanding and Predicting Culture Process" in Japan

Pharmco employees started gaining understanding of Japanese culture by gathering and understanding cultural generalities. . . . Employees became more involved in the learning process by working on the tools to be used as well as applying them in a Japanese context.

Employees gathered information through visits, while in Japan, to museums, theaters, shrines, baseball games, and business meetings. . . . The initial work session was led by the manager-anthropologist but the trainees at the session participated in data entry. . . . After the introduction of the model, the anthropologist made no effort to suggest data classification according to anthropological criteria. Rather, Pharmco employees using the model defined classifications acceptable to and understood by them. For example, in the case of "insider-outsider," discussed under "artifacts" below, the visual artifact was the way people sat at business and dinner tables, with the concept rightly belonging in the cultural logic. Employees, however, skipped the visual and placed the cultural logic in the artifacts section. The point is that they understood what they meant.

The following analysis of Japanese culture used by Pharmco as baseline data is:

Artifacts *How are things classified or what are the artifacts of an agreed classification system?* In Japan there are two basic classification systems commonly used: (1) insider-outsider and (2) front-rear. The insider is determined in the first instance by what Nakane (1970) refers to as a "frame." By frame, she means criteria that classify and identify individuals as part of a group. In business, the most obvious is the identification by company. When introducing oneself, one says, for example, "I am Pharmco's Reeves-Ellington." Japanese frames can also be determined by locality, such as the city in which one is born or family or household affiliations. In all cases frame indicates a criterion that sets a boundary and gives a common basis to a group of individuals who are located or involved in it. Outsiders are all those who are excluded from the frame. Hence, the use of the word "foreigner" (*gaijin*) is frequent in Japan. If one is not part of the frame, i.e., Japanese (insider), then one is a foreigner (outsider) (Nakane 1970).

Front and rear in the Japanese concept are not linear, as in the western world, but circular. The front, which embodies the concept of *tatamae*, is what is seen or what is commonly known, or frontstage, whereas the rear is what is hidden or backstage. This rear embodies the concept of *honne*, commonly referred to as what is "true." In the western world, these two concepts are the flip sides of a coin existing in a dichotomous relationship, but in Japan, the two concepts are a circular continuum. One folds into the next as do the rooms of a house as one walks through it. Outsiders are always kept to the front, whereas insiders are introduced to the rear (Matsumoto 1988).

The artifacts of the classifications are always determined by the situation in which people come together (Hall and Hall 1987). For example, in the inside-outside relationship, obvious manifestations are the family, localities, schools, companies, and associations. Tour groups are formed to make a group of people insiders.

Outsiders are those not in a particular group, e.g., family members are outsiders to the company inside group. On the other hand, fellow employees are typically outsiders to a colleague's family group. In another context, such as going on a trip together, the family and business colleagues could both be insiders, as members of the XYZ tour group. The artifacts of the front and rear classifications can be exemplified by business meetings. Humans typically belong to a complex of groups that can be concentrically layered and are variably mutually inclusive and exclusive. The front artifacts are expressed in how people are arranged at a table and the courtesy that is extended to guests. The rear artifacts are expressed in terms of who is attending and the body language that occurs.

Social Knowledge (*values*) *What are proper principles for behavior? What are the values that drive the categories and artifacts described above?* In Japan, adoption of the classification systems discussed above keeps as many people on the outside as possible. One keeps one's social obligations to a level that encourages self gain but eliminates all that offer less gain than one is required to give. One sees this principle in action in the Tokyo subway system. The proverbial Japanese politeness is totally absent, replaced with a "survival of the fittest" behavior pattern, which is accomplished, in part, by avoiding eye contact, thereby assuring that everyone around stays on the outside.

Keeping people on the outside embodies another principle: Minimize obligations to others. The personal value that drives this principle is the desire and need for personal relationships of a meaningful nature. If too many people are insiders, personal relationships would be weakened and a fundamental value diluted.

There is a third human principle at work: Everyone needs to be an insider somewhere. All Japanese are striving to be an insider in situations that will provide personal gain. In companies, they have a strong sense of being inside: On tour groups, they all do things together as insiders in a travel experience. The driving value that leads Japanese to strive for insider status is the value of acknowledging and accepting mutual interdependencies with others (*amae*) (Doi 1990).

Cultural Logic Social knowledge or values are based on underlying cultural logic around relationships to the environment, the nature of reality, truth, human nature, human activities, human relationships, and use of time. Within a culture, these are all taken for granted, rarely understood, and almost never expressible by those living in the culture, but they are of utmost importance to foreigners wishing to live and work in that culture. An explanation of Japanese cultural logic is contained in Table 1.

TABLE 1   Cultural Logic

Environmental relationships

Japanese, as well as other Asians, view the physical environment and human environment as intertwined and not in opposition as do most Christians (Campbell 1960, 1989; Pelzel 1974). As exemplified in Japanese gardens, humans control and shape the environment in ways that suit the artistic feeling of people. The garden denotes the desire for environmental harmony and orderliness.

Nature of truth and reality

Truth and reality are determined by situations and social contexts in which people find themselves (Hall and Hall 1987; Lebra 1976). In a social group, only the insiders determine what is true and real. The accuracy of this determination is based on the degree of harmony and orderliness obtained within the insider group.

Nature of human nature

Humans are driven by emotion and not by logic (Doi 1990b). Mutuality of love and obligation (within the context of the concept of obligation) ties closely with that of hate (Ishida 1974). This mutuality in human relations forces the concept of consensus into human society organization. Since human nature is not believed to be inherently "bad," it is assumed this behavior is caused by ignorance and not evil intent.

Nature of human relationships

Using the concept of relational value orientation (Kluckhohn and Strodbeck 1961), collaterality in human relationships is highly valued. Within this concept is the perception that uncertainty is to be avoided and much effort is put into avoiding it. Within the basic collateral value, there exists a strong power distance within organizations and generational structures (Hofstede 1980).

Nature of human activities

Activity is focused on working toward ideals of harmonious relationships and involves an orientation toward human interdependency (Doi 1990; Lebra 1976; Hayashi 1988). Activity is necessarily done in groups and by groups.

Use of time

Time is polychronic (Hall and Hall 1987). The time system is characterized by the simultaneous occurrence of many things and by a deep involvement with people. There is more emphasis on completing transactions than holding to a schedule. A person confronted with too many subjects to be covered in too short a time chooses to expand the time available to complete the tasks rather than reduce the number of tasks.

THEORY INTO PRACTICE

To get theory into practice, Pharmco decided to learn how to do introductions, meetings, leavings, dinner, and drinking in Japan.

This analysis brings to life Pharmco's learning by relating incidents about just how badly things can go wrong when there is no basis for successful behaviors leading to appropriate judgements in the course of cross-cultural activities. In spite of the mistakes made, Diversity employees were gracious and appreciative of the efforts made to behave properly. They understand that Pharmco, being foreign, will never get it exactly right in Japan—just as the Japanese will never get it exactly right in the United States. Pharmco employees constantly remind themselves that they are involved in a continuous process they may never get entirely "right." There are always new and more subtle nuances to learn.

The Business Card (*meishi*)

During the initial meeting with the Japanese, the first item of business is introductions. (See Table 2.) Proper introductions require proper business cards (*meishi*). The word *meishi* is used by all people in Japan, including foreigners because the two words, business card and *meishi*, refer to the same card but the meaning behind the card is substantially different. For this reason, *meishi* should be prepared in Japan and be ready upon arrival to do business. At the time of presenting the *meishi*, the Japanese expect the viewer of the *meishi* to examine it carefully and to remember both name and title.

Mistreatment of a Japanese businessman's *meishi* will ruin a relationship, whether new or established. Since the *meishi* is an extension of self, damage to the card is damage to the individual. Explaining this to Pharmco staff was not sufficient. They did not

TABLE 2   Introductions at Business Meetings

Artifacts	Social Knowledge	Cultural Logic
Technology • Business cards • *Meishi* Visual behavior • Presentation of *meishi* by presenting card, facing recipient. • Senior people present *meishi* first. • Guest presents first, giving name, company affiliation and bowing. • Host presents *meishi* in same sequence. • Upon sitting at conference table, all *meishi* are placed in front of recipient to assure name use.	• Once given a card is kept—not discarded. • *Meishi* are not exchanged a second time unless there is a position change. • Before the next meeting between parties, the *meishi* are reviewed for familiarization with the people attending the meeting. • The *meishi* provides status for the owner.	Human relations • *Meishi* provide understanding of appropriate relations between parties. • *Meishi* take uncertainty out of relationships. Environment • *Meishi* establish insider/ outsider environment. • *Meishi* help establish possible obligations to environment. Human activity • *Meishi* help to establish human activities.

understand the implications of the *meishi* until two stories were told to help their understanding.

The importance of this point is demonstrated in the following story. A major U.S. company was having problems with one of its distributors, and the parties seemed unable to resolve their differences. The president of the U.S. company decided to visit Japan, meet with his counterpart in the wholesaler organization, and attempt to resolve their differences. The two had not met previously and, upon meeting, each followed proper *meishi* ritual. The American, however, did not put the Japanese counterpart's *meishi* on the table; instead he held on to it. As the conversation became heated, the American rolled up the *meishi* in his hand. Horror was recorded on the face of the Japanese businessman. The American then tore the *meishi* into bits. This was more than the Japanese could stand; he excused himself from the meeting. Shortly afterward the two companies stopped doing business with each other.

How Japanese use the *meishi* also helped Pharmco staff understand its importance. Japanese companies value a high degree of consistency in those with whom they work and in the handling of personnel within a company. Failure to demonstrate consistency toward internal employees indicates a probable inconsistency in relationships outside the company. The *meishi* can provide the Japanese executive with some indication of a company's attitude toward its employees. The Pharmco employees learned this lesson with a particularly painful outcome at a meeting with a senior Japanese executive. After the Pharmco team explained the purpose of the visit, this executive took a number of *meishi* from his desk. As he turned each of them up, he asked, "I see that I met with Mr. Hansen of your company ten years ago. Where is he now?" Then came the next card. "I see I met with Mr. Harman of your company eight years ago. Where is he now?" The questioning went through eight separate *meishi*. The Pharmco team leader responded each time that the particular person was no longer with the company. At the end, the Japanese executive said, "People are not treated well in your company. In our company, people do not leave until retirement." The meeting was not successful.

With this background, Pharmco staff visiting Japan have a good understanding of the *meishi* and treat it and its presentation with the respect Japanese expect.

The Conference Table

As soon as introductions are complete both sides take a seat at the conference table. In Japan, there are no round tables at business meetings. The expression "head of the table" is meaningless in a Japanese context. Understanding conference table arrangements (Table 3) leads to a successful meeting.

Seating is highly ritualistic and stylized. The power position is flanked by advisors; next come suppliers of data and information, should they be requested; and finally interested parties are seated at the extremities of the conference table (Figure 1). The person in the power seat performs all ritualistic duties for the side represented. That person directs all comments or questions to particular members of his team who are best qualified

TABLE 3   Conference Seating Arrangements

Artifacts	Social Knowledge	Cultural Logic
Technology • Rectangular table Visual behavior • Hosts on one side of the table and guests on the other. • Guests are framed by most attractive background. • The power seat is in the middle of the table. • Junior people are closest to the door.	• Set seating allows all parties social/business understanding. • Person responsible for success has the authority. • Guests are treated as customers.	Human relations • Seating arrangements allow established order to be known, allowing a proper order and power structure to function between people. Reality and truth • Responsibility and authority are combined for success. • The inside and outside are maintained at the conference table. Environment • Used to honor customers and guests. • Used to maintain inside-outside definitions.

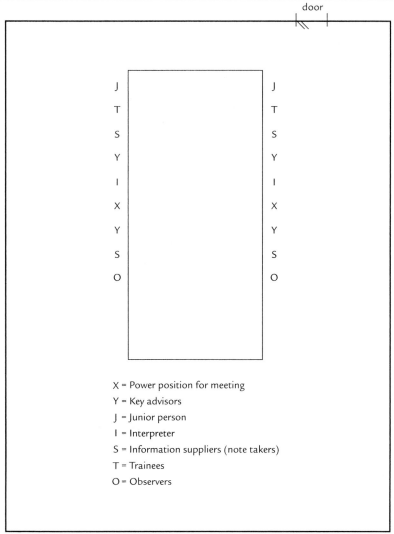

X = Power position for meeting
Y = Key advisors
J = Junior person
I = Interpreter
S = Information suppliers (note takers)
T = Trainees
O = Observers

FIGURE 1   Meeting room

TABLE 4   Leaving the Conference

Artifacts	Social Knowledge	Cultural Logic
Visual behavior	• Politeness demands guests be treated as though they were visiting the Japanese at home.	Environment
• Ritualistic thank yous end the meeting while all are seated.		• Guests are under control while in the insider environment. They are left only when they achieve the outside environment.
• Conclusion of exchange means guests initiate standing. All arise.		Truth and reality
• Power person stays with guests until they are off company premises.		• All exchanges assure a smooth transition from one status to another.
• Bows start upon arising and continue each time one of either side leaves.		Human relations
		• All structured interactions require a host and a guest role.

to answer them and also functions as the go-between for his team and the other side.

Contrary to usual western practice, the person in the power seat is not necessarily the most senior person present. Rather, the person designated as the official contact for his company or the person most knowledgeable about the subject matter to be discussed takes the seat. The Japanese want the powerful person to be the one who can accomplish the business at hand.

Not understanding this point led to Pharmco embarrassment. Pharmco managers believed at first that the senior person present always occupied the power seat. This assumption was based on meetings between senior managers of the companies who were addressing subject matter only they could decide. When Pharmco's R&D senior manager led Pharmco's initial discussions with Diversity regarding research philosophy and programs, he correctly took the power seat. At a subsequent meeting, called to address program execution, the senior R&D manager again took the power seat. The Japanese body language indicated he should not be there. A new lesson was learned that day: expertise and subject matter, not status, determine the occupant of the power seat. In the case of program execution, the Pharmco power seat occupant should have been the senior scientist for toxicology, not the head of R&D. By taking the power seat, the R&D manager offended the Japanese scientist because he had less status and therefore felt ineffectual. The meeting was inconclusive.

Knowing who is in the power seat offers insights to the other side's agenda. At a negotiating meeting between Diversity KK and Pharmco, the Pharmco team expected the meeting to be a confirmation of work done. When the meeting started, however, the Diversity power seat was occupied by an attorney, not the familiar businessman known by Pharmco. Pharmco immediately excused themselves for a few minutes. In private caucus, the team discussed the change of people and

decided that major changes in the contract under negotiation were about to be introduced. This proved to be a correct interpretation. Even this short notice helped the Pharmco team stay in control of unfolding events. At the conclusion of the meeting, leaving is as ritualistic as arriving. Table 4 provides a grasp of the ritual.

At the conclusion of a business meeting, both sides stand up to leave; the host leads the guests out of the conference room; the host's team escorts the guests to the elevator; the entire team, excluding the host, leaves the guests as the elevator doors close, both sides bowing profusely; the host joins his guests in the elevator. The remaining host and his guests then go to the front door of the office, where, if a car has been arranged, the host will get into the car if there is room and accompany his guests back to their hotel. If no car is arranged, the host will stay with the guests until a taxi is found and the guests are safely in it and driving off. The host will remain at the curb, bowing, until the taxi is well into the traffic. The guests keep eye contact, heads nodding and arms waving until the car leaves the curb.

The respect ritualistically shown is based on the status of the individual's company, not on that of the individual. By showing this level of courtesy, the hosts expect the guests to recognize that they have an obligation to reciprocate in the future, when he is on their turf.

Once Pharmco staff understood the social importance of what the Japanese were doing in seeing them off, they immediately instituted the same policy of courtesy for the Japanese when they visited the Pharmco facilities.

Going out to Dinner

When foreigners are invited to dinner, they must be prepared to express a preference for the nationality of food to be eaten; in Japan, a preference for Japanese is obligatory because it demonstrates a willingness to engage in things "Japanese." The Japanese restaurant is likely to be more comfortable and offer more privacy than others, thus creating a better relationship. A Japanese menu includes raw fish. The Japanese host will inevitably ask "Do you like raw fish?" The answer is "yes." Accepting what is offered is a necessity for relationship building in Japan, but it does not include the necessity of eating everything. Being a guest is a simple task as all that is necessary is responding to what the Japanese host suggests or discusses. The intricacies of the organization are the responsibility of the hosts.

Hosting a dinner is much more difficult than being a guest. The host is responsible for assuring a successful relationship-building event. Hosting requires an understanding of Japanese social knowledge if the event is to be successful. Three principles of social knowledge are at work in dinner meetings: (1) have an environment that permits individual members of the companies to start to become acquainted and either start building a relationship or support and maintain one; (2) provide a setting and a meal befitting the guests' social position and thereby show that the host respects this position; and (3) send indirect signals of the status of the relationship in terms of the locale and quality of food. The meal can offer a form of celebration, a basis of apology[1] or just a feeling of comfort. The atmosphere created at dinner should be relaxed and enjoyable. The host is responsible for the comfort of the guests and, should that comfort be threatened for any reason, the host must make certain that conviviality is restored.

Execution of these social values requires one to know when to host, how to select the right guests, how to select a proper restaurant, how to assure that the meal is a proper one, how to keep the conversation in an acceptable mood and assure that the event starts and ends within a culturally acceptable time frame.

Determination of who hosts must be settled well in advance of the date of the dinner. The decision should not be left open until the close of a formal business meeting. If one side has an apology to make or if they have a difficult request, then they should certainly offer to host. For dinners following routine meetings, Pharmco works on the basis that if the meetings are in Japan, then the Japanese host, and if they are in the United States, Pharmco hosts. This works well. If, however, the Japanese are insistent upon acting as host, it is best to follow their lead.

The attendees of any particular dinner must correlate to reciprocal status of individuals from both companies. Therefore the attendees must be agreed upon well in advance of the dinner. Any changes of attendee by one side must be announced well in advance of the dinner. For one side to change the status level of attendance

at the last minute causes problems for the other. If the side making changes lowers the level of attendance, the other side has two problems to sort out. First, is a *honne* message being sent and why? For example, Japanese companies have been known to use this type of last-minute change as a way to tell the other company that they want to downgrade the existing relationship between the two companies. Second, how can a Japanese manager explain such changes to his superior? If, on the other hand, the level of attendance is increased at the last minute, the other might not be able to reciprocate, leading to embarrassment and a weakening of friendly relations. Attendance, once set, should not change.

The class of the restaurant must be in keeping with the status of the senior member of the party being invited, for Japanese executives have a clear understanding of where their status allows them to dine. Selection of a restaurant considered below a Japanese guest's status results in the guest losing face with his colleagues. Anticipation of this problem makes the Japanese uncomfortable during the meal, precluding the building of good social relationships. An example demonstrates the point.

Pharmco headquarters decided that the cost of entertaining in Tokyo was too high and dictated that cheaper places be found. The dictum was followed and, on the occasion of the next business meeting with a middle manager of Diversity, disaster resulted. When the guest arrived, his first comment was that one of his subordinates often brought suppliers to the restaurant. Pharmco had clearly insulted him in the choice of eating establishment, causing Pharmco managers to spend the rest of the night apologizing. Trying to rectify the situation, the next time they hosted the manager, Pharmco managers went to a very exclusive place. The first comment received was, "the president of our company likes this restaurant but I have never been here." This time, Pharmco embarrassed the Diversity manager by taking him to a location beyond his status, causing him to explain to his colleagues the next day why he was there.

Avoiding these problems requires only that foreigners ask a Japanese for a restaurant preference. The answer will be "no," followed by a comment indicating a restaurant in which he has never eaten but would like to do so. If this approach fails, a visit to the social director of the hotel in which the foreigner is staying will yield dividends. By showing the director the card of the individual to be entertained, she will make appropriate selections, based on the *meishi* information of the name of the company and the title of the person. She never errs in judgement.

Selection of the restaurant leads to the selection of a suitable menu, which is done by the host in advance

TABLE 5   Going to Dinner

Artifacts	Social Knowledge	Cultural Logic
Physical • Guests • Restaurant • Meals • Transportation Visual behavior • Hosting • Guesting • Timing to eat	• Relationship building is purpose of eating. • Status is honored by correct dinners. • Dinner group has some "insider" attributes.	Use of time • Time at dinners is effective use of time for relations. Relationships • Identifies how two companies view people's position in hierarchy. • Confirms status matching through acceptance or nonacceptance of invitations.

and must reflect the status of the guests and the nature of the occasion. For example, if it is a dinner just to end the day, a simple meal is in order. If the relationship is particularly strong, a stop in a noodle shop can be totally appropriate. If the dinner is one of celebration or a form of apology, however, a more elaborate meal is required. As with the choice of a restaurant, use Japanese expertise. A visit to the restaurant with the guest's business card and a discussion of the room and the meal with the majordomo of the restaurant (a discussion that should also cover who will attend and the purpose of the meal) assures a proper menu and setting.

When Pharmco management decided to enter a strategic alliance with Diversity KK, they had to inform Nippon Pharmaceutical, a potential partner, that they had decided not to work with them. The business aspects of the decision were discussed with Nippon Pharma at their offices, but then at dinner the relationship aspects of the decision were covered. The choice of location and meal was more elaborate than would normally be the case, given the state of the relationship. At the end of the meal, the Nippon Pharma representatives complimented Pharmco on their ability to be a good Japanese host.

Conversation at dinners does not include heavy business negotiations under any but the most unusual circumstances. Talk focuses on recreational activities, current politics, travel, or other "cocktail party" chat. The point of conversation, as well as of the food, is to put everyone at ease. Failure to follow this principle can cause discomfort.

At a dinner hosted by Diversity management, a Pharmco manager discussed matters relating to fundamental changes in the Japanese health care system. He did not notice that the Japanese were becoming upset until one of them exploded that "these matters were not the business of foreigners and they should not express opinions. Rather they should wait to be taught the right way to do business by the Japanese." While

the foreigner thought himself at fault by not avoiding the delicate subject matter, he received an extensive apology by a colleague of the Japanese who expressed such a forceful opinion. He said "As host, I should not permit such things to happen!"

In Japan, dinners are arranged for the end of the business day, which is around 6:30 p.m. The foreign host should plan to invite his guests for a 7 p.m. dinner, as doing so will give them a half an hour to get to the restaurant. Always offer an exact time. The American habit of "let's make it around 6:30 to 7" is not acceptable. The host always should arrive a few minutes early and be there to greet his guests. At the close of the meal, the host walks the guest to the front of the restaurant, where he has had the restaurant arrange transportation. The host stands at the curb and stays there, preferably bowing or waving, until the guests have been driven off. Table 5 summarizes the critical cultural factors concerning dinner engagements.

Drinking in Bars

Going out to drink after dinner is the first opportunity for colleagues of different companies to have the chance to behave as a set of "insiders." It also provides a setting in which anyone of the group can express a *honne* sentiment. Drinking provides the foreigner a sense of how relationship-building is progressing between his company, himself and his Japanese counterparts. Therefore, ethnographic understanding of ritual drinking is imperative (Table 6).

"Know how to sing" was the key learned by Pharmco management before going out drinking after dinner. Drinking in Karaoke bars is the ultimate socializing and relationship-building mechanism with and among Japanese. Power and social distance are almost completely broken down at the bars. The president as well as the most junior person present will sing, tell

TABLE 6   Going Out Drinking

Artifacts	Social Knowledge	Cultural Logic
Physical • Karaoke bars • Tabs • Female social managers Visual behavior • Singing • Joking • Honest opinion	• Freedom of speech acceptable. • Drunken behavior acceptable. • Place to get things "off the chest." • Everyone can be an "insider."	Human relations • Provides a time for *honne* talk. • Fills the need for business associates to be a set of "insiders." Environment • Setting is outside a traditional "insider" setting, allowing a new set of "insiders" to be formed on "neutral" ground. Reality and truth • Feelings (reality) must be expressed and understood (truth) by an insider group.

jokes, and generally relax. Although there is still not a round table, all the people together act as though they are at one. The environment has also changed substantially from that of the office. The bar is smaller than the office, and women are an important addition as they are to provide conversation and pour the drinks.[2] The tables are laid out so that there is little structure in the physical environment. A basic assumption is that this is the one place in the entire social milieu where uncertainty is acceptable. The assumption is that, with drink, it is totally acceptable to say what is on your mind to whomever you want. A further assumption is that whatever is said cannot be held against a person after leaving the bar.

Being there makes one an insider for the time spent together in the bar. "Insidership" is created only if the proper bar is chosen—one befitting the status of the group. Unlike choosing a restaurant, however, the foreigner must ask his Japanese associates for advice as to where to go, for they know that the foreigner lacks the knowledge to make a proper selection. A Pharmco executive experienced near-disaster the one time he selected a bar without consulting a Japanese businessman. He had found the hotel social relations director helpful with restaurants so [he] thought that person would be a good source of information for bars. He was not. As soon as he walked in the bar recommended by the director, he knew there was a problem: Except for one or two Japanese, only foreigners were present; the bar was almost empty; and the hostesses ranged in age from 40 to 50—far too old for the tastes of the Japanese guests. Fortunately, relationships between the Pharmco executive and his Japanese guests [were] strong enough for everyone to get a good laugh from the situation. He is still periodically reminded of the incident.

Business is usually not done at the bar, where drinking offers the Japanese an opportunity to express *honne* opinions about his relationships with colleagues, both foreign and Japanese. These opinions are tolerable as they are expressed when the person expressing them is acceptably drunk. Within the drinking context, everyone is in the same social circle. For this reason, one must constantly be alert for signals that might indicate something is on a colleague's mind. At one drinking session, a Pharmco manager felt that something was bothering his Japanese counterpart but, as the evening wore on, nothing was said. Just before it ended, the Japanese manager put his face down on the table and muttered that he had something important to say. The American leaned forward and asked what it was. All the Japanese said was "Your Johns-san is an asshole." Nothing more was said and the subject was never raised again. The American assumed that just stating the opinion was enough to relieve the tension the Japanese had. The opinion was not reported to Johns. The next business day discussions with the Japanese gentlemen were more relaxed than had been previously experienced.

PHARMCO BUSINESS IMPROVEMENTS

Three critical factors were deemed necessary for the program to be judged a success: (1) effective working relationships with Japanese executives; (2) shortened project times; and (3) improved financial returns. The project is successful based on these factors (Table 7) and is in the process of being applied to other countries.

Before learning the methodologies and skills outlined in this paper, Pharmco executives avoided travel to Japan and working with Japanese whenever possible. Fifty Pharmco executives have been through the training program. Before the program, they were asked to evaluate their comfort level of working with Japanese and their enjoyment of business trips to Japan. The

TABLE 7   Critical Factors Outcome

Effective working relationships

1. Pharmco employees are more self-assured when meeting Japanese in Japan.

2. Their Japanese counterparts state they prefer working with Pharmco over other foreign companies.

Shortened project times

1. Prior to introducing the cultural material, projects between Pharmco and Diversity averaged 15 months to completion.

2. Projects run by executives applying cultural methodologies shortened project completion times to an average of 8 months, while all others remain at 15 months.

Improved financial returns

1. Financial returns based on contracts negotiated by personnel not exposed to the cultural material average gross income of 6% of sales.

2. Financial returns of contracts negotiated by personnel applying the anthropological techniques provide gross income equal to 18% of sales.

rating scale was 1 to 10 with 1 expressing no comfort and no enjoyment to 10 expressing total comfort and enjoyment. The average score was 3 with a range of 1 to 5. After exposure to the concepts, tools, and material, the average score increased to 6, with a range of 5 to 9. The final measurement was based on 15 executives who used the concepts and tools in their next series of meetings. The average score of this group was 8, with a low score of 5 and a high score of 10. Before the program, most employees wanted to be accompanied to Japan by a person experienced in Japan. After the exposure, almost all are comfortable making these trips on their own. This willingness to work in and with Japan has improved the personal effectiveness of all these employees working on Japanese projects.

Late delivery of projects was costly to Pharmco and discouraged Diversity managers from working with their Pharmco counterparts. In one case the delays were estimated to cost Pharmco $90 million over a ten-year period. The delays were of a nature that a competitor entered the market with a similar product, thereby denying innovator status to Pharmco. The improved delivery times are helping both Diversity and Pharmco in gaining valuable marketing time over their key competitors.

SUMMARY

The ability to work with and within a foreign culture requires an organization to adopt and implement an interpretive strategy that permits its practitioners to set out to work proactively within the perceived meaning of the foreign environment. This strategy requires managers to become transformational in order to operate successfully in other social and institutional environments. Successful implementation of such a strategy demands

the use of both business and anthropological tools and skills. By creating a base of these skills and providing a training environment in which employees individually could learn and implement such a strategy, Pharmco achieved dramatic improvements in its Japanese business relationships and business results. This success has led to adapting the training to other countries.

NOTES

1. In Japan, the concept of apology involves a great shame for not having behaved correctly or done something in the right way. To apologize is traumatic for a Japanese.

2. Apologies are necessary to my female colleagues for this chauvinistic viewpoint. It is how things are in Japan, however. I would like to point out that should a female colleague be part of the group visiting the bar, she would be treated as a colleague by her peers and be well received by the employees in the bar.

REFERENCES

Brislin, Richard W., Kenneth Cushner, Craig Cherrie, and Mehalahi Yong. 1986. *Intercultural Interactions: A Practical Guide.* Beverly Hills, CA: Sage.

Campbell, Joseph. 1960. *The Masks of God: Primitive Mythology.* New York: Viking Press.

———. 1989. *The Hero with a Thousand Faces.* New York: Viking Press.

David, Kenneth. 1985. *Participant Observation in Pharmaceutical Field Selling.* Norwich, CT: Norwich Eaton Pharmaceutical Co., Inc.

Doi, Takeo. 1990a. *The Anatomy of Dependence.* Tokyo: Kodansha International.

_____. 1990b. *The Anatomy of Self.* Tokyo: Kodansha International.

Hall, Edward T., and Mildred R. Hall. 1987. *Hidden Differences.* New York: Anchor Press.

Hamada, Tomoko. 1991. *American Enterprise in Japan.* Albany: SUNY Press.

Hayashi, Shuji. 1988. *Culture and Management in Japan.* Tokyo: University of Tokyo Press.

Hofstede, Geert. 1980. *Culture's Consequences: International Differences in Work-Related Values.* Beverly Hills, CA: Sage.

Ishida, Eiichiro. 1974. A Culture of Love and Hate. In *Japanese Culture and Behavior,* Takie Sugiyama Lebra and William P. Lebra, eds. Pp. 27–36. Honolulu: University Press of Hawaii.

Kluckhohn, F. R., and F. L. Strodbeck. 1961. *Variations in Value Orientations.* Westport, CT: Greenwood Press.

Lebra, Takie Sugiyama. 1976. *Japanese Patterns of Behavior.* Honolulu: University Press of Hawaii.

Matsumoto, Michihiro. 1988. *The Unspoken Way.* Tokyo: Kodansha International.

Nakane, Chie. 1970. *Japanese Society.* Tokyo: Charles E. Tuttle Co.

Pelzel, John C. 1974. Human Nature in the Japanese Myths. In *Japanese Culture and Behavior,* Takie Sugiyama Lebra and William P. Lebra, eds. Pp. 3–26. Honolulu: University Press of Hawaii.

Reeves-Ellington, Richard H. 1988. Relationships Between Multinationals and Peasants. Paper presented at the annual meeting of the American Anthropological Association, Chicago.

Reeves-Ellington, Richard H., and Paul Steidlmeier. 1991. *Total Quality, Institutionalism and the Retooling of American Business.* Binghamton, NY: SUNY-Binghamton, School of Management.

19

Family Planning Outreach and Credit Programs in Rural Bangladesh

Sidney Ruth Schuler and Syed M. Hashemi

In many parts of the world, high fertility rates threaten women's health and lead to a variety of negative consequences associated with exploding populations. Many applied anthropologists argue that stabilizing population growth is critical for increased quality of life in developing nations. Yet the paradoxical coexistence of high birthrates in tandem with starvation and poverty is all too common. Governments and nongovernmental agencies spend millions and millions of dollars each year trying to reduce birthrates. Certainly there has been much success, but there is a long way to go.

As we have seen repeatedly, anthropology teaches us of the interrelationships between the various segments of our social order. If we wish to reduce the birthrate, for example, there may be ways that are less intrusive than family planning and that have additional benefits for women and their communities.

Women's participation in the economic sphere is linked to their status in society. Low status, isolation, dependence, and lack of mobility to even visit with other women limit women's opportunities and ability to act in their own interests. Empowering women by enhancing their economic role in society can have many consequences, one of which is an increased use of contraceptives.

This intriguing selection examines the case of a Grameen Bank program that provides loans for poor women in rural Bangladesh.

As you read this selection, ask yourself the following questions:

- Who should make judgments about whether the fertility rate in Bangladesh is too high? And who has the right to implement programs that change the social order?

- How does purdah limit women's access to family planning services?

- What is Grameen Bank's strategy for reducing women's isolation?

- How are economic conditions linked to the use of contraceptives?

- Should family planning workers assist women in using contraceptive methods secretly?

- What do women mean when they say that through Grameen Bank they have "learned to talk"?

The following terms discussed in this selection are included in the Glossary at the back of the book:

dependent variable	qualitative methods
hypothesis	random sample
purdah	TFR (total fertility rate)

I n rural Bangladesh, women's ability to seek out family planning services is limited by their isolation and their economic and social dependence on men. Large numbers of female outreach workers—about 28,000—are being employed by the government and nongovernmental programs to bring family planning

services to women in their homes. Program evaluations and research studies have documented the effectiveness of this strategy, particularly in increasing use of the oral pill and other temporary contraceptive methods. Recent studies show substantial increases in contraceptive use and a decline in estimated fertility rates—from TFR[1] of about 7 in the late 1960s and early 1970s to about 5 in 1989—and attribute this change in large part to the expansion in access to family planning services in recent years, mainly through female

Reprinted with permission of Society for Applied Anthropology from *Human Organization* 54(4): 455–61, 1995.

community-based workers (Cleland et al. 1994; Larson and Mitra 1992; World Bank 1992).

While the intensive door-to-door delivery strategy has been effective in raising levels of contraceptive use from low to moderate levels (e.g., from 19% in 1983 to 40% in 1991), it is obvious that intensification of service delivery can only go so far, and that other strategies will be needed if levels of contraceptive use are to be increased to a level that would stabilize population growth. Improvements in the quality of services are needed, both for achievement of higher levels of contraceptive use, and from the perspective of women's rights to better health and reproductive autonomy. Another strategy would be interventions that increase women's ability to take an active role in getting access to services— for example, programs that strengthen women's economic roles and increase their mobility. This article examines the effects of the Grameen Bank program that provides small loans for women's self-employment activities in rural Bangladesh. Survey and ethnographic research findings are used to analyze the effects of the Grameen Bank, community-based family planning outreach, and women's relative levels of physical mobility on their practice of contraception. The effects of exposure to the Grameen Bank and home visits by family planning workers are compared for members and nonmembers living in Grameen Bank villages.

BACKGROUND

Among the poor in rural Bangladesh, women's lives are severely restricted by their social and economic dependence on men. Because of *purdah* (a system based on an ideology concerned with secluding and protecting women to uphold social standards of modesty and morality) women's contacts with the world outside of the family are extremely limited. Many cannot avail themselves of family planning, health and other services that may be available unless these services are brought to their homes. Bringing services to women in or near their homes is the principal strategy of the Bangladesh Government's family planning program and of many of the nongovernmental organizations providing family planning services in rural areas. As noted above, this strategy has been very effective in increasing contraceptive use.

Grameen Bank is a quasi-governmental organization involved in lending to the poor in nearly half of all villages in rural Bangladesh. Its two million female members (and about two hundred thousand male members) come from landless rural poor families, most of whom have very few assets of any kind. The program attempts to draw women out of isolation by providing them with credit, to enable them to earn a cash income through various types of self-employment activities. In addition to supporting economic activities that require interactions in the public sphere, it increases women's mobility and access to information by requiring that they attend regular meetings. The rituals of membership help women to create a sense of identity outside of the family. Grameen Bank does not provide family planning services. We have argued, based on a previous analysis, that the program influences contraceptive use by strengthening women's economic roles and contributing to their empowerment, increasing their ability to overcome obstacles to use of contraception. The same analysis suggested that BRAC (Bangladesh Rural Advancement Committee), whose program focus is similar but somewhat broader, does not have the same effect on contraceptive use because it is less effective in strengthening women's economic roles and in helping them to establish identities outside of the family (Schuler and Hashemi 1994).

A number of studies (e.g., Koenig et al. 1992) have assessed the effects of family planning outreach on use of contraception in Bangladesh. Two recent studies (Simmons et al. 1988, 1992) argue that the role of the female family planning worker in Bangladesh goes beyond the conventional concept of "supply" of family planning methods and services, so that they function as change agents in the communities where they work. In this article we focus on the effects of credit rather than family planning programs in transforming reproductive norms, and we attempt to highlight the interactive effects of the two types of interventions.

METHODOLOGY

Data Sources

The analysis is based on a survey conducted in late 1992 to measure the impact of participation in credit programs on contraceptive use. It included four separately selected samples. The first two were random samples of Grameen Bank and BRAC members.[2] . . . With a few exceptions, the women in these two samples have been members of the programs for a minimum of 18 months. The third was a comparison group consisting of nonmembers from Grameen Bank villages who would be eligible to join BRAC or Grameen Bank (i.e., poor and functionally landless). The fourth was a second comparison group consisting of women living in villages not served by either program, who would be eligible to join the programs. One adult woman was selected from each household. The interviewers were Bangladeshi women who had previous experience in conducting demographic surveys. They received more training during the process of pretesting the questionnaires. In addition to questions related to contraceptive use, the survey included questions related to women's status within the family and community, their physical mobility and their economic roles. A total of 1305 married women younger than 50 were interviewed.[3]

The data from concurrent ethnographic research in six villages describes the credit programs in operation, from the perspectives of the field research team as well as participants in the programs. The team consisted of six women and six men, all Bangladeshi, most of whom had master's degrees. The team received intensive training in qualitative research methods at the beginning of the project, and the principal investigators provided continuing informal training throughout the study. The male-female team in each village conducted in-depth interviews to document change processes, both in women's roles and status and in norms related to reproduction and use of contraception. This article is based primarily on the survey data, but data from the ethnographic study is taken into account in interpreting the survey results.

Hypotheses

The following analysis is intended to test several specific hypotheses. Underlying all of them is the more general hypothesis that women's isolation, dependence, and lack of mobility inhibit use of contraception, and that a variety of programmatic strategies can be used to lessen these effects. The specific hypotheses are:

1. Home visits by family planning fieldworkers are positively related to contraceptive use.

2. Membership in credit programs and residence in villages where such programs are present increases the likelihood that a woman will use contraception.

3. Women's relative physical mobility is positively related to use of contraception.

4. The higher level of physical mobility of credit program participants does not fully explain their greater propensity to use contraception.

Variables

Dependent Variable   The dependent variable indicates whether or not the respondent is currently using any method of contraception.

Exposure to Credit Programs   These variables indicate whether the respondent was a Grameen Bank member, a nonparticipant living in a Grameen Bank village, or a resident of a comparison village, where no credit program existed.

Control Variables   In order to distinguish between effects of credit program participation per se and effects of other variables that are believed to affect contraceptive use in Bangladesh, several control variables are included. These are respondent's age, whether she ever attended school, number of surviving children, existence of at least one surviving son, existence of at least one surviving daughter, and an indicator of the relative economic level of the respondent's household. The latter is a composite measure based on the number of items owned from the following list: bed, blanket/quilt, shawl/sweater/coat, radio/TV, cow/buffalo.

Indicators of Access to Family Planning Services
We include two indicators of access to family planning services. The first of these is whether the respondent was ever visited by a family planning worker and the second is whether she was visited in the three months prior to the survey. Because of the strong emphasis on community-based services in the Bangladesh family planning program, these are generally thought to be the best indicators of access to family planning services in rural Bangladesh.

Indicators of Women's Physical Mobility   For this analysis we consolidated the variables related to women's mobility to create a single score. In the survey interview the respondent was presented with a list of places (the market, a medical facility, the movies, outside the village) and asked if she had ever gone there. She was given one point for each place she had visited and an additional point if she had ever gone there alone. A dichotomous variable was then created, in which a respondent with a score of 3 or better was classified as "more mobile."

Frequency distributions and means, as applicable, for the dependent and independent variables are presented in Table 1.

STATISTICAL RESULTS

The first section of the analysis compares women living in villages where Grameen Bank is present with women living in villages without a credit program. As Table 1 indicates, there is a dramatic difference in levels of contraceptive use between Grameen Bank members and women living in comparison villages—a difference of 16 percentage points. . . . The presence of the Grameen Bank program in a village has a significant effect on use of contraception, both among members and nonmembers, which is not explained by the effects of outreach. Visits by family planning workers (both recent and "ever") also appear to have strong independent effects, as do age, relative wealth, and presence of a surviving son.

TABLE 1   Characteristics of Study Samples

	GB	GB Non-members	Comparison
% using contraception	59.0	48.0	43.0
Mean age (in years)	31.0	26.0	29.0
Mean no. surviving children	3.5	2.6	3.3
Mean no. surviving sons	1.8	1.3	1.7
Mean no. surviving daughters	1.7	1.3	1.6
% attended school	29.0	18.0	18.0
Mean wealth score	2.5	1.7	1.6
% ever visited by FP worker	83.0	67.0	78.0
% visited in past 3 months	36.0	38.0	35.0
Mean mobility score	2.3	2.1	1.9
Mean duration of membership (in months)	50.0	—	—
N of cases	312	315	424

. . . [Further,] women who are "more mobile" are considerably more likely to use contraception. Sixty percent of the "more mobile" group were using a contraceptive method, compared with 46% of the "less mobile" group. The relatively higher level of mobility of women in Grameen Bank villages explains, at least in part, the higher level of contraceptive use.

COMBINED EFFECTS OF GRAMEEN BANK AND FAMILY PLANNING OUTREACH

Previous studies in Bangladesh have found contact with female family planning workers to be one of the most important determinants of contraceptive use. . . . In general the findings indicate that family planning outreach has a highly significant effect on contraceptive use and that the presence of Grameen Bank in a village has an added effect. However, another dimension is added when contraceptive use rates among women who have/have not been visited by family planning workers are examined separately for each of the three groups (Figure 1).

For the comparison group and for nonmembers in Grameen Bank villages, rates of contraceptive use among women who have been visited by a family planning worker are 21 and 30 points higher, respectively, than for women who have never been visited. However, for members of Grameen Bank, the rate of contraceptive use is consistently high (59%), regardless of whether the women have ever been visited by a family planning worker. This suggests that the

*Difference in CPR for women visited/not visited significant at p<.001 in chi square test.

FIGURE 1   Current contraceptive use—all methods, whether ever visited by FP worker

potential of Grameen Bank to influence contraceptive use is particularly important for women whose access to family planning services is relatively limited. For nonparticipating women in Grameen Bank villages who have been visited by a family planning fieldworker, the rate of contraceptive use is almost as high as among Grameen Bank members in the same communities—58%, compared with 48% for women in the comparison group. For the nonparticipants, the combined effect of the presence of Grameen Bank in a

*Difference in CPR for women visited/not visited significant at $p<.05$ in chi square test.

**Difference in CPR for women visited/not visited significant at $p<.001$ in chi square test. (For GB members difference not significant at $p<.05$ level.)

FIGURE 2   Current contraceptive use—all methods, whether ever visited by FP worker past three months

village and family planning outreach is even more evident when one looks at visits by family planning workers within the past three months (Figure 2). Among women who were not visited within the three months preceding the survey, the rates of contraceptive use are about the same for the comparison group, and about 20 points lower than among Grameen Bank members. The rates of contraceptive use among women who were visited by a family planning worker within the past three months are 9 points higher for Grameen Bank members, 11 points higher for the comparison group, and 32 points higher for Grameen Bank non-members (65%, 50%, and 68%, respectively).

. . . Family planning outreach is an important factor explaining the relatively high level of contraceptive use among nonparticipants in Grameen Bank villages, but . . . the even higher level of contraceptive use among participants is due to other factors.

DISCUSSION AND CONCLUSION

The strong effect of visits by community-based family planning fieldworkers on use of contraception supports the findings of previous research in Bangladesh. Because of their social and economic dependence on men, and their limited physical mobility, most women in rural Bangladesh cannot get access to family planning

methods and services without assistance. As one of the respondents put it,

> I am not allowed to go out and work even though we are so poor that we are sometimes desperate. Neither my husband nor his parents will let me go out to work . . . I had wanted to use family planning before my two daughters were born. I asked my husband several times to bring me a family planning method but he wouldn't listen . . . I am a woman—I could not get it for myself.

The ethnographic study data indicate that men often fail to provide this assistance because they are generally apathetic about fertility control, or because they fear that side effects will lead to economic losses—either by interfering with work or by incurring monetary costs for treatment. Since most women are prevented from working outside of the home, and perceived as economically nonproductive, their husbands and in-laws often feel that it is wrong for them to incur expenses (Schuler et al. 1995).

In this context the presence of a community-based fieldworker, whether employed by the government or a nongovernmental organization, can make a great difference. By providing information and services in the home, they preempt the need for most women to go to clinics or other sources for family planning methods. They provide free pills and suggest things that women can say to persuade their husbands to allow them to use contraception. In cases where persuasion seems unlikely to be effective, they often assist women in using contraceptive methods secretly.

The survey findings suggest that, in addition to "supply-side" strategies, it is possible to influence fertility through programs that decrease women's isolation and their economic dependence on men. Such programs can help women to overcome obstacles to contraceptive use such as lack of mobility, lack of cash, lack of information about contraceptive methods and services, and opposition or lack of cooperation from their husbands and other family members. Grameen Bank strengthens women's economic roles through credit, enabling them to contribute more substantially to their families' support. Even in cases where the woman hands her loan money over to her husband, there is usually some acknowledgment from the family that she is a source of income. Involvement in the program also gives women a socially legitimate purpose to participate in a group outside of the family. The opportunity for involvement in a nonfamily group can be important as a source of identity, new experiences, and ideas.

The ethnographic and the survey findings from this study generally support Grameen Bank's own contention that strengthening women's economic roles

TABLE 2 Comparison of Method Mix in Grameen Bank Villages Versus Comparison Villages (N = 1051)

	Grameen Bank Villages	Comparison Villages
Modern Methods		
Pills	22%	15%
Condom	1%	—
Injectables	5%	1%
IUDs	1%	1%
Female Sterilization	18%	18%
Male Sterilization	2%	3%
Traditional Methods		
Rhythm Method	4%	4%
Withdrawal	1%	—
Abstinence	1%	—
Other	1%	1%
No Method	46%*	56%*

*Totals not equal to 100% because of rounding.

gives them more autonomy and more control over important decisions affecting themselves and their families, as well as contributing to their self-confidence and propensity to plan for the future. It promotes women's relative freedom to move about in public and to travel outside of the village. Where more women are employed outside of the home, and are required to walk along roads or use buses or other forms of transport, it is less difficult for them to travel within and outside of their villages to get services.

Participation in the Grameen Bank program also makes members more experienced in interacting with men outside of the family and with authority figures. Although the interactions that take place in weekly meetings with bank staff clearly cast the women in a subservient role, this nevertheless seems to give them a certain self-confidence. In all interactions with government officials and even representatives of nongovernmental organizations, the poor are in a subservient role, and at least in this case it is the woman rather than her husband who is doing the interacting. Several of the women in our study told our field investigators that through Grameen Bank they had "learned to talk," and now they were not afraid to talk to outsiders. This probably increases their ability to avail themselves of family planning and health services.

Through a combination of intimidation and confidence-building, Grameen helps women to stand up to their husbands. Normally, any savings or asset that a women might have could be legitimately (at least from her husband's point of view) appropriated by him. Having recognized that this would be a central problem in a loan program for women, Grameen Bank tells women what to say when their husbands try to take their loan money. Case studies suggest that women who have developed the self-confidence to try to protect their assets and earnings from their husbands are more likely to take initiative in other areas, such as practicing family planning.

The Grameen Bank program can produce high rates of contraceptive use among members, even if they are not exposed to family planning outreach. The very high rates of contraceptive use among nonmembers in Grameen Bank villages who are visited by a family planning fieldworker suggest that the presence of Grameen Bank's program in a village in combination with family planning outreach can increase use of contraception dramatically, even among women who do not join Grameen Bank. The probable explanation is that reproductive norms are changing in Grameen Bank villages, but that diffusion of innovations takes time. Nonmembers, whose level of dependence on men has not been reduced because they have not participated in the program, typically require the support of family planning workers to follow the reproductive norms that are emerging (Table 2).

In considering the implications of these findings, it is important to avoid overestimating the magnitude of the changes occurring in gender relations. The vast majority of women—including those who participate in the Grameen Bank program—are able to make only small cash or kind contributions to the family's support, and many have little or no control over the income. Only a quarter of the Grameen Bank members in our survey said that their contribution represented half or more of the family's income, and only 7% of the nonmembers in Grameen Bank villages and 4% in comparison villages said this. Socially, and psychologically as well, the typical Grameen Bank member, like other women, is extremely dependent on her husband, and simply has to accept inequities, extreme limitations on her autonomy, and in some cases physical abuse. Watching the realities of poverty and gender-based subordination being played out in social life in the six ethnographic study villages, most of the members of our research team did not expect to find that the small changes occurring in women's lives as a result of Grameen Bank were having a measurable impact on contraceptive use.

Our ethnographic study provided some insight into the processes through which women are asserting themselves in making reproductive decisions, but it also revealed continuing obstacles to increased and more effective fertility control. The most significant of these seems to be fear—related to method side effects, health problems that may be perceived as side effects, and the widespread belief that contraceptive methods cause physical weakness and other problems. In some cases lingering ideas that contraceptive use may be sinful are reinforced when contraceptive users suffer from side effects or experience other types of misfortunes. In addition to physical suffering and even death, contraceptive users and their families fear inability to work, and the possibility that the problems resulting from contraceptive use will require costly medical treatments. Because most women do not have an independent income or control over money, they know that if something happens to them they will be dependent on others—in most cases their husbands—to arrange and pay for medical treatment. Generally the fieldworkers who come to their doors have limited training and are only minimally equipped to treat health problems. Women's restricted physical mobility and their economic dependence on men, as well as their general condition of poverty, limit their ability to seek treatment. In our view, a continuous and increased focus on providing economic opportunities for women and, simultaneously, on improving poor women's access to health services and improving the quality of contraceptive services is needed.

NOTES

1. TFR, or Total Fertility Rate, is the average number of children born to a woman during her lifetime.

2. Since the previous analysis suggested that BRAC does not affect the level of contraceptive use among its members it was excluded from the present analysis.

3. See Schuler and Hashemi 1994 for a more detailed description of the survey methodology.

REFERENCES

Cleland, John, James E. Phillips, Sajeda Amin, and G. M. Kasmal. 1994. The Determinants of Reproductive Change in Bangladesh: Success in a Challenging Environment. World Bank Regional and Sectoral Studies. Washington DC: The World Bank.

Koenig, Michael A., Ubaidur Rob, Mehrab Jali Khan, J. Chakraborty, and Vincent Fauveau. 1992. Contraceptive Use in Matlab, Bangladesh in 1990: Levels, Trends, and Explanations. *Studies in Family Planning* 23(6): 352–364.

Larson, Ann and S. N. Mitra. 1992. Family Planning in Bangladesh: An Unlikely Success Story. *International Family Planning Perspectives* 18(4):123–129.

Mauldin, W. Parker and John A. Ross. 1991. Family Planning Programs: Efforts and Results, 1982–89. *Studies in Family Planning* 22(6):350–367.

Mitra, S. N., Ann Larson, Gilliam Foo, and Shahidul Islam. 1992. *Bangladesh Contraceptive Prevalence Survey. July 1991: Key Findings.* Dhaka: Mitra and Associates.

Schuler, Sidney Ruth and Syed M. Hashemi. 1994. Credit Programs, Women's Empowerment and Contraceptive Use in Rural Bangladesh. *Studies in Family Planning* 25(2):65–76.

Schuler, Sidney Ruth, Syed M. Hashemi and Ann Hendrix. 1995. Bangladesh's Family Planning Success Story: A Gender Perspective. *International Family Planning Perspectives* 27:6.

Simmons, Ruth, Laila Baqee, Michael A. Koenig, and James E. Phillips. 1988. Beyond Supply: The Importance of Female Family Planning Workers in Rural Bangladesh. *Studies in Family Planning* 19(1):29–38.

Simmons, Ruth, Rezina Mita, and Michael A. Koenig. 1992. Employment in Family Planning and Women's Status in Bangladesh. *Studies in Family Planning* 23(2):97–109.

The World Bank. 1992. Population and the World Bank: Implications from Eight Case Studies. Operations Evaluations Department. Washington, DC: The World Bank.

20

Coming of Age in Palo Alto

Katie Hafner

When people imagine anthropologists and anthropological work, they often envision the lone anthropologist living in a grass-roofed hut in the high mountains of New Guinea or in a canvas tent only a stone's throw away from an exciting archaeological dig. These images are not exactly wrong: Anthropologists are still doing such fieldwork in remote places, and such "exotic" work is still necessary for furthering our understanding of humankind. On the other hand, those images are quite incomplete, since many anthropologists work closer to home. Twenty-first-century anthropology encompasses an exceptionally broad range of topics and research settings. Anthropologists are applying the theories and research methods honed in the Australian outback or the Kalahari Desert to modern settings, lending new and innovative insights and creating novel solutions.

When anthropologists describe the continuing processes of culture change, they often begin with an analysis of patterns of technological innovation. So-called traditional societies are sometimes using ancient technologies. In the past two decades, no technological development has been more revolutionary than the Internet; today, it is a technology that we take for granted.

This article profiles several anthropologists who conduct observational research on the social aspects of modern technology and how it is used in people's everyday lives. The title refers both to Margaret Mead's classic anthropological study *Coming of Age in Samoa* and to Palo Alto, California, a part of the famed Silicon Valley and home to numerous successful high-tech companies. The effectiveness of the new technologies from Silicon Valley depends on their acceptability to consumers, so these anthropologists look at consumers in the "natural habitat" of their homes and offices. The anthropologists profiled here work at places like AT&T Labs, Intel, and Media One, using their anthropological training to improve technological products. The concepts and methods of anthropology can be easily applied to both product development and marketing studies for business.

As you read this selection, ask yourself the following questions:

- What does the author mean by "embodied knowledge"?
- How do these observational studies compare with aspects of ethnographic field research?
- How do the anthropologists in this article combine observational studies with ethnographic field research?
- When an anthropologist is employed by a company like Media One, is she or he still doing anthropology?

The following terms discussed in this selection are included in the Glossary at the back of the book:

ethnography
embodied knowledge
observational research

In 1981, while doing postdoctoral field work in cultural anthropology, Bonnie A. Nardi lived with villagers in Western Samoa, trying to understand the cultural reasons that people there have an average of eight children.

Today Dr. Nardi works at AT&T Labs West in Menlo Park, Calif., and has no regrets. She left academia in 1984 and is considered a pioneer among anthropologists who are employed by high-tech companies to examine consumers' behavior in their homes and offices.

"Usually people say, 'What is an anthropologist doing here?'" Dr. Nardi said. "But when I explain that I study how people use technology in order to get new ideas for products and services, it instantly makes sense."

No longer do companies study consumers' psyches only by asking people what they think about technology and how they use it. Now they conduct observational research, dispatching anthropologists to employ their ethnographic skills by interviewing, watching and videotaping consumers in their natural habitats. In the past several years, companies like Apple, Motorola, Xerox and Intel, as well as telecommunications and cable companies, have brought anthropologists into the corporate fold. The goal is to apply what the anthropologists learn to new product concepts. "It's the extreme form of understanding the customer," Dr. Nardi said.

Half of all anthropologists with doctorates are going to work outside universities, said Susan Squires, president-elect of the National Association for the Practice of Anthropology, which represents anthropologists outside academia. High competitive pressure and short product cycles mean that corporate field work is usually much briefer than academic research and fewer people are studied. While the work might not be considered reliable enough to be published in a traditional anthropology journal, companies can use the results to help them make marketing and product-design decisions.

Observational research isn't new for American industry. It can be traced to the 1930's and 1940's, when social scientists began examining productivity during the Depression and World War II, said Marietta Baba, chairwoman of the anthropology department at Wayne State University in Detroit. "They left industry completely in the 60's and 70's," Dr. Baba said. "They came back in the 80's and there has been a slow, steady increase since then." The rise in corporate employment for anthropologists has roughly paralleled a drop in academic opportunities. Hallmark Cards has an anthropologist. The automotive industry employs at least a dozen, and so does Andersen Consulting.

But it is in the high-tech arena, with intense pressure and high rate of product failures, that studying consumers' habits at very close range is currently most popular, Dr. Squires said.

"We go out into the consumer space, into people's homes—we go to where the people are," said Tony Salvador, an experimental psychologist at Intel, where he is called a design ethnographer. "If we're interested in their homes, we go there. If we're interested in what they do on vacation, we go on vacation with them."

Sometimes an ethnographic inquiry will lead to new ways to use an existing technology or will generate new technologies. It was a 1996 study of pager use in rural China, where there is a scarcity of phones, that prompted Motorola to start thinking seriously about two-way paging outside urban markets, said Jean Canavan, an anthropologist who is the manager of culture and technology initiatives at Motorola.

"The context is really critical," Ms. Canavan said. "If we want to develop technologies that really fit into the way people live their day-to-day lives, then we have to understand how people really live."

Many anthropologists work with a concept called embodied knowledge—tacit, nonscientific knowledge—and look for ways to incorporate such information into product design. Embodied knowledge is "basically the intelligence in your muscles," Dr. Nardi said.

"You aren't born knowing how to ride a bicycle," Dr. Baba said. "You don't learn by reading a book. With experience, your body comes to 'know' how to ride a bike."

Paying attention to embodied knowledge helped Matsushita build a better bread maker in 1987. The company sent a team of engineers to be apprenticed for several months to a master bread chef at the Osaka International Hotel in Japan. The magic ingredient turned out to be a special maneuver the chef executed with his hand while kneading the dough, so the engineers figured out how to mimic the movement with the machine.

"Anthropologists are trained in those patient, detailed ways of watching for hundreds of hours and taking everything down in minute detail, which is where the knowledge is—in the tiny details," Dr. Baba said. An understanding of movement skills has helped in the design of things like the computer mouse, joystick and touch screen. The mouse, for instance, lets the hand mimic the way the eyes scan a computer screen.

The social aspects of technology particularly interest anthropologists like the ones in Dr. Salvador's group at Intel. Three and a half years ago, the group was set up when the company began considering other consumer products after releasing its Pentium processor. "It was selling really well into homes, and people were saying we have to build more things for the home," he said. "We thought maybe we should understand more about the home."

The group members embarked on a study of 10 families with young children. They visited each family for an evening, eating dinner with the family and analyzing the organization of the home and the family's daily routine.

Dr. Salvador's group found that the kitchen and family room were the most important rooms in the house. "Very rarely are people alone in those spaces," he said. "Social relationships are very important." Dr. Salvador's findings may not seem like much of an epiphany, but his work has helped lead Intel to look beyond the notion of a PC as a device generally used by someone seated at a desk alone in a room and to understand the importance of whole families using and sharing computing devices.

Anne McClard and Ken Anderson, anthropologists who are married to each other, do similar observational research at Media One, a cable provider that

AT&T recently agreed to purchase. Ms. McClard and Mr. Anderson are part of Media One's Broadband Innovation Group. Their charge is to find new users and new uses for the company's services and, as Ms. McClard put it, "to make broadband living a reality."

To study Internet usage patterns, companies also install tracking systems on subjects' computers. But those kinds of studies are a poor substitute for the serendipitous twists and turns of actual interviews, anthropologists say.

Dr. Nardi said it was also important to couple interviews with observations to pick up on the knowledge and behavior people exhibit but do not think to mention. In her book *Information Ecologies: Using Technology with Heart* (M.I.T. Press, 1999), Dr. Nardi describes a study she did of a broadcast video and audio system in a hospital. She noticed that the surgical staff told jokes during routine parts of an operation. "This became an issue when the multimedia system began to broadcast audio to remote parts of the hospital," she said in an interview. The jokes and banter, she said, relieved tension during lengthy operations. "But no one would ever have said in an interview, 'We tell jokes during surgery,'" she noted.

Dr. Nardi and her colleagues recommended that the hospital add a feature to the system so the surgeons would know whether the audio component was turned on.

Ms. McClard and Mr. Anderson of Media One have had similar experiences. Last summer, they conducted a study called Always On, in which they observed families with cable modem connections, which allow computers to have a constant connection to the Internet at very high speeds, in an effort to understand what it is like to have such a link to the Internet in one's home.

The two anthropologists found that people with constant connections were often unaware of changes in their behavior. For instance, the people would often walk over to the computer to perform tasks like retrieving E-mail even if they were busy with tasks somewhere else. But they hardly notice that they are doing it, Mr. Anderson said.

Such observations by anthropologists can be important for sales later on. When Canon first introduced its color printers for the home market in 1995, said Dr. Squires, who works for GVO, a consumer product consulting company in Palo Alto, Calif., consumers did not know what to do with them. So a team of researchers from GVO went into homes to examine refrigerator doors and bedroom walls for the types of printed material families create and exchange. The result was Canon Creative, the greeting card, T-shirt and poster software that comes bundled with the printers. Sales of the printers took off, Dr. Squires said.

But corporate anthropologists operate under constraints that make their jobs harder. Ms. McClard said the year and a half she took for an academic project seemed like "a real luxury" from the standpoint of the corporate world. A project for, say, Media One lasts just a few months.

So many of those anthropologists find it hard to present their findings, often from limited field samples, in a way that interests the people in the company who plan and design products. "Part of the challenge is telling the story in a way that makes it compelling to people who have the power to develop products," Ms. McClard said.

Ms. McClard and Mr. Anderson videotape most of their interviews. "When engineers see the people talking, they are more convinced than if we told them stuff," she said. "We have to bring the experience alive for people. We don't have the numbers. The only thing we have is the experience of the people we go out to see."

Larry Prusak, executive director of I.B.M.'s Institute for Knowledge Management, a research organization, in Cambridge, Mass., said he believed that the number of anthropologists in industry would continue to grow.

"There's going to be a huge flourishing of industrial anthropologists in the next 20 years," he said, adding that this was especially true in the technology sector because companies were continuing to study technology's potential for mimicking human behavior. "We're in the infancy in this area, and I don't think anyone would tell you differently."

21

Our Babies, Ourselves

Meredith F. Small

Nature or nurture? Genes or environment? A perennial question in anthropology is the relative importance of innate human biology or particular cultural and early-childhood influences in people's social and psychological development. Cross-cultural variation in thought and behavior patterns is the hallmark of human diversity. Most anthropologists believe that there is individual variation within cultural variation. That is, members of a society share ideas of appropriate behavior, including the ways to raise children, and those shared ideas supercede individual variation. The influence of culture on personality development has been a theme in cultural anthropology since the days of Margaret Mead. These questions require us to study child-raising practices in a cross-cultural perspective.

This selection describes how parenting behaviors vary across societies. The way in which we interact with our own babies and children influences the adults they become. Sometimes we use the computer analogy of biology being the hardware (the brain) and culture as the software (the models with which we think and pattern our behavior) to think about nature and nurture. That analogy misses the fact that as babies learn they are physically shaping their neural pathways. With this in mind, the study of parenting and child development is even more important. In this regard, so-called traditional societies might have a lot to teach

us. People may be reticent to learn from others ("If it was good enough for us . . .") or to change behaviors, like extended breast-feeding.

As you read this selection, ask yourself the following questions:

- Why do Americans put babies in their own cribs, or feed them on schedules, or "let them cry it out"? What underlying cultural values might parents be trying to teach?
- How might high infant mortality risk affect parents' behaviors?
- How much stimulation for infants is appropriate? Why did the Dutch mother put her baby down for a nap right after the bath?
- Who is best to take care of a baby? How do people decide that?
- Why do anthropologists report that babies in traditional societies like the !Kung do not cry as much?

The following terms discussed in this selection are included in the Glossary at the back of the book:

adaptation	*socialization*
ethnopediatrics	*weaning*

During one of his many trips to Gusiiland in southwestern Kenya, anthropologist Robert LeVine tried an experiment: he showed a group of Gusii mothers a videotape of middle-class American women tending their babies. The Gusii mothers were appalled. Why does that mother ignore the cries of her unhappy baby during a simple diaper change? And how come that

From Our Babies, Ourselves, Meredith Small, Robert A. LeVine, Sara Harkness, Charles M. Super, Edward Z. Tronick, Ronald G. Barr, Katherine A. Dettwyler, James J. McKenna; NH, pp. 42–51. Reprinted from *Natural History* Oct. 1997; Copyright © Natural History Magazine, Inc.

grandmother does nothing to soothe the screaming baby in her lap? These American women, the Gusii concluded, are clearly incompetent mothers. In response, the same charge might be leveled at the Gusii by American mothers. What mother hands over her tiny infant to a six-year-old sister and expects the older child to provide adequate care? And why don't those Gusii women spend more time talking to their babies, so that they will grow up smart?

Both culture—the traditional way of doing things in a particular society—and individual experience guide parents in their tasks. When a father chooses to pick up his newborn and not let it cry, when a mother

---

GUSII SURVIVAL SKILLS
By Robert A. LeVine

Farming peoples of subSaharan Africa have long faced the grim reality that many babies fail to survive, often succumbing to gastrointestinal diseases, malaria, or other infections. In the 1970s, when I lived among the Gusii in a small town in southwestern Kenya, infant mortality in that nation was on the decline but was still high—about eighty deaths per thousand live births during the first year, compared with about ten in the United States at that time and six to eight in Western Europe.

The Gusii grew corn, millet, and cash crops such as coffee and tea. Women handled the more routine tasks of cultivation, food processing, and trading, while men were supervisors or entrepreneurs. Many men worked at jobs outside the village, in urban centers or on plantations. The society was polygamous, with perhaps 10 percent of the men having two or more wives. A woman was expected to give birth every two years, from marriage to menopause, and the average married woman bore about ten live children—one of the highest fertility rates in the world.

Nursing mothers slept alone with a new infant for fifteen months to insure its health. For the first three to six months, the Gusii mothers were especially vigilant for signs of ill health or slow growth, and they were quick to nurture unusually small or sick infants by feeding and holding them more often. Mothers whose newborns were deemed particularly at risk—including twins and those born prematurely—entered a ritual seclusion for several weeks, staying with their infants in a hut with a constant fire.

Mothers kept infants from crying in the early months by holding them constantly and being quick to comfort them. After three to six months—if the baby was growing normally—mothers began to entrust the baby to the care of other children (usually six to twelve years old) in order to pursue tasks that helped support the family. Fathers did not take care of infants, for this was not a traditional male activity.

Because they were so worried about their children's survival, Gusii parents did not explicitly strive to foster cognitive, social, and emotional development. These needs were not neglected, however, because from birth Gusii babies entered an active and responsive interpersonal environment, first with their mothers and young caregivers, and later as part of a group of children.

---

decides to bottle-feed on a schedule rather than breast-feed on demand, when a couple bring the newborn into their bed at night, they are prompted by what they believe to be the best methods of caregiving.

For decades, anthropologists have been recording how children are raised in different societies. At first, the major goals were to describe parental roles and understand how child-rearing practices and rituals helped to generate adult personality. In the 1950s, for example, John and Beatrice Whiting, and their colleagues at Harvard, Yale, and Cornell Universities, launched a major comparative study of childhood, looking at six varied communities in different regions: Okinawa, the Philippines, northern India, Kenya, Mexico, and New England. They showed that communal expectations play a major role in setting parenting styles, which in turn play a part in shaping children to become accepted adults.

More recent work by anthropologists and child-development researchers has shown that parents readily accept their society's prevailing ideology on how babies should be treated, usually because it makes sense in their environmental or social circumstances. In the United States, for example, where individualism is valued, parents do not hold babies as much as in other cultures, and they place them in rooms of their own to sleep. Pediatricians and parents alike often say this fosters independence and self-reliance. Japanese

parents, in contrast, believe that individuals should be well integrated into society, and so they "indulge" their babies. Japanese infants are held more often, not left to cry, and sleep with their parents. Efe parents in Congo believe even more in a communal life, and their infants are regularly nursed, held, and comforted by any number of group members, not just parents. Whether such practices help form the anticipated adult personality traits remains to be shown, however.

Recently, a group of anthropologists, child-development experts, and pediatricians have taken the cross-cultural approach in a new direction by investigating how differing parenting styles affect infant health and growth. Instead of emphasizing the development of adult personality, these researchers, who call themselves ethnopediatricians, focus on the child as an organism. Ethnopediatricians see the human infant as a product of evolution, geared to enter a particular environment of care. What an infant actually gets is a compromise, as parents are pulled by their offspring's needs and pushed by social and personal expectations.

Compared with offspring of many other mammals, primate infants are dependent and vulnerable. Baby monkeys and apes stay close to the mother's body, clinging to her stomach or riding on her back, and nursing at will. They are protected in this way for many months, until they develop enough motor and cognitive skills to move about. Human infants are at

AN INFANT'S THREE Rs

By Sara Harkness and Charles M. Super

You are an American visitor spending a morning in a pleasant middle-class Dutch home to observe the normal routine of a mother and her six-month-old baby. The mother made sure you got there by 8:30 to witness the morning bath, an opportunity for playful interaction with the baby. The baby was then dressed in cozy warm clothes, her hair brushed and styled with a tiny curlicue atop her head. The mother gave her the midmorning bottle, then sang to her and played patty-cake for a few minutes before placing her in the playpen to entertain herself with a mobile while the mother attended to other things nearby. Now, about half an hour later, the baby is beginning to get fussy.

The mother watches her for a minute, then offers a toy and turns away. The baby again begins to fuss. "Seems bored and in need of attention," you think. But the mother looks at the baby sympathetically and in a soothing voice says, "Oh, are you tired?" Without further ado she picks up the baby, carries her upstairs, tucks her into her crib, and pulls down the shades. To your surprise, the baby fusses for only a few more moments, then is quiet. The mother returns looking serene. "She needs plenty of sleep in order to grow," she explains. "When she doesn't have her nap or go to bed on time, we can always tell the difference—she's not so happy and playful."

Different patterns in infant sleep can be found in Western societies that seem quite similar to those of the United States. We discovered the "three Rs" of Dutch child rearing—*rust* (rest), *regelmaat* (regularity) and *reinheid* (cleanliness)— while doing research on a sample of sixty families with infants or young children in a middle-class community near Leiden and Amsterdam, the sort of community typical of Dutch life styles in all but the big cities nowadays. At six months, the Dutch babies were sleeping more than a comparison group of American babies—a total of fifteen hours per day compared with thirteen hours for the Americans. While awake at home, the Dutch babies were more often left to play quietly in their playpens or infant seats. A daily ride in the baby carriage provided time for the baby to look around at the passing scene or to doze peacefully. If the mother needed to go out for a while without the baby, she could leave it alone in bed for a short period or time her outing with the baby's nap time and ask a neighbor to monitor with a "baby phone."

To understand how Dutch families manage to establish such a restful routine by the time their babies are six months old, we made a second research visit to the same community. We found that by two weeks of age, the Dutch babies were already sleeping more than same-age American babies. In fact, a dilemma for some Dutch parents was whether to wake the baby after eight hours, as instructed by the local health care providers, or let them sleep longer. The main method for establishing and maintaining this pattern was to create a calm, regular, and restful environment for the infant throughout the day.

Far from worrying about "adequate stimulation," these mothers were conscientious about avoiding overstimulation in the form of late family outings, disruptions in the regularity of eating and sleeping, or too many things to look at or listen to. Few parents were troubled by their babies' nighttime sleep routines. Babies's feeding schedules were structured following the guidelines of the local baby clinic (a national service). If a baby continued to wake up at night when feeding was no longer considered necessary, the mother (or father) would most commonly give it a pacifier and a little back rub to help it get back to sleep. Only in rare instances did parents find themselves forced to choose between letting the baby scream and allowing too much night waking.

Many aspects of Dutch society support the three Rs throughout infancy and childhood—for example, shopping is close to home, and families usually have neighbors and relatives nearby who are available to help out with child care. The small scale of neighborhoods and a network of bicycle paths provide local play sites and a safe way for children to get around easily on their own (no "soccer moms" are needed for daily transportation!). Work sites for both fathers and mothers are also generally close to home, and there are many flexible or part-time job arrangements.

National policies for health and other social benefits insure universal coverage regardless of one's employment status, and the principle of the "family wage" has prevailed in labor relations so that mothers of infants and young children rarely work more than part-time, if at all. In many ways, the three Rs of Dutch child rearing are just one aspect of a calm and unhurried life style for the whole family.

---

the extreme: virtually helpless as newborns, they need twelve months just to learn to walk and years of social learning before they can function on their own.

Dependence during infancy is the price we pay for being hominids, members of the group of upright-walking primates that includes humans and their extinct relatives. Four million years ago, when our ancestors became bipedal, the hominid pelvis underwent

a necessary renovation. At first, this new pelvic architecture presented no problem during birth because the early hominids, known as australopithecines, still had rather small brains, one-third the present size. But starting about 1.5 million years ago, human brain size ballooned. Hominid babies now had to twist and bend to pass through the birth canal, and more important, birth had to be triggered before the skull grew too big.

DOCTOR'S ORDERS
By Edward Z. Tronick

In Boston, a pediatric resident is experiencing a vague sense of disquiet as she interviews a Puerto Rican mother who has brought her baby in for a checkup. When she is at work, the mother explains, the two older children, ages six and nine, take care of the two younger ones, a two-year-old and the three-month-old baby. Warning bells go off for the resident: young children cannot possibly be sensitive to the needs of babies and toddlers. And yet the baby is thriving; he is well over the ninetieth percentile in weight and height and is full of smiles.

The resident questions the mother in detail: How is the baby fed? Is the apartment safe for a two-year-old? The responses are all reassuring, but the resident nonetheless launches into a lecture on the importance of the mother to normal infant development. The mother falls silent, and the resident is now convinced that something is seriously wrong. And something is—the resident's model of child care.

The resident subscribes to what I call the "continuous care and contact" model of parenting, which demands a high level of contact, frequent feeding, and constant supervision, with almost all care provided by the mother. According to this model, a mother should also enhance cognitive development with play and verbal engagement. The pediatric resident is comfortable with this formula—she is not even conscious of it—because she was raised this way and treats her own child in the same manner. But at the Child Development Unit of Children's Hospital in Boston, which I direct, I want residents to abandon the idea that there is only one way to raise a child. Not to do so may interfere with patient care.

Many models of parenting are valid. Among Efe foragers of Congo's Ituri Forest, for example, a newborn is routinely cared for by several people. Babies are even nursed by many women. But few individuals ever play with the infant; as far as the Efe are concerned, the baby's job is to sleep.

In Peru, the Quechua swaddle their infants in a pouch of blankets that the mother, or a child caretaker, carries on her back. Inside the pouch, the infant cannot move, and its eyes are covered. Quechua babies are nursed in a perfunctory fashion, with three or four hours between feedings.

As I explain to novice pediatricians, such practices do not fit the continuous care and contact model; yet these babies grow up just fine. But my residents see these cultures as exotic, not relevant to the industrialized world. And so I follow up with examples closer to home: Dutch parents who leave an infant alone in order to go shopping, sometimes pinning the child's shirt to the bed to keep the baby on its back; or Japanese mothers who periodically wake a sleeping infant to teach the child who is in charge. The questions soon follow. "How could a mother leave her infant alone?" "Why would a parent ever want to wake up a sleeping baby?"

The data from cross-cultural studies indicate that child-care practices vary, and that these styles aim to make the child into a culturally appropriate adult. The Efe make future Efe. The resident makes future residents. A doctor who has a vague sense that something is wrong with how someone cares for a baby may first need to explore his or her own assumptions, the hidden "shoulds" that are based solely on tradition. Of course, pediatric residents must make sure children are cared for responsibly. I know I have helped residents broaden their views when their lectures on good mothering are replaced by such comments as "What a gorgeous baby! I can't imagine how you manage both work and three others at home!"

As a result, the human infant is born neurologically unfinished and unable to coordinate muscle movement. Natural selection has compensated for this by favoring a close adult–infant tie that lasts years and goes beyond meeting the needs of food and shelter. In a sense, the human baby is not isolated but is part of a physiologically and emotionally entwined dyad of infant and caregiver. The adult might be male or female, a birth or adoptive parent, as long as at least one person is attuned to the infant's needs.

The signs of this interrelationship are many. Through conditioning, a mother's breast milk often begins to flow at the sound of her own infant's cries, even before the nipple is stimulated. New mothers also easily recognize the cries (and smells) of their infants over those of other babies. For their part, newborns recognize their own mother's voice and prefer it over others. One experiment showed that a baby's heart rate quickly synchronizes with Mom's or Dad's, but not with that of a friendly stranger. Babies are also predisposed to be socially engaged with caregivers. From birth, infants move their bodies in synchrony with adult speech; they are hard-wired to absorb the cadence of speech and the general nature of language. Babies quickly recognize the arrangement of a human face—two eyes, a nose, and a mouth in the right place—over other more Picasso-like rearrangements. And mothers and infants will position themselves face-to-face when they lie down to sleep.

Babies and mothers seem to follow a typical pattern of play, a coordinated waltz that moves from attention to inattention and back again. This innate social connection was tested experimentally by Jeffrey Cohn and Edward Tronick in a series of three-minute laboratory

THE CRYING GAME

By Ronald G. Barr

All normal human infants cry, although they vary a great deal in how much. A mysterious and still unexplained phenomenon is that crying tends to increase in the first few weeks of life, peaks in the second or third month, and then decreases. Some babies in the United States cry so much during the peak period—often in excess of three hours a day—and seem so difficult to soothe that parents come to doubt their nurturing skills or to begin to fear that their offspring is suffering from a painful disease. Some mothers discontinue nursing and switch to bottle-feeding because they believe their breast milk is insufficiently nutritious and that their infants are always hungry. In extreme cases, the crying may provoke physical abuse, sometimes even precipitating the infant's death.

A look at another culture, the !Kung San hunter-gatherers of southern Africa, provides us with an opportunity to see whether caregiving strategies have any effect on infant crying. Both the !Kung San and Western infants escalate their crying during the early weeks of life, with a similar peak at two or three months. A comparison of Dutch, American, and !Kung San infants shows that the number of individual crying episodes are virtually identical. What differs is their length: !Kung San infants cry about half as long as Western babies. This implies that caregiving can influence only some aspects of crying, such as duration.

What is particularly striking about child-rearing among the !Kung San is that infants are in constant contact with a caregiver; they are carried or held most of the time, are usually in an upright position, and are breast-fed about four times an hour for one to two minutes at a time. Furthermore, the mother almost always responds to the smallest cry or fret within ten seconds.

I believe that crying was adaptive for our ancestors. As seen in the contemporary !Kung San, crying probably elicited a quick response, and thus consisted of frequent but relatively short episodes. This pattern helped keep an adult close by to provide adequate nutrition as well as protection from predators. I have also argued that crying helped an infant forge a strong attachment with the mother and—because new pregnancies are delayed by the prolongation of frequent nursing—secure more of her caregiving resources.

In the United States, where the thread of predation has receded and adequate nutrition is usually available even without breast-feeding, crying may be less adaptive. In any case, caregiving in the United States may be viewed as a cultural experiment in which the infant is relatively more separated—and separable—from the mother, both in terms of frequency of contact and actual distance.

The Western strategy is advantageous when the mother's employment outside of the home and away from the baby is necessary to sustain family resources. But the trade-off seems to be an increase in the length of crying bouts.

experiments at the University of Massachusetts, in which they asked mothers to act depressed and not respond to baby's cues. When faced with a suddenly unresponsive mother, a baby repeatedly reaches out and flaps around, trying to catch her eye. When this tactic does not work, the baby gives up, turning away and going limp. And when the mother begins to respond again, it takes thirty seconds for the baby to reengage.

Given that human infants arrive in a state of dependency, ethnopediatricians have sought to define the care required to meet their physical, cognitive, and emotional needs. They assume there must be ways to treat babies that have proved adaptive over time and are therefore likely to be most appropriate. Surveys of parenting in different societies reveal broad patterns. In almost all cultures, infants sleep with their parents in the same room and most often in the same bed. At all other times, infants are usually carried. Caregivers also usually respond quickly to infant cries; mothers most often by offering the breast. Since most hunter-gatherer groups also follow this overall style, this is probably the ancestral pattern. If

there is an exception to these generalizations, it is the industrialized West.

Nuances of caretaking, however, do vary with particular social situations. !Kung San mothers of Botswana usually carry their infants on gathering expeditions, while the forest-living Ache of Paraguay, also hunters and gatherers, usually leave infants in camp while they gather. Gusii mothers working in garden plots leave their babies in the care of older children, while working mothers in the West may turn to unrelated adults. Such choices have physiological or behavioral consequences for the infant. As parents navigate between infant needs and the constraints of making a life, they may face a series of trade-offs that set the caregiver–infant dyad at odds. The areas of greatest controversy are breast-feeding, crying, and sleep—the major preoccupations of babies and their parents.

Strapped to their mothers' sides or backs in traditional fashion, human infants have quick access to the breast. Easy access makes sense because of the nature of human milk. Compared with that of other mammals, primate milk is relatively low in fat and protein but

WHEN TO WEAN

By Katherine A. Dettwyler

Breast-feeding in humans is a biological process grounded in our mammalian ancestry. It is also an activity modified by social and cultural constraints, including a mother's everyday work schedule and a variety of beliefs about personal autonomy, the proper relationship between mother and child (or between mother and father), and infant health and nutrition. The same may be said of the termination of breast-feeding, or weaning.

In the United States, children are commonly bottle-fed from birth or weaned within a few months. But in some societies, children as old as four or five years may still be nursed. The American Academy of Pediatrics currently advises breast-feeding for a minimum of one year (this may be revised upward), and the World Health Organization recommends two years or more. Amid conflicting advice, many wonder how long breast-feeding should last to provide an infant with optimal nutrition and health.

Nonhuman primates and other mammals give us some clues as to what the "natural" age of weaning would be if humans were less bound by cultural norms. Compared with most other orders of placental mammals, primates (including humans) have longer life spans and spend more time at each life stage, such as gestation, infant dependency, and puberty. Within the primate order itself, the trend in longevity increases from smaller-bodied, smaller-brained, often solitary prosimians through the larger-bodied, larger-brained, and usually social apes and humans. Gestation, for instance, is eighteen weeks in lemurs, twenty-four weeks in macaques, thirty-three weeks in chimpanzees, and thirty-eight weeks in humans.

Studies of nonhuman primates offer a number of different means of estimating the natural time for human weaning. First, large-bodied primates wean their offspring some months after the young have quadrupled their birth weight. In modern humans, this weight milestone is passed at about two and a half to three years of age. Second, like many other mammals, primate offspring tend to be weaned when they have attained about one third of their adult human weight; humans reach this level between four and seven years of age. Third, in all species studied so far, primates also wean their offspring at the time the first permanent molars erupt; this occurs at five and a half to six years in modern humans. Fourth, in chimpanzees and gorillas, breast-feeding usually lasts about six times the duration of gestation. On this basis, a human breast-feeding would be projected to continue for four and a half years.

Taken together, these and other projections suggest that somewhat more than two and a half years is the natural minimum age of weaning for humans and seven years the maximum age, well into childhood. The high end of this range, six to seven years, closely matches both the completion of human brain growth and the maturation of the child's immune system.

In many non-Western cultures, children are routinely nursed for three to five years. Incidentally, this practice inhibits ovulation in the mother, providing a natural mechanism of family planning. Even in the United States, a significant number of children are breast-fed beyond three years of age. While not all women are able or willing to nurse each of their children for many years, those who do should be encouraged and supported. Health care professionals, family, friends, and nosy neighbors should be reassured that "extended" breast-feeding, for as long as seven years, appears physiologically normal and natural.

Substantial evidence is already available to suggest that curtailing the duration of breast-feeding far below two and a half years—when the human child has evolved to expect more—can be deleterious. Every study that includes the duration of breast-feeding as a variable shows that, on average, the longer a baby is nursed, the better its health and cognitive development. For example, breast-fed children have fewer allergies, fewer ear infections, and less diarrhea, and their risk for sudden infant death syndrome (a rare but devastating occurrence) is lower. Breast-fed children also have higher cognitive test scores and lower incidence of attention deficit hyperactivity disorder.

In many cases, specific biochemical constituents of breast milk have been identified that either protect directly against disease or help the child's body develop its own defense system. For example, in the case of many viral diseases, the baby brings the virus to the mother, and her gut-wall cells manufacture specific antibodies against the virus, which then travel to the mammary glands and go back to the baby. The docosahexanoic acid in breast milk may be responsible for improved cognitive and attention functions. And the infant's exposure to the hormones and cholesterol in the milk appears to condition the body, reducing the risk of heart disease and breast cancer in later years. These and other discoveries show that breast-feeding serves functions for which no simple substitute is available.

---

high in carbohydrates. Such milk is biologically suitable if the infant can nurse on a frequent basis. Most Western babies are fed in a somewhat different way. At least half are bottle-fed from birth, while others are weaned from breast to bottle after only a few months. And most—

whether nursed or bottle-fed—are fed at scheduled times, waiting hours between feedings. Long intervals in nursing disrupt the manufacture of breast milk, making it still lower in fat and thus less satisfying the next time the nipple is offered. And so crying over food and

BEDTIME STORY

By James J. McKenna

For as far back as you care to go, mothers have followed the protective and convenient practice of sleeping with their infants. Even now, for the vast majority of people across the globe, "cosleeping" and nighttime breast-feeding remain inseparable practices. Only in the past 200 years, and mostly in Western industrialized societies, have parents considered it normal and biologically appropriate for a mother and infant to sleep apart.

In the sleep laboratory at the University of California's Irvine School of Medicine, my colleagues and I observed mother–infant pairs as they slept both apart and together over three consecutive nights. Using a polygraph, we recorded the mother's and infant's heart rates, brain waves (EEGs), breathing, body temperature, and episodes of nursing. Infrared video photography simultaneously monitored their behavior.

We found that bed-sharing infants face their mothers for most of the night and that both mother and infant are highly responsive to each other's movements, wake more frequently, and spend more time in lighter stages of sleep than they do while sleeping alone. Bed-sharing infants nurse almost twice as often, and three times as long per bout, than they do while sleeping alone. But they rarely cry. Mothers who routinely sleep with their infants get at least as much sleep as mothers who sleep without them.

In addition to providing more nighttime nourishment and greater protection, sleeping with the mother supplies the infant with a steady stream of sensations of the mother's presence, including touch, smell, movement, and warmth.

These stimuli can perhaps even compensate for the human infant's extreme neurological immaturity at birth.

Cosleeping might also turn out to give some babies protection from sudden infant death syndrome (SIDS), a heartbreaking and enigmatic killer. Cosleeping infants nurse more often, sleep more lightly, and have practice responding to maternal arousals. Arousal deficiencies are suspected in some SIDS deaths, and long periods in deep sleep may exacerbate this problem. Perhaps the physiological changes induced by cosleeping, especially when combined with nighttime breast-feeding, can benefit some infants by helping them sleep more lightly. At the same time, cosleeping makes it easier for a mother to detect and respond to an infant in crisis. Rethinking another sleeping practice has already shown a dramatic effect: In the United States, SIDS rates fell at least 30 percent after 1992, when the American Academy of Pediatrics recommended placing sleeping babies on their backs, rather than face down.

The effect of cosleeping on SIDS remains to be proved, so it would be premature to recommend it as the best arrangement for all families. The possible hazards of cosleeping must also be assessed. Is the environment otherwise safe, with appropriate bedding materials? Do the parents smoke? Do they use drugs or alcohol? (These appear to be the main factors in those rare cases in which a mother inadvertently smothers her child.) Since cosleeping was the ancestral condition, the future for our infants may well entail a borrowing back from ancient ways.

even the struggles of weaning result from the infant's unfulfilled expectations.

Sleep is also a major issue for new parents. In the West, babies are encouraged to sleep all through the night as soon as possible. And when infants do not do so, they merit the label "sleep problem" from both parents and pediatricians. But infants seem predisposed to sleep rather lightly, waking many times during the night. And while sleeping close to an adult allows infants to nurse more often and may have other beneficial effects, Westerners usually expect babies to sleep alone. This practice has roots in ecclesiastical laws enacted to protect against the smothering of infants by "lying over"—often a thinly disguised cover

for infanticide—which was a concern in Europe beginning in the Middle Ages. Solitary sleep is reinforced by the rather recent notion of parental privacy. Western parents are also often convinced that solitary sleep will mold strong character.

Infant care is shaped by traditions, fads, science, and folk wisdom. Cross-cultural and evolutionary studies provide a useful perspective for parents and pediatricians as they sift through the alternatives. Where these insights fail to guide us, however, important clues are provided by the floppy but interactive babies themselves. Grinning when we talk to them, crying in distress when left alone, sleeping best when close at heart, they teach us that growth is a cooperative venture.

22

Measuring Up to Barbie

Ideals of the Feminine Body in Popular Culture

Jacqueline Urla and Alan C. Swedlund

Cultural ideas about beauty and sexual attractiveness vary across time and between different cultural groups. Feminine ideals of height, weight, appearance, and adornment range from buxom to svelte, from pubescent to maternal, and from scantily clad to ornately garbed. Within this variation, however, some recognizable stereotypes of female beauty have emerged in the postindustrial global culture. Recognizable figures like that of the supermodel, seen from runways in Paris to the cover of magazines in supermarkets, loom large in the definition of women's beauty. Just as recognizable, and particularly American, is the Barbie doll.

Given that Barbie is such an iconic figure, a child's toy, it may be difficult to imagine how she could be a bad girl. Urla and Swedlund discuss Barbie's history and what her plastic frame, boyfriend, and Dream House symbolize. By taking Barbie's measurements and scaling them to life size, they show how unrealistic (even impossible) Barbie really is, especially in comparison with many American women. The authors show that the idea of an "average woman" itself has a history. As a material object of socialization (just like baby dolls that teach mothering) the sexualized Barbie embodies American ideals of femininity, as well as a consumerist model of the "good life" full of fashionable clothing, cars, and swimming pools. Barbie's "hard" body represents self-control and discipline and sexual attractiveness, but not necessarily reproduction or motherhood.

As you read this selection, ask yourself the following questions:

- What does Barbie symbolize for American girls when they make-believe play about the lives of grown-ups? Why is Barbie fun?

- How is Barbie a consumer? Are desired consumption patterns part of gender socialization?

- How might the "beauty myth" be related to the ideas of the "natural tendencies of the body to decay" that Horace Miner described for the Nacirema people (Selection 1)?

- What does the anthropometry experiment tell us? How is culture involved in the definition of "normal"?

- What is the primary measurable difference between Barbie and a "normal" American woman?

The following terms discussed in this selection are included in the Glossary at the back of the book:

anorexia nervosa	*constructions of femininity*
anthropometry	*late capitalism*

I t is no secret that thousands of healthy women in the United States perceive their bodies as defective. The signs are everywhere: from potentially lethal cosmetic surgery and drugs, to the more familiar routines of dieting, curling, crimping, and aerobicizing, women seek to take control over their unruly physical selves. Every year at least 150,000 women undergo breast implant surgery (Williams 1992), while Asian women have their noses rebuilt and their eyes widened to make themselves look "less dull" (Kaw 1993). Studies show the obsession with body size and sense of inadequacy starts frighteningly early; as many as 80% of 9 year old suburban girls are concerned about dieting and their weight (Bordo 1991:125). Reports like these, together with the dramatic rise in eating disorders among young women, are just some of the more noticeable fall-out from what Naomi Wolf calls "the beauty myth." Fueled by the hugely profitable cosmetic, weight loss, and fashion industries, the beauty myth's glamorized notions of the ideal body reverberate back upon women as "a dark vein of self hatred, physical obsessions, terror of aging, and dread of lost control" (Wolf 1991:10).

It is this paradox—that female bodies are never feminine enough, that they require deliberate and oftentimes painful refashioning to be what "nature" intended—that motivates our inquiry into the feminine ideal. Neither universal nor changeless, idealized notions of both masculine and feminine bodies have a long history that shifts considerably across time, racial or ethnic group, class, and culture. Body ideals in twenty-first century North America are influenced and shaped by images from classical or "high art," the discourses of science and medicine, as well as a multitude of commercial interests, ranging from mundane life insurance standards, to the more high-profile fashion, fitness, and entertainment industries. Each has played contributing and sometimes conflicting roles in determining what counts as a desirable body for us today. In this essay, we focus our attention on the domain of popular culture and the ideal feminine body as it is conveyed by one of pop culture's longest lasting and most illustrious icons: the Barbie doll.

Making her debut in 1959 as Mattel's new teenage fashion doll, Barbie rose quickly to become the top selling toy in the United States. Several decades and a women's movement later, Barbie dolls remain one of Mattel's biggest selling items netting over one billion dollars in revenues worldwide (Adelson 1992), or roughly one Barbie sold every two seconds (Stevenson 1991).[1] By the nineties, Mattel was estimating that in the U.S. over 95% of girls between the ages of 3 and 11 own at least one Barbie and that the average number of dolls per owner is seven (Shapiro 1992). Barbie is clearly a force to contend with, eliciting, over the years, a combination of critique, parody, and adoration. A legacy of the post-war era, she remains an incredibly resilient visual and tactile model of femininity for pre-pubescent girls.

It is not our intention to settle the debate over whether Barbie is a good or bad role model for little girls. Though that issue surrounds Barbie like a dark cloud, we are more concerned with how Barbie has been able to survive and remain popular in a period marked by the growth of consumer society, intense debate over gender and racial relations, and changing notions of the body. Our aim, then, is not to offer another rant against Barbie, but to explore how this doll crystallizes some of the predicaments of femininity and feminine bodies in late twentieth-century North America.

A DOLL IS BORN

Parents thank us for the educational values in the world of Barbie . . . They say that they could never get their daughters well groomed before—get them out of slacks or blue jeans and into a dress . . . get them to scrub their necks and wash their hair. Well that's where Barbie comes in. The doll has clean hair and a clean face, and she dresses fashionably, and she wears gloves and shoes that match. (Ruth Handler 1964, quoted in Motz 1987:130)

Legend has it that Barbie was the brainchild of Mattel owner Ruth Handler, who first thought of creating a three dimensional fashion doll after seeing her daughter play with paper dolls. As an origin story, this one is touching and no doubt true. But Barbie was not the first doll of her kind nor was she just a mother's invention. Making sense of Barbie requires that we look to the larger socio-political and cultural milieu that made her genesis both possible and meaningful. Based on a German prototype, the "Lili" doll, Barbie was from "birth" implicated in the ideologies of the cold war and the research and technology exchanges of the military-industrial complex. Her finely crafted durable plastic mold was, in fact, designed by Jack Ryan, well known for his work in designing the Hawk and Sparrow missiles for the Raytheon Company. Conceived at the hands of a military weapons designer-turned-toy inventor, Barbie dolls came onto the market the same year as the infamous Nixon-Khrushchev "kitchen debate" at the American National Exhibition in Moscow. There, in front of the cameras of the world, the leaders of the capitalist and socialist worlds faced off, not over missile counts, but over "the relative merits of American and Soviet washing machines, televisions, and electric ranges" (May 1988:16). As Elaine Tyler May has noted in her study of the Cold War, this much celebrated media event signaled the transformation of American-made commodities and the model suburban home into key symbols and safe-guards of democracy and freedom. It was thus with fears of nuclear annihilation and sexually charged fantasies of the perfect bombshelter running rampant in the American imaginary, that Barbie and her torpedo-like breasts emerged into popular culture as an emblem of the aspirations of prosperity, domestic containment, and rigid gender roles that were to characterize the burgeoning post-war consumer economy and its image of the American Dream.

Marketed as the first "teenage" fashion doll, Barbie's rise in popularity also coincided with and no doubt contributed to the post-war creation of a distinctive teenage lifestyle.[2] Teens, their tastes and behaviors, were becoming the object of both sociologists and criminologists, as well as market survey researchers intent on capturing their discretionary dollars. While J. Edgar Hoover was pronouncing "the juvenile jungle" a menace to American society, we have retailers, the music industry, and movie-makers declaring the 13 to 19 year old age bracket "the seven golden years" (Doherty 1988:51–52).

Barbie dolls seemed to cleverly reconcile both of these concerns by personifying the good girl who was sexy, but didn't have sex, and was willing to spend, spend and spend. Amidst the palpable moral panic over juvenile delinquency and teenagers' new found sexual freedom, Barbie was a reassuring symbol of solidly middle-class values. Popular teen magazines, advertising, television and movies of the period painted a highly dichotomized world divided into good (i.e. middle class) and bad (i.e. working class) kids: the clean-cut college-bound junior achiever versus the street corner boy; the wholesome American Bandstander versus the uncontrollable bad seed (cf. Doherty 1988; and Frith 1981 for England). It was no mystery where Barbie stood in this thinly disguised class discourse. As Motz writes, Barbie's world bore no trace of the "greasers" and "hoods" that inhabited the many grade B films about teenage vice and ruin. In the life Mattel laid out for her in story books and comics, Barbie, who started out looking like a somewhat vampy, slightly Bardot-esque doll, was gradually transformed into a "'soc' or a 'frat'—affluent, well-groomed, socially conservative" (Motz 1987:130). In lieu of back-seat sex and teenage angst, Barbie had pajama parties, barbecues, and her favorite pastime, shopping.

Every former Barbie owner knows that to buy a Barbie was to lust after Barbie accessories: that matching pair of sandals and handbag, canopy bedroom set, or country camper. Both conspicuous consumer and a consumable item herself, Barbie was surely as much the fantasy of U.S. retailers as she was the panacea of middle class parents. For every "need" Barbie had, there was a deliciously miniature product to fulfill it. As Paula Rabinowitz has noted, Barbie dolls, with their focus on frills and fashion, epitomize the way that teenage girls and girl culture in general have figured as accessories in the historiography of post-war culture; that is as both essential to the burgeoning commodity culture as consumers, but seemingly irrelevant to the historical events defining cold war existence (Rabinowitz 1993).

Perhaps what makes Barbie such a perfect icon of late capitalist constructions of femininity is the way in which her persona pairs endless consumption with the achievement of femininity and the appearance of an appropriately gendered body. By buying for Barbie, girls practice how to be discriminating consumers knowledgeable about the cultural capital of different name brands, how to read packaging, and the overall importance of fashion and taste for social status (Motz 1987:131–132). Being a teenage girl in the world of Barbie dolls becomes quite literally a performance of commodity display requiring numerous and complex rehearsals. In making this argument, we want to stress that we are drawing on more than just the doll. "Barbie"

is also the packaging, spin-off products, cartoons, commercials, magazines, and fan club paraphernalia, all of which contribute to creating her persona. Clearly, as we will discuss below, children may engage more or less with those products, subverting or ignoring various aspects of Barbie's "official" presentation. However, to the extent that little girls *do* participate in the prepackaged world of Barbie, they come into contact with a number of beliefs central to femininity under consumer capitalism. Little girls learn, among other things, about the crucial importance of their appearance to their personal happiness and ability to gain favor with their friends. Barbie's social calendar, like her closet, is constantly full, and the stories in her fan magazines show her frequently engaged in preparation for the rituals of heterosexual teenage life: dates, proms, and weddings. A perusal of Barbie magazines, and the product advertisements and pictorials within them, shows an overwhelming preoccupation with grooming for those events. Magazines abound with tips on the proper ways of washing hair, putting on make-up, and assembling stunning wardrobes. Through these play scenarios little girls learn Ruth Handler's lesson about the importance of hygiene, occasion-specific clothing, knowledgeable buying, and artful display as key elements to popularity and a successful career in femininity.

Barbie exemplifies the way in which gender has become a commodity itself, "something we can buy into . . . the same way we buy into a style" (Willis 1991:23). In her insightful analysis of the logic of consumer capitalism, cultural critic Susan Willis pays particular attention to the way in which children's toys like Barbie and the popular muscle-bound "He-Man" for boys link highly conservative and narrowed images of masculinity and femininity with commodity consumption (1991:27). Being or becoming a teenager, having a "grown-up" body, observes Willis, is presented as inextricably bound up with the acquisition of certain commodities, signaled by styles of clothing, cars, music, etc. In play groups and fan clubs (collectors are a whole world unto themselves) children exchange knowledge about the latest accessories and outfits, their relative merit, and how to find them. They become members of a community of Barbie owners whose shared identity is defined by the commodities they have or desire to have. The articulation of social ties through commodities is, as Willis argues, at the heart of how sociality is experienced in consumer capitalism. In this way, we might say that playing with Barbie serves not only as a training ground for the production of the appropriately gendered woman, but also as an introduction to the kinds of knowledge and social relations one can expect to encounter in late capitalist society.

BARBIE IS A SURVIVOR

For anyone tracking Barbie's history, it is abundantly clear that Mattel's marketing strategies have been sensitive to a changing social climate. When the women's movement gained momentum in the seventies, Barbie dolls became a target of criticism (Billyboy 1987; Lord 1994). Mattel responded by giving Barbie new outfits to "reflect the activities and professions that modern women are involved in" (quoted in Harpers, August 2, 1990, p. 20). Just as Barbie graduated from Candy striper and ballerina to astronaut and doctor, Mattel also tried to diversity her lily-white image beginning in 1967 with Barbie's first Black friend, "Colored Francie." With the expansion of sales worldwide, Barbie has acquired multiple national guises (Spanish Barbie, Jamaican Barbie, Malaysian Barbie, etc.).[3] In addition, her cohort of "friends" has become increasingly ethnically diversified, as has Barbie advertising, which now regularly feature Asian, Hispanic and Afro-American little girls playing with Barbie. Today, Barbie pals include a smattering of brown and yellow plastic friends, like Teresa, Kira, and Miko who appear on her adventures and, very importantly, can share her clothes.

Perhaps Mattel's most glamorous concession to multiculturalism was Shani who premiered at the 1991 Toy Fair with great fanfare and media attention. Unlike her predecessors who were essentially "brown plastic poured into blond Barbie's mold," Shani, together with her two friends, Asha and Nichelle (each a slightly different shade of brown), and boyfriend Jamal created in 1992, were decidedly Afro-centric, with outfits in "ethnic" fabrics rather than the traditional Barbie pink (Jones 1991). The packaging also announced that these dolls' bodies and facial features were meant to be more realistic of African American women, although as we will see, the differences, while meaningful, don't preclude interchanging clothes with Barbie. Now Mattel announced, "ethnic Barbie lovers will be able to dream in their own image" (*Newsweek* 1990:48). Multiculturalism cracked open the door to Barbiedom and diversity could walk in as long as she was big busted, slim hipped, had long flowing hair, tiny feet, and was very very thin.[4]

In looking over the course of Barbie's career, it is clear that part of her resilience, continuing appeal and profitability stems from the fact that her identity is constructed primarily through fantasy and is consequently open to change and reinterpretation. As a fashion model, Barbie continually creates her identity anew with every costume change. In that sense, we might want to call Barbie emblematic of the restless desire for change that permeates post-modern capitalist society (Wilson 1985:63). Not only can her image be renewed with a change of clothes, Barbie is also seemingly able to clone herself effortlessly into new identities—"Malibu Barbie"; "Totally Hair Barbie"; "Teen Talk Barbie"; even Afro-centric Shani—without somehow suggesting a serious personality disorder. Since Barbie is a perpetual teenager, Barbie's owners are at liberty to fantasize any number of life choices for her; she might be a high-powered fashion executive or she just might marry Ken and "settle down" in her luxury condo. Her history is a barometer of changing fashions, changing gender and race relations, and a keen index of corporate America's anxious attempts to find new and more palatable ways of selling the beauty myth and commodity fetishism to new generations of parents and their daughters.

What is striking, then, is that while Barbie's identity may be mutable—one day she might be an astronaut, another a cheerleader—*her hyper-slender, big-chested body has remained fundamentally unchanged over the years*—a remarkable fact in a society that fetishizes the new and improved. Barbie, of course, did acquire flexible arms and legs as we know, her face has changed significantly, and her hair has grown by leaps and bounds (Melosh and Simmons 1986). But her body measurements, pointed toes, and proportions have not altered significantly. It is to that body and to the results of our class experiment in the anthropometry of Barbie that we now turn. But before taking out our calipers on Barbie and her friends to see how their bodies measure up, we want to offer a very brief historical overview of anthropometry to help us understand how the notion of the "average" American female, body was debated in post-war United States.

THE MEASURED BODY: NORMS AND IDEALS

> The paramount objective of physical anthropology is the gradual completion, in collaboration with the anatomists, the physiologists, and the chemists, of the study of the normal white man under ordinary circumstances.
>
> —Ales Hrdlicka, 1918

Anthropometry, the science of measuring human bodies, belongs to a long line of techniques of the 18th and 19th centuries—craniometry, phrenology, comparative anatomy—concerned with measuring, comparing, and interpreting variability in the physical dimensions of the human body. Early anthropometry shared with these early sciences the expectation that the body was a window into a host of moral, temperamental, racial, or gender characteristics. It sought to distinguish itself from its predecessors, however, by being more rigorous and standardized in its techniques (Hrdlicka 1939:12). Head shape, especially cranial capacity, was a constant source of special fascination, but by the early part of this century, physical anthropologists, together with anatomists and medical doctors were developing a precise and routine set of measurements for the entire body that they hoped would permit systematic comparison of the human body across race, nationality, and gender.[5]

Anthropometry developed in the United States under the aegis of Ernest Hooton, Ales Hrdlicka, and Franz Boas, located respectively at Harvard, the Smithsonian, and Columbia University. Their main areas of interest were (1) identifying the physical features of racial and or national types, (2) the measurement of adaptation and "degeneracy," and (3) a comparison of the sexes. As is well documented by now, women and non-Europeans did not fare well in these emerging sciences of the body which held white males as the pinnacle of evolution (see the work of Blakey 1987; Gould 1981, Schiebinger 1989; Fee 1979; Russett 1989). Hooton, in his classic book, *Up from the Ape* (1931) regularly likened women and especially non-Europeans of both sexes to non-human primates. Similarly Hrdlicka's 1925 comparative study of male and female skulls went to rather extraordinary lengths to argue that women's brains (presumed at the time to be a sign of intelligence) were actually *smaller* than men's even though his measurements showed females to have a relatively *larger* cranial capacity than that of males.[6]

When it came to defining racial or national types, men, not women, were the most commonly studied.[7] Although Hrdlicka and others considered it necessary to measure both males and females, early physical anthropology textbooks reveal that more often than not it was the biologically male body that was selected to visually represent a particular race or humanity as a whole. Males were, in short, the unspoken prototype, while women's bodies were understood as a sexual subset. Women's bodies were frequently described as deviations from the generic or ideal type: their body fat "excessive"; their pelvis maladaptive to a bipedal (i.e. more evolved) posture; their musculature weak. Scientists seem to agree that what most dictated a woman's physical shape was her reproductive function. All other features were subordinated to and could be explained by this capacity to bear children. Not surprisingly, given this assumption, it was women's, particularly African or non-European women's, reproductive organs, genitalia and secondary sexual characteristics, that were the most carefully scrutinized and measured (see Fausto-Sterling 1995).

In the United States, we begin to find an attempt to scientifically define a normative "American" female body in the late 19th and early twentieth centuries. By the 1860's, Harvard as well as other universities had begun to regularly collect anthropometric data on their male student populations, and in the 1890's comparable data began to be collected from the East Coast women's colleges as well. It was thus upper class, largely WASP, young people who were the basis of some of the early attempts to define the measurements of the "normal" American male and female. By basing themselves in elite colleges, "other" Americans—descendants of African slaves, North American Indians, and the many recent European migrants from Ireland, southern Europe, and eastern Europe—were effectively excluded from defining the norm. Rather, their bodies were more often the subject of racist evolutionary oriented studies concerned with "race crossing," degeneracy, and the effects of the "civilizing" process (see Blakey 1987).

Academia was not the only place where body standards were being developed. By the early part of the twentieth century industry began to make widespread commercial use of practical anthropometry: the demand for standardized measures of the "average" body manifested in everything from designs for labor-efficient workstations and kitchens to standardized sizes in the ready-to-wear clothing industry (cf. Schwartz 1986). Soon insurance companies would enter the scene. Between 1900 and 1920, the first medicoactuarial standards of weight and height began to appear. The most significant of these, the Dublin Standard Table of Heights and Weights, developed in 1908 by Louis Dublin, a student of Franz Boas and statistician for the Metropolitan Life Insurance Company, became the authoritative reference in every doctor's office (cf. Bennett and Gurin 1982:130–138). However, what began as a table of statistical averages soon became a means of setting ideal 'norms'. Within a few years of its creation, the Dublin table shifted from providing a record of statistically "average" weights to becoming a guide to "desirable" weights which, interestingly enough, began to fall notably below the average weight for most adult women. Historian Joan Brumberg points to the Dublin Table, widely disseminated to doctors and published in popular magazines, together with the invention of the personal or bathroom scale, as the two devices most responsible in America for popularizing the notion that the human figure could be standardized and that abstract and often unrealistic norms could be uniformly applied (1988:232–235).

By the 1940's the search to describe the normal American male and female body in anthropometric terms was being conducted on many fronts fueled by a deepening concern about the physical fitness of the American people. Did Americans constitute a distinctive physical type? Were they physically stronger or weaker than their European ancestors? Could they defend themselves in time of war? And who did this category of "Americans" include? Questions such as these fed into an already long-standing preoccupation with defining a specifically American national character and, in 1945, led to the creation of some of the most celebrated and widely publicized life-size anthropometric statues of the century: Norm and Norma, the average American male and female. These statues, sculpted by Malvina Hoffman, were based on the composite measurements of thousands of white eighteen to twenty-five year old subjects. Both figures were put on display, but it was Norma who received the greatest media attention when the Cleveland Health Museum, which had purchased the pair, decided to sponsor a contest to find the woman in Ohio whose body most closely matched the dimensions of Norma. Under the catchy headline, "Are you Norma, Typical Woman?" the publicity surrounding this contest instructed women how to take their measurements for the contest. Within ten days, 3863 women had sent in their measurements to compete for the $100 prize in U.S. War Bonds that would go to the woman who most resembled the average American girl.

Besides bolstering the circulation of the *Cleveland Plain Dealer,* the idea behind the contest was to promote interest in physical fitness. Norma was described in the press as everything the young American woman should be in a time of war: fit, strong-bodied and at the peak of her reproductive potential. Newspaper articles emphasized that women had a national responsibility to be fit if America was to continue to excel after the war. Few contestants apparently measured up to the challenge (Shapiro 1945). Only one percent came close to Norma's proportions. Commenting on the search for Norma, Dr. Gebhard, director of the Cleveland Health Museum, was quoted in one of the many newspaper articles as saying that "if a national inventory of the female population of this country were taken there would be as many "4Fs" among the women as were revealed among the men in the draft" (Robertson 1945:4). The contest provided the occasion for many health reformers to voice their concern about the weakening of the "American stock" and to call for eugenic marital selection and breeding.

Norma and Norman were thus always more than statistical composites; they were prescriptive ideals that, like the college studies that preceded them, erased American's racial and ethnic differences. The "average American" of the post-war period was still imagined as a youthful white body. However, there were competing ideals. Health reformers, educators, and doctors who approved and promoted Norma as an ideal for American women were well aware that her sensible, strong, thick-waisted body differed significantly from the tall, slim-hipped bodies of fashion models in vogue at the time.[8] As the post-war period advanced, Norma would be overshadowed by the array of images of fashion models and pin up girls put out by advertisers, the entertainment industry, and a burgeoning consumer culture. These fashion images were becoming increasingly thin in the sixties and seventies while the "average" woman's body was in fact getting heavier.

THE ANTHROPOMETRY OF BARBIE: TURNING THE TABLES

Anthropometry, like the very notion of a "normal" body it has been used to construct, is part of an unsavory history. Nevertheless, in the contemporary cultural context where an impossibly thin image of women's bodies has become the most popular children's toy ever sold, it strikes us it might just be the power tool we need for destabilizing a fantasy spun out of control. It was with this in mind that we asked students in one of our social biology classes to measure Barbie to see how her body compared to the average measurements of young American women of the same period. Besides estimating what Barbie's dimensions would be if she were life-size, we see the experiment as an occasion to turn the anthropometric tables from disciplining the bodies of living women, to measuring the ideals by which we have come to judge ourselves and others. We also see it as an opportunity for students who have grown up under the regimes of normalizing science, students who no doubt have been measured, weighed, and compared to standards since birth, to use those very tools to unsettle a highly popular cultural ideal.

Our initial experiment involved measuring many Barbies and Kens from different decades as well as some of their friends. Here we will only report on the results for Barbie and Ken from the Glitter Beach collection, as well as Jamal and Shani, Barbie's more recent African-American friends. (See tables 1 and 2.) Mattel had marketed these latter dolls as having a more authentic African-American appearance and a "rounder more athletic" body, and we wanted to test that out.

After practicing with the calipers, discussing potential observational errors, and performing repeated trial runs, we began to record. In scaling Barbie to be life-sized, the students decided to translate her measurements using two standards: (a) If Barbie were a fashion model (5'10") and (b) if she were of average height for women in the United States (5'4"). We also decided to measure Ken, in the same way, using an average male stature, which we designated as 5'8", and the more "idealized" stature for men, 6'. We report here only the highlights of the measurements taken on the newer Barbie and newer Ken, Jamal, and Shani, scaled at the fashion-model height. For purposes of comparison, we include data on average body measurements from the standardized published tables of the 1988 Anthropometric

TABLE 1   Measurements of Glitter Beach Barbie, African-American Shani, and the Average Measurements of the 1988 U.S. Army Women Recruits.[1]

Meas.	Barbie	Shani	U.S. Army "Norma"
Height	5'10"	5'10"	5'4"
Chest Circum.	35"	35"	35.7"
Waist Circum.	20"	20"	31"
Hip Circum.[2]	32.50"	31.25"	38.10"
Hip Breadth	11.6"	11.0"	13.49"
Thigh Circum.	19.25"	20.00"	22.85"

[1]"Norma" is based on 2,208 army recruits, 1,140 of which were white, 922 of which were black.

[2]Hip circumference is referred to as "buttock circumference" in anthropometric parlance.

TABLE 2   Measurements of Glitter Beach Ken, African-American Ken, and the Average Measurements of the 1988 U.S. Army Male Recruits.[1]

Meas.	Ken	Jamal	U.S. Army "Norm"
Height	6'0"	6'0"	5'9"
Chest Circum.	38.4"	38.4"	39.0"
Waist Circum.	28.8"	28.8"	33.1"
Hip Circum.[2]	36.0"	36.0"	38.7"
Hip Breadth	12.2"	12.2"	13.46"
Thigh Circum.	20.4"	20.4"	23.48"

[1]"Norm" is based on 1774 males, 1,172 of which were white and 458 of which were black.

[2]Hip circumference is referred to as "buttock circumference" in anthropometric parlance.

Survey of the Army Personnel. We have dubbed these composites for the female and male recruits "Army Norma" and "Army Norm," respectively.

Both Barbie and Shani's measurements at 5'10" reveal the extreme thinness expected of the runway model. Both dolls have considerably smaller measurements than Army Norma *at all points,* even though they are six inches taller than her. When we scaled the dolls to 5'4"—the same as Army Norma—we can see just how skewed the dimensions are: Barbie's chest, waist, and hip measurements come out as 32"–17"–28," clinically anorectic to say the least. We also wanted to see if Mattel had physically changed the Barbie mold in making Shani. Most of the differences we could find appeared to be in the face. Shani's nose is broader and her lips are slightly larger. The only significant difference we found in the bodies was that Shani's back is arched in such a way that it tilts her buttocks up, producing the visual illusion of a higher, rounder, butt . . . Perhaps this is what Mattel was referring to in claiming that Shani has a realistic or ethnically correct body (Jones 1991).

When it came to the male dolls, we did not find the same kind of dramatic difference between them and Army Norm as we did in the female dolls. As the table shows, Ken and Jamal were largely identical to each other, and they were only somewhat slimmer than the average soldier. Visually Ken and Jamal appear very tight and muscular and "bulked out," while the U.S. Army males tend to carry slightly more fat, judging from the photographs and data presented in the 1988 study.

OUR BARBIES, OUR SELVES

> I feel like Barbie; everyone calls me Barbie; I love Barbie. The main difference is she's plastic and I'm real. There isn't really any other difference.
>
> —Hayley Spicer, winner of Great Britain's Barbie-Look-Alike competition

Our venture into anthropometry revealed that Barbie has a much more "abnormal" body than does Ken. But her hyper-thin body was by no means exceptional. Studies tracking the body measurements of Playboy magazine centerfolds and Miss America contestants show that between 1959 and 1978 the average weight and hip size for women in both of these groups has decreased steadily while the average weight of women was increasing (Wiseman, Gray, Mosimann and Ahrens 1992). A follow up study for the years 1979–1988 found this trend continuing into the eighties: approximately 69% of Playboy centerfolds and 60% of Miss America contestants were weighing in at 15% or more below their expected age and height category. In short, the majority of women presented to us in the media as having desirable feminine bodies, were, like Barbie, well on their way to qualify for anorexia nervosa.

On the surface, at least, it might seem that Barbie's signature thin body would seem at odds with the doll's seemingly endless desire for consumption and self-transformation. Being thin for most women requires repression of desire and self discipline, neither of which are traits we associate with the consummate shopper. And yet, as Susan Bordo (1990) has argued in regard to anorexia, these two phenomena—hyper thin bodies and hyper consumption—are very much linked in advanced capitalist economies which depend upon commodity excess. Bodies, says Bordo, are where the regulation of desire is played out most keenly. The imperative to manage the body and to "be all that you can be"—in fact the idea that you can *choose* the body that you want to have—is a pervasive feature of consumer culture. Keeping control of one's body, not getting too fat or flabby, in other words, conforming to gendered norms of fitness and weight, have become signs of an individual's social and moral worth. But as Bordo, Sandra Bartky (1990), and other feminist scholars have been quick to point out, not all bodies are subject to the same degree of scrutiny or the same repercussions if they fail. It is women's bodies and desires in particular where the structural contradictions—the simultaneous incitement to consume and social condemnation for overindulgence—appear to be most acutely manifested in bodily regimes of intense self-monitoring and discipline. Just as it is women's appearance which is subject to greater social scrutiny, so it is that women's desires, hunger, and appetites are seen as most threatening and in need of control in a patriarchal society.

This cultural context is relevant to making sense of Barbie and the meaning her body holds in late consumer capitalism. In dressing and undressing Barbie, combing her hair, bathing her, turning and twisting her limbs in imaginary scenarios, children acquire a very tactile and intimate sense of Barbie's body. Barbie is presented in packaging and advertising as a role model, a best friend or older sister to little girls. Television jingles use the refrain, "I want to be just like you," while look-alike clothes and look-alike contests make it possible for girls to live out the fantasy of being Barbie. In short, there is every reason to believe that girls (or adult women) link Barbie's body shape with her popularity and glamour.

This is exactly what worries many people. As our measurements show, Barbie's body differs wildly from anything approximating "average" female body weight and proportions. Over the years her wasp-waisted body has evoked a steady stream of critique for having a negative impact on little girls' sense of self-esteem. For example, the release of a Barbie aerobics work-out video for girls in 1992 was met with the following angry letter from an expert in the field of eating disorders:

> I had hoped these plastic dolls with impossible proportions would have faded away in this current health-conscious period; not at all. . . . Move over Jane Fonda. Welcome again, ever smiling breast-thrusting Barbie with your stick legs and sweat-free aerobic routines. I'm concerned about the role model message she is giving our young. Surely it's hard to accept a little cellulite when the culture tells you unrelentingly how to strive for thinness and the perfect body. [Warner 1992)][9]

There is no doubt that Barbie's body contributes to what Kim Chernin (1981) has called "the tyranny of slenderness."[10] But is repression all her hyper-thin body conveys? In her work on how anorectic women see themselves, Susan Bordo writes that, "for anorectics, [the slender ideal] may have a very different meaning; it may symbolize, not so much the containment of female desire, as its liberation from a domestic, reproductive destiny" (Bordo 1990:103).

Similar observations have been made about cosmetic surgery: women often explain their experience as one of empowerment, of taking charge of their bodies and lives (Balsamo 1993; Davis 1991). What does this mean for making sense of Barbie and her long lasting appeal? We would suggest that a sub-text of agency and independence, even transgression, accompanies this pencil-thin icon of femininity. One the one hand, one can argue that Barbie's body displays conformity to dominant cultural imperatives for a disciplined body and contained feminine desires. On the other hand, however, her excessive slenderness can also signify a rebellious manifestation of willpower, a refusal of the maternal ideal, symbolized by pendulous breasts, rounded stomach and hips. Hers is a body of hard edges, distinct borders, and self control. It is literally impenetrable. While the anorectic woman becomes increasingly androgynous the more she starves herself, Barbie, in the realm of plastic fantasy, is able to remain powerfully sexualized with her large gravity-defying breasts, even while she is distinctly non-reproductive. Like the "hard bodies" in fitness advertising, Barbie's body may signify for women the pleasure of control and mastery both of which are highly valued traits in American society and both of which are predominantly associated with masculinity (Bordo 1990:105). Putting these elements together with her apparent independent wealth can make for a very different reading of Barbie than that of bimbo. To paraphrase one Barbie doll owner: she owns a Ferrari and doesn't have a husband; she must be doing something right.[11]

By invoking these testimonies of anorectic women, we are not trying to suggest that playing with Barbie, or trying to become like Barbie, are paths to empowerment for little girls. Rather we want to signal the complex and contradictory meanings that her body has in contemporary American society. And we also want to underscore that our bodies, whatever the reigning ideal might be, continue to function as a vitally important stage on which gender—as well as race and class—conformity and transgression are played out.[12] It is clear that a next step we would want to take in the cultural interpretation of Barbie is an ethnographic study of Barbie doll owners.[13] It is sensible to assume that the children who play with Barbie are themselves creative users who respond variously to the messages about femininity encoded in her fashions and appearance. In the hands of their adult and child owners, Barbies have become Amazon cave warriors, drag queens, dutiful mommies, and evil axe murderers.[14] As we consider Barbie's many meanings, we should also note that the doll has become a world traveler. A product of the global assembly-line, Barbie dolls owe their existence to the internationalization of the labor market and global flows of capital and commodities that today characterize the toy industry as well as other industries in the post-war era. Designed in Los Angeles, manufactured in Taiwan or Malaysia, distributed worldwide, Barbie TM is American-made in name only. Speeding her way into an expanding global market, Barbie brings with her some of the North American cultural subtext we have outlined in this analysis. How this teenage survivor has inserted herself into the cultural landscapes of Mayan villages, Bombay high rises, and Malagasy towns is a rich topic that begs to be explored.

ACKNOWLEDGMENTS

This essay is based on a longer piece of research first published in Urla and Swedlund (1995). Follow-up research we have carried out on the ideal of the thin waist will appear in Orgel, Urla, and Swedlund (in press).

NOTES

1. The statistics and figures provided on sales reflect research carried out in the nineties.
2. While the concept of adolescence as a distinct developmental stage between puberty and adulthood was not new to the fifties, Thomas Doherty (1988) notes that it wasn't until the end of World War II that the term "teenager" became standard usage in the American language.
3. More work needs to be done on how Barbie dolls are adapted to appeal to various national markets. For example, Barbie dolls manufactured in Japan for Japanese consumption are reputed to have noticeably larger, rounder eyes than those marketed in the United States (see Billyboy 1987). For some suggestive thoughts on the cultural implications of the transnational flow of toys like Barbie dolls, TransFormers, and He-Man, see Carol Breckenridge's (1990) brief but intriguing editor's comment to *Public Culture*.
4. On Black Barbies see duCille 1995.
5. Though measurements of skulls, noses, facial angles for scientific comparison had been going on throughout the 19th century, it wasn't until the 1890's that any serious attempts were made to standardize anthropometric measurements of the living body. This culminated in the Monaco agreement of 1906, one of the first international meetings to standardize anthropometric measurement. For a brief review of the attempts to use and systematize photography in anthropometry see Spencer (1992).
6. Hrdlicka argued, rather fantastically, that there was more space between the brain and the cranium in women than in men. Michael Blakey refers to this as Hrdlicka's "air head" hypothesis (1987:16).
7. In her study of 18th century physical sciences, Schiebinger (1993) remarks that male bodies (skulls in particular) were routinely assumed to embody the prototype of their race in the various typologies devised by comparative anatomists of the period. "When anthropologists did compare women across cultures, their interest centered on sexual traits—feminine beauty, redness of lips, length and style of hair, size and shape of breasts or clitorises, degree of sexual desire, fertility, and above all the size, shape, and position of the pelvis" (1993:156). In this way, the male body "remained the touchstone of human anatomy," while females were regarded as a sexual subset of the species (1993:159–60).
8. Historians have noted a long-standing conflict between the physical culture movement, eugenicists and health reformers on the one hand, and the fashion industry on the other that gave rise to competing ideals in American society of the fit and the fashionably fragile woman (e.g. Banner 1983; Cogan 1989).
9. When confronted with these kinds of accusations, Mattel and the fashion industry protest that Barbie dolls, like fashion models, are about fantasy, not reality. "We're not telling you to be that girl" writes Elizabeth Saltzman, fashion editor for *Vogue*. "We're trying to show you fashion" (France 1992:22).
10. In response to this anxiety, Cathy Meredig, an enterprising computer software designer, created the "Happy to be Me" doll. Described as a healthy alternative for little girls, "Happy to be Me" has a shorter neck, shorter legs, wider waist and larger feet, and a lot fewer clothes,

designed to make her look more like the average woman ("She's No Barbie, Nor Does She Care to Be." *New York Times*, August 15, 1991, C-11).

11. "Dolls in Playland." 1992. Colleen Toomey, producer. BBC.

12. For an illuminating case study of race, class, and gender codings of the female body, see Krause 1998.

13. While not exactly ethnographic, Hohmann (1985) offers a socio-psychological study of how children experiment with social relations during play with Barbies.

14. Barbie has become a somewhat celebrated figure among avant-garde and pop artists, giving rise to a whole genre of Barbie satire known as "Barbie Noire" (Kahn 1991; Ebersole and Peabody 1993). On queer appropriations of Barbie and Ken, see Rand (1995).

REFERENCES

Adelson, Andrea. 1992. And Now, Barbie Looks Like a Billion. *New York Times*. Nov. 26. pg. D3.

Balsamo, Anne. 1993. On the Cutting Edge: Cosmetic Surgery and the Technological Production of the Gendered Body. *Camera Obscura* 28:207–238.

Banner, Lois W. 1983. *American Beauty*. New York, Knopf.

Bartky, Sandra Lee. 1990. "Foucault, Femininity, and the Modernization of Patriarchal Power." In *Femininity and Domination: Studies in the Phenomenology of Oppression*. pp. 63–82. New York: Routledge.

Bennett, William and Joel Gurin. 1982. *The Dieter's Dilemma: Eating Less and Weighing More*. New York: Basic Books.

Billyboy. 1987. *Barbie, her Life and Times, and the New Theater of Fashion*. New York: Crown Publishers.

Blakey, Michael L. 1987. Skull Doctors: Instrinsic Social and Political Bias in the History of American Physical Anthropology. *Critique of Anthropology* 7(2):7–35.

Bordo, Susan R. 1990. "Reading the Slender Body." In *Body/Politics: Women and the Discourses of Science*. M. Jacobus, E. Fox Keller, and S. Shuttleworth, eds. pp. 83–112. New York: Routledge.

Bordo, Susan R. 1991. "'Material Girl': The Effacements of Postmodern Culture." In *The Female Body: Figures, Styles, Speculations*. L. Goldstein, ed. pp. 106–130. Ann Arbor, MI: The University of Michigan Press.

Breckenridge, Carol A. 1990. Editor's Comment: On Toying with Terror. *Public Culture* 2(2):i–iii.

Brumberg, Joan Jacobs. 1988. *Fasting Girls: The History of Anorexia Nervosa*. New York: New American Library.

Chernin, Kim. 1981. *The Obsession: Reflections on the Tyranny of Slenderness*. New York: Harper.

Cogan, Frances B. 1989. *All-American Girl: The Ideal of Real Woman-hood in Mid-Nineteenth Century America*. Athens and London: University of Georgia Press.

Davis, Kathy. 1991. Remaking the She-Devil: A Critical Look at Feminist Approaches to Beauty. *Hypatia* 6(2): 21–43.

Doherty, Thomas. 1988. *Teenagers and Teenpics. The Juvenilization of American Movies in the 1950's*. Boston: Unwin Hyman.

DuCille, Ann. 1995. "Toy Theory: Blackface Barbie and the Deep Play of Difference." In, *The Skin Trade: Essays on Race, Gender and Merchandising of Difference*. Cambridge: Harvard University Press.

Ebersole, Lucinda and Richard Peabody, eds. 1993. *Mondo Barbie*. New York: St. Martin's Press.

Fausto-Sterling, Anne. 1995. "Gender, Race and Nation: The Comparative Anatomy of "Hottentot" Women in Europe, 1815–1817." In, *Deviant Bodies: Critical Perspectives on Difference in Science and Popular Culture*. J. Terry and J. Urla, eds. Bloomington: Indiana University Press.

Fee, Elizabeth. 1979. Nineteenth Century Craniology: The Study of the Female Skull. *Bulletin of the History of Medicine* 53:415–433.

France, Kim. 1992. "Tits 'R' Us." *Village Voice*, March 17, p. 22.

Frith, Simon. 1981. *Sound Effects: Youth, Leisures, and the Politics of Rock'n' Roll*. New York: Pantheon.

Gould, Steven Jay. 1981. *The Mismeasure of Man*. New York: Norton.

Hohmann, Delf Maria. 1985. Jennifer and her Barbies: A Contextual Analysis of a Child Playing Barbie dolls. *Canadian Folklore Canadien* 7 (1–2):111–120.

Hooton, E. A. 1931. Up from the Ape. New York: The MacMillan Company.

Hrdlicka, Ales. 1925. Relation of the Size of the Head and Skull to Capacity in the Two Sexes. *American Journal of Physical Anthropology* 8:249–250.

Hrdlicka, Ales. 1939. *Practical Anthropometry*. Philadelphia: Wistar Institute of Anatomy and Biology.

Jones, Lisa. 1991. Skin Trade: A Doll is Born. *Village Voice*. March 26, p. 36.

Kahn, Alice. 1991. A Onetime Bimbo Becomes a Muse. *New York Times*. September 29.

Kaw, Eugenia. 1993. Medicalization of Racial Features: Asian American Women and Cosmetic Surgery. *Medical Anthropology Quarterly* 7(1):74–89.

Krause, Elizabeth. 1998. A Bead of Raw Sweat in a Field of Dainty Perspirers: Nationalism, Whiteness and the Olympic Ordeal of Tonya Harding. *Transforming Anthropology* 7 (1).

Lawson, Carol. 1993. Toys will be Toys: The Stereotypes Unravel. *New York Times*. February 11. C1, C8.

Lord, M. G. 1994. *Forever Barbie: The Unauthorized Biography of a Real Doll*. New York: William Morrow.

May, Elaine Tyler. 1988. *Homeward Bound: American Families in the Cold War Era*. New York: Basic Books.

Melosh, Barbara and Christina Simmons. 1986. "Exhibiting Women's History." In *Presenting the Past: Essays on History and the Public*. Susan Porter Benson, Stephen Brier, and Roy Rosenzweig eds. Philadelphia: Temple University Press.

Motz, Marilyn Ferris. 1983. "'I Want to Be a Barbie Doll When I Grow Up': The Cultural Significance of the Barbie Doll." In, *The Popular Culture Reader,* 3rd ed. Christopher D. Geist and Jack Nachbar, eds. pp. 122–136. Bowling Green: Bowling Green University Popular Press.

Newsweek. 1990. Finally, Barbie Dolls go Ethnic. *Newsweek* (August 13), p. 48.

Orgel, Mary, Jacqueline Urla and Alan Swedlund. In press. Surveying a Cultural Waist-land: Biological Poetics and Politics of the Female Body. In *Anthropology United: Challenging Bio-Social Reductivisms.* Susan McKinnon and Sydel Silverman, eds. University of Chicago Press.

Rabinowitz, Paula. 1993. Accessorizing History: Girls and Popular Culture. Discussant Comments, Panel#150: "Engendering Post-war Popular Culture in Britain and America. Ninth Berkshire Conference on the History of Women. Vassar College, June 11–13, 1993.

Rand, Erica. 1994. "We Girls Can Do Anything, Right Barbie? Lesbian Consumption in Postmodern Circulation." In *Lesbian Postmodern,* ed. Laura Doan, pp. 189–209. New York: Columbia.

Rand, Erica. 1995. *Barbie's Queer Accessories.* Durham and London: Duke University Press.

Robertson, Josephine. 1945. Theatre Cashier, 23, Wins Title of "Norma." *Cleveland Plain Dealer.* September 21, pp. 1, 4.

Russett, Cynthia Eagle. 1989. *Sexual Science: The Victorian Construction of Womanhood.* Cambridge, MA: Harvard University Press.

Schiebinger, Londa. 1989. *The Mind Has No Sex: Women in the Origins of Modern Science.* Cambridge: Harvard University Press.

Schwartz, Hillel. 1986. *Never Satisfied: A Cultural History of Diets, Fantasies and Fat.* New York: The Free Press.

Shapiro, Eben. 1992. 'Total Hot, Totally Cool.' Long-Haired Barbie Is a Hit. *New York Times.* June 22. p. D-9.

Shapiro, Harry L. 1945. Americans: *Yesterday, Today, Tomorrow.* Man and Nature Publications. (Science Guide No. 126). New York: The American Museum of Natural History.

Spencer, Frank. 1992. "Some Notes on the Attempt to Apply Photography to Anthropometry during the Second Half of the Nineteenth Century. In *Anthropology and Photography: 1860–1920.* Elizabeth Edwards, ed. pp. 99–107. New Haven, CT: Yale University Press.

Stevenson, Richard. 1991. Mattel Thrives as Barbie Grows. *New York Times.* December 2.

Urla, Jacqueline and Alan Swedlund. 1995. "The Anthropometry of Barbie: Unsettling Ideals of the Feminine Body in Popular Culture." In *Deviant Bodies: Critical Perspectives on Difference in Science and Popular Culture.* J. Terry and J. Urla, eds. pp. 277–313. Bloomington: Indiana University Press.

Warner, Patricia Rosalind. 1992. Letter to the Editor. *Boston Globe.* June 28.

Williams, Lena. 1992. Woman's Image in a Mirror: Who Defines What She Sees? *New York Times.* February 6. A1; B7.

Willis, Susan. 1991. *A Primer for Daily Life.* London and New York: Routledge.

Wilson, Elizabeth. 1985. *Adorned in Dreams: Fashion and Modernity.* London: Virago.

Wiseman, C., Gray, J., Mosimann, J., and Ahrens, A. 1992. Cultural Expectations of Thinness in Women: An Update. *International Journal of Eating Disorders* 11 (1):85–89.

Wolf, Naomi. 1991. *The Beauty Myth: How Images of Beauty are Used Against Women.* New York: William Morrow.

23

When Brothers Share a Wife

Melvyn C. Goldstein

Marriage is a social institution that formalizes certain aspects of the relationship between males and females. It is an institution that evokes in us deep-seated emotions about questions of right and wrong, good and evil, and traditional versus modern. Within families, arguments may occur about what is appropriate premarital behavior, what is a proper marriage ceremony, and how long a marriage should last. Although these arguments may be traumatic for parents and their offspring, from a cross-cultural perspective, they generally involve minor deviations from the cultural norms. In contrast, anthropology textbooks describe an amazing variety of marriage systems that fulfill both biological and social functions. This selection will show just how different things could be.

Social institutions are geared to operate within and adapt to the larger social and ecological environment. This was the case in the earlier selections on gender roles and family planning; the organization of the family must also be adapted to the ecology. For example, the nuclear family is more adapted to a highly mobile society than is an extended family unit that includes grandparents and others. As society increasingly focuses on technical education, career specialization, and therefore geographic mobility for employment purposes, a system has evolved that emphasizes the nuclear family over the extended family. In a similar way, fraternal polyandry in Tibet, as described in this selection, can meet the social, demographic, and ecological needs of its region.

As you read this selection, ask yourself the following questions:

- What is meant by the term *fraternal polyandry?*
- Is this the only form of marriage allowed in Tibet?
- How do husbands and wives feel about the sexual aspects of sharing a spouse?
- Why would Tibetans choose fraternal polyandry?
- How is the function of fraternal polyandry like that of nineteenth-century primogeniture in England?

The following terms discussed in this selection are included in the Glossary at the back of the book:

arable land	*nuclear family*
corvée	*population pressure*
fraternal polyandry	*primogeniture*
monogamy	

Eager to reach home, Dorje drives his yaks hard over the 17,000-foot mountain pass, stopping only once to rest. He and his two older brothers, Pema and Sonam, are jointly marrying a woman from the next village in a few weeks, and he has to help with the preparations.

Dorje, Pema, and Sonam are Tibetans living in Limi, a 200-square-mile area in the northwest corner of Nepal, across the border from Tibet. The form of marriage they are about to enter—fraternal polyandry in anthropological parlance—is one of the world's rarest forms of marriage but is not uncommon in Tibetan society, where it

From When Brothers Share a Wife, Melvyn Goldstein, NH, pp. 39–48. Reprinted from *Natural History* March 1987; copyright © Natural History Magazine, Inc. 2006.

has been practiced from time immemorial. For many Tibetan social strata, it traditionally represented the ideal form of marriage and family.

The mechanics of fraternal polyandry are simple. Two, three, four, or more brothers jointly take a wife, who leaves her home to come and live with them. Traditionally, marriage was arranged by parents, with children, particularly females, having little or no say. This is changing somewhat nowadays, but it is still unusual for children to marry without their parents' consent. Marriage ceremonies vary by income and region and range from all the brothers sitting together as grooms to only the eldest one formally doing so. The age of the brothers plays an important role in determining this: very young brothers almost never participate in actual marriage ceremonies, although they typically join the marriage when they reach their midteens.

The eldest brother is normally dominant in terms of authority, that is, in managing the household, but all the brothers share the work and participate as sexual partners. Tibetan males and females do not find the sexual aspect of sharing a spouse the least bit unusual, repulsive, or scandalous, and the norm is for the wife to treat all the brothers the same.

Offspring are treated similarly. There is no attempt to link children biologically to particular brothers, and a brother shows no favoritism toward his child even if he knows he is the real father because, for example, his older brothers were away at the time the wife became pregnant. The children, in turn, consider all of the brothers as their fathers and treat them equally, even if they also know who is their real father. In some regions children use the term "father" for the eldest brother and "father's brother" for the others, while in other areas they call all the brothers by one term, modifying this by the use of "elder" and "younger."

Unlike our own society, where monogamy is the only form of marriage permitted, Tibetan society allows a variety of marriage types, including monogamy, fraternal polyandry, and polygyny. Fraternal polyandry and monogamy are the most common forms of marriage, while polygyny typically occurs in cases where the first wife is barren. The widespread practice of fraternal polyandry, therefore, is not the outcome of a law requiring brothers to marry jointly. There is choice, and in fact, divorce traditionally was relatively simple in Tibetan society. If a brother in a polyandrous marriage became dissatisfied and wanted to separate, he simply left the main house and set up his own household. In such cases, all the children stayed in the main household with the remaining brother(s), even if the departing brother was known to be the real father of one or more of the children.

The Tibetans' own explanation for choosing fraternal polyandry is materialistic. For example, when I asked Dorje why he decided to marry with his two brothers rather than take his own wife, he thought for a moment, then said it prevented the division of his family's farm (and animals) and thus facilitated all of them achieving a higher standard of living. And when I later asked Dorje's bride whether it wasn't difficult for her to cope with three brothers as husbands, she laughed and echoed that rationale of avoiding fragmentation of the family land, adding that she expected to be better off economically, since she would have three husbands working for her and her children.

Exotic as it may seem to Westerners, Tibetan fraternal polyandry is thus in many ways analogous to the way primogeniture functioned in nineteenth-century England. Primogeniture dictated that the eldest son inherited the family estate, while younger sons had to leave home and seek their own employment—for example, in the military or the clergy. Primogeniture maintained family estates intact over generations by permitting only one heir per generation. Fraternal polyandry also accomplishes this but does so by keeping all the brothers together with just one wife so that there is only one set of heirs per generation.

While Tibetans believe that in this way fraternal polyandry reduces the risk of family fission, monogamous marriages among brothers need not necessarily precipitate the division of the family estate: brothers could continue to live together, and the family land could continue to be worked jointly. When I asked Tibetans about this, however, they invariably responded that such joint families are unstable because each wife is primarily oriented to her own children and interested in their success and well-being over that of the children of other wives. For example, if the youngest brother's wife had three sons while the eldest brother's wife had only one daughter, the wife of the youngest brother might begin to demand more resources for her children since, as males, they represent the future of the family. Thus, the children from different wives in the same generation are competing sets of heirs, and this makes such families inherently unstable. Tibetans perceive that conflict will spread from the wives to their husbands and consider this likely to cause family fission. Consequently, it is almost never done.

Although Tibetans see an economic advantage to fraternal polyandry, they do not value the sharing of a wife as an end in itself. On the contrary, they articulate a number of problems inherent in the practice. For example, because authority is customarily exercised by the eldest brother, his younger male siblings have to subordinate themselves with little hope of changing their status within the family. When these younger brothers are aggressive and individualistic, tensions and difficulties often occur despite there being only one set of heirs.

In addition, tension and conflict may arise in polyandrous families because of sexual favoritism. The bride normally sleeps with the eldest brother, and the two have the responsibility to see to it that the other males have opportunities for sexual access. Since the Tibetan subsistence economy requires males to travel a lot, the temporary absence of one or more brothers facilitates this, but there are also other rotation practices. The cultural ideal unambiguously calls for the wife to show equal affection and sexuality to each of the brothers (and vice versa), but deviations from this ideal occur, especially when there is a sizable difference in age between partners in the marriage.

Dorje's family represents just such a potential situation. He is fifteen years old and his two older brothers

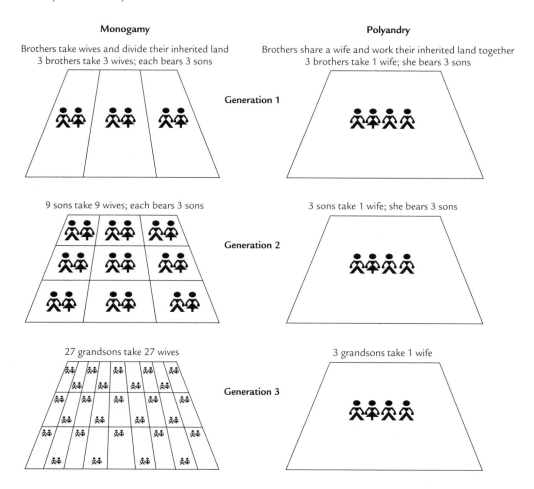

are twenty-five and twenty-two years old. The new bride is twenty-three years old, eight years Dorje's senior. Sometimes such a bride finds the youngest husband immature and adolescent and does not treat him with equal affection; alternatively, she may find his youth attractive and lavish special attention on him. Apart from this consideration, when a younger male like Dorje grows up, he may consider his wife "ancient" and prefer the company of a woman his own age or younger. Consequently, although men and women do not find the idea of sharing a bride or a bridegroom repulsive, individual likes and dislikes can cause familial discord.

Two reasons have commonly been offered for the perpetuation of fraternal polyandry in Tibet: that Tibetans practice female infanticide and therefore have to marry polyandrously, owing to a shortage of females; and that Tibet, lying at extremely high altitudes, is so barren and bleak that Tibetans would starve without resort to this mechanism. A Jesuit who lived in Tibet in the eighteenth century articulated this second view: "One reason for this most odious custom is the sterility of the soil, and the small amount of land that can be cultivated owing to the lack of water. The crops may suffice if the brothers all live together, but if they form separate families they would be reduced to beggary."

Both explanations are wrong, however. Not only has there never been institutionalized female infanticide in Tibet, but Tibetan society gives females considerable rights, including inheriting the family estate in the absence of brothers. In such cases, the woman takes a bridegroom who comes to live in her family and adopts her family's name and identity. Moreover, there is no demographic evidence of a shortage of females. In Limi, for example, there were (in 1974) sixty females and fifty-three males in the fifteen- to thirty-five-year age category, and many adult females were unmarried.

The second reason is also incorrect. The climate in Tibet is extremely harsh, and ecological factors do play a major role perpetuating polyandry, but polyandry is not a means of preventing starvation. It is characteristic, not of the poorest segments of the society, but rather of the peasant landowning families.

In the old society, the landless poor could not realistically aspire to prosperity, but they did not fear starvation. There was a persistent labor shortage throughout Tibet, and very poor families with little or no land and few animals could subsist through agricultural labor, tenant farming, craft occupations such as carpentry, or by working as servants. Although the per person family income could increase somewhat if brothers married polyandrously and pooled their wages, in the absence of inheritable land, the advantage of fraternal polyandry was not generally sufficient to prevent them from setting up their own households. A more skilled or energetic younger brother could do as well or better alone, since he would completely control his income and would not have to share it with his siblings. Consequently, while there was and is some polyandry among the poor, it is much less frequent and more prone to result in divorce and family fission.

An alternative reason for the persistence of fraternal polyandry is that it reduces population growth (and thereby reduces the pressure on resources) by relegating some females to lifetime spinsterhood. Fraternal polyandrous marriages in Limi (in 1974) averaged 2.35 men per woman, and not surprisingly, 31 percent of the females of child-bearing age (twenty to forty-nine) were unmarried. These spinsters either continued to live at home, set up their own households, or worked as servants for other families. They could also become Buddhist nuns. Being unmarried is not synonymous with exclusion from the reproductive pool. Discreet extramarital relationships are tolerated, and actually half of the adult unmarried women in Limi had one or more children. They raised these children as single mothers, working for wages or weaving cloth and blankets for sale. As a group, however, the unmarried women had far fewer offspring than the married women, averaging only 0.7 children per woman, compared with 3.3 for married women, whether polyandrous, monogamous, or polygynous. While polyandry helps regulate population, this function of polyandry is not consciously perceived by Tibetans and is not the reason they consistently choose it.

If neither a shortage of females nor the fear of starvation perpetuates fraternal polyandry, what motivates brothers, particularly younger brothers, to opt for this system of marriage? From the perspective of the younger brother in a landholding family, the main incentive is the attainment or maintenance of the good life. With polyandry, he can expect a more secure and higher standard of living, with access not only to his family's land and animals, but also to its inherited collection of clothes, jewelry, rugs, saddles, and horses. In addition, he will experience less work pressure and much greater security because all responsibility does not fall on one "father." For Tibetan brothers, the question is whether to trade off the greater personal freedom inherent in monogamy for the real or potential economic security, affluence, and social prestige associated with life in a larger, labor-rich polyandrous family.

A brother thinking of separating from his polyandrous marriage and taking his own wife would face various disadvantages. Although in the majority of Tibetan regions all brothers theoretically have rights to their family's estate, in reality Tibetans are reluctant to divide their land into small fragments. Generally, a younger brother who insists on leaving the family will receive only a small plot of land, if that. Because of its power and wealth, the rest of the family usually can block any attempt of the younger brother to increase his share of land through litigation. Moreover, a younger brother may not even get a house and cannot expect to receive much above the minimum in terms of movable possessions, such as furniture, pots, and pans. Thus, a brother contemplating going it on his own must plan on achieving economic security and the good life not through inheritance but through his own work.

The obvious solution for younger brothers—creating new fields from virgin land—is generally not a feasible option. Most Tibetan populations live at high altitudes (above 12,000 feet), where arable land is extremely scarce. For example, in Dorje's village, agriculture ranges only from about 12,900 feet, the lowest point in the area, to 13,300 feet. Above that altitude, early frost and snow destroy the staple barley crop. Furthermore, because of the low rainfall caused by the Himalayan rain shadow, many areas in Tibet and northern Nepal that are within appropriate altitude range for agriculture have no reliable sources of irrigation. In the end, although there is plenty of unused land in such areas, most of it is either too high or too arid.

Even where unused land capable of being farmed exists, clearing the land and building the substantial terraces necessary for irrigation constitute a great undertaking. Each plot has to be completely dug out to a depth of two to two and a half feet so that the large rocks and boulders can be removed. At best, a man might be able to bring a few new fields under cultivation in the first years after separating from his brothers, but he could not expect to acquire substantial amounts of arable land this way.

In addition, because of the limited farmland, the Tibetan subsistence economy characteristically includes a strong emphasis on animal husbandry. Tibetan farmers regularly maintain cattle, yaks, goats, and sheep, grazing them in the areas too high for agriculture. These herds produce wool, milk, cheese, butter, meat, and skins. To obtain these resources, however, shepherds must accompany the animals on a daily basis. When first setting up a monogamous household, a younger brother like Dorje would find it difficult to both farm and manage animals.

In traditional Tibetan society, there was an even more critical factor that operated to perpetuate fraternal polyandry—a form of hereditary servitude somewhat analogous to serfdom in Europe. Peasants were tied to large estates held by aristocrats, monasteries, and the Lhasa government. They were allowed the use of some farmland to produce their own subsistence but were required to provide taxes in kind and corvée (free labor) to their lords. The corvée was a substantial hardship, since a peasant household was in many cases required to furnish the lord with one laborer daily for most of the year and more on specific occasions such as the harvest. This enforced labor, along with the lack of new land and the ecological pressure to pursue both agriculture and animal husbandry, made polyandrous families particularly beneficial. The polyandrous family allowed an internal division of adult labor, maximizing economic advantage. For example, while the wife worked the family fields, one brother could perform the lord's corvée, another could look after the animals, and a third could engage in trade.

Although social scientists often discount other people's explanations of why they do things, in the case of Tibetan fraternal polyandry, such explanations are very close to the truth. The custom, however, is very sensitive to changes in its political and economic milieu and, not surprisingly, is in decline in most Tibetan areas. Made less important by the elimination of the traditional serf-based economy, it is disparaged by the dominant non-Tibetan leaders of India, China, and Nepal. New opportunities for economic and social mobility in these countries, such as the tourist trade and government employment, are also eroding the rationale for polyandry, and so it may vanish within the next generation.

24

Law, Custom,
and Crimes Against Women
The Problem of Dowry Death in India

John van Willigen and V. C. Channa

Anthropologists find many societies with unusual customs, beliefs, and behaviors. Usually they discover, after careful study and reflection, that these perform some useful function within the society, as in the case of polyandry discussed in the previous selection. But is this always the case? Must we assume that simply because a custom exists it is healthy for the members of society? We think not, and the Christians who were fed to lions and the Aztec slaves who were sacrificed to a bloodthirsty god would most likely agree.

Times change; hunters and gatherers plant crops, tribal people rush headlong into peasantry, and small-scale farmers become urban wage earners. Traditions that helped maintain a healthy society in one context may become dysfunctional in another. For better or worse, traditions and beliefs run deep and are almost impossible to unlearn. It is the nature of culture to resist change.

As you will read, the practice of dousing a bride with kerosene and creating a human torch certainly indicates that the payment of dowry is a traditional practice gone awry. That said, what can be done? Laws, even those that carry serious penalties, are light ammunition against the armor of strongly held cultural beliefs. Governments will solve such problems only through public policy based on in-depth cultural understanding.

As you read this selection, ask yourself the following questions:

- What do you think the authors mean when they suggest that dowry death presents a problem for ethnologists because of ethnological theory's functional cast?

- Why does the institution of dowry make college education problematic for some young women?

- What are the present-day approaches to solving the dowry death problem?

- How can women's access to production roles and property, delocalization of social control, and economic transformation affect the problem of dowry death?

- Dowry-related violence in India is related to the economic value of women. What might be said about the relationship between the economic position and the social status of women in America?

The following terms discussed in this selection are included in the Glossary at the back of the book:

caste	ethnology
cultural materialism	peasants
demography	sex roles
dowry	

A 25-year-old woman was allegedly burnt to death by her husband and mother-in-law at their East Delhi home yesterday. The housewife, Mrs. Sunita, stated before her death

Reproduced by permission of the Society for Applied Anthropology, from Van Willigen, John and Channa, V. C., Law, Custom, and Crimes against Women: The Problem of Dowry Deaths in India, SfAA 1991, *Human Organization*, Vol. 50, No. 4, pp. 369–377.

at the Jaya Prakash Narayana Hospital that members of her husband's family had been harassing her for bringing inadequate dowry.

The woman told the Shahdara subdivisional magistrate that during a quarrel over dowry at their Pratap Park house yesterday, her husband gripped her from behind while the mother-in-law poured kerosene over her clothes.

Her clothes were then set ablaze. The police have registered a case against the victim's husband, Suraj Prakash, and his mother.

—*Times of India*, February 19, 1988

This routinely reported news story describes what in India is termed a "bride-burning" or "dowry death." Such incidents are frequently reported in the newspapers of Delhi and other Indian cities. In addition, there are cases in which the evidence may be ambiguous, so that deaths of women by fire may be recorded as kitchen accidents, suicides, or murders. Dowry violence takes a characteristic form. Following marriage and the requisite giving of dowry, the family of the groom makes additional demands for the payment of more cash or the provision of more goods. These demands are expressed in unremitting harassment of the bride, who is living in the household of her husband's parents, culminating in the murder of the woman by members of her husband's family or by her suicide. The woman is typically burned to death with kerosene, a fuel used in pressurized cook stoves, hence the use of the term "bride-burning" in public discourse.

Dowry death statistics appear frequently in the press and parliamentary debates. Parliamentary sources report the following figures for married women 16 to 30 years of age in Delhi: 452 deaths by burning for 1985; 478 for 1986 and 300 for the first six months of 1987 (Bhatia 1988). There were 1,319 cases reported nationally in 1986 (*Times of India*, January 10, 1988). Police records do not match hospital records for third degree burn cases among younger married women; far more violence occurs than the crime reports indicate (Kumari 1988).

There is other violence against women related both directly and indirectly to the institution of dowry. For example, there are unmarried women who commit suicide so as to relieve their families of the burden of providing a dowry. A recent case that received national attention in the Indian press involved the triple suicide of three sisters in the industrial city of Kanpur. A photograph was widely published showing the three young women hanging from ceiling fans by their scarves. Their father, who earned about 4,000 Rs. [rupees] per month, was not able to negotiate marriage for his oldest daughter. The grooms were requesting approximately 100,000 Rs. Also linked to the dowry problem is selective female abortion made possible by amniocentesis. This issue was brought to national attention with a startling statistic reported out of a seminar held in Delhi in 1985. Of 3,000 abortions carried out after sex determination through amniocentesis, only one involved a male fetus. As a result of these developments, the government of the state of Maharashtra banned sex determination tests except those carried out in government hospitals.

The phenomenon of dowry death presents a difficult problem for the ethnologist. Ethnological theory, with its residual functionalist cast, still does not deal effectively with the social costs of institutions of what might be arguably referred to as custom gone bad, resulting in a culturally constituted violence syndrome.

This essay examines dowry and its violent aspects, and some of the public solutions developed to deal with it in India. Our work consists of a meta-analysis of some available literature. We critique the legal mechanisms established to regulate the cultural institution of dowry and the resultant social evils engendered by the institution, and argue that policies directed against these social evils need to be constructed in terms of an underlying cause rather than of the problem itself. We consider cause, an aspect of the problem infrequently discussed in public debate. As Saini asserts, "legal academicians have shown absolutely no interest in the causal roots of dowry as practiced in contemporary India" (1983:143).

THE INSTITUTION

Since ancient times, the marriage of Hindus has required the transfer of property from the family of the bride to the family of the groom. Dowry or *daan dehej* is thought by some to be sanctioned by such religious texts as the *Manusmriti*. Seen in this way, dowry is a religious obligation of the father of a woman and a matter of *dharma* (religious duty) whereby authority over a woman is transferred from her father to her husband. This transfer takes different forms in different communities in modern India (Tambiah 1973). In public discussion, the term "dowry" covers a wide range of traditional payments and expenses, some presented to the groom's family and others to be retained by the bride. Customs have changed through time. The financial burdens of gifts and the dowry payments per se are exacerbated by the many expenses associated with the marriage celebration itself, but dowry payment is especially problematic because of its open-ended nature. As Tambiah notes, "marriage payments in India usually comprise an elaborate series of payments back and forth between the marrying families" and "this series extends over a long period of time and persists after marriage" (1973:92). Contemporary cases such as the death of Mrs. Sunita, often revolve around such continued demands.

A daughter's marriage takes a long time to prepare and involves the development of an adaptive strategy on the part of her family. An important part of the strategy is the preparation for making dowry payments; family consumption may be curtailed so as to allow accumulation of money for dowry. Seeing to marriage arrangements may be an important aspect of retirement planning. The dowries that the family receives on behalf of their sons may be "rolled over" to deal with the daughter's requirements. Families attempt to cultivate in both their sons and daughters attributes that will make them more attractive in marriage negotiations. Many things besides dowry are considered in negotiations: "non-economic" factors have demonstrable effect on the expectations for dowry and the family's strategy concerning the dowry process.

Education is a variable to be considered in the negotiation process. Education of young women is somewhat problematic because suitable husbands for such women must also be college educated. The parents of such young men demand more dowry for their sons. A consideration in sending a young woman to college will therefore be her parents' capacity to dower her adequately so as to obtain an appropriate groom. In any case, education is secondary to a man's earning power and the reputation of a woman's family. Education is, however, important in the early stages of negotiation because of the need to coordinate the level of the education of the men and women. Education qualifications are also less ambiguously defined than other dimensions of family reputation. Physical attractiveness is a consideration, but it is thought somewhat unseemly to emphasize this aspect of the decision.

Advertisements in newspapers are used for establishing marriage proposals (Aluwalia 1969, Niehoff 1959, Weibe and Ramu 1971), but contacts are more typically established through kin and other networks. Some marriages may be best termed "self-arranged," and are usually called "love marriages." In these cases, young men and women may develop a relationship independent of their families and then ask that negotiations be carried out on their behalf by family representatives.

Analysis of matrimonial advertisements shows some of the attributes considered to be important. Listed in such advertisements are education, age, income and occupation, physical attributes, *gotra* (a kind of unilineal descent group) membership, family background, place of residence, personality features, consideration of dowry, time and type of marriage, and language.

Consideration of dowry and other expenditures are brought out early in the negotiations and can serve as a stumbling block. Dowry negotiations can go on for some time. The last stage is the actual "seeing of the groom" and the "seeing of the bride," both rather fleeting encounters whose position at the end of the process indicates their relative lack of importance.

Marriage is a process by which two families mutually evaluate each other. The outcome of the negotiations is an expression of the relative worth of the two persons, a man and a woman, and, by extension, the worth of their respective families. This estimation of worth is expressed in marriage expenditures, of which dowry is but a part. There are three possible types of expenditures: cash gifts, gifts of household goods, and expenditures on the wedding celebration itself. The cash gift component of the dowry goes to the groom's father and comes to be part of his common household fund. The household goods are for use by the groom's household, although they may be used to establish a separate household for the newlyweds. When separate accommodations are not set up, the groom's family may insist that the goods do not duplicate things they already have.

Dates for marriages are set through consideration of horoscopes; horoscopy is done by professional astrologers *(pandits)*. This practice leads to a concentration of marriage dates and consequent high demand for marriage goods and services at certain times of the year. During marriage seasons, the cost of jewelry, furniture, clothes, musicians' services and other marriage related expenditures goes up, presumably because of the concentration of the demand caused by the astrologers.

The expenditures required of the woman's family for the wedding in general and the dowry in particular are frequently massive. Paul reports, for a middle-class Delhi neighborhood, that most dowries were over 50,000 Rs. (1986). Srinivas comments that dowries over 200,000 Rs. are not uncommon (1984).[1]

ETHNOLOGICAL THEORIES ABOUT DOWRY

Dowry had traditionally been discussed by ethnologists in the context of the functionalist paradigm, and much theorizing about dowry appears to be concerned with explaining the "contribution" that the institution makes to social adaptation. The early theoretician Westermarck interpreted dowry as a social marker of the legitimacy of spouse and offspring, and as a mechanism for defining women's social roles and property rights in the new household (Westermarck 1921:428). Murdock suggests that dowry may confirm the contract of marriage (1949). Dowry is interpreted by Friedl as a means to adjust a woman to her affinal home as it rearranges social relationships including the social separation of the man from his parents (1967). Dowry payments are public expressions of the new relationship between the two families, and of the social status of the bride and groom.

Dowry is seen in the social science literature as a kind of antemortem or anticipated inheritance by which a widow is assured of support, and provision for her offspring (Friedl 1967; Goody 1973, 1976). It transfers money to where the women will be and where they will reproduce; as a result, resources are also placed where the children will benefit, given the practice of patrilineal inheritance of immovable, economically valuable property like farm land.

In India, dowry is also seen as an expression of the symbolic order of society. According to Dumont, dowry expresses the hierarchal relations of marriage in India and lower status of the bride (Dumont 1957). The amount of dowry given is an expression of prestige. The capacity to buy prestige through dowry increases the potential for social mobility (Goody 1973). Dowry is a kind of delayed consumption used to demonstrate or improve social rank (Epstein 1960).

There is a significant discontinuity between discussions of dowry in the ethnological theory and in public discourse. Certainly the dowry problem does appear in the writing of contemporary ethnologists, but it is simply lamented and left largely uninterpreted and unexplained.

THE EXTANT SOLUTIONS TO THE PROBLEM

The Dowry Prohibition Act of 1961, as amended in 1984 and 1986, is the primary legal means for regulating the dowry process and controlling its excesses. The laws against dowry are tough. Dowry demand offenses are "cognizable" (require no warrant) and nonbailable, and the burden of proof is on the accused. There are, in fact, convictions under the law.

The act defines dowry as "any property of valuable security given or agreed to be given either directly or indirectly—(a) by one party to a marriage to the other party to a marriage; or (b) by parents of either party to a marriage or by any other person, to either party to the marriage or to any other person" (Government of India 1986:1). The act makes it illegal to give or take dowry, "If any person after the commencement of this act, gives or takes or abets the giving or taking of dowry, he shall be punishable with imprisonment for a term which shall not be less than five years; and with fine which shall not be less than fifteen thousand rupees or the amount of the value of such dowry which ever is more" (Government of India 1986:1). While this section unambiguously prohibits dowry, the third section allows wedding presents to be freely given. Thus the law does not apply to "presents which are given at the time of marriage to the bride (without demand having been made in that behalf)" (Government of India 1986:1). Identical provisions apply to the groom. Furthermore, all such presents must be listed on a document before the consummation of the marriage. The list is to contain a brief description and estimation of the value of the gifts, name of presenting person, and the relationship that person has with the bride and groom. This regulation also provides "that where such

presents are made by or on the behalf of the bride or any other person related to the bride, such presents are of a customary nature and the value thereof is not excessive having regard to the financial status of the person by whom, or on whose behalf, such presents are given" (Government of India 1986:2). Amendments made in 1984 make it illegal for a person to demand dowry with the same penalty as under the earlier "giving and taking" provision. It was also declared illegal to advertise for dowry, such an offense being defined as not bailable, with the burden of proof on the accused person.

This legislation was coupled with some changes in the Indian Penal Code that legally established the concept of "dowry death." That is, "where the death of a woman is caused by any burns or bodily injury or occurs otherwise than under normal circumstances within seven years of her marriage and it is shown that soon before her death she was subjected to cruelty or harassment by her husband or any relative of her husband for, or in connection with, any demand for dowry, such death shall be called 'dowry death,' and such husband or relative shall be deemed to have caused her death" (Government of India 1987:4). The Indian Evidence Act of 1871 was changed so as to allow for the presumption of guilt under the circumstances outlined above. Changes in the code allowed for special investigation and reporting procedures of deaths by apparent suicide of women within seven years of marriage if requested by a relative. There were also newly defined special provisions for autopsies.

To this point, however, these legal mechanisms have proved ineffective. According to Sivaramayya, the "act has signally failed in its operation" (1984:66). Menon refers to the "near total failure" of the law (1988:12). A similar viewpoint is expressed by Srinivas, who wrote, "The Dowry Prohibition Act of 1961 has been unanimously declared to be an utterly ineffective law" (1984:29).

In addition to the legal attack on dowry abuses, numerous public groups engage in public education campaigns. In urban settings, the most noteworthy of these groups are specialized research units such as the Special Cell for Women of the Tata Institute of Social Sciences (Bombay), and the Center for Social Research (New Delhi). Also involved in the effort are private voluntary organizations such as the Crimes Against Women Cell, Karmika, and Sukh Shanti.

These groups issue public education advertising on various feminist issues. The anti-dowry advertisement of the Federation of Indian Chambers of Commerce and Industry Ladies Organization exemplifies the thrust of these campaigns. In the following advertisement, which was frequently run in the winter of 1988 in newspapers such as the *Times of India,* a photograph of a doll dressed in traditional Indian bridal attire was shown in flames.

> Every time a young bride dies because of dowry demands, we are all responsible for her death. Because we allow it to happen. Each year in Delhi hospitals alone, over 300 brides die of third degree burns. And many more deaths go unreported. Most of the guilty get away. And we just shrug helplessly and say, "what can we do?" We can do a lot.
>
> Help create social condemnation of dowry. Refuse to take or give dowry. Protest when you meet people who condone the practice. Reach out and help the girl being harassed for it. Act now.
>
> Let's fight it together.
>
> As parents, bring up educated, self-reliant daughters. Make sure they marry only after 18. Oppose dowry; refuse to even discuss it. If your daughter is harassed after marriage stand by her.
>
> As young men and women, refuse marriage proposals where dowry is being considered. As friends and neighbors, ostracize families who give or take dowry. Reach out to help victims of dowry harassment.
>
> As legislators and jurists, frame stronger laws. Ensure speedy hearings, impose severe punishments. As associations, give help and advice. Take up the challenge of changing laws and attitudes of society. Let us all resolve to fight the evil. If we fight together we can win.
>
> SAY NO TO DOWRY.

Also engaged in anti-dowry work are peasant political action groups such as Bharatiya Kisan Union (BKU). BKU consists of farmers from western Uttar Pradesh whose political program is focused more generally on agricultural issues. The group sponsored a massive 25-day demonstration at Meerut, Uttar Pradesh, in 1988. The leadership used the demonstration to announce a social reform program, most of it dealing with marriage issues. According to news service reports, "The code of social reforms includes fixing the maximum number of persons in a marriage party at 11, no feasts relating to marriage, and no dowry except 10 grams of gold and 30 grams of silver" (*Times of India*, February 11, 1988). Buses plying rural roads in western Uttar Pradesh are reported to have been painted with the slogan "The bride is the dowry." Private campaigns against dowry occur in the countryside as well as among the urban elites, although it is likely that the underlying motivations are quite different.

POLICY ANALYSIS

Our argument is based on the assumption that social problems are best dealt with by policies directed at the correction of causative factors, rather than at the amelioration of symptoms. While current legal remedies directly confront dowry violence, the linkage between cause and the problematic behavior is not made. Here we develop an argument consisting of three components: women's access to production roles and property; delocalization of social control; and economic transformation of society. The pattern of distribution of aspects of the institution of dowry and its attendant problems is important to this analysis. Although dowry practices and the related crimes against women are distributed throughout Indian society, the distribution is patterned in terms of geography, caste rank, socioeconomic rank, urban/rural residence, and employment status of the women. In some places and among some people there is demonstrably more violence, more intensity of dowry practices, and more commitment to dowry itself. Much of the distributional data are problematic in one way or another. The most frequent problem is that the studies are not based on national samples. Furthermore, the interpretation of results is often colored by reformist agendas. There is a tendency to deemphasize differences in frequency from one segment of the population to another so as to build support of dowry death as a general social reform issue. Nevertheless, while the data available for these distributions are of inconsistent quality, they are interpretable in terms of our problem.

Women's Access to Production Roles and Property

Dowry violence is most frequent in north India. Some say that it is an especially severe problem in the Hindi Belt (i.e., Uttar Pradesh, Haryana, Punjab, Delhi, Bihar) (Government of India 1974:75). It is a lesser, albeit increasing problem in the south. There is also a north/south difference in the marriage institution itself. To simplify somewhat, in the north hypergamy is sought after in marriage alliances, in which case brides seek grooms from higher rank descent groups within their caste group (Srinivas 1984). In the south, marriages are more typically isogamous.

The literature comparing north and south India indicates important contrasts at both the ecological and the institutional levels. Based on conceptions developed by Boserup (1970) in a cross-cultural comparative framework on the relationship between the farming system and occupational role of women, Miller (1981) composed a model for explaining the significant north-south differences in the juvenile sex ratio [the ratio of males to females ten years of age and below]. The farming systems of the north are based on "dry-field plow cultivation," whereas in the south the farming systems are dominated by "swidden and wet-rice cultivation" (Miller 1981:28). These two systems make different labor demands. In the wet rice or swidden systems of the south, women are very important sources of labor. In the north, women's involvement in agricultural production is limited. According to Miller, women in the north are excluded from property holding and receive instead a "dowry of movables." In the south, where women are included in the production activities, they may receive "rights to land" (Miller 1981:28). In the north, women are high-cost items of social overhead, while in the south, women contribute labor and are more highly valued. In the north there is a "high cost of raising several daughters" while in the south there is "little liability in raising several daughters." There is thus "discrimination against daughters" and an "intense preference for sons" in the north, and "appreciation for daughters" and "moderate preference for sons" in the south. Miller thus explains the unbalanced-toward-males juvenile sex ratios of the north and the balanced sex ratios of the south (Miller 1981:27–28). The lower economic value of women in the north is expressed in differential treatment of children by sex. Females get less food, less care, and less attention, and therefore they have a higher death rate. In general the Boserup and Miller economic argument is consistent with Engels's thesis about the relationship between the subordination of women and property (Engels 1884, Hirschon 1984:1).

Miller extended her analysis of juvenile sex ratios to include marriage costs (including dowry), female labor participation, and property owning, and found that property owning was associated with high marriage costs and low female labor force participation, both of which were associated with high juvenile sex ratios. That is, the death rate of females is higher when marriage costs are high and women are kept from remunerative employment. Both of these patterns are associated with the "propertied" segment of the population (Miller 1981:156–159). Her data are derived from the secondary analysis of ethnographic accounts. The literature concerning the distribution of dowry practices and dowry death is consistent with these results.

Miller's analysis shows a general pattern of treatment of females in India. Their access to support in various forms is related to their contribution to production (Miller 1981). This analysis does not explain the problem of dowry violence, but it does demonstrate a fundamental pattern within which dowry violence can be interpreted.

The distribution of dowry varies by caste. In her study of dowry violence victims in Delhi, Kumari found that members of the lower ranking castes report less "dowry harassment" than do those in higher ranking castes (Kumari 1988:31). These results are consistent with Miller's argument since the pattern of exclusion of women from economic production roles varies by caste. Women of lower castes are less subject to restrictions concerning employment outside the realm of reproduction within the household. These women are often poor and uneducated, and are subject to other types of restrictions.

In the framework of caste, dowry practices of higher caste groups are emulated by lower caste groups. This process is known as "Sanskritization" and it may relate to the widely held view that dowry harassment is increasing in lower ranking castes. Sanskritization is the process by which lower ranked caste groups attempt to raise their rank through the emulation of higher rank castes. The emulation involves discarding certain behaviors (such as eating meat or paying bride price) and adopting alternatives (Srinivas 1969). Attitudinal research shows that people of the lower socio-economic strata have a greater commitment to dowry than do those of higher strata (Hooja 1969, Khanna and Verghese 1978, Paul 1986). Although the lower and middle classes are committed to dowry, the associated violence, including higher death rates, is more typically a middle class problem (Kumari 1988).

Employment status of women has an effect on dowry. In her survey of dowry problems in a south Delhi neighborhood, Paul (1986) found that the amount of dowry was less for employed middle class women than it was for the unemployed. This pattern is also suggested by Verghese (1980) and van der Veen (1972:40), but disputed by others (Murickan 1975). This link is also manifested among tribal people undergoing urbanization. Tribal people, ranked more toward the low end of the social hierarchy, typically make use of bride price (i.e., a payment to the bride's family) rather than dowry (Karve 1953). As these groups become more integrated into national life, they will shift to dowry practices to emulate high castes while their women participate less in gainful employment (Luthra 1983). Croll finds a similar relationship in her analysis of post-revolutionary China. She says, "it is the increased value attributed to women's labor which is largely responsible for the decline in the dowry" (1984:58).

Both Kumari (1988) and Srinivas (1984) developed arguments based on non-economic factors. Kumari in effect indicated that if dowry could be explained in economic terms, marriage would be simply a calculation of the value of a woman: if the value were high, bride price would be paid, and if the value were low, dowry transactions would occur. This formulation was presented as a refutation of Madan's dowry-as-compensation argument (Kumari 1988). We agree that reducing this practice to purely economic terms is an absurdity. The argument is not purely economic, but it is certainly consistent with a cultural materialist perspective (Harris 1979) in which symbolic values are shaped by an underlying material relationship that is the basis for the construction of cultural reality.

Delocalization of Social Control

Dowry violence is more frequent in cities (Saini 1983). Delhi has the reputation of having a high frequency of problems of dowry (Srinivas 1984:7). The urban-rural distribution pattern may be a manifestation of the effects of the delocalization of dowry. Dowry, when operative in the relationships among local caste groups in related villages, was to an extent self-regulating through caste *panchayats* (councils) and by the joint families themselves. These groups easily reach into peoples' lives. By contrast, the national level laws have inadequate reach and cannot achieve regulation. While in some areas caste groups continue to function to limit abuses, these groups are less effective in urban settings. Population movements and competition with state level social control mechanisms limit the effectiveness of self-regulation. A government commission study of women's status argues "that because of changed circumstances in which a son generally has a separate establishment and has a job somewhere away from home, the parents cannot expect much help from him, and so they consider his marriage as the major occasion on which their investment in his education can be recovered" (Government of India 1974:74). These views are consistent with the research results reported by Paul, who demonstrates that dowry amounts are higher among people who have migrated to Delhi and those who live in nuclear families, because the families in general and the women in particular are less subject to social constraints (Paul 1986). New brides do not seem to have adequate support networks in urban settings.

Economic Transformation of Society

The custom of dowry has been thrown into disarray by inflationary pressures. The consumer price index for urban non-manual workers has increased from its reference year of 1960 value of 100 to 532 for 1984–85 (Government of India 1987). The media of dowry exchange have changed dramatically because of the increasing availability of consumer goods. It has become increasingly difficult to prepare for giving dowry for a daughter or a sister. Sharma argues that, in part, dowry problems are caused by rapid change in the nature of consumer goods which made it no longer possible to accumulate gift goods over a long period as the latest styles in material goods could not be presented (1984: 70–71).

The current regime of individual dowry seeking and giving is constituted as a kind of rational behavior. That is, it is achieved through choice, is consistent with certain values, and serves to increase someone's utility. There are a number of things sought by the groom's family in these transactions. Wealth and family prestige are especially important. The family prestige "bought" with marriage expenditures, which is relevant to both the bride and groom's side in the transaction, is no doubt very much worth maximizing in the Indian context. From the perspective of the bride's family, dowry payments involve trading present consumption for future earning power for their daughter through acquiring a groom with better qualities and connections. In a two-tier, gender segregated, high unemployment, inflationary economy such as that of India, one can grasp the advantage of investing in husbands with high future earning potential. It is also possible to argue that in societies with symbolic mechanisms of stratification, it is expected that persons will attempt to make public displays of consumption in order to improve their overall performance and so to take advantage of the ambiguities of the status hierarchy system. The demand for both symbolic goods and future earnings is highly elastic. Family connections, education, and wealth seem especially important in India, and they all serve as hedges against inflation and poverty. With women having limited access to jobs and earning lower pay, it is rational to invest in a share of the groom's prospects. If you ask people why they give dowry when their daughters are being married they say, "because we love them." On the other hand, grooms' families will find the decision to forgo dowry very difficult.

SUMMARY

The distributional data indicate that the relationship between the way females are treated in marriage and their participation in economic production is consistent with Miller's development of the Boserup hypothesis. It is assumed that the pattern of maltreatment of females has been subject to various controls operating at the levels of family, caste, and community. Urbanization reduces the effectiveness of these mechanisms, thus increasing the intensity of the problem. This trend is exacerbated by the economic transformations within contemporary Indian society. It is our viewpoint that policies developed to reduce dowry-related violence will fail if they do not increase the economic value of women.

The criminalization of dowry may have been a politically useful symbol, but it has not curtailed the practice. As dowry is attacked, the state has not adequately dealt with the ante-mortem inheritance aspect of the custom. If dowry continues to provide a share of the family wealth to daughters before the death of the parents, then legally curtailing the practice is likely to damage the economic interests of women in the name of protecting them. One might argue that the primary legal remedy for the dowry problem actually makes it worse because it limits the transfer of assets to women. Perhaps this is why research on attitudes toward dowry indicates a continued positive commitment to the institution (Mathew 1987). India is a society in which most people (most particularly the elite) have given and received dowry; most people are even today giving and taking dowries. Declaring dowry a crime creates a condition in which the mass of society are technically criminals. The moral-legal basis of society suffers, and communal, parochial, and other fissiparous forces are encouraged.

To be effective, anti-dowry legislation must make sure that the social utility provided by dowry practices be displaced to practices that are less problematic, and that the apparent causes of the practice be attacked. To do so would mean that attempts to eradicate the social evils produced by the dowry institution need to be based on an examination of women's property rights so as to increase their economic access. Traditional Hindu customs associated with inheritance give sons the right from birth to claim the so-called ancestral properties. This principle is part of the Mitakshara tradition of Hindu law, which prevails throughout India except in Bengal, Kerala, Assam, and northern parts of Orissa. These properties are obtained from father, paternal grandfather, or paternal great-grandfather. According to Sivaramayya (1984:71), "The Hindu Succession Act (the law which controls inheritance) did not abrogate this right by birth which exists in favor of a son, paternal grandson and paternal great grandson. The availability of the right in favor of these male descendants only is a discrimination against daughters." The right is derived from ancient texts. According to Tambiah (1973:95), the Dharmasastras provide that it is "essentially males who inherit the patrimony while women are entitled to maintenance, marriage expenses and gifts." While the Hindu Succession Act abrogates much traditional law, it specifically accepts the principle of male birthright to the property of the joint family. That is, "When a male Hindu dies after the commencement of the Act, having at the time of death an interest in a Mitakshara coparcenary property, his interest in the property shall devolve by survivorship upon the surviving members of the coparcenary and not in accordance with this Act" (Government of India 1985:3). The Hindu Succession Act in its most recent form provides for the intestate or testamentary inheritance of a female of a share of the family property. Yet the prior right of males at birth is not abrogated. Hindu males own a share of the family rights at birth; females can inherit it. Testamentary succession overrides the principle of intestate succession, and therefore the interests of females can be usurped simply by writing a will. The other procedures for a female to renounce an interest in family property are very simple. Moreover, according to Sivaramayya (1984:58), "no specific formality is required for the relinquishment of the interest beyond the expression of a clear intention to that effect." Instruments of relinquishment can be and are forged.

The antemortem inheritance function of dowry has been eroded or perhaps supplanted by transfer of goods to the groom's family for their consumption and the expression of the so-called prestige of the family. Indeed social science commentary on dowry in India suggests that this aspect of dowry is relatively unimportant in any case because only a small portion of the total marriage expenditure is under the bride's control. There is evidence that even the clothing and ornaments and other personal property of the bride are being usurped (Verghese 1980). Implementation of a gender-neutral inheritance law as advocated by the Government of India Committee on the Status of Women may serve to increase the economic value of women in general, while it serves as an alternative to the ante-mortem inheritance aspect of dowry. Since dowry constitutes a kind of ante-mortem inheritance, it is logical to change the inheritance laws in conjunction with the restrictions on dowry behavior. Sisters as well as brothers need to have a share in the family wealth from birth, and that right should be associated with legal procedures that increase the difficulty of alienation of property rights. There is no question that such a procedure would serve to erode the stability of the patrilineal family by diluting its economic base.

The Government of India has passed legislation such as the Hindu Succession Act (1956) and the Hindu Adoption and Maintenance Act (1956), both of which inter-alia provide for a woman's right of inheritance from her father. For example, under the Adoption and Maintenance Act, a woman has a claim of rights of maintenance from her husband's father in case she is widowed. Moreover, she has the right to claim inheritance from her deceased husband's estate. In spite of these changes, inheritance provisions are quite different for males and females. The Chief Justice of the Supreme Court of India, Honorable Mr. Justice Y. V. Chandrachud, wrote that in spite of changes, "some inequalities like the right of birth in favor of a son, paternal grandson and paternal great grandson still persist" (1984:vii). Provision of females with equal rights to inherit ancestral property from birth, or from a bequest, or at the death may reduce dowry problems. Furthermore, property that is allowed to remain in the name of the deceased for any length of time, as is frequently the case in India, should revert to the state. As it stands, property may remain in the name of a deceased ancestor, while his descendants divide it informally among themselves.

The establishment of a gender-neutral inheritance law represents a significant shift in public policy. We argue that there is a link between pro-male property laws and violence toward women. While we assert this position, we also need to recognize that the property laws give coherence and stability to an essential Indian institution, the joint family. The Mitakshara principle of male inheritance rights is both a reflection and a cause of family solidarity. Modifying this principle in an attempt to reduce violence toward women could have a deleterious effect on family coherence. In addition, the fundamental nature of these institutions makes it inconceivable that there would be substantial resistance to these changes. Yet if one considers this issue in historic terms, it is apparent that during the 20th century, legal change is in the direction of gender neutrality, a process that started with the Hindu Law of Inheritance (Amendment) Act (1929) and the Hindu Succession Act (1956), and continues through judicial decisions to the present (Diwan 1988:384). As Diwan notes in reference to the changes brought by the Hindu Succession Act of 1956, "the Mitakshara bias towards preference of males over females and of agnates over cognates has been considerably whittled down" (1988:358). Such change is not easy. The changes brought with the Hindu Succession Act in 1956 were achieved only after overcoming "stiff resistance from the traditionalists" (Government of India 1974:135). The same report states, "The hold of tradition, however, was so strong that even while introducing sweeping changes, the legislators compromised and retained in some respects the inferior position of women" (Government of India 1974:135). It must be remembered that the texts that are the foundations of contemporary law include legislation (such as the Hindu Succession Act itself), case law, and religious texts, so that the constitutional question is also a question for religious interpretation, despite the constitutional commitment to secularism.

We are advocating further steps toward gender neutrality of the inheritance laws so that women and men will receive an equal share under intestate succession, and have an equal chance to be testamentary heirs. The law should thus be gender-neutral while still permitting a range of decisions allowing property to stay in a male line if the holder of the property so chooses. The required social adjustment could be largely achieved through the decisions of a family, backed by the power of the state. Families could express their preferences, but the state would not serve to protect the economic interests of males. The process could involve the concept of birthright as well as succession at death. We do not choose to engage those arguments, but do point out that the rapid aging of the Indian population may suggest that a full abrogation of the Mitakshara principle of birthright would be the best social policy because doing so would give older people somewhat greater control over their property in an economy virtually devoid of public investment in social services for older people (Bose and Gangrade 1988, Sharma and Dak 1987).

There are precedents for such policy at the state level. In Andhra Pradesh, the Hindu Succession Act was amended to provide for a female's birthright interest in the Mitakshara property. In Kerala, the Mitakshara property concept was legally abrogated altogether. Other gender asymmetries in the laws of India need to be attacked. The overall goal of policy should be to increase the economic value of women.

Ethnological theory directs our attention to social recognition of marriage and property transfer as functionally important features of the institution. The state can provide a means of socially recognizing marriage through registration and licensure. The law expresses no explicit preference for traditional marriage ritual, and it is possible to have a civil marriage under the provisions of the Special Marriage Act (1954) through registration with a magistrate. Nevertheless, this system co-exists parallel with the traditional system of marriage, which is beyond the reach of state control. Other marriages may be registered under this act if the persons involved so choose, and if a ceremony has been carried out. These special marriages are an alternative to an unregistered marriage.

We conclude that a useful mechanism for state control of dowry problems is the establishment of universal marriage registration, which does not exist at the present time. Marriage registration is also called for by the first Round Table on Social Audit of Implementation of Dowry Legislation (Bhatia 1988), which may serve to provide some monitoring of dowry abuses and perhaps to manifest the state's interest in an effective marriage institution. It would be naive to assume that such a policy would be widely honored, but as it is, low-income persons do not get married because they do not have the resources for marriage under the traditional non-state controlled regime. There are numerous reform groups that organize mass marriage ceremonies of village people so as to help them escape the burden of marriage expenditures. The point is that compliance is a large problem even under current circumstances.

In conclusion, we feel that the causes of the dowry problems are a product of the low economic value of women, loss of effective social control of abuse through delocalization, and pressures caused by economic transformation. The traditional family, caste group, and community controls which have been reduced in effectiveness should be replaced by state functions. The foundation of state control is universal marriage registration and licensure. The impact of the economic value of women on the problem is indicated by the transition from bride price to dowry among tribal people. It is also associated with a reduction in the extent of gainful employment and lower dowry amounts demonstrated for employed women. A broad program to increase the economic value of women would be the most useful means of dealing with the problem of dowry. Further restrictions on dowry without providing for a radically different property right for females is probably not in the interests of Indian women, since dowry represents ante-mortem inheritance. This underlying paradox may explain the commitment to dowry revealed in attitudinal research with Indian women, even though it is also an important feminist issue. The alternatives include the abolishment of the legal basis for the joint family as a corporate unit as has been done in Kerala, or the legal redefinition of the joint family as economically duolineal, as has occurred in Andhra Pradesh.

NOTE

1. For purposes of comparison, a mid-career Indian academic might be paid 60,000 Rs. per year.

REFERENCES

Aluwalia, H. 1969. Matrimonial Advertisements in Panjab. *Indian Journal of Social Work* 30:55–65.

Bhatia, S. C. 1988. Social Audit of Dowry Legislation. Delhi: Legal Literacy Project.

Bose, A. B., and K. D. Gangrade. 1988. *The Aging in India, Problems and Potentialities*. New Delhi: Abhinav.

Boserup, Ester. 1970. *Women's Role in Economic Development*. New York: St. Martin's Press.

Chandrachud, Y. V. 1984. Foreword. In *Inequalities and the Law*. B. Sivaramayya, ed. Pp. iv–vi. Lucknow: Eastern Book Company.

Croll, Elisabeth. 1984. The Exchange of Women and Property: Marriage in Post-revolutionary China. In *Women and Property—Women as Property*. Renee Hirschon, ed. Pp. 44–61. London/New York: Croom Helm/St. Martin's Press.

Diwan, Paras. 1988. *Modern Hindu Law, Codified and Uncodified*. Allahabad: Allahabad Law Agency.

Dumont, Louis. 1957. *Hierarchy and Marriage Alliance in South Indian Kinship*. London: Royal Anthropological Institute.

Engels, Fredrich. 1884. *The Origin of Family, Private Property and the State*. New York: International.

Epstein, T. Scarlett. 1960. Peasant Marriage in South India. *Man in India* 40:192–232.

Friedl, Ernestine. 1967. *Vasilika, A Village in Modern Greece*. New York: Holt, Rinehart and Winston.

Goody, Jack. 1973. Bridewealth and Dowry in Africa and Eurasia. In *Bridewealth and Dowry*. Jack Goody and S. J. Tambiah, eds. Pp. 1–58. Cambridge: Cambridge University Press.

———. 1976. *Production and Reproduction, A Comparative Study of the Domestic Domain*. Cambridge: Cambridge University Press.

Government of India. 1974. *Towards Equality: Report of the Committee on the Status of Women*. New Delhi: Government of India, Ministry of Education and Social Welfare.

———. 1985. The Hindu Succession Act. New Delhi: Government of India.

———. 1986. The Dowry Prohibition Act, 1961 (Act No. 28 of 1961) and Connected Legislation (as on 15th January, 1986). New Delhi: Government of India.

———. 1987. *India 1986, A Reference Manual*. Delhi: Ministry of Information and Broadcasting.

Harris, Marvin. 1979. *Cultural Materialism: The Struggle for a Science of Culture*. New York: Random House.

Hirschon, Renee. 1984. Introduction: Property, Power and Gender Relations. In *Women and Property—Women as Property*. Renee Hirschon, ed. Pp. 1–22. London/New York: Croom Helm/St. Martin's Press.

Hooja, S. L. 1969. *Dowry System in India*. New Delhi: Asia Press.

Karve, Irawati. 1953. *Kinship Organization in India*. Bombay: Asia Publishing.

Khanna, G. and M. Verghese. 1978. *Indian Women Today*. New Delhi: Vikas Publishing House.

Kumari, Ranjana. 1988. Practice and Problems of Dowry: A Study of Dowry Victims in Delhi. In *Social Audit of Dowry Legislation*. S. C. Bhatia, ed. Pp. 27–37. Delhi: Legal Literacy Project.

Luthra, A. 1983. Dowry Among the Urban Poor, Perception and Practice. *Social Action* 33:207.

Mathew, Anna. 1987. Attitudes Toward Dowry. *Indian Journal of Social Work* 48:95–102.

Menon, N. R. Madhava. 1988. The Dowry Prohibition Act: Does the Law Provide the Solution or Itself Constitute the Problem? In *Social Audit of Dowry Legislation*. S. C. Bhatia, ed. Pp. 11–26. Delhi: Legal Literacy Project.

Miller, Barbara D. 1981. *The Endangered Sex, Neglect of Female Children in Rural North India*. Ithaca, NY: Cornell University Press.

Murdock, George P. 1949. *Social Structure*. New York: Macmillan.

Murickan, J. 1975. Women in Kerala: Changing Socioeconomic Status and Self Image. In *Women in Contemporary India*. A. de Souza, ed. Pp. 73–95. Delhi: Manohar.

Niehoff, Arthur H. 1959. A Study of Matrimonial Advertisements in North India. *Eastern Anthropologist* 12:37–50.

Paul, Madan C. 1986. *Dowry and the Position of Women in India. A Study of Delhi Metropolis*. New Delhi: Inter India Publishers.

Saini, Debi. 1983. Dowry Prohibition Law, Social Change and Challenges in India. *Indian Journal of Social Work* 44(2):143–147.

Sharma, M. L. and T. Dak. 1987. *Aging in India, Challenge for the Society*. Delhi: Ajanta Publications.

Sharma, Ursula. 1984. Dowry in North India: Its Consequences for Women. In *Women and Property—Women as Property*. Renee Hirschon, ed. Pp. 62–74. London/New York: Croom Helm/St. Martin's Press.

Sivaramayya, B. 1984. *Inequalities and the Law*. Lucknow: Eastern Book Company.

Srinivas, M. N. 1969. *Social Change in Modern India*. Berkeley, CA: University of California Press.

——. 1984. *Some Reflections on Dowry*. Delhi: Oxford University Press.

Tambiah, S. J. 1973. Dowry and Bridewealth and the Property Rights of Women in South Asia. In *Bridewealth and Dowry*. Jack Goody and S. J. Tambiah, eds. Pp. 59–169. Cambridge: Cambridge University Press.

van der Veen, Klaus W. 1972. *I Give Thee My Daughter—A Study of Marriage and Hierarchy Among the Anavil Brahmins of South Gujarat*. Assen: Van Gorcum.

Verghese, Jamila. 1980. *Her Gold and Her Body*. New Delhi: Vikas Publishing House.

Weibe, P. O. and G. N. Ramu. 1971. A Content Analysis of Matrimonial Advertisements. *Man in India* 51:119–120.

Westermarck, Edward. 1921. *The History of Human Marriage*. London: MacMillan and Co.

25

How Many Fathers Are Best for a Child?

Meredith F. Small

Anthropologists study systems of kinship and marriage in many societies for three reasons: first, these issues are very important to the people themselves; second, kinship and marriage are keys for understanding how contemporary cultures work; and finally, because they give us clues as to what patterns of family organization may have existed over the course of human history. As a great deal of anthropological research has revealed, diverse cultures have many different ways of organizing families.

In the United States, we often think of the "traditional" family as a nuclear family: two married parents with their children. Many people ethnocentrically believe that this is the normal or natural family system. Other types of family organization, such as "blended" families, are often described as recent variants. But in fact, the nuclear family model is just one of the many types of kinship organization humans have used at present and in the past—and it is only a relatively recent development in the broader context of human history.

This selection describes a pattern in some South American societies, in which a woman has intercourse with two or more men during her pregnancy and the resulting child is considered as having multiple fathers. This kinship system, like many others across the world, is quite different from the American model of a "traditional" family. However, as this selection argues, this arrangement helps improve children's likelihood of survival in Barí social communities. In the United States, social scientists have shown that having a father present is beneficial for children's development.

As you read this selection, ask yourself the following questions:

- If one father is good, are two or more better? How many fathers are best for a child?

- Why do the Barí believe a child can have more than one father?

- How do Barí women justify taking lovers during pregnancy?

- From an evolutionary perspective, what is the ideal number of fathers for a child to have in Barí society? Why?

- How is the Barí system similar to and different from the system of frequent divorce and court-enforced "child support" payments in modern American society?

The following terms discussed in this selection are included in the Glossary at the back of the book:

> *multiple paternity*
> *nuclear family*
> *paleoanthropology*

Anthropologist Stephen Beckerman was well into his forties before he finally understood how babies are made. He had thought, as most people do, that a sperm from one man and an egg from one woman joined to make a child. But one summer day, as he and his colleague Roberto Lizarralde lounged around in hammocks, chatting with Rachel, an elderly woman of the Barí tribe of Venezuela, she pointed out his error. Babies, she explained, can easily have more than one biological father. "My first husband was the father of my first child, my second child, and my third child," Rachel said, recalling her life. "But the fourth child, actually, he has two fathers." It was clear that Rachel didn't mean there was a stepfather hanging around or a friendly uncle who took the kid fishing every weekend. She was simply explaining the Barí version of conception to these ignorant anthropologists: A fetus is built up over time with repeated washes of sperm—which means, of course, that more than one man can contribute to the endeavor.

This interview changed not only the way Beckerman and Lizarralde viewed Barí families but also brought into question the very way that anthropologists portray human coupling. If biological fatherhood can be

Reprinted by permission of Meredith Small.

shared—an idea accepted by many indigenous groups across South America and in many other cultures across the globe—then the nuclear family with one mom and one dad might not be the established blueprint for a family that we have been led to expect. If so, the familiar story of traditional human mating behavior, in which man the hunter brings home the bacon to his faithful wife, loses credibility. And if the Barí and other groups work perfectly well with more flexible family styles, the variety of family structures that are increasingly common in Western culture these days—everything from single-parent households to blended families—may not be as dangerous to the social fabric as we are led to believe. People in this culture may simply be exercising the same family options that humans have had for millions of years, options that have been operating in other cultures while the West took a stricter view of what constitutes a family.

Stephen Beckerman folds his 6-foot-4-inch frame into a chair and turns to the mountainous topography of papers on his desk at Pennsylvania State University. Once he manages to locate a map under all the piles, he points to a spot on the border between Venezuela and Colombia where he spent 20 years, off and on, with the indigenous Barí Indians.

The traditional Barí culture, Beckerman explains, has come under attack by outside forces, starting with the conquistadors who arrived in the early 16th century. Today Catholic missionaries interact with the Barí, coal and oil companies are trying to seize their land, and drug traffickers and guerrillas are threats. Western influences are apparent: Most families have moved from traditional longhouses to single-family dwellings, and everyone wears modern Western clothes and uses Western goods. However, the Barí continue to practice their traditions of manioc farming, fishing, and hunting, according to Roberto Lizarralde, an anthropologist at the Central University of Venezuela who has been visiting the Barí regularly since 1960. Lizarralde also says that the Barí still have great faith in traditional spirits and ancestral wisdom, including their notion that a child can have multiple biological fathers.

The Barí believe that the first act of sex, which should always be between a husband and wife, plants the seed. Then the fledgling fetus must be nourished by repeated anointings of semen; the woman's body is viewed as a vessel where men do all the work. "One of the reasons women give you for taking lovers is that they don't want to wear out their husbands," Beckerman says. "They claim it's hard work for men to support a pregnancy by having enough sex, and so lovers can help." Just look, the Barí say. Women grow fat during a pregnancy, while men grow thin from all their work.

Anthropologists study a culture's ideas about conception because those ideas have a profound impact on the way people run their lives. In our culture, for example, conceiving children incurs long-term economic responsibility for both the mother and father. We take this obligation so seriously that when a parent fails to provide for a child, it is usually a violation of law. In the Barí system, when a man is named as a secondary biological father he is also placed under an obligation to the mother and the child. In addition, he is expected to give gifts of fish and game. These gifts are a significant burden because the man must also provide for his own wife and primary children.

Beckerman and his colleagues have discovered that naming secondary fathers has evolutionary consequences. A team of ethnographers led by Beckerman, Roberto Lizarralde, and his son Manuel, an anthropologist at Connecticut College who has been visiting the Barí since he was 5 years old, interviewed 114 Barí women past childbearing years and asked them about their full reproductive histories. "These interviews were a lot of fun," Beckerman says, laughing. "Randy old ladies talking about their lovers." In total, the researchers recorded claims of 916 pregnancies, an average of eight pregnancies for each woman. But child mortality was high—about one-third of the children did not survive to age 15. Naming secondary fathers was a critical factor in predicting which babies made it to adulthood. Secondary fathers were involved in 25 percent of pregnancies, and the team determined that two fathers were the ideal number. Children with one father and one secondary father made it to their teens most often; kids with only one father or those with more than two fathers didn't fare as well. The researchers also found that this decrease in mortality occurred not during the child's life but during fetal development: Women were less likely to have a miscarriage or stillbirth if they had a husband and an additional male contributing food. This result was a surprise because researchers had expected that help during childhood would be more important. "The Barí are not hungry; they are not close to the bone. But it must be the extra fat and protein that they get from secondary fathers during gestation that makes the difference," Beckerman explains as he points to photographs of Barí women who look well nourished, even downright plump.

Barí women seem to use this more flexible system of paternity when they need it. Within families, some children have secondary fathers, while their siblings belong to the husband alone. The team discovered that mothers are more likely to take on a secondary father when a previous child has died in infancy. Manuel Lizarralde claims the strategy makes perfect sense, given the Barí belief that the best way to cure a sick child is for the father to blow tobacco smoke over the child's body. "It is easy to imagine a bereaved mother thinking to herself that if she had only provided a secondary father and so more smoke for her dead child, she might have saved him—and vowing to provide that benefit for her next child."

Beckerman says extra fathers may have always been insurance for uncertain times: "Because the Barí were once hunted as if they were game animals—by other Indians, conquistadors, oilmen, farmers, and ranchers—the odds of a woman being widowed when she still had young children were one in three, according to data we gathered about the years 1930 to 1960. The men as well as the women knew this. None of these guys can go down the street to Mutual of Omaha and buy a life insurance policy. By allowing his wife to take a lover, the husband is doing all he can to ensure the survival of his children."

Barí women are also freer to do as they wish because men need their labor—having a wife is an economic necessity because women do the manioc farming, harvesting, and cooking, while men hunt and fish. "The sexual division of labor is such that you can't make it without a member of the opposite sex," says Beckerman. Initially, the researchers worried that jealousy on the part of husbands would make Barí women reticent about discussing multiple sexual partners. "In our first interviews, we would wait until the husband was out of the house," says Beckerman. "But one day we interviewed an old couple who were enjoying thinking about their lives; they were lying in their hammocks, side by side, and it was obvious he wasn't going anywhere. So we went down the list of her children and asked about other fathers. She said no, no, no for each child, and then the husband interrupted when we got to one and said, 'That's not true, don't you remember, there was that guy . . .' And the husband was grinning."

Not all women take lovers. Manuel Lizarralde has discovered through interviews that one-third of 122 women were faithful to their husbands during their pregnancies. "These women say they don't need it, or no one asked, or they have enough support from family and don't require another father for their child," Lizarralde says. "Some even admit that their husbands were not that happy about the idea." Or it may be a sign of changing times. Based on his most recent visits to the Barí, Lizarralde thinks that under the influence of Western values, the number of people who engage in multiple fatherhood may be decreasing. But his father, who has worked with the Barí for more than 40 years, disagrees. He says the practice is as frequent but that the Barí discuss it less openly than before, knowing that Westerners object to their views. After all, it took the anthropologists 20 years to hear about other fathers, and today the Barí are probably being even more discreet because they know Westerners disapprove of their beliefs.

"What this information adds up to," Beckerman says, "is that the Barí may be doing somewhat less fooling around within marriage these days but that most of them still believe that a child can have multiple fathers."

More important, the Barí idea that biological paternity can be shared is not just the quirky custom of one tribe; anthropologists have found that this idea is common across South America. The same belief is shared by indigenous groups in New Guinea and India, suggesting that multiple paternity has been part of human behavior for a long time, undermining all previous descriptions of how human mating behavior evolved.

Since the 1960s, when anthropologists began to construct scenarios of early human mating, they had always assumed that the model family started with a mom and dad bonded for life to raise the kids, a model that fit well with acceptable Western behavior. In 1981 in an article titled "The Origin of Man," C. Owen Lovejoy, an anthropologist at Kent State University, outlined the standard story of human evolution as it was used in the field—and is still presented in textbooks today: Human infants with their big brains and long periods of growth and learning have always been dependent on adults, a dependence that separates the humans from the apes. Mothers alone couldn't possibly find enough food for these dependent young, so women have always needed to find a mate who would stick close to home and bring in supplies for the family. Unfortunately for women, as evolutionary psychologists suggest, men are compelled by their biology to mate with as many partners as possible to pass along their genes. However, each of these men might be manipulated into staying with one woman who offered him sex and a promise of fidelity. The man, under those conditions, would be assured of paternity, and he might just stay around and make sure his kids survived.

This scenario presents humans as naturally monogamous, forming nuclear families as an evolutionary necessity. The only problem is that around the world families don't always operate this way. In fact, as the Barí and other cultures show, there are all sorts of ways to run a successful household.

The Na of Yunnan Province in China, for example, have a female-centric society in which husbands are not part of the picture. Women grow up and continue to live with their mothers, sisters, and brothers; they never marry or move away from the family compound. As a result, sisters and brothers rather than married pairs are the economic unit that farms and fishes together. Male lovers in this system are simply visitors. They have no place or power in the household, and children are brought up by their mothers and by the mothers' brothers. A father is identified only if there is a resemblance between him and the child, and even so, the father has no responsibilities toward the child.

Often women have sex with so many partners that the biological father is unknown. "I have not found any term that would cover the notion of father in the Na language," writes Chinese anthropologist Cai Hua in his book *A Society Without Fathers or Husbands: The Na of China*. In this case, women have complete control over their children, property, and sexuality.

Across lowland South America, family systems vary because cultures put their beliefs into practice in different ways. Among some native people, such as the Canela, Mehinaku, and Araweté, women control their sex lives and their fertility, and most children have several fathers. Barí women are also sexually liberated from an early age. "Once she has completed her puberty ritual, a Barí girl can have sex with anyone she wants as long as she doesn't violate the incest taboo," Beckerman explains. "It's nobody's business, not even Mom's and Dad's business." Women can also turn down prospective husbands.

In other cultures in South America, life is not so free for females, although members of these cultures also believe that babies can have more than one father. The Curripaco of Amazonia, for instance, acknowledge multiple fatherhood as a biological possibility and yet frown on women having affairs. Paul Valentine, a senior lecturer in anthropology at the University of East London who has studied the Curripaco for more than 20 years, says, "Curripaco women are in a difficult situation. The wives come into the village from different areas, and it's a very patrilineal system." If her husband dies, a widow is allowed to turn only to his brothers or to clan members on his side of the family for a new husband.

The relative power of women and men over their sex lives has important consequences. "In certain social and economic systems, women are free to make mate choices," says Valentine. In these cultures women are often the foundation of society, while men have less power in the community. Sisters tend to stay in the same household as their mothers. The women, in other words, have power to make choices. "At the other extreme, somehow, it's the men who try to maximize their evolutionary success at the expense of the women," says Valentine.

Men and women often have a conflict of interest when it comes to mating, marriage, and who should invest most in children, and the winners have sometimes been the men, sometimes the women. As Beckerman wryly puts it, "Anyone who believes that in a human mating relationship the man's reproductive interests always carry the day has obviously never been married."

The Barí and others show that human systems are, in fact, very flexible, ready to accommodate any sort of mating system or type of family. "I think that human beings are capable of making life extremely complicated. That's our way of doing business," says Ian Tattersall, a paleoanthropologist and curator in the division of anthropology at the American Museum of Natural History in New York City. Indeed, such flexibility suggests there's no reason to assume that the nuclear family is the natural, ideal, or even most evolutionarily successful system of human grouping. As Beckerman says, "One of the things this research shows is that human beings are just as clever and creative in assembling their kin relations as they are putting together space shuttles or symphonies."

26

The Kpelle Moot

James L. Gibbs Jr.

Some scholars argue that law, like marriage, is a major institution found in all societies, although in widely divergent forms. Others argue that law exists only where some individual or group possesses the authority to impose punishments. Debates about what is and what isn't law aside, conflict exists in all societies. Further, all societies have culturally defined mechanisms by which people attempt to settle their differences.

Conflict-management procedures must be geared to meet the needs of particular social systems. In the urban centers of Western society, people live in faceless anonymity. Relations between people can be characterized as single interest. For example, generally a person's landlord is neither kin nor neighbor. The landlord-tenant relationship is not complicated by any other social bonds. A person who has a car accident is unlikely to have run into a friend or a relative. Our legal system, with its narrow focus on the grievance itself, fits our social system of one-dimensional relationships.

In small-scale social systems, people are often involved with one another on multiple levels. A landlord may also be a neighbor and a relative. In such settings, people are born, grow up, grow old, and die in the same community. Because their social relationships are long-term and highly valued, people in such communities need to resolve disputes in a way that maintains good relations.

Today in the United States, government agencies and grassroots organizations are establishing programs—Neighborhood Justice Centers or Dispute Resolution Centers—based on models of consensus and conciliation. According to the *Citizen's Dispute Resolution Handbook*, the potential of local-level conflict resolution was originally recognized in the work of an anthropologist who had described these processes in Africa.

As you read this selection, ask yourself the following questions:

- How are formal courtroom hearings different from moots?
- In what kinds of cases is the formal court effective and in what kinds is it ineffective?
- How is a mediator different from a judge?
- What is the function of the blessing at the beginning of the moot?
- In contrast to the official court, how does the procedure used during the moot facilitate harmony and reconciliation?
- Why does the author consider the moot therapeutic?

The following terms discussed in this selection are included in the Glossary at the back of the book:

clan	multiplex relationships
culture area	palaver
extended family	patrilineal
mediator	single-interest relationship
moot	social control

Africa as a major culture area has been characterized by many writers as being marked by a high development of law and legal procedures.[1] In the past few years research on African law has produced a series of highly competent monographs such as those on law among the Tiv, the Barotse, and the Nuer.[2] These and related shorter studies have focused primarily on formal processes for the settlement of disputes, such as those which take place in a courtroom, or those which are, in some other way, set apart from simpler measures of social control. However, many African societies have informal, quasi-legal, dispute-settlement procedures, supplemental to formal ones, which have not been as well studied, or—in most cases—adequately analysed.

In this paper I present a description and analysis of one such institution for the informal settlement of disputes, as it is found among the Kpelle of Liberia; it is the moot, the *bɛrɛi mu meni saa* or "house palaver."

The Kpelle Moot, from James L. Gibbs, Jr., From *Africa*, vol. 33, no. 1, 1963. Reprinted by permission of the author.

Hearings in the Kpelle moot contrast with those in a court in that they differ in tone and effectiveness. The genius of the moot lies in the fact that it is based on a covert application of the principles of psychoanalytic theory which underlie psychotherapy.

The Kpelle are a Mande-speaking, patrilineal group of some 175,000 rice cultivators who live in Central Liberia and the adjoining regions of Guinea. This paper is based on data gathered in a field study which I carried out in 1957 and 1958 among the Liberian Kpelle of Panta Chiefdom in north-east Central Province.

Strong corporate patrilineages are absent among the Kpelle. The most important kinship group is the virilocal polygynous family which sometimes becomes an extended family, almost always of the patrilineal variety. Several of these families form the core of a residential group, known as a village quarter, more technically, a clan-barrio.[3] This is headed by a quarter elder who is related to most of the household heads by real or putative patrilineal ties.

Kpelle political organization is centralized although there is no single king or paramount chief, but a series of chiefs of the same level of authority, each of whom is superordinate over district chiefs and town chiefs. Some political functions are also vested in the tribal fraternity, the Poro, which still functions vigorously. The form of political organization found in the area can thus best be termed the polycephalous associational state.

The structure of the Kpelle court system parallels that of the political organization. In Liberia the highest court of a tribal authority and the highest tribal court chartered by the Government is that of a paramount chief. A district chief's court is also an official court. Disputes may be settled in these official courts or in unofficial courts, such as those of town chiefs or quarter elders. In addition to this, grievances are settled informally in moots, and sometimes by associational groupings such as church councils or cooperative work groups.

In my field research I studied both the formal and informal methods of dispute settlement. The method used was to collect case material in as complete a form as possible. Accordingly, immediately after a hearing, my interpreter and I would prepare verbatim transcripts of each case that we heard. These transcripts were supplemented with accounts—obtained from respondents—of past cases or cases which I did not hear litigated. Transcripts from each type of hearing were analysed phrase by phrase in terms of a frame of reference derived from jurisprudence and ethno-law. The results of the analysis indicate two things: first, that courtroom hearings and moots are quite different in their procedures and tone, and secondly, why they show this contrast.

Kpelle courtroom hearings are basically coercive and arbitrary in tone. In another paper[4] I have shown that this is partly the result of the intrusion of the authoritarian values of the Poro into the courtroom. As a result, the court is limited in the manner in which it can handle some types of disputes. The court is particularly effective in settling cases such as assault, possession of illegal charms, or theft where the litigants are not linked in a relationship which must continue after the trial. However, most of the cases brought before a Kpelle court are cases involving disputed rights over women, including matrimonial matters which are usually cast in the form of suits for divorce. The court is particularly inept at settling these numerous matrimonial disputes because its harsh tone tends to drive spouses farther apart rather than to reconcile them. The moot, in contrast, is more effective in handling such cases. The following analysis indicates the reasons for this.[5]

The Kpelle berɛi mu meni saa, or "house palaver," is an informal airing of a dispute which takes place before an assembled group which includes kinsmen of the litigants and neighbors from the quarter where the case is being heard. It is a completely ad hoc group, varying greatly in composition from case to case. The matter to be settled is usually a domestic problem: alleged mistreatment or neglect by a spouse, an attempt to collect money paid to a kinsman for a job which was not completed, or a quarrel among brothers over the inheritance of their father's wives.

In the procedural description which follows I shall use illustrative data from the Case of the Ousted Wife:

Wama Nya, the complainant, had one wife, Yua. His older brother died and he inherited the widow, Yokpo, who moved into his house. The two women were classificatory sisters. After Yokpo moved in, there was strife in the household. The husband accused her of staying out late at night, of harvesting rice without his knowledge, and of denying him food. He also accused Yokpo of having lovers and admitted having had a physical struggle with her, after which he took a basin of water and "washed his hands of her."

Yokpo countered by denying the allegations about having lovers, saying that she was accused falsely, although she had in the past confessed the name of one lover. She further complained that Wama Nya had assaulted her and, in the act, had committed the indignity of removing her headtie, and had expelled her from the house after the ritual hand-washing. Finally, she alleged that she had been thus cast out of the house at the instigation of the other wife who, she asserted, had great influence over their husband.

Kɔlɔ Waa, the Town Chief and quarter elder, and the brother of Yokpo, was the mediator of the moot, which decided that the husband was mainly at fault, although Yua and Yokpo's children were also in the wrong. Those at fault had to apologize to Yokpo and bring gifts of apology as well as local rum[6] for the disputants and participants in the moot.

The moot is most often held on a Sunday—a day of rest for Christians and non-Christians alike—at the home of the complainant, the person who calls the moot. The mediator will have been selected by the complainant. He is a kinsman who also holds an office such as town chief or quarter elder, and therefore has some skill in dispute settlement. It is said that he is chosen to preside by virtue of his kin tie, rather than because of his office.

The proceedings begin with the pronouncing of blessings by one of the oldest men of the group. In the Case of the Ousted Wife, Gbenai Zua, the elder who pronounced the blessings, took a rice-stirrer in his hand and, striding back and forth, said:

> This man has called us to fix the matter between him and his wife. May γala (the supreme, creator deity) change his heart and let his household be in good condition. May γala bless the family and make them fruitful. May He bless them so they can have food this year. May He bless the children and the rest of the family so they may always be healthy. May He bless them to have good luck. When Wama Nya takes a gun and goes in the bush, may he kill big animals. May γala bless us to enjoy the meat. May He bless us to enjoy life and always have luck. May γala bless all those who come to discuss this matter.

The man who pronounces the blessings always carries a stick or a whisk (*kpung*) which he waves for effect as he paces up and down chanting his injunctions. Participation of spectators is demanded, for the blessings are chanted by the elder (*kpung namu* or "*kpung* owner*"*) as a series of imperatives, some of which he repeats. Each phrase is responded to by the spectators who answer in unison with a formal response, either *e ka ti* (so be it), or a low, drawn-out *eeee*. The *kpung namu* delivers his blessings faster and faster, building up a rhythmic interaction pattern with the other participants. The effect is to unite those attending in common action before the hearing begins. The blessing focuses attention on the concern with maintaining harmony and the well-being of the group as a whole.

Everyone attending the moot wears their next-to-best clothes or, if it is not Sunday, everyday clothes. Elders, litigants, and spectators sit in mixed fashion, pressed closely upon each other, often overflowing onto a veranda. This is in contrast to the vertical spatial separation between litigants and adjudicators in the courtroom. The mediator, even though he is a chief, does not wear his robes. He and the oldest men will be given chairs as they would on any other occasion.

The complainant speaks first and may be interrupted by the mediator or anyone else present. After he has been thoroughly quizzed, the accused will answer and will also be questioned by those present. The two parties will question each other directly and question others in the room also. Both the testimony and the questioning are lively and uninhibited. Where there are witnesses to some of the actions described by the parties, they may also speak and be questioned. Although the proceedings are spirited, they remain orderly. The mediator may fine anyone who speaks out of turn by requiring them to bring some rum for the group to drink.

The mediator and others present will point out the various faults committed by both the parties. After everyone has been heard, the mediator expresses the consensus of the group. For example, in the Case of the Ousted Wife, he said to Yua: "The words you used towards your sister were not good, so come and beg her pardon."

The person held to be mainly at fault will then formally apologize to the other person. This apology takes the form of the giving of token gifts to the wronged person by the guilty party. These may be an item of clothing, a few coins, clean hulled rice, or a combination of all three. It is also customary for the winning party in accepting the gifts of apology to give, in return, a smaller token such as a twenty-five cent piece[7] to show his "white heart" or good will. The losing party is also lightly "fined"; he must present rum or beer to the mediator and the others who heard the case. This is consumed by all in attendance. The old man then pronounces blessings again and offers thanks for the restoration of harmony within the group, and asks that all continue to act with good grace and unity.

An initial analysis of the procedural steps of the moot isolates the descriptive attributes of the moot and shows that they contrast with those of the courtroom hearing. While the airing of grievances is incomplete in courtroom hearings, it is more complete in the moot. This fuller airing of the issues results, in many marital cases, in a more harmonious solution. Several specific features of the house palaver facilitate this wider airing of grievances. First, the hearing takes place soon after a breach has occurred, before the grievances have hardened. There is no delay until the complainant has time to go to the paramount chief's or district chief's headquarters to institute suit. Secondly, the hearing takes place in the familiar surroundings of a home. The robes, writs, messengers, and other symbols of power which subtly intimidate and inhibit the parties in the courtroom, by reminding them of the physical force which underlies the procedures, are absent. Thirdly, in the courtroom the conduct of the hearing is firmly in the hands of the judge but in the moot the investigatory initiative rests much more with the parties themselves. Jurisprudence suggests that, in such a case, more of the grievances lodged between the parties are likely to be aired and adjusted. Finally, the range of relevance applied to matters which are brought out is extremely broad. Hardly anything mentioned is held to be irrelevant. This too leads to a more thorough ventilation of the issues.

There is a second surface difference between court and moot. In a courtroom hearing, the solution is, by and large, one which is imposed by the adjudicator. In the moot the solution is more consensual. It is, therefore, more likely to be accepted by both parties and hence more durable. Several features of the moot contribute to the consensual solution: first, there is no unilateral ascription of blame, but an attribution of fault to both parties. Secondly, the mediator, unlike the chief in the courtroom, is not backed by political authority and the physical force which underlies it. He cannot jail parties, nor can he levy a heavy fine. Thirdly, the sanctions which are imposed are not so burdensome as to cause hardship to the losing party or to give him or her grounds for a new grudge against the other party. The gifts for the winning party and the potables for the spectators are not as expensive as the fines and the court costs in a paramount chief's court. Lastly, the ritualized apology of the moot symbolizes very concretely the consensual nature of the solution.[8] The public offering and acceptance of the tokens of apology indicate that each party has no further grievances and that the settlement is satisfactory and mutually acceptable. The parties and spectators drink together to symbolize the restored solidarity of the group and the rehabilitation of the offending party.

This type of analysis describes the courtroom hearing and the moot, using a frame of reference derived from jurisprudence and ethno-law which is explicitly comparative and evaluative. Only by using this type of comparative approach can the researcher select features of the hearings which are not only unique to each of them, but theoretically significant in that their contribution to the social-control functions of the proceedings can be hypothesized. At the same time, it enables the researcher to pin-point in procedures the cause for what he feels intuitively: that the two hearings contrast in tone, even though they are similar in some ways.

However, one can approach the transcripts of the trouble cases with a second analytical framework and emerge with a deeper understanding of the implications of the contrasting descriptive attributes of the court and the house palaver. Remember that the coercive tone of the courtroom hearing limits the court's effectiveness in dealing with matrimonial disputes, especially in effecting reconciliations. The moot, on the other hand, is particularly effective in bringing about reconciliations between spouses. This is because the moot is not only conciliatory, but *therapeutic*. Moot procedures are therapeutic in that, like psychotherapy, they re-educate the parties through a type of social learning brought about in a specially structured interpersonal setting.

Talcott Parsons[9] has written that therapy involves four elements: support, permissiveness, denial of reciprocity, and manipulation of rewards. Writers such as Frank,[10] Klapman,[11] and Opler[12] have pointed out that the same elements characterize not only individual psychotherapy, but group psychotherapy as well. All four elements are writ large in the Kpelle moot.

The patient in therapy will not continue treatment very long if he does not feel support from the therapist or from the group. In the moot the parties are encouraged in the expression of their complaints and feelings because they sense group support. The very presence of one's kinsmen and neighbors demonstrates their concern. It indicates to the parties that they have a real problem and that the others are willing to help them to help themselves in solving it. In a parallel vein, Frank, speaking of group psychotherapy, notes that: "Even anger may be supportive if it implies to a patient that others take him seriously enough to get angry at him, especially if the object of the anger feels it to be directed toward his neurotic behavior rather than himself as a person."[13] In the moot the feeling of support also grows out of the pronouncement of the blessings which stress the unity of the group and its harmonious goal, and it is also undoubtedly increased by the absence of the publicity and expressive symbols of political power which are found in the courtroom.

Permissiveness is the second element in therapy. It indicates to the patient that everyday restrictions on making anti-social statements or acting out anti-social impulses are lessened. Thus, in the Case of the Ousted Wife, Yua felt free enough to turn to her ousted co-wife (who had been married leviratically) and say:

> You don't respect me. You don't rely on me any more. When your husband was living, and I was with my husband, we slept on the farm. Did I ever refuse to send you what you asked me for when you sent a message? Didn't I always send you some of the meat my husband killed? Did I refuse to send you anything you wanted? When your husband died and we became co-wives, did I disrespect you? Why do you always make me ashamed? The things you have done to me make me sad.

Permissiveness in the therapeutic setting (and in the moot) results in catharsis, in a high degree of stimulation of feelings in the participants and an equally high tendency to verbalize these feelings.[14] Frank notes that: "Neurotic responses must be expressed in the therapeutic situation if they are to be changed by it."[15] In the same way, if the solution to a dispute reached in a house palaver is to be stable, it is important that there should be nothing left to embitter and undermine the decision. In a familiar setting, with familiar people, the parties to the moot feel at ease and free to say *all* that is on their minds. Yokpo, judged to be the wronged party in the Case of the Ousted Wife, in accepting an apology, gave expression to this when she said:

> I agree to everything that my people said, and I accept the things they have given me—I don't have *anything else* about them on my mind. (*My italics.*)

As we shall note below, this thorough airing of complaints also facilitates the gaining of insight into and the unlearning of idiosyncratic behaviour which is socially disruptive. Permissiveness is rooted in the lack of publicity and the lack of symbols of power. But it stems, too, from the immediacy of the hearing, the locus of investigatory initiative with the parties, and the wide range of relevance.

Permissiveness in therapy is impossible without the denial of reciprocity. This refers to the fact that the therapist will not respond in kind when the patient acts in a hostile manner or with inappropriate affection. It is a type of privileged indulgence which comes with being a patient. In the moot, the parties are treated in the same way and are allowed to hurl recriminations that, in the courtroom, might bring a few hours in jail as punishment for the equivalent of contempt of court. Even though inappropriate views are not responded to in kind, neither are they simply ignored. There is denial of *congruent* response, not denial of *any* response whatsoever. In the *bɛrɛi mu meni saa*, as in group psychotherapy, "private ideation and conceptualization are brought out into the open and all their facets or many of their facets exposed. The individual gets a 'reading' from different bearings on the compass, so to speak,[16] and perceptual patterns . . . are joggled out of their fixed positions. . . ."[17]

Thus, Yua's outburst against Yokpo quoted above was not responded to with matching hostility, but its inappropriateness was clearly pointed out to her by the group. Some of them called her aside in a huddle and said to her:

> You are not right. If you don't like the woman, or she doesn't like you, don't be the first to say anything. Let her start and then say what you have to say. By speaking, if she heeds some of your words, the wives will scatter, and the blame will be on you. Then your husband will cry for your name that you have scattered his property.

In effect, Yua was being told that, in view of the previous testimony, her jealousy of her co-wife was not justified. In reality testing, she discovered that her view of the situation was not shared by the others and, hence, was inappropriate. Noting how the others responded, she could see why her treatment of her co-wife had caused so much dissension. Her interpretation of her new co-wife's actions and resulting premises were not shared by the co-wife, nor by the others hearing a description of what had happened. Like psychotherapy, the moot is gently corrective of behavior rooted in such misunderstandings.

Similarly, Wama Nya, the husband, learned that others did not view as reasonable his accusing his wife of having a lover and urging her to go off and drink with the suspected paramour when he passed their house and wished them all a good evening. Reality testing for him taught him that the group did not view this type of mildly paranoid sarcasm as conducive to stable marital relationships.

The reaction of the moot to Yua's outburst indicates that permissiveness in this case was certainly not complete, but only relative, being much greater than in the courtroom. But without this moderated immunity the airing of grievances would be limited, and the chance for social relearning lessened. Permissiveness in the moot is incomplete because, even there, prudence is not thrown to the winds. Note that Yua was not told not to express her feelings at all, but to express them only after the co-wife had spoken so that, if the moot failed, she would not be in an untenable position. In court there would be objection to her blunt speaking out. In the moot the objection was, in effect, to her speaking *out of turn*. In other cases the moot sometimes fails, foundering on this very point, because the parties are *too* prudent, all waiting for the others to make the first move in admitting fault.

The manipulation of rewards is the last dimension of therapy treated by Parsons. In this final phase of therapy[18] the patient is coaxed to conformity by the granting of rewards. In the moot one of the most important rewards is the group approval which goes to the wronged person who accepts an apology and to the person who is magnanimous enough to make one.

In the Case of the Ousted Wife, Kɔlɔ Waa, the mediator, and the others attending decided that the husband and the co-wife, Yua, had wronged Yokpo. Kɔlɔ Waa said to the husband:

> From now on, we don't want to hear of your fighting. You should live in peace with these women. If your wife accepts the things which the people have brought you should pay four chickens and ten bottles of rum as your contribution.

The husband's brother and sister also brought gifts of apology, although the moot did not explicitly hold them at fault.

By giving these prestations, the wrong-doer is restored to good grace and is once again acting like an "upright Kpelle" (although, if he wishes, he may refuse to accept the decision of the moot). He is eased into this position by being grouped with others to whom blame is also allocated, for, typically, he is not singled out and isolated in being labelled deviant. Thus, in the Case of the Ousted Wife, the children of Yokpo were held to be at fault in "being mean" to their step-father, so that blame was not only shared by one "side," but ascribed to the other also.

Moreover, the prestations which the losing party is asked to hand over are not expensive. They are significant enough to touch the pocketbook a little; for the Kpelle say that if an apology does not cost something other than words, the wrong-doer is more likely to repeat the offending action. At the same time, as we noted above, the tokens are not so costly as to give the loser additional reason for anger directed at the other party which can undermine the decision.

All in all, the rewards for conformity to group expectations and for following out a new behaviour pattern are kept within the deviant's sight. These rewards are positive, in contrast to the negative sanctions of the courtroom. Besides the institutionalized apology, praise and acts of concern and affection replace fines and jail sentences. The mediator, speaking to Yokpo as the wronged party, said:

> You have found the best of the dispute. Your husband has wronged you. All the people have wronged you. You are the only one who can take care of them because you are the oldest. Accept the things they have given to you.

The moot in its procedural features and procedural sequences is, then, strongly analogous to psychotherapy. It is analogous to therapy in the structuring of the role of the mediator also. Parsons has indicated that, to do his job well, the therapist must be a member of two social systems: one containing himself and his patient; and the other, society at large.[19] He must not be seduced into thinking that he belongs only to the therapeutic dyad, but must gradually pull the deviant back into a relationship with the wider group. It is significant, then, that the mediator of a moot is a kinsman who is also a chief of some sort. He thus represents both the group involved in the dispute and the wider community. His task is to utilize his position as kinsman as a lever to manipulate the parties into living up to the normative requirements of the wider society, which, as chief, he upholds. His major orientation must be to the wider collectivity, not to the particular goals of his kinsmen.

When successful, the moot stops the process of alienation which drives two spouses so far apart that they are immune to ordinary social-control measures such as a smile, a frown, or a pointed aside.[20] A moot is not always successful, however. Both parties must have a genuine willingness to cooperate and a real concern about their discord. Each party must be willing to list his grievances, to admit his guilt, and make an open apology. The moot, like psychotherapy, is impotent without well-motivated clients.

The therapeutic elements found in the Kpelle moot are undoubtedly found in informal procedures for settling disputes in other African societies also; some of these are reported in literature and others are not. One such procedure which seems strikingly parallel to the Kpelle berei mu meni saa has been described by J. H. M. Beattie.[21] This is the court of neighbors or rukurato rw'enzarwa found in the Banyoro kingdom of Uganda. The group also meets as an ad hoc assembly of neighbors to hear disputes involving kinsmen or neighbors.[22]

The intention of the Nyoro moot is to "reintegrate the delinquent into the community and, if possible, to achieve reconciliation without causing bitterness and resentment; in the words of an informant, the institution exists 'to finish off people's quarrels and to abolish bad feeling.'"[23] This therapeutic goal is manifested in the manner in which the dispute is resolved. After a decision is reached the penalty imposed is always the same. The party held to be in the wrong is asked to bring beer (four pots, modified downwards according to the circumstances) and meat, which is shared with the other party and all those attending the rukurato. The losing party is also expected to "humble himself, not only to the man he has injured but to the whole assembly."[24]

Beattie correctly points out that, because the council of neighbors has no power to enforce its decision, the shared feast is not to be viewed primarily as a penalty, for the wrong-doer acts as a host and also shares in the food and drink. "And it is a praiseworthy thing; from a dishonourable status he is promoted to an honourable one . . ."[25] and reintegrated into the community.[26]

Although Beattie does not use a psychoanalytic frame of reference in approaching his material, it is clear that the communal feast involves the manipulation of rewards as the last step in a social-control measure which breaks the progressive alienation of the deviance cycle. The description of procedures in the rukurato indicates that it is highly informal in nature, convening in a room in a house with everyone "sitting around." However, Beattie does not provide enough detail to enable one to determine whether or not the beginning and intermediate steps in the Nyoro moot show the permissiveness, support, and denial of reciprocity which characterize the Kpelle moot. Given the structure and outcome of most Nyoro councils, one would surmise that a close examination of their proceedings[27] would reveal the implicit operation of therapeutic principles.

The fact that the Kpelle court is basically coercive and the moot therapeutic does not imply that one is dysfunctional while the other is eufunctional. Like Beattie, I conclude that the court and informal dispute-settlement procedures have separate but complementary functions. In marital disputes the moot is oriented to a couple as a dyadic social system and serves to reconcile them wherever possible. This is eufunctional from the point of view of the couple, to whom divorce would be dysfunctional. Kpelle courts customarily treat matrimonial matters by granting a divorce. While this may be dysfunctional from the point of view of the couple, because it ends their marriage, it may be eufunctional from the point of view of society. Some marriages, if forced to continue, would result in adultery or physical violence at best, and improper socialization of children at worst. It is clear that the Kpelle moot is to the Kpelle court as the domestic and family relations courts (or commercial and labour arbitration boards) are to ordinary courts in our own society. The essential point is that both formal and informal dispute-settlement procedures serve significant functions in Kpelle society and neither can be fully understood if studied alone.[28]

NOTES

1. The field work on which this paper is based was carried out in Liberia in 1957 and 1958 and was supported by a grant from the Ford Foundation, which is, of course, not responsible for any of the views presented here. The data were analyzed while the writer was the holder of a pre-doctoral National Science Foundation Fellowship. The writer wishes to acknowledge, with gratitude, the support of both foundations. This paper was read at the Annual Meeting of the American Anthropological Association in Philadelphia, Pennsylvania, in November 1961.

    The dissertation, in which this material first appeared, was directed by Philip H. Gulliver, to whom I am indebted for much stimulating and provocative discussion of many of the ideas here. Helpful comments and suggestions have also been made by Robert T. Holt and Robert S. Merrill.

    Portions of the material included here were presented in a seminar on African Law conducted in the Department of Anthropology at the University of Minnesota by E. Adamson Hoebel and the writer. Members of the seminar were generous in their criticisms and comments.

2. Paul J. Bohannan, *Justice and Judgment among the Tiv*, Oxford University Press, London, 1957; Max Gluckman, *The Judicial Process among the Barotse of Northern Rhodesia*, Manchester University Press, 1954; P. P. Howell, *A Handbook of Nuer Law*, Oxford University Press, London, 1954.

3. Cf. George P. Murdock, *Social Structure*, Macmillan, New York, 1949, p. 74.

4. James L. Gibbs, Jr., "Poro Values and Courtroom Procedures in a Kpelle Chiefdom," *Southwestern Journal of Anthropology* (in press) [1963, 18:341–350]. A detailed analysis of Kpelle courtroom procedures and of procedures in the moot together with transcripts appears in: James L. Gibbs, Jr., *Some Judicial Implications of Marital Instability among the Kpelle* (unpublished Ph.D. Dissertation, Harvard University, Cambridge, Mass., 1960).

5. What follows is based on a detailed case study of moots in Panta Chiefdom and their contrast with courtroom hearings before the paramount chief of that chiefdom. Moots, being private, are less susceptible to the surveillance of the anthropologist than courtroom hearings; thus I have fewer transcripts of moots than of court cases. The analysis presented here is valid for Panta Chiefdom and also valid, I feel, for most of the Liberian Kpelle area, particularly the north-east where people are, by and large, traditional.

6. This simple distilled rum, bottled in Monrovia and retailing for twenty-five cents a bottle in 1958, is known in the Liberian Hinterland as "cane juice" and should not be confused with imported varieties.

7. American currency is the official currency of Liberia and is used throughout the country.

8. Cf. J. F. Holleman, "An Anthropological Approach to Bantu Law (with special reference to Shona law)" in the *Journal of the Rhodes-Livingstone Institute*, vol. x, 1950, pp. 27–41. Holleman feels that the use of tokens for effecting apologies—or marriages—shows the proclivity for reducing events of importance to something tangible.

9. Talcott Parsons, *The Social System*, The Free Press, Glencoe, Ill., 1951, pp. 314–19.

10. Jerome D. Frank, "Group Methods in Psychotherapy," in *Mental Health and Mental Disorder: A Sociological Approach*, edited by Arnold Rose, W. W. Norton Co., New York, pp. 524–35.

11. J. W. Klapman, *Group Psychotherapy: Theory and Practice*, Grune & Stratton, New York, 1959.

12. Marvin K. Opler, "Values in Group Psychotherapy," *International Journal of Social Psychiatry*, vol. iv, 1959, pp. 296–98.

13. Frank, op. cit., p. 531.

14. Ibid.

15. Ibid.

16. Klapman, op. cit., p. 39.

17. Ibid., p. 15.

18. For expository purposes the four elements of therapy are described as if they always occur serially. They may, and do, occur simultaneously also. Thus, all four of the factors may be implicit in a single short behavioural sequence. Parsons (op. cit.) holds that these four elements are common not only to psychotherapy but to all measures of social control.

19. Parsons, op. cit., p. 314. Cf. loc. cit., chap. 10.

20. Cf. Parsons, op. cit., chap. 7. Parsons notes that in any social-control action the aim is to avoid the process of alienation, that "vicious-cycle" phenomenon whereby each step taken to curb the non-conforming activity of the deviant has the effect of driving him further into his pattern of deviance. Rather, the need is to "reach" the deviant and bring him back to the point where he is susceptible to the usual everyday informal sanctions.

21. J. H. M. Beattie, "Informal Judicial Activity in Bunyoro," *Journal of African Administration*, vol. ix, 1957, pp. 188–95.

22. Disputes include matters such as a son seducing his father's wives, a grown son disobeying his father, or a husband or wife failing in his or her duties to a spouse. Disputes between unrelated persons involve matters like quarrelling, abuse, assault, false accusations, petty theft, adultery, and failure to settle debts. (Ibid., p. 190.)

23. Ibid., p. 194.

24. Beattie, op. cit., p. 194.

25. Ibid., p. 193.

26. Ibid., p. 195. Moreover, Beattie also recognizes the functional significance of the Nyoro moots, for he notes that: "It would be a serious error to represent them simply as clumsy, 'amateur' expedients for punishing wrong-doers or settling civil disputes at an informal, sub-official level." (Ibid.)

27. The type of examination of case materials that is required demands that field workers should not simply record cases that meet the "trouble case" criterion (cf. K. N. Llewellyn and E. A. Hoebel, *The Cheyenne Way*, Norman, Okla., University of Oklahoma Press, 1941; and E. A. Hoebel, *The Law of Primitive Man*, Cambridge, Mass., Harvard University Press, 1954), but that cases should be recorded in some transcript-like form.

28. The present study has attempted to add to our understanding of informal dispute-settlement procedures in one African society by using an eclectic but organized collection of concepts from jurisprudence, ethno-law, and psychology. It is based on the detailed and systematic analysis of a few selected cases, rather than a mass of quantitative data. In further research a greater variety of cases handled by Kpelle moots should be subjected to the same analysis to test its merit more fully.

27

Contemporary Warfare
in the New Guinea Highlands

Aaron Podolefsky

Within political units—whether tribes or nations—there are well-established mechanisms for handling conflict nonviolently. Anthropologists have described a wide range of conflict resolution mechanisms within societies. Between politically autonomous groups, however, few mechanisms exist. Consequently, uncontained conflict may expand into armed aggression—warfare. In both primitive and modern forms, warfare always causes death, destruction, and human suffering. It is certainly one of the major problems confronting humankind.

New Guinea highlanders can tell you why they go to war—to avenge ghosts or to exact revenge for the killing of one of their own. As we have seen in previous selections, people do not seem to comprehend the complex interrelationship among the various parts of their own social system. Throughout the world, anthropologists find that people do not fathom the causes of their own social behavior. If they did, finding solutions would certainly be a far simpler matter.

The leaders of Papua New Guinea see intertribal fighting as a major social problem with severe economic consequences. Although fighting itself may be age-old, the reemergence of warfare in this area in the 1970s appears to have a new set of causes. In this selection, Aaron Podolefsky shows how the introduction of Western goods may have inadvertently resulted in

changes in economic arrangements, marriage patterns, and, ultimately, warfare.

As you read this selection, ask yourself the following questions:

- What is the theoretical orientation (research strategy) of this paper?
- When did tribal fighting reemerge as a national problem in New Guinea?
- How did intertribal marriage constrain the expansion of minor conflict into warfare?
- How has the rate of intertribal marriage changed? Why did it change?
- How are the introduction of Western goods, trade, marriage, and warfare interrelated?

The following terms discussed in this selection are included in the Glossary at the back of the book:

affinal kin	*hypothesis*
aggression	*lineage*
agnates	*multiplex relationships*
blood relatives	*pacification*
cross-cutting ties	*tribe*
cultural materialism	

After decades of pacification and relative peace, intergroup warfare reemerged in the Papua New Guinea highlands during the late 1960s and early 1970s, only a few years before national independence in 1975. Death and destruction, martial law, and delay in highlands development schemes have been the outcome.

Most explanations of the resurgence either posit new causes (such as psychological insecurity surrounding political independence from Australian rule or disappointment at the slow speed of development)

or attribute the increased fighting to relaxation of government controls which suppressed fighting since the pacification process began. None of the explanations thus far advanced has looked at changes in the structure or infrastructure of highlands societies themselves which could account for behavioral changes in the management of conflict.

This paper employs a cultural materialist strategy in which the efficacy of explanatory models is ranked: infrastructure, structure, and superstructure.[1] From a macrosociological perspective, infrastructural changes unintentionally induced during the colonial era resulted

From *Ethnology*, 1984. Reprinted by permission of *Ethnology*.

in changes in the structural relations between groups. These changes reduced existing (albeit weak) indigenous mechanisms constraining conflict. Traditionally, groups maintained differential access to resources such as stone used for axes and salt. Axe heads and salt were produced in local areas and traded for valuables available elsewhere. I argue that the introduction and distribution of items such as salt and steel axes reduced the necessity for trade, thereby altering the need for intertribal marriage as well as reducing extratribal contacts of a type which facilitated marriage between persons of different tribes. The reduction of intertribal marriage, over time, resulted in a decay of the web of affinal and nonagnatic kin ties which had provided linkages between otherwise autonomous tribal political units. Thus, the resurgence of tribal fighting is, in part, a result of the reduction of constraints which might otherwise have facilitated the containment of conflict rather than its expansion into warfare. This view sees warfare as one possible end result of a process of conflict management.

An advantage of this strategy is that it suggests a testable hypothesis which runs counter to conventional wisdom and informed opinion that the rate of intertribal marriage would increase after pacification. Some researchers believed that once tribal fighting ended men would be able to wander farther afield and develop relationships with single teenage girls over a wide area. Pacification, then, might reasonably be expected to result in an increase in intertribal marriage. An increase or lack of change in the rate of intergroup marriage since contact would invalidate the explanation. The hypothesis will be tested on data collected in the Gumine District, Simbu (formerly Chimbu) Province, Papua New Guinea.

BACKGROUND

Warfare in traditional highlands societies has been regarded as chronic, incessant, or endemic, and is said to have been accepted as a part of social living in most areas. Indeed, the pattern of warfare was one of the most continuous and violent on record.

However, hostilities were neither random nor did highlanders live in a perpetual state of conflict with all surrounding groups. Some neighboring groups maintained relations of permanent hostility and had little to do with one another. In contrast, most neighboring tribes intermarried and attended one another's ceremonies.

Pacification was an early goal of the colonial administration. By the end of the 1930s fighting was rare in the vicinity of Simbu province government stations. By 1940 Australian authority was accepted and attacks on strangers and tribal fighting had nearly ended, although the entire highlands was not pacified until the 1960s. This period also witnessed the introduction of Western goods such as salt and the steel axe.

Change came quickly to New Guinea. Sterling writes in 1943: "Headhunters and cannibals a generation ago, most of the natives of British New Guinea have now become so accustomed to the ways of the whites that they have been trained as workers and even to assist in administering the white man's law."

From the end of World War II through the 1970s, educational and business opportunities expanded, local government and village courts were introduced, and national self-government was attained in 1975. Highlanders came to expect that development would lead to material gains.[2]

Tribal warfare began to reemerge as a significant national problem in about 1970, five years before independence. By 1973 the government had become concerned that the situation might deteriorate to a point that they could no longer effectively administer parts of the highlands. In 1972, according to government report, 28 incidents involving 50 or more persons were reported in the Western Highlands District. A decade later, Bill Wormsley (1982) reports 60 fights per year in the Enga Province (the figures are of course not directly comparable). Although the level of fighting declined in Enga during 1980 due to the declaration of a state of emergency, it increased again in 1981 and 1982. Martial law has also been declared in the Simbu Province. Deaths lead to payback killing and to demands for compensation payments. Inflated demands for "excess" compensation further compound the problem.

Of the five major theories of warfare outlined by Koch in 1974 (biological evolution, psychological theories, cultural evolution, ecological adaptation, and social-structure analysis), scholars have used only psychological theories and social-structural analysis to explain the recent emergence of tribal warfare.

Some researchers favor explanations which combine the traditional cultural heritage of violence with issues in development. Others seem to argue that the problem lies in the Enga's perception that the government, especially the courts, has become weaker and that this had led to the breakdown in law and order. Rob Gordon notes, however, that the police force in Enga has increased from 72 in 1970 to 300 in 1981, and that the average sentence for riotous behavior has grown from 3 months in 1970 to 9.6 months in 1978–9 with no apparent deterrent effect. Kiaps (field officers), Gordon suggests, have in fact lost power for several reasons. Most interesting from the perspective of the present analysis involves the kiaps' loss of control over access to goods. He (1983:209) states that "The importance that the Enga attach to trade-goods should not be underestimated." An old Engan is quoted as saying

"The first Kiaps gave beads, salt, steel axes—everyone wanted it so they all followed the Kiap and stopped fighting. We stopped fighting because we did not want to lose the source of these things." I would add that once they "followed the kiaps" for these goods, previous important trade relations no longer needed to be kept up. In a 1980 study, Gordon also acknowledges problems created by intergroup suspicion, generational conflict exacerbated by education, and decline in men's houses and clan meetings. Similarly, Paula Brown (1982a) believes that pacification was a temporary effect in which fighting was suppressed. The Simbu do not see the government as holding power.

Explanations also combine development problems with psychologically oriented theories. Contemporary violence is sometimes thought to be a protest rising out of psychological strain created by the drastic social change of an imposed economic and political system. In a 1973 paper Bill Standish describes the period leading up to independence as one of stress, tension, and insecurity. He argues that the fighting is an expression of primordial attachments in the face of political insecurity surrounding national independence from Australian colonial rule. Paula Brown (1982a, 1982b) suggests that during the colonial period expectations for the future included security, wealth, and the improvement of life. "Disappointment that these goals have not been realized is expressed in disorder." She suggests that what is needed is a political movement rather than the imposition of Western institutions and suppression of fighting.

The present paper cannot and does not formally refute any of these explanations. Indeed, some make a great deal of sense and fill in part of a very complex picture. However, it is difficult to evaluate the validity of these explanations since very little data are presented. For example, Standish (1973) presents no evidence to assess whether, in fact, the level of stress has changed over time (precontact, postcontact, or independence era), or whether stress is associated with fighting or even with differential levels of awareness about independence, the latter likely expressing itself geographically around centers of population and development.

ETHNOGRAPHIC BACKGROUND—THE MUL COMMUNITY

Mul lies approximately 3 miles east of the Gumine District Headquarters and 32 miles south of Kundiawa, the capital of the Simbu province. The Gumine patrol post was established in 1954. During the early 1960s a dirt road was constructed linking Gumine to the capital and within a few years the road was extended through Mul. Lying at an elevation of about 5,500 feet, Mul is the central portion of a larger tribal territory which extends steeply from the southern edge of the Marigl Gorge to elevations of 8 to 9,000 feet.

The area is densely populated. Land is either cultivated or fallow in grass or scrub regrowth. Individually owned trees are scattered and there are a yearly increasing number of coffee trees. With 295 persons per square mile on cultivatable land, this density is high compared with other highland groups (see Brown and Podolefsky 1976).

The people of Mul are Simbus. Social relations and cultural patterns follow in most important respects those extensively documented by Paula Brown in numerous publications. I will describe here only those dimensions of organization most directly relevant to the resurgence of tribal fighting.

Mul residents trace kinship through males, and their social groupings are patrilineal. Hierarchical segments link themselves as father/son, while parallel segments are seen as brothers. Individuals, however, are less concerned with this overall construct and tend to interact in terms of group composition and alignments. The likelihood of an individual conflict escalating into warfare is directly related to the structural distance between conflicting parties.

The largest political group to unite in warfare is the tribe, a group of several thousand individuals. Tribes are segmented into clans whose members see themselves as a unified group. Generally, individually owned plots of land tend to cluster and people can point out rough boundaries between adjacent clans. Plots of land belonging to members of a particular subclan tend to cluster within the clan area. The subclan section (or one-blood group) is the first to mobilize for warfare. The potential for expansion of such conflicts depends to a large degree on whether the relative position of the groups in the segmentary system lends itself to opposing alignments at the higher levels of segmentation and upon the past relations between the groups.

Unlike subclan sections in most highlands societies there is no restriction upon fighting between sections of the subclan. Within the subclan section, however, there are moral restrictions on internal fighting. If comembers become extremely angry they may attack with fists, clubs, or staffs, but not with axes, arrows, or spears. These restrictions are related to the notion that members of the subclan have "one-blood," and that this common blood should not be shed.

Segmentary principles operate in situations of cooperation as well as conflict. Members of a subclan section may enclose garden plots within a single fence and cooperate in the construction of men's houses. Brown (1970:99–103) similarly notes that in the central Simbu transactions between clans and tribes are competitive while those within the clan are reciprocal. Generally speaking, in terms of proximity of land holdings and residence, cooperation in gardening and house construction and the willingness to unite in common defense and ceremonial exchange, the solidarity of a social group is inversely related to the position in the segmentary hierarchy.

Cross-cutting these segmentary principles are a variety of interpersonal ties (e.g., affinal and other non-agnatic relations, exchange ties and personal friendships) which affect behavior in conflict situations. It is these ephemeral or transitory linkages which provide the avenues through which structurally autonomous tribal groups interact.

MARRIAGE AND WARFARE

Marriage and warfare are linked in the minds of New Guinea highlanders. Early writers report indigenous notions that highlanders marry their enemies. The Siane say, "They are our affinal relatives; with them we fight" (Salisbury 1962:25). Enga informants report, "We marry those whom we fight" (Meggitt 1958:278). In an extensive study of Enga warfare, Meggitt (1977:42) supports these assertions by reporting quite strong correlations between rates of intergroup marriage and killing.

While there is little doubt that there is a strong association between marriage and warfare, it is not clear at all that they are causally related in any direct fashion, i.e., warfare causing marriage or marriage causing warfare. It is highly unlikely that warfare causes marriage. Researchers have noted the difficulty in arranging marriages between hostile groups. It is similarly unlikely that marriage causes warfare (although exceptions can certainly be pointed out). While disputes may arise between bride and groom or their families, the relations are generally highly valued and long term. The association between marriage and warfare can be reduced to two separate relationships. First, highlanders most frequently marry their neighbors. Second, highlanders most frequently go to war with their neighbors. This is because in the highlands, where travel is restricted and relations are multiplex, neighbors are the parties most likely to be involved in a dispute. Thus propinquity is causally related to both marriage and warfare; the positive correlation between marriage and warfare is spurious. Indeed, the essence of the argument made here is that if other variables could be "controlled" the association between warfare and marriage would in fact be negative.

The notion that there is no direct (as opposed to inverse) causal relationship between warfare and marriage is critical. Warfare results from precipitating disputes in the absence of sufficiently powerful third party mechanisms and other constraints which control the

dispute. One dimension of constraint stems from marriage links.

In her paper "Enemies and Affines," Paula Brown (1964) carefully describes the relevant social relations among the central Simbu. During wedding ceremonies speeches proclaim that the groups of the bride and groom (consisting of subclansmen, some clansmen, kin, and affines) should remain on friendly terms and exchange visits and food. The marriage creates individual ties and obligations outside the clan which, while not institutionalized, are not wholly voluntary. At various stages in the life cycle payments are obligatory. Given the widely documented emphasis on transaction in highlands social relations, it is important to note that whenever a formal food presentation occurs between clans, the donors and recipients are related to one another through marriage. Extratribal relatives play an important role in conflict situations.

> The prevailing hostility between neighboring tribes gives extratribal relatives a special complex role. Men try not to injure their close kin and affines in any conflict between their agnatic group and the group of their relatives, but they may not attempt to prevent or stop hostilities. In any dealings between neighboring tribes, men with connections in both take a leading part; their political sphere of action encompasses both. When intermediaries and peacemakers are required these men are active (Brown 1964:348).

Thus, in Central Simbu, affines played some role in attempting to prevent warfare and were important in restoring peace. No amount of oral history data will tell us how many wars did not occur due to efforts made through these channels. Nor can such data tell us how many wars were shorter or less intense than they would have been had there been fewer cross-cutting ties. The importance of cross-cutting ties is recognized among the densely populated Enga.

> Even while or after two men or groups fight over an issue, others may intervene to urge negotiation and compromise. . . . Whether, however, noncombatants initiate some kind of conciliation or simply stand by and watch the fighting spread depends on a complex set of conditions . . . relevant factors . . . include, for instance, the importance traditionally ascribed to the object in contention (is it a pig or a sweet potato garden?), the number of antagonists, the kinship, affinal, or exchange connections among some or all of them, and between them and interested noncombatants (Meggitt 1977:12).

Moreover, the frequency of intergroup marriage is related to the expansion or containment of a dispute. That is, the more intermarriage the greater the chance that disputes will be handled without violence or that the violence can be contained.

Especially within the tribe, the supporters of each party include men with affines on the other side, most of whom are on good terms with their in-laws and have no wish to offend them. In such cases some men stay out of the fight while others, while participating, avoid meeting their affines in combat. This may serve to confine interclan conflict. Between tribes, similar serious disputes can more easily lead to fighting because fewer men have close ties which restrain them from supporting their fellow tribesmen (Brown 1964:352).

In sum, while there is an apparent correlation between marriage and warfare, marriage, in fact, establishes a social relationship which acts primarily as a constraint upon the expansion of a dispute. Second, as Meggitt suggests, it is not merely the marriage ties between the two groups, but also between them and their allies, i.e., the web of affinal relations. Third, the frequency of marriage, or density of the web, is related to efficacy of conflict management processes.

CHANGING PATTERN OF INTERTRIBAL MARRIAGE

A null hypothesis that the proportion of intertribal marriages has gone up or remained the same can be rejected ($p < 0.001$) on the basis of the data shown in Table 1. Thus, we tend to believe, based upon these data, that there has in fact been an overall decline in intertribal marriage.

The data reveal a statistically significant change in the marriage pattern in the anticipated direction. Figure 1 describes the proportion of marriage ties within and between tribes, before and after Western influence. Comparing the intertribal (between) and intratribal (within) marriage rates in the precontact sample (labeled before), we see that intertribal marriage was nearly three times as frequent as intratribal marriage. Of the 114 marriage ties recorded in the precontact sample, 85 (75 percent) were between members of different tribes while only 29 (25 percent) were within the tribe. This allowed for a dense network of affinal ties

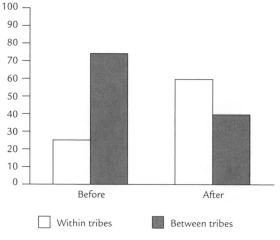

FIGURE 1   Percentage of Marriage Ties

between autonomous political groups. In the recent postcontact period (labeled after), in contrast, the number of intertribal marriages drops below the number of intratribal marriages. Of the 74 marriage ties in the postcontact sample, only 30 (40 percent) were between persons of different tribes while 44 (60 percent) were within the tribe. The intertribal marriage rate in the recent period is nearly half that of the precontact period.

The argument presented in this paper is that the dramatic reduction of intertribal marriage rates had significant implications for the structure of relations between politically autonomous tribal groups.

A Secondary Analysis

Sometimes it is possible to replicate one's findings by performing a secondary analysis on data collected by other researchers.

In 1964, Paula Brown published data on the marriage of some men in the Naregu tribe who live in the central Simbu near the capital of Kundiawa. Data for two clans are divided into previous generations (prior to 1930) and present generation. Brown's categories for marriage ties may be collapsed to match those used above.

What should we expect, a priori? Since Brown did not arrange the data to address this particular question, we expect some differences. Her temporal dichotomy is previous and present generation rather than before and after contact. Europeans did not reach this area until the mid-1930s and Brown's data are dichotomized at 1930. This means that precontact marriages are included in the present generation sample. Neither do Brown's data allow for a decade of transition. Based upon these differences in the data sets, we would expect the difference between the previous and

TABLE 1   Marriage Ties by Time Period

	Before Contact		**After Contact**	
	N	%	N	%
Between tribes	85	75%	30	40%
Within tribes	29	25%	44	60%
Total	114	100%	74	100%

chi squared = 21.86 1 df
$p < 0.001$ (one tail)
phi = .341

TABLE 2   Marriages of Some Men in the Naregu Tribe

	Pre-1930 (Before)		Post-1930 (After)	
	N	%	N	%
Between tribes	154	60%	130	47%
Within tribes	102	40%	144	53%
Total	256	100%	274	100%

chi squared = 8.597 1 df
p < 0.005 (one tail)
phi = .1272

present samples to be less extreme than the difference between the before and after sample in the Mul data (i.e., we expect a lower measure of association).

The data in Table 2 reveal a statistically significant change in the marriage pattern, although the association is lower (as we expected it would be) than in Mul. The between-tribe marriage rate (in the sample) dropped from 60 to 47 percent. This change was sufficient to draw Brown's attention. While the analysis fits our predictions, we cannot be certain that the change in marriage pattern observed by Paula Brown in central Simbu represents the same process occurring in Mul nearly twenty years later. Nevertheless, the analysis is intriguing. I think Brown was observing the initial stages of a process of change initiated by a reduction in the necessity for trade.[3]

TRADE AND MARRIAGE

Given the conventional wisdom that pacification would lead to greater intertribal contact and, therefore, an increase in the rate of intertribal marriage, it remains to be explained why the proportion of intertribal marriages decreased. In other words, what forces or situations affected the marriage pattern?

Interviews with young men of marriageable age and some of the oldest men in the community elicited two different perspectives. (Unfortunately, it was not possible for me, being a male, to maintain serious conversation with women on this topic.) Young men typically explained that they do not find wives from other areas because they are "tired"; they just do not have any desire to travel the long distances to visit women of other areas when there are women close at hand. This emic explanation is not particularly satisfactory from an anthropological perspective.

While the older men could not explain why the distribution of marriages in their younger days differed from that of more recent years, they were able to describe the ways young men and women met prospective spouses from other tribes prior to the coming of Europeans scarcely twenty years earlier. The old men reported that when they were young trade was very important. Salt, stone axes, bird of paradise feathers, shells of different kinds, pandanus oil, carpul fur, and the like were traded between tribes during trading expeditions. Figure 2 maps the trade network as described by the older residents of Mul.

When they were young, the old men reported, they would dress in their finest decorations and travel to the places described in Figure 2. The women at these places, they said, would see them arrayed in all their finery and want to marry them. Of course, the situation may not have been quite this straightforward.

These reports drew my attention to the link between intertribal marriage and trade for scarce necessary and luxury resources. What would be the effect of the introduction of European goods upon trade? And could this affect marriage patterns?

According to the old men, pigs from Mul were traded south to the lower elevation, less densely populated areas in return for bird of paradise feathers and carpul fur (see Figure 2). Some of the fur and feathers were traded for cowrie shells with people from Sina. Cowries, in turn, were traded to the Gomgales for kina shells. Carpul fur and pandanus oil were traded to the east for salt. Finally, some of the fur and feathers obtained from the south and the salt obtained from the east were traded to the northeast for stone axes and small shells, which had in turn been brought in from even further off.

Enter the ubiquitous steel axe; exit the stone axe. No one in Mul today would use a stone axe. Indeed, it was difficult to find someone who recalled how to attach stone to handle. The effect was that the primary reason for trade between the peoples of Mul and Era (i.e., the need for stone axes) was eliminated and the Muls' need for fur, feathers, and salt was reduced (what may have begun to increase was a need for cash). Similarly, salt increasingly became more readily available. Nowadays it can be purchased at the store on the government station or in small trade stores which stock, for example, three bags of salt, two packs of cigarettes, a bit of rice, and two or three tins of mackerel. The availability of salt locally eliminates the need to trade for it and further reduces the need for fur. Thus, two of the five trade routes shown on Figure 2 become totally unnecessary and the usefulness of trade items from a third is reduced.

The elimination of the need to trade for necessary scarce resources allowed some trade relations to atrophy. I use the term *atrophy* since the process was probably one of gradual disuse of trade networks rather than a catastrophic change. The remaining trade relations were reliant upon the need for luxury items such as

FIGURE 2   Traditional Exchange Network

shells and feathers. Scholars who have done long-term research in New Guinea have described the highlanders' declining interest in these decorative items.

With the introduction of Western goods and the reduction of trade, both the need and the opportunity for intermarriage declined. Intertribal marriage was functional in that it facilitated intergroup economic transactions. While there are a range of rights and obligations as well as affective ties which make marriage into neighboring groups preferable, more distant marriages have recognized importance. This same point was made by Roy Rappaport in his study of the Tsembaga Maring:

> While unions between men and women of a single local group are generally preferred, the Tsembaga recognize certain advantages in marriage to members of other local groups . . . unions with groups north of the Sambai River and south of the Bismarks strengthen trading relationships. Bird-of-paradise plumes and shell ornaments are still obtained from these groups and until the 1950s stone axes from the Jimi Valley were traded for salt manufactured in the Simbai Valley (1969:121).

An early paper on the Siani linked trade and marriage directly by focusing on the exchange of nonutilitarian valuables which occurred at marriage and at the rites of passage for children of the marriage (Salisbury 1956). Valuables were traded in from the coast about 70 miles to the northeast. Trading took the form of ceremonial gift exchange between affines. At the

same time, Salisbury reports a statistically significant trend for Siane men to obtain wives from the south and west while their sisters marry into groups from the north and east (the direction from which valuables come).

Even more interesting for the present purpose is Salisbury's report on the effect of the introduction of European wealth goods. The European settlements nearest the Siane were in Goroka and Asaroka, 30 miles to the east and north. Groups nearest these (who were already closer than the Siane to coastal wealth) quickly became wealthy in shells, cloth, and other European goods. Salisbury reports that, as a result of this increased wealth, the movement of women in that direction became more pronounced. He also notes that "Neither the wealth difference nor the movement of women is recognized in Siane ideology."

Thus, Salisbury clearly links marriage patterns to the need to obtain wealth not locally available, although no mention is made of utilitarian goods. While the initial response to "wealthy neighbors" is to increase "wife giving," it is easy to see that once wealth is more evenly (and locally) distributed this reason for marrying out will no longer be of major consequence.

Particularly in the many areas of the highlands where marriages were arranged by families with minimal, if any, consultation with the bride or groom, consideration of trade relations was likely to play a role in the selection of a spouse. Families had an interest in the establishment or maintenance of trade relations.

At the same time that the function of intertribal marriage for maintaining the economic system in terms of access to necessary resources was eliminated, the decline in trade itself reduced the opportunity to make marriage arrangements between non-adjacent groups. Generally speaking, opportunity for marriage is not random but may be structured by factors such as class, caste, religious affiliation, sorority membership, or political borders. Changes in this structure of opportunity may lead to observable changes in marriage patterns. In other words, a change in the visiting (or trading) pattern between autonomous political groups could affect the structure of opportunity. The importance of opportunity remains whether the individuals are free to choose their own mates or whether such choices are made for them.

In central Simbu elders choose a person's spouse for them and, although they can refuse, the bride and groom usually accept even though they may never have met. Brown (1969) reports that some groups do not intermarry because of the lack of opportunity to make arrangements.

Administrative policy and mission influence may have speeded the process. In some areas, such as South Fore or Manga, Australian patrol officers insisted (or at least strongly urged) that brides consent and that women have a right to choose a spouse. Nowadays in central Simbu more marriages are being initiated by the couples themselves. Choice in a mate is likely to further increase the importance of the structure of opportunity.

In sum, the argument here is that the replacement, by Western goods, of resources secured through trade reduced the economic need (function) for intergroup marriage and the opportunity to arrange such marriages. The effects of these changes were not felt immediately because of the extant relations between groups. Over time fewer and fewer intertribal marriages were arranged to replace those of the passing generation. The net effect was a gradual decay of the web of affinal and non-agnatic ties which cut across tribal boundaries.

CONCLUSION

Gordon (1980) has insightfully pointed out that there is very little sense in talking or planning about development if people live in fear of renewed tribal fighting. Moreover, he notes that this is a testing time for anthropologists "who find that their explanatory models are somewhat inadequate." Indeed, few of the explanations begin from a particular theoretical position nor even a unified conceptual model; there is little discussion of the mechanisms by which suggested "causes" result in the behavior being explained; and, little evidence is presented to test the explanations.

In this paper, I have employed a particular theoretic strategy, namely, cultural materialism, in which the efficacy of explanatory models are ranked: infrastructure, structure, and superstructure.

Prior to contact with the outside world, stone axe heads and salt were produced in local areas where these resources were available. Redistribution was accomplished through trade. One of the functions of intertribal marriage was the facilitation of trade between autonomous political groups. With the early introduction of Western goods, particularly steel axes and salt, local production was discontinued and marriage was no longer necessary to maintain these trade relations. As trade was discontinued, so declined the opportunity to make marriage arrangements between non-adjacent groups. Of course, existing marriage ties facilitated continued contact between groups, but probably less frequently, and there was no pragmatic reason for young people to marry others from distant areas. Particularly in the case of women, where such a marriage necessitated a move far from her natal family, there were distinct disadvantages. Thus, as older people died and fewer marriages were arranged between groups, the web of affinal and non-agnatic kin ties decayed. Intertribal marriages provided a linkage through which groups could communicate, and a mechanism and reason for containing conflict. With the decline in intergroup marriage over time, the likelihood of a dispute expanding into full-scale warfare increased.

This explanation began with infrastructural conditions (production) and showed how they were causally related to structural changes (trade relations) which in turn caused further structural changes (the web of kin ties), finally leading to changes in conflict behaviors. I have tried to explain each of the stages in this temporal process, i.e., the relationship between trade and marriage and the relationship between marriage and warfare.

Scientific hypotheses and models can be tested by examining predictions which can be deduced from them. The model which I have outlined predicts the unlikely occurrence that, with pacification and the ability to wander further afield without the threat of life and limb, intertribal marriage actually declined rather than rose as was thought would be the case. The hypothesis was tested on genealogical data collected in this research site as well as on data published earlier from a different area of the Simbu province. This is but a single case study and there is no statistical reason to extend the findings to other areas of the highlands. However, the inability to falsify the hypothesis in this case lends support to the general efficacy of the explanation.

NOTES

1. Financial support from the National Science Foundation (Grant No. BNS76-218 37) is gratefully acknowledged.

2. For a more extensive discussion of this period with special reference to the resurgence of fighting, see Brown 1982a and 1982b.

3. Paula Brown reports (pers. comm.) that recently many Simbu women are marrying outside the Simbu to men they had met in the district or on visits. She notes that there are, now, advantages for older men having a daughter married to a prestigious outsider. Naregu men who migrate probably also marry outsiders.

    Such marriages further the process described here since, although they are extra-tribal, they do not link neighboring potential enemy groups.

REFERENCES

Brown, P. 1964. Enemies and Affines. *Ethnology* 3:335–356.

———. 1969. Marriage in Chimbu. In R. M. Glasse and M. Meggitt (eds.), *Pigs, Pearlshells and Women*, pp. 77–95. Englewood Cliffs, NJ: Prentice-Hall.

———. 1970. Chimbu Transactions. *Man* 5:99–117.

———. 1982a. Conflict in the New Guinea Highlands. *Journal of Conflict Resolution* 26:525–546.

———. 1982b. Chimbu Disorder: Tribal Fighting in Newly Independent Papua New Guinea. *Pacific Viewpoint* 22: 1–21.

Brown, P. and A. M. Podolefsky. 1976. Population Density, Agricultural Intensity, Land Tenure, and Group Size in the New Guinea Highlands. *Ethnology* 15:211–238.

Gordon, R. 1980. Rituals of Governance and the Breakdown of Law and Order in Papua New Guinea. Paper presented at the annual meeting of the American Anthropological Association. Washington, D.C.

———. 1983. The Decline of the Kiapdom and the Resurgence of "Tribal Fighting" in Enga. *Oceania* 53:205–223.

Howlett, D., et al. 1976. *Chimbu: Issues in Development*. Development Studies Centre Monograph No. 4 Canberra.

Koch, K. 1974. *The Anthropology of Warfare*. Addison-Wesley Module in Anthropology No. 52.

Meggitt, M. 1958. The Enga of the New Guinea Highlands. *Oceania* 28:253–330.

———. 1977. *Blood Is Their Argument: Warfare Among the Mae Enga Tribesmen of the New Guinea Highlands*. Palo Alto, CA: Mayfield.

Rappaport, R. 1969. Marriage Among the Maring. In R. M. Glasse and M. Meggitt (eds.), *Pigs, Pearlshells and Women*, pp. 117–137. Englewood Cliffs, NJ: Prentice-Hall.

Salisbury, R. F. 1956. Asymmetrical Marriage Systems. *American Anthropologist* 58:639–655.

———. 1962. *From Stone to Steel*. London: Cambridge University Press.

Standish, B. 1973. The Highlands. *New Guinea* 8:4–30.

Wormsley, W. 1982. Tribal Fighting, Law and Order, and Socioeconomic Development in Enga, Papua New Guinea. Paper presented at the meeting of the American Anthropological Association. Washington, D.C.

28

Life Stories, Disclosure, and the Law

Michelle McKinley

A fundamental idea in anthropology is cultural relativism—that each culture must be understood in its own terms. Anthropologists also argue that people should not judge other cultures but should struggle against their tendencies toward ethnocentrism and cultural bias. Intolerant ethnocentrism, in combination with competition for economic resources is at the root of much political conflict and warfare. This selection shows that because they are people, too, anthropologists are also tempted by ethnocentrism. Anthropologists themselves can bring stereotypes and political ideologies to their fieldwork, even when they are trying to work with and advocate for the rights of disenfranchised peoples.

In this selection, Michelle McKinley describes her work with a refugee who was granted asylum in the United States because of gender persecution in her own country. In essence, McKinley works as a "culture broker" to help serve as a bridge between her client, on one hand, and the courts, on the other. Ultimately, the client's original narrative and the one she ultimately presented in court in her petition for asylum were very different. She did not lie in court; rather, her feelings about her earlier experiences were reinterpreted to reflect what Americans think that she "should" feel.

Applied anthropologists are not simply observers. They have an expert status, access to resources, infor-

mation, and power structures that their research participants or clients do not. Advocating for people from other cultures is not always straightforward, especially when it involves the law.

As you read this selection, ask yourself the following questions:

- Why did the client choose to apply for political asylum in the United States?

- How did her version of her own life story and the version crafted by her anthropologist/advocate differ? Why did they differ?

- Why do you think the client defended arranged marriages even though hers was not successful?

- McKinley writes about her client, "Her actions attest to the fact that human behavior is innovative and situational rather than socially compelled." What does she mean by this?

The following terms discussed in this selection are included in the Glossary at the back of the book:

asylum	refugee
brideprice	situated
culture broker	

THE INSTITUTIONAL CONTEXT OF GENDER BASED IMPACT LITIGATION

It is estimated that while two-thirds of the world's 10 million refugees are women and young girls, more than half the claims for granting refugee status are brought by men. Because the definition of a refugee traditionally applies to an individual who demonstrates a "well founded fear of persecution on account of race, nationality, religion, political opinion or mem-

Michelle McKinley, "Life Stories, Disclosure and the Law," POLAR: *Political & Legal Anthropology Review*, Vol. 20, No. 2: 70–82. © 1997, American Anthropological Association. All rights reserved. Used with permission.

bership in a social group," women have found it difficult to bring *gender*-based persecution claims under the rubric of the five grounds as enumerated in the 1951 Convention (see footnote 1 *supra*).

The reports of genocidal rape as a military strategy in countries as diverse as Bosnia, Peru, El Salvador and Afghanistan have alerted international attention to the plight of women in wartime situations, and sexual persecution of women has begun to receive global condemnation and calls for the prosecution of the perpetrators of such acts. Greater attention has also been focused on quotidian acts of domestic or intimate violence, as recent investigative efforts by international and local human rights organizations have documented a high incidence of battering within the formerly sacrosanct "private" sphere of the home.[1]

A woman's decision to flee gender-based persecution by leaving her homeland, her community and her family is arguably one of the most momentous decisions made during her life. However, should she choose to file an asylum claim, she inevitably faces a host of other instrumental and emotive decisions: how much of her experience to disclose, whom to trust, and in what ways can she best advance her interests.

FROM LIFE STORY TO AFFIDAVIT: NARRATIVE FORMS OF INTERROGATION

The petitioner, a 24 year old Zimbabwean woman, sought political asylum in the United States. The petitioner filed her claim for political asylum based on her membership in a social group that is affected by the persecutory nature of three customs widely practiced throughout *Zimbabwe:* a) arranged marriages, b) payment of brideprice, and c) the offering of young girls as compensation in inter-family disputes. In her testimony, the petitioner stated that her parents arranged her marriage at age 15 to a wealthy Harare businessman, accepting the customary payment of brideprice and subsequent gifts in exchange for their daughter's hand in marriage. The petitioner's parents were involved in an indebted relationship with her husband which predated the marriage, and continued throughout its duration. The couple was never formally married, however, and the petitioner lived in a polygamous situation with 5 other co-wives. The petitioner's husband was extremely abusive. In her testimony, she alleged that her husband raped and beat her continuously throughout their conjugal relationship. When she complained to her parents and other family members about her situation, they urged her to reconcile with her husband, reminding her of his powerful financial position and her limited options for supporting her two children. Because her parents had spent the brideprice and continued to accept gifts and financial favors from her husband, they were obligated to respect his position as her "husband" and refused to provide her with sanctuary. When she appealed to the Zimbabwean authorities, they were reluctant to "meddle" in what they viewed as an exclusively private affair. More importantly, they feared the "reach" or political influence of her husband. In desperation, she escaped to the United States, abandoning her two children. Soon thereafter, she filed her claim for political asylum.

THE BOARD OF IMMIGRATION APPEAL'S ANALYSIS

In assessing the claimant's credibility, the Board of Immigration Appeal (hereinafter the Board) attempted to fit her case into the overall pattern of reported "cultural practices" among the Shona of Zimbabwe to see whether she could legitimately advance a claim of persecution. The Board found that arranged marriages (*kuzvarira*), payments of brideprice (*lobola*), and compensatory bride-bestowal (*ngozi*) were widely practiced among the Shona, and adjudged these in light of extant U.N. Declarations and Conventions as violations of the claimant's human rights. In particular, the Board held that the practice of arranged customary marriages of "child-brides" violated international standards of consensual marriage, the rights of children, and contravened the normative visions of the "family" as defined in the UN Declaration of Human Rights.

ELICITING THE CLIENT'S LIFE STORY

The client reluctantly came to the Legal Services office after a referral by a local immigration attorney. It is important to note her initial reluctance to come to Legal Services, because it indicates that she was in no way disposed to share intimate aspects of her past with the attorneys. Rather, she was induced to file an application for political asylum because it allowed her the opportunity to work legally during the time her claim was pending.

The client recounted the details of her life story with remarkable emotional detachment. In contrast to the passion and wry humor with which she talked about Shona cultural practices, and the post-apartheid dynamics of ethnic politics in her country, she described her personal experiences of rape and intimate abuse hurriedly and with resignation. She was embarrassed by my questions and challenged their relevance to the merits of her case. She remonstrated me for failing to understand the nature of the political situation of poor women in her country. More importantly, she refused to talk about her two children. Sensing her resistance, I pursued other "neutral" lines of questioning— explaining the details of the absurdly bureaucratic asylum process and the important role which her testimony would play in convincing the judge of the merits of her case. I explained that the attorneys were embarking on uncharted territory in gender-based litigation, and outlined the pitfalls and strengths of her case in light of legal precedents and so forth. I reassured her that her lack of corroborating evidence did not imperil her case—that the immigration authorities understood that refugees flee their homelands without elaborate documentation attesting to their persecution. But given the lack of material evidence, her testimony would have to "fit" the reported cultural practices of her country.

I worked with this client on her affidavit for twelve weeks. Throughout the months, I was disturbed by her impassive countenance—I found myself not really believing that she had suffered such incredible abuses because she was so detached. I expected her narrative to mirror the *totality* of her emotional experience.

I assumed that this client had a tumultuous inner life story submerged under the rote incantation of facts she consistently gave. I attributed her passivity to posttraumatic stress, and tried to pierce through her composure by asking the infamous "leading questions." However, I got nothing approximating an emotional response.

She turned out to be a model client in many respects—she was always punctual and willing to work through her affidavit. But I worried about her composure. She spoke about her experience with considerable remove—hardly ever using the first person pronoun. More importantly, she resisted my attempt to shift the narrative from the third to first person when I asked how she felt about arranged marriages or polygamy and the like. Instead, she would respond obliquely, saying "the Shona do this" or "among my people"—so I could never tell if she was angry at her parents or the Zimbabwean authorities, or whether she hated her abusive husband for the things he had done to her. How was I to interpret and narrate her life story when the deeply disturbed and traumatized persona which I expected resolutely refused to emerge? I assumed that the sharing of her experience combating domestic abuse would automatically establish an intimate relationship, and that her rendition of that experience would provide access to a deeper understanding of what "really happened" (Good 1992: 140). In preparing her to testify in front of the judge, the attorneys confronted a genuine dilemma. If she was this resigned to the cultural practices which we claimed were so persecutory—causing her to flee home, community and family—how could we credibly claim that the practices were so oppressive? As a result, I found myself "editing in" sentiments of resentment, vulnerability and loss which *completely* contravened everything she said and certainly contradicted her attitude.

Eight weeks later, I was obliged to read her the drafts of the affidavits which I had written. At one point, I read something to the effect that the desperation of her situation had forced to abandon her two young children—the youngest of whom had barely been weaned. She became furious—asserting with every right—that she had never said that and that I was putting words in her mouth. I feebly responded that I had to inject some sort of subjective element of fear and desperation into the affidavit or that the judge would not believe her story. She retorted that she in fact *despised* her children—that they were symbols of the abuse and oppression she had undergone at the hands of her husband and that she in no way was remorseful that she left them behind. She told me that the scent of her children's excrement made her nauseous ("Their piss smells just like their father's," she said). After this confessional burst, she then retreated into third person by explaining that "among the Shona" children belong to their father's lineage—she would never have any legitimate claim to them in any event.

Clearly, the affidavit could not include this element of her life story—it would completely discredit her testimony and would make the judge think she was merely an unfeeling mother who had abandoned her children to come to Boston to live with her boyfriend (she was in fact living with her boyfriend). Too much rested on the decision to be rendered in this case—it was, in fact, attracting a lot of attention in the immigration field. Therefore, it was necessary to frame the case as one of oppressive gender practices which had driven the client to this drastic measure of abandoning her children.

The attorneys persuaded the client to adopt their version of her story. I do not know whether the final version was a result of consensual negotiations of truth and representation, or whether the asymmetries of the situation caused the client to accept their "expert" version—but in the end her narrative was not the least bit like what it was before. It became transformed into an egocentered, plaintive and apolitical testimonial which blamed her parents, professed a maternal love she decidedly repudiated and personalized the experience of marital rape, brideprice and "child" marriage—all practices to which she had formerly referred in third person. It was an effective appropriation of voice—indeed, she would most likely not have been granted political asylum on the basis of her original narrative. But the point is, *whose narrative was it?*

LIFE STORY TEXTS AND MUTUAL NEGOTIATIONS

A similar negotiation process occurred in the transformation of my client's narrative over the course of twelve weeks. The client was willingly persuaded that her narrative had to be drafted in a way which would persuade the judge of the tragedy of her situation. The attorneys retreated into a "regnant" mode of lawyering, which highlighted their expertise and the client's inexperience and ignorance (Lopez 1992). The client did not resist their regnant lawyering. However, her capitulation was decidedly the result of a bargain. Implicitly, she made it known that we could embellish the details of her story as long as it was expedient to winning her case. This is, after all, what lawyers are trained to do.

In our subsequent meetings, the client no longer contested the ways in which her narrative was framed. She even smiled ironically when I read her lines about how debased she was by the process of being sold for cattle, and how diminished she felt by not being able to choose her own husband. She seemed to think that this was precisely the type of puerile sentimentalism in which Western women indulged. Indeed, she was using the attorneys' skills as instrumentally as we had coopted her story.

Much more was achieved in the two-hour bargaining session than had been achieved in twelve weeks. In retrospect, I see now that I had asked inappropriate questions. I tried consciously to avoid a regnant mode of lawyering by appealing to our commonalities—stressing that we were both immigrant women of color, and so forth. However, given the obvious asymmetries in our situation, my efforts must have seemed banal or hollow at best. But, perhaps more importantly, it is unlikely that the client would have ever divulged anything beyond a formulaic rendition of her life story. As many theorists have noted, the introspective and "confessional" life story is not a universal phenomena.[2] Indeed, the conventional form of autobiography as an ego-centered trajectory through time was not a familiar idiom with which she could articulate her experience.

However, the lawyers' appropriation of the client's narrative raises the question of interpretation and textual representation. The life story "process" was adopted to formulate a credible version of the plight of an African refugee woman which would strengthen the attorneys' position as leading advocates in the field of gender-based litigation. The strategic use of her narrative underscores the fact that life-stories are partial and positioned, and further that they are subject to constant retelling. Moreover, once the narrative is in circulation, its "owner" has no meaningful control over its interpretation, repetition and use.[3]

We can get a deeper sense of the client's emotive experience of motherhood, polygamy, intimate violence and ethnic identity from the ways in which she talked about the details of her life. It was clear that she was resigned to the prospect of arranged marriages, and even pointed out that marriages in African societies are generally regarded as an alliance between two families. She explained repeatedly that arranged marriages have their own protective mechanisms for women who can rely on an extensive network of relations between families in the event of marital insecurity and discontent. She thought that she was fully *entitled* to the "brideprice" which feminists claim as diminishing of personhood. After all, she felt that she had earned the brideprice by securing an education, increasing her status/possibilities for remarriage and maintaining sexual relations with her husband. Indeed, she strongly believed that African women should be able to use the brideprice if they truly "deserved" it.

Moreover, she stressed the important role which her aunts and cousins in Harare played in lending her money to buy her ticket to the United States. Contrary to her final affidavit, she did not blame her parents for committing her into marriage with her husband; as she put it "they were only peasants on his estate— what could they do?"[4]

However, while she professed acceptance to the practice of arranged marriages, in the end, she fled the husband who raped and abused her. In a sense, the most direct route to the client's subjective identity is to look objectively at her actions, rather than to search for an outpouring of emotions through the circuitous life story route. Her actions attest to the fact that human behavior is innovative and situational rather than socially compelled.

NOTES

Acknowledgments: Many thanks to Bartholemew Dean, Kenneth George and Sally Merry for their thoughtful comments and suggestions on earlier drafts of this article.

1. See inter alia Amnesty International, Women on the Front Line: Human Rights Violations Against Women (1991); Amnesty International, Rape and Sexual Abuse: Torture and Ill Treatment of Women in Detention (1992); Women's Rights Project and Asia Watch, Double Jeopardy: Police Abuse of Women in Pakistan (1992); Aron et al Gender Specific Terror of El Salvadoran and Guatemalans: Post-Traumatic Stress Disorder in Central American Refugee Women, 4 WOMEN's STUD. INT'LF.37 (1991); Women's Rights Project & Americas Watch, Criminal Injustice: Violence Against Women in Brazil (1992); Women's Rights Project and Middle East Watch, Punishing the Victim: Rape and the Mistreatment of Asian Maids in Kuwait (1992).

2. In her search for an appropriate discursive tool with which to "write women's lives" Abu-Lughod ultimately rejects the life story model. Abu-Lughod claims that although women may articulate a particular perspective on their experiences as mothers, brides, daughters etc., the life history model, "contribute[s] to a sense of the person at its center as an isolated individual" (Abu-Lughod 1993:31). The Awlad 'Ali women with whom Abu-Lughod works, neither "live nor think of themselves" as isolated individuals. In John Chernoff's study of African musical idioms and aesthetic styles, he writes that the prescribed discursive genre is predicated on syncopation and circumlocution. Straight answers revealing one's thoughts and emotions are crude and prosaic—the elegant speaker is given to circumlocutory and metaphorical digressions (Chernoff 1979).

3. Indeed, the "generic" life history approach (in this case exemplified by Linde) which stresses the social aspect of sharing life histories is analogous to liberal theories of property entitlements: "owning" a life story creates a

foundation for personhood and autonomy, and further, sharing life stories is a priori conditions for intimacy and claims to social group membership.

4. She never came to our sessions without inquiring politely about the health of my son and my parents. She was in constant touch with her parents and faithfully sent them money from her meager earnings. She told me of her plans to bring them here as soon as she could petition for them legally. For obvious reasons, I never asked what her plans were concerning her two children, but I assume that they remain with their father's lineage.

REFERENCES

Appadurai, A. 1991. "Global Ethnoscapes: Notes and Queries for a Transnational Anthropology." Richard Fox, *Recapturing Anthropology: Working in the Present* pp. 191–210. Santa Fe: SAR Press.

Abu-Lughod, L. 1993. *Writing Women's Worlds* Berkeley: University of California Press.

Bauman, R. 1986. *Story, Performance, and Event: Contextual Studies of Oral Narrative.* Cambridge: Cambridge University Press.

Behar, R. 1992. "A Life Story to Take Across the Border: Notes on an Exchange." Rosenwald and Ochberg, *Storied Lives: The Cultural Politics of Self-Understanding,* pp. 108–123. New Haven: Yale University Press.

Chernoff, J. 1979. *African Rhythm and African Sensibility.* Chicago: University of Chicago Press.

Crapanzano, V. 1980. *Tuhami: Portrait of a Moroccan.* Chicago: University of Chicago Press.

Fraser, N. 1989. *Unruly Practices: Power Discourse and Gender in Contemporary Social Theory.* Minneapolis: University of Minnesota Press.

Fuss, D. 1989. *Essentially Speaking: Feminism, Nature & Difference.* New York: Routledge Chapman & Paul.

Good, B. 1994. *Medicine, Rationality, and Experience: An Anthropological Perspective.* Cambridge: Cambridge University Press.

Linde, C. 1993. *Life Stories: The Creation of Coherence.* New York: Oxford University Press.

Lopez, G. 1992. *Rebellious Lawyering: One Chicano's Vision of Progressive Law Practice.* Boulder: Westview Press.

Peacock, James and Dorothy Holland. 1993. "The Narrated Self: Life Stories in Process." *Ethos* 21(4):367–383.

Personal Narratives Group eds. 1989. *Interpreting Women's Lives: Feminist Theory and Personal Narratives.* Bloomington: Indiana University Press.

Rosaldo, R. 1976. "Tukbaw's Story: 'They Listen as He Orates.'" Reynolds and Capps, *The Biographical Process: Studies in the History and Psychology of Religion,* pp. 121–152. The Hague: Mouton.

Salazar, C. 1991. "A Third World Woman's Text: Between the Politics of Criticism and Cultural Politics." Sherna Gluck and Daphne Patai, *Women's Words: The Feminist Practice of Oral History,* pp. 93–106. New York: Routledge, Chapman & Paul.

Tsing, A. 1993. *In the Realm of the Diamond Queen.* Princeton: Princeton University Press.

Walzer, M. 1981. *Spheres of Justice: A Defense of Pluralism and Equality.* New York: Basic Books.

. . . For that, we need to confront two more big issues. First is the acceptance of the possibility of difference. Can we only free Afghan women to be like us or might we have to recognize that even after "liberation" from the Taliban, they might want different things than we would want for them? What do we do about that? Second, we need to be vigilant about the rhetoric of saving people because of what it implies about our attitudes.

Again, when I talk about accepting difference, I am not implying that we should resign ourselves to being cultural relativists who respect whatever goes on elsewhere as "just their culture." I have already discussed the dangers of "cultural" explanations; "their" cultures are just as much part of history and an interconnected world as ours are. What I am advocating is the hard work involved in recognizing and respecting differences—precisely as products of different histories, as expressions of different circumstances, and as manifestations of differently structured desires. We may want justice for women, but can we accept that there might be different ideas about justice and that different women might want, or choose, different futures from what we envision as best (see Ong 1988)? We must consider that they might be called to personhood, so to speak, in a different language.

Reports from the Bonn peace conference held in late November to discuss the rebuilding of Afghanistan revealed significant differences among the few Afghan women feminists and activists present. RAWA's position was to reject any conciliatory approach to Islamic governance. According to one report I read, most women activists, especially those based in Afghanistan who are aware of the realities on the ground, agreed that Islam had to be the starting point for reform. Fatima Gailani, a U.S.-based advisor to one of the delegations, is quoted as saying, "If I go to Afghanistan today and ask women for votes on the promise to bring them secularism, they are going to tell me to go to hell."

One of the things we have to be most careful about in thinking about Third World feminisms, and feminism in different parts of the Muslim world, is how not to fall into polarizations that place feminism on the side of the West. I have written about the dilemmas faced by Arab feminists when Western feminists initiate campaigns that make them vulnerable to local denunciations by conservatives of various sorts, whether Islamist or nationalist, of being traitors (Abu-Lughod 2001). As some like Afsaneh Najmabadi are now arguing, not only is it wrong to see history simplistically in terms of a putative opposition between Islam and the West (as is happening in the United States now and has happened in parallel in the Muslim world), but it is also strategically dangerous to accept this cultural opposition between Islam and the West, between fundamentalism and feminism, because those many people within

Muslim countries who are trying to find alternatives to present injustices, those who might want to refuse the divide and take from different histories and cultures, who do not accept that being feminist means being Western, will be under pressure to choose, just as we are: Are you with us or against us?

My point is to remind us to be aware of differences, respectful of other paths toward social change that might give women better lives. Can there be a liberation that is Islamic? And, beyond this, is liberation even a goal for which all women or people strive? Are emancipation, equality, and rights part of a universal language we must use?

Might other desires be more meaningful for different groups of people? Living in close families? Living in a godly way? Living without war? I have done fieldwork in Egypt over more than 20 years and I cannot think of a single woman I know, from the poorest rural to the most educated cosmopolitan, who has ever expressed envy of U.S. women, women they tend to perceive as bereft of community, vulnerable to sexual violence and social anomie, driven by individual success rather than morality, or strangely disrespectful of God.

BEYOND THE RHETORIC OF SALVATION

Let us return, finally, to my title, "Do Muslim Women Need Saving?" The discussion of culture, veiling, and how one can navigate the shoals of cultural difference should put Laura Bush's self-congratulation about the rejoicing of Afghan women liberated by American troops in a different light. It is deeply problematic to construct the Afghan woman as someone in need of saving. When you save someone, you imply that you are saving her from something. You are also saving her *to* something. What violences are entailed in this transformation, and what presumptions are being made about the superiority of that to which you are saving her? Projects of saving other women depend on and reinforce a sense of superiority by Westerners, a form of arrogance that deserves to be challenged. All one needs to do to appreciate the patronizing quality of the rhetoric of saving women is to imagine using it today in the United States about disadvantaged groups such as African American women or working-class women. We now understand them as suffering from structural violence. We have become politicized about race and class, but not culture.

Could we not leave veils and vocations of saving others behind and instead train our sights on ways to make the world a more just place? The reason respect for difference should not be confused with cultural relativism is that it does not preclude asking how we, living in this privileged and powerful part of the world, might examine our own responsibilities for the situations in which others in distant places have found themselves. We do not stand outside the world, looking out over this sea of poor benighted people, living under the shadow—or veil—of oppressive cultures; we are part of that world. Islamic movements themselves have arisen in a world shaped by the intense engagements of Western powers in Middle Eastern lives.

A more productive approach, it seems to me, is to ask how we might contribute to making the world a more just place. A world not organized around strategic military and economic demands; a place where certain kinds of forces and values that we may still consider important could have an appeal and where there is the peace necessary for discussions, debates, and transformations to occur within communities. We need to ask ourselves what kinds of world conditions we could contribute to making such that popular desires will not be overdetermined by an overwhelming sense of helplessness in the face of forms of global injustice. Where we seek to be active in the affairs of distant places, can we do so in the spirit of support for those within those communities whose goals are to make women's (and men's) lives better (as Walley has argued in relation to practices of genital cutting in Africa, [1997])? Can we use a more egalitarian language of alliances, coalitions, and solidarity, instead of salvation?

Even RAWA, the now celebrated Revolutionary Association of the Women of Afghanistan, which was so instrumental in bringing to U.S. women's attention the excesses of the Taliban, has opposed the U.S. bombing from the beginning. They do not see in it Afghan women's salvation but increased hardship and loss. They have long called for disarmament and for peacekeeping forces. Spokespersons point out the dangers of confusing governments with people, the Taliban with innocent Afghans who will be most harmed. They consistently remind audiences to take a close look at the ways policies are being organized around oil interests, the arms industry, and the international drug trade. They are not obsessed with the veil, even though they are the most radical feminists working for a secular democratic Afghanistan. Unfortunately, only their messages about the excesses of the Taliban have been heard, even though their criticisms of those in power in Afghanistan have included previous regimes. A first step in hearing their wider message is to break with the language of alien cultures, whether to understand or eliminate them. Missionary work and colonial feminism belong in the past. Our task is to critically explore what we might do to help create a world in which those poor Afghan women, for whom "the hearts of those in the civilized world break," can have safety and decent lives.

NOTES

Acknowledgments. I want to thank Page Jackson, Fran Mascia-Lees, Tim Mitchell, Rosalind Morris, Anupama Rao, and members of the audience at the symposium "Responding to War," sponsored by Columbia University's Institute for Research on Women and Gender (where I presented an earlier version), for helpful comments, references, clippings, and encouragement.

REFERENCES

Abu-Lughod, Lila. 1986. Veiled Sentiments: Honor and Poetry in a Bedouin Society. Berkeley: University of California Press.

———. 1995. Movie Stars and Islamic Moralism in Egypt. Social Text 42:53–67.

———. 1998. Remaking Women: Feminism and Modernity in the Middle East. Princeton: Princeton University Press.

———. 2001. Orientalism and Middle East Feminist Studies. Feminist Studies 27(1):101–113.

Ahmed Leila. 1992. Women and Gender in Islam. New Haven, CT: Yale University Press.

Alloula, Malek. 1986. The Colonial Harem. Minneapolis: University of Minnesota Press.

Brenner, Suzanne. 1996. Reconstructing Self and Society: Javanese Muslim Women and "the Veil." American Ethnologist 23(4):673–697.

El Guindi, Fadwa. 1999. Veil: Modesty, Privacy and Resistance. Oxford: Berg.

Fremson, Ruth. 2001. Allure Must Be Covered. Individuality Peeks Through. New York Times, November 4:14.

Global Exchange. 2002. Courage and Tenacity: A Women's Delegation to Afghanistan. Electronic document, http://www.globalexchange.org/tours/auto/2002-03-05_CourageandTenacityeAWomensDele.html. Accessed February 11.

Goldenberg, Suzanne. 2002. The Woman Who Stood Up to the Taliban. The Guardian, January 24. Electronic document, http://222.guardian.co.uk/afghanistan/story/0,1284, 63840.

Hirschkind, Charles, and Saba Mahmood. 2002. Feminism, the Taliban, and the Politics of Counter-Insurgency. Anthropological Quarterly, Volume 75(2):107–122.

Lazreg, Marnia. 1994. The Eloquence of Silence: Algerian Women in Question. New York: Routledge.

MacLeod, Arlene. 1991. Accommodating Protest. New York: Columbia University Press.

Mahmood, Saba. 2001. Feminist Theory, Embodiment, and the Docile Agent: Some Reflections on the Egyptian Islamic Revival. Cultural Anthropology 16(2):202–235.

Mir-Hosseini, Ziba. 1999. Islam and Gender: The Religious Debate in Contemporary Iran. Princeton: Princeton University Press.

Moghissi, Haideh. 1999. Feminism and Islamic Fundamentalism. London: Zed Books.

Najmabadi, Afsaneh. 1998. Feminism in an Islamic Republic. In Islam, Gender and Social Change. Yvonne Haddad and John Esposito, eds. Pp. 59–84. New York: Oxford University Press.

——. 2000. (Un)Veiling Feminism. Social Text 64: 29–45.

Ong, Aihwa. 1988. Colonialism and Modernity: Feminist Re-Presentations of Women in Non-Western Societies. Inscriptions 3–4: 79–93.

——. 1990. State Versus Islam: Malay Families, Women's Bodies, and the Body Politic in Malaysia. American Ethnologist 17(2):258–276.

Papanek, Hanna. 1982. Purdah in Pakistan: Seclusion and Modern Occupations for Women. In Separate Worlds, Hanna Papanek and Gail Minault, eds. Pp. 190–216. Columbus, MO: South Asia Books.

Safire, William. 2001. On Language. New York Times Magazine, October 28: 22.

Spivak, Gayatri Chakravorty. 1988. Can the Subaltern Speak? In Marxism and the Interpretation of Culture. Cary Nelson and Lawrence Grossberg, eds. Pp. 271–313. Urbana: University of Illinois Press.

Strathern, Marilyn. 1987. An Awkward Relationship: The Case of Feminism and Anthropology. Signs 12:276–292.

U.S. Government. 1907. Our Moslem Sisters: A Cry of Need from Lands of Darkness Interpreted by Those Who Heard It. New York: Fleming H. Revell Co.

——. 2002. Electronic document, http://www.whitehouse.gov/news/releases/2001/11/20011117. Accessed January 10.

Walley, Christine. 1997. Searching for "Voices": Feminism, Anthropology, and the Global Debate over Female Genital Operations. Cultural Anthropology 12(3):405–438.

30

The Adaptive Value of Religious Ritual

Richard Sosis

Many anthropologists say that religion and ritual practice are the most fascinating parts of culture. When anthropologists study religion and ritual, however, the questions they ask tend to be very different from those that might concern a theologian, a religious studies scholar, or a potential convert.

Religious beliefs are strongly held because they form the bedrock of the meaning of life; religious rituals reinforce those beliefs. Rather than assessing the truth or falsity of particular religious claims, cultural anthropologists try to understand how religious beliefs and ritual practices shape people's worldviews and their everyday lives. They want to understand those "exotic" beliefs as the believers do. Other anthropologists, especially human behavioral ecologists like the author of this selection, try to explain religion and ritual in a substantially different way. If ritual behaviors are time-consuming, costly, or even painful, then why are they so important roles in most human communities? The author frames this question in evolutionary terms: How might natural selection have favored a human psychology that tends to believe in the supernatural and, by the same token, to engage in costly activities out of commitment to those beliefs?

One possible explanation, the author proposes, has to do with cooperation within a community. If people are linked by a common set of beliefs and a common set of ritual obligations, then they are more likely to cooperate with one another in ways that advance the good of the collective. In this sense, religion and ritual can be described as "adaptive." Religious rituals, the author explains, are thus a form of communication among group members; by participating in rituals, members signal to one another that they identify with the group, that they believe in what it stands for, and that they are prepared to make sacrifices on the group's behalf.

From this perspective, participating in especially challenging forms of ritual behavior—such as praying multiple times each day, carefully controlling one's eating behaviors, dressing in a certain way, or undergoing painful bodily treatments or markings—signals a high level of group commitment. Difficult ritual obligations also deter people with lower levels of commitment ("fakes") from joining the group and "freeloading" on the benefits of group membership. Rituals do not have to have a religious basis in order to have social functions.

While religion and ritual can enhance unity and trust among group members, they can also generate deep-seated animosity toward outsiders. The contemporary world is riddled with religiously motivated conflicts. It becomes much easier to make sense of these conflicts if we keep the double-sided nature of religious affiliation—as a source of unity, on one hand, and as a mechanism of divisiveness, on the other—in mind.

As you read this selection, ask yourself the following questions:

- The author asks, "Why do religious beliefs, practices, and institutions continue to be an essential component of human social life?" How does the author of this selection use his training in behavioral ecology to address this question?

- How have anthropologists' views of the meaning and function of ritual changed since the nineteenth century?

- According to the author, what adaptive problem does ritual behavior solve?

- Within a society, might adherence to religious ritual be more adaptive for some people than others?

- What is the "costly signaling theory of ritual," and what role might it play in the emergence of "demanding religious groups"?

The following terms discussed in this selection are included in the Glossary at the back of the book:

behavioral ecology	kibbutz
commune	natural selection
experimental methods	ritual
functional explanations	signaling theory of ritual
intragroup solidarity	

I was 15 years old the first time I went to Jerusalem's Old City and visited the 2,000-year-old remains of the Second Temple, known as the Western Wall. It may have foreshadowed my future life as an anthropologist, but on my first glimpse of the ancient stones I was more taken by the people standing at the foot of the structure than by the wall itself. Women stood in the open sun, facing the Wall in solemn worship, wearing long-sleeved shirts, head coverings and heavy skirts that scraped the ground. Men in their thick beards, long black coats and fur hats also seemed oblivious to the summer heat as they swayed fervently and sang praises to God. I turned to a friend, "Why would anyone in their right mind dress for a New England winter only to spend the afternoon praying in the desert heat?" At the time I thought there was no rational explanation and decided that my fellow religious brethren might well be mad.

Of course, "strange" behavior is not unique to ultraorthodox Jews. Many religious acts appear peculiar to the outsider. Pious adherents the world over physically differentiate themselves from others: Moonies shave their heads, Jain monks of India wear contraptions on their heads and feet to avoid killing insects, and clergy almost everywhere dress in outfits that distinguish them from the rest of society. Many peoples also engage in some form of surgical alteration. Australian aborigines perform a ritual operation on adolescent boys in which a bone or a stone is inserted into the penis through an incision in the urethra. Jews and Muslims submit their sons to circumcision, and in some Muslim societies daughters are also subject to circumcision or other forms of genital mutilation. Groups as diverse as the Nuer of Sudan and the Iatmul of New Guinea force their adolescents to undergo ritual scarification. Initiation ceremonies, otherwise known as rites of passage, are often brutal. Among Native Americans, Apache boys were forced to bathe in icy water, Luiseno initiates were required to lie motionless while being bitten by hordes of ants, and Tukuna girls had their hair plucked out.

How can we begin to understand such behavior? If human beings are rational creatures, then why do we spend so much time, energy and resources on acts that can be so painful or, at the very least, uncomfortable? Archaeologists tell us that our species has engaged in ritual behavior for at least 100,000 years, and every known culture practices some form of religion. It even survives covertly in those cultures where governments have attempted to eliminate spiritual practices. And,

American Scientist, March 2004, pp. 166–172. Reprinted with permission.

despite the unparalleled triumph of scientific rationalism in the 20th century, religion continued to flourish. In the United States a steady 40 percent of the population attended church regularly throughout the century. A belief in God (about 96 percent), the afterlife (about 72 percent), heaven (about 72 percent) and hell (about 58 percent) remained substantial and remarkably constant. Why do religious beliefs, practices and institutions continue to be an essential component of human social life?

Such questions have intrigued me for years. Initially my training in anthropology did not provide an answer. Indeed, my studies only increased my bewilderment. I received my training in a subfield known as human behavioral ecology, which studies the adaptive design of behavior with attention to its ecological setting. Behavioral ecologists assume that natural selection has shaped the human nervous system to respond successfully to varying ecological circumstances. All organisms must balance trade-offs: Time spent doing one thing prevents them from pursuing other activities that can enhance their survival or reproductive success. Animals that maximize the rate at which they acquire resources, such as food and mates, can maximize the number of descendants, which is exactly what the game of natural selection is all about.

Behavioral ecologists assume that natural selection has designed our decision-making mechanisms to optimize the rate at which human beings accrue resources under diverse ecological conditions—a basic prediction of *optimal foraging theory*. Optimality models offer predictions of the "perfectly adapted" behavioral response, given a set of environmental constraints. Of course, a perfect fit with the environment is almost never achieved because organisms rarely have perfect information and because environments are always changing. Nevertheless, this assumption has provided a powerful framework to analyze a variety of decisions, and most research (largely conducted among foraging populations) has shown that our species broadly conforms to these expectations.

If our species is designed to optimize the rate at which we extract energy from the environment, why would we engage in religious behavior that seems so counterproductive? Indeed, some religious practices, such as ritual sacrifices, are a conspicuous display of wasted resources. Anthropologists can explain why foragers regularly share their food with others in the group, but why would anyone share their food with a dead ancestor by burning it to ashes on an altar? A common response to this question is that people believe in the efficacy of the rituals and the tenets of the faith that give meaning to the ceremonies. But this response merely begs the question. We must really ask why natural selection has favored a psychology that believes in the supernatural and engages in the costly manifestations of those beliefs.

RITUAL SACRIFICE

Behavioral ecologists have only recently begun to consider the curiosities of religious activities, so at first I had to search other disciplines to understand these practices. The scholarly literature suggested that I wasn't 'the only one who believed that intense religious behavior was a sign of madness. Some of the greatest minds of the past two centuries, such as Marx and Freud, supported my thesis. And the early anthropological theorists also held that spiritual beliefs were indicative of a primitive and simple mind. In the 19th century, Edward B. Tylor, often noted as one of the founding fathers of anthropology, maintained that religion arose out of a misunderstanding among "primitives" that dreams are real. He argued that dreams about deceased ancestors might have led the primitives to believe that spirits can survive death.

Eventually the discipline of anthropology matured, and its practitioners moved beyond the equation that "primitive equals irrational." Instead, they began to seek functional explanations of religion. Most prominent among these early 20th-century theorists was the Polish-born anthropologist Bronislaw Malinowski. He argued that religion arose out of "the real tragedies of human life, out of the conflict between human plans and realities." Although religion may serve to allay our fears of death, and provide comfort from our incessant search for answers, Malinowski's thesis did not seem to explain the origin of rituals. Standing in the midday desert sun in several layers of black clothing seems more like a recipe for increasing anxiety than treating it. The classical anthropologists didn't have the right answers to my questions. I needed to look elsewhere.

Fortunately, a new generation of anthropologists has begun to provide some explanations. It turns out that the strangeness of religious practices and their inherent costs are actually the critical features that contribute to the success of religion as a universal cultural strategy and why natural selection has favored such behavior in the human lineage. To understand this unexpected benefit we need to recognize the adaptive problem that ritual behavior solves. William Irons, a behavioral ecologist at Northwestern University, has suggested that the universal dilemma is the promotion of cooperation within a community. Irons argues that the primary adaptive benefit of religion is its ability to facilitate cooperation within a group—while hunting, sharing food, defending against attacks and waging war—all critical activities in our evolutionary history. But, as Irons points out, although everyone is better off if everybody

cooperates, this ideal is often very difficult to coordinate and achieve. The problem is that an individual is even better off if everyone else does the cooperating, while he or she remains at home enjoying an afternoon siesta. Cooperation requires social mechanisms that prevent individuals from free riding on the efforts of others. Irons argues that religion is such a mechanism.

The key is that religious rituals are a form of communication, which anthropologists have long maintained. They borrowed this insight from ethologists who observed that many species engage in patterned behavior, which they referred to as "ritual." Ethologists recognized that ritualistic behaviors served as a form of communication between members of the same species, and often between members of different species. For example, the males of many avian species engage in courtship rituals—such as bowing, head wagging, wing waving and hopping (among many other gestures)—to signal their amorous intents before a prospective mate. And, of course, the vibration of a rattlesnake's tail is a powerful threat display to other species that enter its personal space.

Irons's insight is that religious activities signal commitment to other members of the group. By engaging in the ritual, the member effectively says, "I identify with the group and I believe in what the group stands for." Through its ability to signal commitment, religious behavior can overcome the problem of free riders and promote cooperation within the group. It does so because trust lies at the heart of the problem: A member must assure everyone that he or she will participate in acquiring food or in defending the group. Of course, hunters and warriors may make promises—"you have my word I'll show up tomorrow"—but unless the trust is already established such statements are not believable.

It turns out that there is a robust way to secure trust. Israeli biologist Amotz Zahavi observes that it is often in the best interest of an animal to send a dishonest signal—perhaps to fake its size, speed, strength, health or beauty. The only signal that can be believed is one that is too costly to fake, which he referred to as a "handicap." Zahavi argues that natural selection has favored the evolution of handicaps. For example, when a springbok antelope spots a predator it often *stots*—it jumps up and down. This extraordinary behavior puzzled biologists for years: Why would an antelope waste precious energy that could be used to escape the predator? And why would the animal make itself more visible to something that wants to eat it? The reason is that the springbok is displaying its quality to the predator—its ability to escape, effectively saying, "Don't bother chasing me. Look how strong my legs are; you won't be able to catch me." The only reason a predator believes the springbok is because the signal is too costly to fake. An antelope that is not quick enough to escape cannot

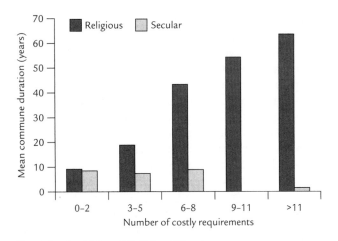

The Adaptive Value of Religious Ritual

Behaviors that are constrained
Consumption of:
coffee, alcohol, tobacco, meat, other foods or beverages

Use and ownership of:
photographs, jewelry, certain technology, other material items

Activities:
monogamous marriage, gambling, communication with the outside, living as a nuclear family, maintaining rights to biological children

Behaviors that are required
trial period for membership, surrender of material belongings, learn a body of knowledge, endure public sessions of criticism, certain clothing styles, certain hairstyles, fasting

imitate the signal because it is not strong enough to repeatedly jump to a certain height. Thus, a display can provide honest information if the signals are so costly to perform that lower quality organisms cannot benefit by imitating the signal.

In much the same way, religious behavior is also a costly signal. By donning several layers of clothing and standing out in the midday sun, ultraorthodox Jewish men are signaling to others: "Hey! Look, I'm a *haredi* Jew. If you are also a member of this group you can trust me because why else would I be dressed like this? No one would do this *unless* they believed in the teachings of ultraorthodox Judaism and were fully committed to its ideals and goals." The quality that these men are signaling is their level of commitment to a specific religious group.

Adherence to a set of religious beliefs entails a host of ritual obligations and expected behaviors. Although there may be physical or psychological benefits associated with some ritual practices, the significant time, energy and financial costs involved serve as effective deterrents for anyone who does not believe in the teachings of a particular religion. There is no incentive for nonbelievers to join or remain in a religious group,

because the costs of maintaining membership—such as praying three times a day, eating only kosher food, donating a certain part of your income to charity and so on—are simply too high.

Those who engage in the suite of ritual requirements imposed by a religious group can be trusted to believe sincerely in the doctrines of their respective religious communities. As a result of increased levels of trust and commitment among group members, religious groups minimize costly monitoring mechanisms that are otherwise necessary to overcome free-rider problems that typically plague communal pursuits. Hence, the adaptive benefit of ritual behavior is its ability to promote and maintain cooperation, a challenge that our ancestors presumably faced throughout our evolutionary history.

BENEFITS OF MEMBERSHIP

One prediction of the "costly signaling theory of ritual" is that groups that impose the greatest demands on their members will elicit the highest levels of devotion and commitment. Only committed members will be willing to dress and behave in ways that differ from the rest of society. Groups that maintain more-committed members can also offer more because it's easier for them to attain their collective goals than groups whose members are less committed. This may explain a paradox in the religious marketplace: Churches that require the most of their adherents are experiencing rapid rates of growth. For example, the Church of Jesus Christ of Latter-day Saints (Mormons), Seventh-day Adventists and Jehovah's Witnesses, who respectively abstain from caffeine, meat, and blood transfusions (among other things), have been growing at exceptional rates. In contrast, liberal Protestant denominations such as the Episcopalians, Methodists and Presbyterians have been steadily losing members.

Economist Lawrence Iannaccone, of George Mason University, has also noted that the most demanding groups also have the greatest number of committed members. He found that the more distinct a religious group was—how much the group's lifestyle differed from mainstream America—the higher its attendance rates at services. Sociologists Roger Finke and Rodney Stark, of Penn State and the University of Washington, respectively, have argued that when the Second Vatican Council in 1962 repealed many of the Catholic Church's prohibitions and reduced the level of strictness in the church, it initiated a decline in church attendance among American Catholics and reduced the enrollments in seminaries. Indeed, in the late 1950s almost 75 percent of American Catholics were attending Mass weekly, but since the Vatican's actions there has been a steady decline to the current rate of about 45 percent.

The costly signaling theory of ritual also predicts that greater commitment will translate into greater cooperation within groups. My colleague Eric Bressler, a graduate student at McMaster University, and I addressed this question by looking at data from the records of 19th-century communes. All communes face an inherent problem of promoting and sustaining cooperation because individuals can free ride on the efforts of others. Because cooperation is key to a commune's survival, we employed commune longevity as a measure of cooperation. Compared to their secular counterparts, the religious communes did indeed demand more of their members, including such behavior as celibacy, the surrender of all material possessions and vegetarianism. Communes that demanded more of their members survived longer, overcoming the fundamental challenges of cooperation. By placing greater demands on their members, they were presumably able to elicit greater belief in and commitment toward the community's common ideology and goals.

I also wanted to evaluate the costly signaling theory of ritual within modern communal societies. The kibbutzim I had visited in Israel as a teenager provided an ideal opportunity to examine these hypotheses. For most of their 100-year history, these communal societies have lived by the dictum, "From each according to his abilities, to each according to his needs." The majority of the more than 270 kibbutzim are secular (and often ideologically antireligious); fewer than 20 are religiously oriented. Because of a massive economic failure—a collective debt of more than $4 billion—the kibbutzim are now moving in the direction of increased privatization and reduced communality. When news of the extraordinary debt surfaced in the late 1980s, it went largely unnoticed that the religious kibbutzim were financially stable. In the words of the Religious Kibbutz Movement Federation, "the economic position of the religious kibbutzim is sound, and they remain uninvolved in the economic crisis."

The success of the religious kibbutzim is especially remarkable given that many of their rituals inhibit economic productivity. For example, Jewish law does not permit Jews to milk cows on the Sabbath. Although rabbinic rulings now permit milking by kibbutz members to prevent the cows from suffering, in the early years none of this milk was used commercially. There are also significant constraints imposed by Jewish law on agricultural productivity. Fruits are not allowed to be eaten for the first few years of the tree's life, agricultural fields must lie fallow every seven years, and the corners of fields can never be harvested—they must be left for society's poor. Although these constraints appear detrimental to productivity, the costly signaling theory of ritual suggests that they may actually be the key to the economic success of the religious kibbutzim.

I decided to study this issue with economist Bradley Ruffle of Israel's Ben Gurion University. We developed a game to determine whether there were differences in how the members of secular and religious kibbutzim cooperated with each other. The game involves two members from the same kibbutz who remain anonymous to each other. Each member is told there are 100 shekels in an envelope to which both members have access. Each participant decides how many shekels to withdraw and keep. If the sum of both requests exceeds 100 shekels, both members receive no money and the game is over. However, if the requests are less than or equal to 100 shekels, the money remaining in the envelope is increased by 50 percent and divided evenly among the participants. Each member also keeps the original amount he or she requested. The game is an example of a common-pool resource dilemma in which publicly accessible goods are no longer available once they are consumed. Since the goods are available to more than one person, the maintenance of the resources requires individual self-restraint; in other words, cooperation.

After we controlled for a number of variables, including the age and size of the kibbutz and the amount of privatization, we found not only that religious kibbutzniks were more cooperative with each other than secular kibbutzniks, but that male religious kibbutz members were also significantly more cooperative than female members. Among secular kibbutzniks we found no sex differences at all. This result is understandable if we appreciate the types of rituals and demands imposed on religious Jews. Although there are a variety of requirements that are imposed equally on males and females, such as keeping kosher and refraining from work on the Sabbath, male rituals are largely performed in public, whereas female rituals are generally pursued privately. Indeed, none of the three major requirements imposed exclusively on women—attending a ritual bath, separating a portion of dough when baking bread and lighting Shabbat and holiday candles—are publicly performed. They are not rituals that signal commitment to a wider group; instead they appear to signal commitment to the family. Men, however, engage in highly visible rituals, most notably public prayer, which they are expected to perform three times a day. Among male religious kibbutz members, synagogue attendance is positively correlated with cooperative behavior. There is no similar correlation among females. This is not surprising given that women are not required to attend services, and so their presence does not signal commitment to the group. Here the

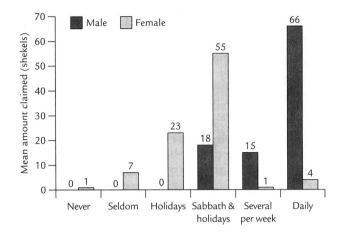

costly signaling theory of ritual provides a unique explanation of these findings. We expect that further work will provide even more insight into the ability of ritual to promote trust, commitment and cooperation.

We know that many other species engage in ritual behaviors that appear to enhance trust and cooperation. For example, anthropologists John Watanabe of Dartmouth University and Barbara Smuts at the University of Michigan have shown that greetings between male olive baboons serve to signal trust and commitment between former rivals. So why are human rituals often cloaked in mystery and the supernatural? Cognitive anthropologists Scott Atran of the University of Michigan and Pascal Boyer at Washington University in St. Louis have pointed out that the counterintuitive nature of supernatural concepts is more easily remembered than mundane ideas, which facilitates their cultural transmission. Belief in supernatural agents such as gods, spirits and ghosts also appears to be critical to religion's ability to promote long-term cooperation. In our study of 19th-century communes, Eric Bressler and I found that the strong positive relationship between the number of costly requirements imposed on members and commune longevity only held for religious communes, not secular ones. We were surprised by this result because secular groups such as militaries and fraternities appear to successfully employ costly rituals to maintain cooperation. Cultural ecologist Roy Rappaport explained, however, that although religious and secular rituals can both promote cooperation, religious rituals ironically generate greater belief and commitment because they sanctify unfalsifiable statements that are beyond the possibility of examination. Since statements containing supernatural elements, such as "Jesus is the son of God," cannot be proved or disproved, believers verify them "emotionally." In contrast to religious propositions, the kibbutz's guiding dictum, taken from Karl Marx, is not beyond question; it can be evaluated by living according to its directives by distributing labor and resources

appropriately. Indeed, as the economic situation on the kibbutzim has worsened, this fundamental proposition of kibbutz life has been challenged and is now disregarded by many who are pushing their communities to accept differential pay scales. The ability of religious rituals to evoke emotional experiences that can be associated with enduring supernatural concepts and symbols differentiates them from both animal and secular rituals and lies at the heart of their efficiency in promoting and maintaining long-term group cooperation and commitment.

Evolutionary research on religious behavior is in its infancy, and many questions remain to be addressed. The costly signaling theory of ritual appears to provide some answers, and, of course, it has given me a better understanding of the questions I asked as a teenager. The real value of the costly signaling theory of ritual will be determined by its ability to explain religious phenomena across societies. Most of us, including ultraorthodox Jews, are not living in communes. Nevertheless, contemporary religious congregations that demand much of their members are able to achieve a close-knit social community—an impressive accomplishment in today's individualistic world.

Religion has probably always served to enhance the union of its practitioners; unfortunately, there is also a dark side to this unity. If the intragroup solidarity that religion promotes is one of its significant adaptive benefits, then from its beginning religion has probably always played a role in intergroup conflicts. In other words, one of the benefits for individuals of intragroup solidarity is the ability of unified groups to defend and compete against other groups. This seems to be as true today as it ever was, and is nowhere more apparent than the region I visited as a 15-year-old boy—which is where I am as I write these words. As I conduct my fieldwork in the center of this war zone, I hope that by appreciating the depth of the religious need in the human psyche, and by understanding this powerful adaptation, we can learn how to promote cooperation rather than conflict.

REFERENCES

Atran, S. 2002. *In Gods We Trust*. New York: Oxford University Press.

Iannaccone, L. 1992. Sacrifice and stigma: Reducing free-riding in cults, communes, and other collectives. *Journal of Political Economy* 100:271–291.

Iannaccone, L. 1994. Why strict churches are strong. *American Journal of Sociology* 99:1180–1211.

Irons, W. 2001. Religion as a hard-to-fake sign of commitment. In *Evolution and the Capacity for Commitment*, ed. R. Nesse, pp. 292–309. New York: Russell Sage Foundation.

Rappaport, R. 1999. *Ritual and Religion in the Making of Humanity*. Cambridge: Cambridge University Press.

Sosis, R. 2003. Why aren't we all Hutterites? Costly signaling theory and religious behavior. *Human Nature* 14:91–127.

Sosis, R., and C. Alcorta. 2003. Signaling, solidarity, and the sacred: The evolution of religious behavior. *Evolutionary Anthropology* 12:264–274.

Sosis, R., and E. Bressler. 2003. Cooperation and commune longevity: A test of the costly signaling theory of religion. *Cross-Cultural Research* 37:211–239.

Sosis, R., and B. Ruffle. 2003. Religious ritual and cooperation: Testing for a relationship on Israeli religious and secular kibbutzim. *Current Anthropology* 44:713–722.

Zahavi, A., and A. Zahavi. 1997. *The Handicap Principle*. New York: Oxford University Press.

31

Hallucinogenic Plants
and Their Use in Traditional Societies

Wade Davis

In Western society, drugs are used for either medicinal purposes or pleasure. Our culture sometimes defines those who use drugs for nonmedicinal purposes as deviant, and we have begun to view the use of drugs as a pathological condition unique in the annals of human history. The illegal use of drugs is considered a major social problem. In Selection 4, an ethnography of "Crack Street," we saw the human dimension of that problem.

The use of drugs is widespread in traditional cultures around the world. However, in traditional societies hallucinogenic plants are used for religious purposes and in ritual settings. Throughout history, people have sought ways to see beyond the normal reality of everyday life. They have endured the risk of poison in experimenting with ways to prepare mind-altering substances. These substances may be smoked, chewed, eaten, sniffed, drunk, rubbed onto the skin or into cuts, or even taken as intoxicating enemas. They have taken these risks, not for pleasure or kicks, but for curing illnesses through magic, divining truth, peering into the future, and making contact with the spirit world. This is serious and important for the people involved.

Another difference highlighted by the comparative study of drug use is the important effect of culture and context on the drug experience. Used in different settings, under different sets of expectations, the same drug may cause very different reactions, from nausea on the one hand to a religious experience on the other. Today we may find it odd that Native Americans

(Amerindians) smoked tobacco to cause giddiness (one of the universal symptoms of ecstasy) and to open the pathways through which shamans disassociated themselves from the normal state of awareness.

In light of America's drug problem, getting a broader historical and comparative vision of the role of drugs in society makes sense.

As you read this selection, ask yourself the following questions:

- Were hallucinogenic plants discovered by chance?
- What is the relationship between medicinal drugs, psychotropic drugs, and poisons?
- What factors influence what an individual sees under the influence of hallucinogens?
- How do ritual and the role of the shamanistic leader create a different context for the use of hallucinogenic drugs in traditional and modern societies?
- Do drug users in our society have their own secular rituals?

The following terms discussed in this selection are included in the Glossary at the back of the book:

Amerindian	*psychoactive drugs*
decoction	*rite of passage*
hallucinogen	*ritual*
indigenous	*sorcery*

The passionate desire which leads man to flee from the monotony of everyday life has made him instinctively discover strange substances. He has done so, even where nature has been most niggardly in producing them and where the products seem very far from possessing the properties which would enable him to satisfy this desire.

From *Cultural Survival* 9(4):2–5, 1985. Reprinted by permission of *Cultural Survival*.

Thus early in this century did Lewis Lewin, perhaps the preeminent pioneer in the study of psychoactive drugs, describe the primal search that led to man's discovery of hallucinogens. Strictly speaking, a hallucinogen is any chemical substance that distorts the senses and produces hallucinations—perceptions or experiences that depart dramatically from ordinary reality. Today we know these substances variously as psychotomimetics (psychosis mimickers), psychotaraxics (mind disturbers) and psychedelics (mind manifesters); dry terms which quite inadequately describe the remarkable effects they have on the human mind. These effects are varied but they frequently include a dreamlike state marked by dramatic alterations "in the sphere of experience, in the perception of reality, changes even of space and time and in consciousness of self. They invariably induce a series of visual hallucinations, often in kaleidoscopic movement, and usually in indescribably brilliant and rich colours, frequently accompanied by auditory and other hallucinations"—tactile, olfactory, and temporal. Indeed the effects are so unearthly, so unreal that most hallucinogenic plants early acquired a sacred place in indigenous cultures. In rare cases, they were worshipped as gods incarnate.

The pharmacological activity of the hallucinogens is due to a relatively small number of types of chemical compounds. While modern chemistry has been able in most cases successfully to duplicate these substances, or even manipulate their chemical structures to create novel synthetic forms, virtually all hallucinogens have their origins in plants. (One immediate exception that comes to mind is the New World toad, *Bufo marinus*, but the evidence that this animal was used for its psychoactive properties is far from complete.)

Within the plant kingdom the hallucinogens occur only among the evolutionarily advanced flowering plants and in one division—the fungi—of the more primitive spore bearers. Most hallucinogens are alkaloids, a family of perhaps 5,000 complex organic molecules that also account for the biological activity of most toxic and medicinal plants. These active compounds may be found in the various concentrations in different parts of the plant—roots, leaves, seeds, bark and/or flowers—and they may be absorbed by the human body in a number of ways, as is evident in the wide variety of folk preparations. Hallucinogens may be smoked or snuffed, swallowed fresh or dried, drunk in decoctions and infusions, absorbed directly through the skin, placed in wounds or administered as enemas.

To date about 120 hallucinogenic plants have been identified worldwide. On first glance, given that estimates of the total number of plant species range as high as 800,000, this appears to be a relatively small number. However, it grows in significance when compared to the total number of species used as food. Perhaps 3,000 species of plants have been regularly consumed by some people at some period of history, but today only 150 remain important enough to enter world commerce. Of these a mere 12–15, mostly domesticated cereals, keep us alive.

In exploring his ambient vegetation for hallucinogenic plants, man has shown extraordinary ingenuity, and in experimenting with them all the signs of pharmacological genius. He has also quite evidently taken great personal risks. Peyote (*Lophophora williamsii*), for example, has as many as 30 active constituents, mostly alkaloids, and is exceedingly bitter, not unlike most deadly poisonous plants. Yet the Huichol, Tarahumara and numerous other peoples of Mexico and the American Southwest discovered that sundried and eaten whole the cactus produces spectacular psychoactive effects.

With similar tenacity, the Mazatec of Oaxaca discovered amongst a mushroom flora that contained many deadly species as many as 10 that were hallucinogenic. These they believed had ridden to earth upon thunderbolts, and were reverently gathered at the time of the new moon. Elsewhere in Oaxaca, the seeds of the morning glory (*Rivea corymbosa*) were crushed and prepared as a decoction known at one time as ololiuqui—the sacred preparation of the Aztec, and one that we now realize contained alkaloids closely related to LSD, a potent synthetic hallucinogen. In Peru, the bitter mescaline-rich cactus *Trichocereus pachanoi* became the basis of the San Pedro curative cults of the northern Andes. Here the preferred form of administration is the decoction, a tea served up at the long nocturnal ceremonies during which time the patients' problems were diagnosed. At dawn they would be sent on the long pilgrimages high into the mountains to bathe in the healing waters of a number of sacred lakes.

Lowland South America has provided several exceedingly important and chemically fascinating hallucinogenic preparations, notably the intoxicating yopo (*Anadenanthera peregrina*) and ebene (*Virola calophylla, V. calophylloidea, V. theiodora*) snuffs of the upper Orinoco of Venezuela and adjacent Brazil and the ayahuasca-caapi-yagé complex (*Banisteriopsis caapi*) found commonly among the rainforest peoples of the Northwest Amazon. Yopo is prepared from the seeds of a tall forest tree which are roasted gently and then ground into a fine powder, which is then mixed with some alkaline substance, often the ashes of certain leaves. Ebene is prepared from the blood red resin of certain trees in the nutmeg family. Preparations vary but frequently the bark is stripped from the tree and slowly heated to allow the resin to collect in a small earthenware pot where it is boiled down into a thick paste, which in turn is sun dried and powdered along with the leaves of other plants. Ayahuasca comes from the rasped bark of a forest liana which is carefully heated in water, again with a number of admixture plants, until a thick decoction is obtained. All three products are violently hallucinogenic and it is of some significance that they all contain a number of subsidiary plants that, in ways not yet fully understood, intensify or lengthen the psychoactive effects of the principal ingredients. This is an important feature of many folk preparations and it is due in part to the fact that different chemical compounds in relatively small concentrations may effectively potentiate each other, producing powerful synergistic effects—a biochemical version of the whole being greater than the sum of its parts. The awareness of these properties is evidence of the impressive chemical and botanical knowledge of the traditional peoples.

In the Old World may be found some of the most novel means of administering hallucinogens. In southern Africa, the Bushmen of Dobe, Botswana, absorb the active constituents of the plant kwashi (*Pancratium trianthum*) by incising the scalp and rubbing the juice of an onion-like bulb into the open wound. The fly agaric (*Amanita muscaria*), a psychoactive mushroom used in Siberia, may be toasted on a fire or made into a decoction with reindeer milk and wild blueberries. In this rare instance the active principals pass through the body unaltered, and the psychoactive urine of the intoxicated individual may be consumed by the others. Certain European hallucinogens—notably the solanaceous belladonna (*Atropa belladonna*), henbane (*Hyoscyamus niger*), mandrake (*Mandragora officinarum*) and datura (*Datura metel*)—are topically active; that is the active principals are absorbed through the skin. We now know, for example, that much of the behavior associated with the medieval witches is as readily attributable to these drugs as to any spiritual communion with the diabolic. The witches commonly rubbed their bodies with hallucinogenic ointments. A particularly efficient means of self-administering the drug for women is through the moist tissue of the vagina; the witches' broomstick or staff was considered the most effective applicator. Our own popular image of the haggard woman on a broomstick comes from the medieval belief that the witches rode their staffs each midnight to the sabbat, the orgiastic assembly of demons and sorcerers. In fact, it now appears that their journey was not through space but across the hallucinatory landscape of their minds.

There is in the worldwide distribution of the hallucinogenic plants a pronounced and significant discrepancy that has only inadequately been accounted for but which serves to illustrate a critical feature of their role in traditional societies. Of the 120 or more such plants found to date, over 100 are native to the Americas; the Old World has contributed a mere 15–20 species. How might this be explained? To be sure it is in part an artifact of the emphasis of academic research. A good many of these plants have entered the literature due to the efforts of Professor R. E. Schultes and his colleagues at the Harvard Botanical Museum and elsewhere, and their interest has predominantly been in the New World. Yet were the hallucinogenic plants a dominant feature of traditional cultures in Africa and Eurasia, surely they would have shown up in the extensive ethnographic literature and in the journals of traders and missionaries. With few notable exceptions, they don't. Nor is this discrepancy due to floristic peculiarities. The rainforests of West Africa and Southeast Asia, in particular, are exceedingly rich and diverse. Moreover, the peoples of these regions have most successfully explored them for pharmacologically active compounds for use both as medicines and poisons. In fact, as much as any other material trait the manipulation of toxic plants remains a consistent theme throughout sub-Saharan African cultures. The Amerindians, for their part, were certainly no strangers to plant toxins which they commonly exploited as fish, arrow and dart poisons. Yet it is a singular fact that while the peoples of Africa consistently used these toxic preparations on each other, the Amerindian almost never did. And while the Amerindian successfully explored his forest for hallucinogens, the African did not. This suggests the critical fact that the use of any pharmacologically active plant—remembering that the difference between hallucinogen, medicine and poison is often a matter of dosage—is firmly rooted in culture. If the peoples of Africa did not explore their environment for psychoactive drugs, surely it is because they felt no need to. In many Amerindian societies the use of plant hallucinogens lies at the very heart of traditional life.

To begin to understand the role that these powerful plants play in these societies, however, it is essential to place the drugs themselves in proper context. For one, the pharmacologically active components do not produce uniform effects. On the contrary, any psychoactive drug has within it a completely ambivalent potential for good or evil, order or chaos. Pharmacologically it induces a certain condition, but that condition is mere raw material to be worked by particular cultural or psychological forces and expectations. This is what our own medical experts call the "set and setting" of any drug experience. *Set* in these terms is the individual's expectation of what the drug will do to him; *setting* is the environment—both physical and social—in which the drug is taken. This may be illustrated by an example from our own country. In the northwest rainforests of Oregon are a native species of hallucinogenic mushrooms. Those who go out into the forest deliberately intending to ingest these mushrooms generally experience a pleasant intoxication. Those who inadvertently consume them while foraging for edible mushrooms invariably end up in the poison unit of the nearest hospital. The mushroom itself has not changed.

Similarly the hallucinogenic plants consumed by the Amerindian induce a powerful but neutral stimulation of the imagination; they create a template, as it were, upon which cultural beliefs and forces may be amplified a thousand times. What the individual sees in the visions is dependent not on the drug but on other factors—the mood and setting of the group, the physical and mental states of the participants, his own expectations based on a rich repository of tribal lore and, above all in Indian societies, the authority, knowledge and experience of the leader of the ceremony. The role of this figure—be it man or woman, shaman, curandero, paye, maestro or brujo—is pivotal. It is he who places the protective cloak of ritual about the participants. It is he who tackles the bombardment of visual and auditory stimuli and gives them order. It is he who must interpret a complex body of belief, reading the power in leaves and the meaning in stones, who must skillfully balance the forces of the universe and guide the play of the winds. The ceremonial use of hallucinogenic plants by the Amerindian is (most often) a collective journey into the unconscious. It is not necessarily, and in fact rarely is, a pleasant or an easy journey. It is wondrous and it may be terrifying. But above all it is purposeful.

The Amerindian enters the realm of the hallucinogenic visions not out of boredom, or to relieve an individual's restless anxiety, but rather to fulfill some collective need of the group. In the Amazon, for example, hallucinogens are taken to divine the future, track the paths of enemies, ensure the fidelity of women, diagnose and treat diseases. The Huichol in Mexico eat their peyote at the completion of long arduous pilgrimages in order that they may experience in life the journey of the soul of the dead to the underworld. The Amahuaca Indians of Peru drink yage that the nature of the forest animals and plants may be revealed to their apprentices. In eastern North America during puberty rites, the Algonquin confined adolescents to a longhouse for two weeks and fed them a beverage based in part on datura. During the extended intoxication and subsequent amnesia—a pharmacological feature of this drug—the young boys forgot what it was to be a child so that they might learn what it meant to be a man. But whatever the ostensible purpose of the hallucinogenic journey, the Amerindian imbibes his plants in a highly structured manner that places a ritualistic framework of order around their use. Moreover the experience is explicitly sought for positive ends. It is not a means of escaping from an uncertain existence; rather it is perceived as a means of contribution to the welfare of all one's people.

32

Culture, Poverty, and HIV Transmission

The Case of Rural Haiti

Paul Farmer

AIDS is currently the deadliest infectious disease in the world, killing over 3 million people every year. While antiretroviral drugs have lengthened the lives of many people infected with HIV, these drugs are expensive, and millions of people who need them still cannot afford them. Without medications, counseling, and support, people living with HIV are likely to infect others and then die.

In the history of this epidemic, anthropologists have played an important role in describing and helping to explain how behavioral practices are related to the transmission of the HIV virus. So, too, have anthropologists helped demonstrate how poverty and other inequalities affect people's likelihood of contracting AIDS in the first place.

In this selection, we learn about the circumstances under which three Haitians developed AIDS, and how circumstances such as poverty and gender inequality put them at dramatically increased risk of infection. Much of the public discourse about AIDS reflects moral judgments about people's lifestyles and places blame for the disease on the sufferers. This selection shows how circumstances beyond individuals' control can place them at risk of infection. Paul Farmer, the author of this selection, is both a physician and an anthropologist, and he has been one of the most prominent and vocal advocates for people whose social and political circumstances place them at increased risk of HIV and other infectious diseases. Students interested in learning more about the work of Paul Farmer might be interested in reading his biography, *Mountains Beyond Mountains*, by Tracy Kidder.

While the biomedical challenge of AIDS is great, the challenge of coping with the human dimensions of AIDS is enormous, requiring resources, compassion, and cross-cultural understanding. Anthropologists have made, and continue to make, important contributions to the efforts of doctors, hospitals, nongovernment organizations, and other people and institutions to cope with the human dimensions of this devastating virus.

As you read this selection, ask yourself the following questions:

- How does poverty affect one's risk of becoming infected with HIV?

- What cultural and political factors influence the distribution of AIDS in Haiti?

- How can HIV infection be seen as *not* the result of bad personal decisions?

- What are some practical suggestions for reducing the human suffering caused by AIDS?

- What does Farmer mean when he says that there is "an AIDS of the North, and an AIDS of the South"?

The following terms discussed in this selection are included in the Glossary at the back of the book:

AIDS	SIDA
epidemic	seropositive
HIV	seroprevalence
medical anthropology	transmission

Haiti, a country of well over seven million inhabitants, is generally considered to be a substantially rural nation,[1] yet few studies of HIV transmission have been conducted in rural parts of the country.

Infections and Inequalities by Paul Farmer. Copyright 1999 by University of California Press. Reproduced with permission of University of California Press in the format Textbook via Copyright Clearance Center.

Early reports by Pape and Johnson, based on small studies conducted in 1986–87, noted that the seroprevalence rate for HIV averaged 3 percent "in rural areas."[2] The seroprevalence in 97 mothers of children hospitalized with dehydration was 3 percent; of 245 unscreened rural blood donors, 4 percent had antibodies to HIV. In an area even more distant from urban centers, only 1 percent of 191 adults who came for immunizations were seropositive. Unfortunately, we know little about the individuals bled for these studies. Just how rural were they? What was the nature of their ties to Port-au-Prince and other high-prevalence cities? How did the seropositive individuals come to be at risk for HIV? How did they differ from seronegative controls? How rapidly was HIV making inroads into the rural population? What, in short, are the dynamics of HIV transmission in rural Haiti?

To understand the rural Haitian AIDS epidemic, we must move beyond the concept of "risk groups" to consider the interplay between human agency and the powerful forces that constrain it, focusing especially on those activities that promote or retard the spread of HIV. In Haiti, the most powerful of these forces have been inequality, deepening poverty, and political dislocations, which have together conspired to hasten the spread of HIV. This chapter details research on HIV transmission in a rural area of Haiti—and also recounts some of the ways such large-scale social forces become manifest in the lives of particular individuals.

AIDS IN A HAITIAN VILLAGE

The setting for the research described here is the Péligre basin of Haiti's Central Plateau, home to several hundred thousand mostly rural people. Although all parts of Haiti are poor, the Péligre basin region and its villages may be especially so.

Before 1956, the village of Kay was situated in a deep and fertile valley in this area, near the banks of the Rivière Artibonite. For generations, the villagers farmed the broad and gently sloping banks of the river, selling rice, bananas, millet, corn, and sugarcane in regional markets. Harvests were, by all reports, bountiful; life then is now recalled as idyllic. With the construction of Haiti's largest hydroelectric dam in 1956, however, thousands of families living in this region were flooded out. The displaced persons were largely peasant farmers, and they received little or no compensation for their lost land.

The hilltop village of Do Kay was founded by refugees from the rising water. The flooding of the valley forced most villagers up into the hills on either side of the new reservoir. Kay became divided into "Do" (those who settled on the stony backs of the hills) and "Ba" (those who remained down near the new waterline). By all standard measures, both parts of Kay are now very poor; its older inhabitants often blame their poverty on the massive buttress dam a few miles away and note bitterly that it brought them neither electricity nor water.

Though initially a dusty squatter settlement of fewer than two hundred persons, Do Kay has grown rapidly in the past decade and now counts about two thousand inhabitants. In spite of the hostile conditions, most families continue to rely to some extent on small-scale agriculture. But many villagers are involved in a series of development projects designed to improve the health of the area's inhabitants. Since 1984, for example, a series of outreach initiatives have complemented the work of our growing team of clinicians, based in Do Kay at the Clinique Bon Sauveur. The most significant efforts were undertaken under the aegis of Proje Veye Sante, the "health surveillance project." Proje Veye Sante, conducted in large part by village-based community health workers from about thirty nearby communities, provides preventive and primary care to close to fifty thousand rural people.

Through Proje Veye Sante, AIDS surveillance began well before the epidemic was manifest in the region. It is thus possible to date the index, or first, case of AIDS to 1986, when a young schoolteacher, Manno Surpris, fell ill with recurrent superficial fungal infections, chronic diarrhea, and pulmonary tuberculosis. Seropositive for HIV, he died a year later.

Although Manno Surpris was from another part of the Central Plateau, it was not long before we began to diagnose the syndrome among natives of Do Kay. The sections that follow offer brief case histories of the first three villagers known to have died of AIDS. None had a history of transfusion with blood or blood products; none had a history of homosexual contact or other "risk factors" as designated by the CDC. They did, however, share two important, if poorly understood, risk factors: poverty and inequality.

Anita

Anita Joseph was born in approximately 1966 to a family that had lost its land to the Péligre dam. One of six children, she briefly attended school until her mother, weakened by the malnutrition then rampant in the Kay area, died of tuberculosis. Anita was then thirteen. Her father became depressed and abusive, and she resolved to run away: "I'd had it with his yelling. . . . When I saw how poor I was, and how hungry, and saw that it would never get any better, I had to go to the city. Back then I was so skinny—I was saving my life, I thought, by getting out of here."

Anita left for Port-au-Prince with less than $3 and no clear plan of action. She worked briefly as a *restavèk*, or live-in maid, for $10 a month but lost this position when her employer was herself fired from a factory job.

Cast into the street, Anita eventually found a relative who took her in. The kinswoman, who lived in a notorious slum north of the capital, introduced her to Vincent, a young man who worked unloading luggage at the airport. Anita was not yet fifteen when she entered her first and only sexual union. "What could I do, really?" she sighed as she recounted the story much later. "He had a good job. My aunt thought I should go with him."

Vincent, who had at least one other sexual partner at the time, became ill less than two years after they began sharing a room. The young man, whom Anita cared for throughout his illness, died after repeated infections, including tuberculosis. Not long after his death, Anita herself fell ill with tuberculosis.

Upon returning to Do Kay in 1987, she quickly responded to antituberculous therapy. When she relapsed some months later, we performed an HIV test, which revealed the true cause of her immunosuppression. Following a slow but ineluctable decline, Anita died in February 1988.

Dieudonné

Dieudonné Gracia, born in Do Kay in 1963, was also the child of two "water refugees." One of seven children, he attended primary school in his home village and, briefly, secondary school in a nearby town. It was there, at the age of nineteen, that he had his first sexual contact. Dieudonné remarked that his girlfriend had had "two, maybe three partners" before they met; he was sure that one of her partners had been a truck driver from a city in central Haiti.

When a series of setbacks further immiserated his family, Dieudonné was forced to drop out of secondary school and also to drop his relationship with the young woman. He returned to Do Kay to work with his father, a carpenter. In 1983, however, the young man decided to "try my luck in Port-au-Prince." Through a friend from Do Kay, Dieudonné found a position as a domestic for a well-to-do family in a suburb of the capital.

While in the city, Dieudonné's sexual experience broadened considerably. He had five partners in little more than two years, all of them close to his own age. Asked about the brevity of these liaisons, Dieudonné favored an economic explanation: "A couple of them let go of me because they saw that I couldn't do anything for them. They saw that I couldn't give them anything for any children."

In 1985, Dieudonné became ill and was dismissed from his job in Port-au-Prince. He returned to Do Kay and began seeing his former lover again. She soon became pregnant and moved to Do Kay as the young man's *plase*, a term designating a partner in a more or less stable conjugal union.[3]

During this interlude, Dieudonné was seen at the Do Kay clinic for a number of problems that suggested immunodeficiency: herpes zoster and genital herpes,

recurrent diarrhea, and weight loss. In the months following the birth of their baby, the young mother fell ill with a febrile illness, thought by her physician to be malaria, and quickly succumbed. Less than a year later, Dieudonné, much reduced by chronic diarrhea, was diagnosed with tuberculosis. Although he initially responded to antituberculous agents, Dieudonné died of AIDS in October 1988.

Acéphie

Acéphie Joseph was born in 1965 on a small knoll protruding into the reservoir that had drowned her parents' land. Acéphie attended primary school somewhat irregularly; by the age of nineteen, she had not yet graduated and decided that it was time to help generate income for her family, which was sinking deeper and deeper into poverty. Hunger was a near-daily occurrence for the Joseph family; the times were as bad as those right after the flooding of the valley. Acéphie began to help her mother, a market woman, by carrying produce to a local market on Friday mornings.

It was there that she met a soldier, formerly stationed in Port-au-Prince, who began to make overtures to the striking young woman from Do Kay. Although the soldier had a wife and children and was known to have more than one regular partner, Acéphie did not spurn him. "What would you have me do? I could tell that the old people were uncomfortable, worried—but they didn't say no. They didn't tell me to stay away from him. I wish they had, but how could they have known? . . . I looked around and saw how poor we all were, how the old people were finished. . . . It was a way out, that's how I saw it."

Within a short time, the soldier fell ill and was diagnosed in the Do Kay clinic with AIDS. A few months after he and Acéphie parted, he was dead.

Shaken, Acéphie went to a nearby town and began a course in what she euphemistically termed a "cooking school," which prepared poor girls for work as servants. In 1987, twenty-two years old, Acéphie went to Port-au-Prince, where she found a $30-per-month job as a housekeeper for a middle-class Haitian woman who worked for the U.S. embassy. She began to see a man, also from the Kay region, who chauffeured a small bus between the Central Plateau and Port-au-Prince.

Acéphie worked in the city until late in 1989, when she discovered that she was pregnant. This displeased both her partner and her employer. Sans job and sans boyfriend, Acéphie returned to Do Kay in her third trimester.

Following the birth of her daughter, Acéphie was sapped by repeated opportunistic infections, each one caught in time by the staff of the clinic in Do Kay. Throughout 1991, however, she continued to lose weight; by January 1992, she weighed less than ninety pounds, and her intermittent fevers did not respond to broad-spectrum antibiotics.

Acéphie died in April 1992. Her daughter, the first "AIDS orphan" in Do Kay, is now in the care of Acéphie's mother. The child is also infected. A few months after Acéphie's death, her father hanged himself.

Sadly, however, this is not simply the story of Acéphie and her family. The soldier's wife, who is much thinner than last year, has already had a case of herpes zoster. Two of her children are also HIV-positive. This woman, who is well known to the clinic staff, is no longer a widow; once again, she is the partner of a military man. Her late husband had at least two other partners, both of them poor peasant women, in the Central Plateau. One is HIV-positive and has two sickly children. The father of Acéphie's child, apparently in good health, is still plying the roads from Mirebalais to Port-au-Prince. His serostatus is unknown.

Individual Experience in Context

When compared to age-matched North Americans with AIDS, Anita, Dieudonné, and Acéphie have sparse sexual histories: Anita had only one partner; Dieudonné had six; Acéphie had two. Although a case-control study by Pape and Johnson suggested that HIV-infected urban men, at least, had larger numbers of partners than our patients did[4] research conducted in Anita's neighborhood in Port-au-Prince suggests that her case is not as unique as it would seem:

> The high seropositivity rate (8%) found in pregnant women 14 to 19 years of age suggests that women [in Cité Soleil] appear to acquire HIV infection soon after becoming sexually active. Moreover, this age group is the only one in which a higher seropositivity rate is not associated with a greater number of sexual partners. Women with only one sexual partner in the year prior to pregnancy actually have a slightly higher prevalence rate (although not significantly so) than the others. This suggests that they were infected by their first and only partner.[5]

The stories of Anita, Dieudonné, and Acéphie are ones that reveal the push-and-pull forces of contemporary Haiti. In all three cases, the declining fortunes of the rural poor pushed young adults to try their chances in the city. Once there, all three became entangled in unions that the women, at least, characterized as attempts to emerge from poverty. Each worked as a domestic, but none managed to fulfill the expectation of saving and sending home desperately needed cash. What they brought home, instead, was AIDS.

How representative are these case histories? Over the past several years, the medical staff of the Clinique Bon Sauveur has diagnosed dozens more cases of AIDS and other forms of HIV infection in women who arrive at the clinic with a broad range of complaints. In fact, the majority of our patients have been women—a pattern rarely described in the AIDS literature. With surprisingly few exceptions, those so diagnosed shared a number of risk factors, as our modest case-control study suggests.

We conducted this study by interviewing the first twenty-five women we diagnosed with symptomatic HIV infection who were residents of Do Kay or its two neighboring villages. Their responses to questions posed during a series of open-ended interviews were compared with those of twenty-five age-matched, seronegative controls. In both groups, ages ranged from 16 to 44, with a mean age of about 27 years. Table 1 presents our findings.

None of these fifty women had a history of prostitution, and none had used illicit drugs. Only two, both members of the control group, had received blood transfusions. None of the women in either group had had more than five sexual partners in the course of their lives; in fact, seven of the afflicted women had had only one. Although women in the study group had on average more sexual partners than the controls, the difference is not striking. Similarly, we found no clear difference between the two groups in the number of intramuscular injections they had received or their years of education.

The chief risk factors in this small cohort seem to involve not number of partners but rather the professions of these partners. Fully nineteen of the women with HIV disease had histories of sexual contact with soldiers or truck drivers. Three of these women reported having only two sexual partners: one a soldier, one a truck driver. Of the women diagnosed with AIDS, none had a history of sexual contact exclusively with peasants (although one had as sole partner a construction worker from Do Kay). Among the control group, only two women had a regular partner who was a truck driver; none reported contact with soldiers, and most had had sexual relations only with peasants from the region. Histories of extended residence in Port-au-Prince and work as a domestic were also strongly associated with a diagnosis of HIV disease.

How can we make sense of these surprising results? In the socio-graphically "flat" region around the dam—after all, most area residents share a single socioeconomic status, poverty—conjugal unions with non-peasants (salaried soldiers and truck drivers who are paid on a daily basis) reflect women's quest for some measure of economic security. In the setting of a worsening economic crisis, the gap between the hungry

TABLE 1   Case-Control Study of AIDS in Rural Haitian Women

Patient Characteristics	Patients with AIDS (N = 25)	Control Group (N = 25)
Average number of sexual partners	2.7	2.4
Sexual partner of a truck driver	12	2
Sexual partner of a soldier	9	0
Sexual partner of a peasant only	0	23
Ever lived in Port-au-Prince	20	4
Worked as a servant	18	1
Average number of years of formal schooling	4.5	4.0
Ever received a blood transfusion	0	2
Ever used illicit drugs	0	0
Ever received more than ten intramuscular injections	17	19

peasant class and the relatively well-off soldiers and truck drivers became the salient local inequality. In this manner, truck drivers and soldiers have served as a "bridge" from the city to the rural population.

Truck drivers and soldiers will soon no longer be necessary components of the rural epidemic. Once introduced into a sexually active population, HIV will work its way to those with no history of residence in the city, no history of contact with soldiers or truck drivers, no history of work as a domestic. But these risk factors—all of which reflect a desperate attempt to escape rural poverty—are emblematic of the lot of the rural Haitian poor, and perhaps especially of poor women.

HIV in a Haitian Village

Extended residence in Port-au-Prince, work as a servant, and sexual contact with nonpeasants—although these risk factors were far different from those described for North Americans with AIDS, they characterized the majority of our male and female patients afflicted with AIDS. The majority of the residents of the area served by Proje Veye Sante shared none of these attributes, however. Did this suggest that few would prove to be infected with HIV? Although a good deal of ethnographic research into the nature of AIDS had already been conducted in the region, no research had addressed the question of HIV prevalence among asymptomatic adults.

Troubled by this lacuna, the staff of the clinic and of Proje Veye Sante established the Groupe d'étude du SIDA dans la Classe Paysanne.[6] GESCAP has a mandate to research the mechanisms by which poverty puts young adults, and especially young women, at risk of HIV infection.[7] With community approval, GESCAP is attempting to illuminate case histories with

serologic surveys, an expanded case-control study, and cluster studies (such as those that revealed how a single HIV-positive soldier came to infect at least eleven natives of the region, one of whom was Acéphie).

After considerable discussion, the members of GESCAP decided to undertake a study of all asymptomatic adults living in Do Kay. The study was to include all members of the community who might plausibly be sexually active (fifteen years and older) and who were free of any suggestion of immunodeficiency; patients with active tuberculosis were excluded from this study. Anyone who was the regular sexual partner of a person with known HIV infection was also excluded.

Of the first one hundred villagers enrolling in the program, ninety-nine were seronegative for HIV.[8] The one young woman with HIV infection, Alourdes, had a history of extended residence in Port-au-Prince and also in 1985 of regular sexual contact with a salaried employee of the national electric company. This man, who had several sexual partners during his tenure in central Haiti, was rumored to have died of AIDS. In 1986, Alourdes had been the partner of a young man from her home village, a construction worker. He later developed tuberculosis, initially attributed to respiratory contact with his wife, who had pulmonary tuberculosis. Both were later found to be infected with HIV; neither had ever had sexual contact outside the Do Kay area. The discovery of HIV infection in Alourdes, who was known to have risk factors as defined in the case-control study, helped to identify the routes of exposure of the couple who had HIV-related tuberculosis.

Such discrete studies do not, however, fully define the nature of the large-scale social forces at work. The discussion in the following sections summarizes the factors that seem to be most significant in the ultimate rate of progression of HIV in rural Haiti. Perhaps an examination of these forces can serve to inform understandings of the dynamics of HIV transmission in other parts of Latin America and also in areas of Asia and Africa where prevalence rates in rural regions are currently low. It is a cautionary tale that argues for aggressive preventive measures:

> If a disaster is to be prevented in rural Haiti, vigorous and effective prevention campaigns must be initiated at once. And although such efforts must begin, the prospects of stopping the steady march of HIV are slim. AIDS is far more likely to join a host of other sexually transmitted diseases—including gonorrhea, syphilis, genital herpes, chlamydia, hepatitis B, lymphogranuloma venereum, and even cervical cancer—that have already become entrenched among the poor.[9]

Only massive and coordinated efforts may yet avert the ongoing disaster that has befallen urban Haiti, Puerto Rico, inner-city North America, Thailand, Brazil, and many nations in sub-Saharan Africa.

THE DYNAMICS OF HIV TRANSMISSION IN RURAL HAITI

Wherever HIV infection is a sexually transmitted disease, social forces necessarily determine its distribution. Cultural, political, and economic factors, while each inevitably important, cannot be of equal significance in all settings. In rural Haiti, we can identify a number of differentially weighted, synergistic forces that promote HIV transmission.

Population Pressures

Haiti, which covers 27,700 square kilometers, is one of the most crowded societies in the hemisphere. In 1980, only 8,000 square kilometers were under cultivation, giving an effective population density of 626 persons per square kilometer. Unfortunately, Haiti's topsoil is now prey to runaway forces that further compound the overcrowding: "The land suffers from deforestation, soil erosion and exhaustion; the country is periodically ravaged by hurricanes which cause enormous damage."[10] As the land becomes increasingly exhausted, more and more peasants abandon agriculture for the lure of wage-labor in cities and towns.

Indeed, one of the most striking recent demographic changes has been the rapid growth of Port-au-Prince. More than 20 percent of the Haitian population now lives in the capital, a city of over 1.5 million. Although this concentration is not impressive by Caribbean standards (more than 30 percent of Puerto Ricans live in San Juan), the rate of growth in Port-au-Prince has been striking: "The urban population was

12.2% of the total in 1950, 20.4% in 1971 and an estimated 27.5% in 1980."[11] Haitian demographers estimate that by the year 2000 urban dwellers will constitute 37 percent of the total population.

As is the case with so many Third World countries, internal migration has played the most significant role in the growth of the capital. Locher estimates that "between 1950 and 1971 rural-urban migration accounted for 59% of Haitian urban growth, while natural population increase accounted for only 8%."[12] Neptune-Anglade has observed that the growth of Port-au-Prince is substantially the result of a "feminine rural exodus," leaving the city approximately 60 percent female.[13] Younger women of rural origin—women like Anita and Acéphie—are most commonly employed as servants.[14] Migrants of both sexes maintain strong ties with their regions of origin. In these respects, the three index cases of AIDS from Do Kay are illustrative of the trends documented by demographers and others who speak of Port-au-Prince as "a city of peasants."

Economic Pressures

Rural Haiti, always poor, has become palpably poorer in recent decades. A per capita annual income of $315 in 1983 masked the fact that income hovered around $100 in the countryside; in the late 1990s the average annual per capita income is down to around $175.[15] Accompanying the population growth and a loss of arable land to erosion and alkalinization has been an inevitable growth in landlessness. All of these factors have inevitably had a devastating effect on agricultural production. For example, Girault typifies the decade preceding 1984 as marked chiefly "by the slowdown of agricultural production and by a decrease in productivity."[16]

This decline has been further compounded by striking rural-urban disparities in every imaginable type of goods and service. In 1984, Girault was able to complain that "Port-au-Prince with 17–18% of the national population consumes as much as 30% of all the food produced in the country and a larger share of imported food."[17] Government statistics reveal that the "Port-au-Prince agglomeration" consumed 93 percent of all electricity produced in the country in 1979. As Trouillot notes, the city "houses 20% of the national population, but consumes 80% of all State expenditures."[18]

In short, current economic conditions push people out of the countryside and into the city or, often enough, out of the country altogether. The Haitian people have long since left behind a peasant standard of living (which did not necessarily mean an exceptionally low one). Whereas Haiti was once a nation with an extremely high percentage of landholders, late-twentieth-century Haiti is increasingly a country of unemployed and landless paupers. When the Population Crisis Committee published its "international index of human suffering" in 1992, based on a variety of measures of human welfare, Haiti had the dubious distinction of heading the list of all countries in this hemisphere. Of the 141 countries studied, only three were deemed to have living conditions worse than those in Haiti—and all three of these countries were at the time being consumed by civil war.[19]

Patterns of Sexual Union

In the numerous studies of conjugal unions in rural Haiti, most have underlined the classic division between couples who are *marye* (joined by civil or religious marriage) and those who are *plase* (joined in a conjugal union that incurs significant and enduring obligations to both partners). *Plasaj* (from French, *plaçage*) has generally been the most common form of conjugal union in rural Haiti, outnumbering marriages by two or three to one.

Early studies usually considered *plasaj* to be polygamous, with one man having more than one *plase* partner. This is often no longer the case, as Moral suggested over three decades ago: "It is 'plaçage honnête'—that is, monogamy—that best characterizes matrimonial status in today's rural society."[20] The reason for this shift toward monogamy, he believed, was the same one that leads many rural people to avoid marriage in the first place: formal unions are costly. "If the considerable growth of *plaçage* is to be explained in part by economic factors," continued Moral, "the form that *plaçage* now takes is greatly influenced by the poverty spreading throughout the countryside."

Allman's review suggests that contemporary sexual unions are considerably more complex than the bipolar model just described. In a survey in which women who had sexual relations with the same partner for a minimum of three months were considered to be "in union," interviews revealed an emic typology with five major categories: three of these—*rinmin*, *fiyanse*, and *viv avèk*—did not usually involve cohabitation and engendered only slight economic support; two others—*plase* and *marye*—were deemed much stronger unions, generally involving cohabitation as well as economic support.[21]

In addition, a number of other sexual practices have often been loosely termed "prostitution," in Haiti a largely urban phenomenon and much understudied.[22] It is clear, however, that unemployed women from rural areas may become involved in occasional and often clandestine sex work (variously described by terms such as *ti degaje, woulman*) when other options are exhausted. There are few avenues of escape for those caught in the web of urban migration, greater than 60 percent unemployment, and extreme poverty.[23]

How are these forms of sexual union related to the dynamics of HIV transmission? To those working in rural clinics, *plasaj* is often implicated in the spread or persistence of sexually transmitted diseases such as gonorrhea and chlamydial disease. Treatment of one or two members of a network is of course inadequate, as even women who have but one sexual partner are indirectly in regular sexual contact with any other *plase* partners of their mate. Regarding HIV, polygamous *plasaj* may be considered a preexisting sociocultural institution that serves to speed the spread of HIV and that constitutes a risk in and of itself, particularly for monogamous women. Women throughout the world bear similar risks—which are compounded wherever gender inequality erodes women's power over condom use.

The unremitting immiseration of Haiti has clearly undermined stable patterns of union such as marriage and *plasaj* by creating economic pressures to which women with dependents are particularly vulnerable. In the wake of these pressures, new patterns have emerged: "serial monogamy" might describe the monogamous but weak unions that lead to one child but last little longer than a year or two. After such unions have dissolved, the woman finds herself with a new dependent and even more in need of a reliable partner.

Equally dangerous, as we have seen, is the quest for a union with a financially "secure" partner. In rural Haiti, men of this description once included a substantial fraction of all peasant landholders. In recent decades, however, financial security has become elusive for all but a handful of truck drivers, representatives of the state (such as soldiers and petty officials), and landholders (*grandòn*). As noted, truck drivers and soldiers are clearly groups with above average rates of HIV infection.

Gender Inequality

"The ability of young women to protect themselves from [HIV] infection becomes a direct function of power relations between men and women."[24] Gender inequality has weakened women's ability to negotiate safe sexual encounters, and this sapping of agency is especially amplified by poverty. The Haitian economy counts a higher proportion of economically active women—most of them traders—than any other developing society, with the exception of Lesotho.[25] It is not surprising, then, that the *machismo* that has so marked other Latin American societies is less pronounced in Haiti.[26] (Even the head of the Duvaliers' dreaded paramilitary force was a woman.) But gender inequality is certainly a force in political, economic, and domestic life. It would be difficult to argue with Neptune-Anglade when she states that, in all regards, rural women "endure a discrimination and a pauperization that is worse than that affecting [rural] men."[27]

Preliminary ethnographic research in the Do Kay area suggests that many rural women do not wield sufficient authority to demand that *plase* partners (or husbands) use condoms. A growing literature documents similar patterns throughout the developing world and in the inner cities of the United States.[28] These considerations lead us to agree with those calling for preventive efforts that are "women-centered." "In societies where the female has a weaker hand," Desvarieux and Pape argue, "effective methods of prevention have a better chance of working if the woman does not have to rely on either the consent or the willingness of her partner."[29]

Other "Cultural" Considerations

Practices such as the widespread and unregulated use of syringes by "folk" practitioners unschooled in aseptic techniques received a fair amount of attention as possible sources of HIV transmission. But far more frequently invoked were "voodoo practices," which played a peculiarly central role in early speculations about the nature of the AIDS epidemic. These speculations, which sparked waves of anti-Haitian sentiment, had the added disadvantage of being incorrect; none of these leads, when investigated, panned out. In urban Haiti, GHESKIO did not even consider these hypotheses worthy of serious investigation.

In our small-scale but in-depth study of AIDS in the Central Plateau, we did not find any strong implication of nonsexual transmission of HIV.[30] Similarly, the Collaborative Study Group of AIDS in Haitain-Americans initiated the first and (so far) only controlled study of risk factors for AIDS among Haitians living in the United States. Compiling data from several North American research centers, the investigators reached the following conclusion: "Folklore rituals have been suggested as potential risk factors for [HIV] transmission in Haiti. Our data do not support this hypothesis."[31] Such hypotheses reflect less an accurate reading of existing data and more a series of North American folk theories about Haitians.[32]

There have been few ethnographic studies of Haitian understandings of AIDS, and most of these have been conducted in Montreal, New York, or Miami. To

my knowledge, the only such study conducted in rural Haiti demonstrated that such understandings were in fact changing, at first quite rapidly. Over time, however, a stable illness representation of *sida*—as AIDS is termed—seemed to evolve.[33]

In the Do Kay region, serial interviews with the same group of villagers permitted us to delineate a complex model of illness causation, one linked fairly closely to understandings of tuberculosis. Villagers often, but not always, cited sorcery in discussions about *sida*, which nonetheless came to be seen as a fatal illness that could be transmitted by sexual contact. Local understandings of *sida* did not seem to affect disease distribution, but certainly they may hamper preventive efforts if not taken into account when designing interventions. Far more disabling, however, has been the nation's political situation.

Political Disruption

It is unfortunate indeed that HIV arrived in Haiti shortly before a period of massive and prolonged social upheaval. Political unrest has clearly undermined preventive efforts and may have helped, through other mechanisms, to spread HIV. Although many commentators observed that political struggles served to divert the public's interest away from AIDS, this was not the case in the Do Kay region. In fact, periods of increased strife were associated with increased public discourse about the new sickness.

But the same political disruptions that may have stimulated commentary about AIDS also served to paralyze coordinated efforts to prevent HIV transmission. For example, although the Haitian Ministry of Health has identified AIDS prevention as one of its top priorities, the office charged with coordinating preventive efforts has been hamstrung by six coups d'état, which have led, inevitably, to personnel changes—and to more significant disruptions. At the time GESCAP was founded, in 1991, *there had been no comprehensive effort to prevent HIV transmission in rural Haiti.* Even in Port-au-Prince, what has been accomplished thus far has often been marred by messages that are either culturally inappropriate or designed for a small fraction of the population (for example, Haitians who are francophone, literate, and television-owning). These messages are especially unsuccessful in rural areas, where even well-funded "social marketing" schemes have had little cultural currency.

A sense of hopefulness, rare in Haiti, returned to the public health community in 1991, when the country's first democratic elections brought to office a social-justice government headed by a progressive priest. A new Ministry of Health promised to make AIDS, tuberculosis, and other infectious pathogens its top priority. But in September of that year, a violent military coup brought a swift end to Haiti's democratic experiment. The impact on the population's health was incalculable.[34]

Political upheaval did not simply hobble coordinated responses to the AIDS epidemic. It has had far more direct effects. One of the most epidemiologically significant events of recent years may prove to be the coup d'état of September 1991. As noted earlier, surveys of asymptomatic adults living in Cité Soleil revealed seroprevalence rates of approximately 10 percent, whereas surveys of asymptomatic rural people were likely to find rates an order of magnitude lower. Following the coup, the army targeted urban slums for brutal repression. A number of journalists and health care professionals estimated that fully half of the adult residents of Cité Soleil fled to rural areas following the army's lethal incursions. It takes little imagination to see that such flux substantially changes the equations describing the dynamics of HIV transmission in rural areas sheltering the refugees.[35] Similar patterns have been noted elsewhere, particularly in sub-Saharan Africa:

> Women living in areas plagued by civil unrest or war may be in a situation of higher risk. In many countries, relatively high percentages of male military and police personnel are infected and their unprotected (voluntary or forced) sexual encounters with local women provide an avenue for transmission. Patterns of female infection have been correlated with the movements of members of the military in parts of Central and Eastern Africa.[36]

Concurrent Disease

The progression of HIV disease depends on host variables such as age, sex, and nutritional status; viral load, CD_4-cell number and function; and concurrent disease. Concurrent illness can alter this progression in at least three ways: first, any serious illness, including opportunistic infections (most notably, tuberculosis), may hasten the progression of HIV disease; second, various diseases can heighten an individual's "net state of immunosuppression," rendering him or her increasingly vulnerable to infection; and, third, certain infections seem to increase the risk of *acquiring* HIV—the point considered here.

Sexually transmitted diseases have been cited as AIDS co-factors in a number of studies, especially those conducted in tropical and subtropical regions.[37] Researchers view STDs as particularly important in the heterosexual spread of HIV, as the virus is less efficiently transmitted from women to men than vice versa. Thus vaginal and cervical diseases—even those as

ostensibly minor as trichomoniasis—may increase the risk of HIV transmission through "microwounds" and even through mere inflammation (as certain lymphocytes are, after all, the target cells of HIV).[38]

Although researchers are now collecting important data about STDs in Port-au-Prince,[39] few studies have focused on rural areas.[40] But there is no evidence to suggest that villagers are more sexually active than their urban counterparts; there is even less evidence to suggest that rural Haitians are more sexually active than age-matched controls from North America. What is evident is that a majority of STDs go untreated—which certainly implies that sores, other lesions, and inflammation will persist far longer in rural Haiti than in most areas of the world.

Other diseases—including leprosy, yaws, endemic syphilis, and various viruses—have been suggested as possible co-factors in "tropical" AIDS, but their roles have not been clarified. It seems safe to add, however, that serious co-infections do enhance the net state of immunosuppression. Similarly, malnutrition clearly hastens the advent of advanced, symptomatic disease among the HIV-infected, although this dynamic may lessen the risk of transmission: the Haitian variant of "slim disease" is now popularly associated with AIDS, and visible cachexia is likely to drive away potential sexual partners.[41]

Access to Medical Services

Finally, in seeking to understand the Haitian AIDS epidemic, it is necessary to underline the contribution, or lack thereof, of a nonfunctioning public health system. Medical care in Haiti is something of an obstacle course, one that places innumerable barriers before poor people seeking care. Failure to have an STD treated leads to persistence of important co-factors for HIV infection; failure to treat active tuberculosis causes rapid progression of HIV disease and death—to say nothing of its impact on HIV-negative individuals, for HIV-infected patients with tuberculosis have been shown to be efficient transmitters of tuberculosis.[42] Contaminated blood transfusions alternate with no transfusions at all. Condoms are often not available even to those who want them. The cost of pharmaceuticals, always prohibitive, has skyrocketed in recent years. Antivirals are in essence unavailable to most Haitians: in February 1990, "local radio stations announced . . . that for the first time, the drug AZT is available in Haiti. It might as well have been on Mars. A bottle of 100 capsules costs $343—more than most Haitians make in a year."[43] Since that time, it has become possible to find newer, highly active antiretroviral agents in Haiti—but for a prince's ransom.

AIDS, ANALYSIS, ACCOUNTABILITY

Identifying and weighting the various social forces that shape the HIV epidemic is a perennial problem, but one too rarely addressed by medical anthropology, which is often asked to elucidate the "cultural component" of particular subepidemics. By combining social analysis with ethnographically informed epidemiology, however, we can identify the most significant of these forces. The factors listed here are differentially weighted, of course, but each demonstrably plays a role in determining HIV transmission in rural Haiti:

1. Deepening poverty
2. Gender inequality
3. Political upheaval
4. Traditional patterns of sexual union
5. Emerging patterns of sexual union
6. Prevalence of and lack of access to treatment for STDs
7. Lack of timely response by public health authorities
8. Lack of culturally appropriate prevention tools

Many of these factors are a far cry from the ones that anthropologists were exhorted to explore—for example, ritual scarification, animal sacrifice, sexual behavior in "exotic subcultures"—during the first decade of AIDS. But the forces underpinning the spread of HIV to rural Haiti are as economic and political as they are cultural, and poverty and inequality seem to underlie all of them. Although many working elsewhere would agree that poverty and social inequalities are the strongest enhancers of risk for exposure to HIV, international conferences on AIDS have repeatedly neglected this subject. Of the hundreds of epidemiology-track posters presented in 1992 in Amsterdam, for example, only three used "poverty" as a keyword; two of these were socioculturally naïve and did not seem to involve the collaboration of anthropologists.

What were anthropologists doing in the early years of AIDS? The mid to late 1980s saw the formation of task forces and research groups as well as an increasing number of AIDS-related sessions at our professional meetings. The central themes of many of the early sessions focused on the "special understanding of sexuality" that was, suggested certain speakers, the province of anthropologists. The scenario most commonly evoked was one in which ethnographers, steeped in local lore after years of participant-observation, afforded epidemiologists and public health authorities detailed information about sexual behavior, childbearing, and beliefs about blood and blood contact. This knowledge transfer was deemed indispensable to determining which "behaviors" put individuals and communities at risk for HIV infection.

Fifteen years into the AIDS pandemic, after at least a decade of social science studies of AIDS, we must ask, How substantial were these claims? How many secret, AIDS-related "behaviors" have we unearthed in the course of our ethnography? Anthropologists deeply involved in AIDS prevention now know that many such claims were immodest. Everywhere, it seems, HIV spreads from host to host through a relatively restricted set of mechanisms. We've also learned that preventive efforts, even the most culturally appropriate ones, are least effective in precisely those settings in which they are most urgently needed. Africa, long a favored proving ground for anthropology, offers the most obvious and humbling example. Haiti offers another.

In the interest of enhancing the efficacy of interventions, it's important to pause and take stock of the situation. How might anthropology best contribute to efforts to prevent HIV transmission or to alleviate AIDS-related suffering? One major contribution would be to help show where the pandemic is going, which leads us back to analytic challenges such as these:

Identifying and differentially weighting the major factors promoting or retarding HIV transmission

Linking the sexual choices made by individual actors to the various shifting conditions that restrict choice, especially among the poor

Understanding the contribution of the culturally specific—not only local sexualities but also kinship structures and shifting representations of disease—without losing sight of the large-scale economic forces shaping the AIDS pandemic

Investigating the precise mechanisms by which such forces as racism, gender inequality, poverty, war, migration, colonial heritage, coups d'état, and even structural-adjustment programs become embodied as increased risk

Anthropology, the most radically contextualizing of the social sciences, is well suited to meeting these analytic challenges, but we will not succeed by merely "filling in the cultural blanks" left by epidemiologists, physicians, scientists, and policy makers. Nor will we succeed without a new vigilance toward the analytic traps that have hobbled our understanding of the AIDS pandemic.[44]

First, we often find widespread, if sectarian, ascription to behaviorist, cognitivist, or culturalist reductionism. Just as many physicians regard social considerations as outside the realm of the central, so too have psychologists tended to reify individual psychology, while economists have reified the economic.

Anthropologists writing of AIDS have of course tended to reify culture. We must avoid confusing our own desire for personal efficacy with sound analytic purchase on an ever-growing pandemic: HIV cares little for our theoretical stances or our disciplinary training. AIDS demands broad biosocial approaches. Jean Benoist and Alice Desclaux put it well:

> The conditions limiting or promoting transmission, illness representations, therapeutic itineraries, and health care practices—none of these subjects are captured by disciplinary approaches. They evade even the distinction between biology and social sciences, so tightly are biological realities tied to behaviors and representations, revealing links that have not yet been fully explored.[45]

Second, much anthropologic analysis focuses overmuch (or exclusively) on local factors and local actors, which risks exaggerating the agency of the poor and marginalized. Constraints on the agency of individual actors should be brought into stark relief so that prevention efforts do not come to grief, as they have to date. To explore the relation between personal agency and supraindividual structures—once the central problematic of social theory—we need to link our ethnography to systemic analyses that are informed by history, political economy, and a critical epidemiology. It is not possible to explain the strikingly patterned distribution of HIV by referring exclusively to attitude, cognition, or affect. Fine-grained psychological portraits and rich ethnography are never more than part of the AIDS story.

Third, the myths and mystifications that surround AIDS and slow AIDS research often serve powerful interests. If, in Haiti and in parts of Africa, economic policies (for example, structural-adjustment programs) and political upheaval are somehow related to HIV transmission, who benefits when attention is focused largely or solely on "unruly sexuality" or alleged "promiscuity"? The lasting influence of myths and immodest claims has helped to mask the effects of social inequalities on the distribution of HIV and on AIDS outcomes.

The recent advent of more effective antiviral therapy could have an enormous impact on what it means to have AIDS at the close of the twentieth century—if you don't happen to live in Africa or Haiti or Harlem. Protease inhibitors and other drugs raise the possibility of transforming AIDS into a chronic condition to be managed over decades, but they also remind us that there are two emerging syndromes: an AIDS of the North, and an AIDS of the South.

Perhaps this does not sound much like an anthropologist speaking. Why talk of latitude (North/South) and class (rich/poor) before speaking of culture? One answer to this question is that, for many of us, the view that AIDS is a culturally constructed phenomenon is not open to debate. AIDS, like sexuality, is inevitably embedded in local social context; representations and responses must necessarily vary along cultural lines. The contribution of cultural factors to the lived experience of AIDS is and will remain enormous. Indeed, the true and vast variation of HIV lies not, as we had been led to believe, in its modes of spread, nor is it found in the mechanisms by which the virus saps the host. The variation of HIV lies, rather, in its highly patterned distribution, in its variable clinical course among the infected, and in the ways in which we respond, socially, to a deadly pathogen.

NOTES

1. In their consideration of unequal exchange and the urban informal sector, Portes and Walton (1982, p. 74) designate Haiti as the most rural of all Latin American nations: in 1950, the nation was described as 88 percent rural; in 1960, 85 percent; in 1970, 81 percent.

2. Pape and Johnson 1988.

3. See Allman 1980 and Vieux 1989 for extended discussions of *plasaj*.

4. See Pape and Johnson 1988.

5. Desvarieux and Pape 1991, p. 275.

6. GESCAP (whose name is translated as "Study Group on AIDS in the Peasant Class") was founded with the generous support of the World AIDS Foundation.

7. Given that the staff of the clinic and of Proje Veye Sante are accountable to the communities served rather than to funding organizations or to research institutions, and given the poverty and non-HIV-related sickness in the region, it is not surprising that research as such is not seen as a high priority. In order to meet our obligations to the community, all serologic studies became part of a *dossier préventif*. This instrument included a series of laboratory examinations (such as hematocrit and RPR), a chest radiograph, and a physical examination. Any abnormal findings were to be pursued aggressively; free dental care was also offered as part of the program. This proposal was presented to members of the community in four different public meetings, engendering considerable enthusiasm for the undertaking.

8. One additional young woman, the regular sexual partner of a truck driver, was also found to be seropositive. She died suddenly during the course of the study, however, less than a week after a negative physical examination. Although the cause of death is unclear—she had explosive, watery diarrhea and presented in shock—she is not considered in this cohort.

9. Farmer 1992, p. 262.

10. Feilden, Allman, Montague, and Rohde 1981, p. 6.

11. Ibid., p. 4.

12. Locher 1984, p. 329.

13. Neptune-Anglade 1986, p. 150.

14. "Note that, in the cities, the [economically] active 10–14-year-old girls are essentially all domestics. . . . These 'restaveks' find themselves at the very bottom of the social hierarchy" (ibid., p. 209). My translation.

15. See Farmer 1988b for a review of data concerning the Haitian economy. In a personal communication on 18 September 1998, a desk officer at the US State Department's Haiti desk offered an annual per capita income estimate of $175 (not adjusted for Purchasing Power Parity); she cited internal IMF memos from April 1998 as her source.

16. Girault 1984, p. 177.

17. Ibid., p. 178. For a critical perspective on more recent "food security" issues, see Woodson 1997.

18. Trouillot 1986, p. 201. My translation.

19. Population Crisis Committee 1992.

20. Moral 1961, p. 173. My translation.

21. Allman 1980.

22. But see Laguerre 1982.

23. This is a cursory discussion of a very complex—and changing—subject. For a more complete discussion of sexual unions in Haiti, see Lowenthal 1984, Murray 1976, Neptune-Anglade 1986, Sylvain-Comhaire 1974, and Vieux 1989.

24. United Nations Development Program 1992, p. 6.

25. See Mintz 1964, Neptune-Anglade 1986, and Nicholls 1985.

26. See Murray 1986.

27. Neptune-Anglade 1986, p. 155. My translation.

28. Maria de Bruyn offers a helpful review of these issues as they affect women in developing countries. She writes: "Even if they dare suggest avoiding risky sexual acts or using condoms, they often encounter male refusal, are accused of adultery or promiscuity (the desire to use condoms being interpreted as evidence of extramarital affairs), are suspected of already being infected with HIV or are said to accuse their partners of infidelity" (1992, p. 256). The mechanisms by which gender inequality conspires with poverty to enhance women's risk for HIV are the subject of Farmer, Connors, and Simmons 1996.

29. Desvarieux and Pape 1991, p. 277.

30. Farmer 1992.

31. Collaborative Study Group of AIDS in Haitian-Americans 1987, p. 638.

32. On American "folk models" of Haitians, see Lawless 1992 and, as related to AIDS, Farmer 1992.

33. The word *"sida"* is derived from the French acronym SIDA, for *syndrome immunodéficience acquise*. The French acronym is commonly rendered as S.I.D.A., SIDA, or Sida; *sida* is the Creole orthography. I have adopted the latter here in order to reflect the substantial difference between the terms as used in different national and cultural settings.

34. See Farmer 1996a for a more complete discussion of "Haiti's lost years."

35. Farmer 1996a examines the effects of the 1991 coup d'état on rates of HIV diagnosis in the Kay region.

36. de Bruyn 1992, p. 253.

37. See, for example, Laga, Manoka, Kivuvu, et al. 1993.

38. Poor young women may be especially at risk of genital trauma: "Non-consensual, hurried or frequent intercourse may inhibit mucous production and the relaxation of vaginal musculature, both of which would increase the likelihood of genital trauma. A lack of control over the circumstances in which the intercourse occurs may increase the frequency of intercourse and lower the age at which sexual activity begins. A lack of access to acceptable health services may leave infections and lesions untreated. Malnutrition not only inhibits the production of mucus but also slows the healing process and depresses the immune system" (United Nations Development Program 1992, pp. 3–4).

39. For example, see Liautaud et al. 1992; Deschamps, Pape, Williams-Russo, Madhavan, Ho, and Johnson, 1993; and Behets, Desormeaux, Joseph, et al. 1995.

40. We do know that in one study of one hundred women presenting to our women's health clinic in 1991 fully 25 percent had trichomoniasis. GESCAP thanks Dr. Anna Contomitros for conducting this study, which included Pap smears. See also Fitzgerald 1996.

41. Data from GHESKIO (e.g., Deschamps et al. 1992) suggest, however, that those ill with HIV disease continue to have sex.

42. DiPerri, Cade, Castelli, et al. 1993.

43. Lief 1990, p. 36.

44. For a review of recent anthropological writings on AIDS, see Farmer 1997b.

45. Benoist and Desclaux 1995, p. 363. My translation.

REFERENCES

Allman, J. 1980. "Sexual Unions in Rural Haiti." *International Journal of Sociology of the Family* 10:15–39.

Behets, F. M. T., J. Desormeaux, D. Joseph, et al. 1995. "Control of Sexually Transmitted Diseases in Haiti: Results and Implications of a Baseline Study Among Pregnant Women Living in Cité Soleil Shantytowns." *Journal of Infectious Diseases* 172 (3): 764–71.

Benoist, J., and A. Desclaux, eds. 1995. *Sida et Anthropologie: Bilan et Perspectives*. Paris: Karthala.

Collaborative Study Group of AIDS in Haitian-Americans. 1987. "Risk Factors for AIDS Among Haitians Residing in the United States: Evidence of Heterosexual Transmission." *Journal of the American Medical Association* 257 (5): 635–39.

de Bruyn, M. 1992. "Women and AIDS in Developing Countries." *Social Science and Medicine* 34 (3): 249–62.

Deschamps, M. M., et al. 1992. "HIV Seroconversion Related to Heterosexual Activity in Discordant Haitian Couples." Poster presented at the Eighth International Conference on AIDS/Third STD World Congress, 19–24 July, Amsterdam. Abstract C1087.

Deschamps, M. M., J. W. Pape, P. Williams-Russo, S. Madhavan, J. Ho, and W. Johnson. 1993. "A Prospective Study of HIV-Seropositive Asymptomatic Women of Childbearing Age in a Developing Country." *Journal of Acquired Immune Deficiency Syndromes* 6 (5): 446–51.

Desvarieux, M., and J. W. Pape. 1991. "HIV and AIDS in Haiti: Recent Developments." *AIDS Care* 3 (3): 271–79.

DiPerri, G., G. P. Cade, F. Castelli, et al. 1993. "Transmission of HIV-Associated Tuberculosis to Health Care Workers." *Infection Control and Hospital Epidemiology* 14:67–72.

———. 1988b. "Blood, Sweat, and Baseballs: Haiti in the West Atlantic System." *Dialectical Anthropology* 13:83–99.

———. 1992. *AIDS and Accusation: Haiti and the Geography of Blame.* Berkeley: University of California Press.

———. 1996a. "Haiti's Lost Years: Lessons for the Americas." *Current Issues in Public Health* 2:143–51.

———. 1997b. "Ethnography, Social Analysis, and the Prevention of Sexually Transmitted HIV Infections Among Poor Women in Haiti." In *The Anthropology of Infectious Disease,* edited by M. Inhorn and P. Brown, pp. 413–38. New York: Gordon and Breach.

Feilden, R., J. Allman, J. Montague, and J. Rohde. 1981. *Health, Population, and Nutrition in Haiti: A Report Prepared for the World Bank.* Boston: Management Sciences for Health.

Fitzgerald, D. 1996. *Final Report HAS: Project 2005.* Boston: Management Sciences for Health.

Girault, C. 1984. "Commerce in the Haitian Economy." In *Haiti—Today and Tomorrow: An Interdisciplinary Study,* edited by C. Foster and A. Valdman, pp. 173–79. Lanham, Md.: University Press of America.

Laga, M., A. Manoka, M. Kivuvu, et al. 1993. "Non-Ulcerative Sexually Transmitted Diseases as Risk Factors for HIV-1 Transmission in Women: Results from a Cohort Study." *AIDS* 7 (1): 95–102.

Laguerre, M. 1982. *Urban Life in the Caribbean.* Cambridge, Mass.: Schenkman.

Lawless, R. 1992. *Haiti's Bad Press.* Rochester, Vt.: Schenkman Books.

Liautaud, B., et al. 1992. "Preliminary Data on STDs in Haiti." Poster presented at the Eighth *International Conference on AIDS/Third STD World Congress,* 19–24 July, Amsterdam. Abstract C4302.

Lief, L. 1990. "Where Democracy Isn't About to Break Out." *U. S. News and World Report,* 12 February, pp. 34–36.

Locher, U. 1984. "Migration in Haiti." In *Haiti—Today and Tomorrow: An Interdisciplinary Study,* edited by C. Foster and A. Valdman, pp. 325–36. Lanham, Md.: University Press of America.

Lowenthal, I. 1984. "Labor, Sexuality, and the Conjugal Contract in Rural Haiti." In *Haiti—Today and Tomorrow: An Interdisciplinary Study,* edited by C. Foster and A. Valdman, pp. 15–33. Lanham, Md.: University Press of America.

Mintz, S. W. 1964. "The Employment of Capital by Market Women in Haiti." In *Capital, Saving, and Credit in Peasant Societies,* edited by R. Firth and B. Yamey, pp. 56–78. Chicago: Aldine.

Moral, P. 1961. *Le Paysan Haïtien.* Port-au-Prince: Les Éditions Fardins.

Murray, G. 1976. "Women in Perdition: Ritual Fertility Control in Haiti." In *Culture, Natality, and Family Planning,* edited by J. Marshall and S. Polgar, pp. 59–78. Chapel Hill: Carolina Population Center, University of North Carolina.

Neptune-Anglade, M. 1986. *"L'Autre Moitié du Développement: A Propos du Travail des Femmes en Haïti."* Pétion-Ville, Haïti: Éditions des Alizés.

Nicholls, D. 1985. *Haiti in Caribbean Context: Ethnicity, Economy, and Revolt.* New York:

Pape, J. W., and W. Johnson. 1988. "Epidemiology of AIDS in the Caribbean." *Baillière's Clinical Tropical Medicine and Communicable Diseases* 3 (1): 31–42.

Portes, A., and J. Walton. 1982. *Labor, Class, and the International System.* New York: Academic Press.

Trouillot, M. R. 1986. *Les Racines Historiques de l'État Duvaliérien.* Port-au-Prince: Imprimerie Henri Deschamps.

United Nations Development Program. 1992. *Young Women: Silence, Susceptibility, and the HIV Epidemic.* New York: UNDP.

Vieux, S. 1989. *Le Plaçage: Droit Coutumier et Famille en Haïti.* Paris: Éditions Publisud.

Woodson, D. 1997. *"Lamanjay, Food Security, Sécurité Alimentaire."* Culture and agriculture 19 (3): 108–22.

33

The Viral Superhighway

George Armelagos

Anthropologists look at human health through the wide-angled lens of our species's long evolutionary history, our biology in a world of microorganisms, and the remarkable medical achievements of our culture. Anthropologists try to see the "big picture."

As recently as the 1970s, epidemiologists—scientists who study the spread of disease—were publicly saying that the age of infectious disease was a thing of the past. At that time, it appeared that the world's major killers, including polio, smallpox, and tuberculosis, were under control—or at least that biomedical science had developed the methods to get them under control. But that has not been the case. Recent decades have seen the emergence of a growing list of new infectious diseases (like HIV/AIDS and SARS) as well as the resurgence of old diseases (like tuberculosis and malaria).

This selection, written by a leading biological anthropologist, shows how pathogenic microorganisms evolve along with humans (and other species) in conjunction with major shifts in patterns of human residence, technological development, and travel. The author identifies three major shifts in the overall pattern of human disease, or "epidemiological transitions," and links them with three major episodes in human prehistory and history.

The first shift involved the domestication of plants and animals that made humans change from nomadic hunting and gathering to sedentary agricultural patterns of residence. The second epidemiological transition was associated with the improvements in nutrition, hygiene, and medicine that accompanied the Industrial Revolution in the nineteenth century and has been characterized by the decline of infectious disease and an increase in chronic disease in the developed world. This second transition has primarily happened in rich countries. The third epidemiological transition, taking place as we speak, is the result of contemporary patterns of globalization, ranging from global warming and other forms of environmental degradation to new patterns of global travel and commerce.

Another major contributor to this third shift is the emergence of drug-resistant strains of common diseases. As the selection illustrates, the pathogens that cause infectious disease, like all other living organisms, are constantly evolving and adapting to new environments. This new development—drug-resistant strains of common microbes—is one of the most frightening possibilities humans now face. However, contemporary human societies can take concrete steps to counter the threats posed by the "viral superhighway." Taking those steps, however, will require concerted effort by political leaders, public health experts, and by all of us.

As you read this selection, ask yourself the following questions:

- How is population health influenced by culture?
- What is an "epidemiological transition"?
- The author describes not one but three epidemiological transitions over the course of human history. When did each of these transitions occur in Europe and the United States, and how can each be explained?
- How is globalization involved in the increasingly rapid spread of infectious disease?
- What steps can we take to protect ourselves, and future generations, against the dangers posed by the widening "viral superhighway"?

The following terms discussed in this selection are included in the Glossary at the back of the book:

"diseases of civilization"   pathogen
epidemiologic transition

229

So the Lord sent a pestilence upon Israel from the morning until the appointed time; and there died of the people from Dan to Beer-sheba seventy thousand men.

—2 Sam. 24:15

Swarms of crop-destroying locusts, rivers fouled with blood, lion-headed horses breathing fire and sulfur: the Bible presents a lurid assortment of plagues, described as acts of retribution by a vengeful God. Indeed, real-life epidemics—such as the influenza outbreak of 1918, which killed 21 million people in a matter of months—can be so sudden and deadly that it is easy, even for nonbelievers, to view them as angry messages from the beyond.

How reassuring it was, then, when the march of technology began to give people some control over the scourges of the past. In the 1950s the Salk vaccine, and later, the Sabin vaccine, dramatically reduced the incidence of polio. And by 1980 a determined effort by health workers worldwide eradicated smallpox, a disease that had afflicted humankind since earliest times with blindness, disfigurement and death, killing nearly 300 million people in the twentieth century alone.

But those optimistic years in the second half of our century now seem, with hindsight, to have been an era of inflated expectations, even arrogance. In 1967 the surgeon general of the United States, William H. Stewart, announced that victory over infectious diseases was imminent—a victory that would close the book on modern plagues. Sadly, we now know differently. Not only have deadly and previously unimagined new illnesses such as AIDS and Legionnaires' disease emerged in recent years, but historical diseases that just a few decades ago seemed to have been tamed are returning in virulent, drug-resistant varieties. Tuberculosis, the ancient lung disease that haunted nineteenth-century Europe, afflicting, among others, Chopin, Dostoyevski and Keats, is aggressively mutating into strains that defy the standard medicines; as a result, modern TB victims must undergo a daily drug regimen so elaborate that health-department workers often have to personally monitor patients to make sure they comply [see "A Plague Returns," by Mark Earnest and John A. Sbarbaro, September/October 1993]. Meanwhile, bacteria and viruses in foods from chicken to strawberries to alfalfa sprouts are sickening as many as 80 million Americans each year.

And those are only symptoms of a much more general threat. Deaths from infectious diseases in the United States rose 58 percent between 1980 and 1992. Twenty-nine new diseases have been reported in the past twenty-five years, a few of them so bloodcurdling

and bizarre that descriptions of them bring to mind tacky horror movies. Ebola virus, for instance, can in just a few days reduce a healthy person to a bag of teeming flesh spilling blood and organ parts from every orifice. Creutzfeldt-Jakob disease, which killed the choreographer George Balanchine in 1983, eats away at its victims' brains until they resemble wet sponges. Never slow to fan mass hysteria, Hollywood has capitalized on the phenomenon with films such as *Outbreak*, in which a monkey carrying a deadly new virus from central Africa infects unwitting Californians and starts an epidemic that threatens to annihilate the human race.

The reality about infectious disease is less sensational but alarming nonetheless. Gruesome new pathogens such as Ebola are unlikely to cause a widespread epidemic because they sicken and kill so quickly that victims can be easily identified and isolated; on the other hand, the seemingly innocuous practice of overprescribing antibiotics for bad colds could ultimately lead to untold deaths, as familiar germs evolve to become untreatable. We are living in the twilight of the antibiotic era: within our lifetimes, scraped knees and cut fingers may return to the realm of fatal conditions.

Through international travel, global commerce and the accelerating destruction of ecosystems worldwide, people are inadvertently exposing themselves to a Pandora's box of emerging microbial threats. And recent rumblings about biological terrorism have highlighted the appalling potential of disease organisms for being manipulated to vile ends. But although it may appear that the apocalypse has arrived, the truth is that people today are not facing a unique predicament. Emerging diseases have long loomed like a shadow over the human race.

People and pathogens have a long history together. Infections have been detected in the bones of human ancestors more than a million years old, and evidence from the mummy of the Egyptian pharaoh Ramses V suggests that he may have died from smallpox more than 3,000 years ago. Widespread outbreaks of disease are also well documented. Between 1347 and 1351 roughly a third of the population of medieval Europe was wiped out by bubonic plague, which is carried by fleas that live on rodents. In 1793, 10 percent of the population of Philadelphia succumbed to yellow fever, which is spread by mosquitoes. And in 1875 the son of a Fiji chief came down with measles after a ceremonial trip to Australia. Within four months more than 20,000 Fijians were dead from the imported disease, which spreads through the air when its victims cough or sneeze.

According to conventional wisdom in biology, people and invading microorganisms evolve together: people gradually become more resistant, and the microorganisms become less virulent. The result is either mutualism, in which the relation benefits both species, or commensalism, in which one species benefits without

This article is reprinted by permission of the New York Academy of Sciences and is from *The Sciences*, January/February 1998 issue.

harming the other. Chicken pox and measles, once fatal afflictions, now exist in more benign forms. Logic would suggest, after all, that the best interests of an organism are not served if it kills its host; doing so would be like picking a fight with the person who signs your paycheck.

But recently it has become clear to epidemiologists that the reverse of that cooperative paradigm of illness can also be true: microorganisms and their hosts sometimes exhaust their energies devising increasingly powerful weaponry and defenses. For example, several variants of human immuno-deficiency virus (HIV) may compete for dominance within a person's body, placing the immune system under ever-greater siege. As long as a virus has an effective mechanism for jumping from one person to another, it can afford to kill its victims [see "The Deadliest Virus," by Cynthia Mills, January/February 1997].

If the competition were merely a question of size, humans would surely win: the average person is 10^{17} times the size of the average bacterium. But human beings, after all, constitute only one species, which must compete with 5,000 kinds of viruses and more than 300,000 species of bacteria. Moreover, in the twenty years it takes humans to produce a new generation, bacteria can reproduce a half-million times. That disparity enables pathogens to evolve ever more virulent adaptations that quickly outstrip human responses to them. The scenario is governed by what the English zoologist Richard Dawkins of the University of Oxford and a colleague have called the "Red Queen Principle." In Lewis Carroll's *Through the Looking Glass* the Red Queen tells Alice she will need to run faster and faster just to stay in the same place. Staving off illness can be equally elusive.

The Centers for Disease Control and Prevention (CDC) in Atlanta, Georgia, has compiled a list of the most recent emerging pathogens. They include:

- *Campylobacter*, a bacterium widely found in chickens because of the commercial practice of raising them in cramped, unhealthy conditions. It causes between two million and eight million cases of food poisoning a year in the United States and between 200 and 800 deaths.

- *Escherichia coli* 0157:H7, a dangerously mutated version of an often harmless bacterium. Hamburger meat from Jack in the Box fast-food restaurants that was contaminated with this bug led to the deaths of at least four people in 1993.

- Hantaviruses, a genus of fast-acting, lethal viruses, often carried by rodents, that kill by causing the capillaries to leak blood. A new hantavirus known as *sin nombre* (Spanish for "nameless") surfaced in 1993 in the southwestern United States, causing the sudden and mysterious deaths of thirty-two people.

- HIV, the deadly virus that causes AIDS (acquired immunodeficiency syndrome). Although it was first observed in people as recently as 1981, it has spread like wildfire and is now a global scourge, affecting more than 30 million people worldwide.

- The strange new infectious agent that causes bovine spongiform encephalopathy, or mad cow disease, which recently threw the British meat industry and consumers into a panic. This bizarre agent, known as a prion, or "proteinaceous infectious particle," is also responsible for Creutzfeldt-Jakob disease, the brain-eater I mentioned earlier. A Nobel Prize was awarded to the biochemist Stanley B. Prusiner of the University of California, San Francisco, for his discovery of the prion.

- *Legionella pneumophila*, the bacterium that causes Legionnaires' disease. The microorganism thrives in wet environments; when it lodges in air-conditioning systems or the mist machines in supermarket produce sections, it can be expelled into the air, reaching people's lungs. In 1976 thirty-four participants at an American Legion convention in Philadelphia died—the incident that led to the discovery and naming of the disease.

- *Borrelia burgdorferi*, the bacterium that causes Lyme disease. It is carried by ticks that live on deer and white-footed mice. Left untreated, it can cause crippling, chronic problems in the nerves, joints and internal organs.

How ironic, given such a rogues' gallery of nasty characters, that just a quarter-century ago the Egyptian demographer Abdel R. Omran could observe that in many modern industrial nations the major killers were no longer infectious diseases. Death, he noted, now came not from outside but rather from within the body, the result of gradual deterioration. Omran traced the change to the middle of the nineteenth century, when the industrial revolution took hold in the United States and parts of Europe. Thanks to better nutrition, improved public-health measures and medical advances such as mass immunization and the introduction of antibiotics, microorganisms were brought under control. As people began living longer, their aging bodies succumbed to "diseases of civilization": cancer, clogged arteries, diabetes, obesity and osteoporosis. Omran was the first to formally recognize that shift in the disease environment. He called it an "epidemiological transition."

Like other anthropologists of my generation, I learned of Omran's theory early in my career, and it soon became a basic tenet—a comforting one, too, implying as it did an end to the supremacy of microorganisms. Then, three years ago, I began working with the anthropologist Kathleen C. Barnes of Johns Hopkins University in Baltimore, Maryland, to formulate an expansion of Omran's ideas. It occurred to us that his epidemiological transition had not been a unique event. Throughout history human populations have undergone shifts in their relations with disease—shifts, we noted, that are always linked to major changes in the way people interact with the environment. Barnes and I, along with James Lin, a master's student at Johns Hopkins University School of Hygiene and Public Health, have since developed a new theory: that there have been not one but three major epidemiological transitions; that each one has been sparked by human activities; and that we are living through the third one right now.

The first epidemiological transition took place some 10,000 years ago, when people abandoned their nomadic existence and began farming. That profoundly new way of life disrupted ecosystems and created denser living conditions that led, as I will soon detail, to new diseases. The second epidemiological transition was the salutary one Omran singled out in 1971, when the war against infectious diseases seemed to have been won. And in the past two decades the emergence of illnesses such as hepatitis C, cat scratch disease (caused by the bacterium *Bartonella henselae*), Ebola and others on CDC's list has created a third epidemiological transition, a disheartening set of changes that in many ways have reversed the effects of the second transition and coincide with the shift to globalism. Burgeoning population growth and urbanization, widespread environmental degradation, including global warming and tropical deforestation, and radically improved methods of transportation have given rise to new ways of contracting and spreading disease.

We are, quite literally, making ourselves sick.

When early human ancestors moved from African forests onto the savanna millions of years ago, a few diseases came along for the ride. Those "heirloom" species—thus designated by the Australian parasitologist J.F.A. Sprent because they had afflicted earlier primates—included head and body lice; parasitic worms such as pinworms, tapeworms and liver flukes; and possibly herpes virus and malaria.

For 99.8 percent of the five million years of human existence, hunting and gathering was the primary mode of subsistence. Our ancestors lived in small groups and relied on wild animals and plants for their survival. In their foraging rounds, early humans would occasionally have contracted new kinds of illnesses through insect bites or by butchering and eating disease-ridden animals. Such events would not have led to widespread epidemics, however, because groups of people were so sparse and widely dispersed.

About 10,000 years ago, at the end of the last ice age, many groups began to abandon their nomadic lifestyles for a more efficient and secure way of life. The agricultural revolution first appeared in the Middle East; later, farming centers developed independently in

China and Central America. Permanent villages grew up, and people turned their attention to crafts such as toolmaking and pottery. Thus when people took to cultivating wheat and barley, they planted the seeds of civilization as well.

With the new ways, however, came certain costs. As wild habitats were transformed into urban settings, the farmers who brought in the harvest with their flint-bladed sickles were assailed by grim new ailments. Among the most common was scrub typhus, which is carried by mites that live in tall grasses, and causes a potentially lethal fever. Clearing vegetation to create arable fields brought farmers frequently into mite-infested terrain.

Irrigation brought further hazards. Standing thigh-deep in watery canals, farm workers were prey to the worms that cause schistosomiasis. After living within aquatic snails during their larval stage, those worms emerge in a free-swimming form that can penetrate human skin, lodge in the intestine or urinary tract, and cause bloody urine and other serious maladies. Schistosomiasis was well known in ancient Egypt, where outlying fields were irrigated with water from the Nile River; descriptions of its symptoms and remedies are preserved in contemporary medical papyruses.

The domestication of sheep, goats and other animals cleared another pathway for microorganisms. With pigs in their yards and chickens roaming the streets, people in agricultural societies were constantly vulnerable to pathogens that could cross interspecies barriers. Many such organisms had long since reached commensalism with their animal hosts, but they were highly dangerous to humans. Milk from infected cattle could transmit tuberculosis, a slow killer that eats away at the lungs and causes its victims to cough blood and pus. Wool and skins were loaded with anthrax, which can be fatal when inhaled and, in modern times, has been developed by several nations as a potential agent of biological warfare. Blood from infected cattle, injected into people by biting insects such as the tsetse fly, spread sleeping sickness, an often-fatal disease marked by tremors and protracted lethargy.

A second major effect of agriculture was to spur population growth and, perhaps more important, density. Cities with populations as high as 50,000 had developed in the Near East by 3000 B.C. Scavenger species such as rats, mice and sparrows, which congregate wherever large groups of people live, exposed city dwellers to bubonic plague, typhus and rabies. And now that people were crowded together, a new pathogen could quickly start an epidemic. Larger populations also enabled diseases such as measles, mumps, chicken pox and smallpox to persist in an endemic form—always present, afflicting part of the population while sparing those with acquired immunity.

Thus the birth of agriculture launched humanity on a trajectory that has again and again brought people into contact with new pathogens. Tilling soil and raising livestock led to more energy-intensive ways of extracting resources from the earth—to lumbering, coal mining, oil drilling. New resources led to increasingly complex social organization, and to new and more frequent contacts between various societies. Loggers today who venture into the rain forest disturb previously untouched creatures and give them, for the first time, the chance to attack humans. But there is nothing new about this drama; only the players have changed. Some 2,000 years ago the introduction of iron tools to sub-Saharan Africa led to a slash-and-burn style of agriculture that brought people into contact with *Anopheles gambiae*, a mosquito that transmits malaria.

Improved transportation methods also help diseases extend their reach: microorganisms cannot travel far on their own, but they are expert hitchhikers. When the Spanish invaded Mexico in the early 1500s, for instance, they brought with them diseases that quickly raged through Tenochtitlán, the stately, temple-filled capital of the Aztec Empire. Smallpox, measles and influenza wiped out millions of Central America's original inhabitants, becoming the invisible weapon in the European conquest.

In the past three decades people and their inventions have drilled, polluted, engineered, paved, planted and deforested at soaring rates, changing the biosphere faster than ever before. The combined effects can, without hyperbole, be called a global revolution. After all, many of them have worldwide repercussions: the widespread chemical contamination of waterways, the thinning of the ozone layer, the loss of species diversity. And such global human actions have put people at risk for infectious diseases in newly complex and devastating ways. Global warming, for instance, could expose millions of people for the first time to malaria, sleeping sickness and other insect-borne illnesses; in the United States, a slight overall temperature increase would allow the mosquitoes that carry dengue fever to survive as far north as New York City.

Major changes to the landscape that have become possible in the past quarter-century have also triggered new diseases. After the construction of the Aswan Dam in 1970, for instance, Rift Valley fever infected 200,000 people in Egypt, killing 600. The disease had been known to affect livestock, but it was not a major problem in people until the vast quantities of dammed water became a breeding ground for mosquitoes. The insects bit both cattle and humans, helping the virus jump the interspecies barrier.

In the eastern United States, suburbanization, another relatively recent phenomenon, is a dominant factor in the emergence of Lyme disease—10,000 cases of which are reported annually. Thanks to modern earth-moving equipment, a soaring economy and population pressures, many Americans have built homes in formerly remote, wooded areas. Nourished by lawns and gardens and unchecked by wolves, which were exterminated by settlers long ago, the deer population has exploded, exposing people to the ticks that carry Lyme disease.

Meanwhile, widespread pollution has made the oceans a breeding ground for microorganisms. Epidemiologists have suggested that toxic algal blooms—fed by the sewage, fertilizers and other contaminants that wash into the oceans—harbor countless viruses and bacteria. Thrown together into what amounts to a dirty genetic soup, those pathogens can undergo gene-swapping and mutations, engendering newly antibiotic-resistant strains. Nautical traffic can carry ocean pathogens far and wide: a devastating outbreak of cholera hit Latin America in 1991 after a ship from Asia unloaded its contaminated ballast water into the harbor of Callao, Peru. Cholera causes diarrhea so severe its victims can die in a few days from dehydration; in that outbreak more than 300,000 people became ill, and more than 3,000 died.

The modern world is becoming—to paraphrase the words of the microbiologist Stephen S. Morse of Columbia University—a viral superhighway. Everyone is at risk.

Our newly global society is characterized by huge increases in population, international travel and international trade—factors that enable diseases to spread much more readily than ever before from person to person and from continent to continent. By 2020 the world population will have surpassed seven billion, and half those people will be living in urban centers. Beleaguered third-world nations are already hard-pressed to provide sewers, plumbing and other infrastructure; in the future, clean water and adequate sanitation could become increasingly rare. Meanwhile, political upheavals regularly cause millions of people to flee their homelands and gather in refugee camps, which become petri dishes for germs.

More than 500 million people cross international borders each year on commercial flights. Not only does that traffic volume dramatically increase the chance a sick person will infect the inhabitants of a distant area when she reaches her destination; it also exposes the sick person's fellow passengers to the disease, because of poor air circulation on planes. Many of those passengers can, in turn, pass the disease on to others when they disembark.

The global economy that has arisen in the past two decades has established a myriad of connections between far-flung places. Not too long ago bananas and oranges were rare treats in northern climes. Now you can walk into your neighborhood market and find food that has been flown and trucked in from all over the world: oranges from Israel, apples from New Zealand, avocados from California. Consumers in affluent nations expect to be able to buy whatever they want whenever they want it. What people do not generally realize, however, is that this global network of food production and delivery provides countless pathways for pathogens. Raspberries from Guatemala, carrots from Peru and coconut milk from Thailand have been responsible for recent outbreaks of food poisoning in the United States. And the problem cuts both ways: contaminated radish seeds and frozen beef from the United States have ended up in Japan and South Korea.

Finally, the widespread and often indiscriminate use of antibiotics has played a key role in spurring disease. Forty million pounds of antibiotics are manufactured annually in the United States, an eightyfold increase since 1954. Dangerous microorganisms have evolved accordingly, often developing antibiotic-resistant strains. Physicians are now faced with penicillin-resistant gonorrhea, multiple-drug-resistant tuberculosis and *E. coli* variants such as 0157:H7. And frighteningly, some enterococcus bacteria have become resistant to *all* known antibiotics. Enterococcus infections are rare, but staphylococcus infections are not, and many strains of staph bacteria now respond to just one antibiotic, vancomycin. How long will it be before run-of-the-mill staph infections—in a boil, for instance, or in a surgical incision—become untreatable?

Although civilization can expose people to new pathogens, cultural progress also has an obvious countervailing effect: it can provide tools—medicines, sensible city planning, educational campaigns about sexually transmitted diseases—to fight the encroachments of disease. Moreover, since biology seems to side with microorganisms anyway, people have little choice but to depend on protective cultural practices to keep pace: vaccinations, for instance, to confer immunity, combined with practices such as hand-washing by physicians between patient visits, to limit contact between people and pathogens.

All too often, though, obvious protective measures such as using only clean hypodermic needles or treating urban drinking water with chlorine are neglected, whether out of ignorance or a wrongheaded emphasis on the short-term financial costs. The worldwide disparity in wealth is also to blame: not surprisingly, the advances made during the second epidemiological transition were limited largely to the affluent of the industrial world.

Such lapses are now beginning to teach the bitter lesson that the delicate balance between humans and invasive microorganisms can tip the other way again. Overconfidence—the legacy of the second epidemiological transition—has made us especially vulnerable to emerging and reemerging diseases. Evolutionary principles can provide this useful corrective: in spite of all our medical and technological hubris, there is no quick fix. If human beings are to overcome the current crisis, it will be through sensible changes in behavior, such as increased condom use and improved sanitation, combined with a commitment to stop disturbing the ecological balance of the planet.

The Bible, in short, was not far from wrong: We do bring plagues upon ourselves—not by sinning, but by refusing to heed our own alarms, our own best judgment. The price of peace—or at least peaceful coexistence—with the microorganisms on this planet is eternal vigilance.

34

A Teaching Framework for Cross-Cultural Health Care

Elois Ann Berlin and William C. Fowkes

Medicine care is just one of the determinants of population health. All societies have medical systems, although sometimes it is difficult to distinguish the beliefs and practices of medicine and religion. While Western biomedicine has the capacity to explain and cure many forms of injury and disease, it is not the only medical system in our own society. Besides a wide range of "complementary and alternative medicines," other medical models include Chinese medicine, the system of Ayurvedic medicine developed in India, the humoral system developed by Galen in ancient Greece, and the hot-cold system common in much of Latin America.

While doctors and nurses are often skeptical of non-Western medical models, they are nonetheless confronted with many patients who take them very seriously. In the United States, biomedical practitioners are increasingly confronted with such traditional or alternative beliefs since so many of their patients are immigrant newcomers with limited exposure to Western medicine. Many patients hide their commitments to non-Western medical ideas and practices, and considerable research has also demonstrated that this form of concealment can lead to incorrect diagnoses, culturally unacceptable forms of treatment, and ultimately patient "noncompliance," sometimes with fatal consequences.

How can doctors and nurses bridge the communication gap between their own medical knowledge, practice, and belief, on one hand, and the beliefs and practices of their patients, on the other? How can they take patients' non-Western medical beliefs seriously without compromising their own beliefs—or their own professional, ethical, and legal responsibilities as medical practitioners? These are not just theoretical questions; for doctors and nurses working in culturally diverse communities, they are both extremely difficult and extremely urgent.

This selection proposes a useful heuristic model, called LEARN, that has proven helpful to many biomedical practitioners serving culturally diverse patient populations. The model relies on five key components

that can be used to help bridge the often vast divides between practitioners and patients. Doctors and nurses are encouraged (1) to *Listen* with sympathy and understanding to their patients' characterizations of the problem, (2) to *Explain* the biomedical perspective on the problem, (3) to *Acknowledge* and discuss differences between the patient's and provider's perspectives, (4) to *Recommend* the appropriate form of treatment in accordance with the biomedical model, and (5) to *Negotiate* a plan of therapy that will be acceptable to both parties.

The LEARN model is not a silver bullet solution to all problems of doctor-patient communication. Yet it offers an important set of concrete, easy-to-apply tools that doctors and nurses can use to avoid alienating their patients—and to avoid creating unnecessary frustration for themselves.

As you read this selection, ask yourself the following questions:

- Why is it important for doctors to know about cross-cultural medicine? After all, isn't medicine a universal science?

- Why is culture a barrier to effective cross-cultural communication? Isn't it just a matter of translation?

- What are some aspects of the cultural beliefs of doctors that can be seen in this selection? Why might patients feel intimidated into not asking questions that are on their mind?

- What is a patient's "explanatory model," and why should a doctor care?

The following terms discussed in this selection are included in the Glossary at the back of the book:

Ayurvedic medicine	*negotiation*
explanatory model	*somatization*
hot-cold humoral system	

Health care providers are finding themselves dealing with increasingly diverse patient populations. Fueled by armed conflict, political unrest and economic instability, the influx of immigrants into the United States is prompting a structural shift in the demographic representation of minorities. The impact is especially acute in states like California, which are subject to secondary migration or relocation after preliminary resettlement. These migration patterns, in combination with reproductive patterns, set a trend that is predictive of what has been termed *minoritization.*

In addition to language and socioeconomic barriers recognized to stand between minority populations and the health care system,[1–3] there is an increasing awareness of the impact of diverse health and disease belief systems on the interaction of health care providers and patients of a different cultural heritage.[4–10]

Overcoming these obstacles is aided by the incorporation of new tolls for cross-cultural communication. At the Family Practice Residency at San Jose Health Center, we have begun to develop a set of guidelines for health care providers in a practice that serves a multicultural patient population. We have structured these guidelines around the following mnemonic:

Guidelines for Health Practitioners: LEARN

L   *Listen* with sympathy and understanding to the patient's perception of the problem

E   *Explain* your perceptions of the problem

A   *Acknowledge* and discuss the difference and similarities

R   *Recommend* treatment

N   *Negotiate* agreement

It should be emphasized that the LEARN model is not intended to replace completely the normal structure of the medical interview. Rather, it is intended as a supplement to history taking. The difference in focus is between a patient's factual subjective report of onset and duration and characteristics of symptoms and a patient's theoretical explanation of the reasons for the problem.

DISCUSSION OF GUIDELINES

Listen

Interview techniques have been proposed that aid in elicitation of a patient's conception of the cause,

process, duration and outcome of an illness as well as healing strategies and resources that the patient considers to be appropriate.[4,6] Understanding a patient's conceptualizations and preferences constitutes the first step. Questions such as, What do you feel may be causing your problem? How do you feel the illness is affecting you? and What do you feel might be of benefit? are examples of the shift in focus.

Explain

Explanation or communication of a "Western medicine" model is the next step. This may be a biomedical model but often the provider is making an educated guess, for example, that a patient's diarrhea is indeed due to an intestinal virus as opposed to toxins from contaminated food or psychosocial stress. In the primary care setting, treatment is frequently initiated without a definite diagnosis or biomedical model. However, it is critical to the success of the interaction that the care-giver have a strategy and that the strategy be conveyed to the patient.

Acknowledge

Acknowledgment of a patient's explanatory model occurs next or is integrated into the previous explanatory step. Based on an understanding of the explanatory models of both patient and provider, areas of agreement can be pointed out and potential conceptual conflicts understood and resolved. Resolution may involve bridging the conceptual gap between disparate belief systems. In many instances there is no therapeutic dilemma involved and a patient's own model can be incorporated into the system of care. If the provider feels that a patient's explanatory model and its consequences may have possible deleterious effects, such as a toxic medicinal substance, then an attempt must be made to market a more appropriate model leading to the next step. An example of a counterproductive explanatory model and resultant intervention is the consumption of pickle brine for hypertension—called "high blood" by some southern blacks. "High blood" is characterized by too much blood and treated by avoiding rich foods and consuming pickle brine, an "astringent" substance. The high sodium content of pickle brine would likely be deleterious in the face of blood pressure elevation.[10]

Recommend

Within the constraints imposed by a patient's and provider's explanatory models, a treatment plan can

From Western Journal of Medicine, 1983, vol. 139, reproduced with permission from the BMJ Publishing Group.

be developed. Patient involvement in the treatment plan is important. This step constitutes an extension of such as effort to include cultural parameters when appropriate culturally relevant approaches can be incorporated into the recommendation to enhance the acceptability of the treatment plan.

Negotiate

Negotiation is perhaps the key concept of the proposed LEARN model. It is necessary to understand a patient's perceptions and to communicate the provider's perspective so that a treatment plan can be developed and negotiated. There may be a variety of options from the biomedical, psychosocial or cultural approaches that could be appropriately applied. The final treatment plan should be an amalgamation resulting from a unique partnership in decision making between provider and patient. A patient can truly be involved in the instrumentation of recovery if the therapeutic process fits within the cultural framework of healing and health.

APPLICATION OF GUIDELINES

To illustrate the application of the LEARN model, we have selected examples from the experiences of our staff and students. We have chosen a separate case to exemplify each concept of LEARN. Although all or most steps in the model are involved in every clinical encounter, the cases were chosen to best illustrate each concept specifically.

Listen

A 28-year-old Vietnamese woman, a social work student, was first seen in the Family Practice Center in autumn of 1982 because of weight loss, mood swings, nervousness, sweaty palms and an increased number of bowel movements. She had lived in the United States for five years. Initially she volunteered that she had been extremely depressed ten years earlier and had once attempted suicide. She had an established diagnosis of retinitis pigmentosa and was legally blind. She was living with her mother and two siblings and was entering college to study social work. On initial examination there were findings consistent with retinitis pigmentosa. Lid lag was also noted. Initial laboratory studies elicited values consistent with mild hyperthyroidism and she was started on a regimen of propranolol hydrochloride taken orally.

She was seen regularly and had a constellation of symptoms including abdominal pain, mute attacks during which she could not open her mouth, twitching and palpitations. After taking propranolol she felt very fatigued and weak and had an episode of syncope after which she refused to take further medication. Additional symptoms developed including squeezing substernal chest pain. Repeat thyroid function testing was normal.

There was no apparent physical explanation for the symptoms and it was felt that she was suffering from anxiety and depression related to her disability and life stress. Supportive approaches were instituted with regular counseling visits. Relaxation training and a life journal were begun. The technique used for relaxation included both breathing exercises and visualization.

Shortly after these measures were instituted the patient presented in a very agitated state and said that the pleasant visual images she attempted to conjure turned "dark and scary." She also related that a childhood diary had been taken from her by one of her sisters and that the contents had been ridiculed. This made it very difficult for her to keep the recommended life journal. At this time, with encouragement, she related some very important events in her childhood. When she was 8 to 10 years of age her affliction was felt by her family to be due to her possession by an evil spirit, and a healer was summoned. The attempt at exorcism failed and this was interpreted as a sign that her illness was a form of punishment for her transgressions in a past life. She was virtually locked away in a back room for several years before the events that led to her immigration.

She stated she no longer held this set of beliefs, but she continued to worry about whether she was a good person. Her physician agreed with her rejection of the ideas held by her family and suggested that her studies in social work and her commitment to help people were indeed evidence of her goodness and worth.

She moved out of her home to campus housing and has improved somewhat. She continues to visit the Family Practice Center for supportive care.

Cultural Context   The medicoreligious beliefs of Vietnam derive from such a variety of sources that specification of exact religious context of the healing rituals of this patient's early life is difficult.

There have been historical interchanges of Ayurvedic medicine, with its roots in Galenic humoral pathology, influenced by Hinduism and Buddhism, especially in Southeast Asia.[11–16] Chinese medicine, which is more closely related to Confucian and Taoist religious philosophies, has made an additional contribution. More recent influences come from Catholicism and Western medicine. Local indigenous beliefs and practices also no doubt exert some influence.[17]

Attribution of illness to possession by spirits or demons is consistent with all of these religious traditions (including Catholicism, at least historically).

Whichever temple and priest or shaman the patient's family applied to for help, her status as a victim of a malevolent source would have been validated by successful exorcism. This would have been confirmed by the return of her eyes to normal appearance. Failure of repeated exorcistic rites to alleviate the symptoms led to the conclusion that her deviant appearance was a mystical mark, a sign of evil committed in a former life. This conclusion transformed her from victim to perpetrator. In a family whose members include all of the living, dead and as yet unborn, the final diagnosis shamed the family in perpetuity. This was the justification for confining the child in the house and restricting her social interactions. The family was, literally, attempting to hide their shame. The psychologic burden that this explanation placed on the patient resulted in somatization of complaints. Mental illness, which bears strong negative sanctions for similar reasons, would have constituted yet another mark against the family.

The patient migrated with her family to the United States when she was an adolescent. The process of acculturation and an alternative biomedical diagnosis provided a context for a change of attitudes and perception of self-worth. Although several people whom the patient had consulted over time (social workers and health care providers) had felt that there was a troubling "cultural component" in her medical history, the patient had never been able to discuss it fully. Careful probing and an open, nonjudgmental attitude on the part of the resident physician allowed the patient to divulge the complete background information and to acknowledge the lingering self-doubt these experiences had produced. She was then able to initiate steps for improvement such as removing herself from the family context, which produced continuing stress and reinforced a negative self-image, and continuing her studies in a helping profession, which confirmed her goodness.

Explain

A 21-month-old Mexican-American male infant with recurrent onset of fever, runny nose and noisy breathing was brought to the clinic by his mother. The mother noted that the child had been sleeping restlessly and making sighing noises while asleep.

On physical examination, he was found to have edematous mucous membranes and mucoid nasal discharge consistent with an upper respiratory tract infection (URI).

The mother stated that she was very concerned because two months earlier the child had had a major motor seizure that she associated with a high fever. She felt that the seizure had precipitated *susto* (fright disease), as evidenced by the sighing and restlessness during sleep, and wanted a regimen to control fever and prevent a worsening of the child's *susto*.

The resident physician discussed upper respiratory tract infections and their effects on breathing. He suggested a decongestant for relief of symptoms. He also confirmed the relationship of fever to seizures and advised continued use of antipyretics. He demonstrated the use of sponge baths to reduce fever and emphasized the importance of fever control in preventing seizures. In addition, he suggested that the mother consult a *curandera* (folk healer) concerning her questions about *susto*. The patient has subsequently been seen for routine visits and has had no further seizures or other significant problems.

Cultural Context   *Susto* is a Latin-American folk illness that is caused by fright.[18–22] The source or cause of fright might be anything from a simple startle response to an encounter with spirits. Children are particularly susceptible to *susto*. Symptoms vary widely, but the sighing and restlessness or poor sleep pattern exhibited by the patient are common manifestations. The mother's explanatory model for this case of *susto* was as follows:

URI → fever → seizures → *susto* → sleep disturbance

The provider was able to give a detailed biomedical explanation of that portion of the patient's explanatory model to which it was applicable and to recommend consultation with a folk specialist for that portion that lay outside the purview of modern medicine.

Acknowledge

A 25-year-old Vietnamese woman was seen for a routine prenatal examination. As part of her evaluation she had blood drawn for laboratory testing. Within the next few days she returned with a variety of symptoms including weakness, fatigue and coryza. She attributed this to having blood removed, feeling that removal of blood weakens the system and causes illness.

Her provider, a Vietnamese physician, was aware of the belief and acknowledged it, but also explained how much blood volume she actually had and gave the example of persons donating blood, a much larger volume, without symptoms.

She was pleased with the explanation, seemed to feel less fearful and her symptoms abated.

Cultural Context   The probable influence of Chinese medicine or Ayurvedic medicine (or both) in Southeast Asia is seen in this patient's response to blood tests. Edwards[23] describes the following physiological process from Chinese medical theory: "The connection between food, [blood], sex and health is found in the transformational formula in which seven units of the precursor yields one unit of the subsequent product:

$$Food \rightarrow blood \rightarrow jing \rightarrow qi \rightarrow shen"$$

Edwards defines the terms as follows: *jing* = "sexual fluid," which is a vital substance; *qi* = "breath" or "life energy" (also written *chi*); *shen* = "ethereal energy." A similar process has been described from Ayurvedic medical theory, which could be outlined as follows:

$$Food \rightarrow chyle \rightarrow blood \rightarrow flesh \rightarrow fat$$
$$bones \rightarrow marrow \rightarrow semen[24]$$

Because several physiological systems are involved in the production, transportation and storage process—that is, digestive, genitourinary, circulatory and respiratory—symptoms can be diffuse and varied. Since all descriptions indicate a geometric reduction between precursor and product, the consequences of interruption of the cycle would increase geometrically in seriousness at each earlier step in the process.

The patient's and the provider's explanatory models were similar in that they both believed blood loss to constitute a potential threat to health. Their explanations differed in the amount of blood that must be lost to pose a problem. By relating the amount of blood removed to the total blood volume and comparing this with the much larger quantities safely removed from blood donors, the physician was able to reassure the patient and to effect alleviation of symptoms.

Recommend

A 38-year-old Mexican-American man was seen in the Family Practice Center for chronic genitourinary problems. He had experienced hematuria and right flank pain two years before. In addition there had been recurrent episodes over 18 years of right flank pain and dysuria, diagnosed as urinary tract infections. He did not use analgesics. Examination of the external genitalia and prostate was unremarkable. He had no abdominal or flank tenderness. Analysis of urine showed 50 to 100 leukocytes per high dry field. An intravenous pyelogram showed a localized hydronephrotic area in the upper pole of the right kidney.

He was seen by a urologist who carried out retrograde pyelograms. These showed a large calyceal diverticulum connected with the right collecting system, with hydronephrosis of the upper pole of the kidney.

Surgical treatment was recommended. The patient expressed considerable reluctance to have an operation.

When questioned by his family physician he expressed concern that his "blood was low" and that he would have trouble going through an operation under the circumstances. His physician discussed the amount of blood that could be expected to be lost with a partial nephrectomy and also the total available blood supply in the body. He suggested that a surgical procedure be delayed for a period to allow the patient to "build up his blood" with appropriate medication. This was quite acceptable to the patient and the consultant urologist.

He subsequently underwent uneventful partial right nephrectomy.

Cultural Context Blood is "hot" according to the hot-cold system of humoral pathology as practiced in Latin America. Blood is also associated with strength, both in the health and the sexual sense. Having a large supply of blood makes one strong and healthy, but is also associated with virility and hence with machismo. Menstrual blood, semen and sexual activity are very hot.[25] Men's blood is hotter than women's blood.

The patient felt a need to build up his blood supply in order to have reserve strength for an operation because he expected a significant amount of blood to be lost during it. He was willing to accept the recommendation that he take iron to help build blood. However, an equally acceptable way to build blood would have been to eat blood products such as fried blood or blood sausage. Organ meats are good for building up strength and blood supply. In the Mexican-American folk system, an abundant and varied diet builds physical reserves, including a healthy supply of blood.

By describing the surgical procedure, including control of bleeding, the resident physician was able to alleviate some of the patient's concerns about blood loss. The provider was then able to recommend a treatment plan acceptable to the patient by prescribing "blood building" medicines and by scheduling the operation following a delay of fixed duration that the patient concurred would be adequate to prepare himself.

Negotiate

A 48-year-old black man was seen because of severe hypertension and congestive heart failure associated with far-advanced renal insufficiency. Initially he was managed conservatively. It became obvious, however, that he had reached a stage at which renal dialysis was his only hope for survival.

When he was approached about the possibility of hemodialysis he declined, stating that he was a devout Christian and felt that the will of God was of prime importance and that he would wait for God's intervention rather than accept dialysis.

His physician acknowledged the importance of God's influence, but suggested that the opportunity for dialysis as a means to control his condition might be the way God had intended for him to survive. Indeed, there was nothing in the Bible that prohibited dialysis and God helps those who help themselves.

The following day the patient consented to hemodialysis and now has a functioning bovine shunt and is doing well.

Cultural Context   The socioreligious context of this patient's explanatory model was fundamentalist Protestantism. The direct intervention and control of health by God is supported in the Old Testament (Exodus 4: 11): ". . . who maketh the dumb or deaf, or the seeing or the blind? Have not I the Lord?" The New Testament contains dozens of examples of the healing powers of Christ.[26] While one common alternative to treatment is faith healing,[27] this patient seemed to be relying on the Old Testament with healing based on direct intervention by God. He suggested that he felt that God did not intend him to die yet and would intervene on his behalf. The provider was able to call on other aspects of Christian beliefs such as "the Lord helps those who help themselves" and that God sometimes works through human agents: "For to one is given by the Spirit the word of wisdom; . . . to another the gift of healing by the same Spirit" (I Corinthians 12:8–9).

The implication was drawn that the physicians and dialysis might be the instruments through which God intended to intervene. Medical intervention was thus translated into a construct that did not violate the tenets of the patient's faith. By using beliefs from the patient's own religious background, the provider was able to negotiate acceptance of recommended biomedical treatment.

SUMMARY AND CONCLUSIONS

Given current demographic trends it is probably unrealistic to assume that health care providers can gain in-depth knowledge about the health-affecting beliefs and practices of every ethnic or cultural group they are likely to encounter in practice. The processes of acculturation, interethnic variation and social change also serve as confounding agents in predicting knowledge, behavior and attitudes. Social class differences, too, provide striking variability. We have, therefore, chosen a process-oriented model by which the cultural, social and personal information relevant to a given illness episode can be elicited, discussed and negotiated or incorporated.

However, it is common in our experience for patients of different beliefs to be reluctant to discuss this problem for fear of criticism or ridicule. It is certainly of value for providers who deal with culturally diverse patients to have some understanding of common basic conceptions of health, illness and anatomy held by these persons. Much work needs to be done in codifying these conceptions and making them available to professionals in medicine.

The foregoing examples serve to illustrate some of the means the members of a family practice residency program have used for enhancing communication and promoting the integration of patient's and providers' perceptions of needs and solutions into the therapeutic process.

NOTES

1. Bullough B, Bullough V: Poverty, Ethnic Identity and Health Care. New York: Appleton-Century-Crofts, 1972.

2. Quesada GM: Language and communication barriers for health delivery to a minority group. Soc Sci Med 1976 June; 10:323–327.

3. Language Access Task Force, Velez M (Chief Author): Health Care for Non-English Speaking Populations: Access and Quality. West Bay Health Systems Agency. San Francisco, Western Center for Health Planning, 1982.

4. Harwood A (Ed): Ethnicity and Medical Care. Cambridge, Mass, Harvard University Press, 1981.

5. Hill CE: A folk medical belief system in the American South: Some practical considerations. South Med 1976 Dec. pp. 11–17.

6. Kleinman A, Eisenberg L, Good B: Culture, illness and care: Clinical lessons from anthropological and cross cultural research. Ann Intern Med 1978; 89:251–258.

7. Martinez RA (Ed): Hispanic Culture and Health Care: Fact, Fiction and Folklore. St Louis, CV Mosby, 1978.

8. Mason JC: Ethnicity and clinical care. Indiana Phys Assist Health Practitioner 1980 Nov; 30:30–39.

9. Muecke MA: Caring for Southeast Asian refugee patients in the USA. Am J Public Health 1983; 73:431–438.

10. Snow LF: Folk medical beliefs and their implications for care of patients: A review based on studies among Black Americans. Ann Intern Med 1974; 81:82–96.

11. Basham AL: The practice of medicine in ancient and medieval India. *In* Leslie C (Ed): Asian Medical Systems. Berkeley and Los Angeles, University of California Press, 1976, pp. 18–43.

12. Burgel JC: Secular and religious features of medieval Arabic medicine. *In* Leslie C (Ed): Asian Medical Systems, Berkeley and Los Angeles, University of California Press, 1976, pp. 44–62.

13. Gard RA: Buddhism. New York, George Braziller, 1962.

14. Obeyesekere G: The impact of Ayurvedic ideas on the culture and the individual in Sri-Lanka. *In* Leslie C (Ed): Asian Medical Systems. Berkeley and Los Angeles, University of California Press, 1976, pp. 201–226.

15. Olness K: Indochinese refugees—Cultural aspects of working with Lao refugees. Minn Med 1979 Dec; 62:871–874.

16. Renou L: Hinduism. New York, George Braziller, 1961.

17. Whitmore JK (Ed): An Introduction to Indochinese History, Culture, Language and Life—For Persons Involved With the Indochinese Refugee Education and Resettlement Project in the State of Michigan, Ann Arbor, Center for South and Southeast Asian Studies, University of Michigan, 1979.

18. Klein J: *Susto:* The anthropological study of diseases of adaptation. Soc Sci Med 1978 Jan; 12:23–28.

19. O'Nell CW, Selby HA: Sex differences in the incidence of susto in the Zapotec Pueblos: An analysis of the relationships between sex role expectations and a folk illness. Ethnology 1968; 7:95–105.

20. O'Nell CW: An investigation of reported "fright" as a factor in the etiology of susto. "Magical Fright." Ethos 1975; 3:41–63.

21. Rubel AJ: The epidemiology of folk illness: Susto in Hispanic America. Ethnology 1964; 3:268–283.

22. Uzzell D: Susto revisited: Illness as a strategic role. Am Ethnol 1974; 1:369–378.

23. Edwards JW: Semen anxiety in South Asian cultures: Cultural and transcultural significance. Med Anthropol, in press.

24. Zimmer HR: Hindu Medicine. Baltimore, Johns Hopkins Press, 1948.

25. Ingham JM: On Mexican folk medicine. Am Anthropol 1970; 72:76–87.

26. Henderson G, Primeaux M: Religious beliefs and healing. *In* Henderson G, Primeaux M (Eds): Transcultural Health Care. Menlo Park, Calif., Addison-Wesley, 1981, pp. 185–195.

27. Baer HA: Prophets and advisers in black spiritual churches: Therapy, palliative, or opiate? Cult Med Psychiatry 1981 Jun; 51:145–170.

In late 2004, camera phones were just hitting the Nigerian market, and I have no doubt they will be all the rage in a very short time.

CONCLUSION

Although it is impossible to pinpoint the origin of the "killer numbers" rumors described at the start of this article, I suggest that their currency and appeal were related to popular discontents about the role of cell phones in highlighting and sometimes aggravating social inequality. Some speculated that the rumors were the work of one provider trying to undermine the business of another (the killer numbers were first associated with the phone numbers of one company, though, in time, it spread to them all). Others argued that the rumors were a form of consumer revenge, with the allegations meant to damage the reputation and profits of companies toward which customers felt increasing anger. Still others suggested that the rumors were started by some among the vast majority of Nigerians who still cannot afford to own cell phones, in order to strike fear into those who were intimidating their economic inferiors with their ostentatious use of this flashy new technology. More important than these theories about origin is the speed with which the rumors spread and the extent to which they captured popular imagination. The fascination they generated reflects the fact that, as happy as most Nigerians are for their newfound access to a modern communications technology, ordinary citizens remain extremely discontented over the extent of inequality in their society. The new technology is being interpreted, to a large extent, in relation to these discontents.

NOTE

1. In 2000, the *New York Times* published an article suggesting the importance of cell phones not only for displaying social status generally, but for the attraction of mates. The newspaper account drew on an article in the journal *Human Nature*, entitled "Mobile Phones as Lekking Devices among Human Males" (Lycett and Dunbar 2000). Regardless of whether one finds a sociobiological argument convincing, the association of cell phones with social status seems to strike a chord across many societies.

REFERENCES

Akinsuyi, Yemi. 2004. "Anxiety Over 'Satanic' GSM Phone Numbers." *This Day* (Nigeria), July 23.

Barber, Karin. 1995. "Money, Self-Realization, and the Person Yoruba Texts." In *Money Matters: Instability, Values and Social Payments in the Modern History of West African Communities*, edited by J. Guyer, 205–24. Portsmouth, NH: Heinemann.

Bearman, Peter. 1997. "Generalized Exchange." *American Journal of Sociology* 102(5): 1383–1415.

Bourdieu, Pierre. 1984. *Distinction: A Social Critique of the Judgement of Taste.* Translated by Richard Nice. Cambridge: Harvard University Press.

Cornwall, Andrea. 2002. "Spending Power: Love, Money, and the Reconfiguration of Gender Relations in Ado-Odo, Southwestern Nigeria." *American Ethnologist* 29(4): 963–980.

Dooring, Nicolas. 2002. "'Kurzm-wird-gesendet'—Abbreviations and Acronyms in SMS Communication (Short-Message-Service)." *Muttersparche.*

Fox, Barry. 2001. "No 2MORO for Text Messaging Lingo." *New Scientist* 171(2298): 24.

Geschiere, Peter and Josef Gugler. 1998. "The Urban-Rural Connection: Changing Issues of Belonging and Identification." *Africa* 68(3): 309–319.

Gugler, Josef. 2002. "The Son of a Hawk Does Not Remain Abroad: The Urban-Rural Connection in Africa," *African Studies Review* 45(1): 21–41.

Ikhemuemhe, Godfrey. 2004. "The Killer Phone Rumour—Operators Cry Foul." *Vanguard* (Nigeria), July 26, 2004.

Lycett, John and Dunbar, Robin. 2000. "Mobile Phones as Lekking Devices among Human Males." *Human Nature* 11(1): 93–104.

Mobile Africa. 2005. "Cellular/Mobile Phone Networks in Africa." http://www.mobileafrica.net/mobile-phone-networks-in-africa.php. Accessed June 7, 2005.

Obadare, Ebenezer. 2004. "The Great GSM (cell phone) Boycott: Civil Society, Big Business and the State in Nigeria." Dark Roast Occasional Paper Series, No. 18. Cape Town: South Africa: Isandla Institute.

PANA (Pan African News Agency). 2005. "Nigeria's Phone Subscriber Base Hits 12 Million." *PanAfrican News Agency Daily Newswire*, May 4.

Smith, Daniel Jordan. 2004. "Burials and Belonging in Nigeria: Rural-Urban Relations and Social Inequality in a Contemporary African Ritual." *American Anthropologist* 106(3): 569–579.

Sylvia, K. N. and Hady, S. W. 2004. "Communication Pattern with SMS: Short Message Service and MMS: Multimedia Message Service as a Trend of Conduct of Modern Teenagers." *International Journal of Psychology* 39(5–6): 289.

Uchendu, Victor. 1965. *The Igbo of Southeast Nigeria.* Fort Worth, TX: Holt, Reinhart, Winston.

36

Just Another Job?

The Commodification of Domestic Labor

Bridget Anderson

For most women, working is a necessity, not an option. There are reasons to celebrate the fact that women have become active participants in the workforce alongside their male counterparts. But this socioeconomic transformation has also created a "double shift" for many women, who work a full day and then return home to the additional unpaid jobs with home, household, and family each night.

Many families try to alleviate this "double shift" by "outsourcing" domestic work to a paid worker. This outsourcing is what the author of this selection means by the "commodification of domestic labor." In other words, domestic labor can be bought and sold like other services or goods. Although domestic labor is an increasingly important commodity in societies throughout western Europe, the United States, and other world regions, it is generally poorly paid. Employers look for potential employees who are willing to work for the lowest wages and, quite frequently, the individuals they hire are migrants from poor, faraway countries.

While the wages middle-income Western families pay their domestic workers may be low by local standards, they are often very high in comparison to wages available in poor countries. As a result, millions of people from countries as diverse as the Philippines, Sri Lanka, Ghana, Nigeria, Columbia, and El Salvador have left their homes and families in order to take their chance of working abroad as a domestic worker. Even educated people with professional experience—among them journalists, teachers, bankers, nurses, and others—are prepared to take on the risks of transnational migration since the benefits are perceived as being so high.

This selection illustrates the difficulties of being a transnational migrant in domestic work. It can be very challenging to work within the intimate space of another person's, or another family's, home—especially within a foreign culture. At the same time is it difficult to live far away from family and friends, including, quite often, one's own children. Relationships between employers and employees are frequently marked by asymmetries of race, nationality, language, class, and citizenship, since many transnational domestic workers have migrated on an undocumented or "illegal" basis. As this selection illustrates, these asymmetries leave transnational domestic workers vulnerable to various forms of discrimination, exploitation, and abuse. Globalization is not just about manufacturing being done in China or call centers in India; globalization hits close to home.

As you read this selection, ask yourself the following questions:

- What is the "commodification of domestic labor"? What factors have contributed to the rise in demand for domestic workers in western Europe?

- Why are so many domestic workers in western Europe transnational migrants from Southeast Asia, West Africa, or eastern Europe?

- From the perspective of the domestic workers the author interviewed, what are the advantages of live-in as opposed to live-out domestic work? What are the disadvantages?

- How do racial stereotypes and other forms of prejudice contribute to the mistreatment of some domestic workers?

- Some employers describe their domestic employees as "one of the family." How might this way of characterizing their employment relationship actually contribute to the exploitation and abuse of the migrant women they employ?

The following terms discussed in this selection are included in the Glossary at the back of the book:

commodification
domestic labor
maternalism

Paid domestic work looks in many ways like just another undesirable job. The hours are long, the pay is low, and the tasks are often regarded as demeaning. The same could be said of hamburger flipping or garbage collection. But there is much to distinguish the culture of domestic labor from other kinds of low-wage work. Significantly, domestic work is deeply embedded in status relationships, some of them overt, but others less so. And these relationships are all the more complex because they fall along multiple axes. They are relationships among women, but often women of different races or nationalities—certainly of different classes. They take place in a space that can be intimate, loving, and private but that can also be a form of social plumage, demonstrating to visitors the home owner's comfort and leisure. And the worker, often a migrant without legal protection or proper papers, may depend on the employer for more than her paycheck, just as the employer depends on the worker for more than her elbow grease.

The demand for domestic workers has been steadily rising in Europe, and although one can point to many economic and demographic forces that may have contributed to this trend—the retrenchment of the welfare state, the rise in the ratio of older to younger people, the feminization of the workforce, the rise in divorce, and the decline of the extended family—they leave a good deal unexplained. For instance, many domestic workers are employed by women who do not work outside their homes. Moreover, many paid domestic workers are cleaners rather than carers. While a working couple might need someone to look after their children or elderly relatives, no one *has* to employ a cleaner in the same way. Ironed clothes, dust-gathering ornaments, polished floors, and clean windows are not necessities; but such markers affirm a household's status by displaying its access to financial and human resources.

The migrant domestic workers I interviewed, many of them through a British support organization called Kalayaan, seemed to spend much of their time servicing lifestyles that their employers would have found difficult and even undesirable to sustain had they undertaken their upkeep themselves. Said Aida, a Filipina live-in in Paris:

> Every day I clean for my madam one pair of riding shoes, two pairs of walking shoes, house shoes. That is every day, just for one person. . . . Plus the children: that's one pair of rubbers and one pair of everyday school shoes. . . . Fourteen pairs of shoes every day. My time is already finished. . . . You will be wondering why she has so many bathrobes, one silk and two cotton. I say, Why does madam have so many bathrobes? Every

day you have to hang them up. Every day you have to press the back because it is crumpled.

Siryani, a Sri Lankan live-in in Athens, recounted, "They have a very big house, and white carpet everywhere. They have three dogs. I hate those dogs with long, long hair. Even one hair will show on the white carpet."

When a cleaner is not enabling her employers to enjoy an extravagant lifestyle or an impractically appointed home (would Siryani's employers have had both white carpet and dogs if they'd had to clean their own home?), she allows her middle-class, female employer to devote "quality" time to her children and husband. In effect, employing a cleaner enables middle-class women to take on the feminine role of moral and spiritual support to the family, while freeing her of the feminine role of servicer, doer of dirty work. The employment of a paid domestic worker thereby facilitates status reproduction, not only by maintaining status objects but also by allowing the worker to serve as a foil to the lady of the house. Simply by hiring a domestic worker, the employer lowers the status of the work that employee does. After all, the employer has better or more lucrative things to do with her time.

Many middle-class, heterosexual couples in the United Kingdom employ a cleaner once they have children, thereby averting gender and generational conflict over domestic work.[1] But there is no total amount of domestic work that can be divided fairly between equal partners or delegated to someone who is paid to do it. When one does not have to do the work oneself, standards change. Eliska, a Czech au pair in the United Kingdom recounted, "Her teenage daughter changes her clothes five, six times a day and leaves them on the floor. I have to pick them up, wash them, iron them, put them away. I cannot tell her, Tasha, you cannot change your clothes so many times. And my employer does not notice."

Economic explanations, then, fail to fully account for the popularity of domestic workers in middle- to upper-class European households, because they fail to consider the status implications of hiring such workers. Similarly, the prevalence of migrant labor in this sector cannot be attributed only to avoidance of tax and national insurance, for there is a supply of cheap, nonmigrant female laborers willing to work off the books. Despite the relatively high wages of Polish workers in Berlin, they still account for a significant proportion of domestic workers. Filipina workers are the most popular in Athens, and they are also the most expensive.

Significantly, migrant workers are more willing than local ones to live with their employers. Live-in workers may be considerably less expensive than live-out workers, in some cases because their board and lodging are set against their wages, but especially because employers get more labor and greater flexibility

From "Just Another Job? The Commodification of Domestic Labor," by Bridget Anderson. Reprinted with permission of the author.

for their money. Whatever hours a live-in nanny and housekeeper is supposed to work, there is virtually no time when she can comfortably refuse to "help" her employer with a household task. Domestic workers and au pairs commonly complain of having to be available at both ends of the day, early in the morning for children and late at night for entertaining guests. It is a question not simply of long hours but of permanent availability. Said Teresa, a Filipina domestic in Athens:

> You're working the minute you open your eyes until the minute you close your eyes. You keep your strength and your body going so that you will finish your work. . . . You keep waiting on your employers until they go to sleep because, although you finish your work, for example you finish ironing everything, putting the children or the elder person to bed, even if you put them to bed at ten o'clock, there are still other members of the family. So you keep on observing, "Oh, can I sleep or maybe they will call me to give them food or to give them a yogurt.". . . And even if you are sleeping you sometimes feel that you are still on duty.

A 1998 survey of thirty-nine Kalayaan members found that although the workers were well organized and belonged to a trade union, only 18 percent worked eight hours or less a day. Nearly 30 percent averaged more than twelve hours a day.

Although the long hours, low pay, and lack of privacy render live-in domestic work extremely unpopular among the population in general, migrants, particularly new arrivals, can find it advantageous: problems of accommodations and employment are solved in one, and the worker can both minimize expenses and acclimatize herself to a new language and culture. Moreover, housing is more than a place to live: it is shelter from the police, and many new arrivals are undocumented and terrified of deportation. Employers appreciate live-in migrants because, unlike local domestic workers, migrants cannot leave their employers to go tend to their own sick children or other family obligations. Undocumented workers in particular have extremely limited access to their own families or, really, to any life outside the employing home.

Such women, however, isolated in private households, without papers or legal protection, are strikingly vulnerable to abuse. Their work can be singularly degrading: cleaning cats' anuses, flushing employers' toilets, scrubbing the floor with a toothbrush three times a day, or standing by the door in the same position for hours at a time. One worker told a researcher of a particularly degrading experience: "We were three Filipinas, she brought us into the room where her guests were, she made us kneel down and slapped each one of us across the face."[2] Sadly, these are not isolated instances. Kalayaan keeps annual figures detailing the kinds of difficulties faced by the workers they register. In 1996–1997, 84 percent reported psychological abuse, 34 percent physical abuse, and 10 percent sexual abuse. Additionally, 54 percent were locked in, 55 percent did not have their own beds, and 38 percent were not fed regularly.

Racial stereotypes play a role both in the abuse of domestic workers and in the selection of migrant workers over local citizens in the first place. Certainly, such stereotypes help manufacture a sense of difference between the female employer and her domestic worker: "other" women are presumed suited to such service work, and these others are so alien that some employers actually fear that the migrants' bodies will contaminate their homes. Workers are typically required to wash their clothes separately from those of the family, and they are given their own cutlery and plates. Said Rose, a Ghanaian domestic worker in Athens, of her employer's family, "The daughter wouldn't even accept water from my hand, simply because I am black." Irene, a Filipina I interviewed in Athens, recounted the following story: "I heard children playing house. One child said, 'I am a Daddy.' The other child said, 'I am a Mummy,' and then, 'She is a Filipina.' So what does the child mean? Even the child knows or is already learning that if you are a Filipina, you are a servant inside the house."

Agencies and employers tend to express preferences for specific nationalities of domestic workers, and these preferences often reflect racial hierarchies that rank women by precise shades of skin color. One volunteer from Caritas, the international Catholic social service and relief agency, in Athens told me, "The Ethiopians are very sweet. They are not like the African Africans, who are ugly." Said a worker at an agency in Barcelona, "Moroccans are difficult to place. . . . Their religion is very different, they observe Ramadan. . . . They are very different, though like Peruvians they are brought up to be servile. . . . Filipinas are easiest to place." And according to a community volunteer in Paris, "You know the black people are used to being under the sun, and the people in France think they are very lazy, they are not going very quick, and you know, another breed, but they are very good with children, very maternal."

Some hierarchies are based on particular national or personal prejudices. Greek employers and agencies tend to frown upon Albanians and Ukrainians. In Paris, many employers evince a preference for Haitians, who are generally darker-skinned than the expressly shunned Moroccans and Algerians. Stereotypes differ across European states, but also across households: one household might display an "eccentric" liking for Congolese, for example, on the basis of household myths of an almost folkloric character. A "bad" experience with a domestic worker might lead a family to generalize about her entire nationality. Consider the comments of this Athens employer:

> I have a problem with women from Ethiopia: they are lazy, and they have no sense of duty, though they are good-hearted. . . . I have a lot of experience. I have had ten girls from Ethiopia. They like to be well-dressed—hair, nails; for that they are good. . . . Then the Albanians—that was terrible. They are liars, always telling lies. And telephone maniacs because they have never had telephones. And they had no knowledge of electrical appliances. For seven months I had that girl. . . . Then I had one from Bulgaria. The Bulgarians are more civilized, more sincere, more concerned about work. But they are very unhappy.

Of course, not all employers are racist or abusive. Some women hire migrants in the hope of helping them. Certainly, migrant workers need the money. Why not match the needs of hard-pressed working mothers, on the one hand, with those of desperate migrants on the other?

Many of the domestic workers I met said that traveling abroad had enabled them to make important contributions to their families back home. But most of the more than four thousand workers at Kalayaan had never intended to come to Britain. Some had migrated first to the Middle East, from where they accompanied their employers to London on business trips or holidays; others had taken jobs in their countries of origin and traveled with their employers to the United Kingdom. While domestic workers who had papers felt that their work brought benefits to their families, others, especially those still undocumented, found the price too high. Said Nora, a Filipina working in London, "My life is worse than before. I'm on this dark road with no way out, that's how I feel. . . . All I want to do is go back home, even though we're very poor. But then, what kind of life will my daughter have?"

Hidden costs become apparent to many workers when they return home. They often feel ill at ease in their home countries, where things have changed in their absence, and where they may feel that they no longer belong. When their families meet them at the airport, these women commonly do not recognize their own kin. They talk of the embarrassment of having sex with husbands who have become virtual strangers, and of reuniting with children who doubt their mothers' love. Often a woman's relatives will have died or moved away. It is thus scarcely surprising that such women are very ambivalent when asked whether they would recommend migration to their daughters. Most migrants would prefer that their daughters did not have to make the choice between hunger and moving abroad.

So is employing a migrant domestic worker an act of sisterhood toward a woman in need or of complicity with abusive power structures? Employers often make contact with Kalayaan after they have seen a television program or read an article exposing the situation of migrant domestic workers in London. They want to help, they explain, and to offer board and lodging in return for "help around the house." A place in a British home is proffered as a kind of charity, and the woman's labor power is a little extra on the side. But even under the best of circumstances, the employer has power over the worker, and this power is greatly increased when the worker is an undocumented migrant. How the employer chooses to exercise that power is up to her.

As Judith Rollins has noted, a kind of "maternalism" sometimes marks these relationships, wherein friendliness between the women works to confirm the employer's sense of her own kindness and of the worker's childlike inferiority.[3] Through kindness, pity, and charity, the employer asserts her power. Nina, an employer in Athens, had hired dozens of migrant domestic workers to care for her very disabled mother over the years, because, she said, "This is the Greek way to help foreigners." She claimed to offer exceptional working conditions (though the wages she told me were extremely low) and a loving household. But her employees, she lamented, have turned out to be gold diggers:

> There is no feeling for what I offer. I'll give you an example of the last woman from Bulgaria. . . . I had a bright idea: "She needs to see her friends." Because I was tired of all the turnover, I gave her Sunday off. . . . Now, every morning, including Sundays, the girl wakes, helps grandmother to the toilet and changes her Pamper. . . . Then she goes, but she must be back before seven P.M. . . . Then after all I do for her, the girl says every Sunday she would like to be back at midnight, and not to do any work—that is, not to change the Pamper in the morning.

This worker was being denied twelve consecutive hours off in a week—an arrangement that would still have placed her hours well above the European legal maximum.

Some employers express their maternalism through gifts, giving their domestic workers mostly unwanted, cast-off household goods. Said Maggie, a Zairean working in Athens, "You need the money to feed your children, and in place of pay they give you old clothes. 'I give you this, I give you this.' They give you things, but me, I need the money. Why? I am a human being."

All of these exercises of power, whether through direct abuse, through the insistence that a worker perform degrading tasks, or through acts of maternalism, expose the relationship between worker and employer as something other than a straightforward contractual one. But that is not the only relationship in the domestic workplace that is fraught with ambiguity and complexity. When we hire someone to care for children or the elderly, we cannot pay simply for the physical labor of care, leaving the emotional labor to those who are genetically linked to those cared for. Magnolia, a Dominican nanny in Barcelona, noted, "Sometimes when they say to me that I should give her lots of love, I feel like saying, well, for my family I give love free, and I'm not discriminating, but if it's a job you'll have to pay me."

Indeed, many parents hire nannies rather than sending their children to day care precisely because they want their children to develop personal, emotional relationships with the people who care for them. But can the emotional labor of care really be bought? The worker may carry out the physical work of care, entering into a sort of intimacy with the children, but her caring engenders no mutual obligations, no entry into a community, and no real human relationship—just money. A worker may care for a child over many years, spending many more hours with that child than the child's natural mother does, but should the employer decide to terminate the relationship, the worker will have no further right to see the child. As far as the employer is concerned, money expresses the full extent of her obligation to the worker. To the worker, this view is deeply problematic; indeed, it denies the worker's humanity and the very depth of her feelings. Juliette, a nanny from Côte d'Ivoire working in Parma, recalled, "I cared for a baby for his first year. . . . The child loves you as a mother, but the mother was jealous and I was sent away. I was so depressed then, seriously depressed. All I wanted was to go back and see him. . . . I will never care for a baby again. It hurts too much."

The idea that the worker can be considered "part of the family" allows some employers to negotiate these difficulties. Interestingly, this language even appears in U.K. immigration legislation with reference to au pairs. But the analogy does not withstand scrutiny. A relative who contracts a long-term illness is not expelled from the family; domestic workers usually are, even if they are given a nice severance package. And although being a part of the family does not entitle the worker to unconditional love or support, it does entitle the employer to encroach on the worker's off-duty hours for "favors." In fact, many employers will invoke either a contractual or a family relationship under different circumstances, depending on what is most convenient. Writes Miranda Miles:

> The disadvantages of being "one of the family" far outweighed the advantages. Wages tended to be lower and erratically paid on the premise that the maid would "understand" their financial situation. Incorporating a domestic worker into the family circle is usually, although not always, a sure way of depressing wages and possibly hiding even the most discreet forms of exploitation involved in the employer-employee relationship.[4]

These are vexed questions, for while informality clearly leaves workers open to exploitation—excessive hours, for instance, or low pay—workers also value having personal relationships with their employers, particularly because domestic work can be highly isolating. In some cases, a woman will decide to work for low wages precisely because she feels that a particular family is "nice" or an employer "treats me as part of the family." Professionalizing employment relations and rendering them more anonymous may therefore introduce new difficulties. Labor is a social, not simply an economic process.

This is not to say that labor contracts for domestic work are not important. We should welcome the emergence of domestic labor into the realm of recognized and productive work. Professionalization is a means of giving respect to domestic workers as workers, as well as of managing the personal relationships that develop from care work.

Certainly, it is possible to argue for the social significance of care work. Changing an elderly person's incontinence pads is surely as important and as deserving of social respect and status as the work of a stockbroker. But the work of cleaners and housekeepers sometimes occupies a more problematic space. Cleaning can be part and parcel of caring, and tidying up for a disabled person, for instance, can be construed as socially valuable. But many cleaners, like those described at the start of this essay, do work that simply expresses the employer's status, leisure, and power. Can such race-, class-, and gender-based divisions be resolved through contracts? Undocumented migrants, for example, cannot draw boundaries or refuse work they find demeaning. They simply do not have the power. The most effective way to protect them is to make sure that they have basic employment rights, as well as access to the means to implement those rights. For migrants, these rights begin with work permits.

Because both the workers and the employers in this sector tend to be women, it is tempting to draw on notions of sisterhood in order to reform the relationships between employers and employees. But the power relations among these women are very complex, to the point where even acts of kindness work to reproduce an employer's status and self-image, and they do not always, in the end, benefit the worker. This does not mean that employers should not respect their domestic workers but, rather, that they should also be aware that the very act of employing a domestic worker weaves them into a status relationship. Real sisterhood, then, should take concerned women beyond their own homes: it means campaigning and organizing around issues of migration and domestic labor, having as an important first demand that domestic work be treated, in the best sense, like just another job.

NOTES

1. Nicky Gregson and Michelle Lowe, *Servicing the Middle Classes: Class, Gender and Waged Domestic Labour in Contemporary Britain* (London: Routledge, 1994).

2. Margaret Healy, "Exploring the Slavery of Domestic Work in Private Households," unpublished M.A. thesis, University of Westminster, 1994.

3. Judith Rollins, *Between Women: Domestic Workers and Their Employers* (Philadelphia: Temple University Press, 1985).

4. Miranda Miles, "Working in the City: The Case of Migrant Women in Swaziland's Domestic Service Sector," in *Gender, Migration and Domestic Service*, ed. Janet Momsen (London: Routledge, 1999).

37

Circumcision, Pluralism, and Dilemmas of Cultural Relativism

Corinne A. Kratz

One of the things about studying anthropology is that we encounter cultural ideas and practices that are very alien to our own. Encountering the "other" can be a challenge in two ways. On an intellectual level, it can be a challenge to understand vastly different cultures and customs—why do people do/believe that? How does it fit within the wider context of their lives? The second of these challenges can be on a personal level, because the beliefs and practices of others might offend our own notions of morality and propriety. Studying and living in other cultures sometimes brings up our own ugly ethnocentrism.

At the same time, it is fair to ask, Are there limits to cultural relativism? Looking cross-culturally, anthropologists can identify some universal (or at least extremely common) elements in cultural codes about proper personal conduct. All societies follow the ethnocentric line of thought that *their own traditions* are correct and right, but at the same time there are gigantic areas of controversy. In a complex society, the laws that are recognized and enforced often reflect the interests of the dominant social group.

The topic of this selection, female circumcision, really bothers some students; they can hardly believe that such cultural practices exist in the twenty-first century. In Africa, female circumcision has been a controversial topic for nearly a century, and there have been repeated international efforts to "eradicate" the custom, as if it were a disease. But this is not simply a medical issue, and to oversimplify the complex issue misses the point.

It is important to recognize that the single term FGM (*female genital modification* or *mutilation*) refers to a wide variety of surgeries with different levels of invasiveness. It is also important to remember that the symbolic and ritual meanings of this practice also vary among cultures. Finally, as students of anthropology, we need to recognize that there are at least two different views of what is at stake here, and, as in many other arenas of public controversy, there is real value to a sympathetic understanding of both sides.

This selection has two parts. The first provides a description of female circumcision in Africa—reporting the "facts" almost as it might be reported in a reference book. The second part discusses the author's strategies for *teaching* about the female circumcision controversy in the college classroom context. This controversy is both local and global—it involves traditional cultures, immigrants, and international nongovernmental organizations (NGOs). Understanding the different dimensions of the argument is an important educational goal; hopefully, it will also challenge you to come to your own well-informed opinion.

As you read this selection, ask yourself the following questions:

- For the women in the societies that practice it, FGM is related to beliefs about aesthetics of the body. Can you think of traditions in your own culture that transform or modify the body for purposes of beauty or identity? (Try relating this to Miner's description of body ritual among the Nacirema in Selection 1.)

- What are the potential health complications of female circumcision? What are the possible social complications of not being circumcised?

- What are the human rights issues involved? Is this a question that local societies should debate themselves, or is international intervention necessary?

- Why does this tradition persist even when it is made against the law? Why would loving parents have this done to their daughters?

- Is the analogy to male circumcision in the West appropriate?

The following terms discussed in this selection are included in the Glossary at the back of the book:

clitorectomy	*infibulation*
FGM	*neocolonial*
human rights	*sunna circumcision*

Differences of social and cultural practice have been a source of both puzzlement and edification around the world and throughout human history, interpreted and treated in vastly different ways in different circumstances.[1] They have been perennial resources through which people form their own identities, defining themselves through contrasts with other cultures. Distinctions in dress, cuisine, language, music, and ritual are particularly common as such markers of identity and difference. When ethnic or religious groups and minorities are reviled, differences in cultural practice have been used to help justify derogatory attitudes and discrimination. In other settings, cultural difference and diversity have been celebrated through various forms of multiculturalism.

With such remarkable diversity in the world, however, situations inevitably arise where incompatible social and cultural values, practices, and aesthetics produce conflict or controversy. How should they be dealt with? Cultural relativism would suggest that each set of practices and understandings is valid within its own circumstances and way of life. Yet plural societies combine and blend different beliefs and practices within the same social settings. Further, certain practices seem to challenge the nonjudgmental tolerance that cultural relativism implies (Shweder 2002) and raise serious questions about how to define human rights and who should define them. To many Americans, for instance, religious practices of discipline and self-mortification might seem extreme when they include self-flagellation, or political martyrdom might be taken as a sign of fanaticism. To people in other parts of the world, on the other hand, certain American economic practices might seem exploitative and certain modes of American dress might be seen as indecent or immoral.

Anthropologists seek to understand cultural production, i.e., how cultural meanings and social worlds continually take shape and change through daily interaction, communication, and exchange, through interpretations of personal and community histories and negotiations of political economic differences. They seek to understand the range of experience, meanings, and values produced by the world's diverse societies and cultures, examining how people perceive and make sense of lives and circumstances as different as those of African pastoralists caught in a long civil war, Chinese women working in a silk factory, men in an urban homeless shelter in the United States, contemporary Australians maintaining complex ritual traditions and fighting for land and mining claims, or radical political activists in Europe (Hutchinson 1996; Rofel 1999; Desjarlais 1997; Dussart 2000; Holmes

2000). In doing so, anthropologists may move beyond simple relativism to develop knowledge and judgments based on pluralism. Philosopher and social theorist Isaiah Berlin describes the distinction between relativism and pluralism (1991:10–11):

> "I prefer coffee, you prefer champagne. We have different tastes. There is no more to be said." That is relativism. . . . [Pluralism is] the conception that there are many different ends that men [sic] may seek and still be fully rational, fully men [sic], capable of understanding each other and sympathising and deriving light from each other, as we derive it from reading Plato or the novels of medieval Japan—worlds, outlooks, very remote from our own.
>
> Members of one culture can, by the force of imaginative insight, understand . . . the values, the ideals, the forms of life of another culture or society, even those remote in time or space. They may find these values unacceptable, but if they open their minds sufficiently they can grasp how one might be a full human being, with whom one could communicate, and at the same time live in the light of values widely different from one's own, but which nevertheless one can see to be values, ends of life, by the realisation of which men [sic] could be fulfilled.

Anthropological research may not be able to resolve conflicts and controversies that emerge from social and cultural difference, but the knowledge produced can provide the foundation of understanding needed for engagement and debate grounded in pluralism. It can help to identify the basic value contradictions and issues at stake as well as the different positions and interests in play. It is also important to pay attention to such controversies and debates themselves as cultural phenomena, analyzing their rhetorics, weighing competing arguments, and placing them within their own social and historical contexts. These analytical skills are important in understanding debates concerning issues of social justice, abortion rights, defining human rights, or controversial practices such as *sati* in India, and they are critical to effective political action related to any of these issues.

This essay considers a widespread cultural practice that has many different forms and meanings throughout the world and a long history of sparking debate and controversy at different times and places: forms of genital modification commonly called circumcision. Vehement debates have swirled around male and female circumcision alike, but the essay focuses particularly on practices of female genital modification because they currently receive the greatest attention and are at the center of recent contention. After outlining the varied practices of female genital modification and some of the meanings associated with them, the essay will turn to controversies and debates about these cultural practices.

Reprinted with permission of Corinne Kratz.

THE VARIED PRACTICES AND MEANINGS OF FEMALE GENITAL MODIFICATION

Female circumcision is a term commonly used to refer to surgical operations performed in over thirty African, Middle Eastern, and Southeast Asian countries, by immigrants from those communities living elsewhere, and for roughly a century (about 1850 to 1950) by physicians in Europe and the United States. As this geographic and historical span suggests, the operations are embedded in a wide range of cultural and historical contexts and can be quite different in definition, meaning, and effect. All involve surgical modification of female genitals in some way, though this ranges from relatively minor marking for symbolic purposes to the most radical operation, infibulation.[2]

The general term *female circumcision* includes at least three clinically distinct kinds of surgery. Clitoridectomy removes all or part of the clitoris and the hood, or prepuce, covering it.[3] The second type, excision, includes clitoridectomy but also removes some or all of the labia minora; all or part of the labia majora might also be cut. The most extreme form of circumcision, infibulation, goes beyond excision.[4] After removing the labia, the sides of the vulva are joined so that scar tissue forms over the vaginal opening, leaving a small gap for urination and menstruation. Infibulated women often require surgical opening to allow first intercourse and birthing; in many cases women are reinfibulated after each childbirth. In addition to these three well-recognized types of female circumcision, a fourth is sometimes included. The mildest form, this involves a symbolic pricking or slight nicking of the clitoris or prepuce. Excision and infibulation are the most widely practiced types of female genital modification. In Africa, infibulation is common primarily in the Horn of Africa (Somalia, Sudan, Djibouti, Ethiopia).

Whether and how circumcision practices affect women's sexuality is much debated. It is important to distinguish sexual desire, sexual activity, and sexual pleasure when considering this question. Sexual desire and sexual activity may not diminish with female genital operations. Evidence about sexual feeling and pleasure is variable, difficult to define or measure, and hard to come by.[5] Euro-American opponents of the practices assert that circumcised women feel no sexual pleasure, but a number of African women disagree with these assertions. Studies suggest that the effect varies widely with type of operation, with prior sexual experience, and other circumstances as well. Some African activists also suggest that the stress on sexual pleasure in anti-circumcision campaigns reflects a recent, primarily Western concept of sexuality.[6]

The operations have also been said to carry a number of health risks. While the range of possible health problems is well known, there has been little epidemiological research to determine how widespread each problem might be in different areas. Immediate risks include infection, shock, excessive bleeding, and urinary retention, risks that are related to hygienic conditions and care during and after the operations. Longer term health problems are most common with infibulation but can be associated with excision as well. Most of these problems are related to heavy scarring and to covering over of vaginal and urinary openings after infibulation: keloid scars, vulvar cysts, retention of urine or menses, painful menstruation, difficulty urinating, and chronic pelvic infections. Clinical studies on the relation between these health problems and genital modification are contradictory, however, and a recent study in Gambia found that many negative consequences commonly cited for the operations were not significantly more common in women who had been cut (Morison et al. 2001).[7]

In many places where female circumcision is practiced, the physical operation is but one moment in an elaborate ceremony that contains many other events. For Okiek people in Kenya, for instance, initiation into adulthood includes circumcision for boys and excision for girls, but the full initiation process continues for several months and includes much more as well: moral teaching, family and community engagement, the negotiation of new social relationships, and important cultural meanings and values. While the operations are a central initiation trial and create a permanent physical mark of adulthood, initiation cannot be reduced to circumcision or excision alone. In many other societies, initiation does not involve circumcision at all.

In every case the purposes and meanings of female genital modification are related to specific cultural understandings of identity, personhood, morality, adulthood, gender, bodily aesthetics, and other important issues. In the Sudan, for instance, it is seen as enhancing a woman's purity, cleanliness, and beauty. For the Kikuyu people of Kenya, circumcision was the foundation of moral self-mastery for women and men alike, performed as part of initiation into adulthood. The age of those circumcised varies widely according to these cultural understandings. In much of Mali and the Sudan, for instance, girls are circumcised at six to eight years, while various communities in Kenya and Sierra Leone perform the operation in the early teens. Yoruba people in Nigeria often circumcise their children at just a few days old, much like male circumcision in the United States and Europe. Circumcision and excision are not connected with initiation for the Yoruba people, but they do relate the operations to moral concepts associated with shame and fertility. Circumcision is not regularly performed after puberty in Africa, where the operation is usually seen as related to a person's social and moral development.[8] The history of female circumcision in Europe and the United States contrasts with most of the world with regard to circumcision age. For roughly a century beginning in the 1850s, clitoridectomy was prescribed for adult women in Europe and the United States as medical treatment for insomnia, sterility, and masturbation (which was defined as an ailment at that time).

Many societies practice male but not female circumcision, but the reverse is rare. Where both are practiced, they can only be understood fully when considered together, in relation to one another. In many societies, cultural meanings and patterns link the two and equate them. A single word refers to both operations in many African languages, and this correspondence is often central to the way their practitioners understand them. The English translation, "female circumcision," maintains this parallel between male and female genital operations, though anticircumcision activists have criticized the term for being misleading (as discussed below).

DEBATES AND CONTROVERSIES ABOUT CIRCUMCISION

Both male and female genital operations have engendered long histories of debate and opposition; these have often involved cross-cultural disagreements about the meaning and worth of the practices. The value of Jewish male circumcision, for instance, was debated in Rome during the first century A.D., and male circumcision has become a topic of heated opposition in the United States again today. The most widespread and vociferous opposition currently centers on female genital modification, but these practices have been the subject of international political controversies and abolition campaigns since at least the 1910s.[9] Contemporary campaigns continue the tradition and rhetoric of colonial and missionary opposition and also build on decades of Africa-based activism. Health consequences have consistently been part of the debate, particularly in relation to infibulation, but the issues have also been defined at times in terms of colonialism, neocolonialism, feminism, sexuality, and human rights.

Controversies can be confusing. Heated arguments based on strong convictions are rarely presented in ways that make clear the different assumptions, perspectives, and interests fueling contention. When controversies cross cultural and national boundaries, they can be very complicated indeed. To begin to understand circumcision debates, it is important to first identify the grounds of controversy: Who is involved, what is it about, and what is at issue. Circumcision controversies concern a wide variety of actors and cross a

number of social and legal arenas, from family and household relations to international tribunals. This renders it impossible to characterize the debates in simple terms. It is inaccurate and misleading to describe them merely as contests of women versus men or Africans versus outsiders.

To understand today's debates, it is helpful to think about them in relation to several contexts. Most central are the sociocultural contexts of the varied practices at issue and the history and contexts of the current controversies themselves. An effective way to highlight the issues and perspectives involved is to consider these contexts comparatively, to relate different situations and practices, or to explore similarities and differences between several controversies (e.g., debates about male and female genital operations, debates that occur at different historical periods, or debates that might concern different practices but are presented in similar ways (such as *sati* in India[10]). Examining cultural practices in context also means identifying the different actors, perspectives, and meanings involved (see below). It is important to recognize that trying to understand unfamiliar practices does not necessarily mean supporting them. However, to oppose or help alter practices that some might consider problematic, it is essential to work *with* the people involved, as equal peers. Such understanding is critical to effective engagement.

One of the best-documented historical examples of circumcision controversy took place in central Kenya during the colonial era. Colonial missionaries and administrators there made judgments about which local customs violated Christian behavior and sought to discourage them. Campaigns to abolish female circumcision in central Kenya were among these efforts. When the Church of Scotland Mission and segments of the Church Missionary Society tried to prohibit the practice in the 1910s and 1920s, Kikuyu female circumcision became connected with the anticolonial movement and defense of cultural tradition (Murray 1974, 1976). Jomo Kenyatta, later president of Kenya, was a prominent opponent of colonial attempts to alter Kikuyu custom. These local protests against abolishing female circumcision provided an impetus for starting independent schools and churches in central Kenya.

Arenas encompassed in this debate, then, included British politics (with pressure from feminist parliamentarians and anticolonial activists), rivalries between Christian denominations with missions in Kenya, the colonial administration in Kenya, and local Kenyan communities. In addition to anticolonial movements and defense of cultural tradition, the debate also became connected with relations of authority between men and women and between women of different generations, and even the introduction of maternity clinics.[11] Since 1979, the Kenyan government has conducted several anticircumcision campaigns that were tinged with Christian and colonial overtones, banning female circumcision in 1982, but with little effect. In 1996, a national organization proposed an alternative initiation ceremony as a substitute. Like Kenya, each country has its own such history of circumcision debates and policies.

To place contemporary controversies in context, we should also consider their own history and the different arenas where debates occur. The debates have been related to feminist movements in various times and places, to colonial administration and missionary campaigns, to Islamic religious movements, and a number of other issues. Arenas of debate shift as different parties become involved. Several decades after the Kenyan controversy, in the late 1950s, international efforts to have the World Health Organization (WHO) address female circumcision were not effective. Later, in the 1970s, a number of publicizing efforts and publications converged to galvanize international attention. These included articles in African publications in the mid-1970s, a press conference held in Switzerland before the WHO assembly in 1977, and publications by Fran Hosken (1979) and Mary Daly (1990) in the United States. The Inter-African Committee on Traditional Practices affecting the Health of Women and Children was formed in Geneva in 1977. A 1979 WHO seminar in Khartoum helped to begin regular discussion of female genital operations by international bodies and at regular conferences. The resurgence of anticircumcision activity in the 1970s was also buoyed by the United Nations Decade of Women (1975–1985).

Since the early 1990s, international debates about female genital modification have again become increasingly heated and highly politicized. Greater media coverage in the 1990s and publicity over legal cases concerning African immigrants in France and the United States brought the debates to a wider public than previously.[12] In the United States, involvement by such well-known figures as novelist Alice Walker also helped to publicize and polarize the debate. A number of African scholars and activists based in the United States (such as Seble Dawit, Salem Mekuria, and Micere Mugo) have been highly critical of the way Walker and others have represented female circumcision in Africa.[13] They argue that Walker and others are engaged in neocolonial depictions that demonize African practitioners, distort the social meanings and contexts involved, portray African women only as victims, ignore decades of activism in Africa, and isolate female circumcision from other issues of women's health, economic status, and education.

Both practices of female genital modification and the arenas of debate have shifted over the years as other circumstances changed and different constituencies became involved. Public health education about the potential risks of the operations has increased in most countries where they are practiced. Similarly, an increasing number of female genital modifications are being performed either by specialists who have received some hygienic training or in health clinics and hospitals. As noted above, alternative rituals have also been proposed in some countries, though it is not clear whether they will be widely adopted. Shifts in practice also include adoption of genital modification by noncircumcising communities (Leonard 1999) and modification of long-standing rituals toward what I call "circumcision by pronouncement" or "performative circumcision," i.e., substituting a verbal formula for actual cutting (Abusharaf 1999:7; Hernlund 1999). There are intense debates among African activists about whether a medicalized, minor form of female genital modification should be promoted as an interim substitute for more severe operations (Obiora 1997; Shell-Duncan 2001). African immigrant communities in Europe and the United States often continue traditional practices in new ways in their new homes. Their preservation of the practices has brought all these debates to the fore in those countries as immigrant communities and their children have grown in recent decades. Sweden, Switzerland, the United Kingdom, and several other European countries passed laws restricting the operations in the 1980s and early 1990s. The United States followed suit in 1997.

CONTEXTS FOR UNDERSTANDING THE DEBATES AND ISSUES

These examples illustrate how many different parties and perspectives can become involved in these controversies. In tracing the shape of today's debates, it is useful to distinguish the following three interacting arenas. The social, cultural, and historical contexts of debates about female and male genital operations can be examined for each:

1. *Home countries* are countries in Africa, the Middle East, and Southeast Asia where circumcising practices have traditional standing. There may be a variety of traditions and practices that include genital modification within each home country and a number of different positions within each community, if the practices are debated.

2. The *United States* and *Europe* are the second arena to consider. These countries also have a history of genital operations for both boys and girls. The histories are related to changing understandings of health, class, ethnicity, gender, and sexuality. In the U.K., for instance, male circumcision had

become a middle-class fashion by the 1920s (Lonsdale 1992:388). In Nazi Germany, it was taken as a mark of Jewish identity. In the United States today, white men are more likely to be circumcised than African Americans or Hispanics; higher education levels are also related to higher circumcision rates (Laumann et al. 1997: 1053–1054). Clitoridectomy was a recognized medical treatment for women in these countries for decades, as noted above. Concern about female genital operations within these countries is now related particularly to immigrants from home countries.

3. The third arena is that of *international campaigns.* Though obviously related to the other two, it is useful to consider how international campaigns differ from debates within the other arenas, how international bodies and action groups establish their legitimacy to intervene in other countries, and how the international arena redefines issues central to particular communities and nations.[14]

In addition to identifying the complex social geographies and range of actors involved, it is equally important to pay attention to the ways that language and rhetoric shape the presentation of issues and convey particular values and judgments. For instance, the growing intensity of the debates became encapsulated in the very terms used for female genital operations between the 1970s and 1990s, illustrating the political divisions and rhetorics involved. *Female circumcision* was the most common term for decades, the English phrase ordinarily used in the debates about British colonial attempts to outlaw female genital operations in Kenya in the 1920s–30s. In the 1970s, anticircumcision activists increasingly criticized the term *female circumcision,* claiming that it condoned a brutal custom by creating what they considered false similarities between male and female circumcision.[15] A more partisan alternative was coined and eventually popularized: *female genital mutilation.*[16] The new term did not attempt impartial description, but condemned the practices through a label that defined them all as intentional mistreatment and disfigurement. Promotion of the new "mutilation" term was part of an escalating anticircumcision campaign that used more sensationalism and gory images.[17] As this term became more common, it was shortened to an acronym, "FGM." Others reject this term as misrepresenting the intentions of African families, criminalizing parents and relatives, and judging them through Euroamerican cultural values.

The increasingly heated and polarized nature of the debate thus became embedded in its very terms. Attempting to find an appropriate phrase, *New York Times* reporter Celia Duggers used the term *genital cutting* in

her late 1996 articles, a term she adopted from demographic and health surveys.[18] A number of other alternative terms also came into use in the mid-1990s, seeking more neutral ground: genital surgery, genital operations, genital modification, and body modification. This last term acknowledges broad similarities among such practices as male and female genital surgeries, genital/body piercing, and other cosmetic surgery. Female circumcision, genital cutting, and FGM remain the most common terms in English, though the acronym FGM has now also been redefined as "female genital *modification*" in efforts to use less polarizing, descriptive language.

Whatever terms are used, the topic at the center of controversy is a generalized category defined and shaped by that very debate. The category is created by extracting and combining fragments from many different cultural practices found in dozens of countries, a variety of practice described above. The fragments all concern genital modification but may share little else. Taken out of their social and cultural contexts, they combine to form a new, abstract category (e.g., "female circumcision"). Scientific, medical language is an important tool in this process. The clinical emphasis makes the general category seem like an objective and universal way to talk about women's bodies, but it also narrows the range of information defined as relevant to the debate. For instance, the physically different operations described above are combined and treated as the same thing, though they vary considerably in extent and effects. The rest of the ceremonies in which the physical operations may be embedded are often ignored.

The terms used in circumcision controversies convey different impressions of the people involved as well. A number of African women and others have objected to the word *mutilation,* for instance, because it misrepresents parents and families. It suggests that they intend harm to their children, likening to child abuse what they themselves might see as a cultural triumph, "carried out for the noblest of reasons, the best of intentions, and in good faith" (Iweriebor 1996). Accounts often demonize women who perform the operations as well. In recent French legal cases, for instance, they were portrayed as avaricious and predatory and received the harshest rulings.

A prominent example concerns the way African or "Third World" women in general are represented as a single, unified group, as seen across a range of sources: news media, informational publicity material produced by action groups, scholarly writing, or novels.[19] This stereotyped concept of "African women" is usually formed by homogenizing divergent circumstances; it assumes women to be a pre-existent, coherent group with shared interests and desires. This requires removing the concept of "woman" from any specific cultural context and isolating it from related notions that help form understandings of gender. How are differences based on nationality, class, ethnicity, religion, education, or age accommodated in this generalized figure and how might these variations affect the debates? The "average" Third World woman that emerges is set in contrast to elite women, though the contrast is often implicit. Elite women are presented as self-conscious, active, choice-making agents. They are not exclusively Western, but also include women born in the Third World who have joined the campaign against female genital modification. Yet African activists consistently protest that their work is rarely recognized when controversies are described. The rhetoric and structure of these controversies might be examined further by looking at how different kinds of men are portrayed, or by considering parallel cases in contemporary campaigns against male genital operations, abortion, or welfare.[20]

These different portrayals of Third World women and other actors in circumcision controversies are often bound up with notions of "progress" and other values as they have been defined in Euroamerican contexts. But conflicting values are the very crux of controversy. Diverse social and political positions inform the perspectives of those involved, but they are also grounded in different cultural frameworks, competing definitions of the practices at issue, and what seem to be irreconcilable values. In seeking to understand circumcision debates, it can be helpful to identify the various positions on each issue, along with the priorities and cultural values associated with each. Issues at stake would include the following:

Human Rights   Circumcision debates presented in human rights terms often emphasize the integrity and inviolability of the human body, sometimes using analogies with torture and child abuse. As noted above, this falsely attributes evil intent to parents and relatives. "Human rights" as a concept is itself under considerable debate. Should social and economic rights be included? Whose values will be enshrined as universal when there are fundamental disagreements (An-Na'im 1992; An-Na'im and Deng 1990)? How might the language of human rights accommodate the diverse people, practices, and circumstances involved?

Self-Determination   The human rights approach does not fit easily with another common way that circumcision debates are framed, in terms of self-determination.[21] However, self-determination can be defined in relation to individuals, families, or communities, each with rather different implications. Upholding family autonomy, community values, or religious freedom would seem to support continuing traditional practices understood as central to personal and community identity. Does this include male and female initiation ceremonies? How does individual self-determination apply in the intricate contexts of family and community relations? How do questions of self-determination apply to children of different ages?

Health Issues and Sexuality   These were discussed earlier in this essay. Both have been central to debates about female genital modification. Questions of sexuality have also figured in opponents' efforts to explain the operations. They commonly assert that male desire to control female sexuality is the origin and reason for all such practices. This universal conspiracy theory, however, does not correspond to what is known about circumcising practices. There is no evidence or discussion of when or how this might have happened in so many places, how this explanation would account for the variety of circumcising practices, why women also staunchly defend them, or how the theory relates to explanations offered by practitioners.[22]

Yet even when the issues and stances in circumcision controversies are delineated, the fact remains that the debates involve fundamentally different perceptions and lived understandings of aesthetics, morality, society, and personhood that come together with questions of authority, class, power, gender, and history.[23] There are no simple, single answers to the issues they raise. They pinpoint a nexus whose very opaqueness of understanding illustrates recalcitrant problems and issues of cultural translation. In this respect, recent circumcision controversies draw attention to the limits and dilemmas of cultural relativism and moral judgments. How are such judgments, choices, and even laws to be made in plural societies (which ultimately means all societies)? Can incommensurable values be accommodated? As Sir Isaiah Berlin noted, "A certain humility in these matters is very necessary" (1991:18).

CULTURAL AND MORAL VALUES: DILEMMAS OF RELATIVISM

Many people would agree that cultural difference and diversity should be recognized, respected, and accommodated. Cultural relativism has fairly wide currency in the United States as a general way to approach cultural difference, though it coexists with popular notions of cultural evolution and civilizational hierarchy. The relativist view that each society's practices and values are valid and understandable in the particular context of their lives may be easiest to hold, however, when applied to distant people or to practices that seem strange but harmless. What happens when people with incompatible practices and values live closely together, when culturally justified practices seem to be physically harmful, or when an overarching national legal system must deal with radically different values? Does cultural relativism imply moral relativism as well?

The controversies over genital operations present such dilemmas and flashpoints. Usually associated with ceremonial performances, the songs, dances, costumes, and other beliefs that give meaning to the ceremonies are readily accepted as part of "tradition," as markers of particular forms of ethnic or religious identity. Scarification or tattooing might also be recognized and appreciated as part of a different aesthetic or religion, so what is different about genital operations? Why are they seen as an exception that raises this moral dilemma? What other practices pose similar dilemmas?

In the last decade, legal cases dealing with African immigrants in the United States and Europe have raised these issues in particularly clear and urgent ways. Examining these cases—particularly court procedure and sections of testimony—provides a way to again consider the different actors and interests involved, this time in situations even closer to home (Kratz 2002). Among the many questions that these cases raise are the following:

- Legislation is written in general terms, intended as applicable to the broadest range of cases. However, laws are interpreted through individual cases and precedents. Should a case about, for instance, Somali immigrants (who practice infibulation for young girls) serve as precedent for families from Sierra Leone (where initiated individuals are older, the operation is less severe, and family relations are quite different)?

- Whose legal rights should be protected and when? Parents' rights to raise their children in accordance with their beliefs and traditions? What if parents disagree? The rights of the girls affected? What if they *choose* to undergo the operation? What if they are minors legally?

- When female genital operations are outlawed, who is legally responsible and liable for prosecution? At different times and places, the accused have included fathers, mothers, initiates, and surgeons. What constructions of actors, intentions, and meanings are involved in each of these scenarios?

- When court proceedings involve immigrants, how are issues of adequate translation and adequate legal representation handled? These were important problems in the way French cases in the 1990s were handled.

- Are judges, juries, lawyers, and those concerned with civil liberties informed about the communities and cultural values involved? For instance, a

lawyer in one case argued that the girls affected would have psychological problems when they realized they were not like other women, but the "other women" assumed in this statement were not women of the immigrant community. In fact, most women in their own ethnic community had had the operation, making the argument one that would more appropriately support the operation (cf. Matias 1996:4).

- How do gendered differences in immigrant experiences influence knowledge about relevant laws and services and the ways people participate in legal proceedings?

These questions raise some of the difficult practical implications of general issues of cultural translation and the moral dilemmas involved. They provide another way to ground the circumcision debates in specific questions and situations. Such groundings provide useful ways to understand and engage with controversies that are puzzling and sometimes troubling in their passions and complexities.

NOTES

1. This paper includes portions of Kratz (1999a) and (1999b) that have been combined, revised, and updated for inclusion here.

2. Wide variation in female genital modification can be found on the African continent alone, where it is practiced across a band of the continent that includes parts of Mauritania, Senegal, Gambia, Guinea-Bissau, Sierra Leone, Liberia, Mali, Burkina Faso, Côte d'Ivoire, Ghana, Togo, Benin, Niger, Nigeria, Chad, Cameroon, Central African Republic, Democratic Republic of the Congo (formerly Zaire), Sudan, Egypt, Eritrea, Ethiopia, Djibouti, Somalia, Kenya, Tanzania, and Uganda. The percentage of women circumcised in each country varies considerably (e.g., 5–10% in Uganda, 25–30% in Ghana, 80% in the Sudan), as does the kind of operation practiced, its cultural and personal significance, and its history. Female circumcision is not practiced at all in some communities within this broad area, but it is commonplace in others. Regional, ethnic, and religious variation in practice is considerable. Christians, Muslims, and followers of traditional religions all might practice forms of female circumcision. Communities have adopted, abandoned, and modified the practices in various ways over the centuries, in keeping with the complex histories of political and religious influence and interaction among societies on the African continent.

3. This is sometimes called *sunna circumcision*, though *sunna circumcision* might also refer to preputial cutting alone. The name *sunna* relates the practice to Islamic traditions, though most Muslim scholars and theologians deny Koranic justification for female circumcision.

4. Infibulation is also called *pharaonic circumcision,* a name originating in beliefs that the practice was part of ancient Egyptian life.

5. See Apena (1996:8); Kratz (1994:345–346); Lyons (1981:507, 510); Obiora (1997:298). Matias (1996:3) and Ogbu (1997:414–415) cite examples where they are seen as enhancing sexuality. Again, the type of operation is critical. Infibulation is more often discussed as reducing desire (Boddy 1989:54), though Obiora (1997:310) cites another study in the Sudan to opposite effect. As for sexual pleasure, according to Gruenbaum (also writing about the Sudan), some infibulated women do have orgasms, perhaps because "many midwives, fearing hemorrhage, leave much of the clitoral (erectile) tissue intact beneath the infibulation when they perform the surgeries" (1996:462). She notes, though, that other infibulated women report finding sex unsatisfying. See also Parker (1995:514); Obiora (1997:308–310); Koso-Thomas (1987:37–42). Several of these sources note that reports of sexual pleasure are related to sexual experience before circumcision as well as other factors.

6. Even in Europe and the United States, the pleasure-oriented definition of sexuality became prominent in recent decades. In this view, recent international debates about female genital operations have taken a form that resonates particularly with recent Western concerns and anxieties (Parker 1995). The paradoxical nature of questions of sexuality can be brought into relief through comparison. Historically, classical theologians and philosophers made parallel claims about men; they promoted male circumcision because it reduces male sexual passion (Boyarin 1992:486–487; Lyons 1981:503–504). Though circumcised men today might not agree, similar assumptions still inform medical research. A study publicized on National Public Radio in 1997 found that circumcised men are more "sexually adventurous," but explained this as compensation for loss of sexual feeling (Laumann et al. 1997). "Adventurousness" was defined through behavioral range and frequencies, suggesting that sexual interest, desire, and activity were actually greater with circumcision. Considering such gender reversals can raise critical questions about all these claims and show that understandings of sexuality are neither universal nor unchanging.

7. Obiora (1997:292) cites studies that show no obstetric or gynecological complication when infibulation is performed at an early age. Parker (1995:514–516) notes that findings in some studies of health risks from other forms of genital operations are not clear, though it is generally accepted that some complications can occur.

8. See Shell-Duncan and Hernlund (2000) for a collection of case studies on female genital modification in various parts of Africa.

9. Far earlier, in the 1820s, circumcising practices were also at the center of debates in the Sudan (Abusharaf 1999).

10. In the Hindu practice of *sati,* a widow immolates herself on her husband's funeral pyre. *Sati* became the subject of considerable debate in India during British colonial rule, leading to abolition in 1829. The *sati* controversy, like debates about female genital operations, involves a wide range of perspectives and has been framed at various times in terms of women's status, issues of tradition, authority, religious rights, personal autonomy, and humanitarianism. Outlawing *sati* did not make it disappear entirely. "Through the 1970s and 1980s . . . [the same time when circumcision controversies were heating up], either incidents of *sati* increased or greater scrutiny was brought to bear on the issue, primarily by women's organizations" (Courtright 1994:47). In September 1987, the case of Roop Kanwar, a young Hindu woman who burned in Rajasthan, galvanized national debate. Nandy (1988) and Mani (1990b) have noted continuities of language and argument between contemporary Indian positions and earlier colonial debates, parallels similar to those in circumcision controversies. Both debates involve "instabilities of perspective, of meaning, of judgment," and provide avenues for considering the "social history of moral imagination" (Geertz 1983:42). See also Mani (1990a), Nandy (1975), and Teltscher (1995:37–72).

11. Different aspects of this debate are described in Murray (1974; 1976), Pederson (1991), and Lonsdale (1992: 388–397). Descriptions of Kikuyu initiation and contemporary women's attitudes can be found in Davison et al. (1989). Thomas discusses debates in nearby Meru, Kenya, and their connections with many other domains of life (1996; 1997).

12. For instance, several 1990s immigration cases and asylum claims in the United States have been based on arguments about the persecution of women through genital operations. Lydia Oluloro, a Nigerian woman, fought deportation on the grounds that she was protecting her daughters from the procedure. Her case was profiled in newspapers and on television in a segment of *Sixty Minutes* in 1994. A woman from Togo, Fauziya Kassindja, was also granted asylum in 1996, and a woman calling herself "Adelaide Abankwah" received asylum in the United States in 1999. Highly publicized cases in France in the 1990s prosecuted immigrant parents and ritual surgeons who continued the practice in their new country (Verdier 1992; Winter 1994). Kratz (2002) analyzes several asylum cases heard in the United States.

13. See for example Dawit (1997).

14. Actors and institutions involved in each arena might include the following. (1) *In each home country:* National governments and politicians' local NGOs and national action groups; international action groups; churches; religious and ethnic communities whose circumcising practice may differ and whose histories of education and involvement with government also differ. Within each circumcising community, differences of age, gender, education, religion, and wealth also influence positions. For instance, a Christian mother, her non-Christian husband, his educated brother, and their school-child daughter might disagree about whether the girl should participate with her friends in initiation ceremonies during a school holiday. Peters (1997:484–486) discusses the different positions within the Togolese family and community in the

asylum case of Fauziya Kassindja as an actual example. See Gruenbaum (1996:463–470) and the film *Bintou in Paris* for other examples. (2) *In the United States and Europe:* Female genital modification was historically recognized as a viable medical procedure in these countries, "cosmetic" labial surgery on women is currently performed, and male circumcision is also widely practiced. Current female genital operations within their borders are usually debated in relation to immigrant families and communities from various "home countries." Some families and communities have lived outside their home countries for quite a while, with some children born and raised in the United States and Europe. Actors involved in these debates include immigrants themselves (again with differences of gender, religion, ethnicity, education, length of residence, etc.); their community organizations and spokespersons; national, state, and municipal governments, judiciaries, and agencies dealing with immigrants (e.g., Immigration and Naturalization Service, Health and Human Services, child welfare services, etc.); national action groups and organizations concerned with women and children; and international action groups. (3) *In international campaigns:* These actors may also be engaged with those in "home countries" and in the United States or Europe, but they reach beyond national boundaries as well. They include international action groups based in various countries; the United Nations, World Health Organization, and related international agencies and NGOs; journalists; religious officials; national governments and politicians who seek conditionality clauses for foreign policy and provision of aid.

15. In many contexts, however, ritual meanings and patterns unite the two for practitioners, who often use a single word for both operations in local languages.

16. Fran Hosken may have coined the term, though I could not verify this. She certainly played a key role in popularizing it through the Women's International Network (WIN) newsletter she wrote. By the time she wrote the Hosken Report in 1979, *female genital mutilation* had become her standard term. Before 1975, she vacillated between that term and *female circumcision*. Mary Daly also used "genital mutilations" in her 1978 book. In the British parliamentary debates about Kenya, the word *mutilation* was used at times to distinguish between two different types of genital operations (infibulation was not at issue in this controversy), but it did not become the primary term of reference (Pederson 1991:666). The Church of Scotland Mission, however, did begin to use the term *sexual mutilation* (Pederson 1991:671).

17. There are striking parallels between these shifts in rhetoric and tactics and the rhetoric of radical anti-abortion organizations such as Operation Rescue.

18. Duggers eschewed the automatic condemnation of "mutilation," the medical implications of "surgery," and what she considered the "mildness" of "female circumcision" (Moses 1997:4).

19. A number of scholarly papers discuss the problems with these generalized images and show how they are constructed; Mohanty (1988) and Stephens (1989) are a good

starting place. Alice Walker's books, *Possessing the Secret of Joy* and *Warrior Marks,* are commonly used as novelistic examples. Walker's representations of African women have also been discussed by a number of scholars; Obiora (1997:323–328) and Mugo (1997) are examples focused on their relation to controversies about female genital modification.

20. Information about campaigns against male genital operations is available from NOCIRC (National Organization of Circumcision Information Resource Centers) or NOHARMM (National Organization to Halt the Abuse and Routine Mutilation of Males). Both can be found through Web searches.

21. Examples of different body modifications illustrate the different kinds and contexts of "choice" involved in self-determination. Operations for breast reduction or enhancement, multiple ear piercings, and body piercings (including genital piercings) are modifications often presented by their American or European practitioners as ways to take control of one's body. These self-definitions are very much like local definitions of female genital operations in initiation, also seen as a sign of self-control, maturity, and both social and personal change. In both cases, the practices are linked to understandings of the body, aesthetics, sexuality, and gender relations, but the understandings are rather different, as are their social and institutional settings.

22. See Gruenbaum (1996:460–463) for further discussion of so-called false consciousness and the costs and benefits of female genital operations for various segments of Sudanese communities.

23. I have talked with many people in the United States who seek a "logical" explanation or rationale for traditions of female genital modification. When I summarize what Okiek in Kenya might say in response—e.g., that initiation is necessary for children to become adults—Americans have a hard time understanding and accepting these as "reasons." What for Okiek are logically satisfying, deeply felt, and natural understandings do not have for Americans the same intuitive sense and resonance. It is equally hard to answer Okiek questions about Americans, whom they sometimes encounter as tourists: Why do the women paint their mouths to look like they drink blood? Why do they walk about without clothing (e.g., in bathing suits)? Don't they feel shame? Why aren't girls initiated— how can they live their entire lives as children?

REFERENCES

Abusharaf, Rogaia Mustafa. 1999. Beyond "The External Messiah Syndrome": What Are Sudanese People Doing to End Ritualized Genital Surgeries? Paper presented at the Annual Meetings of the American Anthropological Association, Chicago. Session on Female Genital Cutting: Local Dynamics of a Global Debate.

An-Na`im, Abdullahi, ed. 1992. *Human Rights in Cross-Cultural Perspectives: A Quest for Consensus.* Philadelphia: University of Pennsylvania Press.

An-Na`im, Abdullahi, and Francis Deng, eds. 1990. *Human Rights in Africa : Cross-Cultural Perspectives.* Washington, DC: The Brookings Institution.

Apena, Adeline. 1996. Female Circumcision in Africa and the Problem of Cross-Cultural Perspectives. *Africa Update* 3(2):7–8 (see below for Web version).

Berlin, Isaiah. 1991. *The Crooked Timber of Humanity.* New York: Alfred A. Knopf.

Boddy, Janice. 1989. *Wombs and Alien Spirits.* Madison: University of Wisconsin Press.

Boyarin, Daniel. 1992. "This We Know to Be Carnal Israel": Circumcision and the Erotic Life of God and Israel. *Critical Inquiry* 18(3):474–505.

Courtright, Paul. 1994. The Iconographies of Sati. In *Sati, the Blessing and the Curse.* Ed. John S. Hawley. New York: Oxford University Press.

Daly, Mary. 1990. African Genital Mutilation: The Unspeakable Atrocities. In *Gyn/ecology.* Boston: Beacon Press (originally 1978).

Davison, Jean, with the women of Mutira. 1989. *Voices from Mutira: Lives of Rural Gikuyu Women.* Boulder: Lynn Rienner.

Dawit, Seble. 1997. Letter from a Female Circumcision Activist. *Colloquium: The On-line Magazine of the Case Western Reserve Law Review.* November 1997:*lawwww. cwru.edu/cwrulaw/publications/colloquium/dawitfea.html.*

Desjarlais, Robert. 1997. *Shelter Blues: Sanity and Selfhood Among the Homeless.* Philadelphia: University of Pennsylvania Press.

Dussart, Françoise. 2000. *The Politics of Ritual in an Aboriginal Settlement: Kinship, Gender and the Currency of Knowledge.* Washington, DC: Smithsonian Institution Press.

Geertz, Clifford. 1983. Found in Translation: On the Social History of Moral Imagination. In *Local Knowledge.* New York: Basic Books.

Gruenbaum, Ellen. 1996. The Cultural Debate over Female Circumcision: The Sudanese Are Arguing This One Out for Themselves. *Medical Anthropology Quarterly* 10(4): 455–475.

Hernlund, Ylva. 1999. Ritual Negotiations and Cultural Compromise: An Alternative Initiation in the Gambia. Paper presented at the Annual Meetings of the American Anthropological Association, session on Female Genital Cutting: Local Dynamics of a Global Debate.

Holmes, Douglas R. 2000. *Integral Europe: Fast-Capitalism, Multiculturalism, Neofascism.* Princeton, NJ: Princeton University Press.

Hosken, Fran. 1979. *The Hosken Report.* Lexington, MA: Women's International Network News.

Hutchinson, Sharon. 1996. *Nuer Dilemmas.* Berkeley: University of California Press.

Iweriebor, Ifeyinwa. 1996. Brief Reflections on Clitoridectomy. *Africa Update* 3(2):2 (see below for Web version).

Koso-Thomas, Olayinka. 1987. *The Circumcision of Women: A Strategy for Eradication.* London: Zed Books.

Kratz, Corinne. 1994. *Affecting Performance: Meaning, Movement, and Experience in Okiek Women's Initiation.* Washington, DC: Smithsonian Institution Press.

———. 1999a. Contexts, Controversies, Dilemmas: Teaching Circumcision." In *Great Ideas for Teaching About Africa.* Eds. Misty Bastian and Jane Parpart. Boulder: Lynne Rienner, pp. 103–118.

———. 1999b. Female Circumcision in Africa. In *Africana: Encyclopedia of the African and African American Experience.* Eds. Kwame Anthony Appiah and Henry Louis Gates, Jr. New York: Perseus Publishing. Co-published with CD-ROM version by Microsoft.

———. 2002. Circumcision Debates and Asylum Cases: Intersecting Arenas, Contested Values, and Tangled Webs. In *Engaging Cultural Differences: The Multicultural Challenge in Liberal Democracies.* Eds. Richard A. Shweder, Hazel R. Markus, and Martha Minow. New York: Russell Sage Foundation.

Laumann, E. O., C. M. Masi, and E. W. Zuckerman. 1997. Circumcision in the United States: Prevalence, Prophylactic Effects, and Sexual Practice. *Journal of the American Medical Association* 277(13):1052–1057.

Leonard, Lori. 1999. "We Did It for Pleasure Only": Hearing Alternative Tales of Female Circumcision. Paper presented at the Annual Meetings of the American Anthropological Association, session on Female Genital Cutting: Local Dynamics of a Global Debate.

Lonsdale, John. 1992. Wealth, Poverty, and Civic Virtue in Kikuyu Political Thought. In B. Berman and J. Lonsdale, *Unhappy Valley: Conflict in Kenya and Africa.* London: James Currey.

Lyons, Harriet. 1981. Anthropologists, Moralities, and Relativities: The Problem of Genital Mutilations. *Canadian Review of Sociology and Anthropology* 18(4):499–518.

Mani, Lata. 1990a. Contentious Traditions: The Debate on *Sati* in Colonial India. In *The Nature and Context of Minority Discourse.* Eds. A. JanMohamed and D. Lloyd. Oxford: Oxford University Press.

———. 1990b. Multiple Mediations: Feminist Scholarship in the Age of Multinational Reception. *Feminist Review* 35:24–40.

Matias, Aisha Samad. 1996. Female Circumcision in Africa. *Africa Update* 3(2):3–6.

Mohanty, Chandra. 1988. Under Western Eyes: Feminist Scholarship and Colonial Discourses. *Feminist Review* 30:61–88.

Morison, Linda, Caroline Scherf, Gloria Ekpo, et. al. 2001. The Long-term Reproductive Health Consequences of Female Genital Cutting in Rural Gambia: A Community-Based Survey. *Tropical Medicine and International Health* 6(8):643–653.

Moses, Meredith. 1997. Watching the Watchdog: Female Circumcision in *The New York Times.* Student paper, Emory University.

Mugo, Micere. 1997. Elitist Anti-Circumcision Discourse as Mutilating and Anti-Feminist. *Case Western Reserve Law Review* 47(2):461–80.

Murray, Jocelyn. 1974. The Kikuyu Female Circumcision Controversy, with Special Reference to the Church Missionary Society's "Sphere of Influence." Ph.D. dissertation, University of California, Los Angeles.

——. 1976. The Church Missionary Society and the "Female Circumcision" Issue in Kenya, 1929–1932. *Journal of Religion in Africa* 8(2):92–104.

Nandy, Ashis. 1975. Sati: A Nineteenth Century Tale of Women, Violence, and Protest. In *Rammohun Roy and the Process of Modernization in India*. Ed. V. C. Joshi. Delhi: Vikas Publishing House.

——. 1988. The Human Factor. *The Illustrated Weekly of India*, 17 January, pp. 20–23.

Obiora, L. Amede. 1997. Bridges and Barricades: Rethinking Polemics and Intransigence in the Campaign Against Female Circumcision. *Case Western Reserve Law Review* 47(2):275–378.

Ogbu, M. A. 1997. Comment on Obiora's "Bridges and Barricades." *Case Western Reserve Law Review* 47(2):411–422.

Parker, Melissa. 1995. Rethinking Female Circumcision. *Africa* 65(4):506–524.

Pederson, Susan. 1991. National Bodies, Unspeakable Acts: The Sexual Politics of Colonial Policymaking. *Journal of Modern History* 63:647–680.

Peters, Pauline. 1997. Another Bridge to Cross: Between "Outside" and "Inside." *Case Western Reserve Law Review* 47(2):481–490.

Rofel, Lisa. 1999. *Other Modernities: Gendered Yearnings in China After Socialism*. Berkeley: University of California Press.

Shell-Duncan, Bettina. 2001. The Medicalization of Female "Circumcision": Harm Reduction or Promotion of a Dangerous Practice? *Social Science and Medicine* 52: 1013–1028.

Shell-Duncan, Bettina, and Ylva Hernlund, eds. 2000. *Female "Circumcision" in Africa: Culture, Controversy and Change*. Boulder, CO: Lynne Rienner.

Shweder, Richard. 2002. What About Female Genital Mutilation? And Why Understanding Culture Matters in the First Place. In *Engaging Cultural Differences: The Multicultural Challenge in Liberal Democracies*. Eds. Richard A. Shweder, Hazel R. Markus, and Martha Minow. New York: Russell Sage Foundation.

Stephens, Julie. 1989. Feminist Fictions: A Critique of the Category "Non-Western Woman" in Feminist Writings on India. In *Subaltern Studies VI*. Ed. R. Guha. New York: Oxford University Press.

Teltscher, Kate. 1995. *India Inscribed: European and British Writing on India, 1600–1800*. Oxford: Oxford University Press.

Thomas, Lynn. 1996. "Ngaitana (I will circumcise myself)": The Gender and Generational Politics of the 1956 Ban on Clitoridectomy in Meru, Kenya. *Gender and History* 8(3):338–363.

——. 1997. Imperial Concerns and "Women's Affairs": State Efforts to Regulate Clitoridectomy and Eradicate Abortion in Meru, Kenya, c. 1920–1950. *Journal of African History*.

Verdier, Raymond. 1992. The *Exiseuse* in Criminal Court: the Trial of Soko Aramata Keita. *Passages* 3:1–3 (originally in *Droit et Cultures: Revue semestrielle d'anthropologie et d'histoire*, 1991).

Winter, Bronwyn. 1994. Women, the Law, and Cultural Relativism in France: The Case of Excision. *Signs* 19(4): 939–974.

38

The Price of Progress

John H. Bodley

Anthropologists are not against progress: We do not want everyone to return to the "good old days" of our Paleolithic ancestors. On the other hand, the discoveries of cultural anthropologists have made us painfully aware of the human costs of unplanned social and economic change. Anthropologists do not want our society to plunge blindly into the future, unaware and unconcerned about how our present decisions will affect other people or future generations. Cultures are always changing, and the direction of that change is toward a single world system. Cultures change because a society's economy is pulled into the world economy. "Progress" is a label placed on cultural and economic change, but whether something represents "progress" or not depends on one's perspective.

In this selection, John Bodley reviews some of the unexpected consequences of economic development in terms of health, ecological change, quality of life, and relative deprivation. We have seen this same theme in several previous selections—the invention of agriculture, for example. The benefits of economic development are not equally distributed within a developing society. In this selection, we see the relative costs and benefits of economic progress for some of the most marginalized people of the world—the tribal peoples who have been the traditional focus of cultural anthropology research. We believe that the problems detailed here should make our society think about the way cultural change can make people's lives worse; these are issues of social justice.

Anthropologists have been active in seeking solutions to many serious problems. At the same time, most anthropologists believe that tribal peoples have a right to lead their traditional lifestyles and not to be forced into change. In this regard, an organization called Cultural Survival has been active in the international political arena in protecting the land and rights of native peoples.

As you read this selection, ask yourself the following questions:

- What is meant by quality of life? Why might it increase or decrease for a population?

- What are the three ways in which economic development can change the distribution of disease?

- Why do people's diets change? Do people choose diets and behaviors that are harmful to them?

- What is meant by relative deprivation? Can you think of other examples of this process?

- Are tribal peoples more vulnerable to the negative impact of social and economic change than larger industrial societies?

The following terms discussed in this selection are included in the Glossary at the back of the book:

dental anthropology	*relative deprivation*
ecosystem	*self-sufficient*
ethnocentrism	*swidden cultivation*
nomadic band	*tribe*
population pressure	*urbanization*

In aiming at progress . . . you must let no one suffer by too drastic a measure, nor pay too high a price in upheaval and devastation, for your innovation.

—Maunier, 1949:725

Until recently, government planners have always considered economic development and progress

beneficial goals that all societies should want to strive toward. The social advantages of progress—as defined in terms of increased incomes, higher standards of living, greater security, and better health—are thought to be positive, *universal* goods, to be obtained at any price. Although one may argue that tribal peoples must sacrifice their traditional cultures to obtain these benefits, government planners generally feel that this is a small price to pay for such obvious advantages.

In earlier chapters, evidence was presented to demonstrate that autonomous tribal peoples have not *chosen* progress to enjoy its advantages, but that governments have *pushed* progress upon them to obtain tribal resources, not primarily to share with the tribal peoples the benefits of progress. It has also been shown that the price of forcing progress on unwilling recipients has involved the deaths of millions of tribal people, as well as their loss of land, political sovereignty, and the right to follow their own life style. This chapter does not attempt to further summarize that aspect of the cost of progress, but instead analyzes the specific effects of the participation of tribal peoples in the world-market economy. In direct opposition to the usual interpretation, it is argued here that the benefits of progress are often both illusory and detrimental to tribal peoples when they have not been allowed to control their own resources and define their relationship to the market economy.

PROGRESS AND THE QUALITY OF LIFE

One of the primary difficulties in assessing the benefits of progress and economic development for any culture is that of establishing a meaningful measure of both benefit and detriment. It is widely recognized that *standard of living*, which is the most frequently used measure of progress, is an intrinsically ethnocentric concept relying heavily upon indicators that lack universal cultural relevance. Such factors as GNP, per capita income, capital formation, employment rates, literacy, formal education, consumption of manufactured goods, number of doctors and hospital beds per thousand persons, and the amount of money spent on government welfare and health programs may be irrelevant measures of actual *quality* of life for autonomous or even semiautonomous tribal cultures. In its 1954 report, the Trust Territory government indicated that since the Micronesian population was still largely satisfying its own needs within a cashless subsistence economy, "Money income is not a significant measure of living standards, production, or well-being in this area" (TTR, 1953:44). Unfortunately, within a short time the government began to rely on an enumeration of certain imported goods as indicators of a higher standard of living in the islands, even though many tradition-oriented islanders felt that these new goods symbolized a lowering of the quality of life.

A more useful measure of the benefits of progress might be based on a formula for evaluating cultures devised by Goldschmidt (1952:135). According to these less ethnocentric criteria, the important question to ask is: Does progress or economic development increase or decrease a given culture's ability to satisfy the physical and psychological needs of its population, or its stability? This question is a far more direct measure of quality of life than are the standard economic correlates of development, and it is universally relevant. Specific indication of this *standard* of living could be found for any society in the nutritional status and general physical and mental health of its population, the incidence of crime and delinquency, the demographic structure, family stability, and the society's relationship to its natural resource base. A society with high rates of malnutrition and crime, and one degrading its natural environment to the extent of threatening its continued existence, might be described as at a lower standard of living than is another society where these problems did not exist.

Careful examination of the data, which compare, on these specific points, the former condition of self-sufficient tribal peoples with their condition following their incorporation into the world-market economy, leads to the conclusion that their standard of living is *lowered*, not raised, by economic progress—and often to a dramatic degree. This is perhaps the most outstanding and inescapable fact to emerge from the years of research that anthropologists have devoted to the study of culture change and modernization. Despite the best intentions of those who have promoted change and improvement, all too often the results have been poverty, longer working hours, and much greater physical exertion, poor health, social disorder, discontent, discrimination, overpopulation, and environmental deterioration—combined with the destruction of the traditional culture.

DISEASES OF DEVELOPMENT

> Perhaps it would be useful for public health specialists to start talking about a new category of diseases. . . . Such diseases could be called the "diseases of development" and would consist of those pathological conditions which are based on the usually unanticipated consequences of the implementation of development schemes (Hughes & Hunter, 1972:93).

Economic development increases the disease rate of affected peoples in at least three ways. First, to the extent that development is successful, it makes developed populations suddenly become vulnerable to all of the diseases suffered almost exclusively by "advanced" peoples. Among these are diabetes, obesity, hypertension, and a variety of circulatory problems. Second, development disturbs traditional environmental balances and may dramatically increase certain bacterial and parasite diseases. Finally, when development goals prove unattainable, an assortment of poverty diseases may appear in association with the crowded conditions of urban slums and the general breakdown in traditional socioeconomic systems.

Outstanding examples of the first situation can be seen in the Pacific, where some of the most successfully developed native peoples are found. In Micronesia, where development has progressed more rapidly than perhaps anywhere else, between 1958 and 1972 the population doubled, but the number of patients treated for heart disease in the local hospitals nearly tripled, mental disorder increased eightfold, and by 1972 hypertension and nutritional deficiencies began to make significant appearances for the first time (TTR, 1959, 1973, statistical tables).

Although some critics argue that the Micronesian figures simply represent better health monitoring due to economic progress, rigorously controlled data from Polynesia show a similar trend. The progressive acquisition of modern degenerative diseases was documented by an eight-member team of New Zealand medical specialists, anthropologists, and nutritionists, whose research was funded by the Medical Research Council of New Zealand and the World Health Organization. These researchers investigated the health status of a genetically related population at various points along a continuum of increasing cash income, modernizing diet, and urbanization. The extremes on this acculturation continuum were represented by the relatively traditional Pukapukans of the Cook Islands and the essentially Europeanized New Zealand Maori, while the busily developing Rarotongans, also of the Cook Islands, occupied the intermediate position. In 1971, after eight years of work, the team's preliminary findings were summarized by Dr. Ian Prior, cardiologist and leader of the research, as follows:

> We are beginning to observe that the more an islander takes on the ways of the West, the more prone he is to succumb to our degenerative diseases. In fact, it does not seem too much to say our evidence now shows that the farther the Pacific natives move from the quiet, carefree life of their ancestors, the closer they come to gout, diabetes, atherosclerosis, obesity, and hypertension (Prior, 1971:2).

In Pukapuka, where progress was limited by the island's small size and its isolated location some 480 kilometers from the nearest port, the annual per capita income was only about thirty-six dollars and the economy remained essentially at a subsistence level. Resources were limited and the area was visited by trading ships only three or four times a year; thus, there was little opportunity for intensive economic development. Predictably, the population of Pukapuka was characterized by relatively low levels of imported sugar and salt intake, and a presumably related low level of heart disease, high blood pressure, and diabetes. In Rarotonga,

where economic success was introducing town life, imported food, and motorcycles, sugar and salt intakes nearly tripled, high blood pressure increased approximately ninefold, diabetes two- to threefold, and heart disease doubled for men and more than quadrupled for women, while the number of grossly obese women increased more than tenfold. Among the New Zealand Maori, sugar intake was nearly eight times that of the Pukapukans, gout in men was nearly double its rate on Pukapuka, and diabetes in men was more than fivefold higher, while heart disease in women had increased more than sixfold. The Maori were, in fact, dying of "European" diseases at a greater rate than was the average New Zealand European.

Government development policies designed to bring about changes in local hydrology, vegetation, and settlement patterns and to increase population mobility, and even programs aimed at reducing certain diseases, have frequently led to dramatic increases in disease rates because of the unforeseen effects of disturbing the preexisting order. Hughes and Hunter (1972) published an excellent survey of cases in which development led directly to increased disease rates in Africa. They concluded that hasty development intervention in relatively balanced local cultures and environments resulted in "a drastic deterioration in the social and economic conditions of life."

Traditional populations in general have presumably learned to live with the endemic pathogens of their environments, and in some cases they have evolved genetic adaptations to specific diseases, such as the sickle-cell trait, which provided an immunity to malaria. Unfortunately, however, outside intervention has entirely changed this picture. In the late 1960s, sleeping sickness suddenly increased in many areas of Africa and even spread to areas where it did not formerly occur, due to the building of new roads and migratory labor, both of which caused increased population movement. Large-scale relocation schemes, such as the Zande Scheme, had disastrous results when natives were moved from their traditional disease-free refuges into infected areas. Dams and irrigation developments inadvertently created ideal conditions for the rapid proliferation of snails carrying schistosomiasis (a liver fluke disease), and major epidemics suddenly occurred in areas where this disease had never before been a problem. DDT spraying programs have been temporarily successful in controlling malaria, but there is often a rebound effect that increases the problem when spraying is discontinued, and the malarial mosquitoes are continually evolving resistant strains.

Urbanization is one of the prime measures of development, but it is a mixed blessing for most former tribal peoples. Urban health standards are abysmally poor and generally worse than in rural areas for the detribalized individuals who have crowded into the towns and cities throughout Africa, Asia, and Latin America seeking wage employment out of new economic necessity. Infectious diseases related to crowding and poor sanitation are rampant in urban centers, while greatly increased stress and poor nutrition aggravate a variety of other health problems. Malnutrition and other diet-related conditions are, in fact, one of the characteristic hazards of progress faced by tribal peoples and are discussed in the following sections.

The Hazards of Dietary Change

The traditional diets of tribal peoples are admirably adapted to their nutritional needs and available food resources. Even though these diets may seem bizarre, absurd, and unpalatable to outsiders, they are unlikely to be improved by drastic modifications. Given the delicate balances and complexities involved in any subsistence system, change always involves risks, but for tribal people the effects of dietary change have been catastrophic.

Under normal conditions, food habits are remarkably resistant to change, and indeed people are unlikely to abandon their traditional diets voluntarily in favor of dependence on difficult-to-obtain exotic imports. In some cases it is true that imported foods may be identified with powerful outsiders and are therefore sought as symbols of greater prestige. This may lead to such absurdities as Amazonian Indians choosing to consume imported canned tunafish when abundant high-quality fish is available in their own rivers. Another example of this situation occurs in tribes where mothers prefer to feed their infants expensive and nutritionally inadequate canned milk from unsanitary, but *high status*, baby bottles. The high status of these items is often promoted by clever traders and clever advertising campaigns.

Aside from these apparently voluntary changes, it appears that more often dietary changes are forced upon unwilling tribal peoples by circumstances beyond their control. In some areas, new food crops have been introduced by government decree, or as a consequence of forced relocation or other policies designed to end hunting, pastoralism, or shifting cultivation. Food habits have also been modified by massive disruption of the natural environment by outsiders—as when sheepherders transformed the Australian Aborigine's foraging territory or when European invaders destroyed the bison herds that were the primary element in the Plains Indians' subsistence patterns. Perhaps the most frequent cause of diet change occurs when formerly self-sufficient peoples find that wage labor, cash cropping, and other economic development activities that feed tribal resources into the world-market economy must inevitably divert time and energy away from the production of subsistence foods. Many developing peoples suddenly discover that, like it or not, they are unable to secure traditional foods and must spend their newly acquired cash on costly, and often nutritionally inferior, manufactured foods.

Overall, the available data seem to indicate that the dietary changes that are linked to involvement in the world-market economy have tended to *lower* rather than raise the nutritional levels of the affected tribal peoples. Specifically, the vitamin, mineral, and protein components of their diets are often drastically reduced and replaced by enormous increases in starch and carbohydrates, often in the form of white flour and refined sugar.

Any deterioration in the quality of a given population's diet is almost certain to be reflected in an increase in deficiency diseases and a general decline in health status. Indeed, as tribal peoples have shifted to a diet based on imported manufactured or processed foods, there has been a dramatic rise in malnutrition, a massive increase in dental problems, and a variety of other nutrition-related disorders. Nutritional physiology is so complex that even well-meaning dietary changes have had tragic consequences. In many areas of Southeast Asia, government-sponsored protein supplementation programs supplying milk to protein-deficient populations caused unexpected health problems and increased mortality. Officials failed to anticipate that in cultures where adults do not normally drink milk, the enzymes needed to digest it are no longer produced and milk *intolerance* results (Davis & Bolin, 1972). In Brazil, a similar milk distribution program caused an epidemic of permanent blindness by aggravating a preexisting vitamin A deficiency (Bunce, 1972).

Teeth and Progress

> There is nothing new in the observation that savages, or peoples living under primitive conditions, have, in general excellent teeth. . . . Nor is it news that most civilized populations possess wretched teeth which begin to decay almost before they have erupted completely, and that dental caries is likely to be accompanied by periodontal disease with further reaching complications (Hooton, 1945:xviii).

Anthropologists have long recognized that undisturbed tribal peoples are often in excellent physical condition. And it has often been noted specifically that dental caries and the other dental abnormalities that plague industrialized societies are absent or rare among tribal peoples who have retained their traditional diets.

The fact that tribal food habits may contribute to the development of sound teeth, whereas modernized diets may do just the opposite, was illustrated as long ago as 1894 in an article in the *Journal of the Royal Anthropological Institute* that described the results of a comparison between the teeth of ten Sioux Indians and a comparable group of Londoners (Smith, 1894: 109–116). The Indians were examined when they came to London as members of Buffalo Bill's Wild West Show and were found to be completely free of caries and in possession of all their teeth, even though half of the group were over thirty-nine years of age. Londoners' teeth were conspicuous for both their caries and their steady reduction in number with advancing age. The difference was attributed primarily to the wear and polishing caused by the traditional Indian diet of coarse food and the fact that they chewed their food longer, encouraged by the absence of tableware.

One of the most remarkable studies of the dental conditions of tribal peoples and the impact of dietary change was conducted in the 1930s by Weston Price (1945), an American dentist who was interested in determining what caused normal, healthy teeth. Between 1931 and 1936, Price systematically explored tribal areas throughout the world to locate and examine the most isolated peoples who were still living on traditional foods. His fieldwork covered Alaska, the Canadian Yukon, Hudson Bay, Vancouver Island, Florida, the Andes, the Amazon, Samoa, Tahiti, New Zealand, Australia, New Caledonia, Fiji, the Torres Strait, East Africa, and the Nile. The study demonstrated both the superior quality of aboriginal dentition and the devastation that occurs as modern diets are adopted. In nearly every area where traditional foods were still being eaten, Price found perfect teeth with normal dental arches and virtually no decay, whereas caries and abnormalities increased steadily as new diets were adopted. In many cases the change was sudden and striking. Among Eskimo groups subsisting entirely on traditional food he found caries totally absent, whereas in groups eating a considerable quantity of store-bought food approximately 20 percent of their teeth were decayed. The figure rose to more than 30 percent with Eskimo groups subsisting almost exclusively on purchased or government-supplied food, and reached an incredible 48 percent among the Vancouver Island Indians. Unfortunately for many of these people, modern dental treatment did not accompany the new food, and their suffering was appalling. The loss of teeth was, of course, bad enough in itself, and it certainly undermined the population's resistance to many new diseases, including tuberculosis. But new foods were also accompanied by crowded, misplaced teeth, gum diseases, distortion of the face, and pinching of the nasal cavity. Abnormalities in the dental arch appeared in the new generation following the change in diet, while caries appeared almost immediately even in adults.

Price reported that in many areas the affected peoples were conscious of their own physical deterioration. At a mission school in Africa, the principal asked him to explain to the native schoolchildren why they were not physically as strong as children who had had no contact with schools. On an island in the Torres Strait the natives knew exactly what was causing their problems and resisted—almost to the point of bloodshed—government efforts to establish a store that would make imported food available. The government prevailed, however, and Price was able to establish a relationship between the length of time the government store had been established and the increasing incidences of caries among a population that showed an almost 100 percent immunity to them before the store had been opened.

In New Zealand, the Maori, who in their aboriginal state are often considered to have been among the healthiest, most perfectly developed of peoples, were found to have "advanced" the furthest. According to Price:

> Their modernization was demonstrated not only by the high incidence of dental caries but also by the fact 90 percent of the adults and 100 percent of the children had abnormalities of the dental arches (Price, 1945:206).

Malnutrition

Malnutrition, particularly in the form of protein deficiency, has become a critical problem for tribal peoples who must adopt new economic patterns. Population pressures, cash cropping, and government programs all have tended to encourage the replacement of traditional crops and other food sources that were rich in protein with substitutes high in calories but low in protein. In Africa, for example, protein-rich staples such as millet and sorghum are being replaced systematically by high-yielding manioc and plantains, which have insignificant amounts of protein. The problem is increased for cash croppers and wage laborers whose earnings are too low and unpredictable to allow purchase of adequate amounts of protein. In some rural areas, agricultural laborers have been forced systematically to deprive nonproductive members (principally children) of their households of their minimal nutritional requirements to satisfy the need of the productive members. This process has been documented in northeastern Brazil following the introduction of large-scale sisal plantations (Gross & Underwood, 1971). In urban centers the difficulties of obtaining nutritionally adequate diets are even more serious for tribal immigrants, because costs are higher and poor quality foods are more tempting.

One of the most tragic, and largely overlooked, aspects of chronic malnutrition is that it can lead to abnormally undersized brain development and apparently irreversible brain damage; it has been associated with various forms of mental impairment or retardation. Malnutrition has been linked clinically with mental retardation in both Africa and Latin America (see, for example, Mönckeberg, 1968), and this appears to be a worldwide phenomenon with serious implications (Montagu, 1972).

Optimistic supporters of progress will surely say that all of these new health problems are being overstressed and that the introduction of hospitals, clinics, and the other modern health institutions will overcome or at least compensate for all of these difficulties. However, it appears that uncontrolled population growth and economic impoverishment probably will keep most of these benefits out of reach for many tribal peoples, and the intervention of modern medicine has at least partly contributed to the problem in the first place.

The generalization that civilization frequently has a broad negative impact on tribal health has found broad empirical support (see especially Kroeger & Barbira-Freedman [1982] on Amazonia; Reinhard [1976] on the Arctic; and Wirsing [1985] globally), but these conclusions have not gone unchallenged. Some critics argue that tribal health was often poor before modernization, and they point specifically to tribals' low life expectancy and high infant mortality rates. Demographic statistics on tribal populations are often problematic because precise data are scarce, but they do show a less favorable profile than that enjoyed by many industrial societies. However, it should be remembered that our present life expectancy is a recent phenomenon that has been very costly in terms of medical research and technological advances. Furthermore, the benefits of our health system are not enjoyed equally by all members of our society. High infant mortality could be viewed as a relatively inexpensive and egalitarian tribal public health program that offered the reasonable expectation of a healthy and productive life for those surviving to age fifteen.

Some critics also suggest that certain tribal populations, such as the New Guinea highlanders, were "stunted" by nutritional deficiencies created by tribal culture and are "improved" by "acculturation" and cash cropping (Dennett & Connell, 1988). Although this argument does suggest that the health question requires careful evaluation, it does not invalidate the empirical generalizations already established. Nutritional deficiencies undoubtedly occurred in densely populated zones in the central New Guinea highlands. However, the specific case cited above may not be widely representative of other tribal groups even in New Guinea, and it does not address the facts of outside intrusion or the inequities inherent in the contemporary development process.

ECOCIDE

"How is it," asked a herdsman . . . "how is it that these hills can no longer give pasture to my cattle? In my father's day they were green and cattle thrived there; today there is no grass and my cattle starve." As one looked one saw that what had once been a green hill had become a raw red rock (Jones, 1934).

Progress not only brings new threats to the health of tribal peoples, but it also imposes new strains on the ecosystems upon which they must depend for their ultimate survival. The introduction of new technology, increased consumption, lowered mortality, and the eradication of all traditional controls have combined to replace what for most tribal peoples was a relatively stable balance between population and natural resources, with a new system that is imbalanced. Economic development is forcing *ecocide* on peoples who were once careful stewards of their resources. There is already a trend toward widespread environmental deterioration in tribal areas, involving resource depletion, erosion, plant and animal extinction, and a disturbing series of other previously unforeseen changes.

After the initial depopulation suffered by most tribal peoples during their engulfment by frontiers of national expansion, most tribal populations began to experience rapid growth. Authorities generally attribute this growth to the introduction of modern medicine and new health measures and the termination of intertribal warfare, which lowered mortality rates, as well as to new technology, which increased food production. Certainly all of these factors played a part, but merely lowering mortality rates would not have produced the rapid population growth that most tribal areas have experienced if traditional birth-spacing mechanisms had not been eliminated at the same time. Regardless of which factors were most important, it is clear that all of the natural and cultural checks on population growth have suddenly been pushed aside by culture change, while tribal lands have been steadily reduced and consumption levels have risen. In many tribal areas, environmental deterioration due to overuse of resources has set in, and in other areas such deterioration is imminent as resources continue to dwindle relative to the expanding population and increased use. Of course, population expansion by tribal peoples may have positive political consequences, because where tribals can retain or regain their status as local majorities they may be in a more favorable position to defend their resources against intruders.

Swidden systems and pastoralism, both highly successful economic systems under traditional conditions, have proven particularly vulnerable to increased population pressures and outside efforts to raise productivity beyond its natural limits. Research in Amazonia demonstrates that population pressures and related resource depletion can be created indirectly by official policies that restrict swidden peoples to smaller territories. Resource depletion itself can then become a powerful means of forcing tribal people into participating in the world-market economy—thus leading to further resource depletion. For example, Bodley and Benson (1979) showed how the Shipibo Indians in Peru were forced to further deplete their forest resources by cash cropping in the forest area to replace the resources that had been destroyed earlier by the intensive cash cropping necessitated by the narrow confines of their reserve. In this case, a certain species of palm trees that had provided critical housing materials were destroyed by forest clearing and had to be replaced by costly purchased materials. Research by Gross (1979) and others showed similar processes at work among four tribal groups in central Brazil and demonstrated that the degree of market involvement increases directly with increases in resource depletion.

The settling of nomadic herders and the removal of prior controls on herd size have often led to serious overgrazing and erosion problems where these had not previously occurred. There are indications that the desertification problem in the Sahel region of Africa was aggravated by programs designed to settle nomads. The first sign of imbalance in a swidden system appears when the planting cycles are shortened to the point that garden plots are reused before sufficient forest regrowth can occur. If reclearing and planting continue in the same area, the natural pattern of forest succession may be disturbed irreversibly and the soil can be impaired permanently. An extensive tract of tropical rainforest in the lower Amazon of Brazil was reduced to a semiarid desert in just fifty years through such a process (Ackermann, 1964). The soils in the Azande area are also now seriously threatened with laterization and other problems as a result of the government-promoted cotton development scheme (McNeil, 1972).

The dangers of overdevelopment and the vulnerability of local resource systems have long been recognized by both anthropologists and tribal peoples themselves, but the pressures for change have been overwhelming. In 1948 the Maya villagers of Chan Kom complained to Redfield (1962) about the shortening of their swidden cycles, which they correctly attributed to increasing population pressures. Redfield told them, however, that they had no choice but to go "forward with technology" (Redfield, 1962:178). In Assam, swidden cycles were shortened from an average of twelve years to only two or three within just twenty years, and anthropologists warned that the limits of swiddening would soon be reached (Burling, 1963:311–312). In the Pacific, anthropologists warned of population pressures on limited resources as early as the 1930s (Keesing, 1941:64–65). These warnings seemed fully justified, considering the fact that the crowded Tikopians were prompted by population pressures on their tiny island to suggest that infanticide be legalized. The warnings have been dramatically reinforced since then by the doubling of Micronesia's population in just the fourteen years between 1958 and 1972, from 70,600 to 114,645, while consumption levels have soared. By 1985 Micronesia's population had reached 162,321.

The environmental hazards of economic development and rapid population growth have become generally recognized only since worldwide concerns over environmental issues began in the early 1970s. Unfortunately, there is as yet little indication that the leaders of the now developing nations are sufficiently concerned with environmental limitations. On the contrary governments are forcing tribal peoples into a self-reinforcing spiral of population growth and intensified resource exploitation, which may be stopped only by environmental disaster or the total impoverishment of the tribals.

The reality of ecocide certainly focuses attention on the fundamental contrasts between tribal and industrial systems in their use of natural resources. In many respects the entire "victims of progress" issue hinges on natural resources, who controls them, and how they are managed. Tribal peoples are victimized because they control resources that outsiders demand. The resources exist because tribals managed them conservatively. However, as with the issue of the health consequences of detribalization, some anthropologists minimize the adaptive achievements of tribal groups and seem unwilling to concede that ecocide might be a consequence of cultural change. Critics attack an exaggerated "noble savage" image of tribals living in perfect harmony with nature and having no visible impact on their surroundings. They then show that tribals do in fact modify the environment, and they conclude that there is no significant difference between how tribals and industrial societies treat their environments. For example, Charles Wagley declared that Brazilian Indians such as the Tapirape

> are not "natural men." They have human vices just as we do. . . . They do not live "in tune" with nature any more than I do; in fact, they can often be as destructive of their environment, within their limitations, as some civilized men. The Tapirape are not innocent or childlike in any way (Wagley, 1977:302).

Anthropologist Terry Rambo demonstrated that the Semang of the Malaysian rain forests have measurable impact on their environment. In his monograph *Primitive Polluters,* Rambo (1985) reported that the Semang live in smoke-filled houses. They sneeze and spread germs, breathe, and thus emit carbon dioxide. They clear small gardens, contributing "particulate matter" to the air and disturbing the local climate because cleared areas proved measurably warmer and drier than the shady forest. Rambo concluded that his research "demonstrated the essential functional similarity of the environmental interactions of primitive and civilized societies" (1985:78) in contrast to a "noble savage" view (Bodley, 1983) which, according to Rambo (1985:2), mistakenly "claims that traditional peoples almost always live in essential harmony with their environment."

This is surely a false issue. To stress, as I do, that tribals tend to manage their resources for sustained yield within relatively self-sufficient subsistence economies is not to make them either innocent children or natural men. Nor is it to deny that tribals "disrupt" their environment and may never be in absolute "balance" with nature.

The ecocide issue is perhaps most dramatically illustrated by two sets of satellite photos taken over the Brazilian rain forests of Rôndonia (Allard & McIntyre, 1988:780–781). Photos taken in 1973, when Rôndonia was still a tribal domain, show virtually unbroken rain forest. The 1987 satellite photos, taken after just fifteen years of highway construction and "development" by outsiders, show more than 20 percent of the forest destroyed. The surviving Indians were being concentrated by FUNAI (Brazil's national Indian foundation) into what would soon become mere islands of forest in a ravaged landscape. It is irrelevant to quibble about whether tribals are noble, childlike, or innocent, or about the precise meaning of balance with nature, carrying capacity, or adaptation, to recognize that for the past 200 years rapid environmental deterioration on an unprecedented global scale has followed the wresting of control of vast areas of the world from tribal groups by resource-hungry industrial societies.

DEPRIVATION AND DISCRIMINATION

Contact with European culture has given them a knowledge of great wealth, opportunity and privilege, but only very limited avenues by which to acquire these things (Crocombe, 1968).

Unwittingly, tribal peoples have had the burden of perpetual relative deprivation thrust upon them by acceptance—either by themselves or by the governments administering them—of the standards of socioeconomic progress set for them by industrial civilizations. By comparison with the material wealth of industrial societies, tribal societies become, by definition, impoverished. They are then forced to transform their cultures and work to achieve what many economists now acknowledge to be unattainable goals. Even though in many cases the modest GNP goals set by development planners for the developing nations during the "development decade" of the 1960s were often met, the results were hardly noticeable for most of the tribal people involved. Population growth, environmental limitations, inequitable distribution of wealth, and the continued rapid growth of the industrialized nations have all meant that both the absolute and the relative gap between the rich and poor in the world is steadily widening. The prospect that tribal peoples will actually be able to attain the levels of resource consumption to which they are being encouraged to aspire is remote indeed except for those few groups who have retained effective control over strategic mineral resources.

Tribal peoples feel deprivation not only when the economic goals they have been encouraged to seek fail to materialize, but also when they discover that they are powerless, second-class citizens who are discriminated against and exploited by the dominant society. At the same time, they are denied the satisfactions of their traditional cultures, because these have been sacrificed in the process of modernization. Under the impact of major economic change family life is disrupted, traditional social controls are often lost, and many indicators of social anomie such as alcoholism, crime, delinquency, suicide, emotional disorders, and despair may increase. The inevitable frustration resulting from this continual deprivation finds expression in the cargo cults, revitalization movements, and a variety of other political and religious movements that have been widespread among tribal peoples following their disruption by industrial civilization.

REFERENCES

Ackermann, F. L. 1964. *Geologia e Fisiografia da Região Bragantina, Estado do Pará.* Manaus, Brazil: Conselho Nacional de Pesquisas, Instituto Nacional de Pesquisas da Amazônia.

Allard, William Albert, and Loren McIntyre. 1988. Rôndonia's settlers invade Brazil's imperiled rain forest. *National Geographic* 174(6):772–799.

Bodley, John H. 1983. The World Bank tribal policy: Criticisms and recommendations. *Congressional Record,* serial no. 98-37, pp. 515–521. (Reprinted in Bodley, 1988.)

Bodley, John H., and Foley C. Benson. 1979. Cultural ecology of Amazonian palms. *Reports of Investigations,* no. 56. Pullman: Laboratory of Anthropology, Washington State University.

Bunce, George E. 1972. Aggravation of vitamin A deficiency following distribution of non-fortified skim milk: An example of nutrient interaction. In *The Careless Technology: Ecology and International Development*, ed. M. T. Farvar and John P. Milton, pp. 53–60. Garden City, N.Y.: Natural History Press.

Burling, Robbins. 1963. *Rengsanggri: Family and Kinship in a Garo Village.* Philadelphia: University of Pennsylvania Press.

Crocombe, Ron. 1968. Bougainville!: Copper, R. R. A. and secessionism. *New Guinea* 3(3):39–49.

Davis, A. E., and T. D. Bolin. 1972. Lactose intolerance in Southeast Asia. In *The Careless Technology: Ecology and International Development*, ed. M. T. Farvar and John P. Milton, pp. 61–68. Garden City, N.Y.: Natural History Press.

Dennett, Glenn, and John Connell. 1988. Acculturation and health in the highlands of Papua New Guinea. *Current Anthropology* 29(2):273–299.

Goldschmidt, Walter R. 1952. The interrelations between cultural factors and acquisition of new technical skills. In *The Progress of Underdeveloped Areas*, ed. Bert F. Hoselitz, pp. 135–151. Chicago: University of Chicago Press.

Gross, Daniel R., and Barbara A. Underwood. 1971. Technological change and caloric costs: Sisal agriculture. *American Anthropologist* 73(3):725–740.

Gross, Daniel R., et al. 1979. Ecology and acculturation among native peoples of Central Brazil. *Science* 206(4422):1043–1050.

Hooton, Earnest A. 1945. Introduction. In *Nutrition and Physical Degeneration: A Comparison of Primitive and Modern Diets and Their Effects* by Weston A. Price. Redlands, Calif.: The author.

Hughes, Charles C., and John M. Hunter. 1972. The role of technological development in promoting disease in Africa. In *The Careless Technology: Ecology and International Development*, ed. M. T. Farvar and John P. Milton, pp. 69–101. Garden City, N.Y.: Natural History Press.

Jones, J. D. Rheinallt. 1934. Economic condition of the urban native. In *Western Civilization and the Natives of South Africa*, ed. I. Schapera, pp. 159–192. London: George Routledge and Sons.

Keesing, Felix M. 1941. *The South Seas in the Modern World.* Institute of Pacific Relations International Research Series. New York: John Day.

Kroeger, Axel, and Françoise Barbira-Freedman. 1982. *Culture Change and Health: The Case of South American Rainforest Indians.* Frankfurt am Main: Verlag Peter Lang. (Reprinted in Bodley, 1988:221–236).

Maunier, René. 1949. *The Sociology of Colonies.* Vol. 2. London: Routledge and Kegan Paul.

McNeil, Mary. 1972. Lateritic soils in distinct tropical environments: Southern Sudan and Brazil. In *The Careless Technology: Ecology and International Development*, ed. M. T. Farvar and John P. Milton, pp. 591–608. Garden City, N.Y.: Natural History Press.

Mönckeberg, F. 1968. Mental retardation from malnutrition. *Journal of the American Medical Association* 206:30–31.

Montagu, Ashley. 1972. Sociogenic brain damage. *American Anthropologist* 74(5):1045–1061.

Price, Weston Andrew. 1945. *Nutrition and Physical Degeneration: A Comparison of Primitive and Modern Diets and Their Effects.* Redlands, Calif.: The author.

Prior, Ian A. M. 1971. The price of civilization. *Nutrition Today* 6(4):2–11.

Rambo, A. Terry. 1985. *Primitive Polluters: Semang Impact on the Malaysian Tropical Rain Forest Ecosystem.* Anthropological Papers no. 76, Museum of Anthropology, University of Michigan.

Redfield, Robert. 1962. *A Village That Chose Progress: Chan Kom Revisited.* Chicago: University of Chicago Press, Phoenix Books.

Reinhard, K. R. 1976. Resource exploitation and the health of western arctic man. In *Circumpolar Health: Proceedings of the Third International Symposium, Yellowknife, Northwest Territories*, ed. Roy J. Shephard and S. Itoh, pp. 617–627. Toronto: University of Toronto Press. (Reprinted in Bodley, 1988.)

Smith, Wilberforce. 1894. The teeth of ten Sioux Indians. *Journal of the Royal Anthropological Institute* 24:109–116.

TTR: TTR, United States, Department of the Interior, Office of the Territories. 1953. Report on the Administration of the trust territories of the Pacific Islands for the period of July 1, 1951 to June 30, 1952.

United States, Department of State. 1955. *Seventh Annual Report to the United Nations on the Administration of the Trust Territory of the Pacific Islands* (July 1, 1953, to June 30, 1954).

———. 1959. *Eleventh Annual Report to the United Nations on the Administration of the Trust Territory of the Pacific Islands* (July 1, 1957, to June 30, 1958).

———. 1973. *Twenty-Fifth Annual Report to the United Nations on the Administration of the Trust Territory of the Pacific Islands* (July 1, 1971, to June 30, 1972).

Wagley, C. 1977. *Welcome of Tears: The Tapirape Indians of Central Brazil.* New York: Oxford University Press.

Wirsing, R. 1985. The health of traditional societies and the effects of acculturation. *Current Anthropology* 26: 303–322.

Glossary

acculturation   The process of extensive borrowing of aspects of another culture, usually as a result of external pressure, and often resulting in the decline of traditional culture.

adaptation   The process by which an organism or a culture is modified, usually through selection, enhancing the ability of individuals to survive and reproduce in a particular environment.

adipose tissue   Fat. A physiological mechanism of energy storage; some adipose tissue, especially when deposited on the central body, is associated with chronic diseases.

adjudication   A process of handling disputes in which the ultimate decision is made by a third party appointed by the legal system.

affinal kin   A kin relationship created by marriage.

affines   Individuals related to one another because of marriage between their families; related through marriage rather than birth.

Afrocentric   An explanation based on African origins.

age grade   A social category of people who fall within a particular culturally distinguished age range; age grades often undergo life cycle rituals as a group.

agency   The means, capacity, condition, or state of exerting power.

aggression   A forceful action, sometimes involving physical violence, intended for social domination.

agnates   Individuals sharing a patrilineal kinship tie; people related through the male line.

agnatic   Related through the male kinship line.

agrarian   Relating to agriculture.

agricultural development   Changes in agricultural production intended to improve the system by producing more harvest per unit of land.

AIDS   Acquired immune deficiency syndrome, a fatal disease caused by the human immunodeficiency virus (HIV) and usually transmitted through semen or blood.

Amerindian   Native American populations.

anorexia nervosa   An eating disorder characterized by extreme dieting and a feeling of being fat even though one is underweight.

anthropology   The systematic study of humans, including their biology and culture, both past and present.

anthropometry   Science of the measurement of the human body, including measurement of bones, muscle, fat, and other body tissues.

applied research   Study directed at gaining valid knowledge to help in the solution of human problems.

arable land   Land suitable for cultivation.

arbitration   The hearing and determination of a dispute by a person chosen by the parties or appointed by the legal system with the consent of the parties.

archaeology   The field of anthropology concerned with cultural history; includes the systematic retrieval, identification, and study of the physical and cultural remains deposited in the earth.

argot   A specialized, sometimes secret, vocabulary peculiar to a particular group.

artifact   An object manufactured and used by human beings for a culturally defined goal.

asylum   The process by which immigrants are allowed to remain legally in their host country because of "persecution or a well-founded fear of persecution" in their country of origin.

australopithecine   A member of the genus *Australopithecus*, the hominid ancestors of humans.

Ayurvedic medicine   Traditional medical system of India.

AZT   An antiviral drug used to slow down the replication of HIV, the human immunodeficiency virus that causes AIDS; AZT is very expensive.

basic research   Study directed toward gaining scientific knowledge primarily for its own sake.

big men   Political leaders in tribal-level societies whose status has been achieved and whose authority is limited.

biogenetic   Genetic.

biological anthropology   Subfield of anthropology that studies the biological nature of humans and includes primatology, paleoanthropology, population genetics, anthropometry, and human biology.

biomedicine   Modern medicine as practiced in the United States and Europe; emphasizes the biological causation and remedy for illness.

biophysical diversity   Outward biological appearance resulting from interaction of genes and environment; phenotype.

biotic community   Plants and animals sharing a niche within an ecosystem.

blood relatives   A folk term referring to consanguineal kin, that is, kin related through birth.

brideprice   See *bridewealth*.

bridewealth   The presentation of goods or money by the groom's family to the bride's family at the time of marriage; an economic exchange that legitimates the marriage and offspring as members of the father's patrilineage.

burqa   A head-to-toe veil common in Afghanistan, often made of cotton and covering most of the body, including the face.

bush-fallow   A technique used by horticulturalists that allows a garden plot to return to the wild state after a period of cultivation.

cadastral   A government survey and record-keeping system for recording land ownership and property boundaries.

canton   A small territorial division of a country.

capitalism   An economic system characteristic of modern state societies where land, labor, and capital all become commodities exchanged on the market and in which socioeconomic inequality is a constant feature.

carrying capacity   The maximum population size that can be maintained in a given area without causing environmental degradation of the ecology.

caste   A ranked group, sometimes linked to a particular occupation, with membership determined at birth and with marriage restricted to others within the group.

ceremony   Public events involving special symbols that signify important cultural values or beliefs.

chief   The political leader of a society that is more complex than a tribal society and is characterized by social ranking, a redistributive economy, and a centralized political authority.

chiefdom   A society more complex than a tribal society, characterized by social ranking, a redistributive economy, and a centralized political authority.

CITES   Convention on International Trade and Endangered Species. An international agreement to limit the capture of endangered animals, including whales, and regulate the market for endangered species; related to the International Commission for the Conservation of Atlantic Tunas (ICCAT) that assigns quotas for tuna fishermen.

civilization   The culture of state-level societies characterized by the following elements: (1) agriculture; (2) urban living; (3) a high degree of occupational specialization and differentiation; (4) social stratification; and (5) literacy.

clan   A kinship group whose members assume, but need not demonstrate, descent from a common ancestor.

class   An economically, socially, and politically similar group of people, e.g., middle class.

clines   A gradient of morphological or physiological change in a group of related organisms, usually along a line of environmental or geographic transition.

clitorectomy (clitoridectomy)   Removal of the clitoris.

Clovis point   A large lancelike projectile fluted at the base and flanked at both sides.

clustering   In epidemiology, the concentration of cases by place of residence and time of diagnosis.

cognates   Words that belong to different languages but have similar sounds and meanings.

cognatic kin   Kinship traced simultaneously through the male and female lines in a nonunilineal pattern of descent.

collective behavior   Patterns of social action.

colonialism   The establishment of government of sovereign rule in a territory through political, social, economic, and cultural domination by a foreign power.

commodification   The transformation of a good or service into something that can be bought and sold with money.

communal   Shared with a group.

comparative framework   An analytical approach in anthropology using the comparison of cultures across time and place.

constructions of femininity   The warp in which a given culture defines appropriate ways of thinking and acting for women. See *gender roles*.

consumable commodity   Something that can be bought or sold, and then used up.

consumer society   A characteristic of modern capitalist societies in which the purchase of non-essential material goods and services is an important marker of social status and identity.

contingent truths   Truth based upon the best scientific evidence available at the time and subject to revision as knowledge expands.

conversational analysis   A technique in sociolinguistics that focuses on the social and symbolic attributes of verbal interactions.

corporate culture   The cultural characteristics of a workplace.

corporate kin groups   Social groups, like lineages, that share political responsibilities and access to land; characteristic of tribal societies.

correlate   A variable that stands in a consistent observed relationship with another variable.

correlation   A statistical relationship between two variables.

corvée   A system of required labor; characteristic of ancient states.

creole   A type of language that results from the widespread adoption of a pidgin language as the primary language of a group.

Cro-Magnon   A term broadly referring to the first anatomically modern humans, from roughly 40,000 to 10,000 B.C.; named after a site in southwestern France.

cross-cultural   A standard form of anthropological analysis using the comparison of traditions and practices from different societies.

cross-cultural research   The exploration of cultural variation by using ethnographic data from many societies.

cross-cutting ties   Affinal or trading relationships that serve to counteract the political isolation of social groups in tribal societies.

cross-sectional   Research done across different geographic locales.

cultural anthropology   A field of anthropology emphasizing the study of the cultural diversity of contemporary societies, including their economies, sociopolitical systems, and belief systems.

cultural dissonance   A situation arising from the incompatibility of two or more interacting cultural systems.

cultural evolution   The process of invention, diffusion, and elaboration of the behavior that is learned and taught in groups and is transmitted from generation to generation; often used to refer to the development of social complexity.

cultural ideals   A valued characteristic or belief of a society.

cultural materialism   The idea, often associated with Marvin Harris, that cultural behaviors are best explained in relation to material constraints (including food-producing technology) to which humans are subjected.

cultural pluralism   The simultaneous existence of two or more cultural systems within a single society; multiculturalism.

cultural relativism/cultural relativity   The principle that all cultural systems are inherently equal in value and, therefore, that each cultural item must be understood on its own terms.

cultural reproduction   The process by which cultural behaviors and beliefs are regenerated across generations or spread among people of the same generation; cultural construction creates reality.

cultural values   Ideas, beliefs, values, and attitudes learned as a member of a social group.

culture   Learned patterns of thought and behavior characteristic of a particular social group.

culture area   A largely outmoded idea that the world can be divided into a limited number of geographical regions, each defined by a certain set of cultural features that result from common ecological adaptation or history and are shared by all groups in the region.

culture broker   An individual who attempts to negotiate and translate between two cultural groups, particularly in contexts of miscommunication or potential miscommunication.

culture shock   The experience of stress and confusion resulting from moving one culture to another; the removal or distortion of familiar cues and the substitution of strange cues.

decotion   The extraction of flavor by boiling.

demography   The statistical study of human populations, including size, growth, migration, density, distribution, and vital statistics.

dental anthropology   A specialization within biological anthropology; the study of the morphology of teeth across time and populations.

dependency   A theory of international economic relations in which an economically powerful nation creates ties with other nations in ways that reduce the possibility of economic independence of the poorer nations.

dependent variable   The resultant phenomenon that is explained by its relationship with an independent variable.

dialect   A regional or class-based version of a spoken language, although the difference between dialect and language can be influenced by historical and political considerations.

diffusion   A process of cultural change by which traits of one society are borrowed by another; the spread of cultural traits.

diseases of civilization   Chronic diseases, such as cardiovascular disease and obesity, that characterize the epidemiological profile of modern capitalist societies and are the result of infrequent exercise and high fat diets.

dividual   As opposed to "individual," someone whose identity or selfhood is tied to his or her relationships with other people.

domestic labor   Work performed in the home, such as cooking, cleaning, and taking care of children.

domestication of plants and animals   The invention of farming.

dowry   Presentation of goods or money by the bride's family to the bride, the groom, or the groom's family.

Ebonics   The rule-based and pattern dialect of English spoken by many working-class urban African Americans; black English vernacular.

economy   The production, distribution, and consumption of resources, labor, and wealth within a society.

ecosystem   A community of plants and animals, including humans, within a physical environment and the relationship of organisms to one another.

edutainment   A marketing technique in consumer-oriented societies in which consumerism and education are simultaneously valued.

egalitarian   A society organized around the principle of social equality; characteristic social formation of food foraging groups.

egalitarian society   A society that emphasizes the social equality of members and makes achieved statuses accessible to all adults.

embodied   Human experience inside an individual body and the expression of culture through the body.

embodied knowledge   Knowledge that seems to reside "in the body" and does not require conscious thought (for example, riding a bike).

epidemic   Higher than normal occurrence of a disease in a particular area.

epidemiological transition   The historical change in the primary cause of mortality in a population from infectious disease to chronic disease.

epidemiology   A science that studies the incidence, distribution, and control of disease in a population.

epistemology   The study of the nature of knowledge and its limits.

ergonomics   Human engineering; an applied science concerned with the anthropometric characteristics of people in the design of technology for improved human-machine interaction and safety.

essentialist   A view of reality based on a single inherent fact rather than a socially constructed reality.

essentialize   The assumption that all individuals of the same social category (e.g., class, caste, race, gender) have the same beliefs, values, experiences, and other characteristics.

ethnic groups   A group of people within a larger society with a distinct cultural or historical identity; ethnicity is a common mechanism of social separation in complex, heterogeneous societies.

ethnocentrism   The assumption that one's own group's lifestyle, values, and patterns of adaptation are superior to all others.

ethnocide   The attempt to exterminate an entire ethnic group (similar to genocide).

ethnographic methods   The research techniques of cultural anthropology based on long-term participant observations, yielding a description of another culture.

ethnography   An anthropological method that generally involves living in a place for an extended period of time, participating in and observing daily life, and then writing about the culture or the place.

ethnology   The study and explanation of cultural similarities and differences.

ethnomedicine   The medical theories, diagnosis systems, and therapeutic practices of a culture or ethnic group.

ethnopediatrics   The study of how differing parenting styles affect infant health and growth.

ethos   The worldview of a particular society, including its distinctive character, sentiments, and values.

etiology   The theory of causation of a disease or illness.

eugenics   The genetic improvement of the human race through control of breeding.

Eurocentric   Interpreting the world in terms of Western and especially European values and experiences.

evaluation researcher   A researcher who assesses (evaluates) the impact or outcome of a treatment or program.

evolutionary medicine   An anthropological approach to disease, symptoms, and medical care based upon our evolutionary heritage.

exchange   A social system for the distribution of goods; reciprocity is a widespread system of exchange between social equals while markets act as a mode of exchange between strangers.

excision   One of three forms of female circumcision; includes clitorectomy and removal of some or all of the labia minora and labia majora.

exogamous   Relating to a custom that forbids members of a specific group from selecting a spouse from within that group.

explanatory model   A patient's cognitive scheme for understanding his or her illness.

extended family   A domestic unit created by the linking together of two or more nuclear families.

fallow   The period during which a unit of agricultural land is not cultivated so that nutrients can be restored to the soil.

family of origin   Nuclear family into which an individual is born and in which he or she is reared.

fecundity   A demographic characteristic of a society referring to its overall capacity for reproduction.

feral   Living in, or pertaining to, the wild; without the benefit of society or culture.

feud   A pattern of reciprocal hostility between families or kin groups, usually involving retribution for past wrongs or deaths; such as blood feud.

FGM   Female genital mutilation or female genital modification; *see* sunna circumcision, excision, infibulation.

fieldwork   The hallmark of research in cultural anthropology, it usually involves long-term residence with the people being studied.

fission   The splitting of a descent group—a residential unit based on shared kinship—into two or more new descent groups or domestic units.

focus groups   A research strategy in which an investigator leads a small group in discussion on a particular topic; frequently used in market research.

folk taxonomy   A culture's system of classification or grouping of objects, which can reveal the cognitive categories of that group.

food foragers   People living in a society with an economic pattern harvesting of wild food resources, usually by gathering plants or hunting animals; hunting and gathering.

food scarcity   The lack of sufficient food to meet the energy requirements of a population; may be the result of failed food production or a socially unequal distribution system.

foraging   Hunting and gathering; the original human economic system relying on the collection of natural plant and animal food sources.

fraternal polyandry   An uncommon form of plural marriage in which a woman is married to two or more brothers at one time.

gender   The social classification of masculine or feminine.

gender dimorphism   Physical and physiological differences between males and females; sexual dimorphism.

gender roles   Accepted models of behavior, thoughts, and emotions associated with masculinity and femininity that are culturally defined and learned over the course of one's upbringing and socialization.

genealogy   The systematic study of the consanguineal and affinal kin of a particular person, including his or her ancestors; a common method used in anthropological field studies.

gestation   The carrying of young in the uterus from conception to delivery.

ghetto   A subsection of a city in which members of a minority group live because of social, legal, or economic pressure.

globalization   A contemporary cultural, political, and economic process involving world capitalism by which production and consumption are expanded to be worldwide in scope or application.

Gordian knot   A highly intractable problem or impasse; in Greek legend, a knot tied by King Gordius of Phrygia and cut by Alexander the Great, after an oracle had said it could be untied only by the next ruler of Asia.

hallucinogen   A substance that induces visions or auditory hallucinations in normal individuals.

hearth   The floor of a fireplace.

hierarchy   The categorization of a group of people according to status, whether it be ascribed at birth or achieved. A hierarchy refers to group organized in this way.

HIV   The human immunodeficiency virus that causes AIDS.

holistic   Refers to viewing the whole society as an integrated and interdependent system; an important characteristic of the anthropological approach to understanding humans.

hominid   An erect-walking bipedal primate that is either human, an extinct ancestor to humans, or a collateral relative to humans.

Homo sapiens   Hominid species including modern humans and immediate archaic ancestors (Neandertals).

horticulture   A plant cultivation system based upon relatively low energy input, like gardening by using only the hoe or digging stick; often involves use of the slash-and-burn technique.

hot-cold humoral system   Traditional ethnomedical system of the Indoeuropean world.

human rights   Related to a post–WWII international movement begun by the United Nations and associated with the 1948 International Declaration of Universal Human Rights. The rights enumerated include: equality before the law; protection against arbitrary arrest; the right to a fair trial; freedom from *ex-post-facto* criminal laws; the right to own property; freedom of thought, conscience, and religion; freedom of opinion and expression; freedom of peaceful assembly and association; also included in the document economic, social, and cultural rights as the right to work and to choose one's work freely, the right to equal pay for equal work, the right to form and join trade unions, the right to rest and leisure, the right to an adequate standard of living, and the right to education. During the 1990s, human rights efforts often emphasized women's rights.

human universal   A trait or behavior found in all human cultures.

hunter-gatherers   Peoples who subsist on the collection of naturally occurring plants and animals; food foragers.

hypothesis   A tentative assumption or proposition about the relationship(s) between specific events or phenomena, tentatively set forth as a "target" to be tested.

ideal body images   Culturally defined standards for attractive body shapes.

indigenistas   Individuals and organizations that work on behalf of indigenous people.

indigenous   The original or native population of a particular region or environment.

infanticide   Killing a baby soon after birth.

infibulation   One of three forms of female circumcision; includes circumcisions and excision, followed by the sewing up of the sides of the vulva so that scar tissue covers the vaginal opening, except for a small gap for urination and menstruation; requiring some surgical opening for first intercourse and birth; also called pharaonic circumcision.

infidel   A nonbeliever with respect to a particular religion.

informant   A member of a society who has established a working relationship with an anthropological fieldworker and who provides information about the culture; the subject of intensive interviewing.

institutions   Formal organizations within a society.

intensive interviewing   The ethnographic method of repeated interviews with a single informant.

intercultural communication   The exchange of meanings and messages between people from different societies characterized by different underlying ideas, beliefs, and worldviews; may or may not be complicated by the speaking of different languages.

Islam   The religious faith of Muslims who profess belief in Allah as the sole deity and in Mohammad as the prophet of Allah.

key respondent   A subject that a researcher finds particularly knowledgeable and amenable to multiple interviews.

kinship   A network of culturally recognized relationships among individuals, either through affinial or consanguineal ties.

Koran   The sacred text of Islam.

kula   Traditional long-distance trading network for valuable objects among Trobriand islanders first described by B. Malinowski.

lactose intolerance   The inability of adults to digest milk because they no longer produce the enzyme lactase; a biological characteristic of a large proportion of the world's population.

land concentration   The degree to which land ownership is concentrated among a small number of people in a society.

land tenure   A system of land ownership and inheritance.

language   A rule-based and patterned system of communication.

late capitalism   A form of capitalism emerging in the second half of the twentieth century, characterized by finance capital, globalization, and technological innovation.

latifundistas   Large landowners who use low-cost native labor to make enormous profits.

levirate   The practice by which a man is expected to marry the wife or wives of a deceased brother; commonly found in patrilineal descent systems.

lexicon   The vocabulary set characteristic of a group; argot.

life history   A methodological technique of cultural anthropologists in which a key informant's biography is compiled using multiple interviews.

lineage   Refers to a kin group tracing common descent through one sex from a known ancestor.

linguistic anthropology   A subfield of anthropology entailing the study of language forms across space and time and their relation to culture and social behavior.

linguistic relativity   A principle of anthropological linguistics referring to the fact that all languages are equally adequate as systems of communication.

linguistics   The study of language, consisting of: (1) historical linguistics, which is concerned with the evolution of languages and language groups through time; (2) descriptive linguistics, which focuses on recording and analysis of the structures of language; (3) sociolinguistics, the way in which speech patterns reflect social phenomena; and (4) ethnosemantics, the study of the connection between reality, thought, and language.

literacy   The ability to read; not possible for people who speak unwritten languages.

lithic   Referring to stone, especially with regard to artifacts.

longitudinal   A research strategy that examines changes in a particular group over time.

luxury   A consumer good primarily purchased as a marker of social status.

mana   A supernatural force inhabiting objects or people.

maternalism   Having or demonstrating characteristics associated with mothers and mothering.

matrilineal   Relating to, based on, or tracing descent through the maternal line.

mediator   The role of a disinterested third party in dispute settlement.

medical anthropology   The study of health and medical systems in a cross-cultural perspective; includes the study of biocultural adaptations to disease, ethnomedical systems, and cultural factors in health-seeking behavior.

meritocracy   A system in which advancement is purportedly based upon ability or achievement of the individual.

metalinguistics   Elements of communication beyond verbal speech; includes the use of gesture, personal space, silence, and nonlinguistic sounds.

microeconomics   Small-scale or individual economic decisions and patterns, such as the ways that individuals budget their cell phone expenditures.

micropolitics of social inequality   Small-scale patterns of power between individuals or small groups, the ways that inequalities between people are played out on a personal level.

miscegenation   Marriage or sexual intercourse between a woman and a man of different races, particularly between a white and an African American in the United States.

moiety system   A social system in which the entire group is divided into two kinship units, which are usually based on unilineal descent and exogamous.

monogamy   Marriage between one man and one woman at a given time.

moot   A public hearing or community assembly to decide local problems and administer justice.

morphology   The study of form as structure as opposed to function.

mosque   An Islamic place of public religious worship.

Muslim   An adherent of or believer in Islam.

multiculturalism   A movement to broaden the range of cultures we study, in reaction to the prevailing opinion that the great accomplishments have been made almost exclusively by males of European descent.

multiple paternity   The concept, occurring in several South American cultures, that every man who has intercourse with a woman during her pregnancy contributes to the formation of the child; therefore, a child may have multiple fathers.

multiplex relationships   Complex social relations characterized by multiple patterns of interaction, for example by kinship, business, political party, ethnicity, and religion.

national character studies   Descriptions of the cultural belief and "typical" personality of people from another culture, an approach used by the culture and personality school of anthropology.

negotiation   The use of direct argument and compromise by the parties to a dispute to voluntarily arrive at a mutually satisfactory agreement.

neocolonial   After the age of colonialism, this refers to continued economic and political policies by which a great power indirectly maintains or extends its influence over other areas or people.

Neolithic   A stage in cultural evolution marked by the appearance of ground stone tools and, more importantly, the domestication of plants and animals, starting some 10,000 years ago.

nomadic band   A food-foraging group that moves among a variety of campsites; a society without sedentary villages.

nonreactive measure of behavior   Various methods for collecting social science data that are unobtrusive and unsubjected to bias introduced by the population under study.

norms   Standards of behavior characteristic of a society or social group to which members are expected to conform.

nuclear family   A basic social grouping consisting of a husband and wife and their children, typical of societies with monogamous marriage with the family living at a distance from the parents of the husband and wife.

obesity   A medically defined condition of excessive fat storage.

observational research   Research conducted by documenting what is observed (as opposed to other research techniques such as interviews, questionnaires, or laboratory tests).

origin myth   A story found in most cultures that explains the creation and population of the world.

orthography   The way in which words in a particular language are written phonetically to include sounds (phonemes) not represented in our alphabet; anthropological linguists usually use the International Phonetic Alphabet (IPA).

ovulation   The part of the menstrual cycle in which the egg (ovum) is released and fertilization can occur.

pacification   In tribal areas like New Guinea, the establishment by outside authorities of peace from blood-feud warfare.

palaver   A discussion for purposes of dispute settlement, typically informal and following customary law.

paleoanthropology   The study of human fossil remains.

Paleolithic   Old stone age; the archaeological period that includes the beginning of culture to the end of the Pleistocene glaciation.

paleontology   The study of the fossils of ancient, usually extinct, animals and plants.

paleopathology   The study of disease patterns in extinct populations, primarily through the examination of skeletal remains.

paramount chief   In a ranked society of ascribed statuses, the position at the top of the hierarchy.

participant observation   The primary research method of cultural anthropology, involving long-term observations conducted in natural settings.

parturient   Bringing forth or about to bring forth young.

pathogen   An agent that causes disease.

patriarchy   A form of social organization in which power and authority are vested in the males and in which descent is usually in the male line.

patrilineal   Descent traced exclusively through the male line for purposes of group membership or inheritance.

patrilocal   A postmarital residence rule by which a newly wed couple takes up permanent residence with or near the groom's father's family.

peasants   Rural, agricultural populations of state-level societies who maintain parts of their traditional culture while they are tied into the wider economic system of the whole society through economic links of rent, taxes, and markets.

pedagogy   The methods and techniques of teaching.

physical anthropology   Another term for biological anthropology; includes the study of paleoanthropology, population genetics, human adaptation, and primatology.

Pleistocene   The geological period approximately from 600,000 years ago to 12,000 years ago, characterized by recurrent glaciations.

pollution   The act of defilement, uncleanness.

polyandry   A relatively rare form of plural marriage in which one woman is married to two or more men.

polygamy   A general term for plural marriage, either polygyny or polyandry.

polygyny   A common form of plural marriage in which one man is married to two or more women; in societies that permit polygyny, the majority of marital unions are monogamous. Extended families may be formed through polygyny.

population   In genetics and biological anthropology, a discrete demographic unit often characterized by in-marriage.

population density   The ratio of the number of people per area of land; closely related to carrying capacity.

population pressure   The situation of population growth in a limited geographical area causing a decline in food production and resources and sometimes triggering technological change.

potlatch   A feast given by a Northwest Coast Native American chief often involving competitive gift-giving, first described by Franz Boas.

prehistoric   The time before written records.

primatology   The study of nonhuman primates.

primogeniture   A rule of inheritance in which the homestead is passed down to the firstborn (male) child.

primordial   Belonging to or characteristic of the earliest stage of development; first in sequence of time.

principal investigator   The lead researcher in a large research project.

privilege   A special advantage, immunity, permission, right, or benefit granted to or enjoyed by an individual, class, caste, or race. Such advantage may be held consciously or unconsciously and exercised to the exclusion or detriment of others.

probability sampling   A data collection sampling technique based on the known proportions of various social groups.

proletariat   The working class in a state-level society, usually residing in urban areas.

psychoactive drugs   Chemicals that affect the mind or behavior and that may cause, among other things, hallucinations.

purdah   The Hindu or Muslim system of sex segregation, which is practiced by keeping women in seclusion.

qualitative methods   Research strategies that emphasize description, in-depth interviewing, and participant observation.

quantitative methods   Research methods that translate behaviors or attitudes into reliable and valid numeric measures suitable for statistical analysis for hypothesis testing.

race   A folk category of the English language that refers to discrete groups of human beings who are uniformly separated from one another on the basis of arbitrarily selected phenotypic traits.

radiocarbon dating   A method of absolute dating in archaeology using organic material and based on the decay rate of the radioactive isotope Carbon-14; useful for objects less than 50,000 years old.

random sample   A data sample selected by a method in which all individuals in a population have equal chance of being selected.

reciprocal gift   A mechanism of establishing or reinforcing social ties between equals involving a "present," which is repaid at a later date.

reciprocity   A system of mutual interaction involving the regular exchange of goods or services (for example, inviting someone over for dinner because they previously had you over for dinner).

reforestation   To renew forest cover by seeding or planting.

refugee   According to international law, someone residing outside of his/her country of nationality, or who has no nationality, because of "persecution or a well-founded fear of persecution."

regional economy   As opposed to globalization, this refers to the production, distribution, and consumption of goods and services in a distinct and limited geographical context.

relative deprivation   A concept wherein individuals perceive that they are less well off only in relation to another group or to their own expectations.

religion   Attitudes, beliefs, and practices related to supernatural powers.

REM   Rapid eye movement. The part of the sleep cycle when dreaming is done.

reproductive success   A variable used in Darwinian analyses referring to an individual's overall achievement in reproduction of their own genes (through direct offspring or kin).

rite of passage   Religious rituals that mark important changes in individual status or social position at different points in the life cycle, such as birth, marriage, or death.

ritual   A set of acts, usually involving religion or magic, following a sequence established by tradition.

sample   A subpopulation that is studied in order to make generalizations.

sanctions   Generally negative responses by a social group as a consequence of an individual's behavior; used to maintain social control.

séance   A ritual, usually held at night, designed to promote direct contact between people and spirits.

segmentary system   A hierarchy of more and more inclusive lineages; functions primarily in contexts of conflict between groups.

self-sufficient   Refers to a characteristic of most pre-state societies; the ability to maintain a viable economy and social system with minimal outside contact.

serial monogamy   The marriage of one woman and one man at a time but in a sequence, usually made possible through divorce.

seropositive   Testing positive for a given disease (such as HIV infection) based on a blood test.

seroprevalence   The prevalence (proportion of people infected in a population) of a given disease based on blood tests.

sex   Determined by biological characteristics, such as external genitalia and having XX or XY chromosomes (contrast with *gender*).

sex roles   Learned social activities and expectations made on the basis of gender.

sexual dimorphism   A condition of having the two sexes dissimilar in appearance.

shaman   A part-time religious practitioner typical of tribal societies who goes into trance to directly communicate with the spirit world for the benefit of the community.

shifting agriculture   A form of cultivation (horticulture) with recurrent, alternate clearing and burning of vegetation and planting of crops in the burnt fields.

sickle-cell anemia   An often fatal genetic disease caused by a chemical mutation that changes one of the amino acids in normal hemoglobin; the mutant sickle-cell gene occurs with unusually high frequency in parts of Africa where malaria is present.

SIDA   The Spanish, French, Italian, and Haitian Creole acronym for AIDS.

SIDS   Sudden infant death syndrome—the sudden and unexpected death of an infant, also known as crib death.

single-interest relationship   A relationship based solely on one connection, such as landlord-tenant.

situated   Formed by a given person's experiences, based on context.

slang   A small set of new and usually short-lived words in the vocabulary of a dialect of a language.

slash-and-burn techniques   Shifting form of cultivation (horticulture) with recurrent, alternate clearing and burning of vegetation and planting in the burnt fields; swidden.

social class   In state-level societies, a stratum in a social hierarchy based on differential group access to means of production and control over distribution; often endogamous.

social cohesion   The process by which a social group binds itself together, producing greater cooperation and conformity.

social construction   A reality that is created and agreed on by interpersonal interaction and discourse; opposite of essentialist.

social control   Practices that induce members of a society to conform to the expected behavior patterns of their culture; includes informal mechanisms, like gossip, legal systems, and punishment.

socialization   The development, through the influence of parents and others, of patterns of thought and behavior in children that conform to beliefs and values of a particular culture.

socially validated   Approved or recognized by the culture of a particular social group.

social mobility   The upward or downward movement of individuals or groups in a society characterized by social stratification.

social networks   An informal pattern of organization based on the complex web of social relations linking individuals; includes factors like kinship, friendship, economics, and political ties.

social organization   A culturally inherited system that orders social relations within social groups.

social status   A person's level of prestige in society. Social status is associated with factors like education and employment as well as higher and lower levels of wealth or power. In the United States, for instance, doctors tend to have higher social status than cooks at McDonald's.

social stratification   An arrangement of statuses or groups within a society into a pattern of socially superior and inferior ranks; based on differential access to strategic resources.

society   A socially bounded, spacially contiguous group of people who interact in basic economic and political institutions and share a particular culture; societies retain relative stability across generations.

sociobiology   The study of animal and human social behavior based on the theory that behavior is linked to genetics.

sociocultural   Refers to the complex combination of social and cultural factors.

sociolinguistics   A subfield of anthropological linguistics emphasizing the study of the social correlates to variations in speech patterns.

solidarity   Unity based on community interest, objectives, and culture.

somatic   Having to do with the body.

somatization   The physical expression of psycho-social social problems.

sorcery   The use of supernatural knowledge or power for purposes of evil, for example causing sickness; used to further the sorcerer's individual social goals.

species   The largest naturally occurring population that is capable of interbreeding and producing fully fertile offspring.

spurious   Not an actual or causal relationship, as in the correlation between the number of storks and birthrate.

stasis   A state of equilibrium or balance between opposing forces.

states   A complex society characterized by urban centers, agricultural production, labor specialization, standing armies, permanent boundaries, taxation, centralized authority, public works, and laws designed to maintain the status quo.

status   Position in a social system that is characterized by certain rights, obligations, expected behaviors (roles), and certain social symbols.

stigma   Socially constructed shame or discredit.

stratified societies   A society in which groups experience structured inequality of access not only to power and prestige but also to economically important resources.

stroll   A street where prostitution activity is concentrated.

structure   In anthropology, generally referring to social institutions and patterns of organization.

subculture   The culture of a subgroup of a society that has its own distinctive ideas, beliefs, values, and worldview.

sunna circumcision   One of three forms of female circumcision; this procedure includes clitorectomy (removal of clitoris and hood) and sometimes refers only to the cutting of the hood (prepuce); the name *sunna* relates the practice to Islamic traditions, although most Muslim scholars and theologians deny any Koranic justification for female circumcision.

superstructure   In the theory of cultural materialism, refers to a society's ideology.

sushi   A traditional Japanese food of rice and thinly sliced raw fish and other ingredients rolled in seaweed and artfully presented to the diner, eaten with a horseradish sauce.

swidden cultivation   A tropical gardening system, also known as slash-and-burn horticulture in which forest is cleared, burned, cultivated, and then left for bush-fallow.

symbol   A sign that consistently but arbitrarily represents an object or meaning; the basis of communication within a culture.

syntax   The word order or pattern of word order in a phrase or sentence.

taboo   A supernaturally forbidden act as defined by a culture, violation of which can have severe negative consequences.

TFR (total fertility rate)   The average number of children born to a woman during her lifetime.

time-allocation study   A quantitative method that identifies what people do and how much time they spend doing various activities; useful for cross-cultural comparison.

totem   A symbolic plant or animal associated with a social group (clan) used for identification and religious expression.

transmission   Passing of an infectious agent to an uninfected person from an infected group or individual.

transnational culture   A pattern of cultural beliefs and behaviors characteristic of elites throughout the world and often spread through mass media.

tribe   A relatively small, usually horticultural, society organized on principles of kinship, characterized by little social stratification and no centralized political authority, and whose members share a culture and language.

trophic exchanges   Relationships between organisms having to do with food; eating or being eaten.

universalism   The understanding that certain beliefs, values, rights, or conditions are or should be universal.

urbanization   The worldwide process of the growth of cities at the expense of rural populations.

urban villages   Small (usually segregated) communities of minorities or rural migrants located in cities.

usufruct rights   The legal right of using land (or resources on land) that is not one's private property.

validity   The quality of a measurement tool or variable actually measuring what is intended.

values   The ideas of a culture that are concerned with appropriate goals and behavior.

virilocal residence   Patrilocal postmarital residence.

walkabout   A custom of Australian Aborigines involving a long circular journey to sacred places and a return to home.

war   Violence between political entities, such as nations, using soldiers; to be distinguished from the smaller scale feud.

weaning   Acclimating someone (as a child) to take food other than by nursing.

Western culture   A generic term referring to the common beliefs, values, and traditions of Europeans and their descendants.

worldview   The particular way in which a society constructs ideas of space, time, social relationship, and the meaning of life.

yerba mate   *Ilex Paraguayensis.* A tea made from the small branches and leaves of this species of tree is consumed hot or cold. Widespread use of this refreshment throughout colonial Latin America made it Paraguay's main export for four hundred years.

yerbateros   People who collect yerba mate, usually in uncultivated stands in the tropical forest.

zeitgeist   The general intellectual, moral, and cultural climate of an era.

Index